W9-CJO-208

# Tax Research

## Second Edition

**Barbara H. Karlin, J.D., LL.M. (Taxation), CPA**
Professor, School of Taxation
Vice President for Academic Affairs
Golden Gate University

Prentice
Hall

Upper Saddle River, NJ 07458

**Managing Editor**: Alana Bradley

**Editor-in-Chief**: P. J. Boardman

**Editorial Assistant**: Jane Avery

**Marketing Manager**: Beth Toland

**Marketing Assistant**: Christine Genneken

**Managing Editor (Production)**: John Roberts

**Permissions Coordinator**: Suzanne Grappi

**Associate Director, Manufacturing**: Vincent Scelta

**Production Manager**: Arnold Vila

**Manufacturing Buyer**: Michelle Klein

**Cover Design**: Kiwi Design

**Cover Photo**: Art Wolfe/Getty Images Stone

**Printer/Binder**: Von Hoffmann

Credits and acknowledgments borrowed from other sources and reproduced, with permission, in this textbook appear on page xi.

**Copyright © 2003 by Pearson Education, Inc., Upper Saddle River, New Jersey, 07458**. All rights reserved. Printed in the United States of America. This publication is protected by Copyright and permission should be obtained from the publisher prior to any prohibited reproduction, storage in a retrieval system, or transmission in any form or by any means, electronic, mechanical, photocopying, recording, or likewise. For information regarding permission(s), write to: Rights and Permissions Department.

Pearson Education LTD.
Pearson Education Australia PTY, Limited
Pearson Education Singapore, Pte. Ltd
Pearson Education North Asia Ltd
Pearson Education, Canada, Ltd
Pearson Educación de Mexico, S.A. de C.V.
Pearson Education–Japan
Pearson Education Malaysia, Pte. Ltd

10 9 8 7 6 5 4 3 2 1
ISBN 0-13-044948-2

# CONTENTS

## Chapter Five – How to Discover Relevant Primary Authority: Using Reference Services and Other Secondary Sources

## About the Author

Barbara Karlin has been a professor in the School of Taxation at Golden Gate University since 1986.  She was Dean of the School of Taxation from 1997-2002 as well as Dean of the School of Business from 1999-2002. In 2002 Barbara became the university's Vice President of Academic Affairs.

Barbara has written and presented extensively on the subject of tax research, including presentations at the AICPA Graduate Tax symposium at the 1990 and 1998 meetings.  In addition, she has written and recorded several video tapes on the subject.

Barbara brings practical experience to her teaching and academic administration.  She earned her CPA certificate while working for Coopers & Lybrand in San Francisco, California.  In addition, Barbara holds an LL.M. in Taxation from Golden Gate University and a J.D. from Hastings College of the Law. She earned her bachelor's degree from Stanford University.

As a professor in the School of Taxation, Barbara developed a graduate course that she teaches entirely over the Internet as part of the university's successful online Masters in Taxation program. She helped develop the graduate Tax Research class also offered on the Internet by Golden Gate.

In addition to her work at Golden Gate University, Barbara has been very involved in the accreditation work of the Western Association of Schools and Colleges (WASC).  She was a member on its Substantive Change Committee and continues to serve on accreditation visiting teams when time permits.

# Acknowledgments

When I agreed to write this book, I did not appreciate the immense challenge I was taking on.  Fortunately, response was very good to the first edition, and, thus, this second edition has been a more positive experience!  The patience and support of my children, **Chris and Katie**, as well as that of my husband, **Jeffrey,** allowed me to complete this work during times I should have been spending with them. A special thanks to my colleagues at Golden Gate University who so kindly understood my need to spend long uninterrupted hours focusing on completing this revision – **Esther, Cassandra, Mary, and Paul.**

Golden Gate University is blessed with the commitment of remarkable practitioner-adjunct faculty.  I wish to thank the following adjunct faculty (former and current) and students who agreed to share with the readers  their "practitioner observations."


*Diane M. Comi*, Attorney at Law
*Fred Daily*, Attorney at Law and author
*Robert Evans*, Vice President, Taxes, The Fremont Group
*Elizabeth Fiattarone*, Attorney at Law
*Loella Haskew*, Buckley, Patchen, Riemann & Hall
*Ralph Kuhen*, Hein & Associates, LLP
*Eric Lee*, Deloitte and Touche, LLP
*Dale A. Lottig*, Partner, Deloitte and Touche, LLP
*Brian MacKenzie*, Attorney at Law
*Kirk Paxson*, Attorney, Internal Revenue Service
*Earl Thomas*, Earl Thomas and Associates
*Frederick W. Sroka*, PriceWaterhouseCoopers
*Joseph Stemach*, Internal Revenue Service (retired)
*Stephen J. Swift*, Judge, United States Tax Court

A special thanks to Earl Thomas, Tom Maier, and Kirk Paxson for reviewing and editing the chapter on federal tax procedure. **Alana Bradley** with Prentice Hall – you were wonderful to work with!  I also thank the following reviewers for their constructive and insightful comments for this second edition:

**Larry Crumbley,** Louisiana State University
**Jeffrey Curcio,** Murphy, Austin, Adam & Schoenfeld, LLP
**Frank Fisher**, PriceWaterhouseCoopers
**Margaret Reed**, University of Cincinnati
**Paul Shoemaker,** University of Nebraska
**Gary Slavett**, Internal Revenue Service

## Permissions

All CCH pictures and Web screens are produced with permission from CCH's *Tax Research NetWork*, published and copyrighted by CCH Incorporated, 2700 Lake Cook Road, Riverwoods, Illinois 60015.

All RIA picture and Web screens reprinted with the permission of RIA.

All web screens from Tax Analysts *TaxBase* reprinted with permission from Tax Analysts.

AICPA Statements on Standards for Tax Services (Copyright (c) 2001 by the American Institute of Certified Public Accountants, Inc.) reprinted with permission.

# THE TAX RESEARCH PROCESS

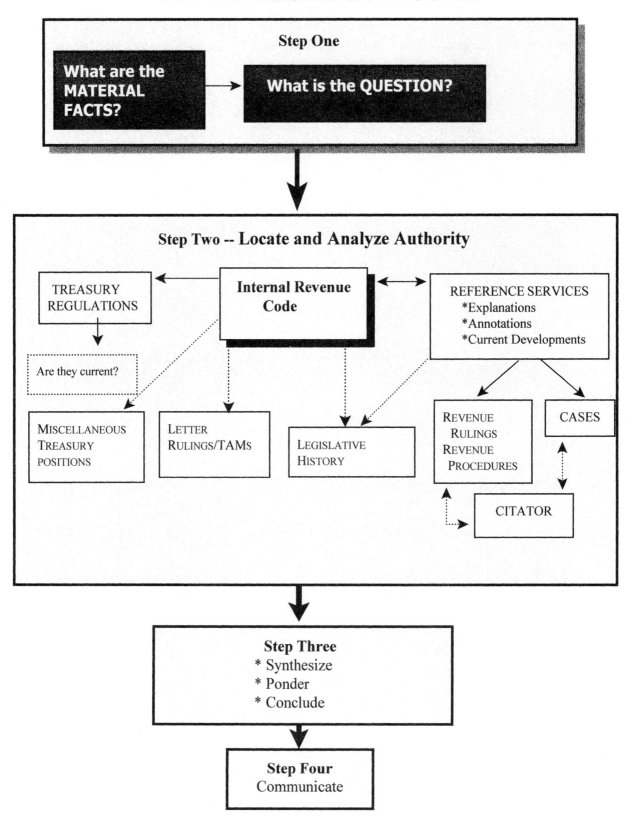

**Step One**

What are the **MATERIAL FACTS?**

**What is the QUESTION?**

**Step Two -- Locate and Analyze Authority**

TREASURY REGULATIONS

**Internal Revenue Code**

REFERENCE SERVICES
*Explanations
*Annotations
*Current Developments

Are they current?

MISCELLANEOUS TREASURY POSITIONS

LETTER RULINGS/TAMs

LEGISLATIVE HISTORY

REVENUE RULINGS REVENUE PROCEDURES

CASES

CITATOR

**Step Three**
* Synthesize
* Ponder
* Conclude

**Step Four**
Communicate

# CHAPTER ONE

# OVERVIEW OF TAX RESEARCH

## *EXPECTED LEARNING OUTCOMES*

Identify the basic tax research steps
Know the importance of determining the research question
Appreciate the significance of gathering all relevant facts
Understand the practical considerations impacting the tax researcher

## *CHAPTER OUTLINE*

Overview
Step One – Gathering Relevant Facts
Step Two – Researching
Step Three – Analyzing
Step Four – Communicating
Practical Considerations in Tax Research
Chapter Summary
Problems

## OVERVIEW

> *Virtually all persons or objects in this country . . . may have tax problems.*
> *Every day the economy generates thousands of sales, loans, gifts,*
> *purchases, leases, wills, and the like, which suggests the possibility of tax*
> *problems for somebody.*
> *U.S. Supreme Court Justice Potter Stewart*

"What are the tax implications?" This question permeates almost every business or investment discussion.  Business decisions are often based on a variety of considerations – some non tax, others tax related. Depending on the particular transaction, tax consequences may completely dictate or only minimally affect the ultimate course of action taken.  For example, tax laws affect such diverse business decisions as: "Should we open an overseas office?" "What discount should we provide for store purchases?" "How much severance should we pay?" "Should I sell my stock in the business?"  Tax considerations also significantly influence many personal decisions: "Should I exercise my stock options now or wait until they fully vest?" "How many days should I rent out my vacation home?" "Should I start gifting property to my children to reduce estate taxes on my death?"

Generally, tax research is necessary to address these questions. The research process begins with someone (perhaps a taxpayer, your employer, or yourself) identifying the need to explore the question "What are the tax implications?"

---

## Practitioner Observation

*Eric Lee, Deloitte & Touche, LL.P*

"No matter how much experience tax professionals possess, they can not know everything about the complex, ever changing tax law. Therefore, what separates the successful tax professionals from those who are not is their ability to effectively and efficiently research tax issues. A parable explains that you can feed a hungry man, but it is better to teach him to fish. Research is the skill tax professionals must master to cure their hunger for tax knowledge."

---

There are four basic steps to the research process: gathering the relevant facts and determining the pertinent tax question; researching available tax resources to determine relevant authority; analyzing the authority you find; drawing a conclusion and communicating your results.

Step One – Gathering Relevant Facts

- Determine the relevant tax question.
- Identify all the material facts.

Step Two – Researching

- Identify and read the pertinent resources.
- Refine the question if necessary and/or obtain additional facts.

Step Three – Analyzing

- Synthesize the information gathered.
- Ponder what you have learned.
- Determine whether there is enough information and authority to render a conclusion.
- Ponder and conclude.

Step Four – Communicating

- Determine the appropriate form of communication.
- Communicate your conclusions.

**Research Steps:**

☞ **gather facts/determine question**

☞ **identify authority**

☞ **analyze and conclude**

☞ **communicate**

The process flowchart at the beginning of each chapter illustrates these steps in the context of the tax resources available. Sometimes there is a tendency to focus solely on the tax research tools and pay little heed to the research process. A good tax researcher understands the process and in this context appreciates what each of the various research tools has to offer. In addition, the process is not simply a mechanical one. Each step requires a large amount of critical reasoning and thinking!

This chapter explores the two stages of Step One in detail: determining the relevant tax question and identifying the relevant facts. The rest of the chapter provides an overview of the remaining steps, which are discussed in depth in the chapters that follow.

## STEP ONE –  GATHERING RELEVANT FACTS

- Determine the relevant tax question.
- Identify all the material facts.

The first phase in the research process consists of two steps: determining the tax question and identifying the relevant facts. Because these first-phase steps appear so straightforward, sometimes researchers do not pay adequate attention to their overriding importance. The first phase sets the foundation for the research process.  You must competently perform each of the first two research steps, or your research results may be significantly flawed.

## Determine the Question

The most critical initial step in the research process is to determine the research question or issue. Prior to achieving a complete understanding of the subject matter, you may initially phrase the question in very general terms: "Are the lottery winnings income?" Or " Is interest paid on a consumer loan deductible?" Regardless of how precisely you frame the initial research question, as you work through the research process and become more informed, you will likely refine, amend, and perhaps add to the question.

> *"If you don't know where you're going, you will probably end up somewhere else."*
>
> by Laurence Johnston Peter, *The Peter Principle* (1969)

For example, you may determine the initial research question is, simply stated, "Is the mortgage interest deductible?"  As you research, you will discover that there are special requirements in order for mortgage interest to be deductible.  For example,  it may need to be "acquisition" debt.   You may further refine your question as  "Is the debt 'acquisition' debt?" As you explore the meaning of the term *acquisition debt*, you discover that the home must be a "qualified residence."  Now you have a new question you must answer: "Is the home a qualified residence?" Consequently, as you frame the initial question, it is important to be mentally flexible enough to feel free to refine or reframe the question.

☛ **As you acquire information, keep your mind open to refine the question.**

Depending on your experience and knowledge of the particular tax area you are researching, you may be able to quickly develop a specific set of relevant, focused research questions.  Even if you are a novice in a particular area, a logical and careful development of the relevant tax question is essential to arrive at a circumspect, professional conclusion.

Tax questions may arise either before or after all facts or events surrounding a particular transaction have occurred. When the question arises before all the facts are established, your research will most often play a significant role in planning a transaction.  In a planning mode, your work may directly affect the taxpayer's actions in establishing a factual "road map" to structuring a transaction in the most tax-wise manner.

In this planning mode, one of the most important gathering aspects is to ascertain what your client wants to accomplish economically or otherwise.  Consequently, the research question may ultimately hinge on how to accomplish the taxpayer's goals most effectively. In a planning situation, the facts are not yet completely established.  For example, perhaps a manager is considering whether to pay year-end bonuses to certain employees.  In addition to determining what facts are already set in stone, it is imperative that you fully understand the goals of the manager.  What the manager wishes to accomplish directly affects how you frame your tax question and, thus, the analysis that follows.

---

## Practitioner Observation

*Robert Evans, Vice President – Taxes, The Fremont Group*

"*In my opinion, the ultimate goal in tax research is to know how to find authorities which will allow your client to get where he/she wants to go with as high a comfort level as possible.  To do this, the professional most often works to present alternatives which tweak the original legal and or/economic deal in order to fit fact patterns in tax authorities which provide the greatest comfort as to the achievability of the desired tax results.*

*The best professionals, therefore, gain the proper understanding of the client's pre-tax economic goals, understand the business deal and the latitude and limitations on potential alterations.  The professional then can present tax alternatives which take all of these pre-tax factors into account.*"

---

Unfortunately, taxpayers do not always call in advance to permit planning considerations.  Frequently, you may only be asked to determine the appropriate way to report a completed transaction on a tax return.  Or you may be required to research a matter to justify or bolster the taxpayer's position taken in a previously filed tax return.  In this type of research role, the existing facts,  rather than the taxpayer's goals, will likely determine the appropriate tax research question.

The best way to start research is to frame an initial research question. Recognize, however, that identifying and refining the tax research question continues throughout much of the research process as you begin to peel back the layers of information and uncover issues.  Of course, you bring to this stage of the process your previous experiences which may impact how you formulate the initial tax question.  You may determine later that you have posed a question too narrowly drawn. Framing the question too narrowly often results in the failure to properly address the ultimate research question.  Initially, you may have missed the key question altogether.  Be open to changing or adding to your research question as you move through the process.

Always try to take the proverbial "step back" after you have commenced your research, and consider whether your question as initially framed continues to be relevant as you explore applicable tax laws.  A good researcher should try to maintain a professional and detached outlook. Also recognize the value of discussing the facts and question with other colleagues when this option is available.  They may provide you with further insight.

---

**EXAMPLE 1: Framing the Research Question**

Taxpayer is taking courses toward an M.B.A. degree.  Taxpayer was employed by an accounting firm and decided to take a leave of absence in order to attend graduate school full-time.  Taxpayer would like to know if she can deduct her tuition expenses.

In this situation, perhaps the most general question is "Are tuition expenses deductible?"  Some may initially believe that there may be a problem because Taxpayer is working toward a degree.  This may result in framing the initial question too narrowly.  For example, "Does the fact that Taxpayer is working toward a degree prohibit her from taking the deduction?"  This may be an appropriate initial question, but if it is the only one researched, the general question regarding the deductibility of the tuition expenses will go unanswered.  Actually, current authority indicates that there is a series of questions to be answered before determining the deductibility of the expenses. These questions include "Will the education help improve her current work skills?" "Does the education qualify her for a new business?" Additional thought and analysis expose a potentially missed issue:  "What is the impact of the leave of absence?"

You should always stay focused on the tax question as you perform each research step. Continue to ask yourself "Is this material relevant?" and "What do I hope to learn from reviewing these documents?" There is so much information available, it is easy to get lost reading irrelevant, albeit interesting material. Remaining focused is probably the most difficult challenge for the tax researcher and yet arguably the most important.

*"In a field as complex as the one before us, involving statutory provisions that are so confusingly interrelated and intricate as to be exasperating, it is particularly important not to embark upon any exploration of issues not properly presented." [Van Products, Inc. v. Commissioner, 40 TC 1018, 1028.]*

## Identify the Relevant Facts

You must be aware of at least some of the facts in order to properly determine the appropriate initial question. Yet knowing which facts are relevant and which are not often depends on the tax question. Therefore, the steps in determining the question and identifying the relevant facts are interdependent.

In practice, you are trying to answer a specific question about how the tax laws relate to a specific set of facts. You need to be aware of all the facts that might impact the application of the tax laws. One logical way of distinguishing a relevant fact from an irrelevant one is as follows: A relevant fact is one that, if changed, might alter the application of the tax laws. An irrelevant fact is one that, if altered, will have no impact on the application of the tax laws. If one question is being considered, a particular fact may be relevant. If another question is being asked, that same fact may become irrelevant.

---

**EXAMPLE 2: Relevant Facts**

Client A is 75 years old. If the research question deals with whether a non-Roth IRA distribution must be made, the taxpayer's age is definitely a relevant fact. In this case, the rules differ dramatically depending on the age of the taxpayer. However, if the question is whether the taxpayer must recognize lottery winnings as gross income, the age of the taxpayer is irrelevant. The tax law in this case is the same regardless of the taxpayer's age.

The dictionary defines a fact as something that is real or actual – "information presented as objectively real."[1]  Be careful not to confuse conclusions with the actual facts.  Conclusions result from making a judgment or decision about the facts or the law.  For example, the taxpayer may tell you that his annual salary of $10,000,000 is reasonable. The only facts in this situation are the amount of the salary and that the taxpayer believes it is reasonable.  It is not necessarily a fact that the salary is reasonable.  It is only the taxpayer's conclusion.

---

**EXAMPLE 3: Fact Versus Conclusion**

A taxpayer corporation provides to its key employees a special benefit of free yoga sessions in order to reduce stress.  The taxpayer's president informs you that this is "ordinary" practice in high stress businesses. You decide that in order to determine the deductibility of the yoga expenses to the corporation, you must determine whether this special employee benefit is "ordinary and necessary" to the conduct of the taxpayer's business.

*Actual facts known*:    Key employees receive free yoga sessions.  President believes this is ordinary in the profession.

More facts will likely need to be gathered in order to determine whether the president is correct in concluding that it is an ordinary and necessary business expense for the corporation to provide free yoga classes to employees. You may initially determine that the president's assertions appear reasonable; however, what if you are later informed that the cost of the yoga contract exceeds 10% of the corporation's gross revenue?

---

Identifying all relevant facts sounds like a rather simple step.  However, in practice, this is actually quite difficult. Typically, it is the taxpayer who provides the factual information. Yet the taxpayer does not always know which facts are relevant to the research and which ones are irrelevant.  It is the responsibility of the researcher to ask the necessary questions to uncover all the relevant facts.  This is generally not easy because it often takes familiarity with the tax law or the business of the client to know initially what facts are relevant.

---

[1]*The American Heritage Dictionary of the English Language*, 3rd edition.

To make matters worse, the taxpayer usually communicates the facts orally – on the phone or in a meeting.  Accurately documenting facts related by an oral narrative presents the extra challenge of exercising good listening skills and the need to take quick, rough notes and fill them in later. In practice, you may not have the luxury provided in the classroom of being given a typed list of all the key facts.

There is a variety of methods you can use to gather the facts. In addition to careful listening, always ask questions.  If you do not clearly understand something, make sure to ask sufficient questions to clarify your understanding.  Although your questions should always demonstrate you are listening carefully, it is acceptable to ask many questions. The outset of research is not the time to be bashful or assume you can find the facts in some other way. Asking focused questions is often the best method for gathering the facts.  If the person you are asking does not know the answer, confirm a time when he or she can determine the answer and advise you. Try not to make any factual assumptions without confirming them. Recognize that you may very likely need to ask questions in the future as you discover the need to acquire more specific information.

In addition to asking questions, you can gather pertinent information by examining important documents such as prior tax returns, corporate documents, broker statements, and divorce decrees. Sometimes through your examination, you may notice an inconsistency between what you initially wrote down from your client interview and the information you discern from the documents.  You will need to resolve any inconsistency by asking additional questions.

Whether the taxpayer is a continuing client or a new client may impact your initial fact-gathering process.  Many firms prefer to have the client initially complete a questionnaire that asks detailed tax questions pertinent to most taxpayers.  However, if the client is one whom you have worked with before, this information should already be known or accessible to you.

**The taxpayer often is the person relaying the facts. But does he or she know what facts are relevant?**

*Practitioner Observation*

**Earl Thomas, Earl Thomas & Associates**

*"When you are being asked to research a question, listen carefully to what is being asked of you. Ask questions to clarify the assignment and to establish parameters. Restating the assignment to the requestor in your own words will serve to reinforce your own understanding of the assignment, as well as to satisfy the requestor that you understand the assignment."*

## STEP TWO –  RESEARCHING

■      Identify and read the pertinent resources.
■      Refine the question if necessary and/or obtain additional facts.

When you first learn how to conduct tax research, the amount of different types of resources available to you may be somewhat overwhelming.  A typical tax library – in print or electronic form – presents you with so many options:  IRS rulings, tax forms, case books galore, multi-volumed services all with slightly different titles, and much more.  What should you read first?  Which ones can you really trust?  Which resources are most important? All these issues are addressed in this book. We'll begin with an overview of tax research tools.

As the flowchart depicts at the beginning of the chapter, the research process requires the researcher to scrutinize the Internal Revenue Code, case law, Treasury interpretations, reference services, and other types of documents.  The Internal Revenue Code (referred to as *IRC* or the *Code*) consists of most of the laws regarding federal taxation that Congress has enacted. The IRC is the actual federal tax law and, thus, comprises the heart of tax research.  You will learn all about the IRC and how to analyze the Code in the next chapter.

☞  **Possible resources:**
  * **Code**
  * **Treasury interpretations**
  * **Cases**
  * **Reference services**
  * **Articles**

The Internal Revenue Code is too complicated to stand on its own.  As a result, two different authoritative groups provide their opinions regarding how to properly interpret and apply the IRC –  the Treasury Department and the judiciary.  Because we have so many types of these interpretations, we need special publishing services to help identify and catalogue in a logical manner the interpretations most pertinent to a specific research question.  These are called "reference services."  Without reference services, it would be nearly impossible to discover all the pertinent court cases and Treasury interpretations. Other sources such as textbooks and journal articles are also available to help us understand how to apply the Internal Revenue Code.  Each of these resources is discussed in the following chapters.

Given the tremendous volume of tax resources available, it is easy to be overwhelmed. Nonetheless, you may be learning so much, you may not even realize when you are lost. Getting sidetracked is a fairly common tax research problem.  However, getting lost in the morass of available information is not conducive to time and cost efficiency.  It may be interesting, but the taxpayer is generally not enthusiastic about paying for unproductive time.

You can minimize your chances of wasting time if you stay focused on the research question. As you hunt for relevant material, keep in mind the facts you are working with and the question you are trying to resolve.  You will want to read those authorities with similar facts that specifically address your research question.

## Primary and Secondary Sources of Authority

There are two types of resources available to you in the research process – **primary** and **secondary** sources.  Ideally, the research process involves locating both types of resources. As the name suggests, primary sources are the most authoritative.  The Code is an example of a primary source. Secondary sources usually guide us to the relevant primary sources. In this way they play a useful role in the research process but by themselves are not considered authoritative. Generally you should base your conclusion only on what is learned from the primary sources.

How do you determine whether a particular type of resource is primary or secondary?  One way is to memorize the list of items in each category.  However, a more useful way is to understand that the origin of the resource determines its categorization as primary or secondary. Primary sources are generated by authorized governmental bodies. Therefore, the Code, Treasury interpretations (regulations, revenue rulings, etc.), and judicial interpretations (court cases) are all primary.  The origin of secondary sources is not as official – publishers and authors offer their views regarding the law and produce helpful reference services, magazine articles, and books.  The following chart illustrates the difference between the two types of authority.

☛ **Stay focused on the research question.**

☛ **Primary sources are the most authoritative.**

☛ **Congress, the Treasury, and the courts generate primary sources of authority.**

# PRIMARY SOURCES

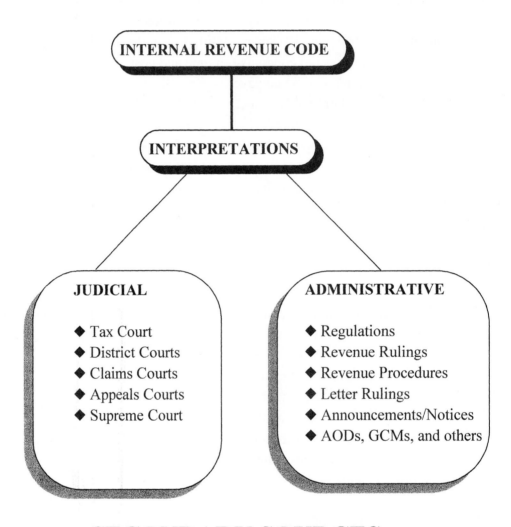

**INTERNAL REVENUE CODE**

**INTERPRETATIONS**

### JUDICIAL

- ◆ Tax Court
- ◆ District Courts
- ◆ Claims Courts
- ◆ Appeals Courts
- ◆ Supreme Court

### ADMINISTRATIVE

- ◆ Regulations
- ◆ Revenue Rulings
- ◆ Revenue Procedures
- ◆ Letter Rulings
- ◆ Announcements/Notices
- ◆ AODs, GCMs, and others

# SECONDARY SOURCES

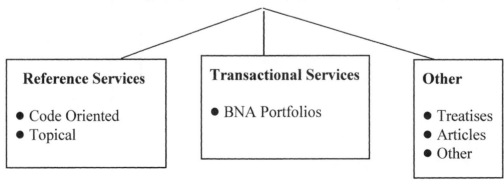

**Reference Services**

- ● Code Oriented
- ● Topical

**Transactional Services**

- ● BNA Portfolios

**Other**

- ● Treatises
- ● Articles
- ● Other

Unfortunately, the research process is more complicated than it might first appear. Not every type of primary source of authority has the same legal weight attached. For example, under federal laws, a United States Supreme Court decision is more significant to the researcher than an IRS private letter ruling, assuming the same legal issue is involved. Chapters Two through Six discuss how to determine the relative weight of primary sources of authority. Bear in mind, however, that no type of secondary source is more authoritative than a primary source of authority.

☛ **Each primary authority carries a different amount of importance.**

## STEP THREE – ANALYZING

- Synthesize the information gathered.
- Determine whether there is enough information and authority to render a conclusion.
- Ponder and conclude.

Locating and analyzing the relevant authority is clearly a critical step in the process of answering a tax question. The next step, however, requires critical thinking. The taxpayer expects more than just a copy of the authority that potentially addresses the issue! You must also critically analyze the information found. What does all the information mean? How does it apply to the client matter under consideration?

☛ **Critical thinking skills are fundamental tools in the research process.**

Your critical thinking skills helped you determine the research question and the appropriate facts. You also applied your analytical skills when you determined the authority that was most relevant to your research question. This next step, however, consists of determining the clearest way to put it all together. Essentially, you have before you the research question, the relevant facts, and the pertinent authority. To answer the research question, you need to synthesize all this information by:

☛ **Some questions have a definite answer, whereas others do not.**

    ✓    Analyzing the importance of each authority relative to the question and facts.
    ✓    Determining the relative significance of each authority vis-a-vis each other.

✓    Applying the reasoning of the authority to your facts.
✓    Reconciling any possible conflicting authoritative positions.
✓    Determining that all authority relied upon is current.

After this analysis, you must ultimately reach a conclusion, even if your conclusion is that there is no definitive answer to the issue presented. Since the tax laws are complex, arriving at a conclusion is often a challenge. Sometimes a research question results in a simple "black and white" answer: "Yes, the salary must be reported as income." Or "No, the demolition expense is not deductible." In these circumstances, you should easily be able to arrive at a cogent and complete conclusion if you carefully performed the necessary research steps.

More complex research questions often give rise to a determination that there is no absolute right or wrong answer. How do you arrive at a conclusion in this case? It is in these "gray" areas that it is hard to stop researching. Nevertheless, there may be instances in which you have found all that is relevant on the issue and still have no definitive answer. It is natural to feel that if you look for it just a little bit longer, perhaps the answer will appear. However, this instinct may be counterproductive if it consumes valuable time with little or no corresponding increase in the accuracy of the findings.

The key to being an excellent tax researcher is knowing the research process well enough to be capable of ascertaining when you have found all the relevant authority. Even if there is no definitive answer, you may conclude it is time to stop looking. At this point, you are left with your ability to reason and work with the authority you did locate to arrive at a well-reasoned conclusion. This being said, you should never mistake your own good judgment as to what you believe is the correct answer as a valid substitute for decisive applicable authority. Your judgment call may be useful, but it is simply

*Practitioner Observation*

*Elizabeth Fiattarone, Attorney at Law*
*"Tax research is about learning a process and learning how to think. There are not black and white absolute answers to most complex tax issues. What a person learns through the process is how to come to a position with respect to any tax issue; and most importantly, the person has the tools to support the answer and make a persuasive argument supporting their position."*

your judgment, and the client should always be informed of that fact. The taxpayer should not rely on your good-faith judgment falsely believing that it represents a conclusion based on applicable law.  We will cover this challenge in more detail in Chapter Six.

---

### Practitioner Observation

*Diane M. Comi, Attorney at Law*

*"Without a clear understanding of tax research methodology and accessing the most effective resource material, tremendous inefficiencies will no doubt occur, causing not only a loss of valuable time but also much frustration.  There are those tax issues for which, no matter how expert the researcher, there is a painful absence of authority or clarity."*

---

## STEP FOUR – COMMUNICATING

- Determine the appropriate form of communication.
- Communicate your conclusions.

All your terrific work to this point doesn't mean much unless you effectively convey your conclusions. This may involve communicating the research conclusion and specific rationale internally to a supervisor or colleague or externally to the client or government representative. At the very minimum, you should always properly document your work in an appropriate manner.

Proper documentation may take the form of a concise memorandum that is simply filed with the rest of the client files. An important factor to carefully consider when communicating and documenting conclusions is the identification of the intended recipient of the communication. Clearly, the method of writing differs depending on the identification of the recipient. In addition, the form of communication should best serve the taxpayer's interests.  For example, while it may be appropriate for you to carefully document your conclusions in an internal file, it may not be helpful to your client's interests in the long term if the memorandum includes concerns regarding your client's position and later is subject to discovery by an adverse party engaged in litigation against your client. Chapter Eight briefly discusses the issue of privilege in the context of a tax client.

There is a variety of external forms your communication may take. Perhaps the client desires that you send a letter conveying all relevant research results. Or perhaps the client engages you to write a letter to a taxing authority advocating the client's position.

☞ **The form of communication varies with each research project.**

Whatever the form, written communication usually involves a reporting of the facts, the research question or issue, and your conclusion and supporting rationale. Thus, your writing includes reporting relevant findings in each one of the research steps previously outlined. The specific, well-reasoned methods of communication are covered in greater detail in Chapter Seven.

In deciding what to communicate to the taxpayer and your method of communication, you must also consider your role as tax advisor. Recall that at times your research involves helping to plan a transaction to best attain the taxpayer's desired results. In this planning mode, your role is that of a creative advisor and educator. You must educate the taxpayer on each available option and its tax consequences. Provide the taxpayer with all the necessary information so that <u>the taxpayer</u> or the authorized representative can make the ultimate decision.

Remember, you communicate the tax analysis – the taxpayer makes the ultimate decision. It is often the case that a taxpayer, fully mindful of adverse tax consequences, appropriately chooses to ignore your best tax-planning advice because other economic or legal concerns were considered of greater importance. For example, you may have advised your client to avoid selling stock because it would result in a large short-term capital gain taxed at maximum tax rates. However, your client may be strapped for cash and simply need to liquidate the investment. Remember that tax consequences are not always the most important taxpayer consideration.

☞ **After being informed of the research results, the taxpayer makes the ultimate decision.**

When your research involves already established facts, you are generally expected to evaluate and communicate the resulting tax consequences.  You may be responsible for communicating the best way to report a transaction on the tax return.  Or you may be asked to be the taxpayer's advocate in discussions with the taxing authority. Obviously the role you are to play determines the method and style of your communication.

It is, therefore, imperative throughout the research process to keep in mind the role you were asked to play – planner or simply advisor regarding a specific set of facts.  This is particularly important as you contemplate how to best communicate your tax analysis. The expectations placed upon you in a planning role may differ substantially from those expected of you when you are simply asked to react to an established set of facts.  As a planner, you are often expected to bring creative ideas to the table. The taxpayer may reasonably expect you to provide more guidance than a simple recitation of the likely tax consequences.

**☞ As a tax planner, creativity is a key skill.**

In addition, your legal responsibility and vulnerability may differ substantially when you act as a planner.  In the planning mode, you may significantly impact the taxpayer's future actions. Consequently, the taxpayer will be understandably vexed if unanticipated negative tax consequences occur as a result of reasonable reliance on your advice.

**☞ A tax planner may shoulder increased vulnerability.**

## Practitioner Observation

*Dale A. Lottig, Partner, Deloitte and Touche, LLP*

*"In our increasingly complex and competitive business environment, the tax researcher is akin to a navigator, steering the business enterprise through the stormy seas of tax regulation toward the safe harbor of a successful tax result."*

## PRACTICAL CONSIDERATIONS IN TAX RESEARCH

To answer the research question, you should always endeavor to follow the process outlined in this chapter: gather the facts and determine the question, identify the relevant authority, analyze your findings, conclude and communicate.  However, within this framework there is a great deal of flexibility calling for judgment and common sense.  Sometimes, you may need to simply check one source to confirm what you already know about the tax rules.  Other times, the process may be extensive and require much time and extensive use of library resources.

A full-fledged research process (as detailed in the flowchart at the beginning of this chapter) in which every source is examined may not be appropriate in all research situations. It is important for you to determine when an exhaustive review is not necessary or prudent. It is careless to take shortcuts out of ignorance only to later discover that, to your embarrassment,  the skipped step would have produced information critical to the client.  However, it is also wise to be cognizant of effective methods of shortening your research in areas of well-settled law.  How detailed your research is may depend on several factors: standards of authority, accuracy, time efficiency, the amount of tax liability involved, and the need to create a proper record of your work.

---

### *Practitioner Observation*

*Frederick W. Sroka, PriceWaterhouseCoopers*

" *The greatest demands facing tax practitioners are not on our technical knowledge, but on our time.  If we spend our time without clear budgets and objectives, then the practice will burn up our energies and talents as surely as a spendthrift burns up money.  If we invest our time wisely with clients, associates, and our families, our intellectual, emotional, and financial net worth will grow.  That's a balanced portfolio I hope to own.* "

---

## Accuracy

Although you should be mindful of the need to be time efficient, you must also give accurate advice to the taxpayer. The bottom line is that the taxpayer expects that the advice you render is correct!  Unfortunately, performing excellent research does not always result in your feeling entirely confident with the research results. Sometimes you get lucky and find the precise answer to a tax question. In this circumstance, you rightfully feel assured that the research results are "correct."  However, when there is ambiguity in the tax laws, you may find a range of possible answers to the question, each with a different tax consequence.  This results in a troublesome reality: One advisor may find a certain set of these possible answers acceptable, whereas another advisor may find a different set acceptable.  And sometimes both may be right!

Against this backdrop of ambiguity and uncertainty, it is sometimes difficult to know when your advice crosses the line of acceptability, invoking ethics and professional responsibility concerns. Must you present to the taxpayer only the most conservative option that renders the greatest tax burden?  Fortunately for the taxpayer, the answer to this is "No."

The famous jurist, Judge Learned Hand, once stated:

> Over and over again courts have said that there is
> nothing sinister in so arranging one's affairs as to
> keep taxes as low as possible.  Everybody does so, rich
> or poor; and all do right, for nobody owes any public
> duty to pay more than the law demands:  taxes are
> enforced exactions, not voluntary contributions.  To
> demand more in the name of morals is mere cant.
> [Commissioner v. Newman, 159 F2d 848 (Ca 2, 1947)]

Obviously,  taxpayers wish to pay the least amount of taxes possible under the law.  The taxpayer expects you to help in this quest. Assisting in appropriate tax planning is quite different from aiding and abetting in tax fraud.  Unfortunately, sometimes no clear litmus test exists to help you determine when your advice is merely reflective of

☛ **The taxpayer expects the advice you render is correct.**

*"Anyone may so arrange his affairs that his taxes shall be as low as possible; he is not bound to choose that pattern which will best pay the Treasury; there is not even a patriotic duty to increase one's taxes."* [Helvering v. Gregory, 1934-1 USTC ¶9180.]

an aggressive interpretation or whether it is simply not in accordance with the law.  The overall complexity of the tax law coupled with this ambiguity may lead to an inherent legal vulnerability for anyone providing tax advice.  Although not determinative, there is a variety of guidelines and standards that provide help in determining how best to approach difficult tax matters.

Generally, you may only sign a tax return or recommend a reporting position that has a "realistic possibility of being sustained on its merits." You may satisfy this standard if you can show that after performing a "reasonable and well-informed analysis" a knowledgeable person in tax law would conclude there is a good chance (one in three) that the position will be upheld.  In making this analysis, the guidelines provide that you may rely only on primary sources of authority.  To avoid monetary penalties imposed on the taxpayer, the position must be supported by "substantial authority."  Consequently, the required accuracy of your work may be, in part, dictated by specific standards. These guidelines and standards are discussed in Chapter Six.

☞ **Would a person knowledgeable in tax law conclude the reported position has a "realistic possibility" of being upheld?**

## Time Efficiency

Whether you work in an accounting or law firm, a taxing agency or a corporation, you are expected to be an efficient tax researcher.  You may be required to precisely record the amount of time spent on a research project. Depending on the firm and its billing practices, you may be required to account for every 10 minutes of billable time!  Tracking time usually serves two purposes: measuring your productivity and providing your employer the information it needs to bill the client.  Depending on whether you are a CPA, an attorney, or other licensed professional, there may also be specific ethical rules of professional responsibility governing tracking and billing time spent on client matters.

☞ **You must record the time spent on each research project.**

How do efficiency concerns affect your decision regarding how extensive your research ought to be? Consider the following practical considerations, and the answer may become clearer.

## Amount Involved

Every transaction involves different dollar amounts and, hence, different exposure.  Buying a company may involve billions of dollars.  Providing subsidized employee parking may involve a few hundred dollars.  Each transaction requires the researcher to address the tax implications.  There is no direct correlation between dollar amounts and ease in determining the tax implications.  Nonetheless, the billion dollar purchase of the company probably warrants more of your research time than the employee parking issue.  The potential financial and tax implications of some transactions may be so immaterial that little research time is justified.  Although some research projects will result in no tax savings, generally, it is a good idea to try, when possible, to avoid sending the taxpayer a bill greater than any potential tax savings your research generates.

Of course, good professional judgment sometimes requires that you perform more work than it is realistic to expect payment for.  Sometimes, an overly cautious client is more concerned with doing everything correctly, no matter how little the risk.  A professional can never suggest it is appropriate to simply ignore legal requirements.  Nonetheless, there is a practical line to draw based on your experience and good judgment.

Clearly, the potential dollar amount at stake may affect the amount of time you spend researching a tax question.   Even small transactions warrant allocating an appropriate amount of research time. Still, not every high-stakes transaction demands a great deal of research. In practice,  most accounting and law firms budget a total number of hours for a research project. Of course, it is often the case that such "budgets" are not right on target!  But they do give you a helpful guide regarding how exhaustive the research effort should be.

As a beginning researcher, if you have concerns regarding the amount of time you are spending on a research project, always consult with your supervisor (when possible) before you spend more time than was initially budgeted.

☛ **The amount of dollars involved in the research question may affect the amount of appropriate research time.**

## Creating a Record

Typically, a myriad of issues arising from the affairs of many clients occupies your day as a tax practitioner. You may spend a few hours in the morning working on Client A's work and then not return to that client's issues until the next week. In the interim, it is easy to forget the details of pending projects or to lose sight of the overall assignment. You may also leave your employer and begin work somewhere else – while the taxpayer remains a client with your original employer. In both instances, it is imperative to maintain complete client files so that you or others may know precisely the status of the client matter.

Complete client files have many benefits. They act as memory refreshers, reminding you of the pertinent facts and any research work you performed for that client. By providing you with a quick reminder of your previous work, well-maintained client files help you become more time efficient. In addition, well-organized, complete client files allow for continuity in the service provided to the taxpayer. Any work done for that client should be well-documented and retrievable even if the personnel engaged on the client matter changes. Appropriate files allow multiple people to quickly understand outstanding client issues and then efficiently work on client matters.

Whether the files are electronic or paper, you should always maintain  a well organized file that contains:

- Tax returns
- Supporting work papers
- Relevant client documents
- Written communications to client
- Summaries of oral communications to client
- Internal communications regarding client matters
- Office memos for each research project
- Supporting documentation for each research memo
- Carryover schedule indicating all return and research issues with possible continuing impact into a subsequent tax year

> " 'The horror of that moment,' the King went on, 'I shall never, never forget!'
> 'You will, though,' the Queen said, 'if you don't make a memorandum of it.'"
>
> By Lewis Carroll in *Alice's Adventures in Wonderland*, Chapter 1.

It is not difficult to prepare complete files, but it requires good organization. As you read useful information, copy it and highlight your copies, or simply summarize it. Then put the summary or copy in the files along with any other related information you find. You will find more information about how to create useful summaries of your work in the following chapters.

## CHAPTER SUMMARY

Your role as tax researcher is varied and complex. You are responsible for determining the tax implications of a taxpayer's situation. Because tax law impacts in some way most business transactions and many personal transactions, effective research skills are critical in today's world.

Sometimes the taxpayer asks you to determine the tax impact of an already existing set of facts. You must analyze the facts and discover all the tax consequences of the situation. Other times, the taxpayer asks you to become involved in helping plan a transaction. As a tax planner, your advice will most likely help determine the actions of the taxpayer. In approaching each step in the research process, it is important to be aware of your role.

The research process consists of four steps:

1. Gathering all the relevant facts and determining the tax question(s).
2. Researching to discover the relevant authority.
3. Analyzing the authority and its impact on the research question; applying your reasoning to the facts and concluding.
4. Communicating your research findings.

The first step in the process is critical to the remainder of the research. It is imperative that you discover all the relevant facts through focused questioning of the taxpayer and by reviewing relevant documents. In order to be most thorough in your fact-finding, you must discern the tax question at issue, recognizing that you may need to add to or refine your original question.

Once you complete Step One, there is a multitude of tools to help you answer your research question. Step Two involves identifying which of these tools are most relevant. The most authoritative types of resources are primary sources. Congress, the Treasury Department, and the courts issue primary authority. Also helpful are secondary sources such as services that refer you to the pertinent primary authority.

Throughout the process, it is critical that you are circumspect regarding what you are doing. Tax research is not simply a mechanical process. It involves a great deal of critical thinking and analysis every step of the way.  The third step of the process requires you to synthesize the authority you discovered and analyze its significance in answering the research question.  Finally, you must arrive at a conclusion regarding the answer(s) to the question.

The last step in the process is to communicate your research findings either internally or externally to the client or taxing agency.

Tax research carries with it several practical realities.  You must be time efficient and take into consideration the dollar amounts involved.  Thorough client files are necessary for a variety of reasons, including ensuring proper documentation of client matters and ease of future review.  In addition, you must try to be as accurate as possible, despite the complexity and ambiguity of the tax laws.   This presents some potential ethical dilemmas for which we have only limited guidelines and standards.

# PROBLEMS

## *KEY CONCEPTS* (1-21)

1.    Define and give an example of the meaning of the following concepts and terms:

    a.    Tax planning
    b.    Fact
    c.    Conclusion
    d.    Relevant fact
    e.    Primary source
    f.    Secondary source
    g.    IRC
    h.    Reference service
    i.    Time budget

2.    What is the purpose of tax research?

3.    Describe the four basic steps in the tax research process.

4.    Why is it so important to determine the research question and, while being flexible to refining the question, remain focused on it throughout your research process?

5.    Why is it important to determine whether you have been asked to act in a planning role when gathering facts and determining the research question?

6.    What is the difference between a fact and a conclusion? Why is it important to recognize the difference?

7.    Does the research question stay the same throughout the research process? Why or why not?

8.    What is the danger of framing the research question too narrowly?

9.    Describe the role of the tax researcher. When does tax research need to be performed? What does the taxpayer usually expect you to do as a tax advisor?

10.    What methods are available to gather relevant facts? Why is it important to be aware of all the facts? What are some of the challenges presented in gathering facts?

11.    What are the two sources of primary authority that provide interpretations of the Internal Revenue Code?

12.    How are reference services useful?

13.    What is the difference between primary and secondary sources? How can you distinguish between the two?

14.    During which steps must you use skills of critical thinking? For each step in which critical thinking is essential, discuss why.

15.    Discuss the variety of forms you may use in communicating the results of your research.

16.    Is it accurate to say that there is only one correct answer to every tax research question? Discuss the reasoning for your response. In what ways does your answer affect how the tax research process is conducted?

17.    When might the tax researcher take on the role of tax advocate?

18.    How can you determine when you are involved in tax planning? What is your role as a tax planner? How does this differ from tax research in which no planning is requested? Why is it important to recognize the difference?

19.    What standards must you abide by when signing a return or recommending a tax return position to a taxpayer? What must you do to satisfy this standard?

20.    What practical considerations does the tax researcher need to be aware of when performing tax research?

21.    What purpose do client files serve? What information should be included in a client file?

## PRACTICAL APPLICATIONS (22-26)

22.    Frame the initial issue(s) arising from the following facts. What additional information would be helpful?

a.      Taxpayer purchases a ticket for the New Jersey lottery. He won $1,000.

b.      Taxpayer paid $5,000 to his former wife.

c.      Taxpayer paid $1,000 to a lawyer for advice.

23.      Mrs. K is a new client. She has recently divorced and has some questions regarding the payments she is receiving from her ex-husband, Mr. K. She tells you that Mr. K is 50 years old and was previously divorced from his first wife. He is a wealthy doctor. Mrs. K received $10,000 a month from Mr. K. She asks you whether she has to pay taxes on the $10,000.

     a.      What additional questions do you need to ask Mrs. K before you begin your research?

     b.      What additional potential sources of information or documents might you want to ask for?

     c.      Which of the preceding facts are relevant? Which are irrelevant?

     d.      Is there a chance that you will need to ask more questions at a later point in time? Why or why not?

     e.      What is the first question you will try to answer in your research? How does your initial question change when you discover in your research that if the $10,000 is considered "alimony," it must be included in Mrs. K's taxable income. You also learn that any amounts that are considered "child support" will not be taxable to Mrs. K. Please comment.

     f.      What do you believe is the taxpayer's desired result? Why is this important? How does it affect your role as tax advisor?

     g.      Is this a planning research type of situation? How do you know?

     h.      What if, instead of $10,000, the monthly amount Mrs. K receives from Mr. K totals $100. How does this affect the tax research?

24.      A yaxpayer works for a law firm. You are working on her tax return. She tells you that she does not have any receipts for her daily parking because the firm pays the parking lot directly for an annual spot for her. She tells you not to worry about it because she knows that employees do not have to pay tax on the value of parking privileges.

     a.      What is your role in this situation?

     b.      How does your role affect the four steps in the research process?

     c.      What are the questions you need to ask the taxpayer?

     d.      What is your research question initially?

     e.      After you speak to her initially, you discover that the Internal Revenue Code does not consider a partner in a firm to be an employee.

i.     How does this new information affect your research?

ii.    Are there some additional questions you now need to ask?  What is the danger here of failing to gather all the relevant facts?

iii.   Does this information change or add to your initial research question?

iv.    You explain to her that, given the facts, she will need to report as income the value of the parking. She tells you just to forget she told you about the parking. Without getting into detail, what issues does this raise?

25.    You are asked to supervise a new hire in your firm's tax department.  The person has been working on the tax return of a corporation that is a new client of the firm.  Help the person put together the client files.  How many and what files would you advise?  What should be included in each file?  (Address this question ignoring the issue as to whether the file is electronic or paper.) Because you are the person's mentor, make sure to explain your reasoning.

26.    In the past 10 years, a taxpayer purchased 100 shares of a particular mutual fund at varying times and prices.  He sold 70 shares on a specific date this year. He seeks your advice regarding the tax impact of the sale.

a.    What is your initial role here?

b.    How might your role change in the future?

c.    What facts must you uncover?

d.    What are some ways you can discover the relevant facts?

e.    What do you think is the research question/issue?

## *INTEGRATED CASE STUDIES* (27- 42)

*You will find the following case studies at the end of each chapter.  The facts will remain the same, although additional facts may be added in subsequent chapters.  Use the knowledge and skills you have learned in this chapter to address the case studies.  Save your notes and answers so that, as you study each chapter, you will be able to refine and add to your research results.*

27.    *Case Study A – Disability Payments*

Mr. Top received $25,000 in disability payments while he was recuperating from heart surgery.  Mr. Top, age 65, is a business consultant and works out of the home. You are asked to prepare this taxpayer's return.

a.    What is your initial research question or issue?

b.    Do you need additional facts or information to answer this question?  If so, what?

c.    In Step Two of your research – identifying and locating authority – you discover the following rules:

* Disability payments received when the taxpayer paid the premiums on the disability insurance are generally excluded from taxable income.

* Disability payments received when an employer paid for the premiums must usually be included as taxable income unless special requirements are satisfied (which the taxpayer fails).

Does this additional information change any of your answers in parts a and b?

d.    You assume that Mr. Top is self-employed since he works out of the home.  What is your initial conclusion to your research question?

e.    In reality, Mr. Top simply telecommutes and is an employee with a large corporation.  The corporation has always paid for the disability insurance of its employees.  How does the discovery of this new fact impact the initial conclusion you drew in part d?  What is the danger of assuming something without confirmation?

f.    Do you have an initial belief regarding the tax treatment in this circumstance?

28.    *Case Study B – Bonus Payments*

Sue is 30 years old and is president and a 51% shareholder of C Corporation. She informs you that C Corporation has 10 shareholders, all unrelated. Other than herself, no shareholder owns more than 10% of the company's stock. Sue plans to recommend to the board of directors that it authorize the payment of a bonus to her and three other top employees. She asks you, as the company's tax advisor, to counsel her on what the company needs to do so that the company can get a deduction for the planned bonus payments.

a.    What additional questions should you ask Sue before you begin your research?

b.    Can you think of any other potential sources of information that you might want to consider?

c.    In addition to asking Sue questions, how else might you discover some of the pertinent facts?

d.    Which of the preceding facts are relevant? Which are irrelevant?

e.    Is it likely that you will need to ask more questions at a later point? Why or why not?

f.    What is the first question you will try to answer in your research? How does your initial question change when you discover that in order for a bonus to be deductible, the employee's salary plus bonus must be considered "reasonable?" In addition, you learn from your client that the company is an accrual basis taxpayer.

g.    What is the taxpayer's desired result? Why is this important? How does it affect your role as tax advisor?

h.    Is this a planning research type of situation? How do you know?

i.    Sue tells you that she is considering paying a $100 bonus to each employee. Does this affect the tax research?

j.    Is it part of your responsibility to decide how much the bonuses should be? Why or why not?

29.    *Case Study C –  Changing Headquarters*

A taxpayer wants to change his company's headquarters – a t10-story building. The company currently owns the building outright.  The taxpayer has identified some potentially more suitable properties.  One of the possible properties is a single story building on a large, attractive lot.  The other property consists of a two-building complex, with retail shops on the ground floor of one building and residential rental property in a portion of the other building.  The taxpayer asks you to help him.

a.    What is your role as a researcher in this situation?  What are your responsibilities in each of the stages of the research process you are going to undertake?

b.    Assume that a colleague provides you with only the preceding facts.  He explains that the taxpayer is a very busy person with little patience. The client has arranged to meet with you and expects you to be fully prepared with the questions you want addressed and any additional information he will need to get for you.  Prepare for this meeting.  Make sure to have your initial list of questions and any additional questions you may want to ask depending on the client's answers.

c.    Knowing only the information provided previously, what possible research questions and issues can you spot?

d.    Before you attend the meeting with the client, you briefly refresh your memory about the rules related to selling and exchanging business property.  The parts of the law you find most pertinent are:

* Demolition expenses of buildings are not deductible.

* The sale of business property will usually trigger a taxable gain or a potentially deductible loss.  Relevant factors in determining whether something will trigger a gain or a loss include original purchase price, improvements, depreciation taken, and sales price of the property.

* The exchange of business property instead of the sale and purchase can result in no taxable gain or loss.

Does this additional information affect the questions you plan to ask?  How?  Does it affect the tax research issues you initially spotted?  Why?

e.    Role-play the initial meeting with the client. Have someone in your class play the client, and you play the researcher. How, if at all, did your research question change as a result of the client's responses? Was this simply a mechanical process? How did your critical thinking skills impact your selection of initial questions and responses to the client?

30.    *Case Study D – Damage Payments to Dentist*

Dr. Tooth is a 40-year-old dentist in Small Town, USA. He graduated from dental school five years ago and has had a thriving practice ever since. At the end of last year, however, Dr. Tooth had an ugly billing disagreement with a patient. The patient, a well-known wealthy entrepreneur, in retribution, maliciously spread a rumor that Dr. Tooth was a carrier of a serious infectious disease. This rumor destroyed Dr. Tooth's patient base, as most of his patients quickly switched dentists. As a result of the stress of losing his business, the cruel gossip that resulted from the rumor, and the financial strain caused by this situation, Dr. Tooth began to suffer from severe migraine headaches, loss of appetite, and significant facial twitches. Dr. Tooth sued the patient for defamation and intentional infliction of emotional distress. He won a jury verdict and has since recovered $3,600,000 in damages from the patient. Dr. Tooth has asked you to determine the appropriate tax treatment of this award.

a.    What additional questions do you need to ask Dr. Tooth before you begin your research?

b.    What additional potential sources of information should you ask for?

c.    Which of the preceding facts are relevant? Which are irrelevant?

d.    Is there a chance that you will need to ask more questions at a later point? Why or why not?

e.    What is the first question you will try to answer in your research? Are there any additional issues that you can identify at this time?

f.    After further discussions with the client, you discover that the $3,600,000 award was broken into the following categories. How does your initial question change?

i.    $1,000,000 lost wages. This was calculated on the basis that, in addition to the one year of wages lost since the date of the defamation, he has lost the ability to earn future wages in Small Town.

    ii.       $50,000 reimbursement for medical expenses incurred in consulting a neurologist, internist, and psychologist.

    iii.      $20,000 for future medical expenses anticipated.

    iv.      $30,000 reimbursement for attorney's fees paid.

    v.       $2,000,000 in punitive damages. The jury determined that the action of the patient was so malicious and heinous that the patient should be monetarily punished for his actions.

    vi.      $300,000 for pain and suffering.

    vii.     $200,000 to compensate Dr. Tooth for the emotional distress he suffered.

g.      Through your interview with the client you discover that, out of the award, he had to pay his attorney $50,000. Does this new fact impact your research?

h.      What is the taxpayer's desired result? Why is this important? How does it affect your role as tax advisor?

i.       Is this a planning research type of situation? How do you know?

31.    *Case Study E –  Housing Expenses*

Ellie Executive lives in Florida with her family in a home bequeathed to her by her parents when they passed away. This year her employer assigned her to a position in London. The assignment is for a minimum of four years. Because she grew up in the house, Ellie would like to keep it and rent it out. There is no mortgage on the home, so renting will create a positive cash flow situation for her. Her employer will be providing her with a housing allowance to cover her London housing costs. Ellie believes the house has a fair market value of at least $500,000. Ellie wants to make sure that if she ends up selling it, she will not have any taxable income from the sale. She has asked for your guidance.

a.      What additional questions do you need to ask the client before you begin your research?

b.      What additional potential sources of information might you want to ask for?

c.      Which of the preceding facts are relevant? Which are irrelevant?

    d.      Is there a chance that you will need to ask more questions at a later point?   Why or why not?

    e.      What is the first question you will try to answer in your research? Are there any additional issues that you can identify at this time?

    f.      What is the taxpayer's desired result? Why is this important?  How does it affect your role as tax advisor?

    g.      Is this a planning research type of situation? How do you know?

32.    *Case Study F – Retirement Contributions*

Tom Speeder is a new client.  From reviewing his client questionnaire, you were able to gather the following facts. He is 50 years old and was recently hired as a middle-level manager with a car manufacturer.  Tom's salary for the current year is $200,000.  In his initial meeting with you, Tom indicates that he would like you to look into an idea he has that will help him maximize his investment portfolio. He tells you that his new company offers its employees the ability to participate in a Section 401(k) plan. He believes it would be to his benefit to maximize his contribution to the company's 401(k) plan that provides for matching employer contributions up to $3,000 annually.  The plan provides for a maximum annual employee contribution of no greater than that provided by the IRC.

It is January, and Tom has indicated to you that he would like to accelerate the maximum contributions to the plan by contributing his entire monthly paycheck until he funds the entire amount.  He believes that such an arrangement will maximize the growth of his portfolio since the earnings are tax free from an earlier time frame than if he spreads the contributions out over the year.

    a.      Are there any additional questions you should ask the client before you begin your research?

    b.      What additional potential sources of information might you want to ask for?

    c.      Which of the preceding facts are relevant?  Which are irrelevant?

    d.      Is there a chance that you will need to ask more questions at a later point?   Why or why not?

e. What is the first question you will try to answer in your research? Are there any additional issues that you can identify at this time?

f. What is the taxpayer's desired result? Why is this important? How does it affect your role as tax advisor?

g. Is this a planning research type of situation? How do you know?

33. *Case Study G – Golf Ball Business*

Toby Power, a fellow Illinois resident, is a new client. Prior to her telephone call this morning (late November), all you really knew about Toby was that for the past five years she has been earning a living as a respected golfing instructor at a local club. She just called you to discuss a transaction she has entered into. You learn from your initial conversation with her that she and a group of friends formed a corporation for which the group will own 100% of the stock.

The corporation will be in the business of selling golf balls that it guarantees are indestructible and, because they glow in water and shade, cannot be lost. Toby transferred an office building to the corporation in return for her 20% stock ownership interest. Her eight other friends transferred primarily manufacturing equipment and cash for their evenly divided 80% interest. Toby has owned the office building for seven years and currently owes several hundred thousand dollars on two mortgages on the building. She estimates the fair market value of the building is about $1,000,000.

Toby informs you that her previous tax advisor, about whom she has nothing but negative things to say, counseled her that in order to avoid paying taxes on the transfer of the building to the corporation, she had to also transfer to the corporation a personal promissory note of $100,000. All of this occurred last year. She wants to know if the transaction was handled correctly, or if she needs to worry.

a. Are there any additional questions you should ask the client before you begin your research?

b. What additional potential sources of information might you want to ask for?

c. Which of the preceding facts are relevant? Which are irrelevant?

    d.      Is there a chance that you will need to ask more questions at a later point?   Why or why not?

    e.      What is the first question you will try to answer in your research? Are there any additional issues that you can identify at this time?

    f.      Is this a planning research type of situation? What do you believe the client wants?

34.    *Case Study H – Private School Expenses*

Mr. and Mrs. Worried, long time clients, have come to you for help.  Their 13-year-old son has recently been expelled from the public junior high school because of severe behavioral problems, culminating in a physical attack on a teacher and threats of future violence.  The son has been seeing a psychologist once a week but with no apparent positive results.  The Worrieds would like to send their son to a private school that can provide the type of psychological help they believe he needs.  The son's psychologist agrees that placement in a special school is imperative if there is ever to be a chance that the son will be a functioning member of society.

The Worrieds tell you that they are concerned because, although they have identified several potential schools, they do not have the financial resources necessary to pay the tuition and other additional costs.  Their insurance does not cover any of the costs.  However, the Worrieds believe that they may be able to afford the expenses if they can take them as a tax deduction.  They ask you for your opinion.

    a.      Are there any additional questions you should ask the clients before you begin your research?

    b.      What additional potential sources of information might you want to ask for?

    c.      Which of the preceding facts are relevant?  Which are irrelevant?

    d.      Is there a chance that you will need to ask more questions at a later point?   Why or why not?

    e.      What is the first question you will try to answer in your research? Are there any additional issues that you can identify at this time?

f.      What are the taxpayers' desired result? Why is this important?  How does it affect your role as tax advisor?

g.      Is this a planning research type of situation? How do you know?

h.      Do you have an initial belief regarding the tax treatment in this circumstance?

35.     *Case Study I – Deadly Fire*

Early this year, a taxpayer was clearing dry brush from behind his Malibu home in California.  He became frustrated with how long it was taking using his clippers.  He decided instead to light the brush on fire, believing this would be safe because it was an overcast day.  The taxpayer brought out a fire extinguisher in case the fire got out of control.  Unfortunately, some wind kicked up and fanned the fire out of control.  The fire completely consumed both his house and his neighbor's house.  The two children staying in the neighbor's house died of smoke inhalation.  The taxpayer was charged with negligent homicide.  The trial is pending.

The taxpayer wishes to take a casualty loss deduction for the loss of his house, which was worth an estimated $1,000,000 at the time of the fire.  The taxpayer purchased the home for $900,000 only six months earlier.  Insurance has refused to compensate for the loss under the circumstances. The taxpayer is currently out on bail. He is the brother of one of your very significant clients who has asked you to provide tax advice to the taxpayer.

a.      Are there any additional questions you should ask the client before you begin your research?

b.      What additional potential sources of information might you want to ask for?

c.      Which of the preceding facts are relevant?  Which are irrelevant?

d.      Is there a chance that you will need to ask more questions at a later point?   Why or why not?

e.      What is the first question you will try to answer in your research? Are there any additional issues that you can identify at this time?

f.      What is the taxpayer's desired result? Why is this important?  How does it affect your role as tax advisor?

g.    Is this a planning research type of situation? How do you know?

h.    Do you have an initial belief regarding the tax treatment in this circumstance?

36.    *Case Study J – Airline Costs*

A major airline manufacturer was found to be in violation of FAA safety rules and was forced to install additional safety devices in each of its planes within the next six months. The airline company projects the cost of this upgrade to be several million dollars, consisting of lost profits while the planes are on the ground, labor costs, and the cost of parts.  In addition, the airline spent $100,000 in attorney's fees in an unsuccessful fight to have the requirement waived. The CFO of the company wishes to know whether any or all of these costs can be deducted.

a.    Are there any additional questions you should ask the client before you begin your research?

b.    What additional potential sources of information might you want to ask for?

c.    Which of the preceding facts are relevant?  Which are irrelevant?

d.    Is there a chance that you will need to ask more questions at a later point?   Why or why not?

e.    What is the first question you will try to answer in your research? Are there any additional issues that you can identify at this time?

f.    What is the taxpayer's desired result? Why is this important?  How does it affect your role as tax advisor?

g.    Is this a planning research type of situation? How do you know?

h.    Do you have an initial belief regarding the tax treatment in this circumstance?

37.    *Case Study K – Vacation Home*

Mr. Z own three homes.  He lives in the San Francisco home full time.  The other two he and his wife vacation in each year.  He is considering replacing the house he has in Palm Springs, California, with another house in the same area.  The new home is a little larger and has a floor plan he prefers.  The two Palm Springs properties have almost the same fair market value.  Mr. Z would like to know if he can exchange the properties instead of selling the one he has now and then buying the new one.  He has a lot of built-up appreciation in the current Palm Springs home, and he doesn't want to have to pay taxes on it.  Someone told him at a cocktail party that he can avoid paying taxes if he does an "exchange."

Mr. Z and his wife own the homes outright.  There is no mortgage on the property.  They use the property occasionally.  This last year they vacationed at the home for about two or three weeks – they aren't sure of the exact days.  They have never rented the property and refuse to rent either the old or new property.  They don't need the money and don't like strangers in their house.

Mr. and Mrs. Z explain that they hold each of their vacation homes for two purposes.  One reason is to provide nice vacation opportunities. Another key reason for owning the homes is for their investment value.  Mr. Z chooses only homes in areas where he believes there are high appreciation possibilities.

Can Mr. Z take advantage of the tax-free exchange rules in the IRC?  How will you advise him?

a.     Are there any additional questions you should ask the client before you begin your research?

b.     What additional potential sources of information might you want to ask for?

c.     Which of the preceding facts are relevant?  Which are irrelevant?

d.     Is there a chance that you will need to ask more questions at a later point?   Why or why not?

e.     What is the first question you will try to answer in your research? Are there any additional issues that you can identify at this time?

      f.        What is the taxpayer's desired result? Why is this important?  How does it affect your role as tax advisor?

      g.        Is this a planning research type of situation? How do you know?

      h.        Do you have an initial belief regarding the tax treatment in this circumstance?

38.     *Case Study L –  Property Easement*

A developer acquired a parcel of unimproved real property that she would like to develop. Although the land is currently zoned for commercial use, the developer would prefer not to begin development until an adjoining city street is widened.  With a wider street, her development can include a landscaped public entrance and lighting. Without the widening, the development will have only one entrance that is neither as accessible nor as attractive.

The city plans to widen the street in order to build bike paths, which are now required in its new city plan.  It will be easier for the city to widen the street if it acquires an easement across the developer's property.  The developer is interested in providing this easement to the city.  However, before she acts, the developer would like assurance that she will receive a charitable deduction for the value of the easement.  She has asked you to request a letter ruling on this matter.

      a.        Are there any additional questions you should ask the client before you begin your research?

      b.        What additional potential sources of information might you want to ask for?

      c.        Which of the preceding facts are relevant?  Which are irrelevant?

      d.        Is there a chance that you will need to ask more questions at a later point?   Why or why not?

      e.        What is the first question you will try to answer in your research? Are there any additional issues that you can identify at this time?

      f.        What is the taxpayer's desired result? Why is this important?  How does it affect your role as tax advisor?

g.      Is this a planning research type of situation? How do you know?

h.      Do you have an initial belief regarding the tax treatment in this circumstance?

39.     *Case Study M – Interest Payment*

A taxpayer is president of a company. He is very wealthy and has a good deal of assets. He went to Bank 1 in January, Yr.1, to borrow $1,000,000. The taxpayer used the loan proceeds to purchase stock. The loan was secured by the stock purchased. The terms of the loan are that it is an interest-only loan, with interest to be paid annually on the anniversary of the loan. The rate is 10% per annum (simple) interest on the original loan face amount.

In November of Yr. 1, the taxpayer realized that he did not have the liquid funds to pay the $100,000 of interest due in January. He had sufficient assets, but, due to the business environment, he determined that the smartest economic move to make would be to borrow the $100,000 rather than to liquidate one of his investments. So he went to Bank 2 and borrowed $100,000. This loan was secured by assets other than his stock and was a regular amortizing loan. Interest was 9%. Upon receipt of the loan proceeds on December 1, Yr. 1, taxpayer deposited the proceeds into his regular checking account in Bank 3. The proceeds remained in the checking account for the entire month of December. The balance of the checking account during the month of December ranged from $100,000 to $115,000.

On January 2 of Yr. 2, the taxpayer wrote a check from his Bank 3 checking account to Bank 1 in full payment of the interest due. On his tax return for Yr. 2, the taxpayer took a deduction of $100,000 as an investment interest expense under Section 163. He had sufficient investment income to cover the deduction. The IRS has indicated it plans to disallow the interest deduction because the IRS believes it has never actually been paid as is required by the Code. The taxpayer would like you to see what the IRS is talking about and whether it has any grounds for its position.

a.      Are there any additional questions you should ask the client before you begin your research?

b.      What additional potential sources of information might you want to ask for?

c.      Which of the preceding facts are relevant? Which are irrelevant?

     d.      Is there a chance that you will need to ask more questions at a later point?   Why or why not?

     e.      What is the first question you will try to answer in your research? Are there any additional issues that you can identify at this time?

     f.      What is the taxpayer's desired result? Why is this important?  How does it affect your role as tax advisor?

     g.      Is this a planning research type of situation? How do you know?

     h.      Do you have an initial belief regarding the tax treatment in this circumstance?

40.     *Case Study N – Racing Car Expenses*

A taxpayer is a partner in an accounting firm.  He has always enjoyed auto racing as a hobby.  Now that his children are grown, he has decided to devote more time to auto racing.  He recently purchased a racing car for $50,000 and has entered several races.  He recently raced in his first competitive race and placed fourth, resulting in winnings of $5,000.  He expects to incur a number of expenses related to his racing: auto maintenance, storage, transportation, and so on.  He would like your advice as to how to proceed so that he can depreciate his car and deduct all of these expenses.

     a.      Are there any additional questions you should ask the client before you begin your research?

     b.      What additional potential sources of information might you want to ask for?

     c.      Which of the preceding facts are relevant?  Which are irrelevant?

     d.      Is there a chance that you will need to ask more questions at a later point?   Why or why not?

     e.      What is the first question you will try to answer in your research? Are there any additional issues that you can identify at this time?

     f.      What is the taxpayer's desired result? Why is this important?  How does it affect your role as tax advisor?

g.       Is this a planning research type of situation? How do you know?

h.       Do you have an initial belief regarding the tax treatment in this circumstance?

41.   *Case Study O – Retainer Fee*

Big Company paid $100,000 at the beginning of the year to a large law firm to retain its services should they be needed during the course of the year.  The law firm specializes in real estate law and is considered the best firm in this field.  Big Company feared that one of its competitors would engage the law firm. This would prevent Big Company from being able to use the firm's services because of conflict-of-interest rules that preclude a firm from representing different clients with actual or potentially adverse legal interests. To prevent this, Big engaged the firm and paid the retainer fee.  Occasionally, Big asked the firm to perform legal work in areas where Big's in-house lawyers were not as well equipped.  It is now December, and it is clear that a substantial amount of the initial retainer will not be used to pay for legal services rendered.  The retainer agreement provides in this case that any unused amount shall be returned to Big, with interest, at year-end.

Big Company is a longtime client of yours.  It has asked you to look into whether any of the retainer fee will be deductible.  It wishes to have this advice before the beginning of next year when it will determine whether to pay another $100,000 retainer to the law firm for the year.

a.       Are there any additional questions you should ask the client before you begin your research?

b.       What additional potential sources of information might you want to ask for?

c.       Which of the preceding facts are relevant?  Which are irrelevant?

d.       Is there a chance that you will need to ask more questions at a later point?   Why or why not?

e.       What is the first question you will try to answer in your research? Are there any additional issues that you can identify at this time?

f.      What is the taxpayer's desired result? Why is this important?  How does it affect your role as tax advisor?

g.      Is this a planning research type of situation? How do you know?

42.     *Case Study P – Sunk Development Costs*

Gobble Corporation purchased 400 acres in Green City to build a private golf course and residences.  The land cost $10,000,000. Gobble planned high quality, large houses that would sell for an average of $700,000.

It believed that the city's general plan allowed for this development.  Gobble spent in excess of $1,000,000 in fees to pay architects and civil engineers and for all necessary environmental studies and approvals.  Two years ago, Gobble's development proposal was approved by the city council in a 5-4 vote.

Two months after the vote, the membership in the council changed dramatically.  The major election issue was growth versus no growth.  The city voted strongly for a no-growth slate.  Given the strong community sentiment, the new city council voted to disregard the earlier vote and alter the city's general plan to prohibit such a large development. They decided to defeat the development proposal.

As a result, Gobble sued the city for unreasonably interpreting its planning documents and reversing its initial approval of the project, all to the grave detriment of Gobble.  Litigation has consumed almost two years and cost a total of $500,000.

Gobble's CFO has come to you to help with the company's tax return preparation. Gobble would like to deduct all the costs incurred in this transaction, including the $1,000,000 paid for the land acquisition.

a.      Are there any additional questions you should ask the client before you begin your research?

b.      What additional potential sources of information might you want to ask for?

c.      Which of the preceding facts are relevant?  Which are irrelevant?

d.      Is there a chance that you will need to ask more questions at a later point?   Why or why not?

e.      What is the first question you will try to answer in your research? Are there any additional issues that you can identify at this time?

f.      What is the taxpayer's desired result? Why is this important?  How does it affect your role as tax advisor?

g.      Is this a planning research type of situation? How do you know?

h.      Do you have an initial belief regarding the tax treatment in this circumstance?

# THE TAX RESEARCH PROCESS

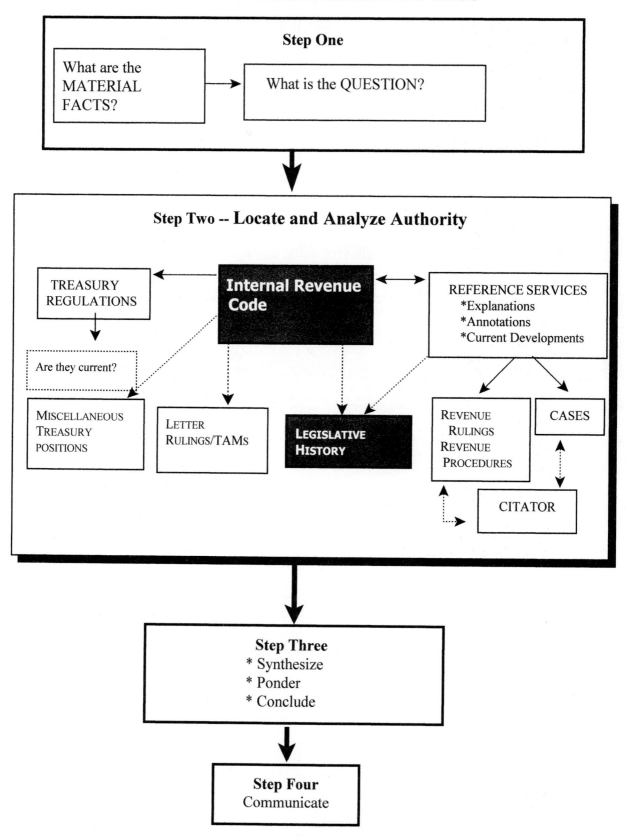

## Step One

| What are the MATERIAL FACTS? | → | What is the QUESTION? |

## Step Two -- Locate and Analyze Authority

TREASURY REGULATIONS

Internal Revenue Code

REFERENCE SERVICES
*Explanations
*Annotations
*Current Developments

Are they current?

MISCELLANEOUS TREASURY POSITIONS

LETTER RULINGS/TAMs

LEGISLATIVE HISTORY

REVENUE RULINGS REVENUE PROCEDURES

CASES

CITATOR

## Step Three
* Synthesize
* Ponder
* Conclude

## Step Four
Communicate

# CHAPTER TWO

# THE INTERNAL REVENUE CODE

*EXPECTED LEARNING OUTCOMES*

- Understand the use of the Internal Revenue Code
- Understand how Congress initiates statutory tax laws and amends the Code
- Know how to find legislative history
- Appreciate the organization of the Code
- Know how to properly cite the Code
- Know how to locate and analyze Code provisions

*CHAPTER OUTLINE*

- Overview
- Origin of the Internal Revenue Code and the Legislative Process
- Organization of the Code
- How to Cite the Code
- Analyzing Code Provisions
- Accessing the Code
- Chapter Summary
- Problems

## OVERVIEW

With the material facts at hand, you are now ready to begin Step Two of the research process – identifying and reviewing the authority relevant to your research question. The most significant resource in this process is the text of the statutory law itself – the Internal Revenue Code (IRC or the Code).

The Internal Revenue Code is a compilation of most of the tax statutes enacted by Congress. Ultimately, the tax researcher's job is to determine how the IRC applies to a particular situation. If the Code does not provide a definitive answer to the research question, you may need to turn to other legal authority, such as Treasury and judicial interpretations.

You may wish to begin your hunt for relevant authority with careful reading of the Internal Revenue Code, since it is the central source of authority of federal tax laws.  The flowchart at the beginning of this chapter illustrates the order of the research process.  However, it is also acceptable to begin tax research with a secondary source, such as a reference service, before commencing research in the Code itself. Whatever the order of research chosen, in most cases, you will ultimately need to carefully read the pertinent provisions in the IRC during this second stage of the research process.

☞ **The Internal Revenue Code is the central source of federal tax law.**

## ORIGIN OF THE INTERNAL REVENUE CODE AND THE LEGISLATIVE PROCESS

The states approved the Sixteenth Amendment to the United States Constitution in 1913. The amendment provides that:

*The Congress shall have power to lay and collect taxes on incomes, from whatever source derived, without apportionment among the several States, and without regard to any census or enumeration.*

Although Congress created a federal income tax soon after the passage of the Sixteenth Amendment, it was not until 1939 that the federal tax provisions were compiled into one distinct body of laws called the Internal Revenue Code.  Prior to 1939, each Revenue Act included all tax provisions, new and old.  Thus, whenever Congress amended the tax laws, it reenacted the entire set of tax laws, new and old.  The 1939 Code contained all applicable tax provisions in effect at that time. Subsequent amendments to the 1939 Code could then be made without the need for Congress to reapprove the entire Code.

☞ **The first Internal Revenue Code was enacted in 1939.**

Congress amended the Code numerous times and in 1954 adopted an entirely new Code.  In addition to a number of technical changes, the 1954 Code rearranged the numbering and structure of the Code into its current format.  In 1986, after hundreds of Code amendments, Congress again changed the name of the 1954 Internal Revenue Code to the "Internal Revenue Code of 1986" as a result of

☞ **The current Code is based on the organization and structure of the 1954 Code.**

the Tax Reform Act of 1986.  However, in contrast to the numerical and structural changes made in adopting the 1954 Code, the organization of the 1986 Code has remained substantially the same since 1954.

**How the Code Is Amended – The Legislative Process**

Over the years, Congress has amended the IRC many times. In fact, during the 1990s alone, Congress revised the IRC by passing over 48 different acts.  Particularly because each congressional change creates additional potential tax resources, it is important that you understand the basic legislative process involved in amending the Code.

Proposals for possible amendments to the Code originate from a variety of sources –  the president, Treasury Department officials, individual members of Congress, and interested parties such as the AICPA and the ABA.   However, the United States Constitution requires that any proposed change to the IRC must originate in the House of Representatives.  The **House Ways and Means Committee** is the specific House of Representatives committee responsible for developing and proposing tax bills. Once this committee develops a proposed bill, a **committee report** is generated that describes the proposed changes to the IRC.  Committee reports are a part of what is referred to as **legislative history** and are considered primary authority.

Next, the proposed tax bill moves to the full floor of the House of Representatives for debate and ultimately the House members  vote to pass or "kill" the bill.  Congress maintains records of these floor discussions,  although they are not a common source of information for the researcher because few libraries carry them. The debates (or hearings) do become part of the *Congressional Record*, which is included in some of the electronic legal libraries such as *Lexis-Nexis* and *Westlaw.*  Another potential source of this material is the Internet at www.gpo.ucop.edu. This address provides a gateway to the Government Printing Office and its database called "GPO Access." This database contains the full text of many items including the "Historical Congressional Record Index" and the "Historical History of Bills" since 1983.

> ☛ **The U.S. Constitution requires all amendments affecting tax laws begin in the House of Representatives.**

If the House approves the bill, the bill is assigned a number, for example, H.R. 2000. The text of the House bill then moves to the Senate, specifically, the **Senate Finance Committee**. This committee is responsible for marking up the House bill before passing its version on to the full floor of the Senate for debate and vote. The Senate assigns the bill its own Senate number. The Senate Finance Committee generates its own committee report which may also be a useful source for the tax researcher.

Even if the Senate approves the Senate bill, it is often quite different from the House proposal. A third committee – the **Conference Committee** – attempts to reach agreement and resolve outstanding differences between the two bills. The Conference Committee is comprised of designated members of both the House Ways and Means and Senate Finance committees. If the Conference Committee is able to reconcile the differences and reach a compromise, a final bill results. The Conference Committee generates a third type of committee report.

If a bill emerges from the Conference Committee, it is sent to the floors of the House and the Senate for approval or disapproval. If approved, the bill is delivered to the president for signature or veto. Once the bill is passed, it becomes an "act" and is assigned a number and often, a name. All or most of the of the provisions in a Federal Tax Act are incorporated into the Code. However, sometimes special transitional laws and provisions are not codified as Code amendments. Such uncodified provisions may involve a provision exempting a particular corporation or group of persons from the application of the Code amendment. Usually, the two main publishers of the IRC provide these uncodified laws following each Code section under the heading "Amendments." This does not make these laws less authoritative, just harder to find.

**The Senate Finance Committee considers all tax bills generated by the House.**

**The Conference Committee attempts to reach a compromise when the House and Senate bills differ.**

## THE FEDERAL TAX LEGISLATIVE PROCESS

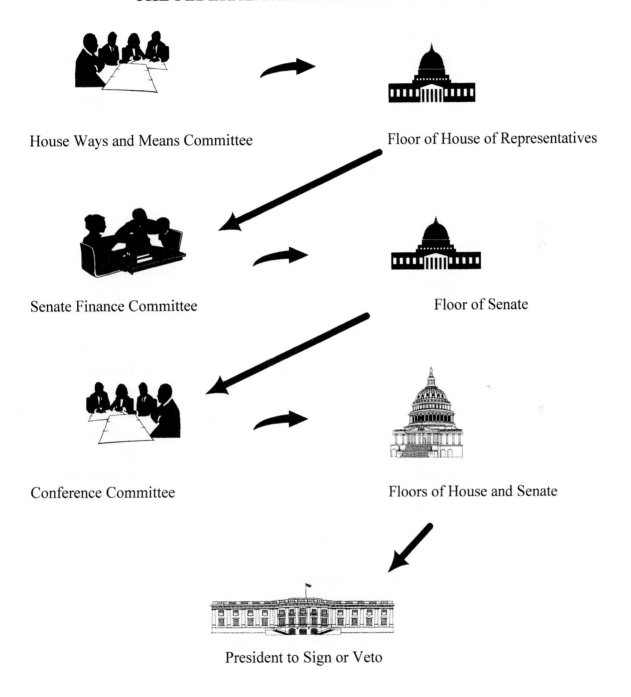

House Ways and Means Committee

Floor of House of Representatives

Senate Finance Committee

Floor of Senate

Conference Committee

Floors of House and Senate

President to Sign or Veto

Another Congressional committee – the **Joint Committee on Taxation** – generally plays a significant role in the process described. This committee should not be confused with the Conference Committee. The Joint Committee is not responsible for developing the legislation. It is a nonlegislative committee established by the Internal Revenue Code [IRC §§8002-8005] .

The staff of the Joint Committee on Taxation works with the congressional legislative counsel and staffs of the House Ways and Means and Senate Finance committees to draft the bills and the committee reports. During discussions in the House and Senate, members of Congress focus primarily on concepts rather than the precise statutory language. The two committees leave to their respective legislative counsel the responsibility of drafting the bill language to reflect the concepts agreed upon. The staff of the Joint Committee on Taxation also assumes primary responsibility for drafting the committee reports to reflect each committee's actions.

In addition, the staff of the Joint Committee on Taxation often provides a useful "General Explanation" of new laws soon after their enactment. This explanation is also often referred to as the "**Blue Book**" because of the blue cover of the paperback publication. The Blue Book is considered primary authority. The Joint Committee is also charged with investigating the administration of the tax system and proposing methods for tax simplification.

☛ **The Joint Committee on Taxation is different than the Conference Committee.**

☛ **The Blue Book provides potentially useful explanations of a new act.**

### How Legislative History Can Be Helpful to the Researcher

It is good practice to be aware of tax legislative activity in order to properly counsel taxpayers and assist in planning. There are many available sources of information regarding pending tax legislation. Both of the two major tax reference services (Commerce Clearing House and Research Institute of America) include a "New" or "Pending" legislation section that summarizes current legislative activity. *Tax Notes*, a weekly publication by a third publisher, Tax Analysts, also provides information regarding current congressional debates and hearings. Similar information is available in a daily newsletter entitled "Daily Tax Report" published by the Bureau of

National Affairs.

Once a tax act has been enacted, it frequently contains language difficult to comprehend. Particularly when new tax provisions are enacted, Treasury interpretations, court cases, and other authority may not be available to provide further insight as to the precise meaning or application of a new Code provision. Legislative history and the Blue Book may provide helpful guidance.

Committee reports may offer some insight into the legislative rationale for adopting a particular provision. They may provide additional information regarding the manner in which the new provision should be applied. Although it is generally unlikely that committee reports will definitively answer every research question, sometimes they provide useful information. The Blue Book is often more complete and provides the greatest amount of guidance regarding new provisions since it is written after their passage and with the intent to provide more detail about the new laws.

When using the committee reports, be sure to read and consider the appropriate committee report. First, review the Conference Committee Report. Often the Conference Committee Report will direct you to the most relevant committee report – either the House Ways and Means or the Senate Finance Committee Report. Remember, the Conference Committee is the compromise committee that attempts to reconcile the two House and Senate bills. Usually, the Conference Committee chooses either the House or the Senate's provision and, thus, follows that particular committee report. If, for example, the Conference Committee Report indicates that it followed the House provision, you must carefully review the House Ways and Means Committee Report. In this situation, you may not need to give credence to the Senate Finance Committee's report, since it may describe provisions that were not a part of the approved legislation.

Less frequently, the Conference Committee resolves conflicting provisions between the House and Senate bills by drafting a new set of provisions. If this is the case, your legislative history review must include a complete analysis of the Conference Committee Report.

☞ **Legislative history and the Blue Book are the only resources available concerning new Code amendments.**

☞ **When examining legislative history, make sure to study the appropriate committee report.**

## How to Research Legislative History

In order to locate relevant committee reports, it is helpful to understand the numbering system applicable to federal tax acts.  Once signed, a legislative act is assigned a two-part number. For example, the 1997 Taxpayer Relief Act is "P.L. 105-34."  "P.L." stands for "public law."   The first number ("105") indicates that it was the 105th Congress that passed the act. The second number ("34")  is simply a numerical designation.

The easiest method to determine the date and official name of an act is to look in the back of most volumes of the Internal Revenue Code for a listing of all the acts that have amended the Code.

---

**ILLUSTRATION**: (Taken from Internal Revenue Code published by CCH)

### PUBLIC LAWS AMENDING THE INTERNAL REVENUE CODE

| Public Law No. | Popular Name | Enactment Date |
|---|---|---|
| 101-194 | Ethics Reform Act | 11-30-89 |
| 101-221 | Steel Trade Liberalization Program Implementation Act | 12-12-89 |
| 101-234 | Medicare Catastrophic Coverage Repeal Act of 1989 | 12-13-89 |
| 101-239 | Omnibus Budget Reconciliation Act of 1989 | 12-19-89 |
| 101-280 | | 5-4-90 |
| 101-380 | Oil Pollution Act of 1990 | 8-18-90 |
| 101-382 | Customs and Trade Act of 1990 | 8-20-90 |
| 101-508 | Omnibus Budget Reconciliation Act of 1990 | 11-5-90 |
| 101-624 | Food, Agriculture, Conservation, and Trade Act of 1990 | 11-28-90 |
| 101-647 | Crime Control Act of 1990 | 11-29-90 |
| 101-649 | Immigration Act of 1990 | 11-29-90 |
| 102-2 | | 1-30-91 |
| 102-90 | Legislative Branch Appropriations Act | 8-14-91 |
| 102-164 | Emergency Unemployment Compensation Act of 1991 | 11-15-91 |
| 102-227 | Tax Extension Act of 1991 | 12-11-91 |
| 102-240 | Intermodal Surface Transportation Efficiency Act of 1991 | 12-18-91 |
| 102-244 | | 2-7-92 |
| 102-318 | Unemployment Compensation Amendments of 1992 | 7-3-92 |
| 102-393 | Treasury, Postal Service, and General Government Appropriations Act, 1993 | 10-6-92 |
| 102-486 | Energy Policy Act of 1992 | 10-24-92 |
| 102-568 | Veterans' Benefits Act of 1992 | 10-29-92 |
| 102-581 | Airport and Airway Safety, Capacity, Noise Improvement, and Intermodal Transportation Act of 1992 | 10-31-92 |
| 103-66 | Omnibus Budget Reconciliation Act of 1993 | 8-10-93 |
| 103-149 | South African Democratic Transition Support Act of 1993 | 11-22-93 |
| 103-178 | Intelligence Authorization Act for Fiscal Year 1994 | 12-3-93 |
| 103-182 | North American Free Trade Agreement Implementation Act | 12-8-93 |
| 103-260 | Airport Improvement Program Temporary Extension Act of 1994 | 5-26-94 |
| 103-272 | | 7-5-94 |
| 103-296 | Social Security Independence and Program Improvements Act of 1994 | 8-15-94 |

Another method of estimating the year of enactment is to apply a bit of mathematical wizardry to the first number of any act. This method will always produce the second year in the two-year Congressional term that passed the act.   For example, if you want to estimate, within a two-year period, the year in which P.L. 105-134 was enacted, perform the following calculation:

| **Method of Conversion:** | First number | = | 105 |
|---|---|---|---|
| | Multiplied by 2 | = | 210 |
| | Minus 112 | = | 98 |
| | Add 1900 | = | 1998 |

Picture reprinted with the permission of RIA.

Usually legislative history is most helpful when there is a new tax act.  In this case, finding the committee reports and the Blue Book is relatively easy.  Each of the major tax publishers publishes the text of the new law, the committee reports, and the Blue Book.  The reports are indexed and cross-referenced so that you can quickly and easily identify the relevant portions.

New legislation and committee reports are also available electronically, both from the fee-based sources discussed later in this chapter and at public Internet addresses.  Some Web addresses that provide the text of recent tax legislation include:

☞   The Library of Congress at www.loc.gov
☞   The Government Printing Office at
      www.gpo.ucop.edu
☞   thomas.loc.gov

☞ **The Internet contains many sources for legislative history.**

## Finding Committee Reports of Older Legislation

Even if the Code provision you are reviewing was enacted years ago, you may still need to consider its legislative history.  This may be appropriate when you have performed almost every step in the research process but are still unable to answer the research question. Perhaps the tax matter you are researching involves a transaction that occurred many years ago when earlier laws applied. This type of legislative history research is a bit more challenging unless your library has a copy of the texts of the applicable committee reports.

All federal tax committee reports are published in *Cumulative Bulletins* which are discussed in greater detail in the next chapter. However, when researching legislative history using the *Cumulative Bulletins*, it can be challenging to find the pertinent portion of the committee reports. Unfortunately, the bulletins provide no index enabling you to quickly find the relevant committee report. To make matters more difficult, the numbering system of federal tax acts does not correlate to the Code's numbering system in the Internal Revenue Code. The same holds true for committee reports. The listing of detailed amendments at the end of each Code section is the best source to obtain the citation to the relevant portion of the legislation. This is discussed later in this chapter.

☛ **The *Cumulative Bulletins* contain legislative history.**

For legislative history prior to the 1954 Code, *Siedman's Legislative History of the Federal Income Tax Laws* includes committee reports, hearings, and debates for selected legislation from 1861 to 1954. This source is organized by federal tax act and contains a detailed index and a useful Code section cross-reference key.

To find legislative history of enacted legislation after 1954, a service published by the Bureau of National Affairs called *Primary Sources* may be helpful. The table of contents is arranged by Code Section. Unfortunately, there is no topical index. Tax Analysts' *Tax Legislative History* provides committee reports for all tax acts since 1985. This excellent resource is only available on CD-ROM and on its Web-based database *TaxBase*. The major tax services (CCH and RIA) provide selected portions of committee reports through their multi-volumed reference services. These are available in paper and electronically.

☛ **Tax Analysts now offers access to all post-1985 committee reports.**

# ORGANIZATION OF THE CODE

In order to be a competent tax researcher, you must fully understand the organization of the Internal Revenue Code.  There are numerous reasons for this.  First, knowledge of the IRC's organization is instrumental in assisting you in determining when your research in the Code is complete.  Second, you will be able to identify more issues as you become more familiar with the Code.  Third, you can realize much greater productivity and avoid wasting time. Absent this fundamental understanding of the Code, you may consume unnecessary time trying to ensure you have not missed anything.

The Internal Revenue Code is a relatively small part of a much bigger set of federal statutory laws called the **United States Code** (the USC).  The USC is broken into divisions called "titles."  The Internal Revenue Code is **Title 26** of the USC.

The IRC is organized using many segments, starting with broad subject matter (for example, income taxes, estate taxes, and excise taxes) and narrowing to specific Code sections.

The segments, from broadest to narrowest, are:

- Title
- Subtitle
- Chapter
- Subchapter
- Part
- Subpart
- Section
- Subsection
- Paragraph
- Subparagraph
- Clause
- Subclause

☛ **Understanding the Code's organization produces increased research efficiency and accuracy.**

☛ **The Internal Revenue Code is Title 26 of the United States Code.**

**ILLUSTRATION: Excerpt from Table of Contents**

---

**ILLUSTRATION: Table of Contents (continued)**

---

In its own peculiar way, the Code is logically organized. Title 26 of the USC is divided into eleven subtitles. Logically, subtitles are divided into chapters covering major topics. Within each chapter, each major topic is generally assigned its own subchapter. Almost all pertinent tax provisions directly on the topic can be found in that subchapter. For example, in Subtitle A, there is a subchapter for determining taxable income (Subchapter B); another for regular corporations (Subchapter C); one for partnerships (Subchapter K); one for trusts (Subchapter J); and so forth.

Sometimes, two subchapters are interrelated, in which case you find the pertinent provisions in both. For example, assume you are interested in reviewing a corporation's ability to deduct employee bonuses. Skimming through the table of contents, it is clear that Subchapter C specifically governs corporate income tax matters. However, Code Section 162 in Subchapter B also appears to be relevant. In this case, you may need to review both subchapters.

Each subchapter has a logical structure using "parts" as the main organizational tool. Within each part, the specific tax provisions lie in the form of "sections." Sections are sequentially ordered within the part. Thus, when Congress passes a new tax law containing a provision relating to a specific part of a subchapter, the provision is placed in the next available Code section number within that part. If there is no unused Code section number within that part, a number is created by putting a capital letter next to the Code section number so that it can remain in the relevant part.

> ☞ **When there are no more numbers available, a new number is created by adding a capital letter**.

Study the table of contents on the preceding pages. The subject of computing taxable income appears well organized. Now study Part IX of Subchapter B. Notice the last several section numbers. They all begin with the number 280 but are followed by a capital letter. Although the sections share the same number, they are not related in any way other than through their common feature of disallowing deductions. The reason for this unusual numbering pattern is that when the current organization of the Internal Revenue Code was established in 1954, each part was allocated a certain amount of unused Code Section numbers in anticipation that Congress would add new tax provisions to the Code in the future. In 1954, Congress apparently did not anticipate that there would be so much activity in the Code involving the disallowance of deductions, so it failed to allocate enough free numbers to Part IX. Little did Congress realize that this area would prove to be among the most active legislative areas in the past four decades.

You may find comfort noting that the organization and logical structure of the Code have remained intact since the enactment of the 1954 Code. Rather than insert extra disallowance tax provisions in the next available section number, the provisions remain within Part IX and are given a created number. Therefore, you can reasonably anticipate that future provisions specifically disallowing deductions will be located in this part. Therefore, when you are researching a possible deduction, there are at least two portions of the Code to review: Subchapter B, Parts V-VIII and Part IX.

Each Code section has its own topical title, which indicates to the reader that the section focuses on a particular topic. For example,

IRC Section 163 is entitled "Interest" and IRC Section 164 is entitled "Taxes." Each section is further divided into categories as follows:

Section [represented by a number and sometimes also with a capital letter – Section **163** or **280A**]

Subsection [represented by a lowercase letter -- Section 163**(a)**]

Paragraph [represented by a number -- Section 163(a)**(1)**]

Subparagraph [represented by an uppercase letter -- Section 163(a)(1)**(B)**]

Clause [represented by a lowercase Roman numeral -- Section 163(a)(1)(B)**(i)**]

Subclause [represented by an uppercase Roman numeral -- Section 163(a)(1)(B)(i)**(II)**]

Note that a particular Code section may be broader in scope than its name or location implies. For example, IRC Section 83 is titled "Property Transferred in Connection with Performance of Services." The section is located in Subchapter B ("Computation of Taxable Income"), Part II ("Items Specifically Included in Gross Income.") This Code Section not only addresses income issues but also provides rules regarding the timing of compensation deductions, a provision that might also logically be placed in Subchapter E entitled "Accounting Periods and Methods of Accounting" (a subchapter of the Code that deals with timing issues).

## HOW TO CITE THE CODE

When referring to the Internal Revenue Code, there is a variety of available options. The context of your communication may determine which is the appropriate option to use. If you are drafting a formal document, such as a court pleading, the citation method may be quite different from the citation style when preparing an internal office memo, since a more formal citation method will likely be required. There are generally no hard and fast rules as to when you must use one citation method versus another. However, once you select a proper citation method, your use of the method should be consistent within the document.

☛ **Each Code section has its own complicated structure.**

☛ **The context of your writing will determine the best citation option.**

Following are various generally acceptable citation methods:

***Formal***:                    26 USC §163.

Title    United    Section 163
         States
         Code

This is a preferred style for court filings.  However, it is not a commonly used form of citation for other purposes.  In addition, always check each particular court's rules prior to filing documents to ensure they are in the proper format.

***Less Formal***:  IRC §163,  or  Code §163, or  IRC Section 163

☛ **The symbol for section (§) is appropriate in most circumstances.**

Notice that the symbol "§" can be used in place of the word "Section."  When citing multiple Code sections, it is also appropriate to use "§§."  For example, Code Sections 701-705 may be cited as "Code §§701-705." When writing a formal document, it is appropriate to spell out the official name of the Code the first time you refer to it. Thus, you may first refer to the Code as "The Internal Revenue Code of 1986, as amended." Because of the length of the cite, it is useful to immediately follow this reference with "(hereinafter referred to as 'IRC' or the 'Code')."  You can then use the less formal methods of citation listed previously in all subsequent references.

Remember that there are many other federal, state, and local "codes" in addition to the Internal Revenue Code.  Your research will occasionally require that you refer to one of the other codes, such as the Federal Bankruptcy Code.  To the extent that other codes are cited, be careful to make sure to distinguish one from the other.  A consistent citation method ensures that there is no ambiguity regarding which code and provision you are referring to.

It is important that the citation be as specific as possible with regard to the issues involved.  If you locate a key provision buried deep within a Code section, it may not be appropriate to simply cite the Code section alone.  You should also cite the specific subsection, paragraph, and so on, until the cite pinpoints the key provision.

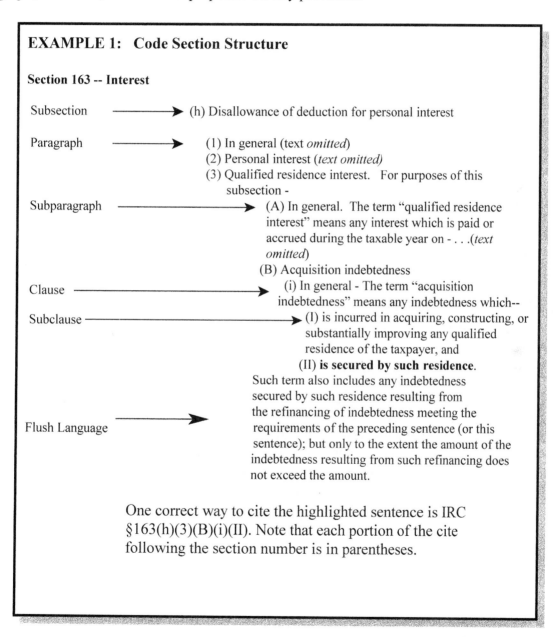

**EXAMPLE 1:   Code Section Structure**

**Section 163 -- Interest**

Subsection ⟶ (h) Disallowance of deduction for personal interest

Paragraph ⟶ (1) In general (text *omitted*)
(2) Personal interest (*text omitted*)
(3) Qualified residence interest.   For purposes of this subsection -

Subparagraph ⟶ (A) In general.  The term "qualified residence interest" means any interest which is paid or accrued during the taxable year on - . . .(*text omitted*)
(B) Acquisition indebtedness

Clause ⟶ (i) In general - The term "acquisition indebtedness" means any indebtedness which--

Subclause ⟶ (I) is incurred in acquiring, constructing, or substantially improving any qualified residence of the taxpayer, and
**(II) is secured by such residence**.

Flush Language ⟶ Such term also includes any indebtedness secured by such residence resulting from the refinancing of indebtedness meeting the requirements of the preceding sentence (or this sentence); but only to the extent the amount of the indebtedness resulting from such refinancing does not exceed the amount.

One correct way to cite the highlighted sentence is IRC §163(h)(3)(B)(i)(II). Note that each portion of the cite following the section number is in parentheses.

Section number citations usually alternate between numbers and letters. But there are some exceptions to this pattern.  For example, IRC Section 212 labels its subsections with numbers rather than letters.  Its first subsection is cited "IRC §212(1)."

Notice that the language after Subclause II in the preceding example (beginning with the language "Such term. . .") does not appear to belong to "Subclause II" because its margins are to the left of the subclause.  Practitioners commonly refer to this as "flush" language. Flush language is not directly preceded with any letter or number reference and is flush against the left margin of the page.  One way to make clear you are referring to this particular text is to refer to it as "the flush language of IRC §163(h)(3)(B)(i)."

☛ **Sometimes it is difficult to determine how to best cite to relevant "flush language."**

## ANALYZING CODE PROVISIONS

> *In my own case, the words of such an act as the Income Tax, for example, merely dance before my eyes in a meaningless procession: cross-reference to cross-reference, exception upon exception – couched in abstract terms that offer no handle to seize hold of – leave in my mind only a confused sense of some vitally important but successfully concealed purport, which it is my duty to extract, but which is within my power, if at all, only after the most inordinate expenditure of time. . .* Judge Learned Hand, *"Thomas Walter Swan," 57 Yale Law Journal. 167 (1947).*

Learning to read and interpret the Internal Revenue Code is definitely a formidable challenge.  Possessing the skill to analyze and apply statutory language sets you apart from other tax practitioners uncomfortable working in the Code.  Among other benefits, this skill enables quick adaptation to Code changes, creative tax planning, better advocacy on behalf of the taxpayer, and more accurate application of the federal tax laws.

The first point to remember is that reading the IRC means you are reading actual federal statutory language.  The Code is not intended to read smoothly like a novel, or even like a technical newspaper or journal.  So be patient.  Speed is not an initial goal when reading the Code; comprehension is.  With practice, you will find yourself more comfortable analyzing Code sections, particularly if you keep in mind the following suggestions.

☛ **Your goal when reading the Code is comprehension.**

## Practitioner Observation

Loella Haskew,
*Buckley, Patchen, Riemann & Hall*

"*Reading the Code is like learning a foreign language. It is a struggle. When I began my career, the Code was the last place I looked for an answer to a tax question. Just after the law changed regarding interest deductions, a client called to ask what would be the tax result of a home mortgage refinance. There was not a lot of commentary because the law was so new. I was forced into reading the Code to find the answer. That is when I realized I was finally fluent. From then on, I knew that pretty much everything else that I read was merely one person's interpretation of the law. I was confident that my interpretation was probably as reasonable as anyone else's.*"

## Getting Started – Finding the Applicable Code Section

You have identified the material facts and the research question. You pick up the IRC to begin your research. But where do you begin? How do you determine what to read? There are four different ways to pinpoint the most applicable Code section.

- ☞ Table of Contents
- ☞ Index
- ☞ Code Section
- ☞ Reference Service

☞ **There are four ways to begin working in the Code.**

If you are unfamiliar with the area of the federal tax law you are researching, one way to begin is to use the detailed table of contents found in the front of the Internal Revenue Code. Because the Code is logically organized, you can find the relevant subtitle, then the relevant chapter, subchapter, part, and so on, until you locate the pertinent Code section(s). This method takes a few minutes but provides you with the added benefit of appreciating the context of the

Code section you are about to read and also allows you to become more familiar with surrounding Code sections.

---

**EXAMPLE 2:  Using the Table of Contents**

Assume the question you are researching deals with the erroneous payment of employment taxes.  Look at the Code's table of contents.  After skimming the table, you will see that Subtitle C is titled "Employment Taxes." After skimming the chapters, you see that Chapter 25 contains a section entitled "Erroneous Payments." Now begin research in this section.

---

The Appendix illustrates how to locate the relevant Code section when using electronic resources.

You should also take advantage of the index provided by the publishers of the IRC.  It is found in the softbound versions of the IRC.  The Code index operates like any other except, instead of referring to a page or paragraph number, it refers directly to the relevant Code section.  The relative disadvantage of using the index to find the key Code section is that it does not provide the contextual comfort that the table of contents provides.  However, you can gain this information simply by going back to the table of contents once you know the Code section to see how the Code section cited by the index fits within the Code's overall organization.

☞ **The index can be an effective way to find the relevant Code sections.**

## ILLUSTRATION:  Excerpt from Commerce Clearing House Index to IRC

# TOPICAL INDEX

*References are to Code Section numbers.*

When you use the index, be patient in searching for the word you are looking for.  The index is somewhat analogous to the Yellow Pages – when looking for a doctor, you may have to look under "physicians," not "doctors."  The same holds true for the index to the Code.  Experience will help, but initially you may need to be creative in determining the appropriate word to look for.

For experienced practitioners, the easiest and quickest route to the relevant Code section may be to bypass both the table of contents and the index and go straight to the key IRC section.  You do this by simply recalling which Code section is relevant.  Of course, this is not always possible.  As you become better acquainted with the Code, make a concerted effort to remember the IRC section numbers you review.  Eventually, your familiarity with the IRC and specific section numbers will speed up your research by helping you quickly focus on the relevant IRC section.

☞ **The quickest route to the relevant Code Section is to know the Code section by recall.**

For practitioners with less experience or familiarity with specific provisions, a reference service may be the most useful method to use in locating the relevant Code sections.  This method is discussed in detail in Chapter Five.

Once you identify the Code section you believe is most relevant to the research question, you are ready to open up the Code, turn to the section and begin.

### Logical Skimming

It is a good research habit to read the entire Code section.  It is ill-advised to stop once you have read part of the Code section and conclude you have the answer to the research question. For example, you may believe that the general rule stated in the Code section resolves the research question.  However, a significant exception to that rule may lurk elsewhere in the Code section or in another provision that is cross-referenced. You must read the entire Code section to discover this. In addition, any provision terminating a Code section is usually near the end of the section.  For example, a Code

☞ **Careful skimming is a time-efficient skill**.

section may state a general rule that appears to resolve the question you are researching. However, the last subsection of the Code section may provide that the provision you seek to rely upon is effective only for tax years ending after December, 31, in year XX. Consequently, although the Code section's general rule may be interesting, it does not apply to the time period under consideration in the transaction you are involved in.

To complete your research in a timely manner and still "read" the entire IRC section requires using a process of skimming and careful reading. Remember the structure of a Code section discussed previously. There may be only one or two subsections pertinent to any given research question. This is why it is critical to read the Code section in the context of the research question. Make sure you are always focused on why you are reading the Code section – to answer a specific question you have. This helps you be an effective and efficient researcher. However, keep in mind that as you examine the Code, the research question(s) may change.

**Stay focused on the research question while examining the Code.**

Code sections contain headings or captions to describe the language in each segment. First, read the subsection heading. Determine whether it is relevant to the research question. If it appears relevant, read the language that follows. Then read the paragraph caption. Only read those paragraphs, subparagraphs, and so on, that appear relevant. Take your time. You will become more adept with experience and greater knowledge. Once you finish the subsection, move to the next Subsection heading. If it is not relevant, skip the entire subsection and review the next subsection heading. Continue this process until you reach the end of the Code section.

**Use the highlighted headings to efficiently skim the Code section.**

---

**EXAMPLE 3:  Logical Skimming**

Assume your research relates to the question of whether free parking provided to an employee by an employer is excludable from taxable income.  Assume you discover that the relevant provision is IRC Section 132.  The first Subsection [132(a)] is titled "Exclusion from gross income."  Clearly, you need to read all of this subsection since it may be directly relevant to the research question. After scanning the subsequent subsections, you will find IRC Section 132(f) entitled "Qualified Transportation Fringe."  Obviously, you should review this subsection and then continue skimming the remainder of the Code section.

---

### Terms of Art

One of the most difficult aspects of the Code is the use of what are commonly called **"terms of art."**  Terms of art are words that have a special meaning when used in the IRC.  This meaning may differ from the usual meaning the words have when used outside the context of federal tax practice.  For example, the word *paid* when used in the Code has a very specific meaning that is not exactly the same as the dictionary's definition.  So, too, with the words *property*, *income*, and *spouse*.  In fact, a sizeable percentage of the words used in the IRC are terms of art.

> The Code is replete with specially defined terms of art.

The Code's use of terms of art requires extreme caution when reading the Code and suspicion of the meaning of each word used.  Some words are easy to identify as terms of art because they have no meaning or application outside of the IRC.  Some examples are *applicable cost recovery method* [IRC §168] and *working condition fringe* [IRC §132(d)]. Once you identify the key words that are potentially relevant to your research question, one of your primary responsibilities becomes trying to discern the IRC's definition of those words.

In fact, most tax research involves attempting to better understand the actual meaning of a word or words in the IRC when considering a certain set of facts. Countless court cases and Treasury interpretations attempt to provide guidance on the meaning of the words *gross income*, *personal injury*, and *principal place of business* just to name a few.

Your first challenge is to identify the key words that apply to your question. The second challenge is to determine their meaning in the context of your taxpayer's facts.

---

**EXAMPLE 4: Identifying the Critical Term of Art**

You determine that your research question is whether the taxpayer, a cash-basis calendar year corporation, can deduct a large bonus to be paid in cash to an employee. In the following pertinent IRC section, the phrase *reasonable allowance for salaries or other compensation* is most critical to your research.

> Sec. 162. Trade or Business Expenses.
> (a) In General - There shall be allowed as a deduction all the ordinary and necessary expenses paid or incurred during the taxable year in carrying on any trade or business, including -
> (1) a **reasonable allowance for salaries or other compensation** for personal services actually rendered; . . .

---

☞ **First identify the words needing clarification in order to be able to answer the research question.**

The relevant words will be different depending upon the taxpayer facts.

---

**EXAMPLE 5: Identifying the Critical Term of Art**

Assume instead that your taxpayer has asked you whether an accounting firm can properly take a deduction for the cost of a trainer used by the firm to help its employees stay in good physical shape. Now the term *ordinary and necessary* would likely require further research.

> Sec. 162. Trade or Business Expenses.
> (a) In General - There shall be allowed as a deduction all the **ordinary and necessary expenses** paid or incurred during the taxable year in carrying on any trade or business, including -

---

☞ **Focus on the research question as you identify the key terms of art.**

Notice that in Examples 4 and 5, the same Code section was the focus of the research.  However, as the facts changed, so too did the key words requiring further definition. Each Code section is filled with terms of art.  One of the most important steps for efficient research is to carefully identify which key words require research.

---

**EXAMPLE 6:  Identifying the Critical "Term of Art"**

Your research question is to determine whether the cost of painting an office building is deductible. The term of art changes again.  Now you must determine whether painting a building is considered an *expense* under Code §162.

> Sec. 162. Trade or Business Expenses.
> (a) In General - There shall be allowed as a deduction all the ordinary and necessary **expenses** paid or incurred during the taxable year in carrying on any trade or business, including -

---

Once you identify the word or words requiring further elaboration, you can begin the process of fully answering the initial question. This step offers many possibilities. Sometimes, the IRC Section itself provides the meaning of the "term of art."  Frequently, when skimming through the Code Section, you will locate a Subsection entitled "Definitions." Carefully study the definitions for the information you are seeking.

☛ **Spend the necessary time to carefully identify the key terms of art relevant to answer the research question.**

☛ **The term of art may be defined within the Code section itself in a subsection called "Definitions."**

---

**EXAMPLE 7:  Defining the Term of Art**

You read IRC §132(f)(1), which provides:

(1) In general.  For purposes of this section, the term "qualified transportation fringe" means any of the following provided by an employer to an employee:
(A) Transportation in a commuter highway  vehicle. . .*language omitted*
(B) Any transit pass
(C) Qualified parking

To find the definition of these terms, you must again skim through IRC §132 until you see IRC §132(f)(5), which reads as follows:

(5) Definitions.  For purposes of this subsection -
(A) Transit pass.  The term "transit pass" means. . .
(B) Commuter highway vehicle. . . . *language omitted.*
(C) Qualified parking. The term "qualified parking"   means.. . . language omitted.

---

At other times, you can find the definition in the sentences of the IRC immediately following the use of the term of art you are trying to understand.  For example, IRC Section 132(a)(1) states that a "no-additional-cost service" fringe benefit will not be included in gross income.  Immediately following IRC Section 132(a) , Subsection (b) defines the term *no-additional-cost service*.

In addition, the Code may cross-reference you to another Code section that provides a more detailed definition of the term. For example, IRC Section 119(d) provides special rules regarding "qualified campus lodging" for employees of an "educational institution."  The term *educational institution* is defined in IRC Section 119(d)(4) as follows: "For purposes of this paragraph, the term 'educational institution' means an institution described in section 170(b)(1)(A)(ii)."

Another place to look for definitions in the Code is IRC Section 7701 which contains definitions of over 50 terms. Some of the

☛ **The term of art may be defined immediately after the word is first used or in a cross-reference.**

terms this section defines include *person, partnership, corporation, foreign, United States,* and *State*.

Sometimes the Code contains definitions for a term but not always in the particular section that uses the term.  The Code's index may also help you locate the definition.

☞ **IRC Section 7701 provides many useful definitions.**

---

**EXAMPLE 8:  Using the Index to Find the Definition to a Term of Art.**

IRC Section 119(a) provides for an exclusion of income for items provided to an "employee," "his spouse," or "any of his dependents."  The term *dependent* is not defined anywhere in the remainder of the Code Section, nor is there a cross-reference.  To locate the definition of *dependent*, look in the Code's index.  There, you will find that IRC Section 152 defines the word.

---

When applying the definition of a term provided in one Code section to its usage in another Code section, you must confirm that the definition is still applicable. Sometimes the same word may have more than one meaning.  For example, the term *wages* is used throughout the Code many times with different meanings. Checking the "limiting language" discussed later will help in this process.

☞ **The index may provide a quick reference to a key definition.**

Unfortunately, the meaning of particular terms of art will frequently remain unclear after reading the pertinent portions of the Code.  When this occurs, you will need to consult some of the interpretations of the Code and continue your steps in the research process as discussed in the following chapters.

☞ **Small words such as *and* can significantly affect the provision's meaning.**

## Connecting Words

Words like *and* and *or,* although not terms of art, play a significant role in the practical application of an IRC provision.  In a provision where two or more requirements are connected by the word *or*, the provision applies as long as any one of those requirements is satisfied.  If the connecting word is *and*, all requirements must be met.

**EXAMPLE 9: The Connecting Word *Or***

Notice the connector utilized in the three key requirements for taking a home office deduction:

> Sec. 280A(c) - Exceptions for Certain Business or Rental Use; Limitation on Deductions for Such Use -
>> (1) Certain Business Use. - Subsection (a) shall not apply to any item.. . . (text omitted) which is exclusively used on a regular basis -
>>> (A) as the principal place of business.. . .*(text omitted)*
>>> (B) as a place of business which is . . .*(text omitted)* trade or business, **or**
>>> (C ) in the case of a separate structure. . .*(text omitted)*

In this Code provision, the specific connector is *or*. It is critical for the tax researcher to notice the *or*. Its presence means that as long as the taxpayer satisfies any one of the three requirements listed, the rule in §280A(c)(1) applies. If the word *and* were inserted in place of *or*, the taxpayer would then be required to satisfy all three requirements.

**EXAMPLE 10: The Connecting Word *And***

The following IRC section uses the connector *and*.

> Sec. 71(b) - Alimony or Separate Maintenance Payments Defined. - For purposes of this section -
>> (1) In general. - The term "alimony or separate maintenance payment" means any payment in cash if -
>>> (A) such payment is received by. . . *(text omitted)*,
>>> (B) the divorce or separation instrument does not. . . *(text omitted)*,
>>> (C ) in the case of an individual legally separated. . . *(text omitted)*, **and**
>>> (D) there is no liability to make. . . *(text omitted)*.

From the use of the connector *and*, you know that all four of the requirements must be met if the payments are to be considered *alimony*.

Sometimes it is difficult to identify the connecting words. Watch for sentences that have both *or* and *and* in them. There is no special approach that eases the complexity when this occurs. Read carefully and slowly. Try to cluster those items connected with an *and* and determine what the *or* is referring to.

---

**EXAMPLE 11:  Combination of Connecting Words**

> Sec. 274(a)(1)(A) - With respect to an activity which is of a type generally considered to constitute entertainment, amusement, or recreation, unless the **taxpayer establishes that the item was directly related to,** <u>or</u> in the case of an item directly preceding or following a substantial and bona fide business discussion (including business meetings at a convention or otherwise), that such item was **associated with,** the active conduct of the taxpayer's trade or business.

In this provision, there are two different types of business activities: those that are directly related to and those that are associated with the business. It takes careful reading to notice the positioning of the word *or* and how it relates to the remainder of the sentence. The provision states that an item needs only to be *associated with* the taxpayer's business when it directly precedes or follows a bona fide business discussion. Otherwise, the item must be "directly related to" the taxpayer's trade or business.

---

**Measuring Words**

When reading the Code, you must also be careful to notice words frequently referred to as "measuring words." These are phrases such as *less than, equal to*, and *greater than*. These words significantly impact the application of a specific provision. However, sometimes it is easy to get so bogged down in the other complexities of the Code that you overlook the measuring words and misapply the Code section.

---

**EXAMPLE 12:  Use of Measuring Words**

A taxpayer uses his vacation home for vacation purposes 14 days a year. He rents the home out at fair rental for 30 days. You have been asked to determine whether the vacation home limitations of IRC Section 280A apply to the taxpayer.  The pertinent language from the section is:

> (1) In general - For purposes of this section, a taxpayer uses a dwelling unit during the taxable year as a residence if he uses such unit (or portion thereof) for personal purposes for a number of days which **exceeds the greater** of -
>> (A) 14 days, or
>> (B) 10 percent of the number of days during such year for which such unit is rented at a fair rental.

The key measuring words here are *exceeds the greater of.*  First, you must determine which is "greater": 14 days or 10% of the rental days.  For the taxpayer, 10% of the rental days totals three days (10% of 30 days). Therefore, 14 days is greater.  Next, the section instructs you to determine if the taxpayer's personal use days (14) exceed the greater number that we already determined was 14.  Since 14 does not exceed 14, the taxpayer is not deemed to have used the "dwelling unit during the taxable year as a residence."

---

## Limiting Language

Almost every provision in the Code includes language informing the reader of its scope. Thus, you frequently see *for purposes of* followed by one of the types of organizing divisions in the Code: title, subtitle, chapter, subchapter, and so on.

You must understand the scope of a provision in order to fully understand its effect. After all, you may discover that the scope is so limited that the provision does not apply  to the research question.  For example, a provision that is prefaced with *for purposes of this title* applies to every provision in the Internal Revenue Code.  But a Code section commencing with *for purposes of this section* should generally not be applied to another Code section. The exception to this occurs when a Code section specifically refers to the section with the limiting language.

---

**EXAMPLE 13:  Limiting Language**

The research involves the application of IRC Section 119, which uses the word *dependent* but does not define it. You discover that IRC Section 152(a) provides a definition of the term, as follows:

> IRC Section 152(a) General Definition. - **For purposes of this subtitle**, the term "dependent" means. . .

The limiting language indicates that the definition applies to the Subtitle that includes IRC §152.  Upon reviewing the table of contents, it is clear that this is Subtitle A – Income Taxes.  Next you must determine whether IRC §119 is in the same subtitle.  The table of contents indicates that it is. Therefore, you can apply the meaning you found in IRC §152 to IRC §119. Usually, you will not be able to use this meaning ascribed to the word *dependent* to apply to a Code section outside of Subtitle A.  The definition can be used outside Subtitle A only when a Code section in another Subtitle specifically refers to IRC §152 and the definition of *dependent*, or when other appropriate federal tax laws apply such meaning.

---

## Pinballing

Given the complexity and sheer volume of the Code,  its drafters rely heavily on a technique referred to by some as "pinballing."  When the provisions of one Code section are applicable to another Code section, rather than restating the provisions, a mere reference to the Code section itself is used in place of the words.

---

**EXAMPLE 14:  Pinballing**

The home interest deduction rules in IRC Section 163(h)(4) provide the following:

> (A) Qualified Residence. -
>> (I) In General. - The term "qualified residence" means -
>>> (I) the principal residence (within the meaning of section 121) of the taxpayer,  and
>>> (II) one other residence of the taxpayer which is selected by the taxpayer for purposes of this subsection for the taxable year and which is used by the taxpayer as a residence **[within the meaning of section 280A(d)(1)]**. . . *language omitted.*

When applying this section, you must also read Section 121 and, perhaps, Section 280A(d)(1).  Those sections in turn may refer you to yet other sections.  And so on and so on.  Although a temptation, it is not wise to ignore the reference and try to sneak by without turning to the referenced section.  To do so is to risk applying the Code section incorrectly.

---

**Pronoun He and Gender Issues**

The Code uses the pronoun *he* throughout, whenever referring to an individual.  The reasoning behind this is simply to keep the Code from being any longer than it already is.  Imagine its length if the Code were to use *he/her* throughout.  Similarly, the Code often employs the term *husband* when *wife* may likewise be intended. [See IRC §7701(a)(17), which states that ". . . wherever appropriate to the meaning of such sections, the term 'husband' shall be read 'wife' and the term 'wife' shall be read 'husband.'"]

**"Sunset" Provisions**

Usually, tax provisions in the IRC apply until Congress repeals or amends them in some way.  However, Congress sometimes places a time limitation within the  tax provision itself.  This requires Congress to reenact the law if it wishes to continue the application of the provision.  Often sunset provisions are a method of controlling the fiscal cost that a tax credit, exclusion, or deduction gives rise to.  Sometimes Congress simply allows these types of provisions to expire without any action. At other times Congress decides to reenact the provision. Provisions with an effect for a specified time period are referred to as *sunset provisions*. Note that sunset language usually comprises one of the last Subsections in the Code section.

☛ **Provisions terminating the Code Section are found at the end of the Section.**

---

**EXAMPLE 15: Sunset Provision**

IRC Section 45A contains a sunset provision. This section provides for a certain type of tax credit. The following is the current sunset provision for that section:

> Sec. 45A(f) - TERMINATION. - This section shall not apply to taxable years beginning after December 31, 2003.

---

**Transitional Provisions**

Similar to sunset provisions, a transitional provision often bridges the gap from the expiration date of amended or repealed provisions to the effective date of new provisions. Often taxpayers continue to engage in various taxable transactions regardless of pending legislation. Transitional rules may provide taxpayers a "safe harbor," which places the transaction in a position of avoiding the potentially negative impact of a new law. For example, IRC §163(h)(3)(D)(ii) provides an exception and "safe harbor" for most home mortgages incurred prior to the enactment of the act incorporating the particular provision limiting the type of interest described.

☛ **Watch for special transitional rules.**

## EXAMPLE 16: Transitional Provisions

Notice the potential importance of the following transition language found at IRC Section 163(h)(3)(D).

> (D) Treatment of indebtedness incurred on or before October 13, 1987.
>    (i) In general. In the case of any pre-October 13, 1987, indebtedness—
>       (I) such indebtedness shall be treated as acquisition indebtedness, and
>       (II) the limitation of subparagraph (B)(ii) shall not apply.
>    (ii) Reduction in $1,000,000 limitation. The limitation of subparagraph (B)(ii) shall be reduced (but not below zero) by the aggregate amount of outstanding pre-October 13, 1987, indebtedness.
>    (iii) Pre-October 13, 1987, indebtedness. The term "pre-October 13, 1987, indebtedness" means—
>       (I) any indebtedness which was incurred on or before October 13, 1987, and which was secured by a qualified residence on October 13, 1987, and at all times thereafter before the interest is paid or accrued, or
>       (II) any indebtedness which is secured by the qualified residence and was incurred after October 13, 1987, to refinance indebtedness described in subclause (I) (or refinanced indebtedness meeting the requirements of this subclause) to the extent (immediately after the refinancing) the principal amount of the indebtedness resulting from the refinancing does not exceed the principal amount of the refinanced indebtedness (immediately before the refinancing).

☛ **Because of the numerous amendments to the Code, understanding the transitional rules can be critical.**

## Errors and Omissions

The numerous and frequent Code amendments of Congress have resulted in an increasing amount of numbering and cross-referencing errors. For example, IRS §163(h) contains two paragraphs identified as Paragraph "4." Cross-referencing errors frequently abound until a Technical Correction Act is enacted. A cross-reference, once correct, may become incorrect when the Code section is amended and the numbering is changed. Unfortunately, the legislative staff who draft the actual Code language frequently fail to correct the cross-reference.

☛ **The Code frequently contains typographical and other minor errors needing correction.**

## Use of Historical Notes

Because Congress frequently amends the Internal Revenue Code, it is often useful to investigate a provision's language prior to its revision. Such information can be useful to understand current language as well as to provide helpful guidance regarding transitional rules and effective dates.

**In print**, such information is usually provided following the text of the current Code section in smaller type face under the title "Amendments."

☛ **Historical notes may contain much useful information.**

---

### EXAMPLE 17:  Historical Notes

You can find the following immediately under the provisions of IRC Section 132(a).

**Amendments**

Economic Growth and Tax Relief Reconciliation Act of 2001, June 7, 2001, (2001) **P.L. 107-16, §665(a):**

Act Sec. 665(a) amended Code Sec. 132(a) by striking "or" at the end of paragraph (5), by striking the period at the end of paragraph (6) and inserting ", or", and by adding at the end a new paragraph (7) to read as above.

**The above amendment applies to years beginning after December 31, 2001.**

Economic Growth and Tax Relief Reconciliation Act of 2001, June 7, 2001, (2001) **P.L. 107-16, §901, provides:**

**SEC. 901. SUNSET OF PROVISIONS OF ACT.**

(a) IN GENERAL.--All provisions of, and amendments made by, this Act shall not apply--

(1) to taxable, plan, or limitation years beginning after December 31, 2010.

Notice that the amendments follow a reference to P.L. 107-16, §§665 and 901. This represents the public law that changed the provisions. The Sections are act sections (not the IRC section). You will find this information useful if you need to go back and review the congressional history of the Act.

☛ **The reference to the P.L. section does not correlate to the numbering of the Code itself.**

**Electronically**, the historical information can be found by referring to the Code section itself. Each element of the Code section, including its history, is a separate entry that is easily accessed.

## ACCESSING THE CODE

You can access the Internal Revenue Code in a variety of ways. It is available in:

- ▸ print with annotations
- ▸ full-text softbound
- ▸ selected softbound sections
- ▸ electronically on CD-ROM
- ▸ electronically via modem
- ▸ electronically via the Internet

The simplest and most time-efficient way to access the IRC for many tax practitioners is to use the softbound, full-text, print version. Most tax practitioners have a copy of the softbound Code on their desks for quick and easy access. For many, the books are easier to skim and refer to than the electronic format.

In addition to the softbound Codes, you can access the Code in print using the annotated Codes available with multivolume reference services. In these services, the publishers annotate each Code section. Chapter Five discusses these services in more detail. Two of the largest and most well known tax publishers, Commerce Clearing House (CCH) and Research Institute of America (RIA), produce the Code in both the softbound and annotated formats.

The following chart compares each of the print sources of the IRC.

| PRINT SOURCES OF THE INTERNAL REVENUE CODE | | | |
|---|---|---|---|
| PAPER | | | |
| FORMAT | DESCRIPTION | ADVANTAGES | CHALLENGES |
| **Softbound**<br>CCH | ♦ Two volumes of unabridged Code text<br>♦ Historical notes following each Code subsection<br>♦ Index at the end of each volume<br>♦ Table of contents at the beginning of the first volume<br>♦ Available in abridged or full-text format<br>♦ Reissued twice a year. Each issue requires a new purchase. | ♦ Portable<br>♦ Easiest to read<br>♦ Kept current<br>♦ Relatively inexpensive | ♦ Cannot perform electronic searches |
| RIA | ♦ One volume of unabridged Code text<br>♦ Historical notes following each code subsection<br>♦ Index at beginning of volume<br>♦ Table of contents following index<br>♦ Available in abridged or full-text format<br>♦ Reissued twice a year. Each issue requires a new purchase. | | |
| **Hardbound**<br>CCH<br>RIA<br>Mertens | Separate full-text volumes as part of multivolume reference service. Every Code section also separately included in text of reference service volumes | ♦ Kept current | ♦ Not easily portable<br>♦ Cannot perform electronic searches |

You can also access the entire text of the Code electronically. You can find the Internal Revenue Code on CD-ROM and via the Internet. The following chart provides more information about these sources. Commerce Clearing House, Research Institute of America, Lexis-Nexis and Tax Analysts all offer full-text electronic tax databases. Chapter Five discusses each of these proprietary services in more depth.

In addition, the public has free access to the full text of the Internal Revenue Code over the Internet. Individuals, educational institutions, and the government all provide full-text copies of the Code on the Internet. Commerce Clearing House now also offers free access to the Code. Be careful when using the public Internet for research if the provider is not the government or an established tax publisher. The Code language posted may be outdated and, therefore, unreliable. In addition, sometimes the text is not converted to readable text accurately. It is not unusual to find typographical errors and incorrect placement of text in the versions of the IRC made available to the public over the Internet. See the following chart for more information about these sites.

| ELECTRONIC SOURCES OF THE INTERNAL REVENUE CODE | | | |
|---|---|---|---|
| **FORMAT** | **DESCRIPTION** | **ADVANTAGES** | **CHALLENGES** |
| **CD-ROM**<br><br>CCH<br>RIA<br>Kleinrock<br>Tax Analysts | Each contains the full text of the Code on one disk. Accessible using either table of contents or searching capabilities. Depending on the contract purchased, revised disks provided either on a monthly, semiannua,l or annual basis. | ◆ Ability to electronically "search" through the Code for a word or words. If unable to identify the key Code section using the table of contents or the index, an electronic search may prove useful.<br>◆ Updating abilities of the CD-ROM.<br>◆ Word processing opportunities. You are able to cut and paste into your word processing document.<br>◆ Makes cross-referencing easier because you usually are able to quickly move from a cite in the middle of a sentence directly to the provision cited. | ◆ Reading the IRC is difficult enough; having to read it electronically can make the process more burdensome.<br>◆ Skimming through a Code section may be more difficult.<br>◆ Using the search mechanism may land you in a place in the Code for which you have no idea of the context and the surrounding material. Your comfort that you have found the critical section and read all the relevant surrounding provisions may be reduced as a result.<br>◆ Some CD-ROM products do not have the historical amendments found in the paper products. |
| **Proprietary database via Internet**<br>CCH<br>RIA<br>Lexis- Nexis<br>Tax Analysts | Full-text databases that include a current version of the IRC. Accessible through table of contents or search modes. | Same as CD-ROM but can be more current. | Same as CD-ROM. |

| ELECTRONIC SOURCES OF THE INTERNAL REVENUE CODE | | | |
|---|---|---|---|
| **FORMAT** | **DESCRIPTION** | **ADVANTAGES** | **CHALLENGES** |
| **Public Internet** (see table below) | Full-text databases maintained on the Internet by various organizations, schools, and individuals. | Free access. | ♦ Usually outdated.<br>♦ Often cannot search for key words as you can using the other electronic Code sources.<br>♦ Often cannot pinball rapidly through linking as you can using the other electronic sources.<br>♦ Not always exact copy of the law. |

## INTERNET SITES WITH THE IRC

| ADDRESS | PROVIDER | Table of Contents | Text Links | Key Word Search | Cut and Paste |
|---|---|---|---|---|---|
| tax.cchgroup.com/freecoderegs | Commerce Clearing House | yes | yes | yes | yes |
| www4.law.cornell.edu/uscode/26 | Cornell Law School | yes | yes | yes | yes |
| www.gpo.ucop.edu/catalog/ | Gov't Printing Office via Univ. of California | yes | yes | yes | yes |
| www.fourmilab.ch/ustax/ustax.html | John Walker | yes | yes | yes | yes |
| law.house.gov/ | House of Representatives | no | no | yes | no |

# CHAPTER SUMMARY

After identifying the relevant facts and the research question, one possible first step in finding relevant authority is to turn to the Internal Revenue Code. The Code embodies almost all of the federal tax laws and is the most central authority in federal tax research.

The Code is a codification of all the federal tax acts enacted by Congress and signed into law by the president. It is changed only through Congressional action, which begins in the House

Ways and Means Committee.  Any tax bill making it through the House of Representatives goes to the Senate Finance Committee and, eventually, on to the floor of the Senate.  Usually the Senate and House do not entirely agree on all the changes, so the two bills go to a Conference Committee that attempts to resolve the differences.  A final proposed bill then goes to the House and Senate for delivery to the president for approval or veto.  Each of these steps produces committee reports that are useful to the researcher in determining the intent of Congress and the application of the tax provisions.

You can most easily locate committee reports of recent bills in the softbound books printed by each of the major tax publishers, which contain the text of the bill and all the committee reports.  All post-1985 legislative history is available through a service provided by Tax Analysts. You can review older legislative history in either the Cumulative Bulletins or over the Internet.  In addition to the legislative committee reports, the Staff of the Joint Committee on Taxation "Blue Book" provides useful interpretive guidance regarding new tax laws.

Researching the Code requires an appreciation for its organization and structure. The Code is broken down into many topically oriented divisions, the most focused one being the "section."  Code sections are numbered sequentially with no duplicate numbering. This logical numeric organization enables the researcher to find the most pertinent portion of the Code by using the table of contents.  In addition, you can usually find the key Code section by using the index available.

You must read the Code carefully and deliberately.  When studying the Code, you must be aware of all the words that have  meanings other than their everyday meanings.  You must identify the key terms of art pertinent to the research question and then attempt to find their definitions in the context of the taxpayer's facts.  This will require further study of the Code section and will often result in research outside of the Code.

In addition to terms of art, you must be on the alert for measuring words  – *no more than, greater than, less than*, and so on. –  as well as words that limit in some way the application of the provision (*for purposes of. . .*).  Be careful to notice whether two or more requirements are connected with an *and* or an *or*.  When a Code section refers to another section, even in mid-sentence, it is important to read the cross-referenced Code section, even though this "pinballing" style is often time-consuming and hard to follow.

Because termination or sunset provisions are usually at the end of a Code section, it is important to always logically skim through the entire Code section, even though you may feel you have already found an answer. This is particularly true given the poor internal organization of most Code sections.

Finally, when reading a Code section, it is helpful to be aware of the history of amendments made to the particular section.  Such information can be useful in providing guidance regarding effective dates as well as more substantive information.

The Internal Revenue Code is available in a variety of forms.  For those who prefer to read the Code like a book, they can find the full text in both softbound desktop volumes as well as hardbound volumes that are part of a larger reference service.  In addition, the Code is available electronically on a variety of CD-ROM sources and on the Internet.  Each format has advantages and challenges.

# PROBLEMS

## *KEY CONCEPTS*  (1– 17)

1.      Define and discuss the following terms:

        a.      Legislative Committee Reports
        b.      The Joint Committee on Taxation
        c.      The Blue Book
        d.      USC
        e.      Title 26
        f.      Flush language
        g.      Sunset provisions
        h.      Terms of art
        i.      IRC Section 7701
        j.      Limiting language
        k.      Transitional provisions

2.      Explain the role of the following committees in the tax legislative process: House Ways and Means, Senate Finance, Conference Committee.

3.      What resources are generated by the legislative process?  In what way are resources useful?

4.      How can you become informed regarding current congressional activity in tax legislation?

5.      Where can you find committee reports of new legislation?  How do you find committee reports reflective of prior older legislation?

6.      Discuss how the Internal Revenue Code is organized.  Why is it important to understand its organization?

7.      Give examples of three methods of citing the Internal Revenue Code.

8.      What topic is covered in the following portions of the IRC?

    a.      Subtitle F, Chapter 61, Subchapter A
    b.      Subtitle C, Chapter 21, Subchapter A, Section 3102
    c.      Subtitle H, Chapter 95
    d.      Subtitle A, Subchapter E, Part II, Subpart C

9.      Name three ways to identify which part of the Internal Revenue Code is relevant in a research project.

10.     What is the connecting word in the following Code excerpt?  How does the meaning change if the connecting word is changed?

**Section 162(e)**

(e) Denial of deduction for certain lobbying and political  expenditures

(1) In general - No deduction shall be allowed under subsection (a) for any amount paid or incurred  in connection with -

(A) influencing legislation,

(B) participation in, or intervention in, any political campaign on behalf of (or in opposition to) any candidate for public office,

(C) any attempt to influence the general public, or segments thereof, with respect to elections, legislative matters, or referendums, or

(D) any direct communication with a covered executive branch official in an attempt to influence the official actions or positions of such official.

11.     What is the official name of the Federal Tax Act P.L. 104-168?  When did this act become law?  How did you find the answer?

12.     What is the official name of the Federal Tax Act 107-16?  When did this act become law?  How did you find the answer?

13.     When can historical notes to a Code section be helpful?

14.     Name all the different sources for reading the Internal Revenue Code.  What are the major advantages and challenges for each different type of source?

15. Locate IRC Section 162 and answer the following. IRC Section 162 is part of which:

    a.    Title
    b.    Subtitle
    c.    Chapter
    d.    Subchapter

16. Locate IRC Section 162 and answer the following:

    a.    What subsections does it include?
    b.    What paragraphs does Subsection (d) include?
    c.    What subparagraphs does Section 162(d)(3) include?

17. In general, what does IRC Section 7805 provide?

## PRACTICAL APPLICATIONS (18-55)

18. Correctly cite the highlighted sentence in the following excerpt from the Internal Revenue Code.

**Section 280G - Golden Parachute Payments**
(a) General rule - No deduction shall be allowed under this chapter for any excess parachute payment.
(b) Excess parachute payment - For purposes of this section -
  (1) In general - The term "excess parachute payment" means an amount equal to the excess of any parachute payment over the portion of the base amount allocated to such payment.
  (2) Parachute payment defined
    (A) In general - The term "parachute payment" means any payment in the nature of compensation to (or for the benefit of) a disqualified individual if -
      (i) such payment is contingent on a change -
        (I) in the ownership or effective control of the corporation, or
        (II) in the ownership of a substantial portion of the assets of the corporation, and
      (ii) the aggregate present value of the payments in the nature of compensation...*(language omitted)*.
    (B) Agreements - The term "parachute...*(language omitted)*.
    (C) Treatment of ...*(language omitted)*...pursuant to -
      (i)an agreement entered into within 1 year before the change described in subparagraph (A)(i), or
      **(ii)an amendment made within such 1-year period of a previous agreement, ...***(language omitted)*.

19.    Correctly cite the highlighted sentence in the following excerpt of the IRC.

> **Section 460 - Special Rules For Long-Term Contracts**
> (a) Requirement That Percentage of Completion Method Be Used. - In the case of any long-term contract, the taxable income from such contract shall be determined under the percentage of completion method...*(language omitted)*
> (b) Percentage of Completion Method. -
> (1) Requirements of Percentage of Completion Method. - Except as provided in paragraph (3), in the case of any long-term contract with respect to which the percentage of completion method is used -.
> (A) the percentage of completion shall be determined by comparing costs allocated to the contract ...*(language omitted),* and
> (B) upon completion of the contract (or, with respect to any amount properly taken into account after completion of the contract, when such amount is so properly taken into account), the taxpayer shall pay ... *(language omitted).*
> **In the case of any long-term contract with respect to which the percentage of completion method is used, except for purposes of applying the look-back method of paragraph (2), any income under the contract...*(language omitted).***
> (2) Look-Back Method. - The interest computed under the look-back method of this paragraph shall be determined by - *(language omitted).*

20.    Using the Code index, identify the key Code section(s) addressing the following:

    a.    Corporation's ability to deduct mining and exploration costs.
    b.    Taxation of Social Security benefits of nonresident aliens.
    c.    Definition of *Head of Household.*
    d.    Valuation of a gift.
    e.    Sick pay benefits of employees.
    f.    Deductibility of face lift.
    g.    Bad debt reserves.
    h.    Statute of limitations for filing an amended return.
    i.    Withholding requirements for tip income.
    j.    Penalties for tax fraud.

21.    Identify the subtitle that addresses Estate and Gift Taxes.

22.    Identify the subtitle, chapter and subchapter that covers the federal income taxation of insurance companies.  What section defines an insurance company?

23. Using the Code's table of contents, identify the applicable Code section(s) for each of the following topics:

    a. Tax on prohibited transactions of pension plan fiduciaries.
    b. Definition of the Generation Skipping Tax.
    c. Definition of *adjusted basis* in determining gain from sale of asset.
    d. Taxation of contributions made to a partnership.
    e. Limitations on assessment and collection.

24. Using the Code's table of contents, identify the applicable Code section(s) for each of the following topics:

    a. Deduction of interest paid on loans used for education.
    b. Deduction of corporation's start-up and organizational expenses.
    c. Deduction of interest expense attributable to the rental of a person's vacation home.
    d. Definition of a *foreign corporation.*
    e. Payment of estimated income tax.

25. Find the following Code sections in both print and electronic versions. Compare the ease of locating and examining the sections. What topics do the sections address?

    a. IRC §280G
    b. IRC §3102
    c. IRC §68

26. Study the following Code sections. Provide examples of each of the tools discussed in this chapter regarding analyzing the Code (e.g., terms of art, limiting language, measuring words, numbering system, etc.).

    a. IRC §1223
    b. IRC §117
    c. IRC §1239

27.    Study the following Code sections.  Provide an example of each of the tools discussed in this chapter regarding analyzing the Code (e.g., terms of art, limiting language, measuring words, etc.).

     a.     IRC §179
     b.     IRC §280F
     c.     IRC §168

28.    Give an example of a Code provision with the limiting language *For purposes of this Section*. How does it affect the application of the provision you found? (Use a provision other than the example given in this chapter.)

29.    Give an example of a Code provision with limiting language other than *For purposes of this Section*.  How does the limitation affect the application of the provision you found?

30.    IRC Section 172(a) addresses a possible deduction for a "net operating loss."  Read IRC Section 172(a).  Where in this section is the term *net operating loss* defined?

31.    IRC Section 168(b)(3)(B) refers to *Residential rental property*.  What is the definition of this term?

32.    This year, Sam's employer, a privately held company, gave Sam 10 shares of stock as a way of saying "thank you" for all his hard work.  The fair market value for the 10 shares totals $10,000. Sam paid nothing for the stock. The only requirement of the company is that Sam may not be convicted of a crime. If he is convicted, ownership of the stock reverts back to the company. Sam wants to know if he has to recognize the $10,000 in income this year.

In researching in the IRC, you discover that Section 83(a) is the critical Code section. The following excerpts from this Code section appear relevant:

> **Section 83 - Property Transferred in Connection with the Performance of Services**
> (a) General rule
> If, in connection with the performance of services, property is transferred to any person other than the person for whom such services are performed, the excess of -
> (1) the fair market value of such property (determined without regard to any restriction other than a restriction which by its terms will never lapse) at the first time the rights of the person having the beneficial interest in such property are transferable or are not subject to a substantial risk of forfeiture, whichever occurs earlier, over

(2) the amount (if any) paid for such property, shall be included in the gross income of the person who performed such services in the first taxable year in which the rights of the person having the beneficial interest in such property are transferable or are not subject to a substantial risk of forfeiture, whichever is applicable. The preceding sentence shall not apply if such person sells or otherwise disposes of such property in an arm's length transaction before his rights in such property become transferable or not subject to a substantial risk of forfeiture.

(b) Election to include in gross income in year of transfer

(1) In general

Any person who performs services in connection with which property is transferred to any person may elect to include in his gross income for the taxable year in which such property is transferred, the excess of -

(A) the fair market value of such property at the time of transfer (determined without regard to any restriction other than a restriction which by its terms will never lapse), over

(B) the amount (if any) paid for such property. If such election is made, subsection (a) shall not apply with respect to the transfer of such property, and if such property is subsequently forfeited, no deduction shall be allowed in respect of such forfeiture.

(2) Election

An election under paragraph (1) with respect to any transfer of property shall be made in such manner as the Secretary prescribes and shall be made not later than 30 days after the date of such transfer. Such election may not be revoked except with the consent of the Secretary.

(c) Special rules

For purposes of this section -

(1) Substantial risk of forfeiture

The rights of a person in property are subject to a substantial risk of forfeiture if such person's rights to full enjoyment of such property are conditioned upon the future performance of substantial services by any individual.

(2) Transferability of property

The rights of a person in property are transferable only if the rights in such property of any transferee are not subject to a substantial risk of forfeiture.

(3) Sales which may give rise to suit under section 16(b) of the Securities Exchange Act of 1934

So long as the sale of property at a profit could subject a person to suit under section 16(b) of the Securities Exchange Act of 1934, such person's rights in such property are

(A) subject to a substantial risk of forfeiture, and

(B) not transferable.

What language in IRC §83(a) is critical to your understanding of the tax impact to your taxpayer? Is there a definition of these terms anywhere in the Code Section? Is the definition sufficient to enable you to answer your client's question, or will you need to pursue further the meaning of the terms?

33.  In problem 32, assume that Sam receives cash instead of stock. Now, what is the key term of art?

34.    What subchapter of Chapter 1, Title A, addresses the following topics?

     a.    Trust income tax
     b.    Partnership tax
     c.    Corporate tax
     d.    Calculation of individual taxable income

35.    Locate the committee reports that reflect the legislative history of IRC Section 7436. Which committee report offers the most authoritative value? Why? Describe the process used to find the committee reports.

36.    Sam must travel 100 miles once a week to receive intense medical treatment from the State University hospital. Insurance does not cover a night in the hospital even though he is physically unable to make the long trip home. Therefore, each week, Sam spends the night in a hotel near the hospital. The room costs $75 for the evening. How much of this cost qualifies as a deductible medical expense?

37.    Mary receives an award of a personal computer from her employer in recognition of her outstanding work developing a new office management process. All employees were considered for this award, which is valued at $3,000. How much of the award is taxable to Mary?

38.    Your client is the trustee of an irrevocable intervivos trust. On behalf of the trust, the trustee in the current year purchases $50,000 in depreciable property. Is the trust entitled to take a Code Section 179 deduction for the expenditure? Do you have all the necessary facts to answer this question? Provide support for your answer.

39.    Code Section 1033(h) provides for a potential non-recognition event of the receipt of insurance proceeds for unscheduled personal property destroyed in a residentially declared disaster. When was this provision added to the Code? By what act and act section? What is its effective date?

40.    Briefly summarize two tax provisions currently pending before Congress or the president. Describe the process you employed in locating these.

41.    When did costs incurred in searching for a new residence cease being deductible as moving expenses?

42.    IRC Section 121 excludes up to $250,000 in gain from the sale or exchange of a taxpayer's principal residence, assuming all the requirements are satisfied. Answer the following questions regarding this Code Section.

    a.    If all the requirements are met, is a taxpayer required to exclude up to $250,000 in gain?

    b.    A taxpayer's residence is burned down as a result of an accidental fire. Does this Code section apply?

    c.    A taxpayer sold his principal residence for a $250,000 gain on May 8, 1997. He immediately purchased another principal residence, which he sold on July 1, 1998, realizing a $100,000 gain. Assuming he satisfied all other Code Section 121 requirements, will he be able to exclude the $100,000 gain?

43.    A taxpayer sold his principal residence on May 6, 1997. Do the current provisions in Code Section 121 apply?

    a.    What were the provisions in this section before the $250,000 exclusion was enacted? To whom did the section apply? What was the excluded amount?

    b.    Locate and summarize the legislative history for the provision amending the provisions of IRC Section 121 to allow for a $250,000 exclusion. Describe the steps you took to arrive at your answer.

44.    Review Code Section 2001. Summarize the provisions put forth in P.L. 107-16 regarding the rate of estate taxes.

***Using just the Internal Revenue Code, answer the following questions, making sure to cite the provision or provisions of the IRC that provide the answer. Explain your answers in as much depth as possible.***

45.    A taxpayer is a 30-year-old junior high school history teacher in Maine. Her classes focus on the history of the Roman Empire. She plans on tracing the expansion of the Roman Empire by, on her own time, traveling through each of the countries in which the Romans held power. This trip will be costly and she would like to take the expense as an educational deduction.

a.      What are the relevant facts?  Are there additional questions you need to ask?
        What facts, if any, are not relevant?

b.      What is the research question or issue?

c.      Does the Code help answer the research question?  What Code sections apply and
        why?

46.     The new CFO of C Corporation has asked you if C Corporation needs to be directly
        concerned with the passive loss limitations.  There are 10 unrelated shareholders in the
        company, each of whom owns 10% of the outstanding stock.  Assume the corporation is
        neither a personal service corporation nor a Subchapter S corporation.

a.      Before researching, what do you think are the relevant facts?  Is there additional
        information you think you may need?

b.      Before researching, what is the research question or issue?

c.      What provisions can you find in the Code to help address the issue?  After reading
        the Code provision(s), how does your initial research question change?  What is
        your answer to the research question?  Show all of your reasoning.

47.     The governor of your state wants to deduct the expenses he incurs in his position as
        governor.  Using the Internal Revenue Code as your only source, determine whether the
        activities of a governor can constitute a "trade or business."

48.     Z Corporation has identified the property at 123 Street as an ideal place for its new office
        building.  The company would like to buy the property, demolish the building and build a
        new building. The cost of demolition will be approximately $500,000. Z's president asks
        whether the company can deduct this cost or at least depreciate it over time.  What is your
        response and why?

49.     Z corporation provides free parking only to its president.  Parking costs other employees
        $175 a month.  What is the tax impact to the president?

50.	Tom owns two houses. He lives in one of them on a full-time basis. The other one he uses 30 days of the year and rents it to strangers for 10 days a year. There is an original mortgage amount on his principal residence of $200,000, on which he paid $20,000 in interest this year. His second home has an original mortgage amount of $100,000, on which he paid $10,000 in interest this year.

    a.	How much of the interest is deductible?

    b.	What if Tom uses the second house only 14 days a year and he never rents the house out?

    c.	What if the original mortgage was acquired in 1984 and was for a total purchase price of $2,000,000? Assume for this question that the current balance on the mortgage is $1,500,000. Also assume there is no second home.

51.	Sue owns a vacation home. Will her cousin's free personal use of the home be considered as "personal use" by Sue for purposes of the vacation home deduction rules?

52.	If Sue rents her vacation home to her nephew at fair rental value, will his use of the home be considered "personal use" for purposes of the vacation home deduction rules?

53.	John owes Mark $50,000. For business reasons, Mark tells John that he will consider the debt fully paid if John pays him $30,000 in cash. John does so. Under IRC Section 61(a)(12), the $20,000 of debt relieved is generally taxable income to John. Answer the following questions after considering the following additional information you gather.

John's financial balance sheet immediately before the relief of debt reflects the following:

| | |
|---|---|
| Cash | $50,000 |
| Depreciable property (FMV) | $235,000 (Basis = $100,000) |
| Total debt (before relief) | $300,000 |

    a.	How much does John have to recognize in gross income in the year of the debt relief?

    b.	If John has no other "tax attributes," what impact does the relief of debt have on the basis of John's depreciable assets?

c.      What would be the impact if John has a net operating loss carryover from a prior year of $50,000?

54.    Taxpayer is a tax associate at a local CPA firm.  During the year, he took two graduate tax courses. Under his firm's Educational Assistance Program, his firm reimbursed his tuition costs of $3,000.  Is Tony required to recognize the $3,000 in income?  Assume the Educational Assistance Program meets any applicable requirements.

55.    Susan leases office space from Realty Corporation. Susan is a seamstress and uses the office to meet with clients and sew.  She has no employees.  Susan pays to the Realty Corporation monthly lease payments of $3,000.  Recently, Susan had to stop working for an extended period of time due to a back injury sustained while skiing.  As a result, she was unable to pay the $3,000 lease payments for the past two months.  Susan has returned to work but knows it will take several months to begin bringing in the revenue she did before her injury.  Realty Corporation has decided to "forget" the $6,000 Susan owes. She has been a good tenant for many years and brings client traffic that benefits the other tenants.  What is the tax impact to Susan of Realty's decision?

## INTEGRATED CASE STUDIES  (56-71)

*The following case studies are the same as those at the end of the previous chapter. The facts are the same, although you may have discovered additional facts since your initial meeting with the client. Use the knowledge and skills you have learned in this chapter to address the case studies. Use your work in Chapter 1 as the starting point.*

56.    *Case Study A – Disability Payments*

Mr. Top received $25,000 in disability payments while he was recuperating from heart surgery.  Mr. Top, age 65,  is an employee with a large corporation providing general business consulting services. The corporation has always paid for the disability insurance of its employees. Mr. Top telecommutes and works out of the home. From further conversations with the client, you discover that only $10,000 of the disability payments received by Mr. Top arise from a disability policy paid for by his employer under a group disability policy.  The remaining $15,000 was paid on a separate policy that Mr. Top purchased some time ago.  Mr. Top has been paying semiannual premiums on the separate individual policy. You are asked to prepare Mr. Top's return.

a.      What Code section addresses the research question?

b.      Does your study of the relevant Code section help you to refine or add to the initial research question(s)?

c.      Does the Code adequately address the research question?  If so, what are your conclusions, and on what are they based?

d.      Are there questions remaining that require further research?

57.    *Case Study B – Bonus Payments*

Sue is 30 years old and is president and a 51% shareholder of C Corporation.  She informs you that C Corporation has 10 shareholders, all unrelated. Other than herself, no shareholder owns more than 10% of the company's stock. Sue plans to recommend to the board of directors that it authorize the payment of a bonus to her and three other top employees. She asks you, as the company's tax advisor, to counsel her on what the company needs to do so that the company can get a deduction for the planned bonus payments.

After further discussions with Sue, you learn that the company's business is commercial real estate development.  The company had net revenues last year totaling $10,000,000. The company is an accrual-basis taxpayer, and each of the intended recipients employs the cash-basis method of tax accounting.  She would prefer the bonuses to actually be paid next year but deducted by the company this year.  One of the intended recipients is Sue's executive assistant, who is not currently a shareholder in the company.  Sue would like the bonus to equal 100% of each recipient's current salary.  The current salaries of the intended recipients are as follows:

| | |
|---|---|
| President | $500,000 |
| Executive Assistant | $100,000 |
| Chief Financial Officer | $300,000 |
| Vice President of Operations | $250,000 |

The CFO and vice president of operations are shareholders in the company, each owning 10% of the stock.

Sue indicated to you that she believes the annual salaries are comparable or, perhaps, a little on the high side when compared to her company's competitors. You also learn that the company regularly pays out dividends to shareholders and plans to continue to do so.

    a.        What Code section addresses the research question?

    b.        Does your study of the relevant Code section help you to refine or add to the initial research question(s)?

    c.        Does the Code adequately address the research question?  If so, what are your conclusions, and on what are they based?

    d.        Are there questions remaining that require further research?

58.    *Case Study C – Changing Headquarters*

A taxpayer, a calendar-year corporation, wants to change its company's headquarters – currently consisting of a 10-story building. The company owns the building outright.  The taxpayer has identified some potentially more suitable properties.  One of the possible properties is a single-story building on a large, attractive lot.  The other property consists of a two-building complex, with retail shops on the ground floor of one building and residential rental property in a portion of the other building.

After further discussions with the client and a review of relevant documents, you discover the following additional facts: Each of the new properties has a fair market value that slightly exceeds that of the current 10 story building.  The taxpayer would demolish the single-story building if it purchases that property.  The company would then build a specially designed building on the lot.  The sellers of both properties appear to be interested in entering an exchange transaction whereby the company's property would be exchanged for one of the other properties.

    a.        What Code section addresses the research question?

    b.        Does your study of the relevant Code section help you to refine or add to the initial research question(s)?

c.     Does the Code adequately address the research question?  If so, what are your conclusions, and on what are they based?

d.     Are there questions remaining that require further research?

59.   *Case Study D – Damage Payments to Dentist*

Dr. Tooth is a 40-year-old dentist in Small Town, USA.  He graduated from dentistal school five years ago and has had a thriving practice ever since.  At the end of last year, however, Dr. Tooth had an ugly billing disagreement with a patient.  The patient, a well-known, wealthy entrepreneur, in retribution, maliciously spread a rumor that Dr. Tooth was a carrier of a serious infectious disease. This rumor destroyed Dr. Tooth's patient base, as most of his patients quickly switched dentists.  As a result of the stress of losing his business, the cruel gossip that resulted from the rumor, and the financial strain caused by this situation, Dr. Tooth began to suffer from severe migraine headaches, loss of appetite, and significant facial twitches.  Dr. Tooth sued the patient for defamation and intentional infliction of emotional distress.  He won a jury verdict and has since recovered $3,600,000 in damages from the patient. This award was broken into the following categories.

    i.      $1,000,000 lost wages.  This was calculated on the basis that, in addition to the one year of wages lost since the date of the defamation, he has lost the ability to earn future wages in Small Town.

    ii.     $50,000 reimbursement for medical expenses incurred in consulting a neurologist, internist, and psychologist.

    iii.    $20,000 for future medical expenses anticipated.

    iv.    $30,000 reimbursement for attorney's fees paid.

    v.     $2,000,000 in punitive damages.  The jury determined that the action of the patient was so malicious and heinous that the patient should be monetarily punished for his actions.

    vi.    $300,000 for pain and suffering.

    vii.   $200,000 to compensate Dr. Tooth for the emotional distress he suffered.

Through your interview with the client, you discover that he had to pay his attorney $50,000, which was paid out of the award.

a.     What Code section addresses the research question?

b.      Does your study of the relevant Code section help you to refine or add to the initial research question(s)?

c.      Does the Code adequately address the research question?  If so, what are your conclusions, and on what are they based?

d.      Are there questions remaining that require further research?

60.    *Case Study E - Housing Expenses*

Ellie Executive lives in Florida with her family in a home bequeathed to her by her parents when they passed away.  This year her employer assigned her to a position in London.  The assignment is for a minimum of four years.  Because she grew up in the house, Ellie would like to keep it and rent it out.  There is no mortgage on the home, so renting will create a positive cash flow situation for her.  Her employer will be providing her with a housing allowance to cover her London housing costs.  Ellie believes the house has a FMV of at least $500,000.  Ellie wants to make sure that if she ends up selling it, she will not have any taxable income from the sale.  She has asked for your guidance.

After talking with Ellie Executive further, you become aware of the following additional facts:

- Ellie is not certain what she and her husband will do at the end of the four-year London assignment.  She may return to Florida but she also might take another international assignment, since her children are now adults. Ellie plans to continue paying the following expenses while the house is rented:

    * $400 a month for a weekly gardener
    * $500 a month for a weekly housecleaner
    * Approximately $200 a month in utility and maintenance expenses
      (electricity, garbage, and water)

- Ellie anticipates that she can lease the house fully furnished for $2,500 a month.

- Ellie's parents died in 1991 when the FMV of the house was $300,000. They purchased the house in 1950 for $10,000. Her parents spent a total of $20,000 in home improvement costs. Ellie substantially redecorated the house in 1992, spending $65,000 in renovating two bedrooms, two bathrooms, and replacing the roof. In addition, Ellie paid $5,000 for a new perimeter fence and $10,000 to a landscape architect to redesign the yard.

a.  What Code section addresses the research question?

b.  Does your study of the relevant Code section help you to refine or add to the initial research question(s)?

c.  Does the Code adequately address the research question?  If so, what are your conclusions, and on what are they based?

d.  Are there questions remaining that require further research?

61.  *Case Study F – Retirement Contributions*

Tom Speeder is a new client.  From reviewing his client questionnaire, you were able to gather the following facts. He is 50 years old and was recently hired as a middle-level manager with a car manufacturer.  Tom's salary for the current year is $200,000.  In his initial meeting with you, Tom indicates that he would like you to look into an idea he has that will help him maximize his investment portfolio. He tells you that his new company offers its employees the ability to participate in a Section 401(k) plan. He believes it would be to his benefit to maximize his contribution to the company's 401(k) plan that provides for matching employer contributions up to $3,000 annually.  The plan provides for a maximum annual employee contribution of no greater than that provided by the IRC.

It is January, and Tom has indicated to you that he would like to accelerate the maximum contributions to the plan by contributing his entire monthly paycheck until he funds the entire amount.  He believes that such an arrangement will maximize the growth of his portfolio since the earnings are tax free from an earlier time frame than if he spreads the contributions out over the year.

After further discussions with Tom, you discover that in addition to his salary he receives the following employment benefits:

- $100,000 group term insurance for which the employer pays the premiums (totaling $200/year).
- Health insurance, for which the employer pays the $100 in monthly premiums.
- As part of the company's Employee Educational Assistance Plan, tuition payments to a local university for one academic course a year to be chosen by the employee. For the current year, Tom plans to take a course on "Organizational Behavior" that he is interested in and believes will help him better understand his work environment. The university offers both undergraduate and graduate courses in this subject. Tom may take either and will wait to determine which is offered at the more convenient time.

a.    What Code section addresses the research question?

b.    Does your study of the relevant Code section help you to refine or add to the initial research question(s)?

c.    Does the Code adequately address the research question? If so, what are your conclusions, and on what are they based?

d.    Are there questions remaining that require further research?


62.    *Case Study G – Golf Ball Business*

Toby Power, a fellow Illinois resident, is a new client. Prior to her telephone call this morning (late November), all you really knew about Toby was that for the past five years she has been earning a living as a respected golfing instructor at a local club. She just called you to discuss a transaction she has entered into. You learn from your initial conversation with her that she and a group of friends formed a corporation for which the group will own 100% of the stock.

The corporation will be in the business of selling golf balls that it guarantees are indestructible and, because they glow in water and shade, cannot be lost. Toby transferred an office building to the corporation in return for her 20% stock ownership interest. Her eight other friends transferred primarily manufacturing equipment and cash for their evenly divided 80% interest. Toby has owned the office building for seven years and currently owes several hundred thousand dollars on two mortgages on the building. She estimates the fair market value of the building is about $1,000,000.

Toby informs you that her previous tax advisor, about whom she has nothing but negative things to say, counseled her that in order to avoid paying taxes on the transfer of the building to the corporation, she had to also transfer to the corporation a personal promissory note of $100,000. All of this occurred last year. She wants to know if the transaction was handled correctly or if she needs to worry.

Through further discussions and review of pertinent documents, you discover the following additional facts:

- Toby purchased the office building seven years ago for $500,000. She paid $100,000 in cash and $400,000 using a note (Note A) secured by the property.
- Two years ago, the fair market value of the property escalated to $1,200,000. Toby took out a second mortgage on the property in the amount of $300,000 (Note B). She used the borrowed funds to purchase a vacation home in Nevada.
- At the time of the property's transfer to the corporation, the building's fair market value was $1,000,000, determined by an assessor.
- At the time of the property's transfer to the corporation, Note A had an outstanding balance of $310,000. Note B had a balance of $100,000.
- Toby has made no improvements on the property. She has taken approximately $100,000 in depreciation deductions on her tax return.
- The terms of the promissory note Toby gave to the corporation were that she pay the note off over a period of 20 years, paying a single annual payment in the amount of $6,000 ($5,000 principal; $1,000 interest). The first payment is to be made on the anniversary date of the note – September 1. Toby paid the first installment which was due a few months ago.

a.      What Code section addresses the research question?

b.      Does your study of the relevant Code section help you to refine or add to the initial research question(s)?

c.      Does the Code adequately address the research question? If so, what are your conclusions, and on what are they based?

d.      Are there questions remaining that require further research?

63.    *Case Study H – Private School Expenses*

Mr. and Mrs. Worried, longtime clients, have come to you for help.  Their 13-year-old son has recently been expelled from the public junior high school because of severe behavioral problems, culminating in a physical attack on a teacher and threats of future violence.  The son has been seeing a psychologist once a week  but with no apparent positive results.  The Worrieds would like to send their son to a private school that can provide the type of psychological help they believe he needs.  The son's psychologist agrees that placement in a special school is imperative if there is ever to be a chance that the son will be a functioning member of society.

The Worrieds tell you that they are concerned because, although they have identified several potential schools, they do not have the financial resources necessary to pay the tuition and other additional costs.  Their insurance does not cover any of the costs.  However, the Worrieds believe that they may be able to afford the expenses if they can take them as a tax deduction.  They ask you for your opinion.

a.    What Code section addresses the research question?

b.    Does your study of the relevant Code section help you to refine or add to the initial research question(s)?

c.    Does the Code adequately address the research question?  If so, what are your conclusions, and on what are they based?

d.    Are there questions remaining that require further research?

64.    *Case Study I – Deadly Fire*

Early this year, a taxpayer was clearing dry brush from behind his Malibu home in California.  He became frustrated with how long it was taking using his clippers.  He decided instead to light the brush on fire, believing this would be safe because it was an overcast day.  The taxpayer brought out a fire extinguisher in case the fire got out of control.  Unfortunately, some wind kicked up and fanned the fire out of control.  The fire completely consumed both his house and his neighbor's house.  The two children staying in the neighbor's house died of smoke inhalation.  The taxpayer was charged with negligent homicide.  The trial is pending.

The taxpayer wishes to take a casualty loss deduction for the loss of his house, which was worth an estimated $1,000,000 at the time of the fire. The taxpayer purchased the home for $900,000 only six months earlier. Insurance has refused to compensate for the loss under the circumstances. The taxpayer is currently out on bail. He is the brother of one of your very significant clients, who has asked you to provide tax advice to the taxpayer. After review of pertinent documents, you conclude that his "adjusted gross income" will be $200,000 for the year before considering the loss.

a.      What Code section addresses the research question?

b.      Does your study of the relevant Code section help you to refine or add to the initial research question(s)?

c.      Does the Code adequately address the research question? If so, what are your conclusions, and on what are they based?

d.      Are there questions remaining that require further research?

65.     *Case Study J – Airline Costs*

A major airline manufacturer was found to be in violation of FAA safety rules and was forced to install additional safety devices in each of its planes within the next six months. The airline company projects the cost of this upgrade to be several million dollars, consisting of lost profits while the planes are on the ground, labor costs, and the cost of parts. In addition, the airline spent $100,000 in attorney's fees in an unsuccessful fight to have the requirement waived. The CFO of the company wishes to know whether any or all of these costs can be deducted.

a.      What Code section addresses the research question?

b.      Does your study of the relevant Code section help you to refine or add to the initial research question(s)?

c.      Does the Code adequately address the research question? If so, what are your conclusions, and on what are they based?

d.      Are there questions remaining that require further research?

66.    *Case Study K – Vacation Home*

Mr. Z owns three homes. He lives in the San Francisco home full time. The other two he and his wife vacation in each year. He is considering replacing the house he has in Palm Springs, California, with another house in the same area. The new home is a little larger and has a floor plan he prefers. The two Palm Springs properties have almost the same fair market value. Mr. Z would like to know if he can exchange the properties instead of selling the one he has now and then buying the new one. He has a lot of built-up appreciation in the current Palm Springs home, and he doesn't want to have to pay taxes on it. Someone told him at a cocktail party that he can avoid paying taxes if he does an "exchange."

Mr. Z and his wife own the home outright. There is no mortgage on the property. They use the property occasionally. This last year they vacationed at the home for about two or three weeks – they aren't sure of the exact days. They have never rented the property and refuse to rent either the old or new property. They don't need the money and don't like strangers in their house.

Mr. Z explains that he holds each of his vacation homes for two purposes. One reason is for vacations for him and his wife. Another key reason for owning the homes is for their investment value. He chooses only homes in areas where he believes there are high appreciation possibilities.

Can Mr. Z take advantage of the tax-free exchange rules in the IRC?

a.    What Code section addresses the research question?

b.    Does your study of the relevant Code section help you to refine or add to the initial research question(s)?

c.    Does the Code adequately address the research question? If so, what are your conclusions, and on what are they based?

d.    Are there questions remaining that require further research?

67. *Case Study L – Property Easement*

A developer acquired a parcel of unimproved real property that she would like to develop. Although the land is currently zoned for commercial use, the developer would prefer not to begin development until an adjoining city street is widened. With a wider street, her development can include a landscaped public entrance and lighting. Without the widening, the development will have only one entrance that is neither as accessible nor attractive.

The city plans to widen the street in order to build bike paths, which are now required in its new city plan. It will be easier for the city to widen the street if it acquires an easement across the developer's property. The developer is interested in providing this easement to the city. However, before she acts, the developer would like assurance that she will receive a charitable deduction for the value of the easement. She has asked you to request a letter ruling on this matter.

a.     What Code section addresses the research question?

b.     Does your study of the relevant Code section help you to refine or add to the initial research question(s)?

c.     Does the Code adequately address the research question? If so, what are your conclusions, and on what are they based?

d.     Are there questions remaining that require further research?

68. *Case Study M – Interest Payment*

A taxpayer is president of a company. He is very wealthy and has a good deal of assets. He went to Bank 1 in January, Yr. 1 to borrow $1,000,000. The taxpayer used the loan proceeds to purchase stock. The loan was secured by the stock purchased. The terms of the loan are that it is an "interest only" loan, with interest to be paid annually on the anniversary of the loan. The rate is 10% of the principle.

In November of Yr. 1, the taxpayer realized that he did not have the liquid funds to pay the $100,000 of interest due in January. He had sufficient assets, but, due to the business environment, he determined that the smartest economic move to make would be to borrow the $100,000 rather than to liquidate one of his investments. So he went to Bank

2 and borrowed $100,000. This loan was secured by assets other than his stock and was a regular amortizing loan. Interest was 9%. Upon receipt of the loan proceeds on December 1, Yr. 1, the taxpayer deposited the proceeds into his regular checking account in Bank 3. The proceeds remained in the checking account for the entire month of December. The balance of the checking account during the month of December ranged from $100,000 to $115,000.

On January 2, Yr. 2, the taxpayer wrote a check from his Bank 3 checking account to Bank 1 in full payment of the interest due. On his tax return for Yr. 2, the taxpayer took a deduction of $100,000 as an investment interest expense under Section 163. He had sufficient investment income to cover the deduction.

In your research, you discover that Bank 1 owns 90% of the stock of Bank 2. You are able to talk with the client and learn that he was entirely unaware of the relationship. In fact, the loan documents were entirely different and did not make any reference to any relationship. The IRS has indicated it plans to disallow the interest deduction because the Service believes it has never actually been paid as is required by the Code. The taxpayer would like you to see what the IRS is talking about and whether it has any ground for its position.

a.      What Code section addresses the research question?

b.      Does your study of the relevant Code section help you to refine or add to the initial research question(s)?

c.      Does the Code adequately address the research question? If so, what are your conclusions, and on what are they based?

d.      Are there questions remaining that require further research?

69.    *Case Study N – Racing Car Expenses*

A taxpayer is a partner in an accounting firm. He has always enjoyed auto racing as a hobby. Now that his children are grown, he has decided to devote more time to auto racing. He recently purchased a racing car for $50,000 and has entered several races. He recently raced in his first competitive race and placed fourth, resulting in winnings of $5,000. He expects to incur a number of expenses related to his racing: auto maintenance, storage, transportation, and so on. He would like your advice as to how to proceed so that he can depreciate his car and deduct all of these expenses.

    a.       What Code section addresses the research question?

    b.       Does your study of the relevant Code section help you to refine or add to the initial research question(s)?

    c.       Does the Code adequately address the research question?  If so, what are your conclusions, and on what are they based?

    d.       Are there questions remaining that require further research?

70.      *Case Study O – Retainer Fee*

Big Company paid $100,000 at the beginning of the year to a large law firm to retain its services should they be needed during the course of the year.  The law firm specializes in real estate law and is considered the best firm in this field. Big Company feared that one of its competitors would engage the law firm. This would prevent Big Company from being able to use the firm's services because of conflict-of-interest rules that preclude a firm from representing different clients with actual or potentially adverse legal interests. To prevent this, Big engaged the firm and paid the retainer fee.  Occasionally, Big asked the firm to perform legal work in areas where Big's in-house lawyers were not as well equipped.  It is now December, and it is clear that a substantial amount of the initial retainer will not be used to pay for legal services rendered.  The retainer agreement provides in this case that any unused amount shall be returned to Big, with interest, at year-end.

Big Company is a longtime client of yours.  It has asked you to look into whether any of the retainer fee will be deductible to it. It wishes to have this advice before the beginning of next year when it will determine whether to pay another $100,000 retainer to the law firm for the year.

    a.       What Code section addresses the research question?

    b.       Does your study of the relevant Code section help you to refine or add to the initial research question(s)?

    c.       Does the Code adequately address the research question?  If so, what are your conclusions, and on what are they based?

d.      Are there questions remaining that require further research?

71.     *Case Study P – Development Costs*

Gobble Corporation purchased 400 acres in Green City to build a private golf course and residences.  The land cost $10,000,000. Gobble planned high quality, large houses that would sell for an average of $700,000.

It believed that the city's general plan allowed for this development.  Gobble spent in excess of $1,000,000 in fees to pay architects and civil engineers, and for all necessary environmental studies and approvals.  Two years ago, Gobble's development proposal was approved by the city council in a 5 - 4 vote.

Two months after the vote, the membership in the council changed dramatically.  The major election issue was growth versus no growth.  The city voted strongly for a no growth slate.  Given the strong community sentiment, the new city council voted to disregard the earlier vote and alter the City's general plan to prohibit such a large development. They decided to defeat the development proposal.

As a result, Gobble sued the city for unreasonably interpreting its planning documents and reversing its initial approval of the project, all to the grave detriment of Gobble.  Litigation has consumed almost two years and cost a total of $500,000.

Gobble's CFO has come to you to help with its tax return preparation.   Gobble would like to deduct all the costs incurred in this transaction, including the $1,000,000 paid for the land acquisition.

a.      What Code section addresses the research question?

b.      Does your study of the relevant Code section help you to refine or add to the initial research question(s)?

c.      Does the Code adequately address the research question?  If so, what are your conclusions, and on what are they based?

d.      Are there questions remaining that require further research?

# THE TAX RESEARCH PROCESS

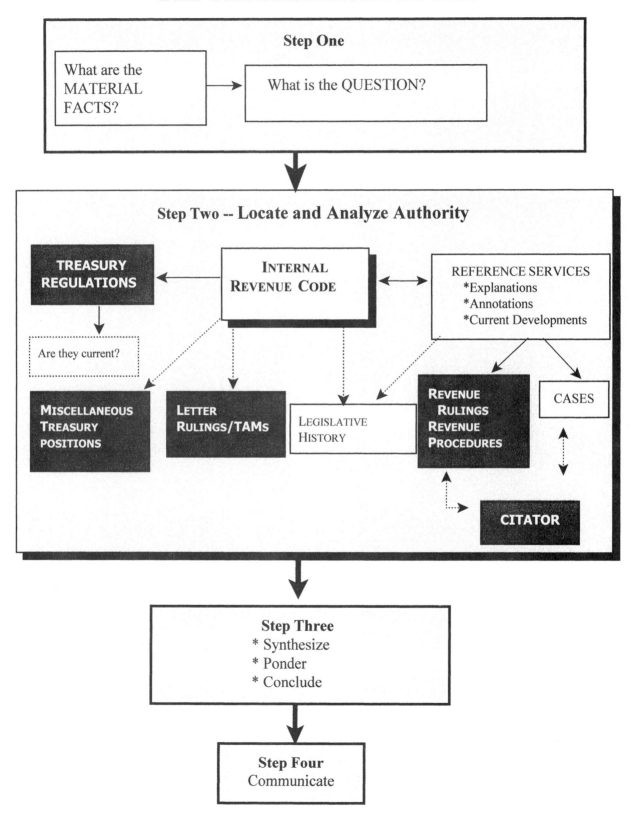

# CHAPTER THREE

# TREASURY INTERPRETATIONS

## *EXPECTED LEARNING OUTCOMES*

- Identify the various administrative interpretations of the Code
- Determine the level of authority of each major type of interpretation
- Identify the various ways of accessing each major type of interpretation
- Know how to determine the validity of each interpretation
- Become adept at citing Treasury interpretations

## *CHAPTER OUTLINE*

- Overview
- Treasury Regulations
- Revenue Rulings
- Revenue Procedures
- Letter Rulings and Technical Advice Memoranda
- Other Types of Treasury Interpretations
- Chapter Summary
- Problems

## OVERVIEW

As you learned from the previous chapter, the Internal Revenue Code is a complex Congressional creation, replete with terms of art and other ambiguous language. Frequently, even a careful analysis of the relevant Code provisions does not render an answer to the research question. Often examination of the Code simply results in refining or adding to the research question. As the chapter flowchart indicates, you may choose to turn to a secondary source such as a reference service for help at this point.

Reference services help direct you to two types of potentially useful primary resources: Treasury interpretations and judicial interpretations. Chapter Five addresses how to use these reference services to locate the pertinent Treasury interpretations and judicial interpretations. This chapter focuses on each type of authority issued by the Treasury Department.

The authority of the Treasury Department to issue Code interpretations is granted by Congress pursuant to IRC §7805(a).  That section provides that ". . . the Secretary shall prescribe all needful rules and regulations for the enforcement of this title . . ."  The Treasury Department issues several types of releases in order to fulfill its responsibility to provide interpretive guidance of the Code.  Most Treasury Department issuances are considered primary authority.  Each, however, provides a different level of reliability and authority.  The key types of Treasury interpretations are:

☛ **Treasury interpretations differ in their weight of authority**.

❑    Regulations
❑    Revenue Rulings
❑    Revenue Procedures
❑    Letter Rulings

## TREASURY REGULATIONS

The primary mechanism the Treasury Department employs to offer potentially helpful interpretations of the Code are Regulations.  The Secretary of the Treasury has charged the Internal Revenue Service (a branch of the Treasury Department) with the responsibility of enforcing regulations.

Treasury regulations attempt to clarify the provisions of a particular Code section.  Regulations generally expand upon and explain a particular Code provision.  They are generally more readable than the statutory language of the IRC, although they often raise complicated new tests and considerations not made clear by the Code.  Typically, regulations address a particular Code provision from a general vantage point – not how it might apply to a specific set of facts.  The most helpful regulations also offer several examples of how the Code section might be applied in different factual situations.

☛ **Regulations attempt to explain the provisions of a Code section.**

It is fair to say that the Treasury Department has not been entirely successful in providing clarity through its regulations.  Sometimes regulations offer no additional useful information and merely repeat the exact language of the Code provision.  In addition, the Treasury has not issued regulations on every Code section. Even when you find a regulation for the relevant Code section, frequently it does not address the part of the section for which you are seeking interpretive guidance.

Even more challenging, regulations are often outdated. As Congress amends the Code more and more frequently, it becomes increasingly difficult for the Treasury Department to issue regulations for the new or amended provisions. The Treasury Department has not even been able to replace regulations that discuss repealed or amended laws.

☞ **Treasury regulations are frequently outdated.**

Even with these drawbacks, because of the possible guidance they may offer, it is usually important to examine the regulations.

There are three types of regulations:

- ❑ Final Regulations
- ❑ Proposed Regulations
- ❑ Temporary Regulations

## Final Regulations

Final regulations frequently provide an authoritative and useful tool to help in understanding the IRC. Regulations have the full force and effect of law as long as they are "reasonable and consistent interpretations" of the Code. Therefore, final regulations may bind both the IRS and the taxpayer. If the regulations directly speak to a taxpayer's facts, it is highly likely that the IRS will apply the regulations.

☞ **A Final regulation is like law if it is a reasonable and consistent interpretation of the Code section.**

The example on the next page illustrates a final regulation that provides more guidance than simply restating the Code provision. In addition to explanatory language, the Regulation provides an example illustrating the application of Code §109. Following the text of the regulation, note that the date for adoption is indicated.

# ILLUSTRATION: IRC Section 109 reads as follows:

## IMPROVEMENTS BY LESSEE ON LESSOR'S PROPERTY

Gross income does not include income (other than rent) derived by a lessor of real property on the termination of a lease, representing the value of such property attributable to buildings erected or other improvements made by the lessee.

**Treas. Reg. §1.109-1 Exclusion from gross income of lessor of real property of value of improvements erected by lessee.**

→ statutory language

(a) Income derived by a lessor of real property upon the termination, through forfeiture or otherwise, of the lease of such property and attributable to buildings erected or other improvements made by the lessee upon the leased property is excluded from gross income. However, where the facts disclose that such buildings or improvements represent in whole or in part a liquidation in kind of lease rentals, the exclusion from gross income shall not apply to the extent that such buildings or improvements represent such liquidation. The exclusion applies only with respect to the income realized by the lessor upon the termination of the lease and has no application to income, if any, in the

→ additional interpretive guidance

form of rent, which may be derived by a lessor during the period of the lease and attributable to buildings erected or other improvements made by the lessee. It has no application to income which may be realized by the lessor upon the termination of the lease but not attributable to the value of such buildings or improvements. Neither does it apply to income derived by the lessor subsequent to the termination of the lease incident to the ownership of such buildings or improvements.

(b) The provisions of this section may be illustrated by the following example:

→ example

*Example.* The A Corporation leased in 1945 for a period of 50 years unimproved real property to the B Corporation under a lease providing that the B Corporation erect on the leased premises an office building costing $500,000, in addition to paying the A Corporation a lease rental of $10,000 per annum beginning on the date of completion of the improvements, the sum of $100,000 being placed in escrow for the payment of the rental. The building was completed on January 1, 1950. The lease provided that all improvements made by the lessee on the leased property would become the absolute property of the A Corporation on the termination of the lease by forfeiture or otherwise and that the lessor would become entitled on such termination to the remainder of the sum, if any, remaining in the escrow fund. The B Corporation forfeited its lease on January 1, 1955, when the improvements had a value of $100,000. Under the provisions of section 109, the $100,000 is excluded from gross income. The amount of $50,000 representing the remainder in the escrow fund is forfeited to the A Corporation and is included in the gross income of that taxpayer. As to the basis of the property in the hands of the A Corporation, see §1.1019-1.

→ TD and date issued

**.01 Historical Comment:** Proposed 6/26/56. Adopted 12/28/56 by T.D. 6220.

Infrequently, courts have held certain regulations to be unreasonable and, therefore, not binding. When this occurs, sometimes the Treasury Department will immediately concede the regulation is invalid. However, without a Supreme Court decision rendering a regulation invalid, the IRS is not legally bound to stop enforcing the regulation in those jurisdictions that are not bound by the court's decision. For example, a decision of the Federal District Court in New York determining a regulation invalid does not require the Treasury to abandon that same regulation in California.

Although possible, it is with risk that a taxpayer directly violates the interpretation set forth in a regulation that has not been invalidated by at least one court. In fact, the Code provides for the possible imposition of a monetary penalty on a tax preparer who intentionally disregards a regulation, revenue ruling, or IRS notice. [IRC §6694(b)]. This is discussed in more detail in Chapter Eight.

Final regulations are released by the Treasury Department through **treasury decisions**. (TDs). The treasury decisions often include **preambles** that may provide useful introductory and contextual information about the specific regulation. Although their formal authority is unclear, preambles are widely viewed as useful sources of information.

Sometimes a Code section specifically states that the details of the provisions will be "as the Secretary shall by Regulations prescribe." Regulations written with this type of Code directive are sometimes referred to as "legislative" regulations. Regulations written to interpret a Code section without this directive are sometimes referred to as "interpretive" regulations. Neither the Code nor the regulations formally categorize regulations into these two categories. The practical difference between the two categories lies in the different legal standard courts may apply in determining whether to invalidate a regulation. Although it may be helpful to recognize when you are examining a "legislative" regulation, it is most important that you be aware that any final regulation has the full force of law if it is consistent with and a reasonable interpretation of the Code provision.

> *"A preamble will frequently express the intended effect of some part of a regulation. As a statement of intent that represents an institutional viewpoint, such a document might be helpful in interpreting an ambiguity in a regulation."* *[Armco, Inc.,* 87 TC 865, 868.]

There is usually a gap of time between the date of the enactment of a Code provision and the release of interpreting final regulations. Final regulations are presumed to have retroactive application unless otherwise provided by the IRS [IRC §7805(b)]. Sometimes courts have denied retroactive application of regulations when there is evidence of the IRS abusing its discretion. In addition, at times, the legislative provisions provide that any regulations issued will have only prospective authority.

## Proposed Regulations

The law requires all regulations to be published first in a proposed format for a minimum of 30 days. This provides an opportunity for interested parties to comment before the proposed regulations become final. Many groups are interested in reviewing proposed regulations – notably the American Institute of Certified Public Accountants (AICPA), the American Bar Association (ABA), and other professional groups and trade organizations.

**☞ All regulations are proposed for at least 30 days.**

Proposed regulations may remain in this proposed status for an unlimited period of time. In fact, the IRS may never finalize them. Some proposed regulations have remained in proposed form for over 20 years! However, this usually does not occur. Generally, the IRS ultimately issues final regulations, often reflecting the comments made while in proposed form.

Generally, proposed regulations do not carry the same authority as final regulations. Courts often do not place much, if any, weight on proposed regulations. However, they are still considered to be somewhat authoritative for purposes of the "substantial authority" rules discussed later in Chapter Six. In some cases, the tax court has held that a taxpayer was reasonable in relying on the proposed regulations given the absence of any more authoritative guidance. As a tax researcher, it is important to recognize that proposed regulations may provide some guidance, but you should be wary about relying on them too heavily.

**☞ Proposed regulations generally offer little authoritative value.**

## Temporary Regulations

Regulations are also issued in temporary form. While temporary, they are also proposed and, thus, open for comment and revision. Notably, temporary regulations differ from regular proposed regulations because they are considered to be authoritative and binding. The Treasury may issue temporary regulations if it finds that the requirements of prior public notice are "impracticable, unnecessary, or contrary to the public interest."

Although a bit confusing, this dual nature of a temporary regulation makes practical sense. Imagine that a new Code section has just been enacted. On its own, the section's correct application may be unclear. In this case, it may be ill-advised or unreasonable to require taxpayers to wait for the issuance of proposed regulations, a process that may take months or years. It may be appropriate for the Treasury to issue temporary regulations providing authoritative guidance to the taxpayer. Although temporary regulations are still in proposed form to permit interested parties the opportunity to discuss and perhaps influence them, temporary regulations are nonetheless authoritative.

Generally, temporary regulations are authoritative until they are superseded by final regulations. However, the Taxpayer Bill of Rights, enacted pursuant to the Technical and Miscellaneous Revenue Act of 1988, provides that temporary regulations automatically expire three years from the date of issuance. The Treasury issues final regulations once it refines the temporary regulations as it deems appropriate. To the extent the final regulations differ from the temporary regulations, the provisions of the temporary regulations remain authoritative for transactions occurring while the regulations were in effect.

## Organization of Regulations

Regulations are organized following the numbering system of the IRC. Remember, the IRC is a part of the larger United States Code. There are regulations explaining other titles of the United

**☛ Temporary regulations provide authoritative guidance while they are being finalized.**

**☛ Regulations are organized around the IRC numbering system.**

States Code.  For example, there are regulations interpreting the Bankruptcy Code and the Federal Criminal Code.   All of these regulations are part of the United States Code of Federal Regulations.  Because the IRC is Title 26 of the United States Code, you can find Treasury regulations in the same title of the Code of Federal Regulations.

☞ **Treasury regulations are found in Title 26 of the Code of Federal Regulations.**

A Treasury regulation cite consists of three parts which are separated by a decimal and a hyphen as illustrated here

Treasury Regulation §1.163-10(a)(2)(B)

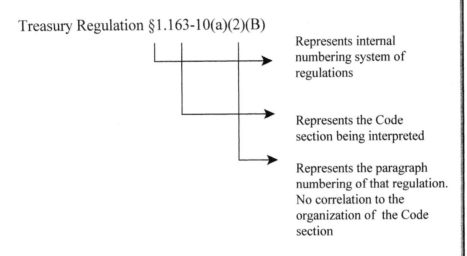

Represents internal numbering system of regulations

Represents the Code section being interpreted

Represents the paragraph numbering of that regulation. No correlation to the organization of the Code section

The number preceding the decimal point in the regulation cite generally indicates the type of regulation as well as its general subject. The number between the decimal and the hyphen represents the IRC section interpreted by the regulation.  The following table indicates the significance of some of the numbers commonly found to precede the decimal point.

☞ **The numbering of Treasury regulations provide information about their type.**

| | |
|---|---|
| 1 | Final income tax regulations |
| 5 -18, 35, 305 | Temporary regulations |
| 301 | Final procedural and administrative regulations |

Unfortunately, the numbering system is not consistently applied.  Therefore, it is not at all uncommon to find temporary regulations with the prefix "1" and a "T" somewhere in the cite to indicate the regulation is temporary.  The best way to determine the type of regulation is to examine the language immediately preceding type.

## Citing the Regulations

Like the Code, regulations may be cited in a variety of appropriate ways. The most formal method is often seen in court documents. This, however, is not the most common method employed by tax practitioners. The two methods are illustrated as follows.

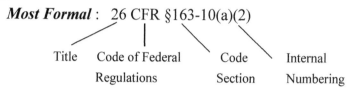

*Most Formal* :   26 CFR §163-10(a)(2)

Title    Code of Federal      Code         Internal
          Regulations        Section       Numbering

*Most Common:*   Treas. Reg. §1.163-10(a)(2)

If the regulation is proposed or temporary, the correct way to cite it is to simply add "Prop." or "Temp." prior to the word "Treas." For example, the following is a correct citation of a temporary regulation: Temp. Treas. Reg. §5f.103-2(h).

It is advisable to cite a regulation in as specific a manner as possible in order to identify the exact source of authority you are relying on.   If the key pertinent provision is buried deep within a regulation section, it is not appropriate to simply cite the entire regulation.  You should also refer to the specific paragraph number of the regulation to best identify the particular relevant portion.

☛ **Treasury regulation cites contain the related Code section number.**

☛ **Be specific when citing a provision of a Treasury Regulation.**

---

**EXAMPLE 1:  Citing a Regulation Section**
The most common method of citing the bolded provisions is
Treas. Reg. §1.83-7(b)(1).

**Treas. Reg. Sec. 1.83-7 Taxation of nonqualified stock options**.
(a) In general.  If there is granted. . .*(language omitted)*
(b) Readily ascertainable defined--
 (1) **Actively traded on an established market.** . . .*(language omitted)*

You can access Treasury regulations in a variety of sources. The Treasury first issues final Treasury regulations as **Treasury decisions** or TDs.  In addition to the text of the regulation, a TD contains the preamble describing the reasons for the Regulation and some of its provisions.  The TD is published in the *Federal Register,* which can be found in any law library.  In addition, the IRS publishes each TD in the ***Internal Revenue Bulletin*** (IRB).  The IRB is published on a weekly basis and is compiled semiannually in a hardbound service called the ***Cumulative Bulletin***.

Although you can access regulations through the *Federal Register*, IRB, or *Cumulative Bulletin*, they are also available in many other sources.  Just as the Code is available in various published media, regulations are available in multi-volume hardbound reference services and in a multi-volume softbound format, as well as electronically in either CD-ROM, modem-accessed, or Internet-accessed formats.

In paper format, an efficient method of accessing the regulations is through softbound regulation books published by either Commerce Clearing House (CCH) or Research Institute of America (RIA).  Most tax practitioners should have a copy of these softbound regulations on their desks for quick and easy access.  In many cases, the books are easier than the electronic format to skim and read.  This source provides the regulations in a sequential order by Code section being interpreted.

Both publishers generally issue the softbound regulations every six months.  Because regulations are frequently issued and amended, it is important to always have on hand the most current edition of these softbound regulations and check more frequently updated services for changes to regulations that you are relying on.

In addition, you can access the entire set of Treasury regulations electronically using one of the many CD-ROM sources or through a fee-based online service provided by CCH, RIA, Lexis-Nexis, or Tax Analysts. Each of these proprietary services is discussed in more depth in Chapter Five. The Appendix illustrates in detail how to locate regulations using these services.

☞ **Final regulations are issues as Treasury decisions.**

Picture reprinted with the permission of RIA

in more depth in Chapter Five. The Appendix illustrates in detail how to locate regulations using these services.

It is much easier to electronically locate a particular Treasury regulation if you know the specific regulation cite. When you are aware of the cite, a simple entry onto the service's "search" template will result in accessing the document. The appendices contain illustrations of this process.

You can also access the full-text of the Treasury regulations free of charge over the Internet. Beware, however, when using this source. The language posted is frequently outdated and, therefore, unreliable. In addition, sometimes the text is not converted into computer language accurately. The Appendix provides information regarding some of these Internet sources.

## Reliability of Regulations

There is one critical step you must take after finding a regulation that appears to directly address the research question. You must confirm that the regulation is "consistent" with the current Internal Revenue Code. Unfortunately, as noted earlier, a substantial percentage of final regulations are obsolete. When Congress amends the Code, the Treasury frequently is unable to amend the interpreting regulations to reflect the legislative changes. This has resulted in a large percentage of the regulations being inconsistent with the Code and, therefore, not authoritative or useful.

To better appreciate how this happens, it is helpful to understand how regulations are written. Each year, the Treasury prepares a list of regulation projects. Treasury staff are assigned to each project. Once they write the regulation, the staff moves to other regulation projects. No one is continuously assigned to a particular regulation section to ensure it is updated as Congress amends the Code section. Thus, there are regulation sections that fail to reflect as many as the past 16 tax acts!

*". . .while agencies are bound by those regulations that are issued within the scope of their lawful discretion . . .they cannot be bound by regulations that are contrary to law. Otherwise, the Secretary of the Treasury would effectively be empowered to repeal taxes that the Congress enacts."* [U.S. Supreme Court Justice Scalia *United States v. Burke,* 504 U.S. 229, 245 (1992)]

Obviously, you cannot rely on a regulation that does not reflect a change in the Code and is no longer consistent with the Code section. Sometimes the inconsistency is simply a difference in dollar amounts, in which case the remainder of the regulation is probably still authoritative. At other times, the very essence of the Code section may have been amended, completely eliminating any authority of the old regulation. Good researchers learn to avoid falling into the trap of relying on an obsolete regulation.

Sometimes simply being aware of the danger of obsolete regulations is all that is needed. For example, if the Code language says one thing and the regulation language says something quite different, you must apply the Code since it represents statutory law. However, you can take some concrete steps to ensure you do not rely on an obsolete regulation. The steps differ depending on the format you are using to read the regulations.

*Hardbound* – The hardbound reference services contain large bold warnings before each regulation provision not reflecting current law. The warning refers the reader to the public law that changed the Code section and that the regulation fails to reflect. The softbound regulations published by Research Institute of America (RIA) provide the same caution.

---

**ILLUSTRATION: Excerpt from RIA's *United States Tax Reporter***

**[¶482.01]   Reg. §1.48-2   New section 38 property.**

→   **Caution:** *The Treasury has not yet amended Reg § 1.48-2 to reflect changes made by P.L. 101-508, P.L. 99-514, P.L. 98-369, P.L. 97-248.*
   **(a) In general.** Section 48(b) defines "new section 38 property" as section 38 property—
   **(1)** The construction, reconstruction, or erection of which is completed by the taxpayer after December 31, 1961, or
   **(2)** Which is acquired by the taxpayer after December 31, 1961, provided that the original use of such property commences with the taxpayer and commences after such date.
   In the case of construction, reconstruction, or erection of such property commenced before January 1, 1962, and completed after December 31, 1961, there shall be taken into account as the basis of new section 38 property in determining qualified investment only that portion of the basis which is properly attributable to construction, reconstruction, or erection after December 31, 1961. See §1.48-1 for the definition of section 38 property.
   **(b) Special rules for determining date of acquisition, original use, and basis attributable to construction, reconstruction, or erection.** For purposes of paragraph (a) of this section, the principles set forth in paragraph (a)(1) and (2) of § 1.167(c)-1 shall be applied. Thus, for example the following rules are applicable:
   **(1)** Property is considered as constructed, reconstructed, or erected by the taxpayer if the work is done for him in accordance with his specifications.
   **(2)** The portion of the basis of property attributable to construction, reconstruction, or erection after December 31, 1961, consists of all costs of construction, reconstruction, or

With some extra effort, you can discover exactly what impact the public law has on the Code section in order to determine the authority of the regulation. Using the knowledge gained from the last chapter, study the historical notes that follow the Code section. Pay particular attention to the public law not reflected in the regulation and determine how it impacts the reliability of the regulation.

***Softbound*** – Both RIA and Commerce Clearing House (CCH) publish softbound volumes of the regulations. Those published by CCH do not have the same helpful warnings as you find in the hardbound version. When using the CCH softbound regulations, you must take an extra step. In the front of the first volume of the regulation set, there is a Table entitled "Law Changes Not Yet in the Regulations." This table lists each regulation that has become partially or wholly obsolete since the publication of the particular set of regulations. If you purchase a new set when they are available (twice a year), this table will be current at least up to the last six months. Following is an excerpt from this table.

---

### EXAMPLE 2: "Law Changes Not Yet in the Regulations" – CCH

| Regulations Section | Public Law Making Changes Not Reflected | Regulations Section | Public Law Making Changes Not Reflected |
|---|---|---|---|
| 1.0-1 | 99-514 | 1.42-2 | 101-239, 103-66 |
| 1.1-1 | 95-600, 97-34, 97-488, 99-514, 100-647, 103-66 | 1.44A-1—1.44A-3 | 98-369 (redesignated Code Sec. 44A as 21), 99-514, 100-485, 104-188 |
| 1.1(i)-1T | 100-647, 101-508, 105-34, 105-206 | 1.44A-4 | 98-369 (redesignated Code Sec. 44A as 21), 99-514, 104-188 |
| 1.2-1 | 99-514 | 5c.44F-1 | 98-369 (redesignated Code Sec. 44F as 30), 99-514 (redesignated Code Sec. 30 as 41) |
| 1.2-2 | 93-597, 94-569, 97-448, 98-369, 99-514 | | |
| 1.3-1 | 94-12, 94-164, 94-455, 95-30, 95-600, 96-222, 97-34, 99-514 | 1.46-1 | 100-647, 101-239, 101-508 |
| 1.11-1 | 94-164, 94-455, 95-30, 95-600, 97-34, 98-369, 99-514, 100-203, 100-647 | 1.46-2 | 96-222, 96-223, 97-34, 97-248, 98-369, 101-508, 97-354, 98-369 |
| | | 1.46-3 | 97-34, 98-369, 99-514, 100-647, 101-508 |
| 1.21-1 | 95-30, 95-600, 97-34, 98-369 (redesignated Code Sec. 21 as 15), 99-514, 100-647 | 1.46-4 | 97-34, 98-369, 99-514, 100-647, 101-508 |
| 1.25-1T | 99-514, 100-647, 101-239 | 1.46-5 | 97-34, 98-369, 100-647, 101-508 |
| 1.25-2T | 99-514, 100-647, 101-239, 104-188, 105-206 | 1.46-6 | 98-369, 99-514, 101-508 |
| | | 1.47-1 | 97-34, 97-248, 98-369, 98-443, |

Review the table. Find Treas. Reg. §1.42-29. The table indicates that this particular regulation has not been updated for Public Laws 101-239 and 103-66. Before relying on this particular regulation section, you should read the historical notes following IRC Code §42 under P.L. 101-239 and P.L. 103-66 to ascertain what effect, if any, the unreflected change may have upon Treas. Reg. §1.41-9. Note that the table is only as current as your regulation volume.

*Electronic* – In the electronic context, each publisher provides a different method of flagging the potential unreliability of a regulation provision, usually with some type of caution sign.

**Commerce Clearing House –** *Tax Research NetWork*

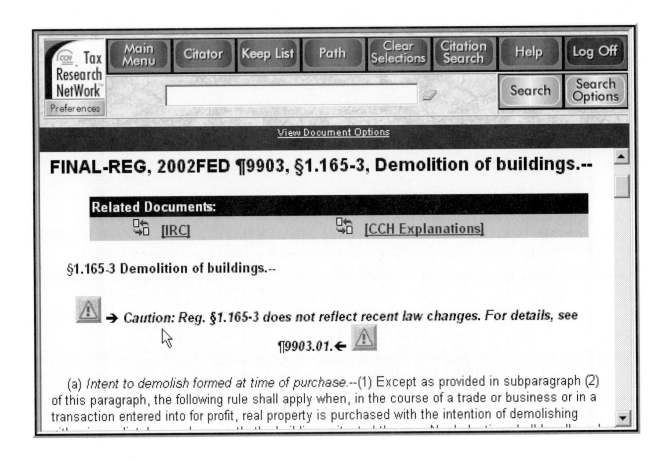

Unfortunately, when accessing the Treasury regulations over the public Internet, there is no such warning mechanism. If this is your source, you will need to follow up by using one of the other tools to check the reliability of the regulation.

Sometimes the regulations fail to provide all the information necessary to thoroughly address the research question. When this occurs, you will need to examine another source.

## REVENUE RULINGS

**Revenue rulings** differ substantially from regulations. Rather than provide generic interpretive guidance about a Code provision, revenue rulings are like mini-cases, often providing an analysis of a transaction and the relevant tax laws. They address the Code's application in a specific, unnamed, hypothetical taxpayer's situation. Revenue rulings are issued by the National Office of the IRS, sometimes in response to taxpayer inquiries, court decisions, or simply out of a perceived need for additional guidance.

Revenue rulings generally all follow the same format. Each includes the following:

- ◆ **Issue.** The IRS states the question needing clarification.

- ◆ **Facts.** Unlike cases, the facts are stated in an anonymous fashion: no dollar amounts, no names.

- ◆ **Law and Analysis.** The IRS sets forth the relevant provisions from the Code, regulations, prior revenue rulings, and case law.

- ◆ **Holding.** The IRS states how it will apply the law to the facts and resolves the issue stated.

- ◆ **Effect on Other Documents.** Any impact on a previously issued revenue ruling is noted here with an explanation.

☛ **Be careful when examining regulations using the public Internet - there may not be a warning when a regulation is obsolete.**

☛ **Revenue rulings address specific taxpayer factual scenarios.**

**ILLUSTRATION: The following illustrates a typical revenue ruling.**

**Revenue Ruling 97-9**
*[Code Sec. 213]*

ISSUE

Is an amount paid to obtain a controlled substance (such as marijuana) for medical purposes, in violation of federal law, a deductible expense for medical care under §213 of the Internal Revenue Code?

FACTS

Based on the recommendation of a physician, *A* purchased marijuana and used it to treat *A*'s disease in a state whose laws permit such purchase and use.

LAW AND ANALYSIS

Section 213(a) allows a deduction for uncompensated expenses of an individual for medical care to the extent such expenses exceed 7.5 percent of adjusted gross income. Section 213(d)(1) provides, in part, that "medical care" means amounts paid for the cure, mitigation, and treatment of disease. However, under §213(b) an amount paid for medicine or a drug is an expense for medical care under §213(a) only if the medicine or drug is a prescribed drug or insulin. Section 213(d)(3) provides that a "prescribed drug" is a drug or biological that requires a prescription of a physician for its use by an individual.

Section 1.213-1(e)(2) of the Income Tax Regulations provides, in part, that the term "medicine and drugs" includes only items that are "legally procured." Section 1.213-1(e)(1)(ii) provides that amounts expended for illegal operations or treatments are not deductible.

Rev. Rul. 78-325, 1978-2 C.B. 124, holds that amounts paid by a taxpayer for laetrile, prescribed by a physician for the medical treatment of the taxpayer's illness, are expenses for medicine and drugs that are deductible under §213. The revenue ruling states that the laetrile was purchased and used in a locality where its sale and use were legal.

Rev. Rul. 73-201, 1973-1 C.B. 140, holds that amounts paid for a vasectomy and an abortion are expenses for medical care that are deductible under §213. The revenue ruling states that neither procedure was illegal under state law.

*A*'s purchase and use of marijuana were permitted under the laws of *A*'s state. However, marijuana is listed as a controlled substance on Schedule I of the Controlled Substances Act (CSA), 21 U.S.C. §§801-971. 21 U.S.C. §812(c). Except as authorized by the CSA, it is unlawful for any person to manufacture, distribute, or dispense, or possess with intent to manufacture, distribute, or dispense, a controlled substance. 21 U.S.C. §841(a). Further, it is unlawful for any person knowingly or intentionally to possess a controlled substance except

---

**ILLUSTRATION:    Revenue Ruling 97-9** (continued)

as authorized by the CSA. 21 U.S.C. 844(a). Generally, the CSA does not permit the possession of controlled substances listed on Schedule I, even for medical purposes, and even with a physician's prescription.

Notwithstanding state law, a controlled substance (such as marijuana), obtained in violation of the CSA, is not "legally procured" within the meaning of §1.213-1(e)(2). Further, an amount expended to obtain a controlled substance (such as marijuana) in violation of the CSA is an amount expended for an illegal treatment within the meaning of §1.213-1(e)(1)(ii). Accordingly, *A* may not deduct under §213 the amount *A* paid to purchase marijuana.

HOLDING

An amount paid to obtain a controlled substance (such as marijuana) for medical purposes, in violation of federal law, is not a deductible expense for medical care under §213. This holding applies even if the state law requires a prescription of a physician to obtain and use the controlled substance and the taxpayer obtains a prescription.

EFFECT ON OTHER DOCUMENTS

Rev. Rul. 78-325 is obsoleted. Subsequent to the issuance of Rev. Rul. 78-325, the courts have upheld the Food and Drug Administration determination that generally prohibits interstate commerce in laetrile under the Food, Drug, and Cosmetic Act, 21 U.S.C. §§331 and 355(a). *See United States v. Rutherford*, 442 U.S. 544 (1979); *Rutherford v. United States*, 806 F.2d 1455 (10th Cir. 1986). Thus, notwithstanding state and local law, laetrile cannot be legally procured within the meaning of §1.213-1(e)(2). Accordingly, amounts paid to obtain laetrile are not deductible under §213.

Rev. Rul. 73-201 is clarified to reflect that the medical procedures at issue in that revenue ruling are not illegal under federal law.

DRAFTING INFORMATION

The principal authors of this revenue ruling are *(names omitted)*.

---

**Accessing Revenue Rulings**

Generally, the best method to effectively discover any relevant revenue ruling is through a reference service. This method is discussed in Chapter Five. There may be times when you wish to narrow your search to only revenue rulings. In this case, there is an additional useful source entitled *IRS Bulletin Index-Digest System*, which the Government Printing Office publishes. This provides the ability to identify most revenue rulings and revenue procedures by

Code section. The *IRS Bulletin Index-Digest System* summarizes each revenue ruling and revenue procedure and organizes them by Code section. In addition, relevant revenue rulings can be identified through the use of the *Digest's* topical index.

Revenue rulings are first issued in the *Internal Revenue Bulletin* (IRB). Once the IRB is bound into the *Cumulative Bulletin* (CB), you can locate revenue rulings in this source. The binding on each volume identifies the year covered and spectrum of revenue rulings it contains. To locate a revenue ruling, you simply need to know its number.

Revenue rulings consist of a two-part number as follows:

Rev. Rul. 2002 - 5

Assigned number in order of issuance for that year

Year of issuance

☛ **Revenue rulings are published in the weekly IRB and the hard-bound *Cumulative Bulletin*.**

Because the revenue ruling number indicates the year of the ruling, you can use this information to select the appropriate volume of the *Cumulative Bulletin*.

Once you locate the correct *Cumulative Bulletin* volume, it is not safe to assume that the revenue rulings are in numerical order. Revenue rulings are placed in the *Cumulative Bulletin* by Code section order. Therefore, it is best to use the table of contents at the very front of the bulletin. This directs you to the page number where the revenue ruling can be found.

**Proper Citation of Revenue Rulings**

Although you can easily locate a revenue ruling with just its number, it is generally not appropriate to cite one in this way. Proper citation includes both the revenue ruling number and information regarding the IRB or CB volume and page. When a revenue ruling is first issued, the appropriate cite is to the *Internal Revenue Bulletin*. Once it is placed in the *Cumulative Bulletin*, the appropriate cite is to the *Cumulative Bulletin*. The following illustrates the citation methods.

***Internal Revenue Bulletin***:

Rev. Rul. 99-100, I.R.B. 1999-20, 15

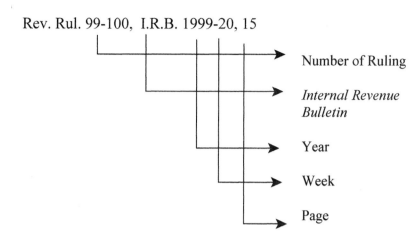

Number of Ruling

*Internal Revenue Bulletin*

Year

Week

Page

An appropriate revenue ruling cite includes the reference to the IRB or CB.

***Cumulative Bulletin***:

Rev. Rul. 83-137, 1983-2 C.B. 15

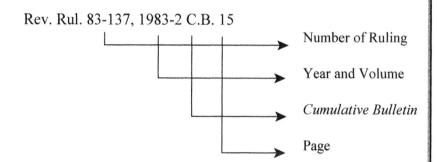

Number of Ruling

Year and Volume

*Cumulative Bulletin*

Page

## Authority of Revenue Rulings

When you discover a potentially relevant revenue ruling, it is important to determine whether it is authoritative. Revenue rulings are not as authoritative as Treasury regulations due to their factual nature. The closer the research facts are to those in the revenue ruling, the more authoritative the revenue ruling is. A revenue ruling that addresses the same research question and involves a very similar factual situation offers significant potential authority. Any material difference in the facts usually diminishes the authoritative value of a revenue ruling.

Absent a decision to risk litigation, it is ill-advised to take a position clearly contrary to a revenue ruling that addresses the same research issue with substantially the same material facts. To do so risks monetary penalties, discussed further in Chapter Eight.

Revenue rulings offer less authority than regulations.

One very important step remains before concluding that a revenue ruling is reliable authority.  You must confirm that no subsequent Revenue Ruling has affected its authority. This step is called "citating" and is discussed later.

## How to Ensure Reliability

Before relying on a revenue ruling, it is <u>essential </u>to check and confirm that the revenue ruling reflects the current position of the IRS. At least three possible subsequent events may have occurred that impact its reliability.

☞ **A revenue ruling that appears authoritative may in reality provide no authority.**

- The issuance of a later revenue ruling modifying or superseding the revenue ruling.

- A decision by a court questioning or invalidating the authoritative value of the ruling.

- An amendment to a Code section addressed in the revenue ruling clearly impacting the reasoning or authoritative value of the ruling.

A revoked revenue ruling has no authority regarding transactions occurring after the date of the new revenue ruling.  In addition, at times, the IRS has retroactively revoked the authority of a revenue ruling, entirely eliminating any authority of the earlier ruling.

A court decision that takes a position contrary to a revenue ruling is not binding on the IRS outside of the court's jurisdiction. Nonetheless, awareness of the court decision may impact the research conclusion.

☞ **Courts are not bound by revenue rulings.**

Clearly, a revenue ruling made obsolete by legislative action has no authoritative value regarding transactions falling within the new Code provisions.

The IRS does not remove revoked or obsolete rulings from the IRB or *Cumulative Bulletin*.  Therefore, failure to confirm that the revenue ruling is still reliable may result in an incorrect conclusion.

Determining the current authoritative value of a revenue Ruling is quite a bit easier than doing the same for a regulation. Remember that the final portion of a revenue ruling describes its impact on any previously issued ruling. Thus, any superseded revenue ruling is actually cited in the one more recently issued. The two major tax publishers, Commerce Clearing House (CCH) and Research Institute of America (RIA), use this system to create an excellent resource called the *citator*.

The citator works by listing all cases, revenue rulings, and revenue procedures that have ever cited the revenue ruling you wish to rely on. To create the citator, the publishers perform electronic searches through all cases, revenue rulings, and procedures searching for all rulings, procedures, and cases cited. This search results in a list of cases and rulings that have previously cited any particular document. The citator is simply a compilation of these lists.

At times, the publishers of the citators edit the list of cases and rulings. This may result in a slight difference between the list results of the various citators. Each publisher represents that its list is more comprehensive than its competitors. You will need to decide which citator is best for you.

The citator does not identify all the documents that may be logically related to the one you are checking. The list of documents in a citator entry includes only documents that actually cite the revenue ruling you are checking. Nor will the citator identify a Code amendment potentially affecting the reliability of the revenue ruling, unless the text of the amendment specifically refers to the ruling. The Code itself is the best source to learn whether it has changed the effect of a ruling. Therefore, it is important to understand that the citator offers a very specific, but limited, benefit: to indicate if the IRS or the courts amended or superseded the authority of a previously issued revenue ruling or procedure.

You can access the citator lists in print or electronically. If you use a hard copy, you must go to the "Finding List" in the citator to

**☛ The citator indicates whether the IRS or courts amended the authority of a ruling or procedure.**

**☛ The citator will not alert the researcher if a Code amendment renders a revenue ruling obsolete.**

locate the revenue rulings.  In this numerically ordered list, you can look up a revenue ruling and determine if it has been impacted in any way by a subsequent revenue ruling or court decision.

---

**EXAMPLE 3:  Citing a Revenue Ruling**

Revenue Ruling 78-325 directly addresses the research question.  You plan to base your conclusion on the ruling. You check the citator to confirm the ruling has not been superseded or otherwise affected by a subsequent ruling.  When citing the ruling, you find the following in each of the citators:

> **CCH-CITATOR, 98FED, Main Finding Lists, Rev. Rul. 78-325**
> **Rev. Rul. 78-325, 1978-2 CB 124**
> ANNOTATED AT  98FED ¶12,543.012; ¶12,543.60, 1978 CCH ¶6874
>> Obsoleted by:
>> Rev. Rul. 97-9

The preceding citator listing indicates that you cannot rely on the revenue ruling because it was made obsolete.   Instead, you must examine Rev. Rul. 97-9 to determine whether it has been superseded by a subsequent ruling.   This is what you find when you look up Rev. Rul. 97-9 in the citator.

> **CCH-CITATOR, 98FED, Main Finding Lists, Rev. Rul. 97-9**
> Rev. Rul. 97-9, IRB 1997-9, February 13, 1997
> ANNOTATED AT  ........... 98FED ¶7324.35; ¶12,543.012; ¶12,543.0671;
> ¶12,543.60, 1997 CCH ¶46,284
>  Clarifying:
> Rev. Rul. 73-201
> Obsoleting:
> Rev. Rul. 78-325

This citator entry indicates that there are no subsequent rulings impacting the authority of Revenue Ruling 97-9.  It also confirms the ruling's impact on other previous rulings. Chapter Five explains the meaning of the annotation references at the beginning of this entry.

---

The ability to cite documents electronically significantly simplifies this process. Electronic citating generates the same information as provided in hard copy. The electronic citator is an electronic reflection of the hard copy document. Thus, it is generally no more current. However, electronic citing enables quick electronic access to those documents citing the one you are checking. This enables you to more quickly determine the revenue ruling's reliability. Using the print citator, thorough citing can be quite onerous.

Generally, the electronic products (CCH and RIA) enable you to discover the reliability of a revenue ruling or another "citatable" document using two different methods. One method involves going into the electronic citator and entering the revenue ruling cite. Another method allows you to determine the reliability of the revenue ruling while reading the ruling. If you are reading a revenue ruling electronically, both of the services allow you to click on the "citator" button, which takes you directly to the citator page for that ruling. The Appendix provides detailed illustrations on the electronic citing process.

### ILLUSTRATION: Commerce Clearing House *Tax Research NetWork*

The relevant entry in the citator appears on the screen as follows.

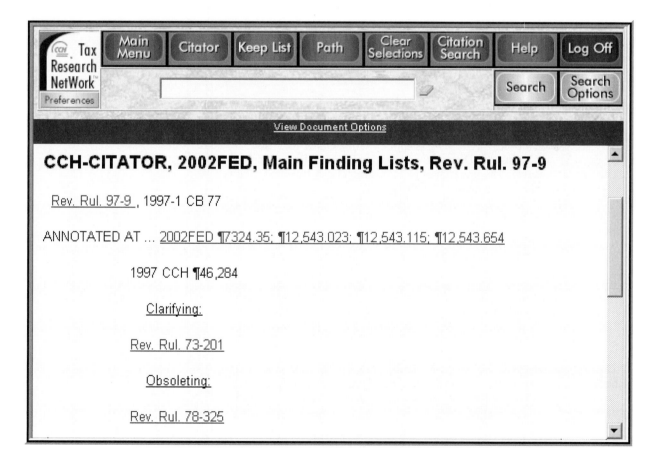

## REVENUE PROCEDURES

The National Office of the IRS also publishes official guidelines regarding procedural matters. These are called **revenue procedures**. Revenue procedures are usually not fact specific but offer important procedural information. For example, there are revenue procedures on such topics as accounting method changes, procedures regarding tax treaty interpretation, and procedures for obtaining letter rulings.

Revenue procedures usually follow a format similar to revenue rulings. Lengthy procedures begin with a table of contents, followed by a discussion of any changes since the last version of the procedure. The detailed procedural information follows.

☞ **Revenue procedures are procedural guidelines published by the IRS.**

---

**ILLUSTRATION:  Revenue Procedure 89-7**

**Commissions: Dismissal pay.**--Dismissal pay, that is, pay by an employer to an employee whose services are ended independently of his will or wishes, is counted as wages for social security purposes.

SECTION 1. BACKGROUND

Rev. Proc. 89-3, page 761, this Bulletin sets forth areas in which advance rulings or determination letters will not be issued by the Internal Revenue Service. Section 5 of Rev. Proc. 89-3 is entitled "Area Under Extensive Study In Which Rulings Or Determination Letters Will Not Be Issued Until The Service Resolves The Issue Through Publication Of A Revenue Ruling, Revenue Procedure, Regulations Or Otherwise.;"

SEC. 2. PROCEDURE

Rev. Proc. 89-3 is hereby amplified by adding to section 5 the following new section: Sections 3121 and 3306. Definitions.

Whether payments made to former employees in the event of a plant closing, layoff, or reduction in force are wages for purposes of the Federal Insurance Contributions Act (FICA) and the Federal Unemployment Tax Act (FUTA).

SEC. 3. EFFECTIVE DATE

This revenue procedure will apply to all ruling requests on hand in the National Office on January 17, 1989, the date of publication of this revenue procedure in the Internal Revenue Bulletin, as well as to requests received thereafter.

SEC. 4. EFFECT ON OTHER REVENUE PROCEDURES
Rev. Proc. 89-3 is amplified.

← Areas where IRS will not issue a ruling.

← Changes to previously issued procedure.

← Effect on previously issued procedures.

Note that revenue procedure 89-7, illustrated, does not address the substantive issue of whether certain payments made to former employees in the event of a plant closing, layoff, or reduction in force are wages for purposes of the Federal Insurance Contributions Act and the Federal Unemployment Tax Act.  Rather, the revenue procedure simply addresses whether the IRS will issue a letter ruling or determination letter regarding such payment.  Contrast this "procedural" guidance to a revenue ruling that would discuss the substance of the particular issue.

Reference services should alert you to any relevant revenue procedures.  To locate a potentially helpful revenue procedure, you follow the same procedure used to locate a revenue ruling.  Similar to revenue rulings, the IRS publishes revenue procedures in the IRB and *Cumulative Bulletin*.  If you have only the revenue procedure number and not the remainder of the cite, make sure to use the *Cumulative Bulletin* table of contents.  Be sure you examine the list of revenue procedures and not the list of revenue rulings.  Distinguishing between the list of rulings and procedures can be tricky since the numbering system for both is the same.

**☞ Reference services will refer you to a potentially useful revenue procedure.**

When you discover a revenue procedure on point, use the citator to ensure its reliability in the same fashion you used it for checking the reliability of a revenue ruling.

**☞ Use the citator to ensure reliability of a revenue procedure.**

Revenue procedures are cited just like revenue rulings, except that instead of "Rev. Rul.," the cite is "Rev. Proc."  The following illustrates a reference to a revenue procedure:

Rev. Proc. 95-1, 1995-1 C.B. 10

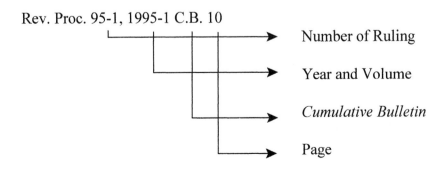

Number of Ruling

Year and Volume

*Cumulative Bulletin*

Page

## LETTER RULINGS AND TECHNICAL ADVICE MEMORANDA

In addition to revenue rulings, the National Office of the IRS issues documents called **letter rulings** and **technical advice memoranda**. These documents read like a revenue ruling; however, they are less authoritative. The IRS issues letter rulings (also referred to as *private letter rulings*) in response to a specific taxpayer's letter outlining a proposed transaction and requesting clarification as to the application of particular federal tax laws to the transaction. A technical advice memorandum (TAM) is a response to a request by an IRS District Director or an appeals officer who has a question that develops during an audit requiring a high level of technical expertise and consistent approach.

☛ **Letter rulings may provide advance comfort to a taxpayer planning a transaction.**

Taxpayers submit letter ruling requests in order to acquire greater comfort about the tax consequences of a planned transaction. If the IRS indicates in the letter ruling that the taxpayer will receive the type of tax treatment desired, the taxpayer is then more comfortable going ahead with the transaction. Because of this, taxpayers frequently request a letter ruling. As a result, the IRS response to a request often takes several months, sometimes years.

In addition, there are many topics on which the IRS will not issue a ruling. The IRS often chooses to refuse to issue letter rulings in areas involving what it believes to be settled law. In essence, the argument is that if the law is clear on a particular point, there is no need to issue hundreds of rulings restating the obvious. Of course, what is obvious to one party may not be as apparent to another. Consequently, taxpayers engaged in complex transactions are often denied the comfort of a letter ruling because the IRS has announced its unwillingness to issue further rulings in a particular area.

☛ **The IRS will not issue letter rulings in a number of areas.**

Every year, the IRS provides guidance regarding the requirements for submitting a letter ruling request, the requisite fees, and other details. The first revenue procedure issued each year provides this guidance. Note that the IRS often issues revenue procedures to describe circumstances pursuant to which it may be willing to issue a letter ruling. The IRS is under no specific duty to issue letter rulings to a taxpayer, and it may condition the issuance of letter rulings on the taxpayer's satisfaction of standards and tests that may go well beyond the requirements of the Code or other applicable tax laws. In essence, the IRS, through a revenue procedure, may require a taxpayer to do more than what is generally necessary in order to obtain a letter ruling.

It is very important to understand that letter rulings and TAMs have limited authoritative value. The IRS indicates that they provide authority only to the taxpayer for which the letter ruling or TAM was issued. Nonetheless, letter rulings and TAMs are considered authority. A variety of court cases have indicated that letter rulings are helpful in generally determining the position of the IRS. Therefore, if there is no other relevant authority, and a letter ruling appears to provide helpful guidance, you may use it, with caution, in arriving at a research conclusion.

---

**ILLUSTRATION: Letter Ruling**

**LTR-RUL, UIL No. 513.00-00 Unrelated v. not unrelated trade or business, Letter Ruling 200204051, November 1, 2001**
CCH IRS Letter Rulings Report No. 1300, 1-30-02

Relevant IRC §

**Uniform Issue List Information:**
UIL No. 0513.00-00

Unrelated v. not unrelated trade or business

[Code Sec. 513 ]

This is in reply to your request for rulings regarding the federal tax consequences associated with the transactions described below . . .*language omitted.*

Facts → O is a T nonprofit corporation and is recognized as exempt from federal income tax under section 501(a) of the Internal Revenue Code as an . . .*language omitted.*

You state that recent terrorist activities have caused massive collateral damage to the V metropolitan area. . .*language omitted.*

Section 513(a) of the Code provides that the term unrelated trade or business means. . . *language omitted.*

Law → Section 1.513-1(a) of the Income Tax Regulations (the Regulations) provides, in general, as used in section 512 , the term "unrelated business taxable income". . . *language omitted.*

Rev. Rul. 71-29 , 1971-1 C.B. 150 provides that a grant to a. . . *language omitted.*

Conclusion → Accordingly, we rule that providing ferry service in the manner and for the purposes described in your ruling request will . . . *language omitted.*

This ruling is based on the understanding that there will be no material changes in the facts upon which it is based.

This ruling is directed only to the organization that requested it. Section 6110(k)(3) of the Code provides that it may not be used or cited as precedent.

Because the IRS did not intend for these documents to be employed as citable authority, prior to 1974, the IRS did not make them available to the public. This is why letter rulings used to be referred to as private letter rulings. However, with the passage of the Freedom of Information Act in the late 1960s, the IRS was required to begin releasing to the public letter rulings. There is no official government source for the letter rulings and TAMs. However, they are now accessible in electronic form through the private tax publishers.

**Reference services do not refer to most letter rulings.**

Unfortunately, perhaps because of their limited research value, the tax reference services usually do not alert you to all relevant letter rulings and TAMs. This can be a severe limitation if a taxpayer is engaged in a "cutting edge" transaction and you are unable to easily locate pertinent authority. To find all relevant letter rulings, you must perform an extra research step. Notice on the research process flowchart at the beginning of this chapter where this step occurs. Generally, you should seek relevant letter rulings and TAMs when nearing the end of the research process.

Each of the tax publishers provides access to letter rulings or TAMs electronically, either in CD-ROM format or through fee-based online access. Chapter Five provides detailed information regarding researching using the electronic reference services. However, the process for finding relevant letter rulings is a distinct step in the research process and, therefore, best to learn separately.

Performing an electronic search for a Code Section is the most efficient method of finding a relevant letter ruling or TAM. Because letter rulings always contain the cite to each Code section being interpreted, you should be able to discover all relevant letter rulings and TAMs through a search. Chapter Five provides detailed information about electronic searches. The Appendix contains step-by-step illustrations on how to electronically locate letter rulings and TAMs.

**Finding a private letter ruling through electronic searching is most efficient.**

## How to Cite Letter Rulings

If there is a letter ruling or TAM you wish to cite in a document, the rules are not as rigid as those previously discussed. There are no official citation standards for this type of document.  The official citation source for the legal community (*The Bluebook: A Uniform System of Citation,* published by Harvard Law Review Association) suggests that letter rulings and TAMs should be cited as follows:

☞ **There is no one way to cite a letter ruling.**

- Letter Ruling:  P.L.R. 2001-52-012
  (November 30, 2002)

- Technical Advice Memo:  T.A.M. 2002-02-005
  (January 20, 2002)

Frequently, you will see these documents cited without the hyphens separating the numbers.  In addition, the preface for a letter ruling may also be *LTR* or the term spelled out.  More important is the significance of the numbers.  Whether the reference is to a letter ruling or a TAM, the elements of the cite are:

☞ **The cite contains no reference to volume or page.**

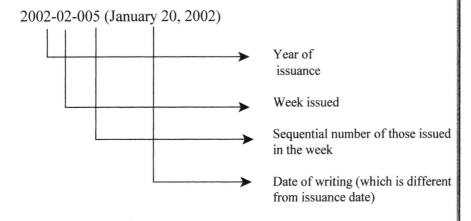

2002-02-005 (January 20, 2002)

→ Year of issuance

→ Week issued

→ Sequential number of those issued in the week

→ Date of writing (which is different from issuance date)

## OTHER TYPES OF TREASURY INTERPRETATIONS

The IRS issues interpretive guidance in a variety of forms, although the types discussed to this point are those most frequently used.  Occasionally, you may find one of the following useful:

❏    Field service advice memoranda
❏    Chief counsel orders and notices
❏    General counsel memoranda
❏    Treasury Department news releases
❏    IRS announcements/notices
❏    IRS publications
❏    Actions on decisions
❏    Acquiescences and nonacquiescences
❏    *Internal Revenue Manual*
❏    IRS forms and instructions

**Field service advice memoranda (FSAs)** are similar to letter rulings.  However, the Office of Chief Counsel issues FSAs in response to requests from IRS personnel such as revenue agents and field attorneys.  The IRS states that FSAs are intended only to assist in resolving matters.  They do not represent the IRS's final position on matters.

**Chief Counsel orders and notices** provide notice of the positions of the Office of the Chief Counsel who is responsible for administering the IRS's revenue rulings and revenue procedures.  These orders are for internal purposes only and provide no authoritative value for the researcher.

The IRS Office of the Chief Counsel publishes **General Counsel Memoranda** (GCMs) as internal guidance to the IRS for preparing external documents such as revenue rulings and letter rulings.  These memoranda provide an indication regarding the IRS's position in an upcoming revenue ruling.  Because they are intended as internal documents, GCMs are not binding authority and are not officially published but are available due to the Freedom of Information Act.

☞ **Field service advice memoranda are similar to letter rulings except that they are issued by the Chief Counsel.**

**ILLUSTRATION: General Counsel Memorandum**

GCM 39867
Date Numbered: December 18, 1991

      Internal Control Number: TR-58-12-90
      Br6:RLOldak

Uniform Issue List Information:
    UIL No. 0501.03-33
    Exemption from tax on corporations, certain trusts, etc.
    - Religious, charitable, etc., institutions and community chest
    -- Lessening the burdens of government

[Code Sec. 501]
An organization that plans, organizes, . . . *(facts omitted)*
(Name omitted)
Assistant Commissioner
(Employee Plans and Exempt Organizations)

Attention: Director, Exempt Organizations Technical Division

    This responds to your memorandum dated March 28, 1990, submitting for our concurrence or comments a proposed ruling letter to the above organization.

ISSUE

    Whether an organization that plans, organizes, promotes, prepares for and participates in the inauguration of a state governor, including activities which are not available to the general public, qualifies for exemption as an organization described in I.R.C. §501(c)(3).

CONCLUSION

    We agree with your conclusion that the Committee does not qualify for exemption as an organization described in section 501(c)(3). However, we would base this conclusion on the following: . . .*(discussion omitted)*

---

**ILLUSTRATION:** (continued)

FACTS

The ***** (Committee) was incorporated in ***** "to plan, organize, promote, prepare for and participate in the inauguration of  ***** as the Governor the State of ***** and to receive and maintain a fund or funds of personal property for such purpose, with the means of providing facilities, equipment and other property and services necessary to properly carry out the inauguration." *(Text omitted)*

ANALYSIS

Section 501(a) provides an exemption from federal income tax for organizations described in subsection 501(c)(3). . . .*(facts omitted)*

Treas. Reg. 1.501(c)(3)-1(a)(1) provides . . . *(Text omitted)*

GCM 39347, EE-118-79 (Oct. 20, 1982), held that in determining whether an organization lessens the burdens of government a two-step analysis is required . . .*(Text omitted)*

In *Columbia Park & Recreation Association v. Commissioner*, 88 T.C. 1, 18-21 (1987). . . *(Text omitted)*

Accordingly, based both on . . . *(Text omitted)* we concur in your proposed adverse ruling to the Committee with respect to its section 501(c)(3) status.

---

**Treasury Department news releases** provide general information to the public regarding recently published regulations and IRS forms and instructions. The news releases generally do not provide significant substantive information and are not usually considered authoritative.

The National Office of the IRS issues **announcements and notices** at times when the IRS believes it is necessary to quickly provide interpretive guidance to the public. Often the texts of the announcements and notices become revenue rulings. These are authoritative documents similar in weight to a revenue ruling or procedure. The IRS publishes them in the *Federal Register* and *Internal Revenue Bulletin*. Notices are also published in the *Cumulative Bulletin*; announcements are not. Both are generally available in paper and electronic versions.

---

**ILLUSTRATION:   Notice**

Notice 2002-7,  January 24, 2002.

**Disaster relief: Terrorist attacks: Retirement plans: Extensions: Presidentially declared disasters.**--The IRS has provided relief with respect to employee benefit plans for affected taxpayers who are unable to meet their federal tax obligations due to the September 11, 2001, terrorist attacks. . . . *(language omitted)*

A. For all plans:

1. If the dates described in §412(c)(10) or 412(m) of the Code and §302(c)(10) or 302(e) of ERISA for making contributions fell within the period beginning on September 11, 2001, and ending on September 23, 2001, then the date such contributions must be made is postponed to September 24, 2001. . .*(language omitted)*

---

☞ **Notices enable the IRS to provide speedy guidance when needed.**

The IRS publishes another type of interpretation to provide guidance to the general public – **IRS publications**. The IRS writes publications in general terms, using more understandable language than in other types of interpretations. The IRS annually updates many of the publications such as Publication 17, *Your Federal Income Tax*. Others are updated as needed. Publications are not listed in the regulations as types of documents that provide substantive authority. They do not bind the IRS. Thus, although they may be helpful to the lay person, they are generally not particularly useful to the tax researcher. However, in practical terms, they may be very helpful in determining the best way to report a particular transaction to the IRS. Publications are available through each of the major tax publishers both in paper and electronic versions.

☞ **IRS publications are generally intended to serve the lay public rather than tax practitioners.**

Another type of internal IRS communication comes in the form of **actions on decisions** (AODs), which are sometimes prepared by the IRS when it loses a tax case in court. An AOD summarizes the case and recommends what action the IRS should take: agree with the decision (issue an acquiescence) or disagree (issue a nonacquiescence). The IRS publishes AODs in the *Internal Revenue Bulletin*. They can also be found in CCH's *IRS Positions*.

## ILLUSTRATION: AOD

HAROLD L. AND TEMPLE M. JENKINS V. COMMISSIONER

File No:AOD/CC-1984-022
March 23, 1984

Decision: C.A. 6th., Docket No.: 3354-79, November 3, 1983, T.C. MEMO 1983-667, 23 TN 175     ← *Case decision IRS is discussing*

Internal Control No.: CC:TL
Br4:DCFegan

Uniform Issue List Nos: 0162.01-17     ← *Code section at issue*
0162.29-00

ISSUE

Whether Conway Twitty is allowed a business expense deduction for payments to reimburse the losses of investors in a defunct restaurant known as Twitty Burger, Inc. 0162.01-17; 0162.29-00.

DISCUSSION

The Tax Court summarized its opinion in this case with the following "Ode to Conway Twitty":

"Twitty Burger went belly up
But Conway remained true
He repaid his investors, one and all
It was the moral thing to do.
His fans would not have liked it
It could have hurt his fame
Had any investors sued him
Like Merle Haggard or Sonny James.
'When it was time to file taxes
Conway thought what he would do
Was deduct those payments as a business expense
Under section one-sixty-two.
In order to allow these deductions
Goes the argument of the Commissioner
The payments must be ordinary and necessary
To a business of the petitioner.
Had Conway not repaid the investors
His career would have been under cloud,
Under the unique facts of this case

*Held: The deductions are allowed."*

**ILLUSTRATION:** (continued)

Our reaction to the Court's opinion is reflected in the following 'Ode to
Conway Twitty: A Reprise':
Harold Jenkins and Conway Twitty
They are both the same
But one was born
The other achieved fame.
The man is talented
And has many a friend
They opened a restaurant
His name he did lend.
They are two different things
Making burgers and song
The business went sour
It didn't take long.
He repaid his friends
Why did he act
Was it business or friendship
Which is fact?
Business the court held
It's deductible they feel
We disagree with the answer
But let's not appeal.

RECOMMENDATION

Nonacquiescence. ←————————

Reviewers: . . . (*names omitted*)

IRS's conclusion
whether it will
follow the
decision
in future cases.

When the Tax Court issues a regular decision contrary to the
IRS's position, the IRS may choose to issue internal communications
indicating its acceptance or nonacceptance of the court's decision. An
**acquiescence** indicates that the Service will not continue to pursue its
position taken in the litigation leading to the decision. An
acquiescence does not necessarily indicate approval of the court's
rationale. A **nonacquiescence** indicates that it is the IRS's intention
to continue applying its previous position regardless of the court
decision.

☞**Nonacquiescence
means the IRS
plans to continue
its position
regardless of the
court decision.**

Acquiescences and nonacquiescences are published in the
*Internal Revenue Bulletin* and the *Cumulative Bulletin*, usually in the

form of a revenue ruling.  In addition, each citator provides information as to whether the IRS issued an acquiescence.

---

### ILLUSTRATION: Nonacquiescence

**Rev. Rul. 85-143, 1985-2 CB 55**

**Section 104.--Compensation for Injuries or Sickness**

*26 CFR 1.104-1: Compensation for injuries or sickness.*

**[IRS Headnote] Damages; libel suit.--**
The Service will not follow the opinion of the United States Court of Appeals in *Roemer v. Commissioner,* 716 F.2d 693 (9th Cir. 1983), *rev'g* 79 T.C. 398 (1982), relating to the taxability of compensatory damages awarded in a libel suit. The Service will follow the decision of the Tax Court in *Roemer.*
[Text]
The Internal Revenue Service will not follow the opinion of the United States Court of Appeals in *Roemer v. Commissioner,* 716 F.2d 693 (9th Cir. 1983), *rev'g* 79 T.C. 398 (1982). The Service will follow the decisions of the Tax Court in *Roemer.*

In *Roemer,* the taxpayer was an insurance broker who had operated his own insurance business in California for many years. By the mid-1960's, the taxpayer enjoyed an excellent reputation in the community, both personally and professionally, and earned a high income from his insurance business. Until 1965, the taxpayer sold primarily casualty insurance. At that time, the taxpayer had an opportunity to expand into the life insurance business. In connection with that opportunity, the taxpayer applied for an agency license from *IC,* a life insurance company. *IC* ordered a credit report on the taxpayer from *X,* a credit bureau. . . .(language omitted.)

---

← **Notice that the IRS indicates it will not follow the court's decision.**

The Internal Revenue Service provides to its employees a manual containing the IRS's procedures, policies, and operational guidelines.  This is called the ***Internal Revenue Manual*** (IRM).  The IRM is available in print and electronically.  Generally, the IRM does not offer authoritative guidelines; however, it may sometimes help to clarify the IRS's position regarding a certain Code provision or Treasury interpretation.

☞ **The IRM is written for IRS employees.**

Of course, the Internal Revenue Service also publishes its official interpretation of the correct application of the federal tax laws through its tax forms and related instructions.  At times, you may find these forms quite instructive.  They are not, however, considered to be authoritative or binding.

The following table provides examples of the citation method for some of these Treasury interpretations.

| Document | How to Cite |
|---|---|
| Field Service Advice | FSA 2001-51-100 |
| General Counsel Memoranda | G.C.M. (42789) or Gen. Couns. Mem. 42,789 [sequential number with no relation to year or code section] |
| IRS Announcements/Notices | Announcement/Notice 84-9, 1984-1 IRB 3 |
| Treasury Department News Releases | IR-88-35 (Feb. 19, 1988) |
| IRS Publications | IRS Publication 17 |
| Actions on Decisions | A.O.D. 1998-150 [year and sequential number] |

## CHAPTER SUMMARY

The Treasury Department provides a variety of documents indicating its position regarding the appropriate application of the Internal Revenue Code.  Each type of interpretation varies in the amount of authoritative value it offers the researcher.  Final treasury regulations may provide a great deal of authority if the regulation is a current interpretation of the Code.  Before relying on a regulation, you must take steps to ensure that its authority has not been impacted by a change in the Code.

Revenue rulings also may provide strong authority.  Unlike the more generic regulations, revenue rulings generally provide Treasury guidance regarding a specific set of facts. Revenue procedures provide similar authority in procedural areas.  Before relying on either a revenue ruling or a revenue procedure, you must confirm that no later rulings or procedures have impacted the one you wish to rely on.  To ensure their reliability, you must "cite" the document.

There are several additional forms of Treasury interpretations.  The following table summarizes those discussed in this chapter.

| Type | Description | Level of Authority | Method of Citation | Electronic Sources |
|---|---|---|---|---|
| Regulations | Final, proposed, and temporary regulations. Descriptive narrative explaining the general application of a Code section.  Issued by U.S. Treasury Department as treasury decisions (TDs). | Like law as long as they are reasonable and consistent with the Code. | Treas. Reg. §1.162-5<br><br>Prop. Reg. §30.280A<br><br>Temp. Reg. §15.132 | CD-ROM and Internet |
| Revenue Rulings | How the Code applies to a specific set of facts. Issued by National Office of IRS. | Authoritative if taxpayer facts are materially the same as those in the ruling. | Rev. Rul. 98-5, IRB 1998-15,20<br><br>or<br><br>Rev. Rul. 97-50, 1997-2 CB 400 | CD-ROM and Internet |
| Revenue Procedures | Procedural guidelines provided by National Office of IRS. | Authoritative if relevant. | Rev. Proc. 99-5, 1999-4, IRB 50<br>or<br>Rev. Proc. 96-1, 1996-1 CB 5 | CD-ROM and Internet |
| Letter Rulings | How the Code applies to a specific set of facts. Issued by the National Office of the IRS to the taxpayer requesting the ruling. | Binding only on the IRS with respect to the taxpayer who requested the ruling.  Of very limited authority to other taxpayers even if  facts are same as those in the ruling. | Letter Ruling 98-34-210<br>or<br>Letter Ruling 9834210 | CD-ROM and Internet |
| Technical Advice Memoranda<br><br>and<br><br>Field Service Advice Memoranda | How the Code applies to a specific set of facts. Issued by the National Office of the IRS (TAM) or Office of the Chief Counsel (FSA) internal personnel in response to their request for guidance during an audit. | Binding only on the IRS with respect to the taxpayer who requested the ruling.  Of very limited authority to other taxpayers even if facts are same as those in the TAM or FSA. | Technical Advice Memoranda 97-23-400<br>or<br><br>FSA 9723400 | CD-ROM and Internet |

| Type | Description | Level of Authority | Method of Citation | Electronic Sources |
|---|---|---|---|---|
| Determination Letters | Letters issued by a district IRS office applying National Office IRS policies to a specific factual situation. | Similar to letter rulings. | | Internet |
| IRS Announcements/ Notices | Issued prior to a revenue ruling or procedure when immediate guidance is necessary.  Usually later embodied in a revenue ruling.  Issued by National Office of IRS. | Same as for revenue rulings and revenue procedures. | Announcement 2002-7, 2002-3 IRB 10 | Internet |
| General Counsel Memoranda | Internal communication within IRS regarding recommended action on revenue rulings, letter rulings, etc. | Same as letter rulings. | G.C.M. (42789) or Gen. Couns. Mem. 42,789 | Internet |
| Actions on Decisions | Internal communication within IRS recommending action to be taken as a result of loss of IRS in court case. | Not authoritative. | A.O.D. 1998-150 [year and sequential number] | Internet |
| Acquiescences/ nonacquiescence | Internal communication within IRS indicating the IRS's reaction to an adverse tax court decision. An acquiescence indicates the IRS's intent to  adopt the court's position. | Not binding on IRS or taxpayer. | Issued and cited as a revenue ruling. | Internet |
| IRS Publications | Guidelines published by National Office of IRS for the purpose of informing the general public about how the tax laws are to be applied. | Not authoritative. | IRS Publication 17 | CD-ROM and Internet |

# PROBLEMS

## *KEY CONCEPTS* (1-22)

1.    Define and discuss the following terms:

    a.    proposed regulations
    b.    temporary regulations
    c.    final regulations
    d.    preamble to regulations
    e.    26 CFR
    f    *Internal Revenue Bulletin*
    g    *Cumulative Bulletin*
    h.    revenue rulings
    i.    revenue procedures
    j.    Citator
    k.    private letter rulings
    l.    technical advice memoranda
    m.    field service advice memoranda
    n.    determination letters
    o.    General Counsel memoranda
    p.    IRS announcements
    q.    IRS news releases
    r.    IRS publications
    s.    actions on decisions
    t    acquiescence/nonacquiescence

2.    Discuss why the researcher must pay close attention to Treasury interpretations, even if there is a court case that is helpful to the taxpayer.

3.    When should the researcher turn to the Treasury regulations for guidance?  Can the researcher always count on the Treasury regulations to help answer the research question? Why or why not?

4.    How is it possible to have a regulation conflict with a Code section?

5.    What steps must the researcher take to ensure the reliability of a regulation?

6. List four sources where you can access the full text of a Treasury regulation. Compare the sources. What are their advantages and disadvantages?

7. How are Treasury regulations and revenue rulings different?

8. When does a revenue ruling provide the greatest amount of authority to the researcher?

9. What are the central components of a revenue ruling?

10. What do the elements of the following revenue ruling cites represent?

Rev. Rul. 97-54, 1997-1 C.B. 25
Rev. Rul. 99-20, I.R.B. 1999-5, 10

11. Describe the process you must take to ensure the reliability of a revenue ruling.

12. Does the citator inform you of all documents that are related to the research issue? Why or why not?

13. What is the difference between a letter ruling and a revenue ruling?

14. Describe how to locate the revenue rulings that interpret a specific Code section when you do not wish to use a reference service.

15. What do the elements in the following letter ruling cite represent?

PLR 2000-45-300 (August 10, 2000)

16. When is it advisable to research letter rulings and technical advice memoranda? How do you find which letter rulings are relevant to your question?

17. Why is it usually more prudent to electronically search the letter ruling database for a Code section or regulation section cite rather than a key word?

18. What is the significance of an acquiescence? Nonacquiescence? When are they issued?

19. What are the differences between the Code and the regulations?

20.    What are the differences between a revenue ruling and a revenue procedure?

21.    How does the IRS indicate its opinion about a court decision?

22.    How can you determine whether the IRS has acquiesced to a court decision?


## *PRACTICAL APPLICATIONS* (23-63)

23.    Correctly cite the highlighted portion of the following regulation:

Treas. Reg. Section 132-5 - Working Condition Fringe

(a) In general –(1) Definition.  Gross income does not include . . .*(text omitted)*

(i) A service or property offered by an employer in connection . . .*(text omitted)*

(ii) If, under section 274 or any other section, certain . . .*(text omitted)*

(iii) An amount that would be deductible by the employee under . . .*(text omitted)*

(iv) A physical examination program . . .*(text omitted)*

(v) A cash payment made by an  . . .*(text omitted)*

   (A) Use the payment for expenses in connection with . . .*(text omitted)*

   (B) **Verify that the payment is actually used for such expenses, and**

   (C) Return to the employer any part of the payment not so used.

24    Indicate what information the Treasury regulations provide regarding the application of the following Code section.

   a.    IRC Section 162(a), particularly the language "ordinary and necessary."
   b.    IRC Section 183, particularly the language "engaged in for profit."
   c.    IRC Section 280A.

25.    What is the correct cite for Revenue Ruling 96-150, which is found on page 225 of the second *Cumulative Bulletin* volume for 1996?

26.    What is the correct cite for Revenue Procedure 99-5, which is found on page 10 of the fifth *Internal Revenue Bulletin* issued in 1999?

27.     Correct and complete the following cites:

    a..    R.R. 95-20, 1 C.B. 163
    b.    Rev. Ruling 91-14, 1991 CB 18
    c.    Rev. Rul. 72-604
    d.    Rev. Rul. 57-441, 1957-50 IRB 2
    e.    R.P. 2002-1
    f    Rev. Procedure 96-1, 1996-1, 385 CB

28.     Citate the following revenue rulings.  What is the status of each?

    a.    Rev. Rul. 71-301, 1971-2 CB 256
    b.    Rev. Rul. 62-199
    c.    Rev. Rul. 87-41, 1987-1 CB 296
    d.    Rev. Rul. 54-14

29.     Citate the following revenue procedures.  What is the status of each?  If another revenue procedure has made it obsolete, continue citing until you find the one most current revenue procedure.

    a.    Rev. Proc. 96-1
    b.    Rev. Proc. 79-63, 1979-2 CB 578
    c.    Rev. Proc. 87-41
    d.    Rev. Proc. 98-5

30.     Briefly describe the facts, issues, and IRS's holding for each of the following revenue rulings.  Discuss whether each is still authoritative. (If incomplete cite is provided, complete the cite.)

    a.    Rev. Rul. 69-608
    b.    Rev. Rul. 95-58
    c.    Rev. Rul. 69-494, 1969-2 CB 88
    d.    Rev. Rul. 57-374, 1957-2 CB 69

31.    Briefly describe the subject covered in the following revenue procedures.  Discuss whether each is still authoritative.

    a.      Rev. Proc.2002-12
    b.      Rev. Proc. 98-1
    c.      Rev. Proc. 95-35
    d.      Rev. Proc. 75-21, 1975-1 CB 715

32.    Indicate the *Cumulative Bulletin* volume and page number for the following revenue rulings and revenue procedures.  What is the topic of each?

    a.      Rev. Proc. 86-15
    b.      Rev. Rul. 85-87
    c.      Rev. Rul. 2001-60
    d.      Rev. Proc. 96-9

33.    Your supervisor tells you that a revenue ruling was issued in 1979 regarding constructive receipt of income when nonnegotiable time deposit certificates are involved.  To what revenue ruling is your supervisor referring?

34.    Correct and complete the following cites:

    a..     R.R. 95-20, 1 C.B. 163
    b.      Rev. Ruling 91-14, 1991 CB 18
    c.      Rev. Rul. 72-604

35.    Study Rev. Proc. 98-25, and answer the following questions:

    a.      Briefly describe the procedure's contents and topic.
    b.      What effect does the procedure have on prior revenue procedures?
    c.      Is the procedure still authoritative?  Describe how you determined this.

36.    You wish to rely on Treas. Reg. §1.165-7(b) regarding the calculation of casualty losses. What public laws have amended IRC §165 that are not reflected in this particular regulation?  Specifically, how do these changes impact the regulation section? What authority supports your position?

37.    You wish to rely on Treas. Reg. §1.163-10T. What public laws have amended IRC §163 that are not reflected in this particular regulation? Generally, how do these changes impact the regulation section? Is this a final or temporary regulation? How long has it been in temporary status? Has a final regulation covering the same Code provisions been issued?

38.    Read and summarize Announcement 98-18.

39.    Read and summarize Notice 99-37.

40.    Read and report on Letter Ruling 200203010. What were the facts before the IRS? What Code section was addressed? How did the IRS rule?

41.    Read and report on Letter Ruling 9827040. What were the facts before the IRS? What Code section was addressed? How did the IRS rule?

42.    Read and report on Letter Ruling 200204007. What were the facts before the IRS? What Code section was addressed? How did the service rule?

43.    Read and report on Letter Ruling 9822009. What were the facts before the IRS? What Code section was addressed? How did the IRS rule?

44.    Study and describe Revenue Procedure 89-14.

    a.    What is its purpose?
    b.    What information does it provide?
    c.    Is it still reliable authority? If not, what changes were made by subsequent Treasury interpretations?

45.    Citate and determine the reliability of the following:

    a.    Rev. Rul. 56-136
    b.    Rev. Rul. 62-180
    c.    Rev. Rul. 62-213

46.    Citate and determine the reliability of the following:

    a.     Rev. Proc. 86-15

    b.     Rev. Proc. 67-6

    c.     Rev. Proc. 74-17

47.    Did the IRS acquiecse to the results in *Mary Furner,* 393 F.2d 292 (CA 7, 1968)?  How did you determine this?  If the IRS did respond to the case, where is the response located?

48.    Did the IRS acquiesce to the results in *Roemer*, 716 F.2d 693 (CA 9, 1983)?  How did you determine this?  If the IRS did respond to the case, where is the response located?

49.    Did the IRS acquiesce to the results in *George Gross*, 23 TC 756 (1955)?  How did you determine this?  If the IRS did respond to the case, where is the response located?

50.    Did the IRS acquiesce to the results in *Warren Jones Company vs. Commissioner,* 60 TC 663 (1973)?  How did you determine this?  If the IRS did respond to the case, where is the response located?

51.    Describe the content of Letter Ruling 200205008.

52.    What is the correct cite for Revenue Ruling 2002-4, which is found on  page 398 of the fourth *Internal Revenue Bulletin* for the year?

53.    What revenue rulings have been issued in the past two years addressing the following Code sections?

    a.     IRC Section 162

    b.     IRC Section 351

    c.     IRC Section 280A

54.    What letter rulings or TAMs have been issued since 1995 regarding the following topics?

    a.     Casualty losses as provided for in IRC §165(c)(3)

    b.     Involuntary conversions under IRC §1033

    c.     Investment interest deductions under IRC §163

55. You wish to rely on Treas. Reg. §1.117. What public laws have amended Code section 117 which are not reflected in this regulation? Generally, how do these changes impact the regulation section? Is this a final or temporary regulation?

56. What treasury decision issued Treas. Reg. §1.117-2?

57. What treasury decision issued Treas. Reg. §1.83-7?

58. Client has been paying what he thinks is "alimony" to his ex-wife since 1994. He is a new client of yours and when reviewing the divorce decree, you see that the decree is silent about the impact on the requirement to make payments should his ex-wife die. Both are California residents. What is the impact of the silence on the categorization of his payments as "alimony"? Use just the IRC and the regulations. Do you need additional information to adequately address the question?

59. This year a taxpayer paid $2,000 for extensive liposuction surgery. Insurance did not cover this expense. Using just the IRC and Treasury regulations, determine whether this can be considered a potentially deductible medical expense.

60. Your client wishes to revoke its S Corporation election. Using just the IRC and Treasury regulations, determine what your client needs to do.

61. A taxpayer is stationed at the military base at Ford Ord, California. This base was one of those selected for closure. As a result, taxpayer was transferred to a base in Virginia. The taxpayer received the following reimbursement from the government:

> * $10,000 dislocation allowance to help with the move
> * $500 temporary lodging for five days
> * $2,000 reimbursement for two months lease payments before permanent housing
>   was found

Using only the Code, Treasury regulations, revenue rulings, and revenue procedures, determine how much, if any, the taxpayer must recognize in gross income as a result of the reimbursements.

62.    Using just the IRC and the Treasury regulations, address the following research question: A taxpayer studies tax law at a university on a part-time basis. He works full-time in the tax department of a large accounting firm and anticipates that the classes will help him become more productive and efficient in his work. Unfortunately, his employer, although supportive of his attending classes, is not reimbursing the taxpayer for any of the $10,000 tuition costs. Can the taxpayer take a deduction for his educational expenses? Do you feel you can adequately answer this question using only the Code and Treasury regulations?

63.    Address the following question using only the IRC, the Treasury regulations, and Rev. Rul. 85-121, 1985-2 C.B. 57.

>    A taxpayer worked for ABC Corporation for 15 years. Unfortunately, this year the company experienced some financial difficulties and laid off the taxpayer. The company has a very generous health insurance program that provides coverage to all employees, even those who have retired or been laid off within the last two years. The company continues to pay all health insurance premiums for the employee's health insurance even while he is not working because of the layoff. Prior to being laid off, the company never included in the taxpayer's income the value of the health premiums. The taxpayer remains available to return to work when his position is reopened.

a.    Must the taxpayer who was laid off include in income the amount of the premiums paid since his layoff?

## *INTEGRATED CASE STUDIES* (64-79)

*The following case studies are the same as those at the end of the previous chapter. Use the knowledge and skills you have learned through this chapter to address the case studies. If previously assigned a case study, use your work in Chapter 1 and Chapter 2 as the starting point.*

64.    *Case Study A – Disability Payments*

Mr. Top received $25,000 in disability payments while he was recuperating from heart surgery. Mr. Top, age 65, is an employee with a large corporation providing general business consulting services. The corporation has always paid for the disability insurance of its employees. Mr. Top telecommutes and works out of the home. From further conversations with the client, you discover that only $10,000 of the disability payments received by Mr. Top arise from a disability policy paid for by his employer under a group disability policy. The remaining $15,000 was paid on a separate policy that Mr. Top purchased some time ago. Mr. Top has been paying semiannual premiums on the separate individual policy. You are asked to prepare Mr. Top's return.

a.     Do the Treasury regulations provide further guidance in this situation?

b.     Do the Treasury regulations help to refine or add to the initial research question(s)?

c.     Do the regulations adequately address the research question? If so, what are your conclusions, and on what are they based?

65.    *Case Study B – Bonus Payments*

Sue is 30 years old and is president and a 51% shareholder of C Corporation. She informs you that C Corporation has 10 shareholders, all unrelated. Other than herself, no shareholder owns more than 10% of the company's stock. Sue plans to recommend to the board of directors that it authorize the payment of a bonus to her and three other top employees. She asks you, as the company's tax advisor, to counsel her on what the company needs to do so that the company can get a deduction for the planned bonus payments.

After further discussions with Sue, you learn that the company's business is commercial real estate development. The company had net revenues last year totaling $10,000,000. The company is an accrual-basis taxpayer, and each of the intended recipients employs the cash-basis method of tax accounting. She would prefer the bonuses to actually be paid next year but deducted by the company this year. One of the intended recipients is Sue's executive assistant, who is not currently a shareholder in the company. Sue would like the bonus to equal 100% of each recipient's current salary. The current salaries of the intended recipients are as follows:

| | |
|---|---|
| President | $500,000 |
| Executive Assistant | $100,000 |
| Chief Financial Officer | $300,000 |
| Vice President of Operations | $250,000 |

The CFO and vice president of operations are shareholders in the company, each owning 10% of the stock.

Sue has indicated to you that she believes the annual salaries are comparable or, perhaps, a little on the high side when compared to her company's competitors. You also learn that the company regularly pays out dividends to shareholders and plans to continue to do so.

a. Do the Treasury regulations provide further guidance in this situation?

b. Do the Treasury regulations help to refine or add to the initial research question(s)?

c. Do the regulations adequately address the research question? If so, what are your conclusions, and on what are they based?

66.    *Case Study C – Changing Headquarters*

The taxpayer, a calendar-year corporation, wants to change its company's headquarters currently consisting of a 10-story building. The company owns the building outright. The taxpayer has identified some potentially more suitable properties. One of the possible properties is a single-story building on a large, attractive lot. The other property consists of a two-building complex, with retail shops on the ground floor of one building and residential rental property in a portion of the other building.

After further discussions with the client and a review of relevant documents, you discover the following additional facts: Each of the new properties has a fair market value that slightly exceeds that of the current 10-story building. The taxpayer would demolish the single-story building if the company purchases that property. The company would then build a specially designed building on the lot. The sellers of both properties appear to be interested in entering an exchange transaction whereby the company's property would be exchanged for one of the other properties.

  a.    Do the Treasury regulations provide further guidance in this situation?

  b.    Do the Treasury regulations help to refine or add to the initial research question?

  c.    Do the regulations adequately address the research question? If so, what are your conclusions, and on what are they based?

67.    *Case Study D – Damage Payments to Dentist*

Dr. Tooth is a 40-year-old dentist in Small Town, USA. He graduated from dental school five years ago and has had a thriving practice ever since. At the end of last year, however, Dr. Tooth had an ugly billing disagreement with a patient. The patient, a well-known wealthy entrepreneur, in retribution, maliciously spread a rumor that Dr. Tooth was a carrier of a serious infectious disease. This rumor destroyed Dr. Tooth's patient base, as most of his patients quickly switched dentists. As a result of the stress of losing his business, the cruel gossip that resulted from the rumor, and the financial strain caused by this situation, Dr. Tooth began to suffer from severe migraine headaches, loss of appetite, and significant facial twitches. Dr. Tooth sued the patient for defamation and intentional infliction of emotional distress. He won a jury verdict and has since recovered $3,600,000 in damages from the patient.

i.    $1,000,000 lost wages. This was calculated on the basis that, in addition to the one year of wages lost since the date of the defamation, he has lost the ability to earn future wages in Small Town.

ii.   $50,000 reimbursement for medical expenses incurred in consulting a neurologist, internist, and psychologist.

iii.  $20,000 for future medical expenses anticipated.

iv.   $30,000 reimbursement for attorneys fees paid.

v.    $2,000,000 in punitive damages. The jury determined that the action of the patient was so malicious and heinous that the patient should be monetarily punished for his actions.

vi.   $300,000 for pain and suffering.

vii.  $200,000 to compensate Dr. Tooth for the emotional distress he suffered.

Through your interview with the client, you discover that he had to pay his attorney $30,000, which was paid out of the award.

a.    Do the Treasury regulations provide further guidance in this situation?

b.    Do the Treasury regulations help to refine or add to the initial research question?

c.    Do the regulations adequately address the research question? If so, what are your conclusions, and on what are they based?

68.    *Case Study E – Housing Expenses*

Ellie Executive lives in Florida with her family in a home bequeathed to her by her parents when they passed away. This year her employer assigned her to a position in London. The assignment is for a minimum of four years. Because she grew up in the house, Ellie would like to keep it and rent it out. There is no mortgage on the home, so renting will create a positive cash flow situation for her. Her employer will be providing her with a housing allowance to cover her London housing costs. Ellie believes the house has a FMV of at least $500,000. Ellie wants to make sure that if she ends up selling it, she will not have any taxable income from the sale. She has asked for your guidance.

After talking with Ellie Executive further, you become aware of the following additional facts: Ellie is not certain what she and her husband will do at the end of the four-year London assignment. She may return to Florida but she also might take another international assignment, since her children are now adults. Ellie plans to continue paying the following expenses while the house is rented:

* \* $400 a month for a weekly gardener
* \* $500 a month for a weekly housecleaner
* \* Approximately $200 a month in utility and maintenance expenses (electricity, garbage, and water)

Ellie anticipates that she can lease the house fully furnished for $2,500 a month. Ellie's parents died in 1991 when the FMV of the house was $300,000. They purchased the house in 1950 for $10,000. Her parents spent a total of $20,000 in home improvement costs. Ellie substantially redecorated the house in 1992, spending $65,000 in renovating two bedrooms, two bathrooms, and replacing the roof. In addition, Ellie paid $5,000 for a new perimeter fence and $10,000 to a landscape architect to redesign the yard.

a.  Do the Treasury regulations provide further guidance in this situation?

b.  Do the Treasury regulations help to refine or add to the initial research question?

c.  Do the regulations adequately address the research question?  If so, what are your conclusions, and on what are they based?

69.  *Case Study F – Retirement Contributions*

Tom Speeder is a new client.  From reviewing his client questionnaire, you were able to gather the following facts. He is 50 years old and was recently hired as a middle-level manager with a car manufacturer.  Tom's salary for the current year is $200,000.  In his initial meeting with you, Tom indicates that he would like you to look into an idea he has that will help him maximize his investment portfolio. He tells you that his new company offers its employees the ability to participate in a Section 401(k) plan. He believes it would be to his benefit to maximize his contribution to the company's 401(k) plan that provides for matching employer contributions up to $3,000 annually.  The plan provides for a maximum annual employee contribution of no greater than that provided by the IRC.

After further discussions with Tom, you discover that in addition to his salary he receives the following employment benefits:

* $100,000 group term insurance for which the employer pays the premiums (totaling $200/year)
* Health insurance, for which the employer pays the $100 in monthly premiums
* As part of the company's Employee Educational Assistance Plan, tuition

payments to a local university for one academic course a year to be chosen by the employee. For the current year, Tom plans to take a course on "Organizational Behavior" that he is interested in and believes will help him better understand his work environment. The university offers both undergraduate and graduate courses in this subject. Tom may take either and will wait to determine which is offered at the more convenient time.

a.      Do the Treasury regulations provide further guidance in this situation?

b.      Do the Treasury regulations help to refine or add to the initial research question?

c.      Do the regulations adequately address the research question? If so, what are your conclusions, and on what are they based?

70.    *Case Study G – Golf Ball Business*

Toby Power, a fellow Illinois resident, is a new client. Prior to her telephone call this morning (late November), all you really knew about Toby was that for the past five years she has been earning a living as a respected golfing instructor at a local club. She just called you to discuss a transaction she has entered into. You learn from your initial conversation with her that she and a group of friends formed a corporation for which the group will own 100% of the stock.

The corporation will be in the business of selling golf balls that it guarantees are indestructible and, because they glow in water and shade, cannot be lost. Toby transferred an office building to the corporation in return for her 20% stock ownership interest. Her eight other friends transferred primarily manufacturing equipment and cash for their evenly divided 80% interest. Toby has owned the office building for seven years and currently owes several hundred thousand dollars on two mortgages on the building. She estimates the fair market value of the building is about $1,000,000. Toby informs you that her previous tax advisor, about whom she has nothing but negative things to say, counseled her that, in order to avoid paying taxes on the transfer of the building to the corporation, she had to also transfer to the corporation a personal promissory note of $100,000. All of this occurred last year. She wants to know if the transaction was handled correctly or if she needs to worry. Through further discussions and review of pertinent documents, you discover the following additional facts:

- Toby purchased the office building seven years ago for $500,000. She paid $100,000 in cash and $400,000 using a note (Note A) secured by the property.

- Two years ago, the fair market value of the property escalated to $1,200,000. Toby took out a second mortgage on the property in the amount of $300,000 (Note B). She used the borrowed funds to purchase a vacation home in Nevada.
- At the time of the property's transfer to the corporation, the building's fair market value was $1,000,000, determined by an assessor.
- At the time of the property's transfer to the corporation, Note A had an outstanding balance of $310,000. Note B had a balance of $100,000.
- Toby has made no improvements on the property. She has taken approximately $100,000 in depreciation deductions on her tax return.
- The terms of the promissory note Toby gave to the corporation were that she pay the note off over a period of 20 years, paying a single annual payment in the amount of $6,000 ($5,000 principal; $1,000 interest). The first payment is to be made on the anniversary date of the note – September 1. Toby paid the first installment, which was due a few months ago.

a.      Do the Treasury regulations provide further guidance in this situation?

b.      Do the Treasury regulations help to refine or add to the initial research question?

c.      Do the regulations adequately address the research question? If so, what are your conclusions and on what are they based?

71.    *Case Study H – Private School Expenses*

Mr. and Mrs. Worried, longtime clients, have come to you for help. Their 13-year-old son has recently been expelled from the public junior high school because of severe behavioral problems, culminating in a physical attack on a teacher and threats of future violence. The son has been seeing a psychologist once a week but with no apparent positive results. The Worrieds would like to send their son to a private school that can provide the type of psychological help they believe he needs. The son's psychologist agrees that placement in a special school is imperative if there is ever to be a chance that the son will be a functioning member of society.

The Worrieds tell you that they are concerned because, although they have identified several potential schools, they do not have the financial resources necessary to pay the tuition and other additional costs. Their insurance does not cover any of the costs. However, the Worrieds believe that they may be able to afford the expenses if they can take them as a tax deduction. They ask you for your opinion.

a.    Do the Treasury regulations provide further guidance in this situation?

b.    Do the Treasury regulations help to refine or add to the initial research question?

c.    Do the regulations adequately address the research question?  If so, what are your conclusions, and on what are they based?

72.    *Case Study I – Deadly Fire*

Early this year, a taxpayer was clearing dry brush from behind his Malibu home in California.  He became frustrated with how long it was taking using his clippers.  He decided instead to light the brush on fire, believing this would be safe because it was an overcast day.  The taxpayer brought out a fire extinguisher in case the fire got out of control.  Unfortunately, some wind kicked up and fanned the fire out of control.  The fire completely consumed both his house and his neighbor's house.  The two children staying in the neighbor's house died of smoke inhalation.  The taxpayer was charged with negligent homicide.  The trial is pending.

The taxpayer wishes to take a casualty loss deduction for the loss of his house, which was worth an estimated $1,000,000 at the time of the fire.  The taxpayer purchased the home for $900,000 only six months earlier.  Insurance has refused to compensate for the loss under the circumstances. The taxpayer is currently out on bail. He is the brother of one of your very significant clients who has asked you to provide tax advice to the taxpayer.

a.    Do the Treasury regulations provide further guidance in this situation?

b.    Do the Treasury regulations help to refine or add to the initial research question?

c.    Do the regulations adequately address the research question?  If so, what are your conclusions, and on what are they based?

73.    *Case Study J – Airline Costs*

A major airline manufacturer was found to be in violation of FAA safety rules and was forced to install additional safety devices in each of its planes within the next six months. The airline company projects the cost of this upgrade to be several million dollars, consisting of lost profits while the planes are on the ground, labor costs, and the cost of parts. In addition, the airline spent $100,000 in attorney's fees in an unsuccessful fight to have the requirement waived. The CFO of the company wishes to know whether any or all of these costs can be deducted.

a.      Do the Treasury regulations provide further guidance in this situation?

b.      Do the Treasury regulations help to refine or add to the initial research question?

c.      Do the regulations adequately address the research question? If so, what are your conclusions, and on what are they based?

74.     *Case Study K – Vacation Home*

Mr. Z owns three homes. He lives in the San Francisco home full time. The other two he and his wife vacation in each year. He is considering replacing the house he has in Palm Springs, California, with another house in the same area. The new home is a little larger and has a floor plan he prefers. The two Palm Springs properties have almost the same fair market value. Mr. Z would like to know if he can exchange the properties instead of selling the one he has now and then buying the new one. He has a lot of built-up appreciation in the current Palm Springs home, and he doesn't want to have to pay taxes on it. Someone told him at a cocktail party that he can avoid paying taxes if he does an "exchange."

Mr. Z and his wife own the home outright. There is no mortgage on the property. They use the property occasionally. This last year they vacationed at the home for about two or three weeks – they aren't sure of the exact days. They have never rented the property and refuse to rent either the old or new property. They don't need the money and don't like strangers in their house. Mr. Z explains that he holds each of his vacation homes for two purposes. One reason is for vacations for him and his wife. Another key reason for owning the homes is for their investment value. He chooses homes only in areas where he believes there are high appreciation possibilities. Can Mr. Z take advantage of the tax-free exchange rules in the IRC? How will you advise him?

a.      Do the Treasury Regulations provide further guidance in this situation?

b.      Do the Treasury Regulations help to refine or add to the initial research question?

c.     Do the regulations adequately address the research question? If so, what are your conclusions, and on what are they based?

75.    *Case Study L – Property Easement*

A developer acquired a parcel of unimproved real property that she would like to develop. Although the land is currently zoned for commercial use, the developer would prefer not to begin development until an adjoining city street is widened. With a wider street, her development can include a landscaped public entrance and lighting. Without the widening, the development will have only one entrance that is neither as accessible nor as attractive.

The city plans to widen the street in order to build bike paths which are now required in its new city plan. It will be easier for the city to widen the street if it acquires an easement across the developer's property. The developer is interested in providing this easement to the city. However, before she acts, she would like assurance that she will receive a charitable deduction for the value of the easement. She has asked you to request a letter ruling on this matter.

a.     Do the Treasury regulations provide further guidance in this situation?

b.     Do the Treasury regulations help to refine or add to the initial research question?

c.     Do the regulations adequately address the research question? If so, what are your conclusions, and on what are they based?

76.    *Case Study M – Interest Payment*

A taxpayer is president of a company. He is very wealthy and has a good deal of assets. He went to Bank 1 in January, Yr. 1, to borrow $1,000,000. The loan proceeds were used to purchase stock. The loan was secured by the stock purchased. The terms of the loan are that it is an interest only loan, with interest to be paid annually on the anniversary of the loan. The rate is 10% per annum (simple) interest on the original loan amount.

In November of Yr. 1, the taxpayer realized that he did not have the liquid funds to pay the $100,000 of interest due in January. He had sufficient assets, but, due to the business environment, he determined that the smartest economic move to make would be to borrow the $100,000 rather than to liquidate one of his investments. So he went to Bank 2 and borrowed $100,000. This loan was secured by assets other than his stock and was a regular amortizing loan. Interest was 9%. Upon receipt of the loan proceeds on December 1, Yr. 1, taxpayer deposited the proceeds into his regular checking account in Bank 3. The proceeds remained in the checking account for the entire month of December. The balance of the checking account during the month of December ranged from $100,000 to $115,000.

On January 2, Yr. 2, taxpayer wrote a check from his Bank 3 checking account to Bank 1 in full payment of the interest due. On his tax return for Yr. 2, taxpayer took a deduction of $100,000 as an investment interest expense under Code Section 163. He had sufficient investment income to cover the deduction.

In the course of your research, you discover that Bank 1 owns 90% of the stock of Bank 2. You are able to talk with the client and learn that he was entirely unaware of the relationship. In fact, the loan documents were entirely different and did not make any reference to any relationship. The IRS has indicated it plans to disallow the interest deduction because it believes it has never actually been paid as is required by the Code. The taxpayer would like you to consider this development raised by the IRS and analyze and whether it has any ground for its position.

a.      Do the Treasury regulations provide further guidance in this situation?

b.      Do the Treasury regulations help to refine or add to the initial research question?

c.      Do the regulations adequately address the research question? If so, what are your conclusions, and on what are they based?

77.    *Case Study N – Racing Car Expenses*

A taxpayer is a partner in an accounting firm. He has always enjoyed auto racing as a hobby. Now that his children are grown, he has decided to devote more time to auto racing. He recently purchased a racing car for $50,000 and has entered several races. He recently raced in his first competitive race and placed fourth, resulting in winnings of $5,000. He expects to incur a number of expenses related to his racing: auto maintenance, storage, transportation, and so on. He would like your advice as to how to proceed so that he can depreciate his car and deduct all of these expenses.

a.    Do the Treasury regulations provide further guidance in this situation?

b.    Do the Treasury regulations help to refine or add to the initial research question?

c.    Do the regulations adequately address the research question?  If so, what are your conclusions, and on what are they based?

78.    *Case Study O – Retainer Fee*

Big Company paid $100,000 at the beginning of the year to a large law firm to retain its services should they be needed during the course of the year.  The law firm specializes in real estate law and is considered the best firm in this field. Big Company feared that one of its competitors would engage the law firm. This would prevent Big Company from being able to use the firm's services because of conflict-of-interest rules that preclude a firm from representing different clients with actual or potentially adverse legal interests. To prevent this, Big engaged the firm and paid the retainer fee.  Occasionally, Big asked the firm to perform legal work in areas where Big's in-house lawyers were not as well equipped.  It is now December, and it is clear that a substantial amount of the initial retainer will not be used to pay for legal services rendered.  The retainer agreement provides in this case that any unused amount shall be returned to Big, with interest, at year-end.

Big Company is a long-term client of yours.  It has asked you to look into whether any of the retainer fee will be deductible to it.  It wishes to have this advice before the beginning of next year when it will determine whether to pay another $100,000 retainer to the law firm for the year.

a.    Do the Treasury regulations provide further guidance in this situation?

b.    Do the Treasury regulations help to refine or add to the initial research question?

c.    Do the regulations adequately address the research question?  If so, what are your conclusions, and on what are they based?

79.   *Case Study P – Development Costs*

Gobble Corporation purchased 400 acres in Green City to build a private golf course and residences.  The land cost $10,000,000. Gobble planned high-quality, large houses that would sell for an average of $700,000.

It believed that the city's general plan allowed for this development.  Gobble spent in excess of $1,000,000 in fees to pay architects and civil engineers for all necessary environmental studies and approvals.  Two years ago, Gobble's development proposal was approved by the city council in a 5-4 vote.

Two months after the vote, the membership in the council changed dramatically.  The major election issue was growth versus no growth.  The city voted strongly for a no-growth slate.  Given the strong community sentiment, the new city council voted to disregard the earlier vote and alter the city's general plan to prohibit such a large development. They decided to defeat the development proposal.

As a result, Gobble sued the city for unreasonably interpreting its planning documents and reversing its initial approval of the project, all to the grave detriment of Gobble. Litigation has consumed almost two years and cost a total of $500,000.

Gobble's CFO has come to you to help with its tax return preparation.  Gobble would like to deduct all the costs incurred in this transaction, including the $1,000,000 paid for the land acquisition.

a.   Do the Treasury regulations provide further guidance in this situation?

b.   Do the Treasury regulations help to refine or add to the initial research question?

c.   Do the regulations adequately address the research question?  If so, what are your conclusions, and on what are they based?

# THE TAX RESEARCH PROCESS

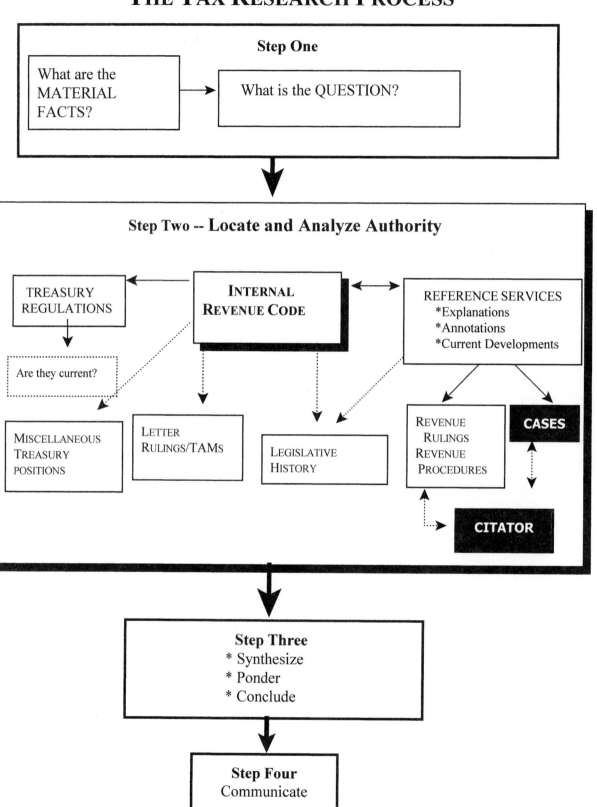

**Step One**

What are the MATERIAL FACTS?

What is the QUESTION?

**Step Two -- Locate and Analyze Authority**

TREASURY REGULATIONS

**INTERNAL REVENUE CODE**

REFERENCE SERVICES
*Explanations
*Annotations
*Current Developments

Are they current?

MISCELLANEOUS TREASURY POSITIONS

LETTER RULINGS/TAMs

LEGISLATIVE HISTORY

REVENUE RULINGS REVENUE PROCEDURES

**CASES**

**CITATOR**

**Step Three**
* Synthesize
* Ponder
* Conclude

**Step Four**
Communicate

# CHAPTER FOUR

# JUDICIAL INTERPRETATIONS

## *EXPECTED LEARNING OUTCOMES*

- Identify the various kinds of federal tax cases
- Determine relative authority of relevant cases
- Become familiar with appropriate case citation
- Analyze a case efficiently and effectively
- Locate and understand relevant cases
- Determine case reliability and relevance

## *CHAPTER OUTLINE*

- Overview
- Courts with Jurisdiction over Federal Tax Laws
- Federal Court Decisions and Their Authoritative Value
- Analyzing and Briefing a Case
- Where to Find Cases
- Ensuring Reliability – Using the Citator
- Chapter Summary
- Problems

## OVERVIEW

The third prong of potential tax authority consists of judicial interpretations or case law. When locating and analyzing authority, in addition to statutory authority and Treasury interpretations, you frequently must examine a number of court cases. Identifying which cases to study usually results from careful review of "annotated" or summarized cases found in a secondary source, such as a reference service. A full discussion of available reference services is covered in the next chapter. This chapter will help you understand how judicial interpretations play an integral part in the research process.

Judicial interpretations are somewhat analogous to the Treasury's revenue rulings in that they apply the federal tax laws to a particular set of facts. However, cases originate from an entirely different branch of government – the judicial branch. In addition, whereas Treasury interpretations represent an effort to provide guidance to the public, judicial interpretations represent a binding resolution to a conflict between the IRS and a taxpayer.

Court cases generally arise from a dispute between the IRS and the taxpayer regarding the appropriate tax return treatment of an event or transaction. For example, the taxpayer may take a particular position regarding the appropriate tax treatment when filing the tax return. Or the taxpayer may simply neglect to file a return. To result in litigation, the IRS must first select the return for audit. Litigation may result if the IRS and the taxpayer fail to agree on the appropriate treatment of the item at issue during the audit process. If the taxpayer chooses to file suit, a published court decision may arise from the dispute.

The sequence of events from the inception of the taxpayer controversy to the publication of a court decision may often take several years from start to finish. Often the IRS may choose not to audit a tax return until immediately prior to the date the statute of limitations runs (usually three years from filing date). The audit process itself may take a number of years. The litigation process also usually takes a good deal of time. (Chapter Eight discusses this process in more detail.)

When examining a relatively new Code provision, do not expect to find an abundance of relevant cases. It frequently takes five years or more from the date of a Code amendment to the time a court has the opportunity to rule on its application. In addition, it is not uncommon for the court to issue a decision interpreting a Code section already amended by Congress by the date of the decision. Consequently, be mindful of cases that render decisions on tax laws already repealed, superseded, or amended.

When studying case law, you may note that frequently the dollar amounts involved appear to be small relative to the cost and effort involved in pursuing the issue in the court system. The taxpayer's decision to litigate may be based on several non monetary factors and may even be based on issues of principle rather than dollars. Bear in mind that the authority of a court decision is not affected by the dollar amounts involved.

Not all taxpayer litigation results in the issuance of a published decision. In fact, a good percentage of court cases are not published. Publication is usually left to the discretion of the presiding Chief Justice and his staff. The guidelines and rationale regarding whether or not to publish are beyond the scope of this text. However, it is important to be aware of the fact that "unpublished" decisions are often rendered. Unpublished court decisions may not be accessed, which means that they generally have no authoritative value in the tax research process.

# COURTS WITH JURISDICTION OVER FEDERAL TAX LAWS

In total, five different courts decide matters relevant to federal tax laws. All but one of these courts also issue decisions on a variety of non tax criminal and civil issues. In fact, in most of these courts, only a small proportion of the total cases involves tax issues. The United States Tax Court is the one exception. It addresses only tax issues. Chapter Eight details the steps required when litigating a tax issue and discusses the factors a taxpayer will want to consider when selecting the appropriate court.

The following chart displays the federal courts and their relative weight of authority.

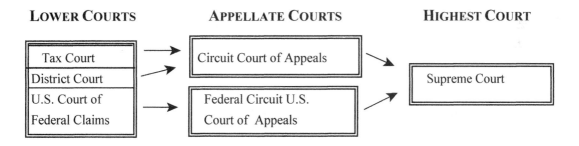

## The Lower Federal Courts

A taxpayer wishing to litigate with the IRS generally may elect among one of three lower courts in which to file suit. They are:

- United States Tax Court
- United States District Court
- United States Court of Federal Claims

Taxpayers often elect to file in the United States **Tax Court** because it is the only federal court with jurisdiction over tax matters that does not require prepayment of the alleged tax due. Taxpayers, however, do not have the right to a jury in this court. Tax court decisions are particularly instructive because of the specialized nature of the court and its judges.

The tax court only issues tax decisions. The president of the United States appoints the tax court judges, usually selecting from longtime tax practitioners. Tax Court judges serve for a renewable term of 15 years. As expected with this expertise on the bench, Tax Court decisions tend to reflect a level of tax sophistication and expertise.  Chapter Eight discusses in more detail the issues involved in determining whether to file in Tax Court.

The Tax Court is located in Washington, DC.  However, Tax Court judges travel to hear cases throughout the country.  One judge hears the case and issues an initial decision that is shared with the remainder of the tax court judges.  Sometimes the court determines that the issue in controversy warrants discussion and review by the entire body of tax court judges.  This is referred to as an ***en banc*** decision. In light of the substantial tax expertise of the Tax Court judges, an *en banc* Tax Court decision may provide compelling authority.

The tax court issues two types of decisions – regular and memorandum.  ***Regular*** Tax Court decisions usually address fresh questions regarding the Code – issues and areas not yet explored by the court. The court publishes decisions in ***memo*** form when the tax issues involved are simply factual variations on issues of law already clearly decided.  Because of the nature of the issues examined, regular tax court decisions carry slightly more authoritative value than memo decisions.

Prior to 1944, the Tax Court was named the *Board of Tax Appeals*.  When researching older case law, you may see the reference *BTA*, which is a reference to the precursor of the Tax Court.  Although the Tax Court and the BTA are distinguishable in many ways, such distinctions are not meaningful to a researcher.  An old BTA case, if representative of current law, is still good authority.

The **United States District Courts** also render decisions involving tax issues.  Each state has at least one United States District Court.  Bear in mind that the federal courts are different and distinct from state courts, which often also have courts called *District Courts*. Some of the more populated states, such as California, have more than one U.S. District Court, each with its own geographical area of taxpayer jurisdiction.  In order to file suit in this court, taxpayers must first pay the tax assessed by the IRS.  However, taxpayers sometime choose to litigate in the U.S. District Court because of the opportunity for a jury trial.  (The rules regarding filing in district court are addressed in more detail in Chapter Eight.)

District courts exercise jurisdiction over many types of criminal and civil cases, with only a small percentage of them involving federal tax matters.  In fact, U.S. District Court judges may often not be particularly well informed regarding federal tax laws, although they or their staff certainly must do their homework prior to rendering a decision.  Consequently, U.S. District Court decisions frequently offer a less sophisticated tax analysis.  Nonetheless, these cases represent reliable authority equal in weight to tax court cases.

**United States Court of Federal Claims** cases are probably the least common among lower courts issuing tax decisions. The U.S. Court of Federal Claims (Claims Court) exercises a more limited jurisdiction than U.S. District Courts. The Claims Court handles cases involving matters for which the U.S. Constitution or a federal statute requires monetary payment. Tax cases represent one of the main areas of federal law considered by the Claims Court. Like the tax court, the Claims Court is based in Washington DC, with its judges traveling to hear cases. The judges are said to "ride the circuit."

Similar to U.S. District Court cases, the taxpayer must first pay the alleged tax deficiency in order to file an action in the Claims Court. In light of the advance payment and the fact that there is no right to a jury, the Claims Court is the least common court chosen for filing suit by the taxpayer. However, taxpayers may choose to file suit in the Claims Court when the taxpayer believes that the court's previous decisions are in favor of the taxpayer's position.

## The Appellate Courts

The appeals process creates the second layer of court cases involving federal tax matters. Regardless of whether the U.S. Tax Court, U.S. District Court, or U.S. Claims Court was the chosen lower court venue, the losing party in the lower court may appeal to the appropriate **appellate court**. The appellate system divides the country into 11 geographic territories called *circuits*. In addition, the District of Columbia is its own circuit. The appealing party files suit in the circuit with jurisdiction over the state the taxpayer resided in at the time the questioned transaction took place. Appeals from the U.S. Claims Court are made to the United States Court of Appeals for the Federal Circuit.

## JURISDICTION OF CIRCUIT COURTS OF APPEAL

1<sup>st</sup> Circuit: Maine, Massachusetts, New Hampshire, Puerto Rico, Rhode Island

2<sup>nd</sup> Circuit: Connecticut, New York, Vermont

3<sup>rd</sup> Circuit: Delaware, New Jersey, Pennsylvania, Virgin Islands

4<sup>th</sup> Circuit: Maryland, North Carolina, South Carolina, Virginia, West Virginia

5<sup>th</sup> Circuit: Louisiana, Mississippi, Texas

6<sup>th</sup> Circuit: Kentucky, Michigan, Ohio, Tennessee

7<sup>th</sup> Circuit: Illinois, Indiana, Wisconsin

8<sup>th</sup> Circuit: Arkansas, Iowa, Minnesota, Missouri, Nebraska, North Dakota, South Dakota,

9<sup>th</sup> Circuit: Alaska, Arizona, California, Guam, Hawaii, Idaho, Montana, Nevada, Oregon, Washington

10<sup>th</sup> Circuit: Colorado, Kansas, New Mexico, Oklahoma, Utah, Wyoming

11<sup>th</sup> Circuit: Alabama, Florida, Georgia

Circuit for the District of Columbia

Usually, the circuit court either **upholds**, **modifies,** or **reverses** the lower court decision. Because the appellate court normally does not engage in fact-finding (but instead relies on the written lower court record in rendering its decision and oral arguments), it may decide to **vacate** the lower court decision and **remand** (send back) the case for further lower court review and consideration.

The decision of the Circuit Court of Appeals represents much greater authority than the lower court decision that triggered the appeal.  Generally, the Circuit Court's decision supersedes the lower court's analysis. You remain interested in the lower court decision only when the Circuit Court upholds the lower decision and simply defers to the lower court's reasoning.  You might also choose to rely on the lower court's decision when it addresses a tax issue not taken to the Circuit Court on appeal.

### The United States Supreme Court

United States Supreme Court decisions represent the highest and most authoritative case law governing federal tax matters.  The losing party at the appellate level has the right to request (but not require) the Supreme Court to hear the case.  The requesting party files a special application called a ***writ of certiorari*** requesting a hearing. ***Cert granted*** indicates that the Supreme Court agreed to hear the case. ***Cert denied*** denotes that the decision at the appellate level is final.  The Supreme Court grants *cert* to a very small percentage of the requests it receives, typically in situations in which two circuits are in disagreement.  Tax cases represent a very small percentage of the overall caseload of the Supreme Court.

If the Supreme Court hears the case, it generally either upholds or reverses the appellate court's decision.  Once the Supreme Court hears a case, both the lower court and the appellate court's decisions usually lose their authoritative value.  Sometimes, however, only one of the issues involved in a lower court decision is appealed.  In this circumstance, the lower court's holding regarding the issue not appealed may still be authoritative.

## FEDERAL COURT DECISIONS AND THEIR AUTHORITATIVE VALUE

The question before a court exercising jurisdiction over federal tax matters is essentially the same as that posed to a tax researcher – "How does the federal tax law apply to the specific set of facts?"  In arriving at their decisions, judges consider applicable authority, weigh that authority, and render a decision. When there is a jury, the jury may decide on the material facts. The judge will decide matters that involve questions of law. The court's basic judgment process is no different from the process the tax researcher should use in answering a tax question.

In general, federal judges examine the same three prongs of authority – the Code (and its legislative history), Treasury interpretations, and other applicable judicial interpretations. Occasionally, judges even look at the fourth prong – secondary sources – for guidance.

At the core of judicial decision making is the doctrine of *precedential authority* or *stare decisis*. Generally speaking, a **precedent** is a previous case decided by the court or by another court possessing appellate jurisdiction over the court reviewing the matter. The application of the precedence doctrine results in a court system in which a court that decided an earlier case must follow that case, or, if it disagrees with its earlier decision, **overrule** it. Other courts in the same jurisdiction are also expected to abide by the previous case. For example, the Ninth Circuit Court of Appeals must follow all of its previously published decisions. If the court no longer agrees with the decision it previously issued, when the same issue comes before the court again, it may overrule its previous decision. Once overruled, the precedential value of the earlier case disappears.

Note that overruling an earlier case does not directly impact either party in the earlier case. The earlier case, now overruled, has already been decided and is final between those parties. However, controversies arising in the future regarding the issues decided in the new case will be subject to the new precedential authority.

Under the doctrine of *stare decisis*, a court is bound by decisions issued by the higher court in its jurisdiction. Therefore, all lower and appellate courts must abide by an applicable U.S. Supreme Court decision. Likewise, each U.S. District Court must follow the holding of the applicable Circuit Court of Appeals. This rule also applies to the Tax Court. According to the *Golsen* case (*Jack Golsen*, 54 TC 742), the Tax Court must follow the ruling of the Circuit Court of Appeals with jurisdiction over the taxpayer.

**EXAMPLE 1: Application of *Stare Decisis***

```
  ┌──────────────────────────────┐       ┌──────────────────────────┐
  │   2ⁿᵈ Circuit Court of Appeals│       │                          │
  │                              │       │ 1ˢᵗ Circuit Court of Appeals│
  │      ┌──────────────────┐    │       │                          │
  │      │  NY District Court│    │       │                          │
  │      └──────────────────┘    │       │                          │
  └──────────────────────────────┘       └──────────────────────────┘
```

A District Court in New York is considering the deductibility of an expenditure of a New York taxpayer.  The 2ⁿᵈ Circuit Court of Appeals (to which New York belongs) previously disallowed the deduction in a similar case.  However, a recent 1ˢᵗ Circuit Court decision allowed the deduction in a case with very similar facts, upholding a District Court decision in Maine.  Under the doctrine of *stare decisis*, The District Court in New York must follow the decision of the 2ⁿᵈ Circuit Court of Appeals.

**EXAMPLE 2:  Application of the *Golsen* Rule**

```
  ┌──────────────────────────────┐       ┌──────────────────────────┐
  │                              │       │                          │
  │   5ᵗʰ Circuit Court of Appeals│       │ 9ᵗʰ Circuit Court of Appeals│
  │                              │       │                          │
  └──────────────────────────────┘       └──────────────────────────┘

               ┌──────────────────┐
               │    Tax  Court     │
               └──────────────────┘
```

The Tax Court is considering the deductibility for an expenditure of a taxpayer residing in Texas. The Court of Appeals for the 5ᵗʰ Circuit (to which Texas belongs) previously disallowed the deduction in a similar case.  However, the 9ᵗʰ Circuit Court of Appeals allowed the deduction in a case it recently decided.  Under the *Golsen* rule, the Tax Court must follow the holding in the 5ᵗʰ Circuit and disallow the deduction if it finds the facts to be materially the same as those in the 5ᵗʰ Circuit Court decision. Had the taxpayer resided in California, the Tax Court would have been obliged to follow the 9ᵗʰ Circuit Court decision and allow the deduction.

The doctrine of *precedential authority* requires courts to follow prior cases only to the extent the issues and material facts of the prior case are essentially the same as those involved in the case before the court. To the extent a court finds a material difference in the facts, the court may reach a different conclusion, so long as its conclusion is not inconsistent with the previous ruling's decision. Therefore, when analyzing a case, you should carefully note instances in which the court distinguishes the facts before it from the facts involved in a previous decision.

Although courts may examine case law issued outside their jurisdiction, such cases are not considered precedents. Thus, the courts are not obligated to follow these decisions. It is not uncommon to find one court questioning or criticizing a decision rendered by another court outside its jurisdiction. This sometimes results in different holdings on similar tax issues at both the District and Circuit Court of Appeals levels. As noted earlier, it is also in these circumstances that the Supreme Court may decide to grant *certiorari* and step in to resolve the conflicting decisions with a uniform rule of law.

In deciding cases, judges sometimes hypothesize about how the court would rule if a different set of facts or issues were before it. This type of discussion in a court holding is called **dictum**. Although dictum may be highly informative as to what the court may consider important as a basis for future decisions, it is not authoritative and has no precedential value. It merely represents an observation by the court not central to the actual holding. Nonetheless, it is not uncommon for subsequent courts to refer to dictum and sometimes apply it as the basis for their decision.

## Relative Authority of Decisions

In the search for authority, you will frequently discover not just one but several cases that appear relevant. To complicate matters, often the court decisions conflict with each other. As a researcher endeavoring to arrive at a well-reasoned conclusion, you may be caught in a conundrum as to what your conclusion should be based on. There is no easy answer. The next step in the research process is to analyze and synthesize the authority you have located. You must carefully study each document and attempt to determine its relative authoritative weight. When examining each applicable authoritative case, consider the following factors:

√    **Level of Authority** – What court issued the decision? Rank the decisions of the court in an order that assigns the highest authoritative value to the highest applicable court.

√ **Jurisdiction of the Court** – Does the court have jurisdiction over the taxpayer if the taxpayer were to litigate the issue under consideration? If not, even though an appellate court may have rendered a relevant decision, a lower court decision issued in the taxpayer's district may be more authoritative. Frequently, no appellate case was issued by a court possessing jurisdiction over your taxpayer. Then the remaining factors become critical.

√ **Factual Similarity** – How similar are the taxpayer's facts to those in the court case? If there are differences, are the differences material to the court's reasoning in rendering a decision? Would the difference between your taxpayer's facts and those in the case likely result in a different decision by the court? How?

This exercise of judgment and analytical thinking is the most important factor in determining the relative weight of the authority. To use judicial interpretations most effectively, you must carefully analyze the similarities and differences between your facts and those in a judicial decision. Obviously, the more similar the facts are to your taxpayer's situation, the more authoritative value the case offers. A difference in one material fact may render the authority of little value.

In this portion of your analysis, consider how the court would likely hold if it addressed the facts you are being asked to consider. Apply the reasoning of the court to the taxpayer's facts. Do any of the factual differences appear to potentially alter how the court would hold?

√ **Code Section at Issue** – Be careful to examine the Code provision applicable to the taxable year the transaction at issue took place. Compare the Code's language for that taxable year to the Code's current language. Note that any difference may significantly impact the usefulness of the case. Likewise, even if the case deals with a Code provision for the 1939 Code, if the language has remained the same, the case will likely still retain its authority. Examine how close the case's issues are to the issues in the research question.

√ **Logic of Analysis** – How well reasoned is the analysis presented in the court's decision? If the court decision has no precedential authority over your taxpayer, you are not obligated to follow it. If the analysis is not supported by clear logic or reasoning, it is possible that the courts having jurisdiction over your taxpayer will not arrive at the same conclusion of the case you are reviewing.

Ultimately, considering the importance of one case decision versus another and contrasting such decisions with the Code and other authority involves experience and good judgment. If you are unsure how to proceed, it is often helpful if you have the opportunity to discuss your reasoning with colleagues.

> ## Practitioner Observation
>
> *Ralph Kuhen, Partner, Hein & Associates, LLP*
>
> *"When performing tax research, you must always temper you initial euphoria when finding that perfect case because you are not quite done. There are a few more relevant considerations - jurisdiction of the court, level of authority, existence of conflict in the circuit courts...."*

## ANALYZING AND BRIEFING A CASE

You can waste precious time reading cases inefficiently. Analyzing cases can be tedious and time consuming. It is tempting to look for an easy shortcut. Nonetheless, it is important to train yourself to engage in case analysis in a logical and circumspect manner. You may discover in the course of your practice that summaries of cases written by others often fail to capture the gist of the matter decided. Consequently, do not make the mistake of relying on a summary of a case presented by a colleague or a reference service in reaching a conclusion. Summaries are useful in helping you determine whether the case is relevant to your research. However, once you decide the case may be applicable, read it in its entirety!

Understanding the basic structure of a court decision should help you analyze cases more effectively and efficiently.

Every case contains the following elements:

- Case title
- Housekeeping notations
- Information about legal representation of the parties
- Description of the facts
- Identification of the key issues
- Court's opinion

As you begin to study a case, keep in mind the reason you are reviewing it in the first place.  Presumably, you have located the case because the facts involved or issues raised are in some way similar to those framed by your research question.  The reason you are reading the case affects, in part, how you read it.

If you are reviewing a case to gain an understanding of the judge's decision regarding the appropriate application of the law in a specific situation, sometimes it makes sense to initially skim the facts.  Read enough of the facts to gain a basic understanding of the key "**material**" facts – those that materially affect the court's decision. The court's recitation of the facts can be quite lengthy, often filled with immaterial detail. Initially skimming the facts may save time and precious client dollars.  It is not necessary that you understand all the details if you believe them immaterial to the court's ultimate decision. You can always go back to pick up more facts if and when you believe further review is warranted.  Upon analyzing a case, you may also realize that you need to gather additional facts from your client.

Once you have a basic appreciation of the facts, review the judge's discussion of the issues before the court.  Is the court addressing issues relevant to the research question?  If so, move to the key part of the case – the opinion.  Focus on the opinion.  It is critical that you understand both the court's reasoning and holding.  Often the judge will repeat the key issues in stating the ultimate ruling.  It is wise to carefully study this portion of the case, including the footnotes.  Be careful to determine when the court is issuing its holding as opposed to merely expressing its views in dictum.

In addition to the official text of the holding, some tax case publishers provide helpful aids to assist your review of cases.  One useful aid consists of a case summary referred to as a *headnote*.  A headnote is a brief summary of the decision made by the court.  Often one case involves a number of legal issues.  Therefore, a case may have a number of headnotes. Headnotes are found prior to the beginning of the text of the case decision after the case name. Headnotes are helpful in a number of ways.  First, they may help you initially determine whether the case is pertinent enough to warrant studying its full text. Second, headnotes usually provide you with a road map of the case, quickly informing you of what to expect in a full reading of the decision.

Other tools used by publishers to simplify the process of reading a case include breaking the court's decision  into the key issues addressed.  Before the text of the case, the publisher summarizes and numbers each key issue. Throughout the text of the case, as that issue is discussed, the publisher inserts the number in parentheses to alert you to the fact that the discussion relates to this issue.

## ILLUSTRATION: Tax Court Case

Name of case → *Estate of Dorothy M. Walsh, Deceased, Charles E. Walsh, Personal Representative v. Commissioner*

Case cite

Docket No. 15150-97., 110 TC --, No. 29., Filed June 15, 1998

[Appealable, barring stipulation to the contrary, to CA-8.--CCH.]

*[Code Sec. 2056 ]*

Headnote → [Estate tax: Marital deduction: Power of appointment: Terminable interest.] H and W formed a trust to hold their property during their lives. The trust agreement provided that the property would pass to two trusts (A and B) upon the death of the first spouse, and that the surviving spouse, while competent, was entitled during life to A's income and corpus. (*Language omitted*). *Held:* The incompetency provisions in the trust agreement take the property passing to A outside the requirements for the marital deduction; the surviving spouse's power of appointment is not exercisable by the surviving spouse alone and in all events, as is required by sec. 2056(b)(5), I.R.C., and the regulations thereunder.

Attorneys → Thomas J. Shroyer, Robert B. Firing, Nicky R. Hay, and Steven Z. Kaplan, 1 Minneapolis, Minn., for the petitioner. John C. Schmittdiel, for the respondent.

Opinion →

### OPINION

Judge →

LARO, Judge:

Facts → This case was submitted to the Court without trial. See Rule 122. The Estate of Dorothy M. Walsh, Deceased, Charles E. Walsh, Personal Representative, petitioned the Court to redetermine respondent's determination of a $291,651 deficiency in Federal estate tax. We must decide whether certain property is eligible for the marital deduction under section 2056(a). We hold it is not.

Unless otherwise indicated, section references are to the applicable provisions of the Internal Revenue Code. Rule references are to the Tax Court Rules of Practice and Procedure. Decedent references are to Dorothy M. Walsh. Estate references are to the decedent's estate.

*Background*
All facts have been stipulated and are so found. The stipulation of facts and the exhibits submitted therewith are incorporated herein by this reference. (...*facts omitted*)

*Discussion*

We must decide whether the property passing to Trust A qualifies for the marital deduction under section 2056. Section 2056 provides in part:

SEC. 2056. BEQUESTS, ETC., TO SURVIVING SPOUSE.

(a) Allowance of Marital Deduction.--* * * the value of the taxable estate shall, except as limited by subsection (b),.. . .(*language omitted*)

An interest is usually not terminable when the surviving spouse receives a life estate and a general power of appointment over it. Sec. 2056(b)(5); *Estate of Meeske v. Commissioner* [Dec. 35,987], 72 T.C. 73, 77 (1979), affd. sub nom. *Estate of Laurin v. Commissioner* [81-1 USTC ¶13,398], 645 F.2d 8 (6th Cir. 1981). ...(*language omitted*)

Decision ⟶    For the foregoing reasons, we sustain respondent's disallowance of the estate's marital deduction. In so doing, we have considered all arguments made by the parties, and, to the extent not discussed above, find them to be irrelevant or without merit.

To reflect respondent's concessions,

Order to be ➤    *Decision will be entered under Rule 155.*
entered under
Rule 155

## Frequently Used Terms Found in Cases

When studying cases, you often confront a number of unfamiliar legal terms. A general understanding of some of these terms should help ease your way through a case.

- **Appellant** – The party filing the suit. In the higher courts, the appellant will be the party who lost in the lower court.

- **Concurring opinion** – When more than one judge participates in a decision, it is possible for a judge to agree with the court's ultimate conclusion but not with the court's reasoning. The judge who agrees with the conclusion but wishes to suggest an alternate rationale may write a concurring opinion. If you wish to cite language from a concurring opinion, you must identify it as such and identify the judge who wrote it. Concurring opinions do not represent binding authority, but they are informative and provide an alternative analytical viewpoint.

- **Dissenting opinion** – When more than one judge participates in a decision and the vote is not unanimous, the dissenting judge(s) may write a dissenting opinion. If you wish to refer to a dissenting opinion, you must cite it as such and be aware that dissenting opinions have no authoritative value. However, if there is a significant percentage of judges dissenting, this can weaken the authority of the court's holding and indicate a possibility of new precedent in the future with a changing court.  Dissenting opinions offer an interesting and alternative analysis of an issue.

- **En banc** – An *en banc* decision is a decision rendered by all of the judges in a particular court. Supreme Court decisions are always *en banc*.  But all other courts usually designate one judge or a panel of judges to hear the case and render a decision.  Sometimes, however, the issue is controversial or important enough to warrant participation by the entire body of judges. In these circumstances, it is not uncommon for some judges to disagree with either the holding or its reasoning. Then the case may include concurring and dissenting opinions.

- **Per curiam** – A decision rendered by all the judges of the court as a unanimous decision.

- **Petitioner** – Same as appellant – the party filing suit.

- **Pro se** – A term that indicates the party is representing himself or herself.

- **Respondent** – The party who is being sued.  In the lower courts this is always the IRS Commissioner.  In the higher courts, the respondent will be the party who won in the lower court.

- **Rule 155** – Frequently, there is a note at the end of Tax Court decisions indicating that the decision is to be "entered under Rule 155."  This simply means that the Tax Court has not determined the actual dollar effect of its determination. The IRS must apply the Tax Court decision and determine the monetary implications to the taxpayer involved.  For example, the court may hold that a deduction is allowed in a case.  If the Tax Court requires the application of Rule 155, the amount of the deduction is left to the IRS to calculate applying the reasoning of the court.

## Briefing Cases

You must often study a number of cases to fully consider one research question. While examining a case, it may be easy to remember what the case is about, how the court ruled, and why. But after studying several other cases, it is just as easy to forget pertinent information regarding the first case you read. There are two useful techniques to help you avoid wasting time having to unnecessarily reread cases. The traditional method is called *briefing* a case. This involves writing up a "brief" summary of the key elements of the case – its facts, issues, conclusion, and reasoning.

An alternative to briefing a case is simply to use modern day technology – a copy machine or printer and a highlighter! After copying the case, you can highlight the material case facts and holdings and place this in the research files.

You may choose to brief only those cases that seem particularly relevant to your research question. The key to writing a good brief is to keep in mind the reason for your brief – to enable you to quickly remember everything important about the case <u>and</u> to save time by allowing you to avoid reading the case again. Therefore, the brief should be short enough to accomplish this – writing a brief as long as the case itself obviously defeats the intended purpose. However, the brief must also be thorough enough to convey the pertinent information.

A brief should follow the same format as Revenue Rulings and cases – facts, issue, conclusion, and reasoning. Some choose to employ the acronym *FIRAC* as a method of recollection. *FIRAC* stands for facts, issue, reasoning, analysis, and conclusion. Whatever the name and order you choose to employ in writing a brief, each brief should include every element. In Chapter Seven, you will discover that this same format is appropriate for other forms of analytical writing as well.

A brief should be separated by headings into the following parts:

☛ **Case Name and Cite** – You must identify the case you are summarizing. Proper identification through appropriate citation ensures that you will have all the necessary information to cite the case should this be necessary in a more formal document.

☛ **Case Facts** – You should make a brief but complete list of all <u>material</u> facts. Courts usually provide you with pages of facts, but only some may be material to the decision. Include only those that you believe are material to the court's decision. You can note relevant facts in a numbered list, even if listed in incomplete sentences. Artful prose conveyed in complete sentences is not generally necessary.

☛ **Issue before the Court** – Remember, the issue before the court is to determine the appropriate application of the federal tax laws to a specific situation. In this portion of the brief, discuss what Code Section the court is interpreting and what the salient issue is. It may be that the court considers it necessary to clarify the meaning of a word or phrase. Or, the court may simply apply an established doctrine to the facts before it. You should indicate in this portion of the brief what the court is trying to determine.

☛ **Conclusion of the Court and Its Reasoning** – How did the court ultimately rule regarding the issue identified? For example, did the court permit the taxpayer the disputed deduction? Did it require an amount to be included in income? Noting the court's conclusion is the easiest part of the brief. However, you must also address the court's reasoning in arriving at its conclusion. Why did the court arrive at its conclusion? Upon what authority did the court base its conclusion? Arguably, the court's reasoning is the most important part of the brief.

---

**ILLUSTRATION: Case Brief (fictitious case)**

*Happy v. Commissioner*, 90 F2d 33; 100-2 USTC ¶500

**Facts:**   * TP purchased a houseboat as his only home in 1990.
* The houseboat had one bedroom, a kitchen, bathroom, and living room.
* Purchase price was $100,000.
* TP sold boat for $200,000 in 1998.

**Issue:** IRC §121 provides for an exclusion of income from the gain on the sale of a taxpayer's "principal residence" as long as it was used as the principal residence for at least 2 of the last 5 years. The question before the 9th Circuit Court of Appeals was whether a house boat can be considered a taxpayer's "principal residence."

**Conclusion and Reasoning:** The 9th Circuit Court of Appeals upheld the Tax Court's decision that a taxpayer's principal residence may take various forms. The court cited *Oceanic Homes v. Commissioner*, 70 U.S. 224 (1935), which defined a principal residence as "any dwelling place consisting of the elements necessary to provide shelter." The court stated that the houseboat had sleeping quarters, bathroom facilities, and cooking facilities and, thus, satisfied this definition.

---

# WHERE TO FIND CASES

Unlike Treasury interpretations, identifying relevant case law usually requires the use of a reference service. This process is discussed in the next chapter. However, once you identify the cases you wish to study, you can locate them in both print and electronic media.

When cases are published, they are printed in an "**official reporter**." There is an official reporter for each court with jurisdiction over federal tax matters. For example, all United States Supreme Court cases are published in the *United States Reporter*, which is the official reporter for the Supreme Court. The official reporter for U.S. District Court cases is called the *Federal Supplement*. The official reporter for U.S. appellate court decisions is the *Federal Reporter*.

Every official reporter (except the one for the Tax Court) includes all cases that the particular court heard and decided, not just those cases involving federal tax controversies. Consequently, since the majority of cases in the official reporters are not tax related, **unofficial case reporters** are produced by two of the tax publishers. These unofficial reporters are solely devoted to reproducing tax-related cases. As a practical matter, the official reporters require more updating and a great deal more shelf space than unofficial reporters.

Of course, since the Tax Court's jurisdiction is solely related to federal tax matters, its cases are, in all events, strictly related to federal tax controversies. Consequently, there is no need for an unofficial reporter of Tax Court regular decisions. However, oddly enough, there is no official reporter for Tax Court memorandum cases.

You can find tax cases in both official and unofficial comprehensive case reporters. The two publishers that produce unofficial casebooks containing only tax cases are Research Institute of America (RIA) and Commerce Clearing House (CCH). Both RIA and CCH sift through the official reporters for cases involving tax matters and reproduce the text in their own respective separate updated services. RIA publishes a case law series entitled *American Federal Tax Reports* and *American Federal Tax Reports 2nd Series*. ( referred to in this text as the "**AFTR**") and CCH publishes its comparable service entitled *United States Tax Cases* (commonly referred to as the "**USTC**"). One important point to note (as illustrated by the following chart) is that, despite their all-inclusive sounding names, neither AFTR nor USTC report Tax Court cases. Both RIA and CCH publish separate unofficial reporters for Tax Court cases.

One important limitation to note regarding unofficial reporters is that occasionally a case involving federal tax matters may **not** be reported in an unofficial tax reporter. This rare occurrence may transpire when the particular tax matter is implicated in another specialized field of law and subject to the jurisdiction of a federal court that does not have primary jurisdiction over tax matters. For example, federal bankruptcy cases often decide matters involving priorities of tax liens and other procedural and substantive issues in a bankruptcy matter. Federal bankruptcy cases are reported in official and non tax unofficial reporters. However, unofficial reporters may provide limited coverage of bankruptcy court cases. Therefore, be careful when dealing with bankruptcy tax issues or other highly specialized areas of federal tax law.

The following chart illustrates the official and unofficial reporters that contain federal tax cases:

| TYPE OF CASE | OFFICIAL REPORTER | UNOFFICIAL REPORTERS |
|---|---|---|
| Tax Court Regular | Tax Court Reports (T.C.)<br><br>Board of Tax Appeals (BTA) for cases issued prior to 1942 | * CCH Tax Court Reporter (vol. 2)<br><br>* RIA Tax Court Reports |
| Tax Court Memorandum | No official reporter | * CCH Tax Court Reporter (vol. 1)<br><br>* RIA Tax Court Reports |
| District Court | Federal Supplement Reporter (F. Supp.)<br>Federal Supplement Report 2d (F. Suppl 2d) | * American Federal Tax Reports (AFTR) – published by RIA<br><br>* United States Tax Cases (USTC) – published by CCH |
| Claims Court | United States Court of Federal Claims Reporter (Fed. Cl.) – since 1992<br><br>Prior to 1992:<br>  * United States Claims Court Reporter (Cl.Ct.) – 1982-1992<br>  * Federal Reporter – 1960-1982 | * American Federal Tax Reports (AFTR) (published by RIA)<br><br>* United States Tax Cases (USTC) -- published by CCH |

| TYPE OF CASE | OFFICIAL REPORTER | UNOFFICIAL REPORTERS |
|---|---|---|
| Appellate Courts | Federal Reporter (F.; F.2d; F.3d) | * American Federal Tax Reports (AFTR) – published by RIA<br><br>* United States Tax Cases (USTC) – published by CCH |
| Supreme Court | United States Reports (U.S.) | * American Federal Tax Reports (AFTR) – published by RIA<br><br>* United States Tax Cases (USTC) -- published by CCH<br><br>* Supreme Court Reporter (S.Ct.) -- published by West |

## Citing Cases

All references to cases will have the name of the case and most likely other pertinent information indicating where you can locate the case. A reference to a case is called a *cite*. There are several ways to cite the variety of court cases, particularly since every case is published in both an official and unofficial reporter. However, every cite contains a few common elements:

- case name
- volume of reporter
- abbreviation of reporter name
- page or paragraph number on which the case begins
- deciding court and the year of decision

Whether you decide to use a case's official or unofficial cite depends on the context in which you are working and to whom you are writing. As noted earlier, when writing a court brief or legal document, it is generally most appropriate to use the citation to the official reporter. However, when corresponding with someone who does not have access to a full law library but instead uses unofficial tax reporters, it is helpful to also cite the unofficial reporter citation. When a citation includes a case reference to more than one reporter, it is called a **parallel** citation.

Whichever source is referenced, one rule remains constant. A complete cite always begins with the case name, either underlined, capitalized, or italicized, followed by the reporter information. For every civil court case except the Tax Court, the case name consists of two parts: the taxpayer's last name and "Commissioner." For Tax Court cases, the first and last name of the taxpayer is sufficient. It is interesting to note that in older cases, the Commissioner's actual name was used. Therefore, you will find a number of cases with a respondent named "Helvering" or "Glenn." Both were prior IRS Commissioners.

In criminal tax cases, the case name consists of the United States versus the taxpayer, since federal criminal cases are technically brought by the U.S. Department of Justice criminal tax division.

**EXAMPLES**:

Non-tax court civil cases:    *Hills v. Commissioner*, reporter information
Tax Court cases:              *Henry Hills,* reporter information
Criminal tax cases:           *U.S. v. Hills*, reporter information

The following chart illustrates the remainder of the cite for each official and unofficial reporter containing tax cases:

| TYPE OF CASE | OFFICIAL CITE FOLLOWING CASE NAME | UNOFFICIAL CITE FOLLOWING CASE NAME |
|---|---|---|
| Tax Court Regular | **Temporary:**<br>100 TC __, No. 5 (1992)<br>&#x2198;       &#x2198;<br>volume     decision number<br><br>**Permanent**:<br>100 TC 405 (1992)<br>&#x2198;     &#x2198;<br>volume   1st page of case | Not appropriate |
| Tax Court Memorandum | There is no official source for Tax Court Memorandum decisions | **\* CCH:**<br>  70 TCM 500 (1998)<br>  &#x2198;     &#x2198;<br>volume   1st page of case<br><br>**\* RIA:**<br>1998 P-H Memo TC ¶98,005<br>&#x2198;       &#x2198;<br>volume    case paragraph |
| District Court | 800 F. Supp. 300 (1992)<br>&#x2198;     &#x2198;<br>volume   1st page of case | **\* CCH** – *United States Tax Cases* (USTC):<br><br>  92-2 USTC ¶500 (SDNY, 1992)<br>  &#x2198;    &#x2198;   &#x2198;<br>year-volume  case  abbrev. for<br>             para.   district<br>                    (in this case<br>                    the Southern<br>                    District Federal<br>                    Court, New<br>                    York)<br><br>**\* RIA** – *American Federal Tax Reports* (AFTR):<br><br>  50 AFTR2d 92-6000 (SDNY, 1992)<br>  &#x2198;    &#x2198;   &#x2198;<br>volume   year- 1st  abbrev. for<br>          page of  district (in<br>          case    this case,<br>                 the Southern<br>                 District Federal<br>                 Court, New<br>                 York) |

| TYPE OF CASE | OFFICIAL CITE FOLLOWING CASE NAME | UNOFFICIAL CITE FOLLOWING CASE NAME |
|---|---|---|
| Claims Court | 10 Fed.Cl. 200 (1992)<br>↘        ↘<br>volume    1st page of case | * **CCH** – *United States Tax Cases (*USTC):<br><br>92-2 USTC ¶500 (Cls. Crt. 1992)<br>↘            ↘        ↘<br>year-volume   case    Claims Court<br>            para.<br><br>* **RIA** – *American Federal Tax Reports* (AFTR):<br><br>50 AFTR2d 92-6000 (Cls. Crt. 1992)<br>↘            ↘        ↘<br>volume      year- 1st   Claims Court<br>            page of case |
| Appellate Courts | 100 F.2d 500 (1992)<br>↘        ↘<br>volume    1st page of case | * **CCH** – *United States Tax Cases* (USTC):<br><br>92-2 USTC ¶500 (CA 2, 1992)<br>↘            ↘        ↘<br>year-volume   case    2nd Circuit<br>            para.    Court of<br>                    Appeals<br><br>* **RIA** – *American Federal Tax Reports* (AFTR):<br><br>50 AFTR2d 92-6000  (CA 2, 1992)<br>↘            ↘        ↘<br>volume      year- 1st   2nd Circuit<br>            page of case   Court of<br>                    Appeals |

| TYPE OF CASE | OFFICIAL CITE FOLLOWING CASE NAME | UNOFFICIAL CITE FOLLOWING CASE NAME |
|---|---|---|
| Supreme Court | 50 U.S. 200 (1992)<br><br>↘    ↘<br>volume   1st page of case | * **CCH** – *United States Tax Cases* (USTC):<br><br>92-2 USTC ¶500 (S.Ct., 1992)<br>↘   ↘   ↘<br>year-volume  case  Supreme Court<br>               para.<br><br>* **RIA** – *American Federal Tax Reports* (AFTR):<br><br>50 AFTR2d 92-6000 (S.Ct., 1992)<br>↘   ↘   ↘<br>volume   year- 1$^{st}$   Supreme<br>         page of case  Court |

When first referring to a case, you must include at least one of the complete cites indicated in the preceding chart. However, when you wish to refer to the same case again, you may frequently avoid rewriting the full cite by instead using one of the following terms:

*Id*. – This term is used only when there is no intervening cite between the place you now wish to cite your document and the last time it was cited. You should use *Id* only after a sentence – not within a sentence itself. It must also be italicized or underlined.

---

**EXAMPLE 3: Use of *Id*.**

"The Tax Court in *Happy v. Commissioner*, 92 TC 400 (1998), held that all taxpayers must smile when paying their taxes. The Tax Court judge stated: 'In order to reduce nationwide tension, all taxpayers must smile when signing their tax returns.' *Id*. at 405."

The use of the term *Id*. here indicates that the immediately preceding cite (*Happy v. Commissioner*, 92 TC 400) is also an appropriate cite for the quotation. The reference to "405" indicates that the specific quotation is on page 405 of the *Happy* case.

***Supra*** – Use *Supra* when you have previously cited the case in full but you have cited
other documents in between the initial full citation and the latest reference to the
case. The term *Supra* cannot stand on its own. When you use the term, start off
the cite with the case name and then use *Supra*. The term takes the place of the
remainder of the cite. You may use *Supra* mid sentence or after a sentence.
Alternatively, a common style that may be adopted is to use footnote citations in
which all citations appear as footnotes (on the same page) or as endnotes (at the
end of the letter or memorandum).

---

**EXAMPLE 4: Use of Supra**

"The court in *Happy v. Commissioner*, 92 TC 400 (1998), held that all
taxpayers must smile when paying their taxes. However, the Treasury
Department recently issued a revenue ruling indicating that it will not follow
the court's decision. Rev. Rul. 98-50, 1998-1 CB 10. It is not clear why the
Internal Revenue Service so vigorously refused the judge's decision in
*Happy* in light of the court's statement that: 'In order to reduce nation- wide
tension, all taxpayers must smile when signing their tax returns.' *Happy v.
Commissioner, Supra* at 405."

The use of the term *Supra* here indicates that the writer has provided the
full citation to *Happy v. Commissioner* earlier in the discussion.

---

## Finding a Case When You Know the Cite

It is easy to locate a case when you know not only its name but also its full cite. In print,
you simply need to locate the appropriate reporter volume and turn to the cited page or paragraph
number. Therefore, the only challenge is finding a library containing the particular reporter
referenced.

Electronically, case law is available through fee-based libraries and the public Internet.
At this point, the public Internet provides a fairly thorough collection of case law. (See the
Appendix for gateway Internet addresses.) However, for easier and more reliable access to cases,
it is best to use one of the fee-based services. Whether in CD-ROM or over the Web, retrieving
the text of

a case involves entering the case cite either on a search template or as otherwise prompted by the particular search program. Once you provide the full cite, the program provides the text of the case.

The ease of this process differs with each electronic service. Some services require an understanding of the specific citation method – the syntax of a cite. For example, you may need to use appropriate periods and spacing. Others build this detail into their systems so that you simply need to be aware of the key cite elements. They ask you to essentially "fill in the blank." The Appendix provides step-by-step examples of this process.

## Finding Parallel Cites to a Case

Electronic libraries enable you to find a case regardless of the particular reporter your cite uses. However, moving seamlessly through a paper library is not as simple. How do you find a case if the only cite you have is to a case reporter not available in your library? Fortunately, the process is not too difficult.

**Converting from USTC to AFTR** – The RIA reference service titled *U.S. Tax Reporter* includes a table of cases in its second volume. Cases are listed in alphabetical order by taxpayer name. Next to the name of the case are all the possible cites to the case. (See the illustration on the next page.) You can find a similar list of cases and cites in RIA's other reference service – *The Federal Tax Coordinator,* volume 2.

Another method is to look up the case name in the RIA citator, discussed later in this chapter. Next to the case name you will find the AFTR cite.

***Converting from AFTR to USTC*** – The AFTR provides information regarding the year the case was decided. For example, the AFTR cite, *Richey v. US.*, 72 AFTR2d 93-6674 indicates that the case was published in the AFTR in 1993, and therefore likely decided that year. Now go to the second volume of the 1993 USTC and turn to the Table of Cases at the back of the book. Look up the case name and locate the case's comparable CCH reference – the USTC volume and paragraph number. Another method is to look up the case name in the CCH Citator. This will provide you with the CCH cite.

### Finding a Case When You Have Only the Case Name

Your partner asks you to read the "*1210 Colvin Ave* case." No one can tell you anything more about the case. How do you find the case under these circumstances? There are a number of ways, depending on whether you use an electronic or paper library.

### *In Print*

With a paper library, an appropriate method for locating a case is through the Citator – a service described in detail later in this chapter. Another way is to find the Table of Cases in one of the two RIA reference services. You can locate this table in volume 2 of both the RIA *Federal Tax Coordinator* and the RIA *United States Tax Reporter*. CCH's reporter does not have a comparable table.

---

**ILLUSTRATION: Table of Cases Using RIA**

The following is an excerpt from RIA *United States Tax Reporter* Table of Cases. Skim through the list (which is in alphabetical order) until you locate the "Colvin Ave" case name. Next to the name, note that the table provides you with both the RIA and CCH cites to the case. In addition, the paragraph notation following the cites refers you to the location in the full *Reporter* where this case is discussed.

111 West 16 St. Owners, Inc., (1988) 90 TC 1243
..62,415
112 West 59th St. Corp. v Helvering (1933) 13
AFTR 513, 68 F2d 397, 3 USTC ¶1181 ..79,007.11
112 West 59th St. Corp. v Helvering (1931) 23
BTA 767 ..79,007.11
1148 Fifth Ave. Corp. (See 550 Park Ave. Corp.)
115 Inc. (See M. S.C. Holding Co.)
117 Corp. (See Bing & Bing, Inc.)
1180 East 63rd St. Bldg. Corp., (1949) 12 TC 437
..615.127(15); 1115.01(25); 79,007.08(10)
1210 Colvin Ave., Inc. v U.S., (1981, DC NY) 48
AFTR 2d 81-5137, 81-1 USTC ¶9474 ..15,635(5)
1220 Realty Co., The, *62,067 ..1625.326(25);
1635.020(5)
1220 Realty Co., The v Comm., (1963, CA6) 12
AFTR 2d 5581, 322 F2d 495, 63-2 USTC ¶9703
..1625.326(25); 1635.020(5)

Official citation, followed by AFTR and USTC cites.

RIA Reporter Paragraph that discusses the *Colvin* case

---

### *Electronically*

Finding the text of a case when you do not have its cite is also quite easy electronically. The search mechanism for the electronic services enables you to cause the computer to perform a search through either the entire applicable database or just a selected portion of it. The search request may be framed in broad terms by requiring the computer to search through all the cases in its database, or the search may be more narrowly focused – perhaps by framing your request to search in the database comprised only of Supreme Court cases. Deciding the breadth and scope of the search request often depends on how much information you already have regarding the particular case you are seeking.

Once you identify the relevant portion of the database you wish to search, you can be even more specific in your search. Most of the electronic products allow you to indicate whether you want to search through the text of every case or just the titles – called a segment search. To find the text of a case for which you know only the name, you need only search through the case titles. For this process, it is advisable to use the last name of the taxpayer as your search query. By performing your search in this way, the computer should take you directly to the case or provide a very short list of cases with each such case name listed, from which you can then select the one you are trying to locate. The Appendix provides several illustrations of this process.

The following chart summarizes and compares the various vehicles for accessing cases:

| SOURCES OF TEXTS OF CASES | | |
|---|---|---|
| **PAPER** | | |
| FORMAT | DESCRIPTION | ADVANTAGES |
| CCH | ♦ Found in *United States Tax Cases*<br>♦ Issued twice a year. | ♦ Historically has included more cases |
| RIA | ♦ Found in *American Federal Tax Reports* (AFTR)<br>♦ Cases are broken down into major issues with each major issue having its own numbered headnote. | ♦ Offers the use of a better citator<br>♦ Includes an informative headnote system |
| **ELECTRONIC ACCESS** | | |
| FORMAT | DESCRIPTION | ADVANTAGES |
| **CD-ROM**<br>CCH<br>RIA<br>Tax Analysts | ♦ Depending on the contract purchased, revised disks provided either on a monthly, semiannual, or annual basis. | ♦ Word processing opportunities. You are able to cut and paste into your word processing document.<br>♦ Relatively quick access<br>♦ Potentially complete library of cases at your desk<br>♦ Searching capabilities |
| **Public Internet** | ♦ Access to a fairly complete selection of cases. (See following chart containing selected Internet addresses) | ♦ Free access |
| **Fee-Based Internet**<br>CCH<br>RIA<br>Lexis-Nexis<br>Westlaw | ♦ Access to tax case library through purchase. Access to Internet required. No additional software necessary. | ♦ Word processing capabilities<br>♦ Quick access<br>♦ Completely portable tax library<br>♦ Searching capabilities<br>♦ Linking capabilities |

## SELECTED PUBLIC INTERNET SITES TO CASES

| ADDRESS | PROVIDER | Comments |
|---|---|---|
| findlaw.com | FindLaw Internet Legal Resources | Contains all Supreme Court cases from 1893 on, as well as Circuit Court of Appeals cases. Only includes a few District Court Cases. Does not include any Tax Court cases. You can search its database by name as well as citate the Supreme Court cases. |
| www.abanet.org/tax/sites.html | American Bar Association Tax Section | Comprehensive Web site that contains links to sites containing case law and other primary authority. No direct links to Tax Court authority. |
| www.uscourts.gov | Federal Judiciary | Contains Supreme Court, Appellate Court, District Court and Bankruptcy Court cases. |
| www.ustaxcourt.gov | The U.S. Tax Court | Contains full text of all tax court decisions. You can locate relevant cases through search, indication of case name and by deciding judge. |

# ENSURING RELIABILITY– USING THE CITATOR

In the previous chapter you learned to use the citator to ensure the reliability of a revenue ruling, revenue procedure, and other Treasury interpretations. This same process is equally important when you are considering whether it is appropriate to rely on a court case. You certainly do not want to discover, after you counsel the taxpayer, that the case on which you based your conclusion was overruled, modified, or otherwise has lost its authoritative validity. You must make a determination that all authority relied on is reliable <u>before</u> making a research conclusion and that you have considered all relevant authority.

As Chapter Three discussed, both Research Institute of America (RIA) and Commerce Clearing House (CCH) publish a citator to help confirm reliability. In addition, another source – *Shepard's* – provides similar information. Unlike the citators, this service covers all case law, not just tax cases. The concept is exactly the same as the citator – it provides a list of all cases that have cited the one you are checking. *Shepard's*, however, differs in a few significant ways. In paper, *Shepard's* refers only to cases by their cite and excludes all case names. In addition, *Shepard's* only recognizes a Tax Court Memo case by its official number, not by either the CCH or RIA cite.

## Organization of the Citators

Most citators are organized around the taxpayer's last name. The citator lists all published cases in alphabetical order by taxpayer last name. Both official and unofficial cites follow each case name to enable you to ensure you have the correct case. This is particularly important when the taxpayer's name is a common one. Notice that the citator provides a wonderful source for finding the complete cite and the official cite to any case – all you need to know is the taxpayer's name. Once you find the case name, below the name you will find a list of all the cases that have cited the case in question. The list is organized by type of court case and within that, by year.

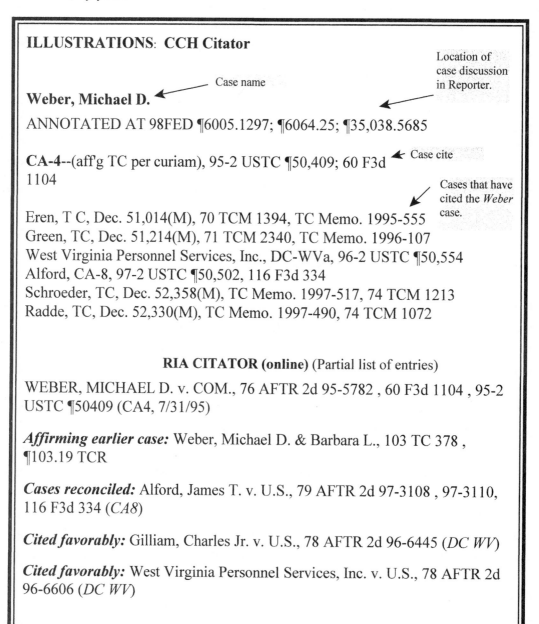

**ILLUSTRATIONS: CCH Citator**

Case name → Location of case discussion in Reporter.

**Weber, Michael D.** ←

ANNOTATED AT 98FED ¶6005.1297; ¶6064.25; ¶35,038.5685

**CA-4**--(aff'g TC per curiam), 95-2 USTC ¶50,409; 60 F3d ← Case cite
1104

Cases that have cited the *Weber* case.

Eren, T C, Dec. 51,014(M), 70 TCM 1394, TC Memo. 1995-555
Green, TC, Dec. 51,214(M), 71 TCM 2340, TC Memo. 1996-107
West Virginia Personnel Services, Inc., DC-WVa, 96-2 USTC ¶50,554
Alford, CA-8, 97-2 USTC ¶50,502, 116 F3d 334
Schroeder, TC, Dec. 52,358(M), TC Memo. 1997-517, 74 TCM 1213
Radde, TC, Dec. 52,330(M), TC Memo. 1997-490, 74 TCM 1072

**RIA CITATOR (online)** (Partial list of entries)

WEBER, MICHAEL D. v. COM., 76 AFTR 2d 95-5782 , 60 F3d 1104 , 95-2
USTC ¶50409 (CA4, 7/31/95)

*Affirming earlier case:* Weber, Michael D. & Barbara L., 103 TC 378 ,
¶103.19 TCR

*Cases reconciled:* Alford, James T. v. U.S., 79 AFTR 2d 97-3108 , 97-3110,
116 F3d 334 (*CA8*)

*Cited favorably:* Gilliam, Charles Jr. v. U.S., 78 AFTR 2d 96-6445 (*DC WV*)

*Cited favorably:* West Virginia Personnel Services, Inc. v. U.S., 78 AFTR 2d
96-6606 (*DC WV*)

It is important to realize that the same case name may have as many as three court decisions – lower court, court of appeals, and the United States Supreme Court. Actually, there may be even more decisions if an appellate court later remands a case back to a lower court for further determinations. Although each case may display the same taxpayer name, the rest of the cite is obviously different. For example, if a subsequent case cited only the Supreme Court's version of the case in question, the citator will list it only under the Supreme Court cite.

**ILLUSTRATION:  CCH Citator**

Assume you wish to rely on the *Glenshaw Glass* case decided by the Supreme Court.  Notice that the citator entry for the case has three separate bullets, one for each court that addressed the *Glenshaw Glass* facts.  The cases that follow each bullet are those that cited the particular *Glenshaw* decision.

*Glenshaw Glass Supreme Court cite.*

**Glenshaw Glass Co.** (See also Goldman Theatres, Inc.)
ANNOTATED AT 98FED ¶5504.012; ¶5900.03; ¶5900.124; ¶8476.4162

* **SCt**--(rev'g CA-3), 55-1 USTC ¶9308; 348 US 426; 75 SCt 473; Ct D 1783; 1955-1 CB 207

*Cases that cited the Glenshaw Glass Supreme Court decision.*

Schleier, SCt, 95-1 USTC ¶50,309, 115 SCt 2159
Burke, SCt, 92-1 USTC ¶50,254, 112 SCt 1867, 504 US 229
Wesson, CA-5, 95-1 USTC ¶50,186, 48 F3d 894
Houston Industries Inc., FedCl, 94-2 USTC ¶50,526, 32 FedCl 202
Taggi, CA-2, 94-2 USTC ¶50,470, 35 F3d 93
Hawkins, CA-9, 94-2 USTC ¶50,386, 30 F3d 1077
Reese, CA-FC, 94-1 USTC ¶50,232, 24 F3d 228
Bennett, FedCl, 94-1 USTC ¶50,044, 30 FedCl 396
Collins, CA-2, 93-2 USTC ¶50,486, 3 F3d 625

*Glenshaw Glass 3rd Circuit cite.*

* **CA-3**--(aff'g TC), 54-1 USTC ¶9328; 211 F2d 928

Rev. Rul. 57-1 , 1957-1 CB 15
Obear-Nester Glass Co., CA-7, 54-2 USTC ¶9675, 217 F2d 56
Basle, TC, Dec. 22,559(M), 16 TCM 745, TC Memo. 1957-169
Silverman, TC, Dec. 22,543, 28 TC 1061
Geer, TC, Dec. 22,530, 28 TC 994
Teleservice Co., TC, Dec. 22,229, 27 TC 722
Lanman & Kemp-Barclay & Co. of Colombia, TC, Dec. 21,794, 26 TC 582
Draper, TC, Dec. 21,701, 26 TC 201
Bloom, TC, Dec. 21,600(M), 15 TCM 210, TC Memo. 1956-49
Jackson, TC, Dec. 21,591, 25 TC 1106
Pellar, TC, Dec. 21,347, 25 TC 299
Henshaw, TC, Dec. 20,635, 23 TC 176
Obear-Nester Glass Co., TC, Dec. 19,915, 20 TC 1102
Rev. Rul. 56-177

*Cases that cited the Glenshaw Glass 3rd Circuit decision.*

* **TC**--Dec. 19,146; 18 TC 860; NA. 1953-1 CB 7

*Glenshaw Glass Tax Court cite.*

Merrill, CA-9, 54-1 USTC ¶9275, 211 F2d 297
Brown-Forman Distillers Corp., TC, Dec. 23,805, 33 TC 87
Goldman Theatres, Inc., TC, Dec. 19,401, 19 TC 637
General American Investors Co., TC, Dec. 19,372, 19 TC 581

When accessing the citator electronically, the citator provides a list of all the cases published in the AFTR, USTC or Tax Court Reports since 1954 citing the case in question. When using the print citator or Shepard's, the information is organized by time period. You will find the case you are citing listed in alphabetical order in each citator volume issued since the date of the decision. However, the only cases listed as citing the case in question will be those decided during the time frame indicated on the volume's outside binding.

---

**EXAMPLE 5: Selecting the Appropriate Citator Volume**

Assume you are citing the *Michael Weber* case decided in 1995.
Using the RIA citator, you have several bound volumes to choose from. One covers cases decided between 1863 and 1954. Clearly, you do not need to review this volume since the *Weber* case was not yet decided when this volume was produced. You will want to select the volume covering cases decided in 1995 and more recently.

Using the CCH citator, you will examine the main citator volume, and then check the quarterly updates that are located in the same volume.

---

Therefore, when using the print citator, you may need to consult several volumes before you complete the process. Using the electronic citator collapses these steps into one.

## Information Provided by the Citator

With case law, the citator provides you the same type of information it does for revenue rulings – a list of all cases and Treasury interpretations that have cited the case in question. Once you identify these, you must determine their impact. Was the case overruled on appeal? Was the case questioned by a later decision with respect to another taxpayer? Was it further explained?

The RIA citator and *Shepard's* provide you with a useful beginning point for answering this critical question by providing a notation indicating why the case was cited. In print, to determine the meaning of the notation, you must refer to the glossary in the front of the citator. Electronically, the notation is spelled out clearly. The citator published by CCH does not provide this information.

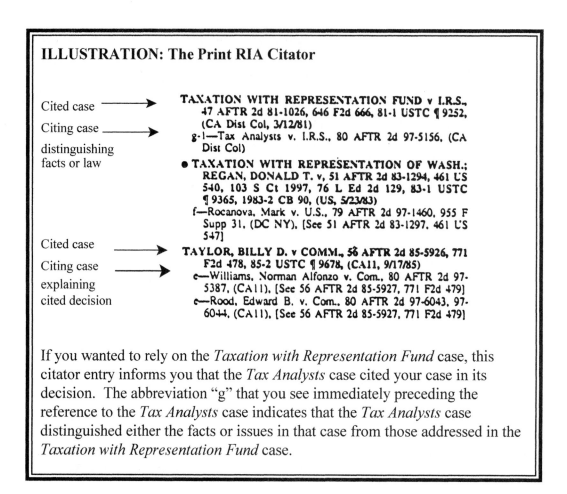

ILLUSTRATION: The Print RIA Citator

Cited case →

Citing case →
distinguishing
facts or law

TAXATION WITH REPRESENTATION FUND v I.R.S.,
47 AFTR 2d 81-1026, 646 F2d 666, 81-1 USTC ¶ 9252,
(CA Dist Col, 3/12/81)
g-1—Tax Analysts v. I.R.S., 80 AFTR 2d 97-5156, (CA
Dist Col)

● TAXATION WITH REPRESENTATION OF WASH.;
REGAN, DONALD T. v, 51 AFTR 2d 83-1294, 461 US
540, 103 S Ct 1997, 76 L Ed 2d 129, 83-1 USTC
¶ 9365, 1983-2 CB 90, (US, 5/23/83)
f—Rocanova, Mark v. U.S., 79 AFTR 2d 97-1460, 955 F
Supp 31, (DC NY), [See 51 AFTR 2d 83-1297, 461 US
547]

Cited case →

Citing case →
explaining
cited decision

TAYLOR, BILLY D. v COMM., 56 AFTR 2d 85-5926, 771
F2d 478, 85-2 USTC ¶ 9678, (CA11, 9/17/85)
e—Williams, Norman Alfonzo v. Com., 80 AFTR 2d 97-
5387, (CA11), [See 56 AFTR 2d 85-5927, 771 F2d 479]
e—Rood, Edward B. v. Com., 80 AFTR 2d 97-6043, 97-
6044, (CA11), [See 56 AFTR 2d 85-5927, 771 F2d 479]

If you wanted to rely on the *Taxation with Representation Fund* case, this citator entry informs you that the *Tax Analysts* case cited your case in its decision. The abbreviation "g" that you see immediately preceding the reference to the *Tax Analysts* case indicates that the *Tax Analysts* case distinguished either the facts or issues in that case from those addressed in the *Taxation with Representation Fund* case.

Some citators provide additional useful information regarding the history of a case. For example, some indicate whether the Supreme Court granted a writ of certiorari or whether the losing party filed an appeal.

It is important to appreciate the limitations of both citators and *Shepard's*. First, the services list only resources actually citing the case you are checking. The citator will not generally provide any information regarding Code changes that might render the case obsolete. Remember again why you read case law – to help you interpret a part of the IRC. Never read case law in a vacuum without beginning or ending in the IRC. Using the citator will not help you avoid relying on a case made obsolete by Congress. It helps you only when the case was made obsolete by another court.

In addition, the citator and *Shepard's* are not able to inform you of potentially relevant court decisions made in the most current two or three months. There is a time lag between the case decision and its inclusion in the citator or *Shepard's*. Therefore, it is possible that a

Supreme Court case overruled your case, but when you check the citator – even the current supplement issued just yesterday – the Supreme Court decision is not listed. Checking the citator or *Shepard's* only provides comfort up to about the last two or three months. To complete the check, you will need to review the current developments of a reference service. Do not be caught making the mistake of believing that because you cited something electronically, that you have checked for cases decided up through the last 24 hours. The same time lag that exists in paper also exists electronically.

### How to Use the Information in the Citator

What do you do when the citator indicates the case was cited in many subsequent cases? Must you read all these cases? No, not necessarily. Remember, your purpose in using the citator is to provide assurance that the case on which you wish to base your decision is still good authority. However, you should scan the other cases to carefully consider whether these other cases include facts that are more on point with those involving the transaction you are considering. It is also helpful to consider the particular jurisdictions of the cases. It is important that you locate a relevant case applicable to the jurisdiction to which your client is subject. For example, if you represent a California taxpayer, a relevant Ninth Circuit Court of Appeals decision is a better case to cite than a Second Circuit Court of Appeals decision.

It is a good idea to read the most recent cases that cited the case you wish to rely upon. If a recent case simply explains the cited case and supports its conclusion, you probably do not need to worry that it was overruled by a prior case. Courts do not tend to cite a case after it has been overruled. Note the date of the case that most recently cited the case. If it has been several years since it was last cited, you should be on the alert and read the last few cases citing the case. There are normally only two reasons to explain the lack of cites – either the case just is not determinative of issues frequently litigated or the case was overruled.

Next, read all the Supreme Court cases and any appellate decisions in your circuit that the citator refers you to. Depending on the number, you may wish to read every appellate decision. There is no hard-and-fast rule regarding the number of cases listed in the citator you should read. Again, if you focus on the reason why you are citing, you should reach a point where you are comfortable that you have reviewed enough cases and are finished citing.

### How to Access the Citator

As with all tax resources, the citator is available in print and electronically. Other than a few stylistic differences, generally, the information is the same in each format. Electronic citating is probably more efficient. Not only is it quicker to find the case you are checking, but also

because of the use of linkable hypertext, you are able to quickly review those cases that have cited your case in order to appropriately determine their impact.

---

**Practitioner Observation**
Brian MacKenzie, Attorney at Law

*"Efficient use of tax research time is critical to cost control and client service. Computerized tax research services increase productivity and efficiency dramatically, especially when citing or shepardizing, which is both time consuming and prone to error when researching with paper products.*

---

You can access a citator electronically using two different methods. Both RIA and CCH enable you, through their Web-based services, to immediately turn to the applicable citator entry directly from the case you are reading. You can also cite a case by bringing up a template and entering the case cite. The Appendix provides step-by-step instructions of both these methods.


## CHAPTER SUMMARY

In the course of your research as a tax practitioner, you will discover many instances in which neither the Code nor the Treasury regulations fully address the specific research question. There are many circumstances in which the Code provides no guidance for various federal tax matters. Consequently, another major source of authority to turn to consists of judicial interpretations.

Cases may be considered the judicial equivalent of Treasury revenue rulings. Federal tax cases generally apply the Code and other applicable federal tax authority (including prior case law precedents) to a specific taxpayer's situation. You generally discover what cases and revenue rulings address the research question through the use of reference services, discussed in the following chapter.

Controversy and disagreement between the IRS and the taxpayer generate a court decision. The taxpayer, unhappy with the results of an IRS audit, files suit in one of the three lower division trial courts of original jurisdiction: the Tax Court, U.S. District Court, or the U.S. Claims Court. Case law results.

The next level of case law – the U.S. Circuit Court of Appeals – results when the losing party in the lower court files an appeal that is heard and determined by the appellate court. The appellate court generally either reverses, upholds, or modifies the lower court decision. An appellate court may also simply vacate a lower court decision and remand the case back to the lower court for further determinations consistent with the appellate court's specific directions and instructions. Supreme Court cases are the most authoritative form of case law and arise when the losing party at the appellate level files a *Writ of Certiorari* which in its sole discretion is granted by the Supreme Court.

You frequently need to examine many cases during the research process. A key judgmental challenge is to determine which at cases you may appropriately rely on. In reviewing and "weighing" case authority, the pertinent factors include the level of the court (lower court versus appellate court), the location of the taxpayer involved and the appropriate court jurisdiction applicable, and the similarity of the facts and issues before the court.

A critical final step before you rely on a particular case is to citate the case to ensure it has not been overruled or seriously undermined by subsequent court cases. You can do this by using either the CCH or RIA citator, or by using Shepard's. Although available in print, electronic citing is typically more efficient for an experienced computer user. Once you discover all the cases that have cited your case, you must read the most recent ones to confirm they did not overrule or significantly question the court's ruling. You should exercise good judgment and common sense in reading or simply scanning other cases citing your case to make sure you have conducted a full and thorough review.

# PROBLEMS

## *KEY CONCEPTS* (1-21)

1.    Define and discuss the following terms:

    a.       Case law
    b.       Lower courts
    c.       Tax Court
    d.       Federal District Court
    e.       Claims Court
    f.       Circuit Courts
    g.       Tax Court Memoranda
    h.       Tax Court Regular Decisions
    i.       Writ of Certiorari
    j.       Overruling a case
    k.       Reversing a decision
    l.       Vacating a decision
    m.       Remanding a case
    n.       "Golsen" rule
    o.       USTC
    p.       AFTR
    q.       Rule 155
    r.       en banc
    s.       Respondent
    t.       Pro se
    u.       Dicta
    v.       Parallel cite
    w.       Citating

2.    Discuss the impact of the Supreme Court denying "cert" versus granting "cert."

3.    Is it possible to find two cases, both involving nearly identical facts, in which the courts issue opposite conclusions? Why? How do you decide which case to use in your research? Assuming you decide which case to utilize, should you ignore the other case?

4.    What factors do you use to determine which cases are important to your research?

5.    Explain the difference between an "official" reporter and an "unofficial reporter." Please provide "official" and "unofficial" cites for each of the following cases.

    a.       U.S. Tax Court
    b.       U.S. District Court

c.      U.S. Appellate Court

d.      U.S. Supreme Court

6.      What are the two federal tax case services?  What benefit do they provide to the tax practitioner?  Are all cases related to federal tax matters always listed in the two federal tax case services?

7.      What steps must the researcher take to ensure the reliability of a court case?

8.      Where can the decisions of all Federal tax cases, other than the Tax Court, be found?

9.      How do you determine whether a case is under appeal or if a Writ of Certiorari has been filed?

10.      If you locate an appellate court decision, are there circumstances in which you may need to study the lower court's opinion?

11.      Discuss the structure of a court case.  Briefly describe the steps you take to most efficiently read a case.

12.      What is a headnote?  How is a headnote useful to a tax researcher?

13.      What do *Id.* and *Supra* mean?  When is it appropriate to use each term?

14.      What is the difference between dictum and a court's holding?

15.      What is the difference between overruling a case and reversing a decision?

16.      What is precedential authority?

17.      Discuss what information a citator provides.  Compare and contrast two of the citator resources available.  Why is citing a case critical?

18.      The following is an entry in the CCH Citator for the *Arkansas Best* case.  What information does it provide regarding the case?  Which of the citing cases might you want to read?  Why?

.CCH-CITATOR, 98FED, Main Citator Table, Arkansas Best Corp.

ANNOTATED AT 98FED ¶10,550.598; ¶16,753.377; ¶32,222.012; ¶32,222.024; ¶32,222.6865; ¶32,222.6935

l SCt--(aff'g CA-8), 88-1 USTC ¶9210; 485 US 212; 108 SCt 971; 1988-2 CB 314

Andrew Crispo Gallery, Inc., CA-2, 94-1 USTC ¶50,097, 16 F3d 1336
Kraft, Inc., FedCl, 94-1 USTC ¶50,080, 30 FedCl 739
Stokely-Van Camp, Inc., CA-FC, 92-2 USTC ¶50,459, 974 F2d 1319
Carmel, BC-DC-Ill, 92-1 USTC ¶50,042, 134 BR 890
***cases omitted*
Federal National Mortgage Association, TC, Dec. 49,102, 100 TC 541
Tway, TC, Dec. 49,040(M), 65 TCM 2655, TC Memo. 1993-212
Marrin, CA-2, 98-2 USTC ¶50,490
***cases omitted*
Swartz Jr., Floyd E., CA-8, 89-1 USTC ¶9354, 876 F2d 657
Circle K Corp., ClsCt, 91-1 USTC ¶50,260, 23 ClsCt 161
O'Rourke, TC, Dec. 46,491(M), 59 TCM 228, TC Memo. 1990-161
Michelson, TC, Dec. 46,329(M), 58 TCM 1219, TC Memo. 1990-27
***cases omitted*

- **CA-8**--(aff'g and rev'g TC), 86-2 USTC ¶9671; 800 F2d 215

Swartz Jr., Floyd E., TC, Dec. 44,343(M), 54 TCM 1153, TC Memo. 1987-582
Buehler, John F., TC, Dec. 44,135(M), 54 TCM 232, TC Memo. 1987-416
Gold Kist Inc., TC, Dec. 50,718, 104 TC 696

- **TC**--Dec. 41,581; 83 TC 640

Cassuto, TC, Dec. 45,968, 93 TC 256
Recklitis, TC, Dec. 45,154, 91 TC 874

19.    What do the elements of the following cites represent?

    a.    *Orange Tangerine*, 101 TC 59 (1991)
    b.    *Rotten Apricot*, 90 TCM 3000 (1998)
    c.    *Rotten Apricot*, RIA T.C. Memo Dec. ¶97,200 (1997)
    d.    *Apple v. Commissioner*, 72-2 USTC ¶198 (CA 9, 1972)
    e.    *Plum v. Commissioner*, 5 AFTR3d 97-200 (S.Ct., 1997)

20.    Identify the U.S. Circuit Court of Appeals that has authority over the following states:

    a.    Hawaii
    b.    Texas
    c.    Illinois
    d.    Florida

21.    Identify the U.S. Circuit Court of Appeals that has authority over the following states:

    a.    New Jersey
    b.    California
    c.    Colorado
    d.    Arkansas

## PRACTICAL APPLICATIONS (22-44)

22.     Correct the following citations using whatever sources you think would be helpful. Indicate the sources used.

    a.    Charles Chapman 74ustc, 9233
    b.    Sutherland Lumber-Southwest, 88 AFTR2d (2001)
    c.    Champion Spark Plug Co. 30, Tax Court, 298

23.     Locate and read the case at 101 TC 537.

    a.    What is the complete cite to the case?
    b.    Which party is filing suit?
    c.    What court issued the holding?
    d.    Did the taxpayer have an attorney serving as his representative?
    e.    Where was the taxpayer located?
    f.    In what year did the transaction in question occur?
    g.    When was the decision rendered?
    h    What were the dollar amounts involved?
    i.    What Code section(s) was at issue?
    j.    For whom did the court rule?
    k.    Who was the judge issuing the opinion?
    l.    Citate the case in the CCH and RIA Citator.  Is the ruling still authoritative with respect to similar facts and issues?  Compare the information each citator provided you.

24.     Locate and read the *Pettet* case at 97-2 USTC ¶50,948 (EDNC, 1997)

    a.    What is the complete cite to the case?
    b.    Which party is filing suit?
    c.    What court issued the holding?
    d.    Did the taxpayer have an attorney serving as his representative?
    e.    Where was the taxpayer located?
    f.    In what year did the transaction in question occur?
    g.    When was the decision rendered?
    h    What were the dollar amounts involved?
    i.    What Code section was at issue?
    j.    For whom did the court rule?
    k.    Who was the judge issuing the opinion?
    l.    Is this case still authoritative with respect to similar issues and facts? How did you determine your answer?

25.    Locate and read the *Follum* case at 80 AFTR2d 97-7779 (CA 2, 1997)

    a.    What is the complete cite to the case?
    b.    Which party is filing suit?
    c.    What court issued the holding?
    d.    Did the taxpayer have an attorney serving as his representative?
    e.    Where was the taxpayer located?
    f.    In what year did the transaction in question occur?
    g.    When was the decision rendered?
    h    What were the dollar amounts involved?
    i.    What Code section was at issue?
    j.    For whom did the court rule?
    k.    Who was the judge issuing the opinion?
    l.    Is this case still authoritative with respect to similar issues and facts? How did you determine your answer?

26.    Locate and read the case at 109 TC --, No. 14.

    a.    What is the complete cite to the case?
    b.    Which party is filing suit?
    c.    What court issued the holding?
    d.    Did the taxpayer have an attorney serving as his representative?
    e.    Where was the taxpayer located?
    f.    In what year did the transaction in question occur?
    g.    When was the decision rendered?
    h    What were the dollar amounts involved?
    i.    What Code section was at issue?
    j.    For whom did the court rule?
    k.    Who was the judge issuing the opinion?
    l.    Is this case still authoritative with respect to similar issues and facts? How did you determine your answer?

27.    Locate and read the case at 95-2 USTC ¶50,508.

    a.    What is the complete cite to the case?
    b.    Which party is filing suit?
    c.    What court issued the holding?
    d.    Where was the taxpayer located?
    e.    In what year did the transaction in question occur?
    f.    When was the decision rendered?
    g.    What were the dollar amounts involved?
    h.    What Code section was at issue?

    i.        For whom did the court rule?

    j.        Who was the judge issuing the opinion?

    k.       Was there a concurring opinion written? If so, by whom?

    l.        Was there a dissenting opinion written?  If so, by whom?

    m.     Is this case still authoritative with respect to similar issues and facts? How did you determine your answer?

28.     Locate and read the case at 2 USTC ¶814; 284 US 1.

    a.       What is the complete cite to the case?

    b.       Which party is filing suit?

    c.       What court issued the holding?

    d.       Where was the taxpayer located?

    e.       In what year did the transaction in question occur?

    f.        When was the decision rendered?

    g.       What were the dollar amounts involved?

    h.       What Code section was at issue?

    i.        For whom did the court rule?

    j.        Who was the judge issuing the opinion?

    k.       Was there a concurring opinion written? If so, by whom?

    l.        Was there a dissenting opinion written?  If so, by whom?

    m.     Is this case still authoritative with respect to similar issues and facts? How did you determine your answer?

29.     Find the following cases using only the following information. Use whatever print or electronic source you believe will be helpful.  Provide the complete cite to the case and the ruling judge.

    a.       *Quaschnick* (tax court case)

    b.       *Furey* (A case involving IRC Section 6662)

    c.       *Allied-Signal, Inc* (Decided around 1995 by an Appellate Court)

    d.       *Burke* (A Supreme Court case on IRC Section 104)

30.     Locate *John F. Tupper*, 134 F.3rd 444 (CA 1, 1998).  Study the case, and answer the following questions:

    a.       What is the parallel cite to one of the unofficial reporters?

    b.       What were the material facts in the case?

    c.       What was the issue before the court?

    d.       What was the taxpayer's position regarding the issue?  Upon what authority was the taxpayer relying?

e.    What was the IRS's position regarding the issue? Upon what authority was the IRS relying?

f.    How did the court hold? What was its reasoning and upon what authority did it rely?

g.    Is this case still authoritative with respect to similar issues and facts? How did you determine your answer?

31.    Locate *Brinley v. Commissioner*, 782 F.2d 1326. Study the case and answer the following questions:

a.    What is the parallel cite to one of the unofficial reporters?

b.    What were the material facts in the case?

c.    What was the issue before the court?

d.    What was the taxpayer's position regarding the issue? Upon what authority was the taxpayer relying?

e.    What was the IRS's position regarding the issue? Upon what authority was the IRS relying?

f.    How did the court hold? What was its reasoning and upon what authority did it rely?

g.    Is this case still authoritative with respect to similar issues and facts? How did you determine your answer?

32.    Locate *Corn Products Refining Co. v. Commissioner*, 350 US 46 (S.Ct., 1955).

a.    What is the parallel cite to one of the unofficial reporters?

b.    What were the material facts in the case?

c.    What was the issue before the court?

d.    What was the taxpayer's position regarding the issue? Upon what authority was the taxpayer relying?

e.    What was the IRS's position regarding the issue? Upon what authority was the IRS relying?

f.    How did the court hold? What was its reasoning and upon what authority did it rely?

g.    Is this case still authoritative with respect to similar issues and facts? How did you determine your answer?

33.    Have any appellate courts cited *Ruth Bohan v. Commissioner*, 456 F.2d 851? If so, in which cases and from what circuit?

34. Read the following cases in addressing the following questions:

> *Henry Hills*, 76 TC 484
>
> *Henry Hills v. Commissioner*, 691 F2d 997; 82-2 USTC ¶9669; 50 AFTR2d 82-6070
>
> *Miller v. Commissioner*, 733 F2d 400; 84-1 USTC ¶9451; 53 AFTR2d 84-1252

a. What court decided each case?

b. What are the material facts in each of these cases? What facts are not material?

c. What is the Code section at issue in each of these cases? What is the specific issue the facts raise about the Code section language?

d. In each case, what was the court's conclusion? List three different sources the courts used in arriving at this conclusion. How did these sources support the courts' conclusions? How did the courts deal with previous court cases?

e. Using the cases cited previously, the Internal Revenue Code and the Treasury regulations, address the following research question.

> Corporation X suffered $10,000 in flood damage to its office building. Although the damage was covered by the company's property and casualty insurance policy, the company decided not to file an insurance claim for the loss because it feared the policy might be canceled in the future as a result of making this small claim for losses. The company would like to take a deduction for the $10,000 on its tax return. The Vice President asks your advice.

f. How are the facts in Corporation X's situation different from those in the cases you read? Are the differences material?

35. Read *Weil v. Retirement Plan Administrative Committee*, 55 AFTR2d 85-404; 1985-1 USTC ¶9164 and address the following questions:

a. What court decided the case?

b What are the material facts? What facts are not material?

c. What is the Code section at issue?

d. What was the court's conclusion? List the sources the courts used in arriving at this conclusion.

e.    Using the *Weil* case, the Internal Revenue Code, and the Treasury regulations, address the following research question.

Last year, Company X underwent a reorganization that involved moving its corporate headquarters from New York to California. Last year the company had 375 employees. At the present time (December), the company employs only 280 people. Of the 95 reduced positions, 42 were duplicate job positions and, therefore, were eliminated as part of the reorganization. The reduction also included 27 people who retired or voluntarily resigned. The remaining 26 positions were employees who were offered positions in California but chose not to relocate. Does this reduction of employees constitute a partial termination of their pension plan?

36.    Read and brief the following two cases.

*N.E. Soliman v. Commissioner*, 113 S.Ct. 701;  93-1 USTC ¶50,014;
        71 AFTR2d 93-463
*N.E. Soliman v. Commissioner*, 935 F2d 52; 91-1 USTC ¶50,291; 67 AFTR2d
        91-1112

a.    Were the judges in the Supreme Court decision unanimous or split?  How do you know?
b.    What does Revenue Ruling 94-24, 1994-1 CB 87 add to your understanding of this Code provision and the *Soliman* case?
c.    Read IRC §280A(c)(1)(A).  Has Congress amended this provision since *Soliman* and the revenue ruling?  In what way?  How do the changes affect the authority of the *Soliman* case? Can you imagine factual situations in which *Soliman* might still apply?

37.    Read and brief the following:

*Roemer v. Commissioner*, 716 F2d 693; 83-2 USTC ¶9600; 52 AFTR2d 83-5954
*Threlkeld v. Commissioner*, 848 F2d 81; 88-1 USTC ¶9370; 61 AFTR2d 88-1285
Rev. Rul. 85-143, 1985-2 CB 55
*E.E. Schleier v. Commissioner*, 115 S.Ct. 2159; 95-1 USTC ¶50,309; 75
        AFTR2d 95-2159

a.    Carefully read IRC §104(a).  How did Congress respond to the forgoing court and Treasury positions?  How does this affect the authority of the previously-referenced court cases and revenue ruling?

38. You have been asked to find the complete cite for the Supreme Court case called *Duberstein v. Commissioner*. Provide the official cite and two unofficial cites. What was the Code section at issue in the case?

39. In *Board v. Commissioner*, 51 F2d 73; 2 USTC ¶763; 10 AFTR 192, the losing party filed a *Writ of Certiorari* with the Supreme Court. Was *cert* granted? If you wanted to rely on this case, how would your knowledge of the case history impact you?

40. Assume you have access only to an electronic library. Use one of the electronic databases to locate the following cases. Read only the case headnote and summarize:

    a.    *Davis v. U.S.*, 495 U.S. 472; 90-1 USTC ¶50,270; 65 AFTR2d 90-1051

    b.    B. Tudyman (You don't know anything more about this case.)

    c.    *Sanford Reffett*, 39 TC 869

41. Assume you have access only to an electronic library. Use one of the electronic databases to locate the following cases. Read only the case headnote and summarize:

    a.    *Daniel E. Godfey v. Commissioner* (Tax Court memo case in 1998)

    b.    *John DiFronzo v. Commissioner*

    c.    *Huffman v. Commissioner*, 67 TCM 2237 (1991)

42. Assume you have access only to an electronic library. Use one of the electronic databases to locate the following cases. Read only the case headnote and summarize:

    a.    68 TCM 917 (1994)

    b.    100 TC 124 (1993)

    c.    *Commissioner v. Matheson*, 82 F.2d 380 (CA 5, 1936)

43. Study the *D.M. Clanton* case.

    a.    What court issued the decision?

    b.    Was the taxpayer represented by an attorney?

    c.    What were the material facts of the case?

    d.    What was the issue before the court?

    e.    What was the taxable year in which the transactions at issue occurred?

    f.    When was the case decided?

    g.    What was the court's ruling?

    h.    What did the court base its ruling on?

    i.    Do you agree with the court's decision?

    j.    What judge(s) wrote the ruling?

k.    Who was the losing party?  Did the losing party appeal?
l.    What other courts have cited this case?

44.    Citate the following cases.  What is the status of each?  Using the RIA citator, list five cases in which each has been cited. Without reading the citing cases, did each of the subsequent cases follow or question the court's decision?  Now use the CCH citator and citate the same cases.  Compare the information you obtain from each citator.

a.    *Eisner v. McComber* (Supreme Court)
b.    *Davis v. U.S.*, 495 U.S. 472; 90-1 USTC ¶50,270; 65 AFTR2d 90-1051
c.    *Sanford Reffett*, 39 TC 869


## INTEGRATED CASE STUDIES *(45-60)*

*The following case studies are the same as those at the end of the previous chapter. Use the knowledge and skills you have learned through this chapter to address the case studies. If previously assigned a case study, use your work in Chapters 1 through 3.*

45.    *Case Study A – Disability Payments* (No additional work can be done until the next chapter.)

46.    *Case Study B – Bonus Payments*

Sue is 30 years old and is president and a 51% shareholder of C Corporation.  She informs you that C Corporation has 10 shareholders, all unrelated. Other than herself, no shareholder owns more than 10% of the company's stock. Sue plans to recommend to the board of directors that it pay a bonus to her and three other top employees. She asks you, as the company's tax advisor, to counsel her on what the company needs to do so that the company can get a deduction for the planned bonus payments.

After further discussions with Sue, you learn that the company's business is commercial real estate development. The company had net revenues last year totaling $10,000,000. The company is an accrual basis taxpayer, and each of the intended recipients are cash basis.  She would like the bonuses to actually be paid next year but deducted by the company this year.  One of the intended recipients is Sue's executive assistant who is not currently a shareholder in the company. Sue would like the bonus to equal 100% of each recipient's current salary. The current salaries of the intended recipients are as follows:

| President | $500,000 |
| Executive Assistant | $100,000 |
| Chief Financial Officer | $300,000 |
| Vice Presidentof Operations | $250,000 |

The CFO and Vice President of Operations are shareholders in the company, each owning 10% of the stock.

Sue had indicated to you that she believes the annual salaries are comparable or a little on the high side compared to her company's competitors.  You also learn that the company regularly pays out dividends and plans to continue to do so.

Your supervisor said she is aware of a case named *Mayson Manufacturing* that may provide some help. (Read any additional cases that the *Mayson* case leads you to.)

a.      Does the case address the research question(s)?

b.      As a result of studying the case, do you believe there are additional facts you should seek?

c.      Are there questions remaining that require further research?

47.   *Case Study C – Changing Headquarters* (No additional work can be done until the next chapter.)

48.   *Case Study D – Damage Payments to Dentist*

Dr. Tooth is a 40-year-old dentist in Small Town, USA.  He graduated from dental school five years ago and has had a thriving practice ever since.  At the end of last year, however, Dr. Tooth had an ugly billing disagreement with a patient.  The patient, a well-known wealthy entrepreneur, in retribution, maliciously spread a rumor that Dr. Tooth was a carrier of a serious infectious disease. This rumor destroyed Dr. Tooth's patient base, as most of his patients quickly switched dentists.  As a result of the stress of losing his business, the cruel gossip that resulted from the rumor, and the financial strain caused by this situation, Dr. Tooth began to suffer from severe migraine headaches, loss of appetite, and significant facial twitches.  Dr. Tooth sued the patient for defamation and intentional infliction of emotional distress.  He won a jury verdict and has since recovered

$3,600,000 in damages from the patient.

- ▸ $1,000,000 lost wages. This was calculated on the basis that, in addition to the one year of wages lost since the date of the defamation, he has lost the ability to earn future wages in Small Town.
- ▸ $50,000 reimbursement for medical expenses incurred in seeing a neurologist, internist, and psychologist.
- ▸ $20,000 for future medical expenses anticipated.
- ▸ $30,000 reimbursement for attorney's fees paid.
- ▸ $2,000,000 in punitive damages. The jury determined that the action of the patient was so malicious and heinous that he should be monetarily punished for his actions.
- ▸ $300,000 for pain and suffering.
- ▸ $200,000 to compensate Dr. Tooth for the emotional distress he suffered.

Through your interview with the client, you discover that, out of the award, Dr. Tooth had to pay his attorney $30,000.

Your supervisor said she is aware of a case named *Threlkeld* that may provide some help. (Read any additional cases that the *Threlkeld* case leads you to.)

a.    Does the case address the research question(s)?

b.    How similar to the facts in Dr. Tooth's case are the facts in this case?

c.    As a result of studying the case, do you believe there are additional facts you should seek?

d.    Are there questions remaining that require further research?

49.    *Case Study E – Housing Expenses* (No additional work can be done until the next chapter.)

50.    *Case Study F – Retirement Contributions* (No additional work can be done until the next chapter.)

51.   *Case Study G – Golf Ball Business*

Toby Power, a fellow Illinois resident, is a new client. Prior to her telephone call this morning (late November), all you really knew about Toby was that for the past five years she has been earning a living as a respected golfing instructor at a local club. She just called you to discuss a transaction she has entered into. This is what you learned from your initial conversation with her. She and a group of friends formed a corporation for which the group will own 100% of the stock.

The corporation will be in the business of selling golf balls that it guarantees are indestructible and, because they glow in water and shade, cannot be lost. Toby transferred an office building to the corporation in return for her 20% stock ownership interest. Her eight other friends transferred primarily manufacturing equipment and cash for their evenly divided 80% interest. Toby has owned the office building for seven years and currently owes several hundred thousand dollars on two mortgages on the building. The fair market value of the building she estimates is about $1,000,000.

Toby informs you that her previous tax advisor, about whom she has nothing but negative things to say, counseled her that, in order to avoid paying taxes on the transfer of the building to the corporation, she had to also transfer to the corporation a personal promissory note of $100,000. All of this occurred last year. She wants to know if the transaction was handled correctly or if she needs to worry.

Through further discussions and review of pertinent documents, you discover the following additional facts:

- Toby purchased the office building seven years ago for $500,000. She paid $100,000 in cash and $400,000 using a note (Note A) secured by the property.
- Two years ago, the fair market value of the property escalated to $1,200,000. Toby took out a second mortgage on the property in the amount of $300,000 (Note B). She used the funds to purchase a vacation home in Nevada.
- At the time of the property's transfer to the corporation, the building's fair market value was $1,000,000, determined by an assessor.
- At the time of the property's transfer, Note A had an outstanding balance of $310,000. Note B had a balance of $100,000.
- Toby has made no improvements on the property. She has taken approximately $100,000 in depreciation deductions on her tax return.
- The terms of the promissory note Toby gave to the corporation were that she pay the note off over a period of 20 years, paying a single annual payment in the amount of $6,000 ($5,000 principal; $1,000 interest). The first payment is to be made on the anniversary date of the note – September 1. Toby paid the first installment, which was due a few months ago.

Your supervisor said she is aware of a case named *Peracchi* that may provide some help. (Read any additional cases that the *Peracchi* case leads you to.)

   a.    Does the case address the research question(s)?

   b.    How similar to the facts in Toby's care are the facts in this case?

   c.    As a result of studying the case, do you believe there are additional facts you should seek?

   d.    What questions remain that require further research?

52.  *Case Study H – Private School Expenses* (No additional work can be done until the next chapter.)

53.  *Case Study I – Deadly Fire* (No additional work can be done until the next chapter.)

54.  *Case Study J – Airline Costs* (No additional work can be done until the next chapter.)

55.  *Case Study K – Vacation Home* (No additional work can be done until the next chapter.)

56.  *Case Study L – Property Easement*

A developer acquired a parcel of unimproved real property that she would like to improve. Although the land is currently zoned for commercial use, the developer would prefer not to begin development until an adjoining city street is widened. With a wider street, her development can include a landscaped public entrance and lighting. Without the widening, the development will have only one entrance, which is neither as accessible nor as attractive.

The city plans to widen the street in order to build bike paths which are now required in its new city plan. It will be easier for the city to widen the street if it acquires an easement across developer's property. Developer is interested in providing this easement to the city. However, before she acts, developer would like assurance that she will receive a charitable deduction for the value of the easement. She has asked you to request a letter ruling on this matter.

Your supervisor said she is aware of a Tax Court case named *DeJong* that may provide some help.

   a.    Does the case address the research question(s)?

b.  How similar to the facts in the developer's are the facts in this case?

c.  As a result of studying the case, do you believe there are additional facts you should seek?

d.  What questions remain that require further research?

57.  *Case Study M – Interest Payment*

A taxpayer is president of a company. He is very wealthy and has a good deal of assets. He went to Bank 1 in January, Yr. 1, to borrow $1,000,000. He used the proceeds of the loan to purchase stock. The loan was secured by the stock purchased. The terms of the loan are that it is an interest only loan, with interest to be paid annually on the anniversary of the loan. The rate is 10% per annum (simple) interest on the original loan amount.

In November of Yr. 1, the taxpayer realized that he did not have the liquid funds to pay the $100,000 of interest due in January. He had sufficient assets but, due to the business environment, he determined that the smartest economic move to make would be to borrow the $100,000 rather than to liquidate one of his investments. So he went to Bank 2 and borrowed $100,000. This loan was secured by assets other than his stock and was a regular amortizing loan. Interest was 9%. Upon receipt of the loan proceeds on December 1, Yr. 1, the taxpayer deposited the proceeds into his regular checking account in Bank 3. The proceeds remained in the checking account for the entire month of December. The balance of the checking account during the month of December ranged from $100,000 to $115,000.

On January 2, Yr. 2, the taxpayer wrote a check out of his Bank 3 checking account to Bank 1 in full payment of the interest due. On his tax return for Yr. 2, taxpayer took a deduction of $100,000 as an investment interest expense under Section 163. He had sufficient investment income to cover the deduction.

In your research, you discover that Bank 1 owns 90% of the stock of Bank 2. You are able to talk with the client and learn that he was entirely unaware of the relationship. In fact, the loan documents were entirely different and did not make any reference to any relationship. The IRS has indicated it plans to disallow the interest deduction because it Service believes it has never actually been paid as is required by the Code. The taxpayer would like you to see what the IRS is talking about and whether it has any ground for its position.

a.  Your supervisor said she is aware of a Tax Court case named *Burgess* that may provide some help.

      b.        Does the case address the research question(s)?

      c.        How similar to the facts in taxpayer's case are the facts in this case?

      d.        As a result of studying the case, do you believe there are additional facts you should seek?

      e.        What questions remain that require further research?

58.    *Case Study N – Racing Car Expenses* (No additional work can be done until the next chapter.)

59.    *Case Study O – Retainer Fee* (No additional work can be done until the next chapter.)

60.    *Case Study P - Development Costs*

Gobble Corporation purchased 400 acres in Green City to build a private golf course and residences. The land cost $10,000,000. Gobble planned high-quality, large houses that would sell for an average of $700,000.

It believed that the city's general plan allowed for this development. Gobble spent in excess of $1,000,000 in fees to pay architects and civil engineers, for all necessary environmental studies and approvals. Two years ago, Gobble's development proposal was approved by the city council in a 5-4 vote.

Two months after the vote, the membership in the council changed dramatically. The major election issue was growth versus no growth. The city voted strongly for a no-growth slate. Given the strong community sentiment, the new city council voted to disregard the earlier vote and alter the city's general plan to prohibit such a large development. They decided to defeat the development proposal.

As a result, Gobble sued the city for unreasonably interpreting its planning documents and reversing its initial approval of the project, all to the grave detriment of Gobble. Litigation has consumed almost two years and has cost a total of $500,000.

Gobble's CFO has come to you to help with its tax return preparation. Gobble would like to deduct all the costs incurred in this transaction, including the $1,000,000 paid for the land acquisition.

Your supervisor said she is aware of a Tax Court case decided in the 1960s named *Willis* that may provide some help.

a.      Does the case address the research question(s)?

b.      Are the facts in the case similar to those of Gobble?

c.      As a result of studying the case, do you believe there are additional facts you should seek?

d.      Are there questions remaining that require further research?

# THE TAX RESEARCH PROCESS

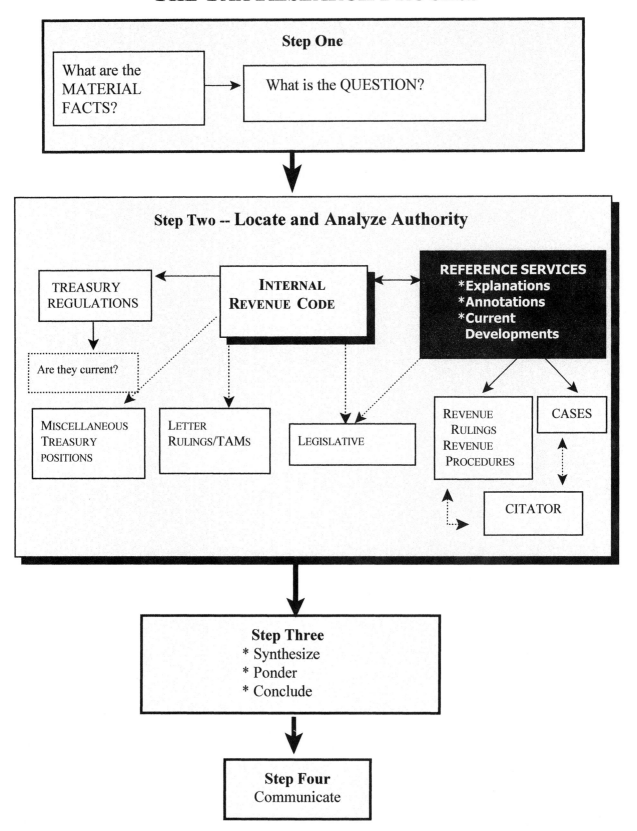

# CHAPTER FIVE

# HOW TO DISCOVER RELEVANT PRIMARY AUTHORITY: USING REFERENCE SERVICES AND OTHER SECONDARY SOURCES

## *EXPECTED LEARNING OUTCOMES*

- Understand the role of secondary sources in the research process
- Identify the various types of secondary sources
- Be able to use each major type of reference service in both paper and electronic resources
- Determine when the tax researcher is best served using one reference service over another (or one medium over another)
- Understand how to proceed after consulting a secondary source

## *CHAPTER OUTLINE*

- Overview
- Introduction to Reference Services
- Code-Oriented Reference Services
- Topically Structured Reference Services
- Electronic Searching
- Special Tools Available with Electronic Services
- Other Secondary Resources
- Chapter Summary
- Problems

## OVERVIEW

You have learned how to analyze and value the three prongs of primary authority that are useful in seeking answers to research questions. First, you considered in Chapter Two the relevant federal statutory laws embodied by the Internal Revenue Code. Second, Chapter Three presented the various Treasury interpretations available. Finally, Chapter Four provided a summary of the source and nature of applicable federal tax judicial decisions and interpretations.

However, a logical gap in your knowledge remains. You now need to know how to identify all the pertinent cases and Treasury interpretations (other than the regulations) that are relevant to your research question.

Fortunately, there is an excellent selection of secondary sources to help summarize and identify relevant authority. Recall that primary federal tax law authority arises from Congressional legislative action, Treasury Department release of interpretations, and court adjudication of federal tax controversies. On the other hand, however, the secondary sources discussed in this chapter are written by various private tax publishers and experts. Secondary sources are works that help us understand the law even though they are not authoritative interpretations.

☞ **Secondary sources are necessary to help you discover relevant authority.**

Potentially useful secondary sources are plentiful. The key sources include:

❏    Reference services

❏    Treatises and textbooks

❏    Journal articles and tax conference materials

❏    Annual tax summaries

# INTRODUCTION TO REFERENCE SERVICES

☞ **Reference services are usually the best tool for identifying relevant authority.**

Reference services act as road maps helping to identify relevant primary authority. The major reference services are designed to furnish two tools:

■    Explanations
■    References

*Explanations:* Each reference service provides a narrative explanation of the Code section or topic under discussion.   Although not authoritative, this explanation helps provide a general understanding of the topic, which may help you as you examine the more complicated case law and Treasury interpretations.  Thorough explanations often summarize the Code provision and provide a brief analysis of the key issues surrounding the provision.  In addition, the explanations often discuss recent cases or Code amendments.  One limitation of reference service explanations is that they often merely restate provisions in the Code or Treasury regulations without, in some instances, providing the more detailed analysis that may be found in journals and treatises.  This is often the case when the issue you are researching is a "cutting-edge" issue not yet examined by the Treasury or the courts.

**Explanations often provide useful analysis. However, this is not authority upon which you can rely.**

*References:*  The main purpose of a reference service should be to provide the citations to cases, revenue rulings and revenue procedures that interpret the Code section under discussion.  In addition, the service should refer you to the other types of primary sources – letter rulings, IRS notices, and so on – on a selective basis when the editors believe such a reference may be particularly useful.  Consequently, reference services often are not particularly useful if you need to thoroughly research letter rulings.  In this case, it is wise to directly research letter rulings using the techniques discussed in Chapter Three.

## Types of Reference Services

There are two different categories of reference services – **Code oriented** and **topic oriented**.  Those structured around the IRC are organized by Code section.  For each Code section, there is a  brief explanation followed by a list of references to the primary law, usually referred to as **annotations**.  The topically structured services provide more lengthy explanations and typically refer you to the primary authority through footnotes rather than annotations.

**There are two types of reference services:  Code oriented and topic oriented.**

When you are ready to review the material in a reference service, you will want to determine which type will be most helpful to begin your research. Topical services are better suited in some circumstances; Code-oriented services are better in others. There is no hard-and-fast rule regarding which type of service is best for a particular type of research project. Personal preference often drives the decision. However, there are a few commonsense factors to help in your decision.

☞ **Personal preference and the type of research project will help you select the reference service best suited for your research.**

> ▸ **Are you unaware of the Code section that applies, or are you uncomfortable with the complexity of the Code Section you are researching? Is Code analysis new to you?** In this case, you may find the topically structured services more helpful to you because they tend to contain more extensive explanations. This type of service provides a lengthier contextual discussion of the relevant authority. Many researchers find the analysis to be a bit easier to understand compared to the Code-oriented services.

> ▸ **Are you reasonably familiar with the Code section? Do you simply want to find out if there is a helpful case or revenue ruling on the specific research question?** In this case, you may find the Code-oriented services a better source for quickly finding what you are looking for. You may even choose to skip the explanation and go straight to the list of relevant annotations.

There is a choice of publishers for each category of reference service. The two central publishers are:

☞ **CCH and RIA are the two key publishers of reference services.**

- Commerce Clearing House (CCH)
- Research Institute of America (RIA)

Although these services differ slightly in their organization and attributes, the fundamental steps for their efficient use are quite similar. Several additional publishers offer alternative reference resources – Bureau of National Affairs (BNA), Westlaw, Lexis-Nexis and Tax Analysts.  The services are available in a paper, CD-ROM, and over the Internet.

In the following discussion, you will learn methods for using each of the major types of reference services using both print and electronic media.  In addition, you will learn some of the differences between the providers so that you can make an informed choice when selecting which one you wish to use.

## CODE-ORIENTED REFERENCE SERVICES

There are two major reporter services organized around the IRC.  They are CCH's *Standard Federal Tax Reporter* and RIA's *United States Tax Reporter*.  Both are organized in a similar fashion and contain the following segments for each Code Section:

☞ **CCH and RIA are organized in a similar fashion.**

- Text of Code Section
- Text of legislative history excerpts
- Text of related Treasury regulations
- Explanation of Code section
- Table of topics for which there is an interpretive case or revenue ruling
- Brief description of each interpretative case or revenue ruling, followed by the complete citation to that authority

The order in which the two services present the preceding material differs slightly. RIA's service provides the foregoing items grouped together under the applicable Code section. When using this service, you must skim all the material to locate relevant entries. CCH's service organizes the materials a bit differently – by issue within each Code section.  Therefore, if you know the specific research issue within the Code section, you have the option to isolate only the material relevant to the research issue.  For example, in a complicated Code section, the material is presented to you in the services in the following manner.

☞ **CCH divides each Code section material by issue.  RIA does not.**

### RIA *United States Tax Reporter:*

- Text of Code section
- Text of related regulations
- Text of legislative history excerpts
- Explanations of Code section
- Table of topics
- Annotations

Picture printed with permission from CCH.

### CCH *Standard Federal Tax Reporter:*

- Text of Code section
- Text of legislative history excerpts
- Contents for topic 1
  - ▸ Text of regulations dealing with topic 1 of Code section
  - ▸ Explanation of rules for topic 1
  - ▸ Table of topics for interpretations of topic 1
  - ▸ Annotations for topic 1
- Contents for topic 2
  - ▸ Text of regulations dealing with topic 2 of Code section
  - ▸ Explanation of rules for topic 2
  - ▸ Table of topics for interpretations of topic 2
  - ▸ Annotations for topic 2

Picture printed with permission from the RIA .

When deciding to use a Code-oriented reference service, you often will employ the following basic steps whether you access the service in paper or through electronic means.

**Step 1:**    Identify the relevant volume (or electronic topic)

**Step 2:**    Locate the relevant text within that volume or topic

| Step 3: | Determine what portion of the Code section coverage to review |
|---|---|
| Step 4: | Study the pertinent portion |
| Step 5: | Check current developments |
| Step 6: | Examine the relevant primary authority |

## Step 1: Identify the relevant volume

You may identify the research question and read the relevant Code section(s) and Treasury regulations before using a reference service. Or you can use a reference service to begin your research and read the Code and regulations within a service. To locate the volume that discusses the relevant Code section(s), you may wish to use the index. Another effective method of locating the pertinent discussion involves "browsing" through the service. In print, you begin this by examining the helpful notations on the outside binding of each volume listing the Code section coverage and topic for each bound volume. You can perform the same steps when accessing the services electronically.

### *Using the Index*

Each service contains a detailed **index** that refers to the potentially relevant authoritative text. Both services divide the text by paragraph number(s). The index refers to all paragraph number(s) in which the index word is used. Using the paragraph information, you can easily locate the pertinent volume containing the discussion.

Often an index topic refers to multiple places where the service discusses the topic. Consequently, it sometimes takes a few tries before you locate the most relevant portion of the particular reference service that addresses the research question. RIA's *United States Tax Reporter* attempts to reduce this challenge by using a paragraph numbering system that includes a reference to the pertinent Code section in the first part of the paragraph number. This enables you to identify the pertinent Code section to which the index is referencing.

☞ **To locate the relevant material, you can use the service's index or table of contents.**

☞ **RIA's service uses a paragraph numbering system containing the Code section number.**

The following two examples illustrate the use of the index using the print services.  The electronic service uses the same index.  The steps necessary to access the electronic index are illustrated in detail in the Appendix.

---

**EXAMPLE 1 :  How to Use the Index in RIA's *United States Tax Reporter* (print service)**

You are researching a question involving annuity contracts and how Code Section 1031 applies to them.  The following excerpt is from the index to RIA's *United States Tax Reporter*.

**Exchange of property**
. acquisition of voting stock . . . . . . . . . . . 3544
. additional first-year depreciation . . . . . *1792.02*
. amount realized . . . . . **10,010(§1001)**; *10,012;* 10,014.01; 10,014.16—10,014.21
. annuity contracts . . . *722.10,* **10,310(§1031)** — *10,312.03;* 10,354
. annuity for property
   *(See Annuities and annuity contracts, sub-head property transferred for)*
. assets of corporation for own stock
   . . . . . . . . . . . . . . . . . . . . 3114.02(e)
. assumption of liabilities . . . . . . . **3570(§357);** **10,310(§1031)**; 3574—3574.04; *10,312—10,312.05;* 10,314.07; 10,314.09; 10,315.07
. . liabilities in excess of basis . . . . **3570(§357);** *3572.01;* 3574—3574.04
. . mortgage . . . . . . . **10,315.07(15), (25), (30)**
. . subject to mortgage . . . . . . . . 10,315.07(10)
. . tax avoidance purposes . . . . . . . . 3574.01(b)
. . taxpayer's liabilities . . . . . . . . . 10,315.07(5)

Notice the number of potentially relevant entries.  Remember that each United States Tax Reporter paragraph number indicates the related Code section.  Thus, you can begin your research by looking at the index entries that include a reference to Code Section 1031.  Be sure to check the Supplementary Index entries.

---

**EXAMPLE 2:  How to Use the Index CCH's *Standard Federal Tax Reporter* (Print service)**

The following entry is an excerpt from CCH's *Standard Federal Tax Reporter*.  Notice that the numbering system does not help you determine which entry relates to Code Section 1031.

**ANNUITIES AND ANNUITY CONTRACTS—**
continued
. death benefits for employees—see
   Employees' death benefits
. definition of . . . . . . . . . . . 6114.015; 6114.20
. delivered outside U.S.
. . withholding of tax at source . . . 35,122.055
. depreciable property . . . . . . . . . . 11,007.11
. . devised property subject to . . . . . . 8470.044
. disability annuities under Foreign Service
   Act, exemption . . . . . . . . . . 6660; 6662.01
. disqualifying payment or settlement
   . . . . . . . . . . . . . . . . . . . . . . . . 6114.0617
. distribution of annuity policies by
   discontinued pension trust . . . . . 17,513.13
. distributions
. . health insurance premiums, distributions
      paying for . . . . . . . . . . . . . . . . . . . 6102
. . insufficient, excise tax imposed . . 35,780—
                                                  35,784.10
. . required, questions and answers by IRS
   . . . . . . . . . . . . . . . . . . . . . . . . . . 18,278
. . retirement plans . 18,207.0565—18,207.064
. . simplified method of taxing . . . . . . . 6102
. . withholding of tax at source . . . 35,122.055
. dividends on policy . . . . . . . . . . . . 6114.38
. dividends received . . . . . . . . . . 6102; 6113
. divorce, domestic relations order . . . . . 6102

. divorce settlements . . . . . . . . . . . 6114.0122
. early distributions—see premature
   distributions under this heading
. early distributions, taxability . . . . 6140.094—
                                                  6140.097
. early withdrawal penalty . . . . . . . . . 6114.67
. early withdrawals—see premature
   distributions under this heading
. elections
. . pre-July 1986 treated as post-June 1986
      investment . . . . . . . . . . . . . . . . 6114.03
. employee death benefits . . . . . . . . . . 6502
. employees' annuities—see Employees'
   annuities
. employees' deductible contributions . . 6102
. employer contributions—see also Employer
   contributions to retirement plans,
   deductibility . . . . . . . . 18,347.01; 18,348.01
. . effect on premiums paid by employee
   . . . . . . . . . . . . . . . . . . . . . . . . . . 6109
. . nondeductible, excise tax imposed
   . . . . . . . . . . . . . . . . . 35,740—35,742.50
. endowment contracts . . . . . . . . 6102; 6102D
. exchange, gain or loss recognition
   . . . . . . . . . . 29,626.042; 31,580—31,582.75
. exchanged for variable annuity . . 31,582.083
. excludable amounts not income . . . . . . 6103
. exclusion ratio . . . . . . . . . . . . . . 6102; 6104

## *Using the Table of Contents*

Although each service provides an index, some researchers choose the relevant text by first selecting the relevant volume of the service.  Whether you use the print or electronic service, you can use the Code section organization to topically move through the service and identify the pertinent discussion.  First, you begin selecting the very broadest topic (for example, Federal taxes).  Then, with each step, you narrow the topic until you arrive at the specific portion of the text you desire.

In print, you do this simply by examining the outside binding of each volume in the service. These bindings note both the central topics discussed as well as the scope of Code Sections covered within the particular bound volume.

When you use either service electronically, usually, the most effective method of locating the relevant material is to "menu walk" or browse through the list of topics.  RIA *CHECKPOINT* specifically allows you to select an option entitled "Table of Contents."  CCH's *Tax Research NetWork* provides you with the opportunity to use the same strategy by "walking" through the topics.  The Appendix provides step-by-step illustrations of this process for each service.

**Be sure to review the Appendix for detailed illustrations of how to electronically perform each research step.**

### Step 2:  Locate the relevant text within that volume

Locating the relevant text within the selected volume should be relatively simple.  Everything is numerically sequenced because the volumes are organized by Code Section.  Each Code section essentially has its own chapter.  In print, chapters are usually divided by tabs, although frequently there is more than one Code section in each tab.  Electronically, the table of contents or topic menus take you step by step to the Code section coverage.

### Step 3:  Determine what portion of Code section coverage to review.

There is abundant information within the service's coverage of each Code section. Whether accessing the service in print or by electronic means, the coverage is the same.  Remember that each service contains the full text of the **Code section**, excerpts of its **legislative history**, complete text of the **regulations,** an **explanation** of the Code section (and sometimes regulations), and **references** to interpretive case law and other primary sources.  Your decision concerning the scope of your analysis depends on your intended purpose for utilizing the service.  Clearly, if you have not yet analyzed the text of the Code section, you may want to read it at this point in your research.  On the other hand, you may have already read the

**Once you locate the Code section coverage, your challenge is to determine what portion will be helpful.**

Code section and companion regulations.  Then, you may choose to skip the Code and regulations and move directly to the applicable explanations and annotations.  Occasionally, you may even choose to skip the explanations.

*Code and Regulations*: You can read the Code section in Code volumes separate from the reference service.  Or, you can read the Code section within the reference service.  There are no advantages or disadvantages to reading the Code section in the reference service as opposed to another source.  It simply may be more convenient for you to read the Code within the service itself.  In regard to regulations, however, remember from Chapter Three that the services provide you with a notation whenever Treasury Regulations do not reflect a change in the Code.  This is one important reason why you might want to use the reference service when reviewing regulations.

☞ **The Code and related regulations are provided in the service as a convenience to you.**

*Legislative History*: Reference services typically contain only selected excerpts of the Committee Reports.  Absent researching a new Code section, usually you will not begin your work in the reference service by reading the legislative history excerpts.  However, you may wish to turn to them when you find little or no interpretive authority elsewhere.

☞ **The services provide only excerpts of the legislative history.**

*Explanations*: The explanation portion of the Code section coverage provides a brief narrative description of the statutory provisions.  The explanations also may identify various issues that have arisen regarding that Code section's application.  The explanations frequently discuss key relevant cases as well as areas for which there is no clear guidance.  Remember that the CCH service organizes the materials for the Code section by topic within the section.  Therefore, explanations are spread throughout the material.  You should find the topic area most relevant within the Code section coverage, and then locate the related explanation.

*Table of Topics with Interpretative Guidance*: This table or list identifies by topic all the areas within the Code section for which there is an applicable case, revenue ruling, revenue procedure, and, occasionally, a letter ruling.  The list acts as a table of contents for the more detailed annotations that follow, which describe the relevant cases and authority. The table of topics is the beginning of the "reference" part of the service.  All cases, revenue rulings, and revenue procedures related to the Code section should contain a reference in the table.  The challenge is in reading the table carefully enough to ensure you find every relevant authoritative source. Regardless of what other portions of the service you read, it is advisable to carefully scan this table.  (There is an illustration of the table on page 250.)

> The table of topics is one of the most useful tools.  It lists the topics addressed by case law and revenue rulings.

Because of its organization, the CCH service frequently includes several tables of topics for one Code section.  It is usually important to review all relevant tables within the Code section material in order to ensure full coverage of the particular topic you are researching.

**Step 4:  Study the pertinent portion**

From your work in the earlier chapters, you are already familiar with examining all the reference service material except the explanations, table of topics, and the annotations.  Studying explanations involves basic analytical review.  When examining the table of topics and the annotations, it is wise to employ a more strategically oriented approach.  Some pointers to follow include:

> When using CCH, it is important to remember you may need to skim through all the topic tables in the Code section coverage.

- ☞ **Stay focused.**  Keep in mind the research question. What are you trying to answer?  What are you specifically seeking to find?

- ☞ **Be open to spotting potentially new issues.**  At first glance, this suggestion appears to directly conflict with staying focused.  However, it is important to be focused while at the same time open to either refining the initial issue you have framed or adding to it.  Often a review of the table of topics and annotations provides information prompting revision of the initial research question.  It is unwise to be so narrowly focused at this step that you close your eyes to all entries except those that appear completely on target.  Likewise, you should not be so indiscriminate that you have difficulty distinguishing between potentially relevant entries and entirely irrelevant ones.

☞ **Carefully skim the table(s).**  Each entry on the table includes a reference to the subparagraph number that houses the annotation. Jot down the most promising references.  Continue skimming the entire table <u>before</u> you turn to the annotations.  What appears relevant at the beginning of the list may be overshadowed in importance by an entry farther down the list.  When you jump off the list to read an annotation immediately after you find the first potentially relevant entry, it is easy to forget to return to the list.  By doing so, you risk missing critical authority.  To avoid this danger, it is usually wise to review the entire table and the related annotations before moving on.

☞ **Using a methodical approach when reviewing the material will help you research efficiently.**

Electronically, you have the option of requiring the computer to perform the task of skimming for you.  By using the **search** function, the electronic services will search through the table and annotations for a word or group of words.  Although skimming is quite efficient and thorough, when faced with a lengthy list, you may prefer employing this computer search method.  Searching is discussed in more detail later in this chapter.

☞ **Examine those annotations you have identified as potentially relevant, using the subparagraph numbers on your list.**  If you noted which entries appear most promising, you may wish to read them first.  Each annotation generally includes a brief explanation of the interpretation, the issue addressed, and its resolution.  You should find the citation to the interpretation at the end of the annotation.  Usually, there is a separate annotation for each case or revenue ruling.  Therefore, sometimes you will see several annotations within the same subparagraph.

☛    **Identify which documents warrant an examination of the full text.  Locate and study these documents.**

The following illustrates steps 3 and 4 when using the print services as well as the necessary analysis when using the electronic services.  The Appendix illustrates this process using electronic tools.

---

**ILLUSTRATION:   RIA's *United States Tax Reporter* (print service)**

You are researching whether a sale of property for cash followed by a leaseback is considered an *exchange* for purposes of Code Section 1031.  You have turned to the tab for Code Section 1031 and located the following list of annotations by issue.

**ANNOTATIONS**

**[¶10,315]   Table of Cases and Rulings by Issue**

"Exchange" defined    ...    ¶10,315.01

(5)   Property transferred for cash and a leaseback
(7)   Exchange v. sale
(10)  Exchange not permitted by State law
(15)  Three-cornered transactions
(20)  Agreement to acquire replacement property from other sources

(22)  Exchanges without legal title
(25)  Exchanges involving co-owners
(27)  Exchanges involving intermediaries
(30)  Exchange of property
(35)  Payment of cash upon an exchange of properties
(40)  Trade-ins

By skimming through the list, it appears that the paragraph located at ¶10,315.01(5) is most on point.  After skimming through the remainder of the list, you determine that there are no other pertinent entries.  You turn to ¶10,315.01(5), which is located in the pages following the list. The annotation you locate follows.

**ILLUSTRATION:   RIA's *United States Tax Reporter* – (print service continued)**

The annotation at ¶10,315.01(5) follows:

**[¶10,315.01]   "Exchange" defined.**

**(5)   Property transferred for cash and a leaseback.** Taxpayer didn't sell property for cash and then lease it back but exchanged it for lease and cash within meaning of nonrecognition provision. After receiving 95 year lease, he was in same economic condition as when he owned property.

> *Century Electric Co. v Comm. (1951, CA8) 41 AFTR 205, 192 F2d 155, 51-2 USTC ¶9482, cert den (3-10-52), aff'g (1950) 15 TC 581.*

Property was sold, not exchanged. Taxpayer received cash equal to value of property along with 30-year leaseback. It could recognize loss since this wasn't merely a change in form of ownership, he lost full ownership of property through transaction.

> *Jordan Marsh Co. v Comm. (1959, CA2) 4 AFTR2d 5341, 269 F2d 453, 59-2 USTC ¶9641, rev'g (1957) TC Memo 1957-237, PH TCM ¶57,237.*

To same effect. Sales price and lease rental were for fair value. Since leasehold lacked capital value, transaction was bona fide sale, not IRC §1031 exchange.

> *Leslie Co. v Comm. (1976, CA3) 38 AFTR2d 76-5458, 539 F2d 943, 76-2 USTC ¶9553, aff'g (1975) 64 TC 247, not acq 1978-2 CB 3.*
> *Crowley, Milner & Co. v. Comm. (1982, CA6) 50 AFTR2d 82-5795, 689 F2d 635, 82-2 USTC ¶9612, aff'g (1981) 76 TC 1030.*

*Contra:* IRS considers transaction IRC §1031 exchange in which boot is received and will not follow result in *Marsh,* above.

> *Rev Rul 60-43, 1960-1 CB 687.*

Parent allowed deduction for sub's loss on sale-leaseback of hotel to parent's other sub. Transaction was for valid business purpose; IRC §1031 didn't apply since lease was for 10 years only.

> *Capri, Inc. (1975) 65 TC 162.*

Transfer of land separate from improvements for cash, with immediate lease-back, was sale not exchange; resulting in deductible loss. Transfer furthered plan of liquidating property holdings; no right of repurchase was included in transaction. Selling price and rental price were fair values.

> *City Investing Co. and Subsidiaries (1962) 38 TC 1, not acq 1963-2 CB 6.*

"Loss" on sale and leaseback for more than 30 years had to be amortized over period of lease including options. No sale took place even though corp. received FMV for building and rental was at going rates. Corp. reserved right to repurchase at fixed amount any time after 5 years.

> *Missouri Pacific Railroad Company v U.S. (1973, Ct Cl) 32 AFTR2d 73-5816, earlier proceedings at (1970) 25 AFTR2d 70-844, 191 Ct Cl 61, 423 F2d 727, 70-1 USTC ¶9285.*

**(7)   Exchange v. sale.** Nonrecognition of gain denied. Taxpayer sold property to corp. and corp. assigned its contracts to buy similar property to taxpayer. Taxpayer bought similar property from 3d parties. Corp. never had title to property taxpayer bought. Sale and repurchase resulted.

> *Carlton, Adm v. U.S., (1967, CA5) 20 AFTR 2d 5376, 385 F2d 238, 67-2 USTC ¶9625, aff'g (1966, DC FL) 17 AFTR 2d 1051, 255 F Supp 812, 66-1 USTC ¶9427 But see ¶10,315.01(22).*

To same effect. Cash, instead of property, was received for property transferred to trusts. Although intent was to use cash to acquire suitable exchange property, totality of transaction didn't result in tax-free exchanges, but in sales and later reinvestments, with taxpayer having constructive receipt of sales proceeds.

Note that there are several different cases and also a revenue ruling within the entry for ¶10,315.01(5). You will read each annotation and select the most relevant entries you believe require further examination. Notice also that the RIA reporter provides complete parallel cites that include a cite to CCH's casebook series (USTC). The CCH reference service does not provide cites to the RIA casebooks (AFTR).

**ILLUSTRATION:  CCH's *Standard Federal Tax Reporter* (print service)**

Your client is the owner of a professional basketball team.  Your client requested that you research whether an upcoming trade of one of the player's contracts will generate taxable income.  Your research leads you to an analysis of the potential application of Code Section 1031.  When skimming the lengthy list of annotations under Code Section 1031, you locate the following:

● ● ● *Annotations by Topic*

| | | | |
|---|---|---|---|
| Assets of business | .0191 | Leasehold | .2035 |
| Assets of parent-subsidiary | .019 | Life estate for remainder | .2037 |
| Automobiles and trucks | .02 | Liquidation | .204 |
| Baseball and football player contracts | .027 | Mortgages | .21 |
| Basis of property received on an exchange (reference to ¶31,506.01 et seq.) | | Oil, gas, and mineral rights (reference to .115) | |
| | | Option exercised | .225 |
| Bonds | .035 | Purpose | .235 |
| Broadcast assets | .0355 | Foreign money | .08 |
| Brokerage commissions (reference to ¶31,515A.07) | | Futures contracts | .082 |
| Bullion | .038 | Guardian's sale and purchase | .083 |
| Cash payment | .04 | Livestock | .10 |
| Contractor's loss | .06 | Memberships | .11 |
| Corporation and shareholder | .061 | Multiparty exchanges (reference to ¶31,521) | |

The entry "Baseball and football player contracts" looks particularly relevant.  After skimming the remainder of the list, you determine this entry to be the most promising.  You turn to the paragraph number 31,508 (identified earlier in the table), subparagraph .027 and find the following annotation.

**.027 Baseball and football player contracts.**—Trades of major league baseball player contracts are like-kind exchanges.
Rev. Rul. 67-380, 1967-2 CB 291.

Similarly, as to trades of professional football player contracts.
Rev. Rul. 71-137, 1971-1 CB 104.

After examining this annotation, you will wish to read and cite both revenue rulings.

## Step 5:  Check current developments

Depending on the medium you use to examine the service, you may need to perform a follow-up step to ensure you have found the most recent authority on the issue.  Electronically, both services identify and include current developments in the body of the discussion, although only RIA does so entirely.  For CCH, developments occurring after the beginning of the calendar year can be found in a separately identified current developments section. Clearly, you want to skim the developments for anything relevant to your question.

In paper, the services differ somewhat in their treatment of current developments.  RIA attempts to integrate the developments into the main volumes of the reporter as they are released. However, you should always check the cross-reference table in the Recent Developments volume (Volume 16 of the *United States Tax Reporter*) for information about developments not yet incorporated into the main portion of the service.  CCH tries to integrate some of the developments but places most of them in a separate section in the last volume of the regular service, labeled *New Matters*.  Electronically, CCH provides a listing entitled *Current Developments*.

In both RIA and CCH, you should check the *Recent Developments* or *New Matters* volume and use the cross-reference table to make sure you read any recent relevant developments. This is critical, particularly when using the CCH service toward the end of the year since most of the year's developments will be discussed only in this section. Both services refer you to paragraphs in the developments volumes through a cross-reference from the relevant paragraph in the main volume. Generally, the cross-reference table also refers you directly to the full text of the development.

---

**ILLUSTRATION:  CCH *Standard Federal Tax Reporter New Matters* (print)**

You are researching whether the home of a teacher can be considered the teacher's business office for purposes of allowing certain Code Section 162 deductions.  You have just completed your research in the main portion of the volume. You turn to the volume labeled *New Matters* and find the following:

| From Compilation Paragraph No. | | | To New Development Paragraph No. |
|---|---|---|---|
| | | **Code Sec. 151—Allowance of deductions for personal exemptions** | |
| 8005 | .092 | *Carter*, TCM—Dependency exemptions denied absent evidence of support | 48,109 |
| | .105 | *Carter*, TCM—Dependency exemptions denied where lodging not provided | 48,109 |
| | .1122 | *Zand* aff'd, CA-11—On another issue | 50,499 |
| | .13 | *Carter*, TCM—Dependency exemptions denied where social security benefits exceeded half of support | 48,109 |
| | | **Code Sec. 162—Trade or business expenses** | |
| 8470 | .3184 | *Podd*, TCM—Deductions denied for consulting fees that were not ordinary and necessary business expenses | 48,097 |
| | .5179 | *Zand* aff'd, CA-11—On another issue | 50,499 |
| | .588 | *Langworthy*, TCM—Estimated business expenses deductible under *Cohan* rule | 48,079 |
| | .591 | *Browne*, TCM (¶47,848)—Taxpayer failed to substantiate entitlement to business deductions. Taxpayer on appeal to CA-11. | |
| | .591 | *Zand* aff'd, CA-11—On another issue | 50,499 |
| 8471 | .1263 | *Kent*, DC Nev.—Business deduction denied for gambling losses | 50,524 |
| 8474 | .2504 | *Goins* aff'd, CA-4 (unpub. op.)—Valid employee business expenses deductible | 50,532 |
| 8476 | .45 | *Zand* aff'd, CA-11—On another issue | 50,499 |
| 8520 | .125 | *Raush*, TCM—Teacher's home was site of primary business activity | 48,111 |
| 8540 | .0367 | *Zand* aff'd, CA-11—On another issue | 50,499 |
| | .0406 | *Nauman, Jr.*, TCM—Automobile expenses incurred regarding minister's uncompensated activities disallowed | 48,078 |

The entry for the *Raush* case, a Tax Court Memorandum decision, appears to be relevant. To locate a discussion of the case, the table directs you to paragraph 48,111, which is located in the pages following the table.  Once you turn to that paragraph, you find the following:

[¶ 48,111(M)]    *Richard Raymond Raush v. Commissioner*, CCH Dec. 52,779(M); Dkt. 3514-97, July 6, 1998, T.C. Memo. 1998-245, opinion by Judge Dinan. [Appealable, barring stipulation to the contrary, to CA-9.—CCH.]

*[Code Sec. 162]*

Deductions: Business expenses: Traveling expenses: Teacher: Primary business activity: Personal preference: Unreported income: Interest: Information returns.—A high school teacher's home was in the city where he conducted his teaching activity, which was his primary business activity, not 200 miles away where he maintained a residence. Although he claimed that he conducted research, writing and other business activities at the location where he maintained the residence, he earned no income from those activities in the year at issue or in the prior and subsequent years and he spent an insubstantial amount of time at that location in relation to the time he spent teaching. Therefore, he was not entitled to a traveling expense deduction in connection with his employment. His residence was maintained out of personal preference, not due to any business necessity. Back reference: ¶ 8520.125.

*[Tax Court Rule 143]*

Information returns, not introduced: Evidence.—A high school teacher was not liable for tax on unreported interest income received from a bank. The IRS attorney stated that she did not intend to introduce into evidence information returns filed by the bank. Since those returns were not made part of the record, there was no evidence of unreported interest income. Back reference: ¶ 43,003.02.

**Step 6**:  **Examine the relevant primary authority**

Once you identify the primary authority that appears most relevant to the research question, you have completed your work in the reference service.  Now, using the skills you learned in the previous chapters, you are ready to examine the cases, revenue rulings, revenue procedures, and any other primary authority the service referred you to.

# TOPICALLY STRUCTURED REFERENCE SERVICES

A topically arranged reference service is simply another available type of reference service. Rather than being organized around the Internal Revenue Code, some reference services are organized by major topic.  The research process is a bit different when using this type of service.  In addition, unlike the Code-oriented services, the organization of each topical service differs.  It is helpful to learn each one separately.

### RIA *Federal Tax Coordinator*

One of the most popular topical reporters is the *Federal Tax Coordinator* published by RIA.  The service is available in both hard-copy and electronic versions.  The electronic version is available on CD-ROM (*On-Point*) and over the Internet (*CHECKPOINT*).  The text of the service is the same regardless of the medium.

☞ **RIA'S** *Federal Tax Coordinator* **is the most popular topical reporter.**

The *Federal Tax Coordinator* covers each major topic entirely through descriptive text, similar to a textbook.  Unlike the Code-oriented services, in the print format of this service, you find the text of the relevant Code sections and regulations in the back of each volume behind an identifying tab.  Instead of using "annotations," the *Coordinator* provides references to primary law throughout the narrative text.  Sometimes the narrative discusses the details of the authority to a greater extent than the Code-oriented annotations.  One cautionary note here is that you should be careful to make sure that the narrative text cites authority for its statements. Sometimes no authority is cited, resulting in the narrative text representing merely the opinion of the author. Other times there is much less information about the authority and simply a reference to a specific source in a footnote.

☞ **Make sure to base your conclusion on primary authority.**

### *Beginning Your Research in RIA's Federal Tax Coordinator*

There are three ways to begin using this reporter – through the index, through major topic groupings, and, when using the electronic service, through an electronic search.

***Using the Index***: You can find the index to this service in the first volume of the print service or through the table of contents in the electronic service. Next to each word in the detailed index is a reference to a volume and paragraph number. When you find the appropriate index reference, you can locate the referenced volume and paragraph. You can use this method with either the hard copy or electronic media. When you locate the index reference electronically, you can click on the *Federal Tax Coordinator* paragraph reference and immediately go to the referenced text. A step-by-step illustration using the electronic service can be found in the Appendix.

---

**ILLUSTRATION:  How to Use the *Federal Tax Coordinator* Index (print)**

You are researching the treatment of production period interest and its calculation. Skimming through the index, you locate the following entry:

### Main Topic Index

Production period interest —Cont'd
. *capitalization, mandatory —Cont'd*
. . *allocation of interest —Cont'd*

. . . period of calculation . . . . . . . . . . . . . . . . L-5927
. . . produce . . . . . . . . . . . . . . . . . . . . . . . L-5930
. . . produced property . . . . . . . . . . . . . . . . L-5926
. . . production expenditures . . . . . . . . . . . . L-5934

This entry informs you that volume "L," paragraph 5927 contains potentially relevant discussion.  Your next step will be to retrieve this volume and locate the specific paragraph number.

---

## *Using the Volume Topic Groupings*

The *Federal Tax Coordinator* is organized by major topic. Therefore, you have the option of skipping the index and simply using its organization as your guide.  In print, the binding of each volume identifies the major topics covered.  Each volume also contains a table of contents.  Electronically, you can replicate the same process, using the table of contents and "walking" through the topics until you arrive at the desired text. You can find detailed examples of this process in the Appendix.

☞ **Use the index or topical indicators on each volume to locate the pertinent material.**

## *Using Electronic Searching*

When accessing the *Federal Tax Coordinator* through electronic means, you have the additional option of locating relevant discussion through electronic searching.  Electronic searching is a literal process – you instruct the computer to find every location of a specific word or combination of words. Thus, the utility of your search primarily depends on how you structure the search.  If your search term is overly broad (for example you search for *depreciation*), you may get thousands of "hits" including an abundance of material with little research value. Alternatively, you may use too narrow of a search term.

Literal searching carries with it the inherent risk that you will inadvertently miss important authority. You may miss relevant authority if you select a search term slightly different than that used in the text of a relevant document. For example, perhaps you search for *home*, but because the key case uses the term *residence* and not *home*, you will miss the key case. Worse, you will likely be unaware you missed important authority because you may otherwise feel you have been extremely thorough in your research. RIA minimizes this risk by providing you with the option of activating its Thesaurus search tool. This tool allows you to choose to search for all synonyms of the search term.

The *Federal Tax Coordinator* provides you the option to locate relevant text through electronic searching. Using RIA *CHECKPOINT* on the Internet, you first must identify what database you wish to search. You will have a wide selection of databases because this vehicle provides you with access to all RIA products. If you wish to use the topically structured RIA *Federal Tax Coordinator*, you will select that as your database. You also have the option of choosing any of the RIA reference services. The Appendix contains a step-by-step illustration of this process.

### Examining the RIA Federal Tax Coordinator

Once you are in the appropriate volume and have found the relevant discussion, skim the material for pertinent text. Because the material is in narrative form, it is fairly easy to read. As you find applicable discussions, jot down the cite to the authority supporting the statement. If you read the service electronically, you may choose to go directly to the reference by clicking on the document icon. You may also decide to save the document you are reading by placing it in the "document folder" provided by the electronic service. This enables you to retrieve the document at any time for further analysis.

☛ **Electronic searching is an another method to locate relevant material. Be aware of this method's inherent risks.**

☛ **You can access the material in the *Federal Tax Coordinator* in a variety of ways.**

**ILLUSTRATION: RIA *Federal Tax Coordinator* (print)**

The following excerpt illustrates a typical discussion in the print version of *Federal Tax Coordinator*. Note that the supporting authority is identified through the use of footnotes that appear at the bottom of each page.

### D-1410. Effect of reasonable compensation rules on professional corporations.

Professional corporations are subject to the same income tax rules as regular corporations. IRS took the position that certain payments made in one case, by a professional corporation to its lawyer-employees exceeded reasonable compensation. The taxpayer contended that applicable state law bars professional corporation dividends. Therefore, all payments from the firm to the lawyers must be reasonable compensation.

The Court of Claims refused to accept the proposition that characterization of payments as reasonable compensation for federal tax purposes is controlled by state law. How the payments are characterized under state law may be a factor to be considered, but it is not a controlling factor. Whether payments are reasonable is a question of fact to be decided on the basis of all the facts and circumstances in each particular case.[33]

33. Isaacson, Rosenbaum, Spiegleman & Friedman, (1979, Ct Cl) 44 AFTR 2d 79-5382, 221 Ct Cl 831, 79-2 USTC ¶9463.
34. U.S. v. Kintner, Arthur R., (1954, CA9) 46 AFTR 995, 216 F2d 418, 54-2 USTC ¶9626, aff'g (1952, DC MT) 42 AFTR 810, 107 F Supp 976, 52-2 USTC ¶9563.

Sometimes, you may find what appears to be a helpful statement in the *Federal Tax Coordinator* but the statement is preceded by an RIA checkmark logo and does not cite to specific supporting authority. Remember that the *Coodinator*, like all secondary sources, is not primary authority and is not itself citable, although numerous judicial opinions have referred to it. Thus, although an editorial statement preceded by the RIA checkmark may be helpful to understand the research question, it may not be clearly supported with absolute certainty by primary authority – the reason why RIA presented it with the checkmark logo. Note that the Federal Tax Coordinator always clearly identifies its editorial expert observations and recommendations by separating them from the rest of the narrative discussion that is specifically supported by primary authority.

☛ **Although helpful, the *Federal Tax Coordinator*, like all other secondary sources, is not primary authority and should not be cited.**

## CCH *Federal Tax Service*

Another topically structured service is CCH's *Federal Tax Service*. This service is now available only on CD-ROM (CCH SmartTax) and on the Web in CCH's *Tax Research NetWork*. If the service were in print, it would fill approximately 20 volumes.

☛ **The *Federal Tax Service* is now only available electronically.**

The *Federal Tax Service* is organized by major topic. The service covers income and estate and gift tax topics. CCH provides explanations and analysis of each topic and provides references through footnotes. A cross-reference to current developments follows each analysis. The *Federal Tax Service* focuses on providing practitioners with practical examples of the application of the tax laws. Several hundred practitioners have contributed to the content of the *Federal Tax Service*, which was previously owned by Matthew Bender.

To access the service through CCH's *Tax Research NetWork*, you select this service from the federal library.  You can then either "walk" through the table of contents, search the service for a key word, or skim the index to the service.

**ILLUSTRATION: CCH *Federal Tax Service***

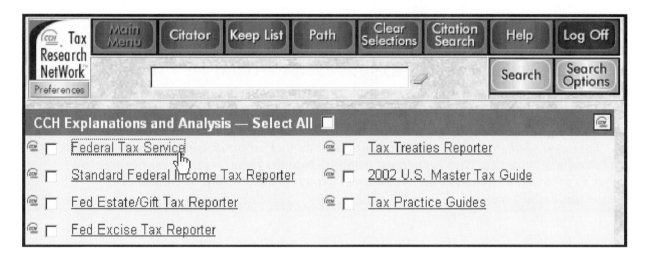

By selecting the topics relevant to your research, you will be able to locate helpful discussion material.

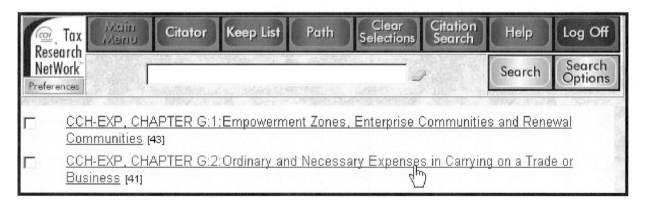

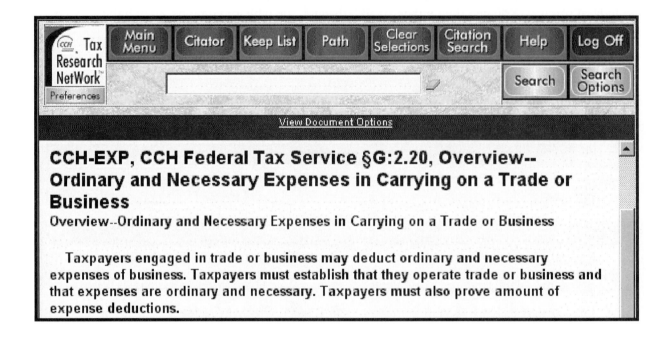

**Tax Analyst's *Federal Tax Baedeker***

In order to assist researchers when using their electronic service called *TaxBase*, Tax Analysts provides a mini-reference service electronically called the *Federal Tax Baedeker*. This brief service is topically structured and enables the researcher to access material through the use of a table of contents. The *Federal Tax Baedeker* provides brief narrative discussion, supported by references to the Internal Revenue Code, Treasury regulations, and revenue rulings. The service doesn't intend to refer to every revenue ruling, just prominent ones. The service does not refer to relevant case law. Relevant cases must be accessed through a different vehicle also located within the *TaxBase*. The Appendix provides a step-by-step example of how to use this service.

## Tax Management Portfolios (BNAs)

Another very helpful topically oriented source is the Tax Management Portfolio service published by the Bureau of National Affairs.  This tool is quite different from the previously discussed topical services. The BNA service consists of individual "portfolios" for a large selection of tax topics and Code Sections.  Although every Code Section does not have a portfolio devoted to it, most receive coverage in at least one portfolio.  Many areas, such as the pension and profit-sharing area, enjoy multiple portfolio coverage.

Where the RIA and CCH services attempt to refer you to every case, revenue ruling, and procedure published, the portfolios (often referred to as "BNAs") provide more selective referencing.  The goal is slightly different than the other services.  Rather than attempting to be a complete encyclopedic reference service, the BNAs are designed to provide an in-depth analysis of each portfolio topic, including the history and background of the topic and an analysis of its application.  You may wish to turn to this service when you determine you need a comprehensive discussion of the research subject.

Unlike the other services, BNAs are individually authored by recognized experts in the particular field of tax law.  Therefore, each portfolio differs somewhat in its content, organization, writing style, and completeness.  The authors select the references they deem appropriate and eliminate those that, in their opinion, are redundant or relatively unimportant.  Notwithstanding, the BNAs often offer a detailed analysis of issues not covered by the more conventional reference services.  Use of BNA portfolios is particularly useful when the topic you are researching is new to you.  The thorough coverage of the topic will enable you to better identify the particular issues needing further clarification.

A convenient feature of the portfolios is their portability, since each portfolio is contained in a slim volume that may easily fit into a briefcase.

☛ **BNA titles include:**
**"Valuation of Publicly Traded Securities"**

**"Grantor Trusts"**

**"Community Property"**

**"Entertainment Expenses"**

**"Tax Crimes"**

**" Real Property Syndications with Limited Partnerships"**

## *How BNAs are organized*

Each BNA portfolio contains the following:

☞ **Current Developments:** The portfolios are updated periodically and contain brief descriptions of developments affecting the portfolio content. It is frequently difficult to determine the date the portfolio was last updated, so be very careful to follow-up your research in a BNA portfolio with research in a reference service to ensure currency of your research results.

☞ **Table of Contents:** This acts as the index for the individual portfolio.  The table lists each paragraph heading so that you can easily find the relevant portion of the portfolio.

☞ **Detailed Analysis:** This portion of the portfolio usually begins with information on the history or background of the topic being discussed.  The remainder of the analysis contains a detailed explanation of the subject in a narrative format.  The narrative discusses and refers to select relevant cases and other primary authority.  Remember, however, that it is not the intent of the portfolio author to address every case or revenue ruling on point.  The best portfolios provide helpful examples of application and discussion in much greater detail than is found in the other services.

☞ **Working Papers:** Working papers are a unique feature of the portfolios and can be extremely helpful.  Here the portfolio author has the opportunity to provide whatever additional practical tools he chooses.  The working papers can be very helpful to practitioners seeking a full understanding of the entirety of a transaction. Working papers may include the

☞ **BNA portfolios are particularly useful when you are looking for a very detailed discussion of a topic's issues and background.**

following:

- sample problems and answers
- flowcharts
- computational worksheets
- completed sample tax returns
- sample draft documents (elections, pension plans, etc.)
- relevant private letter rulings, legislative history, and other primary authority

☛ **Bibliography:** This section lists other sources of information on the topic of the portfolio, such as relevant articles or books.

### *How to Access BNAs*

BNA portfolios are available in print and electronically. They are available on CD-ROM and over the Internet through the Lexis-Nexis service.

Electronically, you must search for key terms to find the relevant portions of a portfolio. Using the print format, it is relatively easy to identify the relevant portfolios. A binder labeled *Tax Management Portfolio Index* contains three different types of indexes: key word, Code section, and major topic. Each index refers you to a portfolio volume number and edition. Because the most efficient use of the portfolios is to locate a portfolio that primarily focuses on the issue you wish to research, the major topic index is often the most helpful. If the research topic is only addressed as a peripheral topic of a portfolio, time efficiency may suggest that you seek another more comprehensive coverage of the issue.

Although tempting, it is not wise to try to discern which portfolio is relevant by simply browsing through the service and looking at each title. There is no logical order to the numbering system. Thus, you may find portfolio number 9 addresses one aspect of partnership taxation and portfolio number 350 addresses yet

**The working papers offer potentially very useful tools.**

**Make sure to use the indexes to locate the most relevant portfolio. The numbering system of the portfolios is entirely random.**

another area in partnership taxation.  Use the index – you will save a good deal of valuable time.

# ELECTRONIC SEARCHING

Generally, a very effective electronic research strategy consists of walking through a particular service topically, in the manner discussed earlier in this chapter.  Because electronic key word searching has the inherent limitation of literal searching, you may unknowingly eliminate potentially important sources through misspelling a word or failing to search for the best terms. Recognizing this limitation, some services have augmented the literal search with tools that lessen this risk.  Nonetheless, if you choose to use electronic searching as your main reference service methodology, be mindful of its inherent risks.

☛ **If you perform an electronic search for the term *home* but the Treasury uses the term *residence*, the search will not identify any potentially relevant Treasury interpretations unless you take advantage of the system's thesaurus.**

## Methods of Electronic Searching

All electronic reference services use one of the two available searching technologies – **folio** searches or **Boolean** searches.  As a researcher, it is useful to understand which search method each service employs and have a basic understanding regarding the differences.  Every service has its own look and feel.  However, if you understand the basics of the two types of search technologies, you should be able to easily adjust to the specific nuances of the service you utilize.

### *Folio Searching*

Some services use the folio method of searching, although most have now moved to some form of Boolean.  Folio searching is the older, simpler and less sophisticated of the two searching forms.  If you instruct the computer to search for one term, the computer searches through the designated database for every instance in which that term appears.  One limitation of this method is that it does not automatically search for the plural form of the word.  To find a plural, you must use a "wildcard" symbol, which alerts the system that you

☛ **Folio and Boolean are the two available search technologies.**

wish to search for anything with the word as its root.

When searching for two or more terms using a folio search system, the system first identifies all the locations of the first term. Then it searches through the entire database again for the second term. Last, it compares the two lists and identifies the documents common to both. The search produces a list of documents containing both terms anywhere in the document but not necessarily located side by

☛ **Each database provides helpful information as to how best to formulate your search to capture your intended results.**

---

**EXAMPLE 3:  Folio Searching**

You want to find all the documents with the phrase *foreign income*. If you put into your search just *foreign income*, you will end up with a list of all documents that have both words in them. The word *foreign* may be at the beginning of the document and *income* at the end. To find those that use the phrase *foreign income*, you must place quotation marks around the search item: "foreign income."

---

side. If you wish to locate only those documents with the terms in a specific order, you must place quotation marks around the words.

In folio searching, it is difficult to search in a more complex manner. For example, it is difficult to search for a phrase and a word at the same time. Thus, in the preceding example, folio searching does not enable you to search for documents containing the phrase *foreign income* and also the term *corporation*.   In folio searching you cannot combine the "or" search and the "and" search. Thus, folio does not enable you to do some of the more intricate searching made necessary by alternative phrases and terms.

### *Boolean Searching*

Most services now use this more sophisticated search technology.  Boolean searching is based on word relationships called "connectors."  When searching for the term *foreign income*, the computer will find only those documents with the two terms side by side.  It will automatically also include any plurals.  If you want to locate all documents with the two terms in the document without regard to their relative proximity, you can search for *foreign and income*. Boolean searching uses the following common connectors: **and**, **or**, within a designated number of words, (for example, "w/10" means "within ten words of one another"). The computer follows the order of the connectors.  In Boolean searching, you are able to search for phrases and individual terms concurrently.  For example, if you want every document that has the words *foreign income* and also the word *corporation*, your search is simply: *foreign income and corporation*.

## ILLUSTRATION:

The following illustrates one method for locating all documents containing the words *professor* and *home office*.

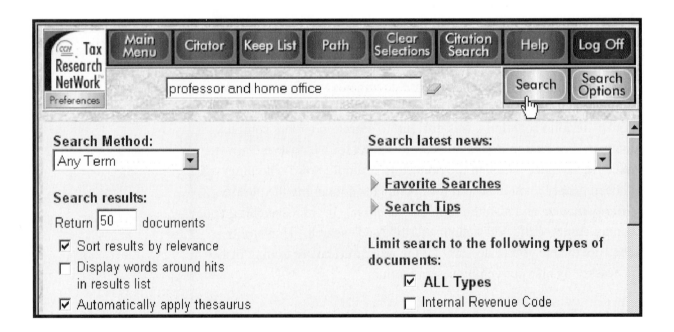

### Plain English Searching

The services have made substantial improvements in their search capabilities so that literal searching is not quite as limiting. For example, assume you instruct the computer to search for the term *professor*. If a document uses the word *teacher*, the search will not automatically reveal that document. However, most of the services now allow for "plain English searching" using a thesaurus that is built into the system. Note in the preceding illustration that a thesaurus is built into the system and is the default option. With a thesaurus, the computer looks for words with a similar meaning to the word used in the search. If however, you intend to limit the search to a specific word and not its synonyms, you can do so by turning off the thesaurus function.

**The thesaurus is an excellent tool to reduce the natural limitations of electronic searching.**

### Segment Searching

Each service enables you to search a certain portion of a group of documents or a particular "library." You may limit your search to just case titles, case text, and so on. This is particularly useful when you know the name of a case but do not possess the proper cite. When you select case titles as your search segment, your search results will contain only those cases with your search request present in the name. This is much more efficient than searching through the texts of all the cases, which would result in a list with all the cases ever citing the one for which you are looking. RIA's *Checkpoint* provides an even simpler method of locating a case through the case name with the use of a simple citation template. The Appendix illustrates how to search for a case in each of the main Internet services when you only have the case name.

**You can search just for a case name when using segment searching.**

## Sources Using Only Electronic Searching

As discussed earlier in this chapter, both the RIA and CCH services enable access through the use of a table of contents. They also contain an optional electronic search tool as a complement to their services. However, some services do not provide a table of contents. Instead, they employ electronic searching as their primary research methodology. The major electronic search-based services are:

☞ **Some resources are available only in an electronic medium.**

- Lexis-Nexis
- Westlaw
- Tax Analysts

### *Lexis-Nexis*

The most widely used of the search-only services is *Lexis-Nexis*. Its database is vast and includes an extensive law and business library. The federal tax library includes all the primary law as well as both RIA reporters (*Federal Tax Coordinator* and *U.S. Tax Reporter*) and the BNA Tax Management Portfolios. In addition, users can purchase libraries that enable access to significant numbers of journal articles, newspapers and other potentially useful secondary sources. This provides access to the *Shepards* method of citing cases and rulings. Lexis-Nexis uses the Boolean search method discussed previously.

☞ **Lexis-Nexis provides an excellent and comprehensive database for the tax researcher.**

Like the RIA and CCH electronic services, Lexis-Nexis is available only on a fee basis over the Internet. The Internet service uses easy-to-understand menus and is, therefore, relatively user friendly. Its address is www.lexis.com.

A Lexis-Nexis search produces a list of all the items containing the search terms. You have the choice of viewing the results in one of the following ways:

- a numbered list of the documents with the search terms
- each document in full text

- each document with just the few sentences before and after the use of the search term. (Referred to as "key words in context method" or KWIC.)

## Westlaw

Westlaw is another research service available on the Internet. Although generally not quite as extensive as the tax database available on Lexis-Nexis, Westlaw provides access to all the primary tax authority as well as news articles. When using this service, you must use searching as your primary method of researching. The service uses the Boolean search technology and allows for "plain English" searching as described previously. Its Internet address is westlaw.com.

## Tax Analysts

Tax Analysts provides a relatively inexpensive tax library through two electronic means: CD-ROM *OneDisc* and the Internet (taxbase.tax.org). The Internet database contains the following:

- Internal Revenue Code and regulations
- Revenue rulings and procedures issued since 1955 Each opinion begins with a summary written by the editors at Tax Analysts.
- Letter rulings and technical advance memoranda from 1980.
- A variety of other documents, such as the *Master Tax Guide*.

In either medium, your key method of research is through searching. However, there is the opportunity to review some material through a topical approach using Tax Analysts' *Tax Baedeker*, discussed earlier.

## Other Search-Based Products

There are and will be more electronic tax databases available

☞ **Westlaw is another service available over the Internet.**

☞ **You can access the database of Tax Analysts by CD-ROM or the Internet.**

to you.  When deciding whether to use an electronic database, you should determine the research methodology you prefer and select the service that best enables you to employ this method.  If you intend to perform searches, consider which search technology you prefer.  With this information and your general tax research knowledge at hand, you should be able to adapt to other electronic tax resources.

## SPECIAL TOOLS AVAILABLE WITH ELECTRONIC SERVICES

Each electronic service offers its own special tools to help make the research process more efficient.   Common to all electronic libraries are the following capabilities:

- **Searching** (discussed in detail previously).

- **Cut and paste** –  The electronic libraries enable you to incorporate a portion or all of the tax resources into your word processing documents.  Some change the document's format once placed into particular word processing formats; others maintain their original format.

- **Hypertext** –   Current hypertext technology allows you to quickly link to another document simply by clicking on the cite, thus significantly expediting the research process.

Some of the services provide additional helpful tools, including:

- **Keep list**.  Sometimes, it is very useful to create an electronic list of the items you find relevant to your research – like putting a "Post-it"™ on those items you want to return to later.  Both CCH's *Tax Research NetWork* and RIA's *Checkpoint* provide this tool.

**Each service provides very useful tools to assist in making the research process most efficient.**

You can add any document you are currently analyzing to your keep list (CCH) or "my folders" folder (RIA) for easy access and/or printing at a later time. To do this, you simply select the appropriate icon while reviewing the document you wish to keep.  The Appendix contains illustrations of this step.

■   **Where am I**?  It is easy to at times find yourself unsure of where you are in the service and how you got there. Both the RIA and CCH electronic services offer a simple tool to enable you to see where you are and where you have been.

## ILLUSTRATION: RIA *CHECKPOINT*

This service provides at the top of the screen a continuous listing of each research step taken to arrive at the current location.

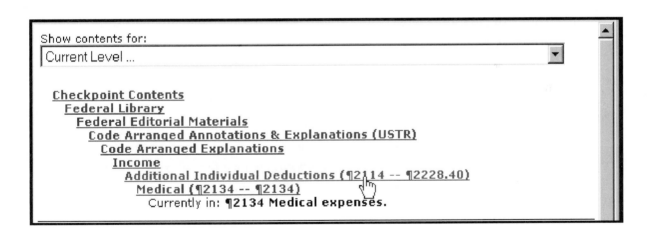

## ILLUSTRATION: CCH's *Tax Research NetWork*

This service also provides a step-by-step indication of the research step taken.

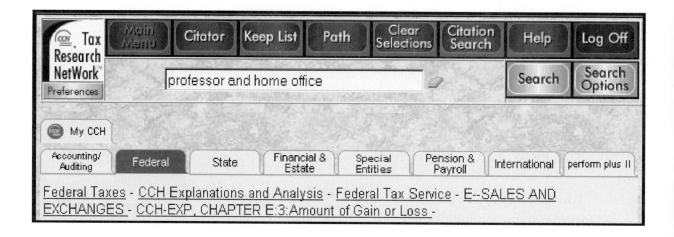

- **Record of all research steps.** Another tool electronic research provides is the ability to create an automatic paper trail of your research steps. This can be placed in your files. It may also be useful for billing purposes or for later reference by other reviewers to avoid unnecessary duplication of prior research efforts.

  In addition to creating a paper trail for your files, a live history of your steps enables you to quickly return to a previous document rather than having to retrace the step. RIA's tool (called *history*) and CCH's tool (called *path*) create a formal path of your research steps. The Appendix provides illustrations of these tools.

# OTHER SECONDARY RESOURCES

In addition to reference services, there are a number of other helpful resources available.  The key ones are:

- Treatises
- Tax summaries
- Journals
- Tax newsletters
- Specialty services

## Treatises

Treatises are texts that discuss a particular topic in detail.  You may be able to address the research question more efficiently by consulting a treatise rather than using a reference service.  Although not designed to refer you to every existing primary authority, a treatise may provide a helpful discussion and description of the key sources of authority on an issue.

**There are many expansive texts on a variety of tax subjects.**

Using a treatise may result in greater efficiency if you later decide to use a reference service.  Or you might go directly to the authority cited in the treatise.  Whatever method you use, remember that treatises age quickly.  Make sure you perform the rest of the research steps to ensure that you do not rely on an outdated authority.

Unfortunately, there is no easy way to acquire a list of all the treatises on a particular topic.  Many tax publishers provide a wide selection of tax books.  Some are written in casebook form and are intended primarily for the student who is learning a topic.  Others are written for the practitioner and are narrative descriptions of the law with cites to authority but no full text of the authority.  Besides going to your local tax library or searching on the Internet, the best way to discover whether there is a useful treatise is to keep a list of titles from each of the main publishers.  Obviously, as you become more of an expert in a particular area, you will become more familiar with the best resources.  Another useful approach is to call a particular trade organization that keeps track of all the current literature in a particular field or to go to one of the useful tax addresses on the Web.  The Appendix lists some of these gateway addresses.  State and local Bar and CPA societies are also resources.

The key publishers of tax treatises include:

***Practitioner Oriented***:

- Warren, Gorham & Lamont
- West Group (combination of Bancroft-Whitney, Clark Boardman Callaghan, Lawyers Cooperative Publishing, Westlaw and West Publishing)
- Matthew Bender
- Harcourt Brace Professional Publishing

***Casebook/Textbook Oriented:***

- Wests/South-Western College Publishing
- Prentice Hall
- Commerce Clearing House
- Irwin/McGraw-Hill

Illustration reprinted with the permission of RIA

☛ **The Web is an excellent place to locate titles of potentially useful treatises.**

## Tax Summaries

Several publishers provide one-volume summaries of the federal tax laws.  RIA's is called the *Federal Tax Handbook*.  CCH's is called the *Master Tax Guide*. Both CCH and RIA publish their one-volume summaries annually.   Having at least one on your desk is good practice. The print versions of the RIA and CCH tax summaries are soft bound and contain significant amounts of useful information, generally including information on basic tax topics.  The entire book attempts to address all of the topics in federal tax – so it is clearly intended to act as a summary rather than an extensive reference source!

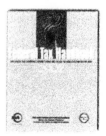

Illustration reprinted with the permission of RIA

Among other things, tax summaries offers a quick reference to the tax tables, depreciation tables, standard deduction amounts, and so on. You may choose to begin your research in this easy-to-read reference guide and use its convenient cross-references to the full reference service. Although convenient in paper, both CCH and RIA also include their tax summaries in their electronic services. In addition, the CCH *Master Tax Guide* is included in the Tax Analysts' *TaxBase*.

 **The *Master Tax Guide* is an easy-to-understand summary of the tax law.**

---

**ILLUSTRATION: CCH's *Master Tax Guide*.** (excerpt)

## GUIDEBOOK, 98USMTG ¶173, Who Is a Head of Household?

### Who Is a Head of Household?

In order to qualify for head of household status, a taxpayer must not be married or a surviving spouse (¶175) at the close of the tax year. In addition, the taxpayer must maintain as his home a household which, for more than one-half of the tax year, is the principal place of abode of one or more of the following:

(1) A son or daughter, grandchild, or stepchild. If one of the above is married at the close of the taxpayer's tax year, the taxpayer must be able to claim the person as a dependent (but not merely by virtue of a multiple support agreement (¶147)). For purposes of this requirement, an adopted child or a foster child that has been a member of the taxpayer's household for the entire year, shall be treated as the taxpayer's child by blood. A taxpayer qualified for "head of a household" status, even though his daughter filed a joint return with her deceased husband, because all parties had lived with the taxpayer during the entire tax year [98FED ¶3240.052].

↑

**Reference to CCH *Standard Federal Tax Reporter***

## Journals

There is a significant amount of wisdom presented in tax journal articles. Although this may not usually be your first step after consulting the Code, you may find that a relevant journal article offers a different perspective regarding a particularly challenging research question. A journal article may be particularly helpful when you are researching a new provision in the law. A journal may be the best place to find nonauthoritative but helpful information.

In print, there are a few indexes available to help you locate articles on your subject. Two of the best are *Federal Tax Articles* (by Commerce Clearing House) and *Index to Federal Tax Articles* (by Gersham Goldstein and published by Warren, Gorham & Lamont).

*Federal Tax Articles* by CCH – This service provides summaries of tax articles published in a wide variety of law journals and business publications. The summaries are organized by Code Section and refer to the source of the article. The service contains two additional indexes to the article summaries. You can locate an article by topic and also by author name. The service consists of several volumes, each covering articles written during a specific period of years. Most often, you will want to focus on current articles and thus will refer to the most current volume.

*Index to Federal Tax Articles* by Warren, Gorham & Lamont – This multivolumed service provides a list of names and cites for a large variety of tax articles published in law school journals and business journals going back as far as 1913. You can find the article listing by looking through either the topical table or by author. The service does not provide content summaries of the articles.

There is a variety of sources for journal articles. They include law reviews, published papers from national conferences, and tax magazines. Most U.S. law schools publish a law review containing scholarly articles on the law. Occasionally, these will include a tax article. In addition, there are a few annual national tax conferences that publish the papers of the presenters. The New York University

Tax Institute is the most well known of these.  In addition, there are many other distinguished university institutes and conferences that publish highly useful materials.

Perhaps most useful are the articles published in the many tax magazines available to us.  The following are some of the publishers and the titles of the magazines:

- Warren, Gorham & Lamont  Some of their titles include:
  - *Business Entities*
  - *Corporate Taxation*
  - *Journal of International Taxation*
  - *Estate Planning*
  - *Real Estate Taxation*
  - *Journal of Taxation*
  - *Taxation of Exempts*
  - *Practical Tax Strategies*
  - *Valuation Strategies*

- AICPA
  - *Journal of Accountancy*
  - *Tax Advisor*

- American Bar Association
  - *The Tax Lawyer*

- Tax Analysts
  - *Tax Notes*

- CCH
  - *Taxes – The Tax Magazine*

**Tax Newsletters**

To help practitioners stay current, a variety of publishers produce newsletters focusing on the current news issues.  The major tax publishers issue daily tax newsletters, including CCH, RIA, and BNA. In addition to the daily newsletters, the publishers provide practitioners with weekly summaries of tax-related topics. Publishers of these weekly newsletters include CCH, RIA, BNA, and Tax Analysts (*Tax Notes*). Monthly newsletters are also available.

Tax newsletters provide information not only on recent court and Treasury interpretations, but also provide interesting information about legislative activity related to taxation. In addition, tax-connected announcements or activities of significant organizations such as the AICPA or ABA may also be discussed. Electronic access provides the ability to review both the tax events of the past 24 hours and those going back several years.

### Specialty Services

In addition to the general reference services discussed earlier in this chapter, the main publishers also produce detailed reference and planning services covering specialized tax areas. Some are available on the publisher's fee-based Internet sites. All are available in print. The specialty services cover such areas as estate planning, financial planning, real estate transactions, partnership taxation, exempt organizations, international tax, and corporate planning.

## CHAPTER SUMMARY

Although secondary authority, reference services usually play a key role in the process of identifying relevant primary authority. There are two major categories of reference services – Code oriented and topic oriented. The Code-oriented services are structured around the IRC. They offer an explanation and list of references referred to as annotations. The topically structured services provide more lengthy explanations and typically refer you to the primary authority through footnotes.

For each research project, it is useful to determine the type of reference service best to begin with. Topical services are often better suited when descriptive guidance about the topic or Code section would be helpful. When simply looking for a quick reference to pertinent cases and revenue rulings, the Code-oriented services may be more efficient.

There are two major reporter services organized around the IRC: the *Standard Federal Tax Reporter* (published by CCH) and the *United States Tax Reporter* (published by RIA). Both are organized in a similar fashion and, for each Code section, the volumes contain the Code text, excerpts of legislative history, related regulations, an explanation, a table of references, and annotations.

To use the Code-oriented services, you can locate the correct volume by either using the index or looking at the print on the outside binding.  In addition, when accessing a service electronically, you can locate the relevant material by using the table of contents or menus.  Next, it is important to identify and examine the pertinent text within the volume.  This usually involves skimming through a table that lists by topic each of the potentially relevant references to primary authority.  After reviewing the pertinent annotations, you select which documents to read in full.

Alternatives to the Code-oriented reference services are those organized by major topic.  One of the most popular topical reporters is the *Federal Tax Coordinator* published by RIA.  This reporter covers each major tax topic through descriptive text.  The *Federal Tax Coordinator* provides references to primary law throughout the narrative text.  Another topically structured secondary source is CCH's *Federal Tax Service*.  This service provides an explanation for each topic.  It is similar to RIA's topical service but available only electron versions.

Yet another very helpful topically oriented source is Tax Analysts' *Federal Tax Baedeker*.  A very comprehensive topical service is published by the Bureau of National Affairs entitled *Tax Management Portfolios*.  This service consists of individual "portfolios" discussing a wide variety of Code Sections and topics.  BNA portfolios are available in hard copy and electronically.

When using one of the reference services electronically, an effective research method is to use the table of contents.  However, each service also provides the option of using electronic key word searching as a research method.  The inherent limitation of electronic word searching is that the searches are literal and, even if you are a very skilled researcher, you run the risk of potentially inadvertently eliminating important sources.

All electronic reference services use one of the two available searching technologies – **Boolean** searches or **folio** searches.  If you understand the basic differences between the two methods, you should be equipped to perform electronic searches on any of the electronic services without much individualized training.

Some services do not enable you to research by walking through all the annotations of a Code Section or through a table of contents.  Instead, they employ electronic key word searching as their sole primary research methodology.  Lexis-Nexis and Westlaw are examples of this type of service.

**Lexis-Nexis** is the most widely used of the search-based services. It has an extensive federal tax library that includes all the primary law as well as both RIA reporters (*Federal Tax Coordinator* and *United States Tax Reporter*) and the BNA Tax Management Portfolios.

When using electronic services, special tools are available to help make the research process more efficient. In addition to providing searching capabilities, electronic research provides the ability to:

- cut and paste from the database to your word processing
- quickly link to another document through hypertext
- create a keep list and a written record of your research steps

When using an electronic secondary source, consider the following elements:

- database/resources
- ease of retrieving a document when you know the cite
- ability to research through using the table of contents
- type of searching capabilities
- ability to check the validity of cites
- the availability of a paper trail

In addition to reference services, there are a number of other helpful resources available to you. The key ones are treatises, tax summaries, journal articles, and specialty services. Treatises are books that discuss a particular topic in detail. They are not designed to refer you to every existing primary authority, but they can provide you with a helpful discussion and description of the key sources of authority. Several publishers provide treatises. Some of the publishers are Warren, Gorham & Lamont, Prentice Hall, Commerce Clearing House, and the Wests Group.

Another helpful secondary source is CCH and RIA's annual summary of tax laws. In one volume, these tools provide you with a helpful summary of the federal tax laws.

You can also find useful analysis in the tax journal articles written by law students and practicing tax experts. You can find journal articles in law reviews, published papers from national conferences, and tax magazines. Other than law schools, the key publishers of tax journal articles are Warren, Gorham & Lamont, the American Institute of Certified Public Accountants, the American Bar Association, and Tax Analysts. Other publishers include state and local tax bar and accountancy organizations, trade groups, and other institutions.

# PROBLEMS

## KEY CONCEPTS (1-22)

1.      Define and give an example of the meaning of the following concepts and terms:

      a.       secondary sources
      b.       reference services
      c.       annotations
      d.       CCH
      e.       RIA
      f.       BNA portfolios
      g.       folio searching
      h.       Boolean searching
      i.       plain English searching
      j.       Lexis-Nexis
      k.       Westlaw
      l.       Tax Analysts
      m.       hypertext
      n.       treatises
      o.       *Master Tax Guide*

2.      What are the two types of information reference services provide?

3.      Why is it unwise to base your research conclusion solely on what you read in a reference service?

4.      What types of primary sources do the reference services refer to?

5.      Should you feel comfortable that the reference service will refer you to every relevant Treasury interpretation?  Why or why not?

6.      What are the factors to consider in selecting the type of reference service that's best for your research project?

7.      What material is covered for each Code section in the Code-oriented services?

8.     List the steps you must take when using a Code-oriented service.

9.     How is CCH's Code-oriented service different from RIA's?

10.    Why is it important to skim through the entire table of annotations before reading the annotations themselves?

11.    What types of topically structured reference services are available to you?

12.    Describe how to find the relevant volume of RIA's *Federal Tax Coordinator*.

13.    How do you find the relevant BNA portfolios?

14.    What information do BNA portfolios offer you?

15.    What are the inherent risks in electronic searching?

16.    What are the two types of electronic search technologies? Describe the major differences between these two types. Provide examples of services using each type.

17.    What is segment searching, and when might it be useful?

18.    Which reference services enable you to use only electronic searching as your main research methodology?

19.    Compare the databases of the Internet services of Lexis-Nexis, RIA (*CHECKPOINT*), CCH, Westlaw, and Tax Analysts.

20.    What are some of the tools available only through electronic research? Which services offer these tools?

21.    In addition to reference services, what other secondary services are available?

22.    Describe how to identify possible tax articles relevant to your research.

## *PRACTICAL APPLICATIONS* (23-42)

23.     You are given a research question concerning making an election to be treated as an *S corporation* for federal tax purposes.  Using the index of the following services, identify the volume and beginning paragraph number containing the relevant information.

a.     *Federal Tax Reporter*, Commerce Clearing House
b.     *United States Tax Reporter*, Research Institute of America
c.     *Federal Tax Coordinator*, Research Institute of America

24.     You are presented with a research question dealing with a partnership issue.  Using only the information provided to you on the outside of each reference service, identify which volume you would use to perform your research.

a.     *Standard Federal Tax Reporter*, Commerce Clearing House
b.     *United States Tax Reporter*, Research Institute of America
c.     *Federal Tax Coordinator*, Research Institute of America

25.     Regarding IRC Section 107, how many annotations are listed in the following services?

a.     *Standard Federal Tax Reporter*, Commerce Clearing House
b.     *United States Tax Reporter*, Research Institute of America

26.     What BNA Tax Management portfolio comprehensively addresses the following subject?  When was it written and by whom?  Identify two items found in the working papers portion of the portfolio.

a.     Community property
b.     IRC Section 179
c.     Irrevocable intervivos trusts
d.     IRC Section 280A

27.     Identify three articles that might be helpful for each of the following topics (provide the name of the article, the author, and the details regarding its location).

a.     Passive loss rules
b.     IRC Section 1031

*Answer the following questions using the primary and secondary sources available to you. If you use an electronic service, make sure to print off your "path" or "history" and include this with your work. You should write an office memorandum for each research question you are assigned. (See Chapter Seven for guidelines on the appropriate format.)*

28.    A taxpayer owns building A, which he uses in his business. He would like to dispose of this building and move to another location to conduct business. He has identified building B as an ideal new location. He already has a buyer for building A. In fact, the taxpayer and the interested buyer, Mr. X, have already signed a sales contract. No conditions of escrow have yet been satisfied. No money has changed hands. Escrow is to close in 60 days.

Someone suggested to the taxpayer that he exchange his property for the one he wants instead of selling his existing property and buying the newly located property. Assuming all parties are willing and ignoring potential value differences, will the nonrecognition provisions of the Code be available to the taxpayer even though he already signed a contract to sell?

29.    A taxpayer is studying for her first CPA exam by taking a preparatory seminar. The seminar costs almost $1,000. The taxpayer currently works in the tax department of an accounting firm that expects her to take and pass the exam. The firm, however, does not reimburse the taxpayer for the costs. Can she take a deduction for the expense?

30.    Corporation X suffered $10,000 in flood damage to its office building. Although the damage is covered by the company's insurance policy, the company decides not to file an insurance claim for the loss because it fears that by making an insurance claim the insurance company may cancel the policy at its next renewal date, thereby precluding coverage for potentially larger future losses. The company would like to take a deduction for the $10,000 on its tax return. Is the company permitted to take the deduction on its federal corporate income tax return for the tax year in which the loss occurred?

31.    A taxpayer studies tax law at a university on a part-time basis. He is diligently working towards a master's degree in taxation. He is employed on a full-time basis in the auditing department of a large accounting firm and anticipates that the classes will help him with his auditing work. He believes the classes will also provide an opportunity for him to work in the tax department of the firm. Unfortunately, his employer, although supportive of his attending classes, is not willing to reimburse the taxpayer for any of the $10,000

tuition costs.

a.     Can the taxpayer take a deduction for his educational expenses?

b.     What if the taxpayer decides to take a leave of absence from his job in order to attend classes full-time?  He anticipates that he will be on a leave for 18 months. He plans on returning to his firm upon completion of his master's degree.

c.     What if, instead of attending tax classes, the taxpayer attends law school on a part-time basis while working at the accounting firm?  He and the firm believe that the law training will be useful to him in his work at the firm.

32.   A taxpayer is an airline attendant for Safe Air.  As part of her job, the company requires her to wear a "uniform" consisting of a specific type of bright yellow shorts and top that she must purchase from a particular department store.  Neither the shorts nor the shirt display any company logo on them.  She is also required to wear a specific brand of high platform shoes.  In order to be sufficiently prepared for travel, the taxpayer purchases three sets of the outfit and two pairs of the shoes.  Although not required, the taxpayer also purchases a bright yellow handbag to match the outfit.  The clothes are suitable for dry cleaning only.  The taxpayer wears these clothes only when working.  She personally believes the outfit is quite unattractive and does not at all conform with her taste in clothing or modern standards of equal respect for gender.  For the current year, the taxpayer spent the following on her work clothes:

| | |
|---|---|
| Purchase of shorts and tops | $350 |
| Shoes | $150 |
| Dry cleaning | $100 |

Are any of these expenses deductible by taxpayer?

33.   A taxpayer plays professional football in New York from July to January.  During that time period,  he lives in his home in New York.  After football season, he lives in a Florida apartment for which he pays monthly rent.  In Florida, the taxpayer works full time as a physical therapist specializing in geriatric care.  He has banking accounts in both locations, is registered to vote in New York, and has a New York driver's license. The taxpayer is single.  He earns $2,000,000 a year from his football job and around $30,000 annually in his physical therapy position.  May the taxpayer deduct any of his living expenses?

34.    Sue paid her attorney $20,000 for his successful work in increasing the alimony payments she is entitled to receive from her ex-husband. Her ex-husband paid almost $15,000 in attorneys fees in an effort to keep the alimony payments at their previous level. What legal expenses, if any, are deductible by Sue? What legal expenses, if any, are deductible by her ex-husband?

35.    Fred is a professional musician. He performs with his electric guitar at various music halls. He has set up a special room in his house that is soundproof and contains a variety of expensive recording and mixing equipment. He uses the room to practice regularly. He does not use the room for anything else. His business records show he paid utilities and maintenance with respect to the room. He believes he should be entitled to deduct his costs, including an appropriate allowance for the depreciation of the room. What is Fred allowed to deduct, and what limitations conceivably apply?

36.    A taxpayer is currently enrolled as a full-time student in a graduate LL.M program in taxation. He graduated from law school in June, studied full-time for the Bar during the summer, and then immediately began the LL.M. classes in September. The taxpayer will pay $15,000 in tuition costs for the program during the current year. The taxpayer's spouse will earn $50,000 in salary income this year. Will the taxpayer be able to deduct any of the LL.M. tuition costs?

37.    New University has come to you seeking advice regarding its obligations to withhold Social Security taxes for the students it employs on a part-time basis. Currently, the university allows any student, full- or part-time, to work for the university no more than nineteen hours a week. In preparation of your meeting with their chief financial officer, prepare an internal office memorandum with your research results.

38.    Mary is a professional tennis player, currently ranked number 10 in the world. She has an endorsement contract with "Boring," the leader in tennis shoe and equipment retail sales whose slogan is "Why do anything if you don't have to?" Under the terms of the contract, Mary is required to wear Boring shoes and tennis attire and also use a Boring racket at all tournament play. As compensation, Boring provides Mary with all the shoes, attire, and rackets she needs, free of charge. What are the tax ramifications of this arrangement to Mary?

39.    Herbert Rain, a popular professional British golfer, has become known for the knickers he wears in each golf tournament. This attire has become his trademark; however, he has no trademark protection under any applicable law. Nor is there any requirement under

golfing rules that he wear anything other than "appropriate attire suitable to the profession." Are the purchase and cleaning costs of the knickers deductible to Mr. Rain?

40. Mr. Future is the president of an established and successful company. The company pays Mr. Future $1,000,000 in salary each year. Mr. Future, a renowned philanthropist, has directed the board of directors to pay him nothing for the year and instead use the $1,000,000 to which he is otherwise entitled to create a scholarship fund. The fund, which he would help oversee, would be used to create scholarships for worthy high school students otherwise unable to afford college. What are the tax ramifications to Mr. Future and to the company?

41. Kay is a member of a gang and has just been convicted by the state of drug possession charges, resisting arrest, and assault and battery. Kay's brother is a longtime client of yours and asks you to prepare Kay's federal income tax return. The district attorney submitted evidence to the court (which you are provided a copy of ) as to the amount of revenue Kay earned the current taxable year in her various criminal activities. Kay believes that she should be able to take a business deduction for her expenses related to engaging in her criminal enterprise, including her illicit drug laboratory costs and attorney defense fees.

42. Jane has a very painful terminal disease and has learned that marijuana may assist in lessening the pain. Jane lives in a state in which it is legal to obtain and use the drug if under the direction of a medical doctor. Jane wonders whether the cost of the marijuana is deductible.

## INTEGRATED CASE STUDIES (43-58)

*The following case studies are the same as those at the end of the previous chapter. Use the knowledge and skills you have learned from this chapter to address the case studies. If previously assigned a case study, use your work in Chapters One through Four.*

43. *Case Study A – Disability Payments*

Mr. Top received $25,000 in disability payments while he was recuperating from heart surgery. Mr. Top, age 65, is an employee with a large corporation providing general business consulting services. The corporation has always paid for the disability insurance of its employees. Mr. Top telecommutes and works out of the home. From further conversations with the client, you discover that only $10,000 of the disability payments received by Mr. Top arise from a disability policy paid for by his employer under a group disability policy. The remaining $15,000 was paid on a separate policy that Mr. Top purchased some time ago. Mr. Top has been paying semiannual premiums on the separate individual policy. You are asked to prepare Mr. Top's return.

a.      What relevant primary authority did you locate?

b.      Does the authority adequately address the research question(s)? If so, what are your conclusions and reasoning upon which they are based?

c.      Were there additional questions that required research beyond a reference service?

d.      What resources did you use in your research?

e.      How much time did you spend on this portion of your research?

44.    *Case Study B – Bonus Payments*

Sue is 30 years old and is president and a 51% shareholder of C Corporation. She informs you that C Corporation has 10 shareholders, all unrelated. Other than herself, no shareholder owns more than 10% of the company's stock. Sue plans to recommend to the board of directors that it authorize the payment of a bonus to her an three other top employees. She asks you, as the company's tax advisor, to counsel her on what the company needs to do so that the company can get a deduction for the planned bonus payments.

After further discussions with Sue, you learn that the company's business is commercial real estate development. The company had net revenues last year totaling $10,000,000. The company is an accrual basis taxpayer, and each of the intended recipients employ the cash-basis method of tax accounting. She would prefer the bonuses to actually be paid next year but deducted by the company this year. One of the intended recipients is Sue's executive assistant, who is not currently a shareholder in the company. Sue would like the bonus to equal 100% of each recipient's current salary. The current salaries of the intended recipients are as follows:

| | |
|---|---|
| President | $500,000 |
| Executive Assistant | $100,000 |

| Chief Financial Officer | $300,000 |
| Vice President of Operations | $250,000 |

The CFO and vice president of operations are shareholders in the company, each owning 10% of the stock.

Sue had indicated to you that she believes the annual salaries are comparable or, perhaps, a little on the high side when compared to her company's competitors. You also learn that the company regularly pays out dividends to shareholders and plans to continue to do so.

a.   What relevant primary authority did you locate?

b.   Does the authority adequately address the research question(s)? If so, what are your conclusions and reasoning upon which they are based?

c.   Were there additional questions that required research beyond a reference service?

d.   What resources did you use in your research?

e.   How much time did you spend on this portion of your research?

45.   *Case Study C – Changing Headquarters*

The taxpayer, a calendar-year corporation, wants to change its company's headquarters – currently consisting of a 10-story building. The company owns the building outright. The taxpayer has identified some potentially more suitable properties. One of the possible properties is a single-story building on a large, attractive lot. The other property consists of a two-building complex, with retail shops on the ground floor of one building and residential rental property in a portion of the other building.

After further discussions with the client and a review of relevant documents, you discover the following additional facts: Each of the new properties has a fair market value that slightly exceeds that of the current 10-story building. The taxpayer would demolish the single-story building if the company purchases that property. It would then build a specially designed building on the lot. The sellers of both properties appear to be interested in entering an exchange transaction whereby the company's property would be exchanged for one of the other properties.

After many discussions with the taxpayer, the company decided to exchange its existing property for the retail and residential building complex.  You assisted the company in structuring the exchange.  Both parties used a "middleman" corporation, to whom the properties were to be initially conveyed.  The agreement with the middleman included the requirement that the taxpayer sell its property to the middleman and then, within 45 days of the initial closing, formally identify which of the two new properties it intended to acquire.  The identified property was also to be sold to the middleman corporation. The corporation would then transfer title to the taxpayer within 180 days after the date of the initial closing.

Unfortunately, the transaction has not proceeded as planned.  The taxpayer transferred its property to the middleman, receiving its FMV of $10,000,000 in cash.  The company formally identified the property with the retail and residential building complex as the property it intended to acquire.  Unfortunately, one week before the 180 days was up, the seller of the property backed out of the arrangement.  The taxpayer is certain it will not be able to identify and cause the transfer of other suitable property within the time limit.

The taxpayer's basis in the 10-story building is only $2,000,000.  The company is concerned  that it will now have to report the $8,000,000 in gain.

a.      What relevant primary authority did you locate?

b.      Does the authority adequately address the research question(s)?  If so, what are your conclusions and reasoning upon which they are based?

c.      Were there additional questions that required research beyond a reference service?

d.      What resources did you use in your research?

e.      How much time did you spend on this portion of your research?

46.    *Case Study D – Damage Payments to Dentist*

Dr. Tooth is a 40-year-old dentist in Small Town, USA.  He graduated from dental school five years ago and has had a thriving practice ever since.  At the end of last year, however, Dr. Tooth had an ugly billing disagreement with a patient. The patient, a well-known wealthy entrepreneur, in retribution, maliciously spread a rumor that Dr. Tooth was a carrier of a serious infectious disease. This rumor destroyed Dr. Tooth's patient base, as most of his patients quickly switched dentists. As a result of the stress of losing his business, the cruel gossip that resulted from the rumor, and the financial strain caused by this situation, Dr. Tooth began to suffer from severe migraine headaches, loss of appetite, and significant facial twitches. Dr. Tooth sued the patient for defamation and intentional infliction of emotional distress. He won a jury verdict and has since recovered $3,600,000 in damages from the patient.

This award was broken into the following categories:

- $1,000,000 lost wages. This was calculated on the basis that, in addition to the one year of wages lost since the date of the defamation, Dr. Tooth has lost the ability to earn future wages in Small Town.
- $50,000 reimbursement for medical expenses incurred in consulting a neurologist, internist, and psychologist.
- $20,000 for future medical expenses anticipated.
- $30,000 reimbursement for attorney's fees paid.
- $2,000,000 in punitive damages. The jury determined that the action of the patient was so malicious and heinous that the patient should be monetarily punished for his actions.
- $300,000 for pain and suffering.
- $200,000 to compensate Dr. Tooth for the emotional distress he suffered.

Through your interview with the client, you discover that he had to pay his attorney $50,000, which was paid out of the award.

a.      What relevant primary authority did you locate?

b.      Does the authority adequately address the research question(s)? If so, what are your conclusions and reasoning upon which they are based?

c.      Were there additional questions that required research beyond a reference service?

d.      What resources did you use in your research?

e.      How much time did you spend on this portion of your research?

47.     *Case Study E – Housing Expenses*

Ellie Executive lives in Florida with her family in a home bequeathed to her by her parents when they passed away. This year her employer assigned her to a position in London. The assignment is for a minimum of four years. Because she grew up in the house, Ellie would like to keep it and rent it out. There is no mortgage on the home, so renting will create a positive cash flow situation for her. Her employer will be providing her with a housing allowance to cover her London housing costs. Ellie believes the house has a FMV of at least $500,000. Ellie wants to make sure that if she ends up selling it, she will not have any taxable income from the sale. She has asked for your guidance.

After talking with Ellie Executive further, you become aware of the following additional facts:

Ellie is not certain what she and her husband will do at the end of the four-year London assignment. She may return to Florida but she also might take another international assignment, since her children are now adults. Ellie plans to continue paying the following expenses while the house is rented:

* $400 a month for a weekly gardener
* $500 a month for a weekly housecleaner
* Approximately $200 a month in utility and maintenance expenses (electricity, garbage, and water)

Ellie anticipates that she can lease the house fully furnished for $2,500 a month.

Ellie's parents died in 1991 when the FMV of the house was $300,000. They purchased the house in 1950 for $10,000. Her parents spent a total of $20,000 in home improvement costs. Ellie substantially redecorated the house in 1992, spending $65,000 in renovating two bedrooms, two bathrooms, and replacing the roof. In addition, Ellie paid $5,000 for a new perimeter fence and $10,000 to a landscape architect to redesign the yard.

a.      What relevant primary authority did you locate?

b.      Does the authority adequately address the research question(s)? If so, what are your conclusions and reasoning upon which they are based?

c.      Were there additional questions that required research beyond a reference service?

d.      What resources did you use in your research?

e.      How much time did you spend on this portion of your research?

48.     *Case Study F – Retirement Contributions*

Tom Speeder is a new client.  From reviewing his client questionnaire, you were able to gather the following facts. He is 50 years old and was recently hired as a middle-level manager with a car manufacturer.  Tom's salary for the current year is $200,000.  In his initial meeting with you, Tom indicates that he would like you to look into an idea he has that will help him maximize his investment portfolio. He tells you that his new company offers its employees the ability to participate in a Section 401(k) plan. He believes it would be to his benefit to maximize his contribution to the company's 401(k) plan that provides for matching employer contributions up to $3,000 annually.  The plan provides for a maximum annual employee contribution of no greater than that provided by the IRC.

It is January, and Tom has indicated to you that he would like to accelerate the maximum contributions to the plan by contributing his entire monthly paycheck until he funds the entire amount.  He believes that such an arrangement will maximize the growth of his portfolio since the earnings are tax free from an earlier time frame than if he spreads the contributions out over the year.

After further discussions with Tom, you discover that, in addition to his salary, he receives the following employment benefits:

* $100,000 group term insurance for which the employer pays the premiums (totaling $200/year)
* Health insurance, for which the employer pays the $100 in monthly premiums
* As part of the company's Employee Educational Assistance Plan, tuition payments to a local university for one academic course a year to be chosen by the employee.  For the current year, Tom plans to take a course on "Organizational Behavior" that he is interested in and believes will help him better understand his work environment.  The university offers both undergraduate and graduate courses in this subject.  Tom may take either and will wait to determine which is offered at the most convenient time.

a.     What relevant primary authority did you locate?

b.     Does the authority adequately address the research question(s)?  If so, what are your conclusions and reasoning upon which they are based?

c.     Were there additional questions that required research beyond a reference service?

d.     What resources did you use in your research?

e.     How much time did you spend on this portion of your research?

49.    *Case Study G – Golf Ball Business*

Toby Power, a fellow Illinois resident, is a new client. Prior to her telephone call this morning (late November), all you really knew about Toby was that for the past five years she has been earning a living as a respected golfing instructor at a local club.  She just called you to discuss a transaction she has entered into. You learn from your initial conversation with her that she and a group of friends formed a corporation for which the group will own 100% of the stock.

The corporation will be in the business of selling golf balls that it guarantees are indestructible and, because they glow in water and shade, cannot be lost.  Toby transferred an office building to the corporation in return for her 20% stock ownership interest.  Her eight other friends transferred primarily manufacturing equipment and cash for their evenly divided 80% interest. Toby has owned the office building for seven years and currently owes several hundred thousand dollars on two mortgages on the building. She estimates the fair market value of the building is about $1,000,000.

Toby informs you that her previous tax advisor, about whom she has nothing but negative things to say, counseled her that, in order to avoid paying taxes on the transfer of the building to the corporation, she had to also transfer to the corporation a personal promissory note of $100,000.  All of this occurred last year. She wants to know if the transaction was handled correctly, or if she needs to worry.

Through further discussions and review of pertinent documents, you discover the following additional facts:

- Toby purchased the office building seven years ago for $500,000. She paid $100,000 in cash and $400,000 using a note (Note A) secured by the property.
- Two years ago, the fair market value of the property escalated to $1,200,000. Toby took out a second mortgage on the property in the amount of $300,000 (Note B). She used the borrowed funds to purchase a vacation home in Nevada.
- At the time of the property's transfer to the corporation, the building's fair market value was $1,000,000, determined by an assessor.
- At the time of the property's transfer to the corporation, Note A had an outstanding balance of $310,000. Note B had a balance of $100,000.
- Toby has made no improvements on the property. She has taken approximately $100,000 in depreciation deductions on her tax return.
- The terms of the promissory note Toby gave to the corporation were that she pay the note off over a period of 20 years, paying a single annual payment in the amount of $6,000 ($5,000 principal; $1,000 interest). The first payment is to be made on the anniversary date of the note – September 1. Toby paid the first installment, which was due a few months ago.

What relevant primary authority did you locate?

a.    Does the authority adequately address the research question(s)? If so, what are your conclusions and reasoning upon which they are based?

b.    Were there additional questions that required research beyond a reference service?

c.    What resources did you use in your research?

d.    How much time did you spend on this portion of your research?

50.    *Case Study H – Private School Expenses*

Mr. and Mrs. Worried, longtime clients, have come to you for help. Their 13-year-old son has recently been expelled from the public junior high school because of severe behavioral problems, culminating in a physical attack on a teacher and threats of future violence. The son has been seeing a psychologist once a week but with no apparent positive results. The Worrieds would like to send their son to a private school that can provide the type of psychological help they believe he needs. The son's psychologist agrees that placement in a special school is imperative if there is ever to be a chance that the son will be a functioning member of society.

The Worrieds tell you that they are concerned, because, although they have identified several potential schools, they do not have the financial resources necessary to pay the tuition and other additional costs. Their insurance does not cover any of the costs. However, the Worrieds believe that they may be able to afford the expenses if they can take them as a tax deduction. They ask you for your opinion.

a.    What relevant primary authority did you locate?

b.    Does the authority adequately address the research question(s)? If so, what are your conclusions and reasoning upon which they are based?

c.    Were there additional questions that required research beyond a reference service?

d.    What resources did you use in your research?

e.    How much time did you spend on this portion of your research?

51.    *Case Study I – Deadly Fire*

Early this year, a taxpayer was clearing dry brush from behind his Malibu home in California. He became frustrated with how long it was taking using his clippers. He decided instead to light the brush on fire, believing this would be safe, because it was an overcast day. The taxpayer brought out a fire extinguisher in case the fire got out of control. Unfortunately, some wind kicked up and fanned the fire out of control. The fire completely consumed both his house and his neighbor's house. The two children staying in the neighbor's house died of smoke inhalation. The taxpayer was charged with negligent homicide. The trial is pending.

The taxpayer wishes to take a casualty loss deduction for the loss of his house, which was worth an estimated $1,000,000 at the time of the fire. The taxpayer purchased the home for $900,000 only six months earlier. Insurance has refused to compensate for the loss under the circumstances. The taxpayer is currently out on bail. He is the brother of one of your very significant clients who has asked you to provide tax advice to the taxpayer.

a.      What relevant primary authority did you locate?

b.      Does the authority adequately address the research question(s)?  If so, what are your conclusions and reasoning upon which they are based?

c.      Were there additional questions that required research beyond a reference service?

d.      What resources did you use in your research?

e.      How much time did you spend on this portion of your research?

52.     *Case Study J – Airline Costs*

A major airline manufacturer was found to be in violation of FAA safety rules and was forced to install additional safety devices in each of its planes within six months.  The airline company projects the cost of this upgrade to be several million dollars, consisting of lost profits while the planes are on the ground, labor costs, and the cost of parts.  In addition, the airline spent $100,000 on attorney's fees in an unsuccessful fight to have the requirement waived. The CFO of the company wishes to know whether any or all of these costs can be deducted.

a.      What relevant primary authority did you locate?

b.      Does the authority adequately address the research question(s)?  If so, what are your conclusions and reasoning upon which they are based?

c.      Were there additional questions that required research beyond a reference service?

d.      What resources did you use in your research?

e.      How much time did you spend on this portion of your research?

53.     *Case Study K – Vacation Homes*

Mr. and Mrs. Z own three homes.  They live in the San Francisco home full time.  Mr. Z and his wife use the other two homes for vacation during the year.  They are considering replacing the house in Palm Springs, California, with another house in the same area. The new home is a little bigger and has a better floor plan. The two Palm Springs properties have almost the same fair market value. Mr. and Mrs. Z would like to know if they can exchange the properties instead of selling the Palm Springs home and buying the new one. They have a lot of built-up appreciation in the current Palm Springs home and don't want to have to pay taxes on it. Someone told Mrs. Z at a cocktail party that she can avoid paying taxes if she and Mr. Z engage in an "exchange."

Mr. Z and his wife own the home outright. There is no mortgage on the property. They use the property occasionally. During last year they vacationed at the home for about two or three weeks – they aren't sure of the exact number of days or precisely how many different times they were there on vacation. They have never rented any of their properties and have no intention of renting the new Palm Springs property. They don't need the money and don't like strangers in their house. Mr. and Mrs. Z explain that they hold each of their vacation homes for two purposes. One reason is for their vacation enjoyment. Another key reason for owning the homes is for their investment value. They choose homes in areas where they believe there are high appreciation possibilities.

Can Mr. and Mrs. Z take advantage of the tax-free exchange rules in the IRC? What would you advise them to do?

a.     What relevant primary authority did you locate?

b.     Does the authority adequately address the research question(s)? If so, what are your conclusions and reasoning upon which they are based?

c.     Were there additional questions that required research beyond a reference service?

d.     What resources did you use in your research?

e.     How much time did you spend on this portion of your research?


54.    *Case Study L – Property Easement*

A developer acquired a parcel of unimproved real property that she would like to develop. Although the land is currently zoned for commercial use, the developer would prefer not to begin development until an adjoining city street is widened. With a wider street, her development can include a landscaped public entrance and lighting. Without the widening, the development will have only one entrance that is not as accessible nor as attractive.

The city plans to widen the street in order to build bicycle paths which are now required in its new city plan. It will be easier for the city to widen the street if it acquires an easement across the developer's property. The developer is interested in providing this easement to the city. However, before she acts, the developer would like assurance that she will receive a charitable deduction for the value of the easement. She has asked you to request a letter ruling on this matter.

a.     What relevant primary authority did you locate?

b.     Does the authority adequately address the research question(s)? If so, what are your conclusions and reasoning upon which they are based?

c.     Were there additional questions that required research beyond a reference service?

d.     What resources did you use in your research?

e.     How much time did you spend on this portion of your research?

55.    *Case Study M – Interest Payment*

A taxpayer is president of a company. He is very wealthy and has a good deal of assets. He went to Bank 1 in January of Yr. 1 to borrow $1,000,000. The loan proceeds were used to purchase stock. Pursuant to a certain stock pledge agreement, the loan was secured by the stock purchased. The terms of the loan are that it is an interest-only loan, with interest to be paid annually on the anniversary of the loan. The rate is 10% per annum (simple) interest on the original loan face amount.

In November of Yr. 1, taxpayer realized that he did not have the liquid funds to pay the $100,000 of interest due in January. He had sufficient assets, but, due to the business environment, he determined that the smartest economic move to make would be to borrow the $100,000 rather than to liquidate one of his investments. So he went to Bank 2 and borrowed $100,000. This loan was secured by assets other than his stock and was a regular amortizing loan. Interest was 9% per annum, compounding semiannually on the outstanding principal loan balance.  Upon receipt of the loan proceeds on December 1, Yr. 1, taxpayer deposited the proceeds into his regular checking account in Bank 3.  The proceeds remained in the checking account for the entire month of December.  The balance of the checking account during the month of December ranged from $100,000 to $115,000.

On January 2, Yr. 2, taxpayer wrote a check authorizing payment of funds from his Bank 3 checking account to Bank 1 in full payment of the interest due.  On his tax return for Yr. 2, taxpayer took a deduction of $100,000 as an investment interest expense under Code Section 163.  He had sufficient investment income to cover the deduction.

In the course of conducting your research, you discover that Bank 1 owns 90% of the stock of Bank 2.  You discuss this fact with the client and learn that he is entirely unaware of the affiliated relationship.  In fact, the loan documents were entirely different and made no reference to any legal relationship between the two banks.  The IRS has indicated it plans to disallow the interest deduction because it believes it has never actually been paid as is required by the Code.  The taxpayer would like you to consider this development raised by the IRS and analyze and report to him whether the IRS has justifiable grounds for its position.

a.    What relevant primary authority did you locate?

b.    Does the authority adequately address the research question(s)?  If so, what are your conclusions and reasoning upon which they are based?

c.    Were there additional questions that required research beyond a reference service?

d.    What resources did you use in your research?

e.    How much time did you spend on this portion of your research?

56.    *Case Study N – Racing Car Expenses*

A taxpayer is a partner in an accounting firm.  He has always enjoyed auto racing as a hobby.  Now that his children are grown, he has decided to devote more time to auto racing.  He just purchased a racing car for $50,000 and has entered several races.  He recently raced in his first competitive race and placed fourth, resulting in winnings of $5,000. He expects to incur a number of expenses related to his racing: auto maintenance, storage, transportation, and so on. He would like your advice as to how to proceed so that he can depreciate his car and deduct all of these expenses.

a.      What relevant primary authority did you locate?

b.      Does the authority adequately address the research question(s)? If so, what are your conclusions and reasoning upon which they are based?

c.      Were there additional questions that required research beyond a reference service?

d.      What resources did you use in your research?

e.      How much time did you spend on this portion of your research?


57.    *Case Study O – Retainer Fee*

Big Company paid $100,000 at the beginning of the year to a large law firm to retain its services should they be needed during the course of the year. The law firm specializes in real estate law and is considered the best firm in this field. Big Company feared that one of its competitors would engage the law firm. This would prevent Big Company from being able to use the firm's services because of conflict-of-interest rules that preclude a firm from representing different clients with actual or potentially adverse legal interests. To prevent this, Big Company engaged the firm and paid the retainer fee. Occasionally, Big Company requests the firm to perform legal work in areas where Big's in-house lawyers are not as knowledgeable. It is now December, and it is clear that a substantial amount of the initial retainer will not be used to pay for legal services rendered. The retainer agreement provides in this case that any unused amount shall be returned to Big, with interest at 3% per annum, at year-end.

Big Company is a long-term client of yours. It has asked you to look into whether any of the retainer fee will be deductible to it. It wishes to receive your advice before the beginning of next year, when it will make a determination whether to pay another $100,000 retainer to the law firm for that year.

a.      What relevant primary authority did you locate?

b.      Does the authority adequately address the research question(s)? If so, what are your conclusions and reasoning upon which they are based?

c.      Were there additional questions that required research beyond a reference service?

d.      What resources did you use in your research?

e.      How much time did you spend on this portion of your research?

58.     *Case Study P – Development Costs*

Gobble Corporation purchased 400 acres in Green City to build a private golf course and 200 executive homes. The land cost $10,000,000. Gobble planned high quality, large (over 5,000 square feet) houses that would sell for an average of $700,000.

Gobble believed that the city's general plan expressly permitted this development. Gobble spent in excess of $1,000,000 in "soft costs" to pay architects and, civil engineers, for all necessary environmental impact studies and approvals. Two years ago, Gobble's development proposal was approved by the city council in a 5 - 4 vote.

Two months after the vote, the membership in the council changed dramatically. The major local election issue was growth versus no growth. The population of the city voted strongly for a no-growth slate of council members. Given the strong community sentiment, the new city council voted to disregard the earlier vote and alter the city's general plan to prohibit such a large development. The council decided to do what was necessary to defeat the development proposal.

As a result, Gobble sued the city. Gobble charged that the city unfairly reneged on its original project approval and abused its discretion by unreasonably interpreting its general plan. Gobble charged that this action caused great harm to Gobble. For the past one and one-half years, the litigation has been ongoing and has cost Gobble a total of $500,000.

Gobble's CFO has come to you to help prepare the company's federal corporation income tax return for the past year and to amend the return for the year before last. Gobble would like to deduct all the costs incurred in this transaction, including the $1,000,000 paid for the land acquisition. The $1,000,000 initial costs were capitalized on the first year's return, which is now the subject of amendment.

a.    What relevant primary authority did you locate?

b.    Does the authority adequately address the research question(s)?  If so, what are your conclusions and reasoning upon which they are based?

c.    Were there additional questions that required research beyond a reference service?

d.    What resources did you use in your research?

e.    How much time did you spend on this portion of your research?

# THE TAX RESEARCH PROCESS

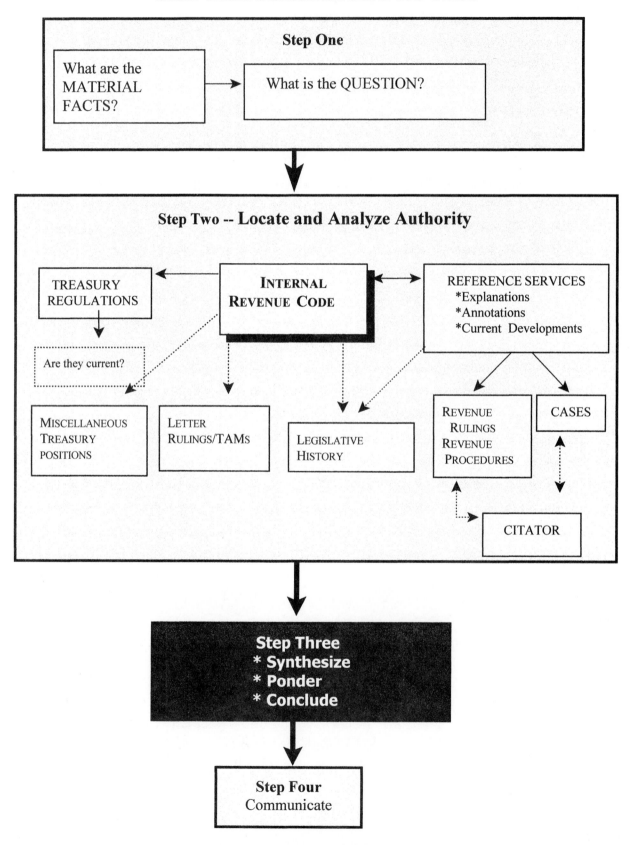

**Step One**

What are the MATERIAL FACTS?

What is the QUESTION?

**Step Two -- Locate and Analyze Authority**

TREASURY REGULATIONS

INTERNAL REVENUE CODE

REFERENCE SERVICES
*Explanations
*Annotations
*Current Developments

Are they current?

MISCELLANEOUS TREASURY POSITIONS

LETTER RULINGS/TAMS

LEGISLATIVE HISTORY

REVENUE RULINGS REVENUE PROCEDURES

CASES

CITATOR

**Step Three**
**\* Synthesize**
**\* Ponder**
**\* Conclude**

**Step Four**
Communicate

# CHAPTER SIX

# CULMINATION OF THE TAX RESEARCH PROCESS

## *EXPECTED LEARNING OUTCOMES*

- Fully understand all steps in the research process
- Know when additional steps must be taken
- Recognize when the research is completed
- Appreciate the formalized ethical standards applicable to the tax researcher

## *CHAPTER OUTLINE*

- Overview
- Review of Research Steps
- Critical Analysis of Authority
- Ethical Guidelines
- Chapter Summary
- Problems

## OVERVIEW

One of the hardest steps in tax research is determining when it is appropriate to conclude your research. It is easy to decide that you are finished in those cases where you find authority that clearly and unequivocally answers the research question – where your comfort level is 100%. But those times are rare. More often than not, you find yourself wondering whether there is something more out there that will provide you with a better, more cogent answer. Yet, as discussed in Chapter One, it is important to be both accurate and efficient. Efficiency requires you to know when to stop researching.

Developing good professional judgment and thoroughly understanding the research process are your primary tools in helping you ascertain when it is appropriate to stop. This knowledge will serve you well when applied in the context of the ethical obligations imposed by various regulatory and professional groups that you or your firm may otherwise be subject to.

# REVIEW OF RESEARCH STEPS

Now that you have studied and practiced each of the research steps separately, it will be helpful to spend a moment reviewing the process as a whole.

## Step One – Gathering Relevant Facts and Determining the Relevant Tax Question

This first phase of the research process is critical to performing efficient research. In this phase, you begin by identifying the relevant facts. You must listen carefully to the taxpayer (or other authorized person instructing you in the project) and clearly ascertain the taxpayer's expectations, concerns, and questions. Methods for gathering all the material facts include requesting the client to complete a written questionnaire, asking questions, and reviewing pertinent documents. Should your firm provide for additional procedures and protocols, you must also consider these.

It is also in this beginning stage of the research process that you begin to formulate the research question. You must determine what issues require clarification. You will often refine and add to the initial research question throughout the research process as you discover additional information and review relevant authority.

## Step Two – Researching: Identifying and Reading Pertinent Resources

Once you identify the initial research question, the next stage in the process involves identifying and locating potentially relevant primary authority. In addition to the Internal Revenue Code, such sources include:

- ▸ Treasury interpretations, including:

  - Treasury regulations
  - Revenue rulings
  - Revenue procedures
  - Letter rulings and technical advice memoranda
  - Actions on decisions
  - Acquiescences and nonacquiescences

☞ **Listen to the taxpayer.**

☞ **Determine relevant facts.**

☞ **Formulate the research question.**

☞ **Identify all relevant authority.**

▸ Judicial interpretations, including the following decisions:

- Tax Court regular decisions
- Tax Court memorandum decisions
- U.S. District Court decisions
- U.S. Claims Court decisions
- U.S. Appellate Court decisions
- U.S. Supreme Court decisions
- Selected court decisions with jurisdiction over federal tax matters, such as the U.S. Bankruptcy Court

As discussed in Chapter Four, secondary sources such as reference services play a significant role in guiding you to the specific documents in the preceding list that may be relevant to the research question.

### Step Three – Analyzing the Authority Gathered and Concluding

This is perhaps the most important and challenging phase of the research process. Each of the previous steps, in addition to requiring critical thinking, involves fairly mechanical, relatively straightforward procedures. This phase of the process requires circumspection and critical analysis.

## CRITICAL ANALYSIS OF AUTHORITY

☛ **The ability to critically analyze the identified authority distinguishes the good tax researcher.**

Up to this point, you have gathered and examined a variety of authority, some of it relevant and some not. Each research project generates a different combination of pertinent authority. In each case, it is your responsibility to analyze the authoritative value of each respective case, revenue ruling, and so on., and weigh that value against all the authority you located. In your analysis, some of the initial questions you may consider include:

### *As to Treasury Interpretations*:

- What, if any, is the Internal Revenue Service's position on the issue?

- Is there any guidance offered by Treasury regulations, revenue rulings, or revenue procedures?

- If there is a revenue ruling on point, how close are the facts of the matter you have been asked to consider to those in the revenue ruling?

- Did you confirm that the Treasury regulation reflects current statutory law?

- Did you citate every relevant revenue ruling and revenue procedure to confirm that the sources of authority you seek to rely on are indeed reflective of current law?

### *As to Applicable Case Law*:

- What court cases address the research question?

- What cases are most similar to your facts?

- If there are any differences between your facts and those of the case, would the court rule differently regarding your facts?

- What particular court decided the case?  In what geographical jurisdiction?

- Is the decided case still subject to appeal, or is there another case in the same or another jurisdiction with the same or similar facts and issues that may be about to be decided by a higher court?

- If there is more than one case on point, which one are the most authoritative?

- Have you citated the cases you believe are important?

You have studied in the previous chapters the relative authority of various Treasury interpretations, and so should be equipped to synthesize and ponder their application to a research question.  The same approach applies to your review of the relative authority of judicial decisions.  The process becomes more

---

*Practitioner Observation*

Joseph Stemach, retired appeals officer, Internal Revenue Service

*" The practitioner must use caution when relying upon case law to support a position. Decisions that appear relevant at first blush most often can be distinguished on their facts.  For example, tax issues involving valuation are fact-specific."*

challenging, however,
when you find that the relevant authority includes both Treasury interpretations and case law.

After gathering authority and studying each document, the research results may fit into one of the following alternative categories:

1.  The Internal Revenue Code clearly and unequivocally addresses the research question.

2.  The Code does not clearly answer the question, and there is no Treasury interpretation or judicial decision addressing the question. Legislative history clearly speaks to the research issue.

3.  An authoritative Treasury interpretation clearly addresses the research question. There is no relevant case law. Or, similarly, the pertinent case law is in full agreement with the Treasury interpretation.

4.  There is no authoritative (or instructive) relevant Treasury interpretation. Judicial decisions, with authority over your client, clearly address the research question. Or, similarly, although there are no court cases with jurisdictional authority over the client, judicial decisions consistently and clearly address the research question.

5.  There is no authoritative (or instructive) relevant Treasury interpretation. Although there is no relevant case with jurisdictional authority over your client, there is case law that addresses the research question. However, the current court decisions of various jurisdictions conflict with one another.

6.  An authoritative Treasury interpretation clearly addresses the research question. Likewise, there are judicial decisions with authority over the client that clearly address the research question. The difficulty is that the Treasury interpretation and court case conflict with each other.

☛ **Research results vary from discovering an unequivocal answer to finding no authority at all. This generates a different level of comfort on the part of the researcher.**

7.    An authoritative Treasury interpretation clearly addresses the research question. There are no relevant cases with jurisdictional authority over the client. However, there is other relevant case law that consistently and clearly addresses the research question. The case law conflicts with the Treasury interpretation.

8.    There is no relevant primary authority of any type.

In addition to the eight preceding scenarios presented, there are obviously other possibilities. At this point, you should be prepared to know how to proceed in the first five situations. However, the last three scenarios are more complicated.

**In scenario 6**, when there is a decision from a court with jurisdiction over your client, this decision will usually have greater authoritative value to you than a conflicting Treasury interpretation. Your analysis must be very thorough, however. Ask yourself – are your client's facts and those involved in the court case materially the same? Certainly, any material difference may have a tremendous impact upon the authoritative value of the court decision. After carefully considering the court's decision, are you sure that you are accurately applying the court's reasoning and conclusion to the client's facts? Have you positively confirmed that the court case is currently reliable authority?

←**Critical analysis when a controlling court case and the Treasury disagree.**

**Scenario 7** presents even greater complexity. If the preferred client position is in line with the Treasury's interpretation, the issue is moot. However, there is some risk when the client prefers to take a position contrary to the Treasury's view and the position is merely supported by court decisions with no jurisdiction over the client's federal tax affairs. The case does not offer "protection" to the client.

←**Critical analysis when a court case with no jurisdiction and the Treasury disagree.**

Consider the impact of taking a position contrary to the IRS. The taxpayer may be subject to an audit and will most likely be unsuccessful in the audit. Armed with the knowledge that there are court cases outside the jurisdiction of the taxpayer that support the taxpayer's position, the client may choose to litigate.

On the other hand, even though the taxpayer may believe his position is entirely correct and would be upheld in court should the issue be litigated, the taxpayer may not wish to undergo the expense, stress, and uncertainty of litigation. It is important to recognize there are practical implications in taking a position with which the IRS does not agree. Therefore, as the taxpayer's advisor, it is important that you explore the defensible options available to the taxpayer, always considering the risks involved with each option.

Remember, you may believe you are right in your reasoning, but litigation is often a proverbial roll of the dice. Ultimately, your client must decide whether this course is reasonable and desirable.

**←Critical analysis when there is no authority on point.**

Perhaps the most uncomfortable situation of all occurs in **scenario 8** when, after you have performed exhaustive research, you conclude that there is no primary authority that addresses the research question. The client expects more from you than a simple "I don't know!" This is particularly true after your client receives a bill for your services. Unfortunately, sometimes what initially appears to be a relatively simple research matter may result in a qualified answer or an ambiguous resolution. Although your options are very limited, you must still use good professional judgment and do your best to address the research question.

First, review the research steps you took to confirm that you have consulted all possible resources. Have you reviewed the legislative history? Did you research the Letter Rulings and Technical Advice Memoranda? You may wish to examine additional secondary resources such as another reference service, treatises, or journal articles.

**☛ Seek the help of another knowledgeable person.**

It may be advisable to pick up the phone and talk to a responsible person in the IRS – perhaps the person who drafted related Treasury Regulations (information provided to you in the Treasury Decision). Or, discuss the matter with a knowledgeable person in your firm. You may also consider contacting a local trade group for information. It is often the case that cutting-edge issues are confronted by many members of the same industry, or by other taxpayers engaged in the same or similar transactions.

Remember that, in all instances, you should keep your client's name and information in the strictest confidence absent receiving express consent from your client to divulge such matters. There is nothing wrong with discussing such matters with the IRS or others on a "no-name" basis. You may pose your questions without identifying the client and base your discussion on hypothetical facts. This is a common approach employed by practitioners. If the IRS official or another person asks you to disclose the name of your client, there is nothing wrong in politely saying: "I'm sorry, I am not at liberty to divulge my client's name or any other information at this time."

Remember that any advice received in this manner, even if given by an IRS official, is not authoritative. In any event, once you have assured yourself that you have sought and received all available and appropriate guidance, you are left only with your judgment and reasoning abilities. The taxpayer still has options.

> ☞ **The ultimate decision rests with the taxpayer.**

The law may be unclear, but you can still review the matter with the client to consider appropriate risks and possible benefits. For example, if the law is unclear and the issue involves a small amount of money, perhaps the client is risk averse and is simply willing to pay the tax. Alternatively, the client may decide to restructure the transaction or simply kill a pending deal. Or perhaps the client is concerned about an audit revealing another questionable transaction involving a potentially substantial tax liability. Different and often competing considerations will usually come into play. Never forget that the ultimate decision rests with the taxpayer. You can endeavor only to give competent, professional advice based on existing laws.

> *"When you know a thing, to hold that you know it; and when you do not know a thing, to allow that you do not know it – this is knowledge."* Confucius, *The Confucian Analects.*

Once you have performed all the research steps, spending more time will not increase your understanding or magically answer an unanswered question. If you can honestly say to yourself that you performed each research step carefully, your research is done. Stop. Confirm that you have maintained a thorough file documenting your research steps and analysis. Then you are ready for the final step – communicating the research results (covered in the next chapter).

## ETHICAL GUIDELINES

All of the critical analysis required in the research process must be performed under the umbrella of ethical guidelines. In real terms, it is clear that many tax questions have a variety of "right" answers. This presents a potential ethical dilemma – what options should you advise the taxpayer about? Are there some that you feel are too aggressive and outside the law?

A variety of interested groups publish both guidelines and

rules intended to govern the tax practitioner's behavior.   Congress, the Treasury Department, the courts, state bars, state departments of Accountancy,  and voluntary membership organizations such as the American Institute of Certified Public Accountants (AICPA) and the American Bar Association (ABA) all provide some guidelines to the researcher and practitioner about how accurate your advice must be and, depending on the particular matter involved or form of communication (i.e., opinion letter, tax return, etc.), what standards apply to issuing such advice. These guidelines include:

☐ Circular 230 (published by the Treasury Department)

☐ AICPA Code of Professional Conduct

☐ AICPA Statements on Standards for Tax Services

☐ Internal Revenue Code Section 6662 and related Treasury regulations

☐ State bar and state accountancy rules of professional responsibility

☛ **There are a number of ethical guidelines that regulate the tax practitioner's actions.**

The Treasury Department provides guidelines that apply to the greatest number of tax researchers.  In Circular 230, the Treasury Department provides rules for all those who "practice before the Internal Revenue Service."  This includes all attorneys, certified public accountants, enrolled agents, and enrolled actuaries.  The circular defines "practicing before the Service" very broadly to include most aspects of  tax practice.  Willful violation of the provisions of Circular 230 may result in the suspension of the practitioner's rights to practice before the IRS.   The relevant specific provisions of Circular 230 are discussed later.

☛ **Circular 230 applies to all those who "practice before the IRS."**

Another source of guidelines comes from two voluntary professional organizations: the AICPA and the ABA.  The AICPA provides the tax practitioner with two sources of guidelines: its Code of Professional Conduct and its Statements on Standards for Tax Services. Both of these standards are now binding on the members of the AICPA; violation results in potential disciplinary proceedings. The Code and standards may be considered by courts in malpractice cases against CPAs.  The ABA offers similar rules in its *ABA Model Rules for Professional Conduct*.  Member violation results in disciplinary proceedings.

☛ **The AICPA and ABA are important sources of professional conduct guidelines.**

Although AICPA and ABA membership is voluntary and their sanctions do not affect nonmembers, the positions promulgated by the two bodies are compelling and play a significant role in the development of rules that impact most tax practitioners. For example, the tax research standards set forth below, although now embodied in Treasury Department Circular 230, originated from the AICPA's and ABA's guidelines on research standards. Therefore, it is important to be aware of the positions of both bodies, even if not a member of either.

Court cases provide another source of information regarding acceptable standards of performance of the tax researcher. The standards suggested by the courts are not contained in one or two simple pronouncements. Instead, they set forth the parameters by which various professionals will be adjudged negligent or liable for malpractice in the course of performing professional services.

**☛ Court cases also provide guidelines.**

Tax malpractice cases are plentiful. They arise in a myriad of circumstances, from drafting defective pension plans to rendering faulty tax opinions giving rise to securities' fraud lawsuits. The impact of being found negligent by a court can be profound. Large monetary awards and even imprisonment are possible consequences of a tax practitioner's negligent or fraudulent behavior. Licensure revocation or suspension proceedings may also be a likely direct result of such court proceedings. At a minimum, a practitioner's reputation may be greatly harmed, resulting in a lower standing in the community, lost referral business, and future impairment of the practice.

## Tax Research Standards

Frequently the results of tax research affect a reporting position on a tax return. The groups discussed earlier provide guidelines and rules that govern each of the following functions:

- ❑     fact gathering
- ❑     researching
- ❑     communicating and advising
- ❑     tax return reporting

### Fact Gathering

Treasury Department Circular 230 provides guidance for the role of fact gatherer. It requires you to make "reasonable inquiries" if taxpayer information appears to be incorrect, inconsistent, or incomplete [§10.34(a)(3)]. Consequently, Circular 230 prohibits tax advisors from pretending they are unaware of significant damaging facts by using language like: "I didn't hear that."

**☞ You must make "reasonable inquiries."**

Likewise, the AICPA's Statements on Standards for Tax Services require you to make "reasonable inquiries" if information furnished appears to be incorrect, incomplete, or inconsistent "either on its face or on the basis of other facts known" to you. The practitioner is also expected to refer to the taxpayer's prior returns if feasible.[SSTS No. 3, *Certain Procedural Aspects of Preparing Returns*].

**☞ You are not required to audit the client's factual representations.**

In addition, when signing a return, you must consider information actually known to you from the tax return of another client if the information is relevant. Otherwise, you may rely on the information the taxpayer provides to you without verification. However, in marked contrast to generally accepted accounting principles and procedures involved in conducting a client audit, there is no requirement that you conduct an audit of your client's factual representations.

### Researching, Advising, and Tax Return Reporting

The Treasury and the professional organizations have made much progress in clarifying to the researcher the standard of care required in reading the laws, advising the taxpayer, and preparing and signing a tax return. At one time, the only real authoritative guidance was that the professional exercise "due diligence" in determining the correctness of the results communicated to the taxpayer [Circular 230, §10.22]. Although this provision remains in the circular, it is not particularly helpful because there is no further description of the meaning of "due diligence."

**☞ "Realistic possibility" is the key standard.**

However, a new standard has emerged that is far more instructive, although still difficult to apply. The tax practitioner must now abide by the "**realistic possibility**" standard. The standard is used in both Circular 230 and Treasury Regulation §1.6694-2(b). The circular specifies that you may not sign a return nor advise a taxpayer to take a position on a return if the position "does not have a realistic possibility of being sustained on its merits." (§10.34) The regulation asserts that the tax preparer is subject to a monetary penalty if a position is taken on a return that does not meet this "realistic possibility" test. This test is also found in both the AICPA and the ABA statements.

The rules provide the opportunity to take a position even when the foregoing test is not met if the position taken is not "frivolous" and is disclosed on the tax return. [Circular 230, §10.34(a)(1)(ii)]. The Statements on Standards defined "frivolous" as a position that is patently improper. [SSTS No. 1].

A position has a "realistic possibility of being sustained on its merits" if a person knowledgeable in tax law, after performing a "reasonable and well-informed analysis," would conclude that the position has "approximately a one in three, or greater, likelihood of being sustained on its merits." [Circular 230, §10.34(a)(4)(i)] In making this determination, you may consider only certain authorities discussed later.

It is important to note that the circular specifically provides that playing the audit lottery and reporting a position with no "realistic possibility" of success with the hope that the return will not be audited is not acceptable behavior. [Circular 230, §10.34(a)(4)(i); Treas. Reg. §1.6694-2(b)] Therefore, be wary of the practitioner who advises: "Don't worry, the IRS will never audit you!" This is not indicative of good, professional judgment. Rather, it is a foolhardy and improper approach.

Treasury Department Circular 230 refers to Internal Revenue Code Section 6662 as an aid in applying the realistic possibility standard. Treasury Regulations interpreting Code Section 6662 provide significant guidance regarding the types of resources you can use to determine whether a position has a realistic possibility of being sustained. Specifically, the Treasury Regulations state that you may use only certain types of authority in the analysis of a position. The following is the list of authorities upon which you are entitled to rely. [Treas. Reg. §1.6662-4(d)(3)(iii)]

- Internal Revenue Code
- Other statutory provisions

☞ **You may be required to disclose a position that does not meet the "realistic possibility" test.**

☞ **Only certain types of authority can be used in meeting the "realistic possibility test."**

- Regulations (final, temporary, and proposed)
- Revenue rulings
- Revenue procedures
- Tax treaties and regulations
- Treasury Department official explanations of treatises
- Court cases
- Committee reports (including explanatory statements of managers)
- Floor statements made prior to bill enactment by manager
- General explanations of tax legislation prepared by the Joint Committee on Taxation (the Blue Book)
- Letter rulings (after 10/31/76)
- Technical advice memoranda (after 10/31/76)
- Actions on decisions (after 3/12/81)
- General counsel memoranda (after 3/12/81)
- IRS information or press releases, notices, announcements
- Other administrative pronouncements published by the IRS in the *Internal Revenue Bulletin*

☞ **Primary sources are the only acceptable sources or authority.**

Notice that the list includes only primary authority. The Treasury regulations do not permit you to base a conclusion on secondary authority. Therefore, reference services, treatises, and journal articles, although helpful, may not be used to satisfy the "reasonable basis" standard. In addition, notice that Treasury publications are not specifically listed as reliable authority. It is unclear whether the IRS considers them as "other administrative pronouncements."

In analyzing this authority, the Treasury regulations indicate that the authoritative value of each type differs "depending on its relevance and persuasiveness, and the type of document providing the authority." An authority that "reaches its conclusion by cogently relating the applicable law to pertinent facts" will carry more weight than one that simply states an unsupported conclusion. In addition, these Regulations go on to indicate that types of authority "from which information has been deleted, such as private letter rulings. . ." is reduced to the extent the missing information is material. [Treas. Reg. §1.6662-4(d)(3)(ii)]

☞ **The authority supporting the position must be "substantial."**

The regulations also impose a separate but related standard in order to avoid monetary penalties for the understatement of income on a tax return. To this end, you must believe there is **substantial authority** supporting the position sought to be taken. What is substantial authority differs somewhat from the "realistic possibility" standard, but it is clearly a much higher standard than is required under the "realistic possibility test." It is also a lower standard than the commonly described criminal standard "beyond a reasonable doubt."

Bear in mind that the federal tax penalty imposed under Code Section 6662 is levied on the taxpayer rather than the researcher. Of course, inevitably a client who has such a penalty imposed on him will likely look to his professional experts for prompt reimbursement. Those interested in the Section 6662 penalty can explore this issue in more detail in Chapter Eight.

## CHAPTER SUMMARY

A good researcher knows when to stop researching. Possessing a good understanding of the research process provides a foundation to enable you to assess whether more steps are necessary or whether your research is complete.

The first phase in the research process involves identifying all pertinent facts and formulating the research question. The next step entails locating and reviewing all relevant authority. A crucial phase in the research process occurs in the third step – the analysis of the authority gathered. Does the authority directly address the research question? What types of authority did you find? How similar are the facts to those involving the taxpayer you represent? Are there material differences? If so, do you believe the material factual differences would give rise to a different court decision if the court decided the merits of your client's case? Do the various authorities present consistent or conflicting positions? If conflicting, which is most authoritative? Do you have enough authority?

Several sources provide guidelines for performing each of the research steps. The key sources of these ethical guidelines are Treasury Circular 230 and the Treasury regulations. When fact gathering, the guidelines state that you must make "reasonable inquiries" if information furnished to you appears to be incorrect, incomplete, or inconsistent with other facts known to you.

The guidelines require you to recommend to the taxpayer only the position that has a "realistic possibility of being sustained on its merits." You satisfy this test if a knowledgeable person in tax law, after performing a "reasonable and well-informed analysis," would conclude that the position has "approximately a one in three, or greater, likelihood of being sustained on its merits." You may sign a return that reports a position failing this test only if you also disclose that such position is being taken on the return and the position is not a frivolous one.

In making the "realistic possibility" determination, you are entitled only to rely on resources listed as authority in the Regulations.  These are almost all of the primary sources of law.  Secondary sources are not authority.  The regulations indicate that each authority must be weighed on the basis of relevance and persuasiveness as well as its form. You can learn about this in greater detail in Chapter Eight and by reading the provisions in Treasury Regulation §1.6662-4(d).

## Summary of Standards for the Tax Researcher

|  | CIRCULAR 230 | AICPA/ABA | REGULATIONS |
|---|---|---|---|
| **To Whom Standards Apply** | Those who practice before the IRS | Members | Everyone |
| **Standards for Gathering Facts** | Must make reasonable inquiries if taxpayer information appears to be incorrect, inconsistent, or incomplete. | Same as Circular 230 | None |
| **Standards for Research** | Realistic possibility standard | Realistic possibility standard | None |
| **Standards for Preparing and Signing Tax Return** | Realistic possibility standard | Realistic possibility standard | Realistic possibility and substantial authority |
| **Possible Impact of Violating Standards** | Inability to practice before the IRS | Loss of membership privilege | Monetary penalties |

# PROBLEMS

## *KEY CONCEPTS* (1-13)

1.    Define and discuss the following terms:

    a. Treasury Circular 230
    b. Practice before the IRS
    c. Tax research standards
    d. Realistic possibility standard
    e. Reasonable inquiry standard
    f. Due diligence

2.    What is the impact of failing to abide by the standards provided in Circular 230?

3.    What is the impact of failing to abide by the standards provided by the AICPA?

4.    What additional guidelines do the Treasury regulations offer?

5.    Compare the guidelines provided by Circular 230, the AICPA, and Treasury regulations. How do they differ?

6.    To whom do the following guidelines apply?

    a.    Circular 230
    b.    AICPA's Statements on Standards for Tax Practice

7.    Why is it important for you to know when your research is complete?

8.    Describe the step of "pondering" your research results. What must you consider?

9.    Assume you complete all the research steps, but you still don't feel comfortable with your conclusion. What do you do?

10.    In reviewing your research results, you find you have a revenue ruling that clearly states your taxpayer cannot do what he wants to do. However, you also found a case (although with no jurisdiction over your taxpayer) that says he can. What do you do? What practical considerations are important?

11.    What are the sources of research guidelines for the tax researcher?

12.    Under what circumstances are you required as a tax researcher to refrain from recommending a certain tax position to a taxpayer?

13.    What is the importance of primary authority?

## PRACTICAL APPLICATIONS (14-24)

14.    Assume that Mrs. K tells you about $10,000 she found in the park. You communicate to Mrs. K that as a result of your research, it is clear that the $10,000 will have to be included in her taxable income based on the fact that even "treasure troves" are gross income. She tells you that she doesn't want to pay taxes on this amount and, therefore, asks you just to pretend that the two of you never had the conversation and that you don't know anything about the $10,000. She tells you that when she gives you all her materials to prepare her tax return, she just won't indicate any receipt of the money. In March, she does just that and omits any information indicating that she found the $10,000. What are your responsibilities in completing her tax return?

15.    Your client is a resident of Florida. He has asked you to research whether he must recognize some of his receipts as income. Your research resulted in locating the following authority:

    * Revenue Ruling that speaks directly to the issue and requires income recognition.

    * U.S. District Court case in Florida (with jurisdiction over your client) that directly addresses the issue and concludes the income may be excluded from taxable income.

    * Ninth Circuit Court of Appeals case that, although the facts are slightly different, concludes the income must be included.

    What will you advise the client?

16.    The only authority you find after an exhaustive research process is a seven-year-old letter ruling. Although the ruling provides few details regarding the transaction the Treasury was reviewing, what is available appears relevant and suggests a position favorable to your client's preferred approach. What do you advise your client?

17.    Your library contains only one of the reference services. It does not contain any case books or the *Cumulative Bulletins*. You do not have access to an electronic library. However, there is a full law library in the city. Your client has requested that you advise her on whether some property she received will need to be recognized in income. The value of the property received is substantial. From your review of the reference service, you believe that she is entitled to exclude the value of the item from income. The reference service provides summaries of several court cases taking this position. What do you do at this point? Why?

18.    You are researching the deductibility of a certain expense. You take the following steps:

Gather facts → Determine issue → Examine annotated reference service → Study the two cases that appeared initially to be on point → Conclude the cases are irrelevant.

You have performed no other research steps or reviewed authority other than that indicated. What additional steps are advisable at this point? Why?

19.    You are researching the deductibility of a certain expense. You take the following steps:

Gather facts → Determine issue → Examine IRC → Examine relevant treatise that seems to adequately answer the research question.

You have performed no other research steps or reviewed authority other than that indicated. What additional steps may be advisable at this point? Why?

20.    You are researching the deductibility of a certain expense. You take the following steps:

Gather facts → Determine issue → Examine annotated reference service → Locate a revenue ruling that appears directly on point and allows the deduction.

You located the revenue ruling as soon as you began researching using the reference service. You did not continue reviewing the reference service once you spotted the revenue ruling cite. You have performed no other research steps or reviewed authority other than that indicated. What additional steps are advisable at this point? Why?

21.    You are researching the deductibility of a certain expense.  You take the following steps:

Gather facts $\rightarrow$ Determine issue $\rightarrow$ Study the IRC $\rightarrow$ Review the related Treasury Regulations $\rightarrow$ Confirm that the helpful regulation still reflects current statutory law $\rightarrow$ Examine Volume 4 of the annotated reference service $\rightarrow$ Thoroughly review that volume and identify two cases that appear directly on point and that allow the deduction $\rightarrow$ Examine the cases and conclude they are applicable.

Are there additional steps remaining in the research process before you advise your client?  If so, what are they?  Why?

22.    You are researching the deductibility of a certain expense.  You take the following steps:

Gather facts $\rightarrow$ Determine issue $\rightarrow$ Study the IRC $\rightarrow$ Review the related Treasury Regulations and determine that there is no tegulation for the relevant Code provision $\rightarrow$ Examine the pertinent volumes of a topical reference service and find no helpful guidance.

How do you proceed?  Are there additional steps remaining in the research process before you advise your client?  If so, what are they?  Why?

23.    Sam works as a professor at Solid University.  He is a significant proponent of Internet education and research.  The university outsources some of its technological work to Tech. Inc.  You are in the process of completing Sam's tax return for the previous year.  Sam and you have been good friends for years.  Sam was sharing his enthusiasm about his job with you and happened to mention that Tech. Inc. recently gave him a new laptop computer valued at $3,500 to "show its appreciation" for his commitment to technological advancement in education.

Sam assumes that the gift was also made because he had recently (and at some personal sacrifice) attended a Technology in Education seminar.  Sam  presented his work along with representatives from Tech. Inc., who proudly held Sam's work out as a product of their collaboration.  Although Sam does not particularly care for Tech. Inc. and does not feel obligated to it in any way (since it is not his employer), Sam gladly accepted the accolades and the computer.  Sam received no appropriate IRS Form 1099 or other income tax reporting forms from Tech. Inc.  What are your responsibilities in completing Sam's tax return?

24.     Your client is a resident of New York. He has asked you to research the possible deductibility of some legal expenses he incurred. In your research, you locate a Tax Court case that allowed a similar deduction to a taxpayer in Montana. You also discovered a revenue ruling indicating that the IRS did not acquiesce to the court decision. You were unable to locate any additional relevant authority. What will you advise the client?

**INTEGRATED CASE STUDIES** (No additional work in this chapter)

# THE TAX RESEARCH PROCESS

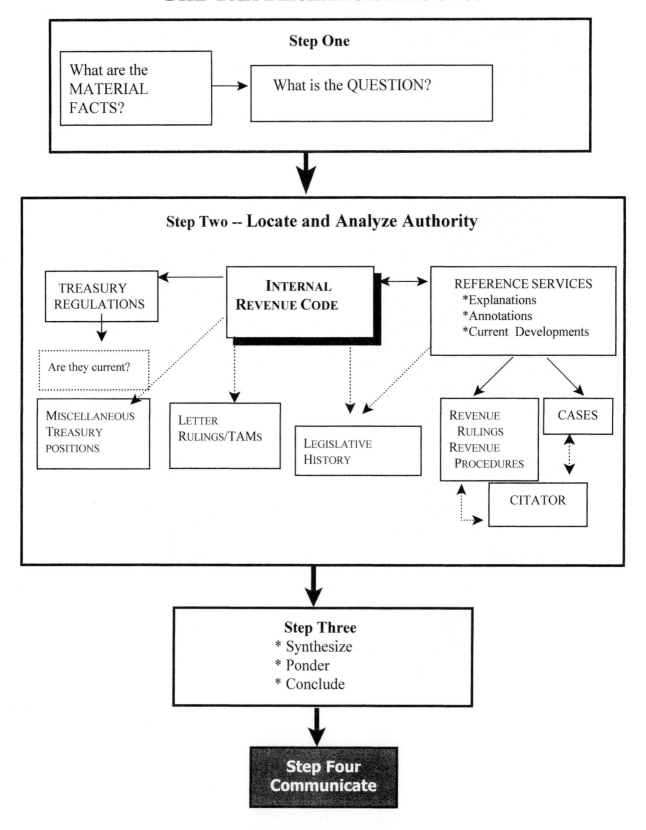

# CHAPTER SEVEN

# COMMUNICATING RESEARCH RESULTS

## *EXPECTED LEARNING OUTCOMES*

- Distinguish among the various forms of tax research communication
- Appreciate the purpose of an office memo, client letter, and protest letter
- Effectively write an office memo, client letter, and protest letter

## *CHAPTER OUTLINE*

- Overview
- Internal Written Communication
- External Written Communication
- Oral Communication
- Chapter Summary
- Problems

## OVERVIEW

Answering the research question is your primary responsibility as a tax researcher. However, to complete your responsibility, you must also effectively communicate your research results.

Communication of tax results may take many forms. It is helpful to separate the types of communication into two broad categories: internal and external communications. Internal communications are those that remain within your office or company – for example, a memo to the file. External communications consist of forms of communication that you make to parties outside of your office or company – perhaps the client or the Internal Revenue Service.

Within these categories, the communication may be oral, written, or both. Effective written communication requires an awareness of the rules of grammar and sentence structure. A discussion of these fundamentals is beyond the scope of this textbook. There are, however, several useful writing resources you may wish to consult. Possible resources include

- *The Elements of Style*, by Strunk and White
- *A Treasury for Word Lovers*, by Freeman
- *Executive's Guide to Effective Speaking and Writing*, by Dyer
- *Effective Writing*, by May

Every situation triggers different requirements regarding the appropriate formality and style of your communication. Even the purpose of your communication will vary. Sometimes it may be simply to inform; at other times, it may be to persuade. In other instances, your advice may take the form of an opinion letter, on which the client and others may rely.

Determining whether your communication will be internal or external, oral or written, formal or informal, educational or persuasive depends upon two factors:

1.    *Who generated the research question? Your client? A colleague?*

Client Generated: When the client directly requests that you find the answer to a tax question, you will ultimately need to communicate your answer to the client, either orally or in writing or both. Generally, your goal here is to educate the client regarding the tax research results. In addition to this external communication, however, you also need to internally document your research and communication using a memo to the files. Be sure to also consider your employer's protocols and procedures regarding appropriate research documentation and file maintenance.

Colleague Generated: A colleague in your firm or company may ask you to perform research, or you may independently determine there is a need to do some research. Either way, you will communicate your research results internally either orally or in a written memo to the file. Typically, the purpose of this type of communication is to create a record of your research results and guide your colleague who may have a broader set of issues under consideration.

2.    *What concern generated the research question? A possible planning idea? A concern for current tax treatment? A request from the audit department regarding tax liability concerns?*

This factor greatly impacts the nature and purpose of the research communication. If the client or colleague presented you with a planning idea, your communication should cover all the various options available to the client along with all of the potential risks. If your research indicates that the client's planned transaction will likely have adverse tax consequences, you should also consider the appropriateness of advising your client as to other possible structures that may be more tax favored and still achieve the intended transaction.  Your purpose is to thoroughly communicate your advice so that the client's future actions are well informed. Remember, however, that colleagues and clients are quite different in their educational backgrounds and sophistication in tax matters. Some clients are highly technically oriented and appreciate knowing all of the technical details raised under applicable tax laws.  Others are either disinterested or unsophisticated and simply want a "yes" or "no" answer (often a difficult answer to provide).

You should also keep in mind that you may reach a solution for a taxpayer that is an excellent result in the short term but imprudent given the client's long-term tax goals.  Each of the matters for which you represent a client may have a bearing on future or past transactions.

Your research may be in response to an audit letter from the Internal Revenue Service. Now your communication goal is to persuade the IRS that your taxpayer's position is correct. You become a client advocate instead of a client educator.

This chapter addresses each type of communication vehicle – its purpose and most effective use.

## INTERNAL WRITTEN COMMUNICATION

Your research will almost always result in the need to internally document your findings. Some exceptions to this general rule may apply where, upon advice of counsel, your client specifically requests that the documentation be kept to a minimum due to concerns regarding discovery of such documentation by third parties.  In any event, assuming this is not at issue, the most efficient method to document your research is to write a memorandum to the file. You may also ultimately distribute this memo in a more formalized format to an office colleague.

An **office memo** to the file serves several very important purposes.  First, it creates a record for you and your firm of your research question, the work you did, your conclusion, and what it was based upon.  This is very useful when you need to refresh your memory in order to communicate your results to the client or a colleague.  You may also find you need this reminder of your work should you need to do follow-up research at a later time.  In addition, you may find such a record helpful to you in case someone asks you a similar tax question.

The office memo also provides a useful tool to others.  Perhaps another colleague takes responsibility for the client.  Your memo provides the potential for continuity in client service. Should the tax treatment of a transaction be audited later, the office memo to the file may provide the person handling the audit with helpful information. Therefore, a well-documented file with appropriate file memoranda is an essential aid for others to become acquainted with client return issues and other matters.

To serve the preceding purposes, the office memo should, at a minimum, include the following items:

- ✓    list of material facts
- ✓    discussion of the tax research question(s) or issue(s)
- ✓    citation to relevant authority
- ✓    discussion of your conclusion and your reasoning to support your conclusion

*FACTS*:  Your memo should be dated and should also indicate who it is from and to whom it is directed.  It should begin with a clear but brief listing of all the material facts. Remember from Chapter One that a relevant or material fact is one that if changed might alter the application of the law.  Your goal in this portion of the memo is to enable you or someone else to quickly learn the relevant facts.  Therefore, do not include those facts that have no impact on the application of the law.  You should include any assumptions you are making regarding the facts and indicate them as such.

You should also state your source of the relevant facts.  Remember that the client usually is entitled to view the file and receive it back in its entirety on request.  Avoid disparaging or confidential remarks.  A colleague might send a copy of your memorandum to your client without your knowledge or consent.

The style you apply to this section depends on whether you wish to be formal or informal. You should always have a heading entitled "facts."  If you choose to write an office memo using a formal style, you will want to use complete and well-written sentences to describe the facts.  If you choose to use a more informal style, you can simply state the facts in a numbered list. This style provides the reader with the ability to quickly review the key facts.  The most appropriate style is generally a matter of personal preference and office practice.

**EXAMPLE 1:  Formal Presentation of Facts**

**DATE:**       November 1, 20XX
**TO:**          Client File
**FROM:**      Tax Researcher

**Facts**:  This year Mr. X won $2 million in the New York lottery.  The state's rules provide that the full amount of the award is to be placed in an escrow account,  which will pay out to Mr. X $200,000 a year for the life of Mr. X or 10 years, whichever is shorter.  Mr. X has no control over the escrow account.  No interest is payable on deferred but unpaid amounts.  Mr. X is currently 80 years old and is a cash-basis taxpayer.

**Notice that this style requires the reader to carefully read each sentence to ascertain the relevant facts.**

**EXAMPLE 2:  Informal Presentation of Facts**

**DATE:**       November 1, 20XX
**TO:**          Client File
**FROM:**      Tax Researcher

**Facts**:
1. Mr. X won $2 million in the NY lottery.
2. State to put $2 million in escrow.
3. Escrow account to pay to Mr. X $200,000/yr for 10 or the rest of his life, whichever is shorter, with no interest payable.
4. TP has no control over the escrow account.
5. TP is 80 yrs old.
6. TP is a cash basis taxpayer.

**Notice that the informal style enables the reader to quickly ascertain the key facts.**

*ISSUE:* In this section of your memo, it is important to clearly identify what your research question is. Here you should indicate what Internal Revenue Code is at issue vis-a-vis the facts. What does the IRC section state? What fact is creating the specific question needing resolution?

---

**EXAMPLE 3: Identification of the Issue**

**DATE:**        November 1, 20XX
**TO:**          Client File
**FROM:**        Tax Researcher

**Facts**: This year Mr. X won $2 million dollars in the New York lottery. The state's rules provide that the full amount of the award is to be placed in an escrow account, which will pay out to Mr. X $200,000 a year for the life of Mr. X or 10 years, whichever is shorter. Mr. X has no control over the escrow account. No interest is payable on deferred but unpaid amounts. Mr. X is currently 80 years old and is a cash basis taxpayer.

**Issues:** Per IRC §61, gross income includes "all income, from whatever source derived." Therefore, lottery winnings are required to be included in federal gross income. However, it is not clear from the Code whether Mr. X is required to recognize all of the $2 million in income in the current year or if it can be spread out over the years of receipt. In addition, the Code is unclear regarding how the placement of the funds into an escrow account impacts the taxability. Is there imputed interest on the award?

---

**Note that in the statement of the issue, the discussion refers to the central Code Section under examination and poses the research questions the facts trigger.**

*CONCLUSION AND REASONING:* It is in this portion of the office memo that you communicate your answer to the research question. This is not as easy as it sounds. Sometimes your research leads you to more than one answer. Perhaps you find a number of possible options available to the client. Whether or not you find a clear answer, you must state your findings and reach a conclusion, even if you conclude that the client has a variety of choices.

Just as critical as your research findings are the logic and analysis you used in arriving at your conclusion. Based on the authority you reviewed, why did you arrive at your conclusion? You should discuss in this section what judicial and/or Treasury interpretations you read that shed some light on the research issue. Your conclusion must be supported by your reasoning. Make sure to include the full cite to each authority you discuss.

When you discuss the authority you used to come to your conclusion, make sure you connect the authority to the facts of your research case. Be careful not to simply discuss each case or Treasury interpretation you found simply by stating "because of the above authority, I conclude. . ."

Instead, as you discuss cases and Treasury interpretations, apply them to your facts. Are the facts in the authority similar to yours? If they are different, do you believe the difference impacts your ability to apply the authority to your situation? Why? If there is some authority that supports your conclusion and some that goes against your conclusion, make sure you discuss both. Do not pretend that negative authority just doesn't exist. You must discuss negative authority and then explain why you believe your conclusion is still correct.

---

**EXAMPLE 4: Discussion of Conclusion and Reasoning**

**DATE:**      November 1, 20XX
**TO:**        Client File
**FROM:**      Tax Researcher

**Facts**: This year Mr. X won $2 million in the New York lottery. The state's rules provide that the full amount of the award is to be placed in an escrow account, which will pay out to Mr. X $200,000 a year for the life of Mr. X or 10 years, whichever is shorter. Mr. X has no control over the escrow account. No interest is payable on deferred but unpaid amounts. Mr. X is currently 80 years old and is a cash basis taxpayer.

**Issues:** Per IRC §61, lottery winnings are required to be included in federal gross income. Is Mr. X required to recognize all of the $2 million in income in the current year or can it be spread out over the years of receipt? How does the placement of the funds into an escrow account impact the taxability? Is there imputed interest on the award?

---

**EXAMPLE 4: Discussion of Conclusion and Reasoning (continued)**

**Conclusion and Reasoning:** Lottery winnings are considered gross income under IRC §61 and do not fall within any income exclusion provision. Regarding the timing of this income, IRC §451 and Treasury Regulation §1.451-1 provide that cash basis taxpayers must include income in the year it is actually or constructively received. Because Mr. X is a cash basis taxpayer, he is required to recognize as gross income the amount of lottery proceeds he actually receives in the year of receipt. Therefore, at a minimum, Mr. X must recognize as taxable income the $200,000 received each year.

Placing the funds in escrow does not appear to alter this conclusion. According to Rev. Rul. 62-74, 1962-1 CB 150 and the Tax Court case of *E. T. Sproull,* 16 TC 244 (1960), the taxpayer must recognize the present value of the future payments only if the taxpayer has control over the escrow or trust account. Therefore, because Mr. X has no control over the escrow account, he will need to recognize income only as he receives it.

Further, no imputed interest is required under the Code because the terms of the award preclude interest and the taxpayer is entitled to funds only at specified future times.

---

**Note in Example 4 that the first portion of the conclusion section states a conclusion and then supports it with a discussion of the relevant authority. However, read the last paragraph of the conclusion again. Do you note something missing? The last paragraph makes an assertion with no supporting authority. The Code section on which the research is based and the reasoning for such a conclusion must be stated.**

Within the general requirements of a statement of facts, issue, conclusion, and reasoning, you have a good deal of flexibility regarding your office memo. People's preferences differ regarding the proper level of formality and the order of the headings. Some people prefer to begin their memo with the conclusion, and then follow with the facts, issue, and reasoning. Others start with the facts. Some combine the conclusion and reasoning; others separate them. These preferences are not significant. The key is to always keep in mind your goal when writing an office memo: to provide a document that will briefly and quickly remind you of the key facts, the research question, your conclusion, and why you arrived at the conclusion.

# EXTERNAL WRITTEN COMMUNICATION

The purpose changes somewhat when the intent is to communicate research results to someone outside the firm or company.  In addition to creating a record of research steps taken, your primary purpose in issuing external communications is either educational or persuasive.  The two most common potential recipients of your external communications are the client and the taxing authority.  Other potential recipients may include other professionals who are seeking clarification of tax matters to help the client structure a transaction.

## Client Letter

A written communication of your research results to the client is commonly called a **client letter**.  The purpose of the client letter is to educate the client regarding the tax issue(s) and your research findings.  You are not the decision maker, simply the educator so that the client can make a well-informed decision.

A form of client letter that expresses specific opinions is known as an **opinion letter**. Generally, the purpose of an opinion is to provide the taxpayer with an opinion supporting a particular transaction (or tax return position).  The express intention of an opinion letter is to enable the taxpayer to fully rely on the opinions expressed in the letter.  Opinion letters are often issued in "**short form**" or in "**long form**."  A long-form letter typically provides a well-reasoned analysis of the facts and applicable laws that form the basis for the opinion(s) expressed. The short form letter simply provides an opinion in most cases.

Arguably, because your research findings are formalized in a written letter to the client, your legal vulnerability is at its highest when writing a client letter.  Particularly with regard to opinion letters, it is often the case that third parties may also rely on the opinion.  It is critical in these circumstances that you perform thorough and accurate research and craft a carefully written letter.  In addition, you should always consider the following guidelines to help lessen your risk and improve the quality of the letter. (Chapter Eight discusses potential applicable penalty provisions.)

*SCOPE OF RESEARCH:*  Always start a client letter with a statement about what you understand the client asked you to do – the scope of your research.  Did the client ask you to look at the possibility of paying a cash bonus?  Or did the client ask you to look at any way of getting cash out to key employees?  This first sentence or two identifies essentially the purpose of the letter.  If your statement of the scope differs from the client's understanding of what was asked of you, the worst that happens is you have to go back and perform more research to satisfy the new scope. However, if you fail to state the scope of your research, it is hard for any possible misunderstanding to come to light at any early stage.

---

**EXAMPLE 5:  Sentences that Limit the Scope of the Opinion in a Client Letter**

Dear Mr. X:

▸      I have researched both the federal and state tax ramifications of your proposed redemption of X Corporation. . . .

▸      As requested, I have analyzed the income tax treatment of expenditures incurred to construct a common play area at Condo Properties.. . .

---

**Note that both preceding examples indicate the parameters the researcher believes the client made when requesting the research.  Should the client believe that the research was to encompass additional analysis, the client now has the opportunity to alert the researcher to this fact.**

*IDENTIFY FACTS:*  Following the scope of your research, you should always recite the pertinent facts as you understand them, from whom the facts were obtained and that any opinions or statements that are expressed rely on these factual assertions.  This is critical because your research results are based on the facts stated.  If there is a misunderstanding of the facts, it may become clear once you present the facts.  Alternatively, if the facts are incorrect but the letter clearly states that someone else provided such factual representations, at least you and your firm are not placed in the undesirable position of directly bearing culpability for a failed letter.  In this circumstance, possible errors in facts should result only in the potential need for you to redo some of your research and amend the letter.  Some firms are so cautious in this regard that letters are first issued in draft form only, clearly marked as such, in order to ensure that the client or others have the opportunity to review and approve the form of the letter before it is finalized.

Although mistakes in facts may mean some of the research you performed may no longer be relevant, the research results will still be correct as they relate to the facts as you stated them to be.  On the other hand, if your understanding of the facts is in error but you fail to restate the facts, you risk stating erroneous research conclusions and may incur legal liability.

---

**EXAMPLE 6: Statement of Facts in Client Letter**

Dear Mr. X:

I have researched both the federal and state tax ramifications of your proposed redemption of X Corporation. . . .

- In order to confirm with you that I completely understand your transactions, I have restated the facts below that I used in my analysis and which your Chief Financial Officer, Michael Money, related to me per his letter to the firm dated month, day, year . . . **OR**

- My understanding of the facts as you described them to me in our September 1, 20XX conference call are as follows:... **OR**

- The facts as I understand them are based on the following documents presented in draft form as follows:

  1.  Draft Loan Agreement dated month, day, year by and between Greedy Bank and Mr. Jones; and
  2.  Draft Deed of Trust dated month, day, year issued by Mr. Jones in favor of Greedy Bank, Greedy Bank Sub, Trustee; and
  3.  Draft Assignment of Rents Agreement dated month, day, year by and between Greedy Bank and Mr. Jones. . ."

---

**Note that, as discussed previously, you have a choice of styles regarding how to present your understanding of the facts. Whatever method you employ, it is important to preface the statement of the facts with the acknowledgment that they are stated <u>as you understand them to be</u>. Similar to the office memo, the facts should be in sufficient detail so that all material elements are restated. This will reveal immediately any factual misunderstanding.**

***BODY OF LETTER***: In the remainder of the letter, communicate all that the client needs to know about what you found through your research.  If you found that the client has more than one option, communicate each option along with any risks that might be involved.  Be careful though.  Clients do not generally want you to write a novel!  Sometimes they may request a letter that is more in the form of a "**white paper**" – a survey of the applicable laws involved in a matter. However, absent such a request, brevity and cogency in writing are important.  You may be an excellent researcher, but remember, the client may see only the letter.  He does not appreciate the many hours of research and analysis culminating in the letter.  If the letter is poorly or sloppily drafted, the client's perception will be that you are a poor researcher.  The client may also be unwilling to pay the related bill.

Again, your purpose in a client letter is to educate the taxpayer. Use language a nontax person can understand.  Unlike the office memo, the client letter should be written in plain language rather than technical tax language.  Try to avoid citing a Code section or case name in the center of a sentence.  Instead, cite to the Code section or other authority in footnotes or in between sentences.  If there are potentially risky positions, make sure that you include enough detail to clearly inform the client of the fact that there is doubt pertaining to positions that are truly risky.

Some practitioners assert that you may appropriately send a client letter without citing any of the authority you found.  As noted previously, short-form opinion letters often are presented in this manner.  However, realize that frequently the client asks another expert to review your letter.  Your letter is often more credible and useful when it contains cites to the relevant authority supporting your statements.

**EXAMPLE 7: Discussion of Opinion**

Dear Mr. X:

I have researched both the federal and state tax ramifications of your proposed redemption of X Corporation . . .

My understanding of the facts as you described them to me in our September 1, 20XX conference call are as follows: . . .

In my opinion, there are many tax considerations you need to be aware of in planning this corporate formation. First, based on the facts you have presented, including your representation that you will control 100% of the company after formation, the incorporation of X corporation should qualify as a tax-free transfer for federal income tax purposes. (IRC §351) Therefore, no gain or loss should result upon formation . . .

The fact that X is contemplating issuing both Class A and Class B voting common stock may be a problem in the incorporation. The law requires that the transferors own at least 80% of the voting stock after the transfer [IRC §368(c)]. The courts have supported this position as well. (See *James Hamrick v. Commissioner*, 60 F.2d. 700.)

An important factor in classifying the notes as debt (in lieu of equity) is the fact that appropriate debt instruments will be employed; interest is required to accrue and be paid on a periodic basis . . . (IRC §385)

Your plan to incorporate may be a good approach to limiting liability for state law purposes while achieving certain tax benefits you desire. It may also be wise as a planning move to consider making an S election. (See IRC §§1361- et seq.) If such an election is made, the corporation will generally not be subject to taxation at the corporate level, although there are a number of circumstances where corporate taxation may occur, including special gains taxes and state franchise taxes, as described further below . . ."

**Note that although the nontechnical language is used, the opinion is nonetheless supported by cites to applicable authority. Because these cites are placed after sentences instead of in the middle of sentences, the citations do not disturb the reading flow.**

When writing an opinion letter, to the extent any statements made are subject to any qualifications, conditions, or other letters or documents, you should state what limitations apply. This is extremely important, because it may absolve you from legal liability downstream. Furthermore, you should state who may rely upon the opinion letter. Consider the following optional statements:

- ***Limit the basis upon which the letter is issued***:

  "The opinions expressed below are based solely on the representations you made in your letter to the undersigned dated month, day, year. Any deviations in facts from the statements made in that letter may result in material modifications to, or revocation of, the opinions expressed herein."

- ***Limit the persons who may properly rely on the letter***:

  "The opinions expressed herein may not be relied on by any other party except Mr. Jones." Or, "No other person is an intended beneficiary of this letter. Any representations to the contrary are prohibited."

- ***Limit the persons who may receive the letter or learn of its contents***:

  "This letter may not be referred to, copied, quoted, or disseminated without the express written consent of the undersigned."

- ***Limit any opinions expressed to ascertainable standards***: (see Chapter Eight for more information regarding these standards).

  "Therefore, based upon the stated facts and the relevant authority cited, a realistic basis exists for taking the charitable contribution deduction . . ."

  "Therefore, based solely on the *Happy* case, there is substantial authority for taking the position that the taxpayer should smile when filing his or her return in the Ninth Circuit and the Second Circuit. (*Id.*) However, the Supreme Court has yet to resolve this issue. The Supreme Court has agreed to review the issue (*Miller*, *Supra*). It is possible that the Court will resolve the issue counter to the *Happy* decision. In such a case, our opinion may be incorrect . . ."

- ■ ***Limit any opinions expressed to the date the letter is issued***:

  "The opinions expressed in this letter are limited to those applicable federal income tax laws that apply as of the date of this letter. Future court decisions or legislative action may defeat the opinions expressed . . ."

- ■ ***Limit your duty to update the letter***:

  "The firm expressly denies any duty to update this letter for subsequent factual developments or changes in applicable laws . . ."

- ■ ***Describe clearly any conditions that the letter is based upon that have not yet occurred***:

  "This letter and the opinions expressed are based upon your representation that you will form the corporation pursuant to all valid state laws and issue the shares in accordance with all applicable laws."

- ■ ***Limit the letter to your role as a tax professional***:

  "Although this letter discusses issues regarding valuation and matters regarding the appropriate calculation of certain liabilities, the firm renders no opinions regarding valuation or accounting matters and does not express any expertise as regards to such matters."

**SUMMARY STATEMENT:** Once you complete your explanation and analysis, end the letter with a brief summary to help the taxpayer focus on the key items in the letter. Then the letter is complete, and you can end with a sentence indicating how you wish to proceed from here.

**EXAMPLE 8:  Summary Statement**

Dear Mr. X:

I have researched both the federal and state tax ramifications of your proposed redemption of X Corporation . . .

My understanding of the facts as you described them to me in our September 1, 20XX, conference call are as follows: . . .

In my opinion, there are many tax considerations you need to be aware of in planning this corporate formation.  First, based on the facts you have presented, including your representation that you will control 100% of the company after formation, the incorporation of X Corporation should qualify as a tax-free transfer for federal income tax purposes. (IRC §351)  Therefore, no gain or loss should result upon formation . . .

The fact that X is contemplating issuing both Class A and Class B voting common stock may be a problem in the incorporation.  The law requires that the transferors own at least 80% of the voting stock after the transfer. [IRC §368(c)] The courts have supported this position as well. (See *James Hamrick v. Commissioner*, 60 F.2d. 700.)

An important factor in classifying the notes as debt (in lieu of equity) is the fact that appropriate debt instruments will be employed; interest is required to accrue and be paid on a periodic basis . . . (IRC §385)

Your plan to incorporate may be a good approach to limiting liability for state law purposes while achieving certain tax benefits you desire. It may also be wise as a planning move to consider making an S election. (See IRC §§1361- et seq.) If such an election is made, the corporation will generally not be subject to taxation at the corporate level, although there are a number of circumstances where corporate taxation may occur, including special gains taxes and state franchise taxes, as described further below . . .

In closing, several issues need to be resolved before we can achieve a tax-free incorporation.  First.... Second....   It may also be wise to obtain a Letter Ruling on this transaction from the IRS in advance.  A favorable ruling will eliminate all doubt as to the tax impact of the proposed transaction.  Let me know if you would like to discuss this option further . . .

**Note that the final paragraph provides you with the ability to nicely summarize for your client your conclusions and any future actions the client may need to consider.**

**Protest Letter to Taxing Authority**

At both the federal and state levels, before final assessment (absent certain "jeopardy assessments" in which collection of the tax may be in jeopardy), the taxing authorities generally provide the taxpayer with one final opportunity to present arguments that the reporting position taken was correct. This final chance is called a **protest letter**. In the federal system, at the conclusion of an audit, if the IRS believes there is a tax owing, the IRS will send the taxpayer a preliminary notice of deficiency. This is often referred to as a "**thirty-day letter**" because the taxpayer has 30 days to file a written protest of the IRS agent's findings. States generally follow similar procedures, providing the taxpayer a specific period of time to protest the initial audit results. Chapter Eight covers this process in greater detail.

The purpose of a protest letter is quite different from that of either an office memo or a client letter. Here the goal is to persuade the IRS (or other applicable taxing agency) that the taxpayer's reporting position in question is correct. The tax researcher now becomes the taxpayer's advocate.

The art of advocacy requires an altogether different tone than the other types of written communication discussed in this chapter. Where the tone in an office memo and client letter is fairly objective and informative, in a protest letter, you need to be more assertive and politely argumentative. Your goal is to convince the reader that the taxpayer's position is correct. As long as you are professionally comfortable that your client has a realistic basis to assert the position, your personal opinion becomes somewhat irrelevant when you are in the role of taxpayer advocate.

*Practitioner Observation*

*Fred Daily*, attorney at law and author of books
including *Stand up to the IRS*, (Nolo Press)  and
*Winning the IRS Game* (Dropzone Press).

"The challenge for a practitioner in written communications with a tax agency is to present the taxpayer's case in such a way that the desired result will naturally flow from the recipient.  Accomplishing this requires pegging the facts to the IRC, Regs or case law.  This should be done in a non-confrontational manner.  For example, in an appeals protest letter, avoid casting aspersions on the Revenue Agent or her work.  Instead, point out the correct tax law to be applied, and allude to the fact that the agent may have overlooked a provision or fact in reaching her decision.  The practitioner is simply helping the Appeals Officer come to the 'right conclusion.'"

The protest letter follows the same basic structure of the office memo and client letter – purpose, facts, issue, conclusion, and reasoning.  However, the role of client advocate often carries with it greater formality, such as the need to obtain and file appropriate powers of attorney forms with the IRS. (See Chapter Eight for more discussion on this topic.)

With the tone of an advocate, you must state that your purpose is to protest the findings of the revenue agent and identify all pertinent facts.  Sometimes, the agent presents incomplete facts that are potentially misleading.  You should present the facts thoroughly and honestly, but in the most favorable light for the taxpayer's position.  It is not your job to represent the IRS position.

## EXAMPLE 9: Posing Facts in a Positive Manner

Assume that Mr. X took a Code Section 162 deduction for expenses (maintenance, depreciation, interest) connected with a home that he owns for investment purposes. He purchased the home five years ago at a cost of $100,000 and has never lived or vacationed in it. He has rented the home out from time to time, although he did not rent it out during the tax year in question. The home was listed with a rental agent, but, because of poor weather, no rental arrangements were made. The home was rented out in subsequent years. The home is presently valued at $500,000. Mr. X's primary reason for owning the home is to ultimately sell it and benefit from its significant appreciation in value since purchase. He also has thoughts that he and his wife may eventually wish to retire and move into the home.

*Presenting the facts in the most __unfavorable__ light to the taxpayer:*

"Mr. X took a Code Section 162 deduction for expenses incurred in connection with a residence in the year 2005. The residence was not rented to any non-family member during the year, or used for any other business purpose."

*Presenting the facts in the most __favorable__ light to the taxpayer:*

"Mr. X purchased residential property in 2000 for $100,000. It is currently valued at $500,000. Since the time of purchase, neither the taxpayer nor his family have ever used the home for personal purposes. The home has frequently been rented to non-family members since the time of purchase at full rental value. During 2005, the home was listed with a rental agent and efforts were continually made to rent out the home. However, due to poor weather during the vacation months, the efforts to rent in 2005 were unsuccessful. The home was rented out in both 2006 and 2007."

Note that the agent presenting the facts in an unfavorable light does not make any misstatements. However, many of the favorable facts are not presented. The presentation of the facts more favorably does not misstate facts either. However, it provides information that helps explain the facts more fully and in a more helpful vein to the taxpayer. The favorable example also omits facts that are best left unstated but that are not material (for example, the future possibility that the taxpayer may use the home for personal purposes).

Although you can presume your reader is a sophisticated tax practitioner with the IRS, you should still carefully explain the issue by identifying the Code Section involved, its requirements, and the question at hand. Then you must carefully and convincingly discuss all relevant authority and explain why an analysis of the authority results in a conclusion that your taxpayer's position was the correct one. You should confront any negative authority and explain why it is inapplicable – either that the facts are distinguishable, or that the reasoning in some way should not apply to your taxpayer.

---

**Example 10: Distinguishing Negative Authority**

(Assume the same facts as in Example 9.)

"Although the court disallowed the expense deduction in *Frank Newcombe*, 54 TC 1298 (1970), the facts were substantially different from those of Mr. X. In the *Newcombe* case, the taxpayer's daughter used the home as her principal residence throughout the year. And unlike Mr. X's situation, the taxpayer never rented out the residence to any non-family member while he owned the property. Clearly, the facts in the *Newcombe* case are so materially different from Mr. X's situation as to render the case entirely inapplicable."

---

Frequently, you will find that you can make alternative arguments in support of the taxpayer. You should present all available arguments, even if they require conflicting assumptions. However, do not weaken the case by presenting obviously erroneous or weak arguments. Just make sure you make a clear transition from one argument to the next so that you do not weaken the force of your arguments.

---

**EXAMPLE 11:  Transition Between Two Arguments**

(Assume the same facts as in Examples 9 and 10.)

**(First argument –  application of Code Section 162)**
"The taxpayer is entitled to a deduction under Code Section 162 because the property was rental property. . . .

**(Transition to second argument – application of Code Section 212)**
Even if you find that the taxpayer did not have a valid business reason for the deduction, it should still be allowed under the principle that the property was held for investment . . ."

---

Each taxing authority spells out in its preliminary notice of deficiency some specific information it expects to see in a responding protest letter.  For instance, the IRS indicates in its thirty-day letter that you must include the following information:

- ✓ a statement that the taxpayer wants to appeal the agent's findings,
- ✓ taxpayer's name and address
- ✓ taxpayer's social security number
- ✓ date and symbols of thirty-day letter
- ✓ tax year(s) involved
- ✓ specific items of adjustment with which the taxpayer does not agree
- ✓ statement of facts
- ✓ explanation of the authority on which the taxpayer is relying
- ✓ a declaration that the information submitted in the protest is truthful. The thirty-day letter provides specific language regarding the declaration of truthfulness.

---

**EXAMPLE 12:  Protest Letter**

December 1, 2007

District Director
Internal Revenue Service

    RE:    Mr X
           Soc. Sec. # 111-11-1111
           Form 1040, Year 2005
           Reference # . . . (symbols on thirty-day letter)

Gentlemen:
    Please find enclosed a copy of your letter dated November 20, 2007, (reference #xxxx), which transmitted a copy of your examining officer's report of November 5 covering her examination of the above-referenced taxpayer.  In the report, the examining agent recommended adjustments to Mr. X's taxable income (loss) in the following amounts:

| Year End | Adjustments |
|---|---|
| December 31, 2005 | $20,000 |

    The taxpayer respectfully protests the proposed adjustments based on the arguments stated below.

---

**EXAMPLE 12: Protest Letter (continued)**

**(Facts)**

The facts involved are as follows.  Mr. X purchased residential property in 2000 for $100,000. It is now valued at $500,000.   Since the time of purchase, neither the taxpayer nor his family has ever used the home for personal purposes.  The home has frequently been rented to non-family members since the time of purchase at full rental value.  During the year 2005, the home was listed with a rental agent and efforts were continually made to rent out the home.  However, due to poor weather during the vacation months, the efforts to rent in 2005 were unsuccessful. The home was rented out in both 2006 and 2007.  Mr. X incurred the following expenses for the property's maintenance. . . .

**(Summary Statement of taxpayer's position)**

Mr. X contends that the above detailed expenses are clearly deductible under IRC Section 162(a) as ordinary and necessary expenses incurred in the conduct of its business. . . .

**(Statement of protest and request for hearing)**

Mr. X  therefore, contends that the disallowances made by the examining agent were in error.  Mr. X requests an oral hearing before the regional director of appeals.

**(Declaration)**

The attached protest was prepared by {name} on the basis of information available to him.  All statements contained therein are true and correct to the best of his knowledge and belief.

---

## Letter Ruling Request

There is one last form of communication in which your research may result.  This is a request to the taxing authority for a letter ruling indicating that the taxing authority agrees with the tax position you are seeking.  Such **letter ruling requests** provide the taxpayer with the opportunity to receive comfort from the taxing authority before proceeding with a specific and potentially risky transaction.  Without a favorable ruling, the taxpayer may decide not to engage in the transaction.  (Refer to Chapter Three for a detailed discussion of letter rulings).

The first revenue procedure each year sets forth the pertinent rules with respect to private letter ruling requests to the IRS.  This revenue procedure lists those subjects for which a request is not permitted and those that have additional rules provided in other revenue procedures.  The revenue procedure may also require that certain factual representations be made under penalty of perjury.  In addition, this revenue procedure provides information regarding the fee the IRS charges for a ruling request.  The revenue procedure also discusses the authority of a ruling.

Except as otherwise stated in the applicable revenue procedures, the structure of a ruling request is no different than the other forms of writing discussed in this chapter.  As is often the case, documentary exhibits may be desirable or required to be attached as exhibits to the ruling request.  The ruling request should contain the following:

- ✓ Identification of the taxpayer (name, address, identification numbers)
- ✓ Statement of the facts (reason for the transaction, description of the transaction, copies of any important relevant documents)
- ✓ Ruling requested (statement of the position that the taxpayer seeks to have affirmed by the IRS)
- ✓ Supporting authority (Expect the reader to be a sophisticated tax person. Therefore, you should feel comfortable to freely cite the Code and other applicable authority.)
- ✓ Penalty of perjury declaration
- ✓ Statement of proposed deletions (Because the ruling will be made public, the taxpayer must formally propose those facts to be deleted from any publication.)

---

**EXAMPLE 13:  Letter Ruling Request**

March 1, 2005

Internal Revenue Service
Associate Chief Counsel


Re:     Mr. X
        Social Security Number 111-11-1111

Dear Sir:

    As the representative for the above-referenced taxpayer, certain rulings regarding the Federal income tax consequences of the following proposed transaction are requested as detailed below.

---

---

**EXAMPLE 13:  Letter Ruling Request (continued)**

**(Statement of Facts)**
Taxpayer proposes the following transaction . . .

**(Ruling Requested)**
The taxpayer respectfully requests that: . . .

**(Supporting Authority)**
The rulings requested are supported by the authorities discussed below . . .

**(Declaration)**
Declaration 1.  "To the best knowledge of the taxpayer, no issue with respect to this ruling request is under examination by any Internal Revenue Service office or has been examined for a return year for which the statute of limitations has not yet expired."

**OR**
Declaration 2. "To the best of the taxpayer's and representative's knowledge, the same issue has not been the subject of a prior ruling by the Service."

**OR**
Declaration 3. "Under penalties of perjury, I declare that I have examined this request, including accompanying documents, and to the best of my knowledge and belief, the facts presented in support of the requested ruling are true, correct, and complete."

**(Power of Attorney)**
A power of attorney (Form 2848) is enclosed. . . .

**(Request for conference if ruling is tentatively unfavorable)**
If there is a question about the probability of a favorable ruling, the taxpayer respectfully requests a conference.

---

# ORAL COMMUNICATION

Frequently, the person you are performing research for wants you to communicate your research results orally.  Simply stated, the client wants you to tell her over the phone what you found.  Sometimes clients do not want to incur the additional expense of having you draft a letter.  Or one of the firm's partners wants you to explain to her in person what you found.  This form of communication obviously carries with it a great deal less formality than written communications.  Clearly, you are not going to tell your client that she "may not quote, refer to, or disseminate to others what you tell her . . ."  Rather than repeating the facts, for instance, you probably will move straight to the issue and your conclusion, with a brief description of your reasoning. In these circumstances, the listener will usually ask questions. You should anticipate these questions and be sure to be polite, even if you believe the questions are unsophisticated.

To most effectively communicate your research results orally, first write an office memo to the file.  This will help you organize your research results.  Then call the client or walk into the partner's office.  Your communication should be based on the research results you detail in your office memo.  If you have put together a memorandum, you may be able to quickly answer the question and mention that you would be delighted to provide a copy of a more detailed, well-reasoned memorandum on the subject should the listener care to study it.

It is important to speak in a way that the client can understand.  Do not talk Code sections as you might if talking to a sophisticated colleague.  After some years of practice, tax practitioners often feel comfortable talking in shorthand jargon.  Just as most of us cannot understand complex medical terms, do not expect others to understand tax language.  Instead of impressing people, it is often a pedantic turnoff.  Avoid using terms of art that only another tax person appreciates. Translate the technical discussion into plain English so that your client can understand.  It is not particularly helpful to your career when your client tells a partner that "Jane is brilliant, but I never know what she's talking about."

If you need to make an oral presentation to a group of people, a few additional suggestions may prove helpful.

√    **Be prepared**. This is the most important ingredient to a successful presentation. Know your material very well so that you can not only give your presentation but also answer questions afterward.  Probably the most critical factor in making a good presentation is the self-confidence you attain from knowing you prepared well for the presentation.

√    **Talk without reading your notes.**  Unfortunately, just knowing your subject doesn't guarantee a good presentation.  One of the most common mistakes is to read from a fully written-out script of what you plan to say.  The idea may initially seem wise.  However, the practical result is that you tend to read your notes, which immediately turns off your listeners.  Instead, prepare your presentation in outline form, without full sentences.  That way, you have a helpful tool to enable you to remember the points you want to make without the temptation or ability to simply read your presentation.

√    **Establish eye contact.**  The old adage that you should find a place on the back wall to look at while giving a talk is bad advice.  When giving a presentation, you need to engage your listeners.  There is no better way to do so than to frequently and meaningfully establish eye contact with each of your listeners.  Don't give your presentation to just one or two people.  That makes everyone feel uncomfortable.  Do share your eye contact with as many as you can.  But make it meaningful.  Quickly shifting from one person to another is distracting.  So talk to one person for a few seconds, then move to someone else in another part of the room.  Try to continue this during the entire presentation, and you will maximize the possibility that everyone will follow your discussion the entire time.

√    **Consider presentation aids**.  Think about whether there is something additional you can do to make the presentation more interesting or educational.  Consider using a slide presentation or an overhead projector to highlight your key points.  Or, illustrate your points using a chalkboard or flipchart.  Handouts are also useful, but be aware of their inherent dangers.  You may want to provide a copy of an outline or white paper to the audience.  However, when your audience is looking down at your handouts, they aren't looking at you.  Therefore, you run the risk of losing your audience unless you use your handouts carefully.

√    **Other suggestions.**  Other obvious and yet difficult to put into practice suggestions are:

- Project your voice so that everyone in the room can hear you.
- Speak at a pace that allows your audience to follow you.
- Try not to fill your natural silent gaps with "ums" or other similar sounds.
- Avoid fidgeting or moving unnaturally. However, do use your hands for occasional emphasis.

# CHAPTER SUMMARY

Finding the answer to the research question is only half of your responsibility. Once you find the answer, you must effectively communicate it. Communications vary depending upon who and what generated the need to research. The different types of communications are:

- Internal or external
- Oral or written
- Formal or informal
- Educational or persuasive

Internal communications are those that generally remain sequestered within your office or company. Typically, this takes the form of an office memo. External communications are made to parties outside of your office or company – the client (client letter) or a taxing authority (protest letter or letter ruling request).

Each of these written types of communication differs in purpose and, therefore, style. External written communications tend to require more formality than the internal office memo. The purpose of the office memo is to create a record of your research so that either you or someone else in your firm can go back, and with relative ease, learn all the important aspects of the research. The fundamental purpose of the client letter is to educate the client about your research findings. The purpose of both the protest letter and the letter ruling request is to persuade the taxing authority that your client's position is correct.

Whatever form your written communication takes, the basic format and structure remain the same. You must always state the relevant facts. This then leads to the need to identify the Code section at issue and the research question. Your conclusion and the supporting reasoning follow.

You will also find that you must communicate your research results orally. It is important that such communications are made after you have carefully written an office memo detailing your research results. Then the office memo can serve as a reminder of what you wish to communicate orally.

When communicating your knowledge of a tax subject or the results of your tax research to a group of people, it is important to be fully prepared and speak using an outline of your points. You want to avoid reading your presentation. Establish good eye contact with your entire audience and consider using presentation aids to enhance your presentation.

## PROBLEMS

### *KEY CONCEPTS* (1-10)

1.    Define and give an example of the meaning of the following concepts and terms:

      a.    Office memo
      b.    Client opinion letter
      c.    Protest letter
      d.    Private letter ruling request
      e.    FIRAC

2.    What are the various types of internal and external written communications?  What factors determine which type of communication is most appropriate?  Why?

3.    What is the purpose of an office memo?  List the main elements.

4.    What are the main elements of a client opinion letter?   Why are client letters the riskiest form of communication for the tax practitioner?

5.    What is the purpose of a protest letter?  How does the purpose impact the style you use in writing one?

6.    What factors must you consider when making an oral presentation?

7.    What is a white paper?

8.    What is the difference between a long form opinion letter and a short form opinion letter?

9.    When would you advise a taxpayer to seek a letter ruling?

10.    Describe two conditions or qualifications in an opinion letter.

## PRACTICAL APPLICATIONS (11-18)

11.     You are reviewing a subordinate's draft client opinion letter. The first sentence states the following:

        "This is in response to your request that we review the tax implications of the transaction you described to us in recent telephone conversations." The letter then begins to address the research findings. In what ways would you correct this?

12.     You are reviewing a subordinate's draft client opinion letter. The first sentence states the following:

        "Our opinion is accurate beyond a reasonable doubt. You may be assured that the positions stated herein will always be correct."

        Please comment.

13.     New University has come to you seeking advice regarding its obligations to withhold Social Security taxes for the students it employs on a part-time basis. Currently, the university allows any student, full- or part-time, to work for the university no more than hours a week. Prepare an opinion letter to the chief financial officer reporting your research results.

14.     Prepare and present an oral presentation to your class providing an overview of a particularly interesting Code section. Some possible ideas include:

        • Home mortgage interest deductions
        • Casualty losses
        • Treatment of stock options and their exercise
        • Treatment of ministers
        • Tax benefit doctrine
        • Educational expense deductions
        • Parachute payments
        • Hobby losses
        • Bad debt deductions
        • Substantiation rules for charitable contributions
        • Medical expenses
        • Child support payments

- Treatment of gain on sale of home
- Involuntary conversions
- U.S. taxation of citizens residing in another country
- Tax preparer penalties
- Business start-up costs

15. Prepare and present an oral presentation to your class on a recent interesting court decision.

16. Prepare and present an oral presentation to your class on a recent interesting letter ruling.

17. Prepare and present an oral presentation to your class on a recent interesting revenue ruling.

18. Prepare and present an oral presentation to your class on a matter involving pending tax legislation.


## INTEGRATED CASE STUDIES (19-34)

*The following case studies are the same as those at the end of the previous chapters. Use the knowledge and skills you have learned through this chapter to address the case studies. If previously assigned a case study, use your work in Chapters One through Six.*

19. *Case Study A - Disability Payments*

Mr. Top received $25,000 in disability payments while he was recuperating from heart surgery. Mr. Top, age 65, is an employee with a large corporation providing general business consulting services. The corporation has always paid for the disability insurance of its employees. Mr. Top telecommutes and works out of the home. From further conversations with the client, you discover that only $10,000 of the disability payments received by Mr. Top arose from a disability policy paid for by his employer under a group disability policy. The remaining $15,000 was paid on a separate policy that Mr. Top purchased some time ago. Mr. Top has been paying semiannual premiums on the separate individual policy. You are asked to prepare Mr. Top's return.

   a.    Write a memo to your supervisor communicating your research results.

   b.    Write a letter to Mr. Top communicating your research results.

20.     *Case Study B - Bonus Payments*

Sue is 30 years old and is president and a 51% shareholder of C Corporation.  She informs you that C Corporation has 10 shareholders, all unrelated. Other than herself, no shareholder owns more than 10% of the company's stock. Sue plans to recommend to the board of directors that it authorize the payment of a bonus to hers and three other top employees. She asks you, as the company's tax advisor, to counsel her on what the company needs to do so that the company can get a deduction for the planned bonus payments.

After further discussions with Sue, you learn that the company's business is commercial real estate development. The company had net revenues last year totaling $10,000,000. The company is an accrual basis taxpayer, and each of the intended recipients employs the cash basis method of tax accounting.  She would prefer the bonuses to actually be paid next year, but deducted by the company this year.  One of the intended recipients is Sue's executive assistant, who is not currently a shareholder in the company. Sue would like the bonus to equal 100% of each recipient's current salary. The current salaries of the intended recipients are as follows:

| | |
|---|---|
| President | $500,000 |
| Executive Assistant | $100,000 |
| Chief Financial Officer | $300,000 |
| Vice President of Operations | $250,000 |

The CFO and vice president of operations are shareholders in the company, each owning 10% of the stock.

Sue had indicated to you that she believes the annual salaries are comparable or, perhaps, a little on the high side when compared to her company's competitors.  You also learn that the company regularly pays out dividends to shareholders and plans to continue to do so.

a.      Write a memo to your supervisor communicating your research results.

b.      Write a letter to the company communicating your research results.

c.      Assume the company proceeds with Sue's plan and declares the bonuses before year-end.  The following year, the company pays the bonuses on March 1. Your firm prepares the tax return, deducting the bonus payments.  The IRS, after an extensive audit, disallows the entire bonus deduction, taking the position that the bonuses were entirely "unreasonable." Write a protest letter to the IRS on behalf of the company.

21.    *Case Study C – Changing Headquarters*

The taxpayer, a calendar-year corporation, wants to change its company's headquarters that currently consisting of a 10-story building. The company owns the building outright. The taxpayer has identified some potentially more suitable properties. One of the possible properties is a single-story building on a large attractive lot. The other property consists of a two building complex, with retail shops on the ground floor of one building and residential rental property in a portion of the other building.

After further discussions with the client and a review of relevant documents, you discover the following additional facts: Each of the new properties has a fair market value that slightly exceeds that of the current 10-story building. The taxpayer would demolish the single-story building if the company purchases that property. The company would then build a specially designed building on the lot. The sellers of both properties appear to be interested in entering an exchange transaction whereby the company's property would be exchanged for one of the other properties.

After many discussions with the taxpayer, the company decided to exchange its existing property for the retail and residential building complex. You assisted the company in structuring the exchange. Both parties used a "middleman" corporation, to whom the properties were to be initially conveyed. The agreement with the middleman included the requirement that the taxpayer sell its property to the middleman, and then, within 45 days of the initial closing, formally identify which of the two new properties it intended to acquire. The identified property was also to be sold to the middleman corporation. The corporation would then transfer title to the taxpayer within 180 days after the date of the initial closing.

Unfortunately, the transaction has not proceeded as planned. The taxpayer transferred its property to the middleman, receiving its FMV of $10,000,000 in cash. The company formally identified the property with the retail and residential building complex as the property it intended to acquire. Unfortunately, one week before the 180 days was up, the seller of the property backed out of the arrangement. The taxpayer is certain it will not be able to identify and cause the transfer of other suitable property within the time limit.

Taxpayer's basis in the ten-story building is only $2,000,000. The company is concerned that it will now have to report the $8,000,000 in gain.

a.      Write a memo to your supervisor communicating your research results.

b.      Write a letter to the taxpayer communicating your research results.


22.     *Case Study D – Damage Payments to Dentist*

Dr. Tooth is a 40-year-old dentist in Small Town, USA. He graduated from dental school five years ago and has had a thriving practice ever since. At the end of last year, however, Dr. Tooth had an ugly billing disagreement with a patient. The patient, a well-known wealthy entrepreneur, in retribution, maliciously spread a rumor that Dr. Tooth was a carrier of a serious infectious disease. This rumor destroyed Dr. Tooth's patient base, as most of his patients quickly switched dentists. As a result of the stress of losing his business, the cruel gossip that resulted from the rumor, and the financial strain caused by this situation, Dr. Tooth began to suffer from severe migraine headaches, loss of appetite, and significant facial twitches. Dr. Tooth sued the patient for defamation and intentional infliction of emotional distress. He won a jury verdict and has since recovered $3,600,000 in damages from the patient.

This award was broken into the following categories:

  i.      $1,000,000 lost wages. This was calculated on the basis that, in addition to the one year of wages lost since the date of the defamation, Dr. Tooth has lost the ability to earn future wages in Small Town.
  ii.     $50,000 reimbursement for medical expenses incurred in consulting a neurologist, internist, and psychologist.
  iii.    $20,000 for future medical expenses anticipated.
  iv.     $30,000 reimbursement for attorney's fees paid.
  v.      $2,000,000 in punitive damages. The jury determined that the action of the patient was so malicious and heinous that the patient should be monetarily punished for his actions.
  vi.     $300,000 for pain and suffering.
  vii.    $200,000 to compensate Dr. Tooth for the emotional distress he suffered.


Through your interview with the client, you discover that he had to pay his attorney

$50,000, which was paid out of the award.

a.      Write a memo to your supervisor communicating your research results.

b.      Write a letter to Dr. Tooth communicating your research results.

c.      Assume that a previous tax advisor signed the client's return reporting none of the damages. Client has just received a letter from the IRS indicating that Dr. Tooth owes substantial taxes on the amount he should have included in income. The IRS's position is that all of the damages award should have been included in gross income. Write a protest letter to the IRS on behalf of Dr. Tooth.

23.    *Case Study E – Housing Expenses*

Ellie Executive lives in Florida with her family in a home bequeathed to her by her parents when they passed away. This year her employer assigned her to a position in London. The assignment is for a minimum of four years. Because she grew up in the house, Ellie would like to keep it and rent it out. There is no mortgage on the home, so renting will create a positive cash flow situation for her. Her employer will be providing her with a housing allowance to cover her London housing costs. Ellie believes the house has a FMV of at least $500,000. Ellie wants to make sure that if she ends up selling it, she will not have any taxable income from the sale. She has asked for your guidance.

After talking with Ellie Executive further, you become aware of the following additional facts:

Ellie is not certain what she and her husband will do at the end of the four-year London assignment. She may return to Florida but she also might take another international assignment, since her children are now adults. Ellie plans to continue paying the following expenses while the house is rented:

   * $400 a month for a weekly gardener
   * $500 a month for a weekly housecleaner
   * Approximately $200 a month in utility and maintenance expenses (electricity, garbage, and water)

Ellie anticipates that she can lease the house fully furnished for $2,500 a month.

Ellie's parents died in 1991 when the FMV of the house was $300,000.  They purchased the house in 1950 for $10,000. Her parents spent a total of $20,000 in home improvement costs. Ellie substantially redecorated the house in 1992, spending $65,000 in renovating two bedrooms, two bathrooms, and replacing the roof. In addition, Ellie paid $5,000 for a new perimeter fence and $10,000 to a landscape architect to redesign the yard.

a.      Write a memo to your supervisor communicating your research results.

b.      Write a letter to Ellie communicating your research results.

24.     *Case Study F – Retirement Contributions*

Tom Speeder is a new client.  From reviewing his client questionnaire, you were able to gather the following facts. He is 50 years old and was recently hired as a middle-level manager with a car manufacturer.  Tom's salary for the current year is $200,000.  In his initial meeting with you, Tom indicates that he would like you to look into an idea he has that will help him maximize his investment portfolio. He tells you that his new company offers its employees the ability to participate in a Section 401(k) plan. He believes it would be to his benefit to maximize his contribution to the company's 401(k) plan that provides for matching employer contributions up to $3,000 annually.  The plan provides for a maximum annual employee contribution of no greater than that provided by the IRC.

It is January, and Tom has indicated to you that he would like to accelerate the maximum contributions to the plan by contributing his entire monthly paycheck until he funds the entire amount.  He believes that such an arrangement will maximize the growth of his portfolio since the earnings are tax free from an earlier time frame than if he spreads the contributions out over the year.

After further discussions with Tom, you discover that, in addition to his salary, he receives the following employment benefits:

*       $100,000 group term insurance for which the employer pays the premiums (totaling $200/year)
*       Health insurance, for which the employer pays the $100 in monthly premiums
*       As part of the company's Employee Educational Assistance Plan, tuition payments to a local university for one academic course a year to be chosen by the employee. For the current year, Tom plans to take a course on "Organizational Behavior" that he is interested in and believes will help him better understand his work

environment. The university offers both undergraduate and graduate courses in this subject. Tom may take either one and will wait to determine which is offered at the most convenient time.

a.      Write a memo to your supervisor communicating your research results.

b.      Write a letter to Tom communicating your research results.

c.      Assume that Tom takes a deduction for the educational expenses on his tax return. The IRS has just sent a letter indicating that it will not allow the deduction. Write a protest letter on behalf of the client.

25.    *Case Study G – Golf Ball Business*

Toby Power, a fellow Illinois resident, is a new client. Prior to her telephone call this morning (late November), all you really knew about Toby was that for the past five years she has been earning a living as a respected golfing instructor at a local club. She just called you to discuss a transaction she has entered into. You learn from your initial conversation with her that she and a group of friends formed a corporation for which the group will own 100% of the stock.

The corporation will be in the business of selling golf balls that it guarantees are indestructible and, because they glow in water and shade, cannot be lost. Toby transferred an office building to the corporation in return for her 20% stock ownership interest. Her eight other friends transferred primarily manufacturing equipment and cash for their evenly divided 80% interest. Toby has owned the office building for seven years and currently owes several hundred thousand dollars on two mortgages on the building. She estimates the fair market value of the building is about $1,000,000.

Toby informs you that her previous tax advisor, about whom she has nothing but negative things to say, counseled her that, in order to avoid paying taxes on the transfer of the building to the corporation, she had to also transfer to the corporation a personal promissory note of $100,000. All of this occurred last year. She wants to know if the transaction was handled correctly, or if she needs to worry.

Through further discussions and review of pertinent documents, you discover the following additional facts:

- Toby purchased the office building seven years ago for $500,000. She paid $100,000 in cash and $400,000 using a note (Note A) secured by the property.
- Two years ago, the fair market value of the property escalated to $1,200,000. Toby took out a second mortgage on the property in the amount of $300,000 (Note B). She used the borrowed funds to purchase a vacation home in Nevada.
- At the time of the property's transfer to the corporation, the building's fair market value was $1,000,000, determined by an assessor.
- At the time of the property's transfer to the corporation, Note A had an outstanding balance of $310,000. Note B had a balance of $100,000.
- Toby has made no improvements on the property. She has taken approximately $100,000 in depreciation deductions on her tax return.
- The terms of the promissory note Toby gave to the corporation were that she pay the note off over a period of 20 years, paying a single annual payment in the amount of $6,000 ($5,000 principal; $1,000 interest). The first payment is to be made on the anniversary date of the note – September 1. Toby paid the first installment which was due a few months ago.

a.  Write a memo to your supervisor communicating your research results.

b.  Write a letter to Toby communicating your research results.

c.  Assume that Toby receives a letter from the IRS indicating that it is treating the transaction as including taxable "boot" equal to $100,000. Write a letter to the IRS protesting this finding.

26.  *Case Study H – Private School Expenses*

Mr. and Mrs. Worried, longtime clients, have come to you for help. Their 13-year-old son has recently been expelled from the public junior high school because of severe behavioral problems, culminating in a physical attack on a teacher and threats of future violence. The son has been seeing a psychologist once a week but with no apparent positive results. The Worrieds would like to send their son to a private school that can provide the type of psychological help they believe he needs. The son's psychologist agrees that placement in a special school is imperative if there is ever to be a chance that the son will be a functioning member of society.

The Worrieds tell you that they are concerned because, although they have identified several potential schools, they do not have the financial resources necessary to pay the tuition and other additional costs. Also, their insurance does not cover any of the costs.

However, the Worrieds believe that they may be able to afford the expenses if they can take them as a tax deduction. They ask you for your opinion.

a.      Write a memo to your supervisor communicating your research results.

b.      Write a letter to the Worrieds communicating your research results.

27.     *Case Study I – Deadly Fire*

Early this year, a taxpayer was clearing dry brush from behind his Malibu home in California. He became frustrated with how long it was taking using his clippers. He decided instead to light the brush on fire, believing this would be safe because it was an overcast day. The taxpayer brought out a fire extinguisher in case the fire got out of control. Unfortunately, some wind kicked up and fanned the fire out of control. The fire completed consumed both his house and his neighbor's house. The two children staying in the neighbor's house died of smoke inhalation. The taxpayer was charged with negligent homicide. The trial is pending.

The taxpayer wishes to take a casualty loss deduction for the loss of his house which was worth an estimated $1,000,000 at the time of the fire. The taxpayer purchased the home for $900,000 only six months earlier. Insurance has refused to compensate for the loss under the circumstances. The taxpayer is currently out on bail. He is the brother of one of your very significant clients who has asked you to provide tax advice to the taxpayer.

a.      Write a memo to your supervisor communicating your research results.

b.      Write a letter to taxpayer communicating your research results.

c.      Assume that your firm agreed to sign the return taking the loss deduction. The taxpayer has just received a letter from the IRS indicating that it is disallowing the deduction. Write a letter to the IRS protesting this finding.

28.     *Case Study J – Airline Costs*

A major airline manufacturer was found to be in violation of FAA safety rules and was forced to install additional safety devices in each of its planes within the six months. The airline company projects the cost of this upgrade to be several million dollars, consisting of lost profits while the planes are on the ground, labor costs, and the cost of parts.  In addition, the airline spent $100,000 in attorney's fees in an unsuccessful fight to have the requirement waived. The CFO of the company wishes to know whether any or all of these costs can be deducted.

a.      Write a memo to your supervisor communicating your research results.

b.      Write a letter to the airline communicating your research results.


29.     *Case Study K – Vacation Homes*

Mr. Z owns three homes.  He lives in the San Francisco home full time.  The other two he and his wife vacation in each year.  He is considering replacing the house he has in Palm Springs, California, with another house in the same area.  The new home is a little bigger and has a floor plan he prefers.  The two Palm Springs properties have almost the same fair market value.  Mr. Z would like to know if he can exchange the properties instead of selling the one he has now and then buying the new one.  He has a lot of built-up appreciation in the current Palm Springs home and he doesn't want to have to pay taxes on it.  Someone told him at a cocktail party that he can avoid paying taxes if he does an "exchange."

Mr. Z and his wife own the home outright.  There is no mortgage on the property.  They use the property occasionally.  This last year they vacationed at the home for about two or three weeks – they aren't sure of the exact days.  They have never rented the property and refuse to rent either the old or new property.  They don't need the money and don't like strangers in their house.

Mr. Z explains that he holds each of his vacation homes for two purposes.  One reason is for vacations for him and his wife. Another key reason for owning the homes is for their investment value.  He chooses homes only in areas where he believes there are high appreciation possibilities.


Can Mr. Z take advantage of the tax-free exchange rules in the IRC?  How will you advise him?

a.      Write a memo to your supervisor communicating your research results.

    b.       Write a letter to Mr. and Mrs. Z communicating your research results.

    c.       Assume that Mr. and Mrs. Z exchange properties in accordance with the nonrecognition provisions.  They file a tax return not reflecting any income from this transaction. The Z's receive a letter from the IRS indicating that it is treating the transaction as taxable. Write a letter to the IRS protesting this finding.

30.    *Case Study L – Property Easement*

A developer acquired a parcel of unimproved real property that she would like to develop. Although the land is currently zoned for commercial use, the developer would prefer not to begin development until an adjoining city street is widened.  With a wider street, her development can include a landscaped public entrance and lighting. Without the widening, the development will have only one entrance that is not as accessible or as attractive.

The city plans to widen the street in order to build bike paths, which are now required in its new city plan.  It will be easier for the city to widen the street if it acquires an easement across the developer's property.  The developer is interested in providing this easement to the city.  However, before she acts, the developer would like assurance that she will receive a charitable deduction for the value of the easement.  She has asked you to request a letter ruling on this matter.

    a.       Write a memo to your supervisor communicating your research results.

    b.       Write a letter ruling request on behalf of the developer.

31.   *Case Study M – Interest Payment*

The taxpayer is president of a company. He is very wealthy and has a good deal of assets. He went to Bank 1 in January Yr. 1 to borrow $1,000,000. He used the proceeds of the loan to purchase stock. The loan was secured by the stock purchased. The terms of the loan are that it is an interest only loan, with interest to be paid annually on the anniversary of the loan. The rate is 10% of the principal.

In November Yr. 1, the taxpayer realized that he did not have the liquid funds to pay the $100,000 of interest due in January. He had sufficient assets, but due to the business environment, he determined that the smartest economic move to make would be to borrow the $100,000 rather than to liquidate one of his investments. So he went to Bank 2 and borrowed $100,000. This loan was secured by assets other than his stock and was a regular amortizing loan. Interest was 9%. Upon receipt of the loan proceeds on December 1, Yr. 1, taxpayer deposited the proceeds into his regular checking account in Bank 3. The proceeds remained in the checking account for the entire month of December. The balance of the checking account during the month of December ranged from $100,000 to $115,000.

On January 2, Yr. 2, taxpayer wrote a check from his Bank 3 checking account to Bank 1 in full payment of the interest due. On his tax return for Yr. 2, taxpayer took a deduction of $100,000 as an investment interest expense under Section 163. He had sufficient investment income to cover the deduction.

In your research, you discover that Bank 1 owns 90% of the stock of Bank 2. You are able to talk with the client and learn that he was entirely unaware of the relationship. In fact, the loan documents were entirely different and did not make any reference to any relationship. The IRS has indicated it plans to disallow the interest deduction because the IRS believes it has never actually been paid as is required by the Code. The taxpayer would like you to see what the IRS is talking about and whether it has any ground for its position.

a.      Write a memo to your supervisor communicating your research results.

b.      Write a letter to the taxpayer communicating your research results.

c.      Write a letter to the IRS protesting its findings.

32.     *Case Study N – Racing Car Expenses*

A taxpayer is a partner in an accounting firm.  He has always enjoyed auto racing as a hobby.  Now that his children are grown, he has decided to devote more time to auto racing.  He recently purchased a racing car for $50,000 and has entered several races.  He recently raced in his first competitive race and placed fourth, resulting in winnings of $5,000.  He expects to incur a number of expenses related to his racing: auto maintenance, storage, transportation, and so on.  He would like your advice as to how to proceed so that he can depreciate his car and deduct all of these expenses.

a.      Write a memo to your supervisor communicating your research results.

b.      Write a letter to the taxpayer communicating your research results.

33.     *Case Study O – Retainer Fee*

Big Company paid $100,000 at the beginning of the year to a large law firm to retain its services should they be needed during the course of the year.  The law firm specializes in real estate law and is considered the best firm in this field.  Big Company feared that one of its competitors would engage the law firm. This would prevent Big Company from being able to use the firm's services because of conflict-of-interest rules that preclude a firm from representing different clients with actual or potentially adverse legal interests.  To prevent this, Big engaged the firm and paid the retainer fee.  Occasionally, Big asked the firm to perform legal work in areas where Big's in-house lawyers were not as well equipped.  It is now December, and it is clear that a substantial amount of the initial retainer will not be used to pay for legal services rendered.  The retainer agreement provides in this case that any unused amount shall be returned to Big, with interest, at year-end.

Big Company is a longtime client of yours.  It has asked you to look into whether any of the retainer fee will be deductible to it. It wishes to have this advice before the beginning of next year when it will determine whether to pay another $100,000 retainer to the law firm for the year.

a.      Write a memo to your supervisor communicating your research results.

b.      Write a letter to Big Company communicating your research results.

34.    *Case Study P – Development Costs*

Gobble Corporation purchased 400 acres in Green City to build a private golf course and residences.  The land cost $10,000,000. Gobble planned high quality, large houses that would sell for an average of $700,000.

Gobble believed that the city's general plan allowed for this development.  Gobble spent in excess of $1,000,000 in fees to pay architects and civil engineers for all necessary environmental studies and approvals.  Two years ago, Gobble's development proposal was approved by the city council in a 5-4 vote.

Two months after the vote, the membership in the council changed dramatically.  The major election issue was growth versus no growth.  The city voted strongly for a no-growth slate.  Given the strong community sentiment, the new city council voted to disregard the earlier vote and alter the city's general plan to prohibit such a large development. They decided to defeat the development proposal.

As a result, Gobble sued the city for unreasonably interpreting its planning documents and reversing its initial approval of the project, all to the grave detriment of Gobble.  Litigation has consumed almost two years and has cost a total of $500,000.

Gobble's CFO has come to you to help with its tax return preparation.  Gobble would like to deduct all the costs incurred in this transaction, including the $1,000,000 paid for the land acquisition.

a.    Write a memo to your supervisor communicating your research results.

b.    Write a letter to Gobble communicating your research results.

c.    Assume that Gobble takes a deduction for all the costs.  Gobble receives a letter from the IRS indicating that it is disallowing the entire deduction. Write a letter to the IRS protesting this finding.

# THE AUDIT PROCESS

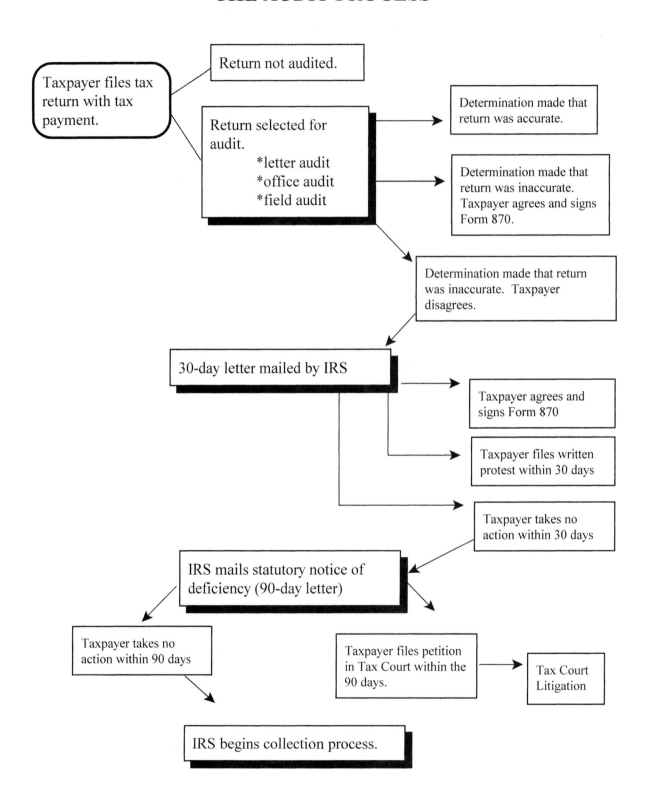

Taxpayer files tax return with tax payment.

Return not audited.

Return selected for audit.
*letter audit
*office audit
*field audit

Determination made that return was accurate.

Determination made that return was inaccurate. Taxpayer agrees and signs Form 870.

Determination made that return was inaccurate. Taxpayer disagrees.

30-day letter mailed by IRS

Taxpayer agrees and signs Form 870

Taxpayer files written protest within 30 days

Taxpayer takes no action within 30 days

IRS mails statutory notice of deficiency (90-day letter)

Taxpayer takes no action within 90 days

Taxpayer files petition in Tax Court within the 90 days.

Tax Court Litigation

IRS begins collection process.

# CHAPTER EIGHT

# OVERVIEW OF TAX PROCEDURE

## *EXPECTED LEARNING OUTCOMES*

- Understand the voluntary nature of federal tax reporting
- Appreciate the basic tax return filing requirements
- Understand the IRS audit and appeals process, refund rights, and generally applicable statutes of limitation
- Appreciate significant IRS powers of summons, levy, and lien
- Recognize available court forums and their benefits and detriments
- Identify tax penalty and interest provisions
- Recognize and maintain available privileges

## *CHAPTER OUTLINE*

- Overview
- Administration of the Federal Tax Laws
- Voluntary Compliance by the Taxpayer – The Tax Return
- Compliance Verification – The IRS Audit Process
- Appeal of Adverse Audit Determination
- Refund Claims
- IRS Collections
- Federal Penalty and Interest Provisions
- Privileged Communications
- Chapter Summary
- Problems

## OVERVIEW

Throughout this text we have emphasized the importance of fully understanding and appreciating how an answer may be found from the variety of primary and other tax authority comprising federal and state tax laws. Research questions do not typically arise in a vacuum but rather result from a variety of communications taking place between the tax advisor and others. Whether the tax practitioner is engaged in preparing a tax return, rendering an opinion, or representing the taxpayer in a tax controversy before the IRS or the courts, the fundamental issue remains the same.  Namely, a well-trained practitioner must always use good, professional judgment and keep at hand all of the technical skills he or she possesses in best representing the taxpayer's interests.

Most tax research determinations ultimately involve taking a particular reporting position on a tax return. This tax reporting position may be audited by the IRS, which may actively seek to defeat the best intentioned plans of the taxpayer. Like any other document, the way in which a return is filed, its timeliness, and proper submission are all important matters that bear on the overall professionalism of the tax practitioner and the persuasiveness of the tax return positions taken. In other words, a tax practitioner may be an expert tax researcher but fall down badly in the process of preparing and filing a tax return, thereby causing great harm to the client.

☛ **Ultimately, a tax return will be filed reflecting the research position taken.**

Understanding the nuances of proper return preparation and filing and the taxpayer's procedural rights and remedies are critical factors in the event that the IRS disagrees with the taxpayer's reporting position on one or more issues.  Although the results of your research may suggest that you have arrived at a correct result favorable to the taxpayer at a particular point in time, years later, the IRS often plays the role of an adverse party, intent on scrutinizing each detail of your earlier determination in order to overturn the reporting position taken.  Recognizing that the IRS, while often helpful, is an adversary subject to specific ground rules will assist you in better representing your client's interests.

☛ **When the IRS disagrees with a return position, it is important to understand the taxpayer's rights.**

This chapter explains the basics regarding the IRS role in administering the provisions of the Internal Revenue Code and other federal tax laws.  Specific rules apply governing the proper filing of all federal tax returns and payment of associated tax liabilities, and this chapter specifically spells out the basic requirements for properly filing a federal income tax return and making appropriate tax payments. However, because the area of federal tax procedure and practice is voluminous, this text endeavors only to summarize such matters.  The IRS audit and appeals process is also discussed, as is the basic procedure for a taxpayer to seek a refund claim and the statute of limitations provisions that apply to limit the time period during which the taxpayer may generally be subject to audit liability or make refund claims.

The process of audit examination is fraught with taxpayer risks but also based on established principles of due process. Understanding the various procedural options available to the taxpayer by way of extensions of time, and appellate rights, including appropriate court selection and potential remedies via compromise offers, are key to a successful result in practicing before the IRS. Furthermore, understanding possible penalty and interest provisions may result in greatly diminishing the adverse financial effects of unexpected tax return liabilities. Finally, throughout these processes, the practitioner must always bear in mind the confidential nature of client and practitioner communications and tax return filings, and the need to preserve and maintain all available privileges that may apply. This chapter discusses the basics regarding all of these issues.

☛ **Successful practice before the IRS requires an understanding of procedural options.**

## ADMINISTRATION OF THE FEDERAL TAX LAWS

The United States Treasury Department is charged with the responsibility of implementing and enforcing the federal tax laws embodied in the Internal Revenue Code. [IRC §7801(a)] The **secretary of the Treasury** Department, as overseer of the IRS, delegates this responsibility to the **Internal Revenue Service commissioner** who, in turn, is appointed by the president of the United States, with the advice and consent of the Senate. [IRC §7802(a)] The commissioner is appointed to a renewable five-year term.

☛ **The U.S. Treasury Department is responsible for implementing the IRC.**

After substantial public debate and congressional testimony regarding perceived abuses by the IRS in enforcing the mandates of the United States tax system, on July 22, 1998, President Clinton signed into law the **Internal Revenue Service Restructuring and Reform Act of 1998** (the "1998 Reform Act"), which anticipated significant change in both the mission and structure of the Internal Revenue Service. The following Senate Committee excerpt from the 1998 Reform Act is particularly informative:

☛ **The 1998 Reform Act significantly restructured the IRS.**

*...The Committee believes that a well-run IRS is critical to the operation of our tax system. Public confidence in the IRS must be restored so that our system of voluntary compliance will not be compromised. The Committee believes that most Americans are willing to pay their fair share of taxes, and that public confidence in the IRS is key to maintaining that willingness.*

*...The Committee...agrees that fundamental change in IRS management and oversight is essential. The Committee believes that a new management structure that will bring greater expertise in needed areas, and more focus and continuity will help the IRS to become an efficient, responsive, and respected agency that acts appropriately in carrying out its functions...*

The 1998 Reform Act directed the IRS to revise its mission statement to provide an emphasis on "serving the public and meeting the needs of the taxpayers." Its previous mission was:

*...to collect the proper amount of tax revenue at the least cost; serve the public by continually improving the quality of our products and services; and perform in a manner warranting the highest degree of public confidence in our integrity and fairness.*

In September 1998, the IRS released its revised mission statement as required by the 1998 Reform Act. The new statement provides that the mission of the IRS is to:

*...provide America's taxpayers top-quality service by helping them understand and meet their tax responsibilities and by applying the tax law with integrity and fairness to all.*

☞ **The 1998 Reform Act resulted in a new, more service-oriented mission for the IRS.**

The new mission statement deliberately emphasizes taxpayer service and does not specifically mention tax collection or law enforcement. While the revised mission statement will not directly change taxpayers' rights or the overall functioning of the IRS, it signals an intent to focus on improved relationships with taxpayers and their advisors.

The 1998 Reform Act also required the IRS commissioner to restructure the IRS in order to improve its orientation toward assisting taxpayers. Prior to the 1998 Reform Act, the IRS was a three-tiered organization comprised of a national office, regional offices and district offices.  The offices were structured on geographical grounds. The national office developed the national IRS policies which were administered at the regional and district levels.  Most taxpayer filings were made at the regional offices while district offices conducted audits and performed other administrative and collection duties.

The 1998 Reform Act directed the IRS commissioner to either eliminate or substantially modify the three-tier structure and replace it with a structure organized around particular groups of taxpayers with similar needs. Accordingly, the IRS commissioner identified four taxpayer types: small businesses, the self-employed, large and mid-sized business and tax-exempt organizations, and wage and investment plans. Each of these taxpayer groups has an operating division devoted to "end-to-end" service of their needs.

In addition, the 1998 Reform Act provided for the establishment within the Treasury Department of an **Oversight Board** to oversee the IRS in the administration, management, conduct, direction and supervision of the application of the revenue laws. Among other responsibilities, the board reviews and approves the strategic plans of the IRS, including its revised organizational structure.  The Oversight Board is to consist of nine members, six of whom are appointed by the president and who are not federal employees. The other members include the secretary of the Treasury, the IRS commissioner, and a full-time IRS employee.

**The 1998 Reform Act resulted in a revision of the IRS internal structure.**

**An Oversight Board oversees the administration of the IRS.**

In addition to the commissioner, the key leadership of the IRS has historically included the **chief counsel** who is the chief law officer for the IRS and acts as the legal advisor to the commissioner, furnishing legal opinions to assist in the preparation of rulings and proposed legislation. The chief counsel is appointed by the president and reports both to the commissioner and to the Treasury general counsel.

The 1998 Reform Act provided for additional important IRS positions, including:

> ▸ **Treasury Inspector General for Tax Administration** Appointed by the president with advice and consent of the Senate. The Inspector is charged with conducting independent audits and investigations relating to Treasury operations to promote efficiency and detect and deter fraud.

☛ **A Treasury inspector general audit Treasury operations to detect and deter fraud.**

> ▸ **National Taxpayer Advocate**. Appointed by the commissioner to assist taxpayers in resolving problems with the IRS, identify areas in which taxpayers have problems dealing with the IRS, propose changes in the IRS administrative practices, and identify potential legislative changes that may help reduce these problems.

> ▸ Taxpayers can request a **taxpayer assistance order (TAO)** if the taxpayer is suffering or will suffer a **significant hardship** as a result of IRS actions. A significant hardship occurs when there is an immediate threat of adverse action, there has been a delay of more than 30 days in resolving the taxpayer's account problems, and the taxpayer will incur significant costs or suffer irreparable harm if relief is not granted.

☛ **Taxpayers may request a taxpayer assistance order if the IRS actions are causing significant hardship.**

## Practitioner Observation

Kirk Paxson, Attorney,
Tax Exempt & Government Entities
Internal Revenue Service

*"When dealing with the Internal Revenue Service, understanding the procedural process is as important as having a well researched position. A tax practitioner may have done an excellent job in researching a particular position, but failing to know how or at what juncture to present that position to the IRS can be detrimental to the client. For example, where the IRS and the practitioner do not agree on the outcome of an audit, when should the practitioner submit his or her position to the IRS Exam Agent? The answer is one of common sense -- as soon as possible so that the IRS can fully understand the client's position. However, there may be instances where for strategic reasons, or due to a clash of personalities, the practitioner may wish to wait to take the case to Appeals. In any event, knowledge of tax procedure as well as tax research is imperative to providing effective tax advice to your clients."*

## VOLUNTARY COMPLIANCE BY THE TAXPAYER – THE TAX RETURN

In marked contrast to many other countries' systems of taxation, the United States tax system is one based on the voluntary compliance of the taxpayer.

### Requirements of a Tax Return

Under the U.S. system of voluntary compliance, the Code requires the taxpayer to self-assess tax liability. The principal tool in this process is the tax return. [IRC §6011] Each major category of taxpayers reports tax information using a return specifically designed for that type of taxpayer or for the type of income, deduction, or credit reported. For example, to report taxable income for each year for federal income tax purposes, individual taxpayers are required to file a tax return on IRS Form 1040, with accompanying specific IRS schedules or taxpayer statements included. Likewise, corporate taxpayers file their annual return information on IRS Form 1120, with accompanying forms.   In addition to federal income tax returns, the Code requires the filing of appropriate estate and gift tax returns, excise tax returns, wage statements, and so on. Not all of the filing requirements relate directly to taxes owing. For example, in order to bolster voluntary compliance, third-party payers of interest and dividends are under a separate and independent duty to file a variety of  information returns, as are pension plans and other parties who are not necessarily directly liable for tax payments.

Pursuant to the United States voluntary tax reporting system, it is incumbent upon taxpayers to file, on a timely basis, all appropriate tax returns. In other words, it is not the responsibility of the IRS to ensure that the taxpayer is provided with the correct forms to file or to alert the taxpayer of relevant filing deadlines. Generally, in order to consider a return filed, the following must be satisfied:

☞ **Taxpayers are responsible for filing appropriate returns under the voluntary compliance system of the United States.**

- ✓    The tax return must be filed using the correct form. [IRC §6011(a)]
- ✓    The return must include sufficient information to compute the tax liability. [IRC §6611(g)]
- ✓    The return must be properly signed under penalty of perjury.

Understandably, the IRS receives thousands of returns each year that are defectively filed, unsigned, or are otherwise deficient in some regard.  A return will not be considered filed if it simply includes the taxpayer's name and address and incomplete information. Nor will a return be considered filed that states that failure to supply the pertinent information is due to an assertion of the taxpayer's "self-incrimination" privilege. [See, for example, *United States v. Sullivan,* 274 US 259 (1927).]  The federal prison population includes many individuals who confuse the voluntary compliance system with an outright constitutional or other privilege to simply avoid declaring or paying federal taxes.

In order to be considered appropriately filed, federal income tax returns must be signed under penalty of perjury in accordance with relevant Treasury regulations. [IRC §6061-§6063] Treasury regulations require that, on an individual return, the individual taxpayer must be the signatory. When the taxpayer is a minor who is unable or legally incompetent to sign the return, the minor's parent or legal guardian must sign on the minor's behalf. On corporate returns, the Code provides that the president, vice president, treasurer, or an authorized officer must sign the return. Partnership returns must be signed by one of the partners.

**In most circumstances, a complete return must be signed by the taxpayer.**

Joint individual tax returns must be signed by both spouses, unless one is too ill to sign. In such a case, the other spouse may sign on behalf of the ill spouse, with a notation indicating whether the signing spouse is the husband or wife.

In only limited cases may someone sign a return for the taxpayer. These include times when the person is indisposed due to illness or is outside the country for at least 60 days prior to the return due date. [Treas. Reg. §1.6012-1(a)(5)] When an agent signs the return, a power of attorney (IRS Form 2848) must be filed with the return.

In most circumstances, Treasury regulations require the return to include a Social Security number (SSN) or taxpayer identification number (TIN). Individuals use their Social Security numbers, while entities must use the taxpayer identification numbers assigned to them by the IRS. (TINs are obtained by filing the IRS Form SS-4 upon or shortly after the entity is formed or commences business operations.)

**The return must usually include a Social Security number or taxpayer identification number.**

Two of the key incentives to the taxpayer for ensuring that tax returns are appropriately filed include:

- Commencing the appropriate **statute of limitations** provisions governing the time period within which the IRS may assess a tax deficiency;

- Avoiding failure to file and other penalties and interest costs that may arise from the taxpayer's failure to file appropriate tax returns and/or pay taxes otherwise due.

General rules regarding the statute of limitations and penalty and interest provisions are addressed later in this chapter.

## How and When the Federal Income Tax Return Must Be Filed

The due date for a federal income tax return depends on the type of tax return involved. Absent appropriate extension filings, calendar-year individual taxpayers must file their tax return on or before April 15 of the year following the tax year. Corporate returns are due one month earlier, on the fifteenth day of the third month following the calendar or fiscal year close. [IRC §6072] When the due date for a return falls on a weekend day or a legal holiday, generally, filing may be made on the next day that is not a weekend day or legal holiday. For example, if April 15 is a Saturday, the due date for calendar-year individual taxpayer returns is the following Monday, April 17. [IRC §7503]

The Code provides for a "reasonable extension of time" for filing a Federal income tax return, not to exceed six months unless the taxpayer is abroad. [IRC §6081] The IRS grants extensions only if the taxpayer appropriately files a proper request for extension prior to the return due date. There are two types of extension requests: automatic and discretionary. By filing IRS Form 4868, individuals are entitled to an automatic four-month extension from the April 15 deadline, making August 15 the due date for the return. Individuals may request an additional discretionary two-month (October 15) extension by filing IRS Form 2688. Similarly, corporations may receive an automatic six-month filing deadline extension by filing IRS Form 7004.

Generally, the tax return is considered filed on the date the return is received by the IRS. However, when the receipt by the IRS occurs after the return's due date, the return will be considered timely filed if the mailing envelope has a postmark date that falls within the required period for filing and the return is deposited in the mail in the United States in an envelope with proper postage and that is properly addressed to the appropriate IRS office. The IRS has designated several courier services for which the "timely mailed, timely filed"

☛ **Taxpayers must pay close attention to return due dates and extension possibilities.**

☛ **Practice Tip**:

*The IRS occasionally loses or misplaces otherwise properly filed tax returns. Because of the importance of assuring that tax returns are filed on a timely basis, it is advisable to mail returns utilizing certified mailing, return receipt requested, noting the certified number on the tax return itself. This procedure enables the taxpayer to document the timely filing of returns with appropriate IRS offices.*

rules will also apply.

The exact date when a return is considered to be filed becomes relevant when there is a possible statute of limitations issue. IRC §7502 and its underlying regulations provide more detailed guidance on this issue.

Taxpayers are now able to file their returns electronically and, for certain types of tax returns, telephonically. The Senate Committee Report (adopted by the Conference Committee) of the 1998 Reform Act states:

> . . .the policy of Congress is to promote paperless filing, with a long range goal of providing for the filing of at least 80 percent of all tax returns in electronic form by the year 2007. . . .

> The Committee believes that the implementation of a comprehensive strategy to encourage electronic filing of tax and information returns holds significant potential to benefit taxpayers and makes the IRS returns processing function more efficient. For example, the error rate associated with processing paper tax returns is approximately 20 percent, half of which is attributable to the IRS and half to error in taxpayer data. Because electronically-filed returns usually are prepared using computer software programs with built-in accuracy checks, undergo pre-screening by the IRS, and experience no key punch errors, electronic returns have an error rate of less than one percent. . . . Senate Committee Report No. 105-174, Act Sec. 2001.

☞ **Electronic filing provides a more efficient system for the IRS.**

Currently, because a signature is required, even though the taxpayer may submit a return electronically, the taxpayer must also submit a paper form [IRS Form 8453] with the taxpayer's signature and other relevant forms (e.g., a W-2 annual wage statement). In the 1998 Reform Act, Congress recognized that this procedure does not necessarily provide for maximum efficiency to the taxpayer and may also create confusion as to when an electronic return is actually filed. Consequently, the 1998 Reform Act requires the secretary of the Treasury to develop procedures to eliminate the need to file a paper form with the taxpayer's signature, and in the meantime, to provide for alternative methods of signing returns. With respect to the issue of a filing date for electronically filed returns, the 1998 Reform Act authorizes the IRS to issue regulations that apply the current filing date rules for paper to electronically filed returns.

## Payment of Taxes

The taxpayer must pay the entire tax liability stated on the tax return by the due date of the return, without regard to any extension. [IRC §6151]  Therefore, the return must include payment for any tax liability unpaid at the time of the filing.  This is the total tax liability less any amount withheld or previously paid in estimated tax payments.  Interest begins to run from the last day the return is due on any amount of tax unpaid.  Of course, the Code and Treasury regulations also provide for much earlier due dates for, among other items,  deposits of estimated taxes and wage withholdings, which carry their own respective severe penalties for failures to meet such deadlines.

**Full payment must accompany a complete tax return.**

The IRS may grant extensions to pay a tax "for a reasonable period not to exceed 6 months," or a longer period for a taxpayer outside the country and 12 months for estate tax due.  [IRC §6161] To request an extension for payment, the taxpayer must file an application for extension in accordance with the regulations before the due date of the payment.  Such application must show that immediate payment would cause "undue hardship" to the taxpayer and must include financial data supporting this claim. [Treas. Reg. §1.6161-1] If the extension is granted, the IRS may require the taxpayer to pay the liability in installments with interest.

**Extensions for payment may be granted when "undue hardship" can be shown.**

## Confidentiality of the Tax Return

Generally, taxpayer returns are confidential documents between the taxpayer and IRS.  [IRC §6103]  However, in certain situations, returns and return information may be disclosed to other federal agencies under certain conditions or any state agency charged with administering state tax laws to the extent such disclosure is necessary to administer those laws.  In addition, a taxpayer's return may be disclosed to a person with a "material interest" as defined in IRC §6103.  For example, federal bankruptcy tax rules also provide circumstances in which one taxpayer (the bankruptcy estate) may obtain access to another taxpayer's return (the bankrupt taxpayer).

Other exceptions to the general confidentiality rule include possible provision to Congressional committees.  Disclosure of taxpayer return information falling outside these exceptions may result in significant fines (up to $5,000) as well as imprisonment.  Federal employees who illegally disclose return information may face criminal charges.  [IRC §7213]  Likewise, the Code prohibits tax return preparers from disclosing any return information.  [IRC §7216]  Notwithstanding the confidential status accorded tax returns under federal tax laws, it is fairly common for taxpayers to voluntarily provide copies of tax returns or tax return information to third parties, such as lenders.

The 1998 Reform Act requires these confidentiality rules be explained in any instruction booklet sent out with individual income tax forms.  In addition, the act requires the Joint Committee on Taxation and the secretary of the Treasury to study the current taxpayer privacy protections, the need for third parties to use tax return information, and the impact on taxpayer privacy of sharing tax return information to enforce state or other laws.

Congressional hearings on abusive IRS practices revealed that some taxpayers appear to have been retaliated against for reporting IRS managerial wrongdoing.  To enable investigation of IRS wrongdoing, a person who has or had access to taxpayer return information is now allowed to disclose this information to Congress

☞ **Generally, the tax return is a confidential document between the IRS and the taxpayer.**

☞ **There are several exceptions to the confidentiality of a tax return.**

or one of its committees when reporting IRS misconduct. [IRC §6103(f)]

In any event, in an age of "identity theft," practitioners should carefully safeguard their clients' tax returns and Social Security numbers by maintaining careful controls over access to confidential client files.

## COMPLIANCE VERIFICATION – THE IRS AUDIT PROCESS

The Internal Revenue Service has broad authority to verify that taxpayers are indeed complying with the provisions of the Internal Revenue Code. It may review returns to verify their accuracy and request the taxpayer provide additional information when it believes this is necessary to substantiate a position on the return. [IRC §7602] An audit may eventually result in the assessment of additional tax. Likewise, as discussed later in this chapter, substantial penalties and interest may be imposed.

When information is not voluntarily provided, the IRS may also find it necessary to summon a taxpayer or other person to force production of relevant information. There are also circumstances in which the IRS may "file" a return on behalf of the taxpayer where no return has been theretofore filed. Predictably, such deemed filings often result in the taxpayer facing a fairly sizable tax liability.

Depending on the tax involved, after the passage of specific statutory time periods, most returns are no longer subject to IRS audit. The provisions governing the time in which otherwise permissible audits and assessments must occur are called the **statutes of limitations** and are covered in a variety of Code sections. [IRC §§6501-6533] In certain fairly esoteric circumstances that go beyond the scope of this text, the statute of limitations will be held not to apply to limit either the IRS or a taxpayer from opening up a prior tax return or issues dealt with therein. These special rules may apply where the taxpayer or the IRS takes an inconsistent position justifying the opening up of an otherwise closed year for statute of limitations purposes. Such provisions are often referred to as **mitigation of**

☞ **The IRS may review returns to verify conformance with the IRC.**

☞ **The IRC imposes a time limit on the IRS and its ability to verify the correctness of a return.**

**statute of limitation** rules. [See IRC §§1311 et seq.] Nonetheless, the general rules governing applicable statutes of limitations are fairly straightforward. However, some of the exceptions are complex and necessarily extend beyond the scope of this text.

In most income tax matters, the IRS may only assess an additional federal income tax within three years of the date a federal income tax return is filed. Since federal income tax returns are considered filed on the due date of the return (determined without regard to extensions of the period for filing) unless filed after the due date, an early filed tax return provides no advantage in "starting the clock" on the applicable statute of limitations. When filed late, the filing date is the date the return was actually delivered to the IRS. The three-year statute of limitations begins the day after the due date or return filing date, whichever is the later relevant date.

☛ **Generally, there is a three-year statute of limitations.**

The statute of limitations increases to six years if the taxpayer omitted income exceeding 25 percent of the gross income reported on the return and the omission is not disclosed in the return. [IRC §6501(e)(1)(A)] This extension has been held not to apply when deductions are overstated but there is not the required omission from gross income. Filing a fraudulent return triggers an unlimited assessment period. In other words, there is no statute of limitations in cases of fraud. This is also true when the taxpayer fails to file a complete return.

☛ **Fraud or omission of greater than 25 percent of gross income may extend the statute of limitations.**

Additional problems may arise when the return filing responsibility rests in the hands of another party. For example, an individual limited partner of a limited partnership may not have access to partnership records or the authority to file a return on behalf of the partnership. If the partnership fails to file a return, and the partnership is subject to the so-called "unified audit" rules, the individual partner may be unpleasantly surprised with a tax deficiency assessment years after the statute of limitations has otherwise run with respect to matters disclosed on his individual federal income tax return.

## The Initial Audit Process

The Internal Revenue Service Center where the tax return is filed typically checks for obvious return flaws such as missing signatures, Social Security numbers, and mathematical errors. Some returns may also trigger scrutiny by the IRS if the return's variables (deductions, type and amount of income, etc.) do not seem to be in line with the norm for the type of taxpayer or business involved. These returns may be audited. The 1998 Reform Act imposes upon the IRS the requirement to set forth in its Publication 1 ("Your Rights as Taxpayer") certain of the criteria and procedures for selecting taxpayers for examination. [1998 Reform Act Sec. 3503]

☞ **Audits vary in their complexity and format.**

The most straightforward audit is performed by an Internal Revenue Service Center and often involves clearly incorrect return positions – erroneous computations, incorrect filing status, inconsistency with information returns such as dividend or interest income returns filed by third-party banks or investment companies on IRS Form 1099, and so on. Typically, the result of this type of audit is the receipt by the taxpayer of an IRS notice proposing a correction in the tax.

☞ **One type simply involves correspondence between the IRS and the taxpayer.**

Another relatively simple type of audit involves the Service Center sending a letter to the taxpayer inquiring about a specific tax return reporting position. The IRS letter asks the taxpayer to provide the requested support for the position within a specified period of time. Once the IRS receives the substantiation, it either proposes changes to the return or terminates the audit. The Internal Revenue Manual suggests that this type of audit is limited to certain types of issues such as minor business expenses and certain itemized deductions such as those for interest, charitable contributions, and education.

☞ **An office audit involves a meeting with an IRS Revenue Agent at the IRS offices.**

Another type of audit, the office audit, requires that the taxpayer meet with a revenue agent at the IRS offices. The taxpayer usually receives a  letter indicating that the taxpayer or the taxpayer's representative must make an office appointment and must bring specific requested records. If the taxpayer is to be represented by another person (attorney, CPA, enrolled agent, or other), the representative must hold a written power of attorney executed by the taxpayer. [IRC §7521(c)]  With 10 days advance notice, either the IRS or the taxpayer may record the interview.  Usually, after all the information has been examined, the taxpayer has a conference with the auditor, during which the IRS agent typically indicates what changes are proposed.

The last type of audit involves a prearranged visit by a revenue agent to the taxpayer's place of business.  "Field examinations" are frequently employed when the audit involves a corporate return. Treasury regulations provide special rules regarding the selection of the location of the examination.

☞ A field audit may be appropriate when a corporate return is involved.

## IRS Audit Determination

The audit process may result in clarification of facts to the extent that the examining revenue agent agrees that the reporting position was accurate.  Likewise, the taxpayer may agree during the audit that adjustments to the tax liability are appropriate.  In this case, the revenue agent completes and the taxpayer signs a form setting forth such adjustments.  By signing this form, the taxpayer consents to the assessment of the stated deficiencies and agrees to forgo the formal assessment process discussed later.  Even when there is agreement, the Internal Revenue Manual requires the agent to write a report of the examination that is reviewed by IRS staff.  The audit is not closed until the taxpayer receives a notice from the IRS that the report was accepted.

The audit process may also result in continued disagreement between the taxpayer and the revenue agent regarding the correctness of a  return position.  When there is partial agreement, the taxpayer signs an IRS form titled "Waiver of Restriction on Assessment and Collection of Deficiency in Tax and Acceptance of Overassessment" – IRS Form 870.  By signing this form, the taxpayer agrees to pay any amount of tax deficiency agreed upon.  In addition, the taxpayer agrees not to contest the deficiency in Tax Court. The taxpayer is still entitled, however, to pursue a refund claim in the United States District Court or the United States Court of Federal Claims.

☞ When there is partial agreement, taxpayer may sign IRS Form 870.

The **revenue agent's report** will indicate those issues where agreement could not be reached and summarize the agent's proposed changes to the return.  The summary of changes and an explanation of the adjustments are sent to the taxpayer in a letter referred to as a **30-day letter**.  This letter informs the taxpayer of his appeal rights if he does not wish to accept the agent's finding.  Upon receipt of this letter, the taxpayer's options include:

> ▸ Accepting the adjustments and signing the enclosed Form 870.  As a result, the taxpayer will receive a bill for the taxes owing.  He may later choose to pursue the matter and file a refund claim.

> ▸ Taking no action.  In this case, the IRS will send to the taxpayer a **statutory notice of deficiency** indicating that tax will be assessed unless the taxpayer files a petition with the United States Tax Court within 90 days of receipt of the notice of deficiency.

> ▸ Filing a written protest to the findings within 30 days of the issuance of the letter. (See Chapter Seven for a discussion regarding protest letters.)   In cases where the proposed assessment is no more than $2,500, an oral protest and request for conference may be allowed.

**Assessment Procedures**

When the IRS determines that the taxpayer owes additional taxes, it begins the formal assessment process by mailing to the taxpayer a **statutory notice of deficiency**. [IRC §6212]  This notice consists of a letter indicating the amount of the deficiency and how it was computed.  The notice is often also referred to as a **90-day letter** because its mailing date begins a 90-day period during which time the taxpayer is entitled to file a petition with the Tax Court. The 90-day period may be expanded to150 days for certain taxpayers who are outside the United States.

☞ **A 30-day letter  from the IRS provides the taxpayer with a number of options.**

☞ **The IRS may send a statutory notice of deficiency indicating it believes taxes are due.**

If the taxpayer does file a petition with the Tax Court within this 90-day period, the IRS may not assess nor attempt to collect a deficiency until the Tax Court renders its decision. [IRC §6213] Generally, as long as the notice is sent to the taxpayer's last known address by certified or registered mail, the 90-day period begins with the mailing date, even if the taxpayer does not actually receive the notice.

The statutory notice of deficiency alerts the taxpayer of his options in addition to petitioning the Tax Court. At this stage in the process, his options are very limited. They are:

> ▸ waiving the right to pursue the issue in Tax Court by completing Form 870. This permits immediate assessment.

> ▸ doing nothing for 90 days from the date of the notice's mailing. The IRS will then assess the tax and send a bill for the deficiency.

There are a few circumstances where the IRS may issue an assessment without first issuing a statutory notice of deficiency. This may occur when the deficiency is the result of a mathematical error on the return. In this case, the IRS must provide the taxpayer with an explanation and 60 days to respond. If the taxpayer protests this "summary" assessment, the IRS must treat its proposed deficiency as a normal proposed deficiency and provide the taxpayer with a Statutory Notice of Deficiency.

An assessment without a statutory notice of deficiency is also provided for when the IRS has reason to believe that collection will be jeopardized by delay. This type of assessment is called either a "termination assessment" or a "**jeopardy assessment**" and may be made only when the taxpayer appears to be ready to flee the country, put his property beyond the reach of the government by removing it from the country or concealing it, or become insolvent. [IRC §6861] In this circumstance, the IRS may issue to the taxpayer a notice and demand to pay tax, and a notice of jeopardy assessment and right of appeal letter. A regular statutory notice of deficiency must be mailed

☛ **The statutory notice of deficiency, or 90-day letter provides the taxpayer with several options.**

☛ **Some situations do not require that a 90-day letter be sent.**

☛ **Jeopardy assessment may be appropriate when the IRS believes collection is at great risk.**

to the taxpayer within 60 days following the jeopardy assessment.

The mailing of a jeopardy assessment entitles the IRS to seize or "levy" taxpayer property in order to satisfy the assessment amount. The IRS may also encumber or place a lien against taxpayer assets. Special rules apply when the taxpayer files for relief with the United States Bankruptcy Court. Because of the seriousness of this type of assessment, the Code requires prior IRS Chief Counsel approval before one may be issued. [IRC §7429] In addition, the taxpayer must receive within five days of such assessment a written statement of the information upon which the secretary relied in issuing the assessment.

> **A jeopardy assessment allows the IRS to take taxpayer property to satisfy the assessment.**

## IRS Investigative Powers

When the IRS is unable through voluntary means to gather all necessary information, the Code provides that the secretary of the Treasury may compel the taxpayer to produce records and testimony. The secretary is entitled to issue a summons to: [IRC §7602(a)(2)]

> **The IRS may summon the taxpayer or another person to determine the correctness of a return.**

- ▸ determine the correctness of a return
- ▸ create a return when none is filed
- ▸ determine the tax liability of any person (including a fiduciary or "transferee") and
- ▸ collect any tax liability

To accomplish this, the Code allows the secretary of the Treasury a broad range of powers, including the right to:

- ▸ examine any records and other relevant material
- ▸ summon the taxpayer to appear and produce records
- ▸ summon any other person deemed appropriate and
- ▸ take relevant testimony of any appropriate person under oath

The summons must generally be served by delivering it to the person to whom it is directed or by leaving it at the person's last known address. [IRC §7603] When a corporation is involved, the summons may be served at a corporate office or upon a person authorized to accept service of process on behalf of the corporation.

The 1998 Reform Act provides that the IRS may contact most third parties after providing reasonable advance notice to the taxpayer that it intends to contact that party.  The taxpayer has a set period of time to defeat or "quash" the summons.  If the taxpayer files such a motion, the third party is prohibited from abiding with the summons until the court rules on the motion.  [IRC §§7602, 7609]

In addition to the power to summons, the Code provides that the IRS may use search warrants to seize property constituting evidence of the commission of a criminal offense. [IRC §7302]  A United States Attorney is authorized to approve Title 26 warrants, which may be issued to search offices, structures, and premises owned or controlled by the target of a criminal investigation.

☛ **Search warrants may also be sought by the IRS when there is evidence of a crime.**

According to the Internal Revenue Manual, a grand jury investigation is appropriate in two tax situations:

☛ **In limited circumstances, a grand jury may become involved.**

  ▸ The relevant facts cannot be gathered in a reasonable time through the normal administrative process or
  ▸ The case has a significant possibility of deterring others and the use of a grand jury will result in a more efficient investigation. [Internal Revenue Manual 9267.21]

The results of grand jury investigations may be disclosed to government personnel who are deemed necessary to assist in enforcing federal criminal law. [Federal Rules of Criminal Procedure 6(e)]  In limited circumstances, the results may also be released to the IRS in civil cases.

## APPEAL OF ADVERSE AUDIT DETERMINATION

If there are unresolved issues following the audit, the taxpayer has a choice as to how to proceed.  He may follow an appeal process within the IRS, appeal outside the IRS to the United States Tax Court, or he may pay the assessment and pursue the issue by filing a refund claim and litigating in either the U.S. District Court or the U.S. Court of Federal Claims.

## Appeal Within the IRS

When the taxpayer files a written protest of the agent's findings, the Appeals Office of the IRS may review the case. It will then likely hold a conference with the taxpayer or taxpayer's representative. The Internal Revenue Manual states that the goal here is to resolve the tax controversy without litigation, in a manner that is fair and that will enhance voluntary compliance and public confidence in the IRS.

☛ **The taxpayer may have an appeals conference in response to a written protest.**

The Appeals Office conference is informal and does not involve sworn testimony under oath. The taxpayer may appear with or without representation or choose to have only his representative appear. Notwithstanding, factual representations may be requested to be submitted in an affidavit. The appeals officer makes his determination based on the revenue agent's report, the taxpayer's written protest, and any evidence and arguments presented at the conference.

The Appeals Office considers the risk of unsuccessful litigation when it makes its decisions regarding a taxpayer protest. The Internal Revenue Manual suggests that the probable result of litigation or substantial uncertainty of the result in litigation should be considered in deciding whether to settle. If the Appeals Office agrees to settle with the taxpayer, the settlement can take a variety of forms. One form of settlement is accomplished through the completion of IRS Form 870, discussed earlier. Another IRS form, 870-AD, is used when neither party agrees to concede their position but both are willing to settle. This form is effective only when accepted by the commissioner of the IRS. Although still the subject of much controversy, several courts have held that this form is by itself insufficient to prevent the taxpayer from claiming a refund. However, the IRS Form 870-AD does generally prevent the IRS from reopening the case absent a showing of fraud or misrepresentation.

Perhaps the most formal method for agreeing to a final settlement with the IRS is to use a **closing agreement,** which is binding on both the IRS and the taxpayer. [IRC §7121]  The Treasury regulations state that a closing agreement is appropriate when: "....there appears to be an advantage in having the case permanently and conclusively closed....and it is determined by the Commissioner that the United States will sustain no disadvantage..." [Treas. Reg. §301.7121-1]  This type of agreement may not be modified or set aside unless one of the specific statutory bases for doing so occurs.

**☛ A closing agreement is binding on both the IRS and the taxpayer.**

The 1998 Reform Act requires the IRS to develop procedures under which either a taxpayer or the Appeals Office may enter into nonbinding mediation when the appeals process results in the inability to settle an issue.  The IRS is also required to begin a pilot binding arbitration program with the expectation that, once refined, such program will be extended to all taxpayers.  [IRC §7123]

**☛ The IRS is to develop mediation and arbitration procedures.**

## Taxpayer Appeals to the Tax Court

The United States Tax Court is the only regular tax trial court in which the taxpayer can seek relief from an asserted tax deficiency without being required to pay the asserted tax deficiency.  This court was created by Congress under Article I of the Constitution, rather than Article III, which established the U.S. District Courts.  Therefore, the Tax Court hears only those types of cases Congress assigned to it when it was created.

**☛ The U.S. Tax Court hears only tax cases.**

Generally, the Tax Court reviews cases involving "deficiencies" where an assessment has not yet been made, unless the assessment is a jeopardy or termination assessment.  The Tax Court may also determine whether there is an overpayment for the year at issue and, thus, a refund warranted. [IRC §6512]  Any decision by the Tax Court is appealable by the losing party to the United States Court of Appeals. (See the following discussion regarding who shoulders the burden of proof in these proceedings.)

Only those admitted to practice before the Tax Court can represent a taxpayer in these hearings. Attorneys can be admitted if they are in good standing with the United States Supreme Court Bar or the bar of the highest court of any state or the District of Columbia. Nonattorneys may only practice before the Tax Court if they pass a comprehensive tax examination.

If the taxpayer chooses to have the Tax Court review his case before the IRS issues a final assessment, he must file a petition with the court within the 90-day period that begins with the issuance of the statutory notice of deficiency. The petition is a formal document and must include all pertinent taxpayer information, the date of the mailing of the statutory notice as well as a copy of that notice, a statement of the facts, and the asserted errors made by the IRS. Once the petition is filed with the Tax Court, the IRS must file an answer within 60 days.

☞ **The taxpayer must file a petition with the Tax Court within 90 days from the date of the Statutory Notice of Deficiency.**

When a case involves a tax liability (plus interest and penalties) amount of $50,000 or less, the taxpayer may request to have the Tax Court decide the case under the "small tax case" procedures. Proceedings here are less formal than in the regular Tax Court cases, with taxpayers frequently representing themselves. Small tax case decisions are also neither appealable nor may they be treated as precedent by other courts. [IRC §7463(a)] The Tax Court must agree with the taxpayer's request to have the case heard under the small tax case procedures.

☞ **The small tax case procedures are available for smaller amounts of taxes at issue.**

A taxpayer may be required to pay up to $25,000 when it is determined that he filed in Tax Court primarily for the purpose of causing a delay or when the taxpayer's position is frivolous or groundless. [IRC §6673] On the other hand, the Code provides for the payment of litigation costs to a taxpayer who "substantially" prevailed with respect to the amount or controversy involved in the litigation. See a more detailed discussion that follows.

# REFUND CLAIMS

The taxpayer may believe that he overpaid his taxes and, thus, is entitled to a refund for the overpayment. A claim for refund may involve an unaudited or audited return. By filing a refund claim, the taxpayer is requesting the IRS examine the information and determine the amount of the overpayment. A refund claim must also be filed before a taxpayer can pursue judicial review of a tax controversy outside of the Tax Court, since only the Tax Court may hear cases in which the taxpayer has not paid the tax deficiency asserted.

The IRS provides specific forms for use in claiming a refund. The specific form used depends on the nature of the taxpayer and the type of refund being claimed. For example, IRS Form 1040X is commonly used by individual taxpayers and IRS Form 1120X by corporate taxpayers. Generally, for a claim for refund to be considered made, the claim must:

**The claim for a refund must be made on the required form and signed.**

1. be in writing
2. specify the grounds upon which the claim is based
3. state the amount of the overpayment and
4. be signed by the taxpayer

A claim for refund must be filed within the later of three years from the date of the return or two years of the time the tax was paid. If the taxpayer files a return or pays the tax due earlier than the due date, for purposes of the statute of limitations, the payment is considered to be paid on the "last possible day." This does not include any filing extensions. [IRC §6511]

**There are time limitations controlling when a refund claim must be filed.**

If the refund claim is filed within three years of the return filing date, the refund amount cannot exceed the total tax paid within the three years preceding the date of the refund claim. When the claim is filed within the two years, the total refund amount is limited to the tax paid during the two years preceding the filing of the claim.

The Code provides that the government must pay interest on a taxpayer overpayment, calculated from the date of overpayment to no more than 30 days prior to the issuance of the check. [IRC §6611]

Special rules apply, however, when the IRS responds to a refund claim within 45 days of the filing of the claim.

When a refund claim is denied, the taxpayer has the option to pursue the refund claim through the court system as discussed in the following pages.

## Tax Litigation

As previously discussed, the taxpayer may seek judicial resolution of a tax controversy before final assessment of a tax deficiency by filing a timely petition in the Tax Court. Another option available to the taxpayer is to pay the assessed tax due and file for a refund in either the United States District Court or the United States Court of Federal Claims (previously titled "Claims Court"). The United States Bankruptcy Court also has limited jurisdiction to resolve certain tax disputes for taxpayers involved in bankruptcy proceedings.
(Also refer to Chapter Four for a discussion of these options.)

In determining the best court in which to adjudicate the issues, the taxpayer may wish to consider the following factors:

✓    Ability to pay tax deficiency. If the taxpayer is unable to pay the deficiency before litigation, the only option available to him is to pursue the issue in Tax Court prior to final assessment. (See preceding discussion.)

✓    Desire for jury trial. The only one of these courts with a right to a trial by jury is the United States District Court.

✓    Legal precedent. The taxpayer may wish to consider the decisions of previous cases in each court and determine which has a case history most favorable to the taxpayer.

☞ **The government must pay interest on a taxpayer overpayment.**

☞ **Taxpayers also have the option to file for a refund in the U.S. District Court or the U.S. Court of Federal Claims.**

✓    Jurisdictional authority.  The U.S. Court of Federal Claims has limited jurisdiction and cannot hear every type of tax case.

✓    Sophistication.  Since the United States Tax Court hears only tax cases, it is often more sophisticated than other courts as to tax matters.  This may be useful where the tax controversy involves complex issues.

In order to file for a refund in either the Federal District Court or Court of Federal Claims, the taxpayer must first file a claim for refund with the Internal Revenue Service.  Any litigation must be based on a ground presented in the denied claim for refund.  [IRC §7422]  Unless the claim is denied, the taxpayer may not file a refund claim in court until six months after the filing of the refund claim with the IRS.  In addition, the taxpayer must file suit within two years of the IRS's mailing of the notice disallowing the taxpayer's refund.  [IRC §6532]

☛ **Taxpayers must first file a refund claim with the IRS before filing suit in a court other than the Tax Court.**

## Burden of Proof

Prior to the 1998 Reform Act, the taxpayer generally carried the **burden of proof** that the position taken on the return was correct.  Burden of proof is a legal concept requiring the party who is subject to carrying the burden of proof to demonstrate, by appropriate evidence, that the particular required standard of proof has been met.  Typically, in civil cases, the party bearing the burden of proof must support his position by a "preponderance" of the evidence.  In contrast, criminal proceedings require that the prosecutor offer proof of guilt "beyond a reasonable doubt" in order to convict. The highest civil standard of proof is "clear and convincing evidence" of the asserted position.  There are other potentially applicable standards such as the requirement that the taxpayer support his position by "substantial" evidence, a lower threshold requirement than the "preponderance" standard.

☛ **Burden of proof indicates which party must demonstrate that the required standard of proof has been met.**

Regardless of which standard applies, it is critical that tax practitioners recognize what the applicable standard is and who shoulders the burden to satisfy the standard.  Depending on the particular claim, during the course of litigation, the burden of proof may shift from one party to another.

The 1998 Reform Act shifts to the IRS the burden of proof in tax litigation with respect to a relevant factual issue as long as the taxpayer presents credible evidence regarding that issue and meets certain requirements. [IRC §7491]  First, the taxpayer must abide with the Code's substantiation and record-keeping requirements.  Second, the taxpayer must cooperate with "reasonable requests" by the IRS for information, documents, witnesses, and so on.  Cooperation includes providing the requested information within a reasonable period of time and reasonably providing assistance to the IRS to access documents and witnesses not within the taxpayer's control.  Third, non-individual taxpayers with a net worth in excess of a certain amount continue to shoulder the burden of proof.

☞ **The taxpayer most frequently shoulders the burden of proof. However, the 1998 Reform Act shifts the burden to the IRS in some circumstances.**

In order to shift the burden to the IRS, the taxpayer must prove that each of the preceding requirements is satisfied.  The burden shifts only if the taxpayer provides evidence with a level of quality that will render it sufficient to serve as the basis for a court decision on the issue absent contrary evidence.  For example, unlikely factual statements, frivolous claims, and "tax protestor-type" arguments will not constitute credible evidence.  The impact of the shift of burden of proof is that when the court believes the evidence is equally balanced, the court must find that the secretary did not satisfy the burden of proof and the court must hold for the taxpayer.

## Attorneys Fees

The Code provides that litigation costs, including attorneys' fees (at a rate of $125 an hour adjusted for inflation), may be awarded to a taxpayer who "substantially" prevailed with respect to the amount or issue of the litigation.  [IRC §7430]  However, such an award will not be granted if the government is able to establish that its position was "substantially justified."  In making this determination, the court

☞ **Courts may award attorneys' fees in limited circumstances.**

must take into account the government's previous success on substantially similar issues in other courts, including other Circuits Courts of Appeals.

In addition, court costs may be awarded when the taxpayer made an offer to the IRS that the IRS rejected and that is greater than or equal to the ultimate court judgment against the taxpayer. In this situation, the Code states that the taxpayer will be treated as the prevailing party.

The Code also provides for the award of attorneys' fees where the taxpayer filed suit for civil damages for unauthorized inspection or disclosure of tax returns and return information.

## IRS COLLECTIONS

The first step in the collection process of assessed tax liability is the mailing of a bill to the taxpayer requesting payment. If the taxpayer does not respond to such mailings, the IRS will send a letter demanding payment within 10 days of receipt. The IRS must send this notice within 60 days after making the assessment. [IRC §6303] If payment is not made within this time, the Code authorizes the secretary of the Treasury to collect the tax by imposing a lien on property and/or levying (seizing) property or rights to property. [IRC §§6321, 6331]

Practically speaking, the IRS typically mails a series of notices to the taxpayer, until finally, one warns that enforcement action may be taken. Each notice must include information regarding the basis for and amounts of tax due, including any interest and penalties. [IRC §§6303, 7521]

If payment is not timely made, a lien will attach to the taxpayer's property. The IRS can establish its priority with respect to the lien by filing a **notice of federal tax lien**. Generally, no court action is required. The types of property potentially subject to a lien are unlimited and may include bank accounts, personal property, real property, and right to income from others. The manner in which liens

☞ **Taxpayers have 10 days to pay assessed taxes from the date of receipt of an IRS demand for payment.**

☞ **The government may attach a lien on a taxpayer's property in certain situations.**

are filed depends on the type of the lien and property involved. The taxpayer has the right to administratively appeal the lien and also to request a withdrawal of the notice of a lien in certain specific circumstances set forth in the Code. [IRC §§6323-6326] Unless removed, the lien continues until the assessed liability is satisfied or becomes unenforceable because the statute of limitations for collection (10 years) has run. [IRC §6322]

The government may also collect taxes through the seizure of the taxpayer's assets. Some assets are exempt from this action, particularly a minimum amount of salaries and wages. [IRC §6334] The IRS must send notice to the taxpayer at least 30 days before levy, containing a statement of the tax to be paid. [IRC §6331] The 1998 Reform Act requires supervisory approval before a notice of lien or levy may be mailed. The supervisor must determine that the action is appropriate given the amount of the tax due and the value of the property subject to seizure.

> ☞ **When a levy is made, the taxpayer must immediately surrender the property for sale.**

The Code provides that when a levy has been made, the taxpayer must surrender the property for immediate sale by the government. [IRC §6332] The taxpayer may retrieve the property prior to sale by paying the tax, interest, and penalties due. The taxpayer may also have a right of redemption with respect to real estate even after the sale has been completed. Failure by the taxpayer to surrender the property renders him subject to additional fines and penalties.

When the government seizes property to pay for delinquent taxes, the IRS must notify the taxpayer of the date and place of the sale and make public this information through notice in a generally circulated newspaper. [IRC §6335] The sale must take place either by public auction or under sealed bids. The sale proceeds are applied first against the expenses of the levy and sale and then against the taxes owing. [IRC §6342]

When the IRS believes it is unlikely that the full tax liability can be collected, it may accept payment of less than the assessed amount – a "compromise" amount. [IRC §7122] Such compromises may occur in situations where there is either doubt as to the liability or, more commonly, doubt as to the collectibility. A taxpayer wishing to make an "**offer in compromise**" must submit the requisite IRS Form 656 along with a detailed financial statement. Typically, the taxpayer must indicate that he would suffer a hardship if the entire amount of the tax were paid. The IRS will examine the taxpayer's property interests and earning potential. If the offer is accepted, the taxpayer agrees to "toll" or suspend the running of the statutory period of limitations on assessment and collection while the offer is pending or the period that any installment remains unpaid. It also requires the taxpayer to abide with all filing and payment requirements for five years. Failure to do so results in a default of the agreement.

## FEDERAL PENALTY AND INTEREST PROVISIONS

As a vehicle to furnish an incentive to taxpayers and their representatives to comply with the tax laws, the Internal Revenue Code provides for an array of penalties for those who fail to do so. The provisions include both civil and criminal penalties that may result in the imposition of monetary fines or, in the case of a criminal conviction, possible imprisonment. A lengthy discussion of each possible penalty is beyond the scope of this text. However, the following discussion summarizes the commonly asserted penalties of which taxpayers and their return preparers need to be aware.

☛ **Taxpayers are subject to a variety of penalty provisions when they fail to comply.**

### Tax Return Preparer Penalties

In addition to the tax return preparation standards and guidelines provided by the Treasury Department under Circular 230, the American Institute of Certified Public Accountants, and the American Bar Association, the Code subjects preparers of income tax returns to penalties for acts of misconduct. To determine whether this type of penalty provision applies, you must first determine that the party involved was a "tax return preparer."

### Definition of a Tax Return Preparer

An *income tax return preparer* is any person who prepares for compensation any return required by Subtitle A of the Code. This includes the preparation of a "substantial portion of a return." [IRC §7701(a)(36)] Whether a portion of the return is "substantial" depends on the return complexity and the tax liability involved. [Treas. Reg. §301.7701-15(b)] The regulations provide a detailed discussion of this topic.

☞ **An income tax preparer is also subject to a variety of penalties.**

An *income tax return preparer* does not include any person who merely types or copies a return, prepares a return for his or her employer, or prepares a return as a fiduciary. The definition does cover those who prepare returns for compensation as an employer, employee, or self-employed. A preparer may also be a corporation or a partnership. A person who prepares a return for no compensation is not a preparer, "even though the person receives a gift of return service or favor." [Treas. Reg. §310.7701-15(a)(4)]

According to the Treasury regulations, return preparation encompasses activities such as providing "sufficient information and advice so that completion of the return . . .is largely a mechanical matter. . .even though that person does not actually place or review placement of information on the return. . ." [Treas. Reg. §301.7701-15(a)] A person who provides advice "directly relevant to the determination of the existence, characterization, or amount of any entry on a return" may be an income tax preparer if that entry is a "substantial portion" of the return. [Treas. Reg. §301.7701-15(a)(2)(ii)and (b)]

The Treasury regulations clearly state that an IRS employee performing his official duties is not a preparer, nor is the person who provides return assistance under a Volunteer Income Tax Assistance program (VITA).

## Required Conduct of Tax Return Preparer

The Code requires the tax return preparer to abide by a number of rules in order to avoid penalties.  The key requirements are discussed here.

✓ *Provide copy of return to taxpayer.*  The Internal Revenue Code requires any income tax return preparer to provide a completed copy of the return to the taxpayer no later than the time when the return is provided to the taxpayer for signature. [IRC §6107]  The preparer must also keep a copy of the return for at least three years after filing.  [IRC §6107]  Failure to comply with this requirement may result in the imposition of a $50 penalty on the preparer, unless the failure was due to "reasonable cause." [IRC §6695(a)-(c)]

✓ *Sign return.*  The preparer must sign the return prior to presenting it to the taxpayer for signature and must include his address and employer ID number, Social Security number, or an alternative number as anticipated by the 1998 Reform Act. [IRC §§6695, 6109]  If there is more than one preparer involved in preparing a return, the person with "the primary responsibility. . . for the overall substantive accuracy of the preparation . . ." must sign the return. [Treas. Reg. §1.6695-1(b)(2)]  Failure to comply with this requirement may result in the imposition of a $50 penalty on the preparer, unless the failure was due to "reasonable cause." [IRC §6695(a)-(c)]

✓ *Accurately report amount of tax liability.*  The tax return preparer is charged with the responsibility of accurately reporting the amount of the taxpayer's tax liability.  If there is an understatement of the liability, the Code may impose a penalty on the preparer.  The amount of the penalty depends, in part, on the role of the preparer in making the understatement.

   ▸ Unrealistic position: The Code provides that if an income tax preparer knew that "any part of any understatement" of tax liability was due to a position

☛ **To avoid penalties, the tax return preparer must abide by a number of requirements.**

☛ **The taxpayer must be given a copy of the return.**

☛ **The preparer must sign the return.**

with no "realistic possibility of being sustained," and that position was not disclosed as such on the return, the preparer is subject to a penalty unless the preparer can show there was reasonable cause for the understatement. [IRC §6694]  In this case, the understatement penalty is $250.  See Chapter Six for a more detailed discussion of "realistic possibility."

☛ **The amount of tax liability must be accurately reported.**

▸  Willful or reckless: If the tax return preparer made a "willful" attempt to understate the liability or displayed a "reckless or intentional disregard" of rules or regulations, a $1,000 penalty may be imposed. The regulations provide that a "willful" attempt to understate tax liability occurs when the preparer disregards information provided by the taxpayer or others in an effort to reduce the taxpayer's tax liability.

▸  Aiding or abetting: Any person who aids or assists in the preparation of a return (or portion of it) with knowledge (or reason to believe) that an understatement of the tax liability will result is subject to a $1,000 penalty ($10,000 in the case of a corporation).  [IRC §6701]  This is similar to the criminal fraud penalty discussed later. However, in a civil case, the required burden of proof is lower than in a criminal situation.  Therefore, under this Code section, the standard of proof requires that only a "preponderance of the evidence" must be shown.

The Internal Revenue Service is allowed to seek an injunction against any income tax return preparer who violates certain provisions, including those discussed previously.  Since practicing before the IRS is a privilege, not a right, the court may ultimately permanently prohibit the preparer from acting as an income tax return preparer.  [IRC §7407]

☛ **The court may permanently prohibit a person from being an income tax return preparer.**

In addition to civil penalties, the Code provides for the imposition of criminal penalties. The circumstances under which these penalties may be imposed on a tax return preparer include:

✓ *Tax evasion*: There is a criminal sanction imposed on "any person" who willfully attempts to evade any tax. [IRC §7201]  This penalty may apply to a number of professionals involved, including the tax advisor and return preparer.  A person convicted of this felony is subject to a fine of up to $100,000 ($500,000 in the case of a corporation) and/or imprisonment of up to five years.

**Criminal penalties may also be imposed.**

✓ *Preparing a fraudulent return*: Criminal sanctions are imposed on any person who "willfully aids or assists in, or . . .counsels, or advises the preparation . . .of a return . . .which is fraudulent or is false as to any material matter." [IRC §7206]  Case law indicates that, generally, there must be evidence that the preparer intended to defraud the government.  When the law is unclear and subject to debate, courts have stated it is difficult to find the requisite fraudulent intent.  As one case stated: "A criminal proceeding . . .is an inappropriate vehicle for pioneering interpretations of tax law." [*Karl L. Dahlstrom*, 713 F2d 1423 (9th Cir. 1983)]

## Taxpayer Interest and Penalty Provisions

The Code also imposes interest and penalties on a taxpayer who fails to comply with the federal tax laws.  Interest on the amount of the assessed tax deficiency generally begins accruing on the date the taxes are due (due date of return) and continues until the taxpayer actually makes payment.  [IRC §6601]  In addition, in many cases, the Code imposes interest on the penalties. The interest rate for tax underpayments is determined by adding three percentage points to the short-term federal rate calculated each quarter. [IRC §7206]  If the interest rate changes, the new rate applies from the date of the change until either the tax is paid or the rate changes again.  Understandably, the calculation of interest can be complex.  The Internal Revenue Service has attempted to aid the practitioner and taxpayer through making software programs and uniform tables available to assist in performing this calculation.

**Taxpayers may be subject to penalties and interest.**

The Code now provides that interest shall not accrue during a delay resulting from the failure of an Internal Revenue Service official to perform a "ministerial or managerial act," as long as the taxpayer did not significantly contribute to the delay. [IRC §6404(e)] This exception applies only to interest accruing after notification of the taxpayer by the IRS regarding an understatement.

The 1998 Reform Act provides that, in most cases, interest shall stop accruing after 18 months from the due date of the return or the date the return was filed unless the taxpayer receives notice from the IRS stating the taxpayer's liability and basis for the liability. Under this provision, the accrual of interest and penalties will start again 21 days after the notice date. [IRC §6404(g)]

**☛ Interest ceases to accrue after 18 months unless the IRS notifies the taxpayer of the tax liability.**

When the taxpayer makes a partial payment to the IRS but does not designate how the payment should be allocated, the IRS has indicated that the payment will first be credited to the tax owing, then to any penalties and finally, to the interest due, all for the earliest tax deficiency then outstanding. [Rev. Rul. 73-305, 1973-2 CB 43]

Some of the civil penalties imposed on the taxpayer for failing to abide by the tax laws include:

✓ *Accuracy-related penalties.* A significant penalty is imposed by the Code on the taxpayer who is found to have understated his tax liability due to one or more of the following reasons. [IRC §6662] The penalty is generally 20 percent of the tax liability underpayment caused by one of the following.

 ▸ Negligence or disregard of the rules or regulations. The Code defines *negligence* to occur when the taxpayer failed to "make a reasonable attempt to comply." *Disregard* is defined to include any careless, reckless, or intentional disregard. [IRC §6662(c)] The Treasury regulations provide that the negligence penalty will apply unless the taxpayer has a "reasonable basis" for the return position taken. This position must have a "realistic possibility of being sustained on its merits," a term also discussed in Chapter Six.

▶ Substantially understated income tax. The Code states that an understatement is *substantial* and, therefore, subject to this penalty when it exceeds the greater of 10 percent of the tax required to be shown on the return or $5,000 ($10,000 for corporations). This penalty is not imposed when the taxpayer can show there was "substantial authority" for the position taken on the return. *Substantial authority* requires reliance on primary authority (as defined earlier in this text). If the taxpayer's position is not supported by *substantial authority*, the penalty can still be avoided if the position has a "reasonable basis" and is disclosed on the return using the appropriate forms. [IRC §6662(d)]

▶ Additional accuracy-related penalties may apply, including cases of substantially misstated valuation, substantially overstated pension liabilities, and substantially understated estate or gift tax valuation.

✓ *Underpayment due to fraud.* The Code imposes a penalty equal to 75 percent of the tax underpayment that is due to fraud. [IRC §6663] For purposes of this provision, fraud occurs when there is an intent to evade tax. The IRS must prove with clear and convincing evidence that the taxpayer acted fraudulently. [IRC §7454] Note that this is a much higher standard than a "preponderance of the evidence" standard but lower than "proof beyond a reasonable doubt."

✓ *Filing a frivolous tax return.* The Code imposes a $500 penalty on any individual taxpayer who files a return that does not contain the necessary information to make an accurate tax assessment and the conduct is due to "a position which is frivolous" or "a desire . . .to delay or impede the administration of Federal income tax laws." [IRC §6702]

**Taxpayers are subject to a penalty when there is a substantial understatement of the tax liability unless the position is supported by "substantial authority."**

✓ *Failure to file.* A penalty of 5 percent of the tax required to be shown on the return will be imposed for each month the return is late. This penalty cannot exceed 25 percent of the tax liability. If the failure to file is due to fraud, the penalty increases to 15 percent per month, up to a total penalty of 75 percent. [IRC §6651]

✓ *Failure to pay tax due.* The Code imposes a penalty equal to one half percent for each month the tax is not paid, up to a maximum of 25 percent. [IRC §6651] Where both the failure to file and failure to pay penalties apply to the same month, the aggregate maximum rate of the penalty is 5 percent for that month.

In addition to the civil penalties outlined previously, the taxpayer may also be subject to criminal penalties, including:

✓ *Willfully failing to file return, supply information, or pay tax.* This liability results when any person "willfully" fails to pay tax required by the Code. This is a misdemeanor that may result in the imposition of a $25,000 (individual taxpayer) or $100,000 (corporate taxpayer) fine and/or imprisonment for up to one year. [IRC §7203]

✓ *Filing fraudulent return.* Any person who willfully files a return known by him to be fraudulent or false as to any material matter may be charged with a misdemeanor and fined up to $10,000 and/or imprisoned for up to one year. [IRC §7207]

# PRIVILEGED COMMUNICATIONS

It is still unsettled who must reveal to the IRS or courts information potentially relevant to a tax return position. The confidentiality of communications between an attorney and client is generally protected by the well established attorney-client privilege. Communications protected under this privilege generally include only

**Taxpayers are also subject to penalties for failing to file a return or failing to pay the tax due.**

**Taxpayers may also be subject to criminal penalties.**

**Taxpayer communications with his attorney are generally privileged.**

advice on legal matters and communications made by a client to the attorney regarding a legal matter.  This privilege has long been recognized as necessary to encourage frank and full disclosure by a client to the representing attorney. The issue of privileged communications is replete with controversy.  Determining what is a "confidential communication," and to whom the privilege applies, has been the subject of many court decisions.

Despite much litigation, prior to the 1998 Reform Act, there was no federal recognition of an accountant-client privilege.  At the state level, only some states recognize an accountant-client privilege as well as the attorney-client privilege.  The 1998 Reform Act extends the attorney-client privilege to any "federally authorized tax practitioner."  This extension applies only to Title 26 issues in noncriminal tax matters before the IRS and noncriminal tax proceedings in federal court brought by or against the United States. [IRC §7525]

**The 1998 Reform Act extended the attorney- client privilege to accountant- client communications.**

The provision defines a "federally authorized tax practitioner" as any individual who is authorized to practice before the IRS.  The protected communication is only with respect to "tax advice," which the Code defines as "advice given by an individual with respect to a matter within the scope of the individual's authority" to practice before the IRS.  The privilege does not apply to any communication to a corporate taxpayer in connection with a tax shelter.

The extension of the privilege does not broaden the regular attorney-client privilege but rather simply expands the type of parties such privilege will apply to.  Thus, the communication must still fall within a class of otherwise "privileged" communications. A protected communication is generally one that is made in confidence for the purpose of receiving tax advice or assistance. It may be oral or written.  It does not cover communications of information that are available through some other nonprivileged means.  Nor does it automatically cover preexisting records delivered to the attorney or accountant. These are privileged only if they would have been privileged in the hands of the taxpayer.

**A protected communication must still fall within the definition of one made in confidence.**

Not all tax-related communications are privileged.  Whether a specific communication is privileged depends on the facts and circumstances surrounding it. One of the key factors is whether the communication was intended to be kept confidential for privilege purposes. The information intended to be included on the tax return, for example, is not intended to be kept confidential and, thus, may not be protected. Generally, then, neither the name of a client nor the fee paid for services is subject to the privilege. However, there are exceptions to this where disclosure of the client's name would also disclose other privileged matters.

An exception to the privilege applies to communications that involve assisting the client in the commission of a crime. This exception applies when there exists two elements:

- ✓ There is evidence that the client was engaged in fraudulent or criminal conduct or was planning it when he sought the advice (or committed it after receiving the advice).

- ✓ There is evidence that the attorney (and, presumably now, also the accountant) assisted in furthering the fraudulent or criminal conduct.

As noted previously, the attorney-client/accountant-client privilege belongs to the client, not the advisor. Therefore, the client may waive the privilege intentionally or unintentionally. Because a privileged communication is one intended to be kept confidential, the privilege generally does not protect communications made while people other than the attorney or accountant are present. In addition, even when the taxpayer intends the communication to be confidential, an eavesdropper is typically allowed to disclose what he heard. Likewise, the taxpayer waives the privilege when he voluntarily discloses the information.

The attorney-client/accountant-client privilege typically applies only to "communications" with the client, not the "work product" of the advisor. Generally, however, the *work product* of an attorney is protected from discovery unless there is a showing that the denial of discovery would prejudice the preparation of the party's case or cause undue hardship. [Federal Rule of Civil Procedures 26(b)(3)] Prior to the 1998 Reform Act, the Supreme Court ruled that without a clear statutory provision, accounting work papers are not privileged. [*Arthur Young & Co.*, 465 US 805 (S.Ct. 1984)] It is unclear whether the extension of the communication privilege to accountants extends to the *work product* of the accountant or audit work papers.

## CHAPTER SUMMARY

It is important for the federal tax researcher to appreciate the role of the IRS in administering the federal tax laws. The Code provides that the United States Treasury Department shall implement and enforce the tax laws it embodies.  The Treasury Department has delegated this authority to the Internal Revenue Service.  Because of a growing concern that the current structure and mode of operations of the IRS are inadequate and do not best serve the tax-paying public, in 1998, Congress enacted legislation directing the IRS to reorganize in order to be better oriented toward providing taxpayer assistance.  As a result, the organization and structure of the IRS have changed in recent years.

It is clear that the United States tax system is based upon voluntary compliance by the public.  The central tool in this system is the tax return that the taxpayer is required to submit according to specific filing requirements.  Each return must contain certain information and be accompanied or preceded by full payment of any tax liability owing.

In order to verify that taxpayers are indeed complying with applicable tax laws, the Internal Revenue Service selects a small percentage of returns to audit.  The IRS performs various types of audits ranging from correspondence audits to field examinations.

If the IRS agent finds that the taxpayer has not fully complied with the tax laws, the IRS will provide to the taxpayer a notice of the agent's findings and the asserted tax deficiency.  The taxpayer may choose to agree with the IRS's position or may appeal the decision by filing a written protest of the findings. After an appeal to the IRS, if the IRS continues to assert a tax deficiency, the taxpayer will receive an assessment for the tax owing unless he files a timely petition in the United States Tax Court.  A decision unfavorable to the taxpayer enables the IRS to proceed with collections.  The IRS may endeavor to collect the tax earlier if it determines the collection may be in jeopardy.

The taxpayer has the right to file a claim asserting that any overpaid taxes must be refunded.  If the IRS rejects a refund claim, the taxpayer may file suit for a refund in either the United States District Court or in the United States Court of Federal Claims.  There are a number of factors the taxpayer should consider in determining which court to select.  In tax litigation, the IRS must carry the burden of proving its position if the taxpayer is able to satisfy certain requirements such as substantiation and cooperation with the IRS.

The Code provides for assessment of numerous interest and penalties in cases of taxpayer or tax return preparer negligence or misconduct.  The provisions include both civil and criminal penalties.  The tax return preparer is subject to a variety of accuracy-related penalties as well as failure to abide with certain ministerial requirements.  Likewise, taxpayers are subject to underpayment penalties as well as penalties for failing to file a return or pay taxes on a timely basis.

# PROBLEMS

## *KEY CONCEPTS* (1-40)

1.   Define and discuss the following terms:

    a.   Internal Revenue Service Restructuring and Reform Act of 1998
    b.   Secretary of the Treasury
    c.   Internal Revenue Service commissioner
    d.   IRS Oversight Board
    e.   Chief counsel
    f.   Treasury inspector general for tax administration
    g.   National taxpayer advocate
    h.   Statute of limitation
    i.   Mitigation of statute of limitation
    j.   IRS audit
    k.   Revenue agent's report
    l.   IRS summons
    m.   Form 870
    n.   Closing agreement
    o.   United States Tax Court
    p.   Statutory notice of deficiency
    q.   Assessment
    r.   Levy
    s.   Offer in compromise
    t.   Income tax return preparer
    u.   Privileged communication

2.   Is the tax system of the United States a self-assessment system?  What does this mean? How is this different from other countries' systems?

3.   What must a completed tax return contain in order to be considered as having been filed?

4.   What incentives does the Code provide to the taxpayer to comply with the tax laws?

5.   When must a calendar-year individual taxpayer file the individual income tax return?

6.   If a corporation's fiscal year closes on June 30, when must it file its income tax return?

7.	If the filing date occurs on a Saturday, when must the return be filed?

8.	An individual taxpayer anticipates that her unpaid tax liability will be approximately $2,000.  She does not have all the information necessary to file the tax return by the due date.  What are her options?

9.	What is the last date an individual calendar-year taxpayer's tax return can be filed if all extension requests are filed and granted?

10.	When may the IRS reveal tax return information to someone other than the person filing the return or his authorized representative?

11.	In general, what is the statute of limitations for an income tax return timely filed on April 15, XXX2?  What if the return is not due until April 15, but the taxpayer files the return on February 1, XXX2?

12.	When might the statute of limitations be longer than the general statute you described in problem 11?

13.	What types of tax return audits does the IRS perform?

14.	What is a "30-day letter?"  What are the taxpayer's options upon receiving such a letter?

15.	What are the potential methods the IRS can use to investigate whether the taxpayer has complied with the tax laws?

16.	When is the IRS entitled to institute a grand jury investigation regarding tax compliance?

17.	What is a "90-day letter?"  What are the taxpayer's options upon receiving such a letter?

18.	When may a taxpayer petition the U.S. Tax Court?  How is this done?

19.	Who may represent a taxpayer in a U.S. Tax Court proceeding?

20.	When may a taxpayer request to have the Tax Court decide a case under the "small tax" case procedures?  Why might the taxpayer choose to make this request?

21.	What is a "jeopardy assessment?"  When may this be appropriate? What does such an assessment entitle the IRS to do?

22.     If a taxpayer disagrees with the position of the IRS and is assessed a tax deficiency, what options are available to the taxpayer?

23.     In order to be considered filed, what must a claim for refund include?

24.     When is the last day a claim for refund can be filed if the tax return was filed on April 15, XX02, and the tax (plus penalties) was paid on December 1, XX06?

25.     When is the last day a claim for refund can be filed when the return was filed and full payment was made on February 15, XX02?  The return was not due until April 15 of that year.

26.     What are the taxpayer's options when a refund claim is denied by the IRS?

27.     If the taxpayer wishes to file suit in court, what factors might the taxpayer consider in selecting which court to petition?

28.     What does it mean to state that a particular party has the "burden of proof"? What are some examples of the level of burden of proof a party may carry?

29.     In tax cases, who carries the burden of proof, the IRS or the taxpayer?

30.     Under what circumstances may attorneys' fees be awarded to a taxpayer?

31.     What are the various methods the IRS may use in attempting to collect taxes assessed?

32.     According to the Treasury regulations, what constitutes "return preparation" for purposes of the penalty provisions?

33.     What are some of the obligations of the tax return preparer?

34.     What are the penalties if the tax return preparer fails to sign a tax return he prepared?

35.     What are the potential penalties for a tax return preparer who signs a return he knew reported a position with no "realistic possibility of being sustained" and fails to disclose this fact on the return?

36.     What are the potential penalties for a tax return preparer who intentionally ignores information reported to him by the taxpayer in an attempt to understate the tax liability

shown on the return?

37.     What are some of the criminal charges a tax return preparer may be subject to? What are the potential consequences if found guilty?

38.     Discuss some of the penalties that can be imposed on the taxpayer for understating his tax liability.

39.     What types of communication may be protected by the attorney-client or accountant-client privilege? What is the philosophical basis for the privilege? Has the accountant-client privilege always existed?

40.     When may a tax-related communication fall outside the protection of the privilege?

# CHAPTER NINE

# STATE TAX RESEARCH

## *EXPECTED LEARNING OUTCOMES*

- Appreciate the need for state tax research
- Understand the basic components of state tax research

## *CHAPTER OUTLINE*

- Overview
- The Basic Components of State Tax Research
- Tools Available for State Tax Research
- Chapter Summary
- Problems

## OVERVIEW

If your work focuses on mastering federal tax law compliance and research, it is easy to forget that there is an entirely separate tax system at the state level. Each state has its own tax code and tax administrative structure that are analogous, but not identical, to the IRS. As a tax practitioner, it is important to keep in mind that if there is an issue as to how the Internal Revenue Code should be applied to a certain transaction, there will likely be a similar state income tax issue as well.

In addition, state and local governments collect numerous other types of taxes such as property taxes, transfer taxes, and sales and use taxes. Transactions such as corporate mergers or real estate like-kind exchanges, which typically may be structured as income tax free on the federal level, may nonetheless give rise to state and local property taxes, transfer taxes, and sales and use taxes.

---

**EXAMPLE 1: Potential Impact of State Taxes**

A party disposing of personal property at a taxable loss for federal income tax purposes may be subject to a stiff sales tax under local laws based upon a percentage of gross receipts received in exchange for the property. Imagine the surprised look on a client's face in a 7% sales tax jurisdiction when he discovers that the personal property acquired for $6,000,000 and sold for $5,000,000, (a $1,000,000 deductible loss for federal income tax purposes under Code Section 165 and applicable state income tax law) is a $350,000 taxable sales tax event ($5,000,000 x 7%) under local sales tax laws!

---

Even experienced practitioners often forget to do an overall "collateral damage" assessment when they are in the throes of reviewing a complicated transaction. Even if you are asked only to review a federal income tax question, always bear in mind that it is prudent to inquire whether the related state and local tax matters are being handled and by whom. Be sure to appropriately document the scope of the project you have been assigned so that you are not later called to task to answer why you did not spot a pressing state or local tax matter. A clear understanding of the laws you are to consider will always help in protecting your client from unintended tax consequences and avoid unexpected professional malpractice.

☛ **Even if asked to review a federal question, inquire whether someone is looking at the state and local tax issues.**

In addition to state tax provisions, the nontax laws of a state may also be pertinent when performing federal tax research. This can give rise to very difficult questions and often incorrect conclusions if care is not taken. Other experts may be required to render legal determinations. Some federal or state tax laws often defer to the provisions of state law to define the legal terms appropriate to a transaction, whereas other tax laws often provide that state nontax laws may be overridden in certain circumstances. For example, there are specific federal tax provisions that apply to transactions involving

☛ **State nontax laws may be important in applying federal tax laws.**

a form of property ownership under some states' laws known as "community property." Code Section 1014(b)(6) provides a highly important basis adjustment related to community property passing at death. It is state law that generally determines the legal character of property and whether it is held as community property.

Alternatively, although the state law characterization of such matters as the nature of property ownership may be important, federal and state tax laws often disregard state nontax law characterization. It is important to note the fact that the Code often deems matters to be the case for tax purposes that are, strictly speaking, not the case for state law purposes. For example, the Code provides a specific definition of "alimony" that for the most part, ignores the categorization of the payments by the state. Likewise, federal tax laws are clear that the mere holder of title to otherwise depreciable property is not necessarily the "economic" owner for federal tax law purposes, thereby denying the state law owner a depreciation deduction. The case law is replete with holdings involving taxpayers who learned they were not entitled to the tax advantages that their state law ownership rights would otherwise suggest were available.

Learning whether particular state laws are important, how they "mesh" with federal and state tax laws, and for what purpose involves attaining an advanced knowledge of particular fields of tax and achieving a well-grounded understanding of the overall legal principles commonly interfacing with such tax areas.

☛ **The Code often ignores state law definitions and determinations. At other times, the Code looks to state law determinations.**

---

*Practitioner Observation*
Stephen J. Swift, United States Tax Court Judge

*"Often in researching Federal tax, relevant state statutory case law material is overlooked. For example, a Federal tax dispute involving property rights might turn on state law."*

Taxation at the state level has grown so complex and important that many practitioners specialize only in state taxation issues, some in property taxes, and others in sales and use taxes.  Even if you enjoy the luxury of having a colleague with such expertise, however, it is still useful to acquire and maintain a general understanding of the state tax research resources available to you. You will then be in a position to know when you need to either perform detailed state tax research and/or seek the aid of a state tax specialist.

## THE BASIC COMPONENTS OF STATE TAX RESEARCH

State tax research can be broken into a number of different topics.  One subset of state tax research involves the taxing relationship between states.  This area concerns constitutional limitations on the states and their authority to impose tax on transactions that are part of interstate commerce.  This is a very active area in the law, particularly now that companies (both domestic and international) do business in multiple states and/or multinationally. How is the income from that company taxed by the states?  What portion of income can each state tax?  When may a company be subject to the myriad of nonincome taxes imposed by state and local governments?  What tax credits or deductions, if any, are available to preclude the double taxation of the same income by one state versus another?

☛ **How does a state tax interstate transactions?**

Another major subset of state tax research consists of each state's specific income or other tax laws.  As noted previously, there is a wide variety of possible taxes a state may levy, all with potential research issues.  Some of the types of state taxes you may need to investigate in your research include:

☛ **What are the state taxation laws?**

- Personal income tax
- Corporate income tax
- Real property tax
- Transfer tax
- Personal property tax
- Inheritance, estate and gift tax

- Sales and use tax
- Special taxes (cigarette, gasoline, alcohol, etc)

It is interesting to note the source of state tax revenues as shown in the following chart. The numbers represent the percentages of total state tax revenue for all 50 states in 2001.

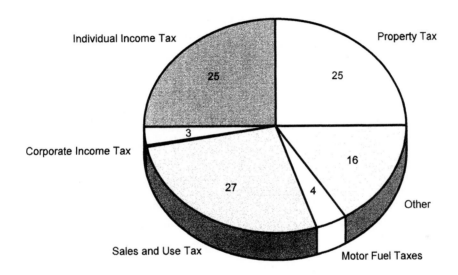

In addition to substantive issues regarding the taxability and measure of a tax, there are procedural and compliance issues to consider. What are the filing requirements? Must a company, with only a bank account in the state, report and pay income tax to that state? Must the federal tax return be attached to a state tax return? Is the state a "piggyback" state that determines taxable income based on federal taxable income, or does it deviate from the federal system requiring separate state taxable income calculations? What are the state's interest and penalty provisions?

Each state has its own administrative taxing structure. The basic common components in each state are:

- Taxing statute (federal analogy – IRC)
- Taxing agency (federal analogy – IRS)
- Court structure (federal analogy – district, appellate, supreme)

It is difficult to generalize beyond this. Each state calls its taxing statute by a different name. For example, California's taxation statutes generally fall into the *Revenue and Taxation Code*. New York's is titled *Tax Law* and Oklahoma's is titled *Oklahoma Tax Code*. Each of these codes differs in organization and content.

In addition, each state gives a different name to its income taxing agency – Department of Revenue Service (Connecticut), Department of Taxation and Finance (New York), Franchise Tax Board (California income tax agency). Other state agencies may collect and enforce other state taxes. For example, the California Employment Development Department enforces state employment tax matters. The structure of each taxing agency is also different.

Even the state court systems differ. Although you will usually find a three-layer system – lower court, appeals court, final court – the states occasionally differ in nomenclature by calling each type of court by a different name. For example, in California, the jurisdictional levels from lowest to highest courts are named: Superior Court, Appellate Court, Supreme Court. However, in New York, the Appellate Court is the highest court.

> ☛ **Each state has taxing statutes and taxing authorities.**

There is nothing in the state court structure completely comparable to the Federal Tax Court; that is, there is no state court totally devoted to the litigation of state tax matters. However, some states have an optional process whereby taxpayers have the opportunity to have a quasi judicial hearing before a group of people other than the taxing agency. This extra step occurs before the taxpayer brings the case to the court system and represents one last chance for the dispute to be resolved without litigation. California's State Board of Equalization is an example of this optional internal appeal structure.

> ☛ **State court structures all differ.**

With all the state tax variations, however, the one common element is that they, in some way, resemble the federal structure. More importantly to the researcher, the states also generally follow, to a considerable extent, the laws set forth by the Internal Revenue Code. Therefore, although each state has its own tax code, most of the states conform entirely or in part to the provisions of the Internal Revenue Code. However, it is still incumbent upon any researcher or practitioner practicing in a particular state to become broadly familiar with the inevitable differences between federal and state laws. Most states' Bar and CPA organizations sponsor annual state tax seminars that are highly useful to tax preparers and others to highlight differences in federal and state taxes.

With this backdrop, when researching state tax law, you first need to determine whether the state tax laws conform with the IRC. You will need to carefully examine whether there are any possible differences between the IRC and the state law. In addition, if the state law does conform to the IRC, it is important to ascertain when the state decided to conform. Often there is a substantial time lag between the time changes are made to the IRC and the when state law changes are made. This is because state law changes must await state legislative approval and the governor's signature. This may result in the need to make adjustments to accurately reflect the state law.

☛ **First, determine whether the state tax law conforms with the IRC provisions.**

---

**EXAMPLE 2: Impact of State and Federal Tax Differences**

Over the years, the federal depreciation system has changed many, many times, requiring different assets placed in service in different taxable years to be accounted for based on different methods of depreciation. The problem becomes nightmarish when it comes to state tax matters and other financial reporting.

For persons conducting business in many states, this has required scores of differing depreciation systems applied to the various assets owned. One system may apply for generally accepted accounting principles ("GAAP" nontax "book" accounting), another depreciation method for federal income tax purposes, and others for state income tax purposes. In this regard, it is no joke when people refer to their second, third, and fourth sets of financial books and records.

# TOOLS AVAILABLE FOR STATE TAX RESEARCH

What tools are available to answer state tax questions? Generally, we have the same types of primary authority for state tax research as we have for federal tax research. The possible tools include:

- Taxing statute
- Administrative interpretations
- Judicial interpretations

In addition to the primary authority available, there are many analogous secondary sources available to help you find the relevant primary authority.

## State Taxing Statute

The state statute can be a more challenging research source than its federal counterpart – the IRC. The reasons for this are many.

First, the numbering system in most states results in section numbers that are often long – often in excess of five digits. Unless you frequently work in the state tax area, it is difficult to remember the pertinent number and, thus, turn quickly to it when you have a question. Typically, the numbering system does not correspond to the IRC. Therefore, even for experienced researchers, it is likely easiest to rely on the index or table of contents. This may prove a bit frustrating for someone who usually works with the IRC and understands its organization.

☛ **The state tax numbering system can be an obstacle for some who wish to quickly refer to the pertinent Code section.**

Second, many state tax codes are organized in a significantly different manner than the IRC. Therefore, if you are accustomed to the IRC's structure, working with the state code can be difficult. Remember, each state tax code was enacted based on each state's legislative mandates and concerns. Obviously, there are very different economic and political issues confronting a low population state such as Wyoming versus its larger cousins in Texas and Illinois. States may also rely on sources of revenue that are highly distinct. For example, the state of Nevada has no individual income tax, relying instead primarily on casino gaming income, sales taxes, and property-based revenues.  Florida and Texas likewise do not levy an individual income tax.  Other states such as New York and California seem abundant in taxes of all kinds.

Finally, if you are primarily a federal tax practitioner, it is not always practical to have an easily accessible copy of the applicable state tax code.  Every tax library should have the code.  However, it may very well be a multivolumed hard copy that is part of a larger service. In paper, two publishers, **Deerings** and **Wests,** publish the full state code – comparable to the United States Code. Of course, the revenue laws make up only a portion of the state code.

☞ **Sometimes it is difficult to have easy access to the state tax code.**

In addition, both Commerce Clearing House (CCH) and Research Institute of America (RIA) have reporter services for each state in which at least one of the volumes contains the tax statutes. You can also generally find the text of state tax law through the Internet.  Many state Web sites now contain full text of their tax statutes as do the fee-based services of either CCH, RIA, Westlaw, and Lexis-Nexis.  The gateway addresses found in the Appendix provide a good starting point for this type of research.

☞ **Many state government Web sites now contain the text of their tax statutes.**

States usually conform at least in part to the federal tax laws. This means that the state actually adopts a provision of the Internal Revenue Code as one of its own taxing provisions.  When this happens, the state statute usually also provides that in applying the provision, the federal interpretations (administrative and judicial) that relate to the IRC section will also apply to the state.

Therefore, even though you may be researching a state tax question, at times you will be using federal tax resources in your research.  However, always check to ensure that the state tax law provision fully conforms to its federal counterpart before relying solely on federal tax authority.  Every now and then a state's Attorney General or other person or court may throw in a monkey wrench by interpreting the state provision in a manner different than the bootstrapped federal provision.  Also, the fact that a state legislature has adopted a particular federal provision as its state law does not ensure that subsequent changes to or interpretations of federal laws will likewise result in state tax law changes or new interpretations.

## Administrative Interpretations

Each state's **administrative interpretations** of the tax laws differ in nature. However, most states do issue interpretive regulations of the state tax laws, as well as interpretations similar in nature and authority to revenue rulings, revenue procedures, and private letter rulings. Again, many of the administrative interpretations you will use to apply state law will actually be the IRS interpretations if the state law conforms to the IRC.

In print, it is becoming increasingly hard to access state administrative interpretations other than the regulations. The best place to access these is electronically through the Internet databases of CCH, RIA, Tax Analysts, Westlaw, and Lexis-Nexis, and state Web sites.

## Judicial Interpretations

There are also **judicial interpretations** of the state tax laws to help you correctly apply the state tax law you have a question about. However, there generally is no state equivalent to the CCH and RIA tax cases (USTC and AFTR services) that report only tax cases. Instead, you will need to access a law library or database that contains all state court cases, including tax cases. Unless you have access to a full paper law library, access through one of the electronic services is likely your best bet.

The citation method is completely analogous to what you have already learned for federal cases. Your case will always have a name, volume number, reporter abbreviation, and page or paragraph number.

As with administrative interpretations, when the state law conforms to the federal law, you may end up using federal case law to address a state tax question.

☛ **When the state statute conforms to the IRC, federal interpretations are usually applicable.**

☛ **When researching state tax case law, electronic databases are most efficient and complete.**

## Secondary Sources

State secondary sources are comparable to federal secondary sources and are available to help determine what relevant primary authority exists. Both CCH and RIA publish reporter services that focus on the issues dealing with the taxing authority of states vis-a-vis each other and the federal government. Commerce Clearing House's reporter is called the *State Tax Cases Reporter*. Research Institute of America publishes a reporter called *State and Local Taxes*.

To aid in locating relevant state regulations and case law, each publisher also publishes separate state tax reporters for each individual state. These are analogous to the federal reporters and contain the text of the code provision, explanations, and annotations. These services are available on the publisher's Internet products.

In addition to the reporters, there are a few other very useful secondary resource tools. Both RIA and CCH publish multistate handbooks annually. RIA publishes the *All States Tax Handbook*. CCH publishes the *State Tax Handbook*. Both are available in softback. This is a terrific resource that provides an abundance of basic information regarding the status of tax laws in all the states. For instance, this handbook contains charts with the following information:

- Names and addresses of all top tax officials and administrative agencies for each state
- Corporate income tax rates, due dates and filing requirements, and consolidated returns information
- States with alternative minimum tax for individuals and/or corporations and the rate
- Multistate income apportionment
- Wage and withholding returns
- Personal income tax rates, exemptions, and filing requirements
- Capital gains rules and rates
- Itemized deductions allowed
- Partnership tax
- Sales and use and property taxes

☛ **The central tax publishers provide full state reporter services.**

- Special taxes

In addition, both Panel Publishers and Commerce Clearing House and RIA produce helpful two-volume services entitled *Multistate Corporate Tax Guide* (Panel), *Multistate Corporate Income Taxes* (CCH), and *Multistate Corporate Income Taxes* (RIA).

For several of the larger states, both CCH and RIA also publish, on an annual basis, a softbound book equivalent to the *Federal Master Tax Guide* discussed in Chapter Five. This state handbook provides a cross-reference table between the federal tax provisions and the state tax provisions so that the researcher can quickly identify which IRC provisions the state conforms to. The book also briefly discusses state provisions which differ from the IRC. It provides a cross-reference to the portion of the full state reporter that addresses the subject. Electronically, RIA provides the ability to create your own state analysis. This excellent tool in RIA *CHECKPOINT*, is called *CompareIt*, and allows you to create a customized state-to-state comparison.

The states with this one-volume summary of the tax rules include California, Florida, Illinois, Massachusetts, Michigan, New Jersey, New York, North Carolina, Ohio, and Pennsylvania. For researchers practicing in or concerned about state tax matters in these states, these books are an essential cross-reference guide to have near at hand!

Although there are not the number of journals devoted to state taxes as you find for federal taxes, Warrem. Gprham & Lamont publishes the *Journal of Multistate Taxation and Incentives*, which provides an analysis of state and local tax developments. This is available in print and via RIA *CHECKPOINT*.

☛ **The state research process may differ from that used to research a federal tax question.**

## Research Process

What process should you use to find an answer to a state tax question? The steps differ depending on whether you are going to use print or electronic tools. In print, unless you are a state tax expert, it is most efficient to use a process quite different from what you are accustomed to when answering a federal tax question.  It is best to use your knowledge of federal taxation as your starting point. The following steps can be used:

√      Determine what IRC section applies to the question.

√      If available, use the summary of state tax law published by RIA or CCH.  In RIA's summary, use either the table of contents or the index to locate the relevant discussion in the text.  In CCH, find the cross-reference table to inform you whether the state conforms to federal law or differs.

---

**ILLUSTRATION: CCH Guidebook to California Taxes**

## PERSONAL INCOME TAX

### FEDERAL-CALIFORNIA CROSS REFERENCE TABLE AND INDEX

Showing Sections of California Personal Income Tax Law (Revenue and Taxation Code) Comparable to Sections of Federal Law (1986 Internal Revenue Code)

| Federal | California | Subject | Paragraph |
|---|---|---|---|
| IRC Sec. 1,3 | Secs. 17041, 17048 | Tax Rates and Tables | ¶ 112 |
| IRC Sec. 2(a) | Secs. 17046, 17142.5 | "Surviving Spouse" Defined | ¶ 104a |
| IRC Secs. 2(b), 2(c) | Sec. 17042 | "Head of Household" Defined | ¶ 110 |
| IRC Sec. 15 | Sec. 17034 | Effect of Changes | ¶ 406 |
| IRC Sec. 21 | . . . | Credit—Child Care | . . . |
| IRC Sec. 23 | Sec. 17052.25 | Adoption Costs Credit | ¶ 128 |
| IRC Secs. 25-30A | Sec. 17039 | Credits—Various | . . . |
| IRC Sec. 31 | Sec. 19002 | Credit—Tax Withheld | ¶ 712a |
| IRC Secs. 32-37 | . . . | Credits—Various | . . . |
| IRC Sec. 38 | Sec. 17053.57 | Community Development Investment Credit | ¶ 145 |
| IRC Secs. 39-40 | . . . | Credits—Various | . . . |
| IRC Sec. 41 | Sec. 17052.12 | Research Expenditures Credit | ¶ 137 |
| IRC Sec. 42 | Sec. 17058 | Low-income Housing Credit | ¶ 127 |
| IRC Sec. 43 | Sec. 17052.8 | Enhanced Oil Recovery Credit | ¶ 140 |
| IRC Sec. 44 | Sec. 17053.42 | Disabled Access Credit | ¶ 129 |
| IRC Sec. 45C | . . . | Clinical Testing Credit | . . . |
| IRC Secs. 51-52 | Sec. 17053.7 | Work Opportunity Credit | . . . |
| IRC Sec. 53 | Sec. 17063 | Minimum Tax Credit | ¶ 139 |
| IRC Secs. 55-59 | Secs. 17062, 18037.5, 18037.6 | Alternative Minimum Tax | ¶ 112a, ¶ 319 |

---

√      Turn to the relevant paragraph in the summary and examine the analysis. Even if the law appears to conform to the IRC, read the explanation to make sure there are no differences you need to be aware of.  If none, then research into federal tax law as you would with a federal tax question.

√    If the law does not conform to the IRC, read the summary explaining the
provision and the differences from the federal law.  The summary will identify the
Code section number of the state provision.

---

## ILLUSTRATION:  CCH Guidebook to California Taxes

### ¶ 128 Adoption Costs Credit

*Law:* Sec. 17052.25 (CCH CALIFORNIA TAX REPORTS ¶ 15-384).
*Comparable Federal:* Sec. 23.
*California Form:* Form 540.

California provides a credit for an amount equal to 50% of the specified costs paid or incurred by a taxpayer for the adoption of any U.S. citizen or legal resident minor child who was in the custody of a state or county public agency. The credit may not exceed $2,500 per child and may be claimed only for specified costs directly related to the adoption.

The adoption cost credit may be claimed only for the taxable year in which the decree or order of adoption is entered; however, the costs that are included may have been incurred in previous taxable years. The credit may be carried over until the total credit of $2,500 is exhausted. Any personal income tax deduction for any amount paid or incurred by the taxpayer upon which the credit is based must be reduced by the amount of the adoption cost credit.

The California credit is similar to the federal tax credit that is available for tax years beginning after 1996, with the following exceptions:

(1) the amount of the California credit is lower (50% of qualifying costs v. the 100% allowed under the federal credit);

(2) the dollar cap on the California credit is lower ($2,500 per child v. the federal limit of $5,000 per child or $6,000 per special needs child);

(3) unlike the federal credit, California's credit is not phased out on the basis of the taxpayer's adjusted gross income;

(4) the expenses that may be claimed for purposes of the federal credit include any reasonable and necessary adoption fees, court costs, attorney fees, and other expenses that are directly related to the adoption proceedings; whereas California specifies that expenses include adoption fees charged by the Department of Social Services or a licensed adoption agency, travel expenses related to adoption, and unreimbursed medical fees related to adoption;

(5) California's requirements concerning the adoptive child's citizenship, residency, and custodial status do not apply for purposes of claiming the federal credit; and

(6) California's credit may be carried over until exhausted, whereas there is a five-year carryover limit on the federal credit.

---

Information regarding the state law cite and location in the state reporter containing more information.

Analysis of federal and state differences

This excerpt illustrates an example of a state provision that is similar to the federal provision, but not identical. The analysis summarizes the differences between the two provisions.

√      In the preceding illustration, you may wish to further explore the law. You have the option at this point of either examining the language of the Code section itself or, by using the summary's cross-reference to the full state tax reporter (either CCH or RIA), studying the pertinent portion of the reporter. In the reporter, you will find an explanation and annotations to case law and other potentially relevant interpretations.

√      Use the annotations to determine what additional resources you need to read. Locate the cases or administrative rulings referred to you by the reporter either in print or electronically.

Electronically, the process is much more straightforward. Although you can electronically imitate the preceding steps on both CCH and RIA, a more effective way to electronically research state tax law is by using the service's state tax table of contents. Tax Analysts and Lexis-Nexis also have complete state tax libraries. The Appendix illustrates in detail each necessary step in the CCH, RIA, and Tax Analysts Internet services.

## CHAPTER SUMMARY

As tax researchers, always remember that client situations may give rise to questions regarding the application of state tax laws. There may be issues concerning which state has the right to tax particular income. There may also be issues simply dealing with how the specific state's tax provisions apply in a particular situation.

Each state has its own tax code and tax administrative structure fairly analogous to the IRS. Each state has a tax statute, an agency to administer the statute, and a judicial system to help apply and interpret the tax laws. The similarity stops there, with each state having different taxing laws and administrative and judicial structures.

There are many tools available to perform state tax research. All of the tools are available in print, although it may be difficult to locate a library with a complete print state tax library. However, you can access all state tax information through the key tax publisher's fee-based Internet research products as well as through each state's Web site.

State tax research is easiest to perform using these electronic resources.  Using the table of contents approach, you can, with relative ease, find all the information you need to answer your state tax question.

## PROBLEMS

### KEY CONCEPTS (1-7)

1. Discuss why it is important to be aware of state tax issues.

2. Describe how nontax state laws may affect federal tax research.

3. Describe the types of tax issues that can arise concerning state taxes.

4. What is the name of your state's general statutory income tax laws?  What agency administers it?

5. Identify your state courts, from the lowest court to the highest.

6. Is there a body in your state between the taxing agency and the courts that can hear and decide tax cases?  If so, what is it called?

7. Locate and identify the secondary sources available to you regarding your state's taxes.

### PRACTICAL APPLICATION (8-21)

8. Does your state conform to the IRC in any way?  If so, name three of the provisions.

9. List all the types of taxes that your state imposes.

10. List the three states with the highest corporate income tax rates.

11. Does Texas impose any of the following taxes?  If so, when must the returns be filed?

    a. Individual income tax
    b. Corporate income or franchise tax
    c. Inheritance tax or estate tax
    d. Generation-skipping transfer tax

e.     Gift tax

12.   Does Iowa have a corporate alternative minimum tax? If so, is it based on federal alternative minimum taxable income or Iowa minimum taxable income?

13.   What are the tax treatment and reporting requirements for partnerships in the following states?

   a.   Michigan
   b.   North Carolina
   c.   Tennessee
   d.   Wyoming

14.   What states require a separate state election to be filed in order to adopt S corporation status?

15.   In general, is a net operating loss (NOL) allowed as a deductible item for individuals in the following states? If so, what are the carryback and carryforward provisions?

   a.   Your state
   b.   New Jersey
   c.   Arizona

16.   Is a net operating loss (NOL) allowed as a deductible item for corporations in the following states? If so, what are the carryback and carryforward provisions?

   a.   Your state
   b.   California
   c.   Louisiana

17.   What is the highest personal individual income tax bracket for the following states?

   a.   Your state
   b.   California
   c.   New York

18.   What states do not have a personal income tax?

19.   In the month of March, what are all the filing dates for individuals and entities in the

following states?

    a.      Arkansas

    b.      Connecticut

    c.      Georgia

20.    A taxpayer purchased his home in 1995 for $100,000. This year he sold it for $250,000 cash. Under federal law, he will be able to avoid paying any taxes on the $150,000 gain because of IRC Section 121. How does your state treat this transaction?

21.    A taxpayer purchased a large copy machine for his business last year. The cost of the machine was $100,000. He made no other purchases of depreciable assets for the year. In your state, how much will he be able to take as a depreciation deduction in the year of purchase?

# APPENDICES

## Databases of CCH, RIA, and Tax Analysts Web-Based Libraries

| | CCH *Tax Research NetWork* | RIA *CHECKPOINT* | TAX ANALYSTS' *TAXBASE* |
|---|---|---|---|
| **Primary Resources** | All | All | All<br>Cases from 1985 only<br>Rev.Ruls/Rev. Procs from 1955 only<br>LTRs from 1980 only |
| **Reference Services** | CCH *Federal Tax Advisor*<br><br>CCH *Federal Tax Reporter*<br><br>CCH *Federal Excise Tax Reporter*<br><br>CCH *Federal Estate and Gift Tax Reporter*<br><br>CCH *Tax Treaties Reporter* | RIA *Federal Tax Coordinator*<br><br>RIA *United States Tax Reporter* | * **Tax Analysts'** *Federal Tax Baedeker*<br><br>* **Tax Analysts'** *Worldwide Tax Treaties* |
| **Other Major Secondary Resources** | * *Master Tax Guide*<br><br>* *Taxes - The Tax Magazine*<br><br>* *The Journal of Retirement Planning*<br><br>* Daily and Weekly Newsletters<br><br>* CCH Citator | * Warren, Gorham and Lamont Treatises<br><br>* *Master Tax Guide*<br><br>* Tax Journals - WGL<br><br>* BNA *Daily Tax Reporter*<br><br>* Tax Dictionary - WGL<br><br>* RIA Citator | * Tax Analysts' Tax Directory<br><br>* Tax Analysts' *Tax Notes* and Tax *Notes Today*<br><br>* Tax Analysts' *Tax Notes International* |

Appendix
B

**Research Using CCH *Internet Tax Research NetWork***

## THE MAIN MENU

**Research Using CCH *Internet Tax Research NetWork***

## THE MAIN MENU

| Practice Aids | |
| --- | --- |
| CCH Client Letter Toolkit | Election and Compliance Toolkit |
| CCH Depreciation Toolkit | IRS Actuarial Factors |
| Tax Rates and Tables | |

**Federal Tax Archives — Select All**

Archived Documents and Reporters

| | | | |
| --- | --- | --- | --- |
| 2001 | 1995 | 1989 | |
| 2000 | 1994 | 1988 | 1982 |
| 1999 | 1993 | 1987 | 1981 |
| 1998 | 1992 | 1986 | 1980 |
| 1997 | 1991 | 1985 | 1979 |
| 1996 | 1990 | 1984 | 1978 |

**Topical Indexes — Select All**

| | |
| --- | --- |
| Federal Income Tax Reporter | Tax Treaties Reporter |
| Internal Revenue Code | Federal Tax Service |
| Federal Excise Tax Reporter | U.S. Master Tax Guide |
| Federal Estate/Gift Tax Reporter | |

Indexes

## Research Using CCH *Internet Tax Research NetWork*
## How to Access a Document for Which You Know the Cite

Appendix B

### THE INTERNAL REVENUE CODE
### AND TREASURY REGULATIONS

**STEP 1:**

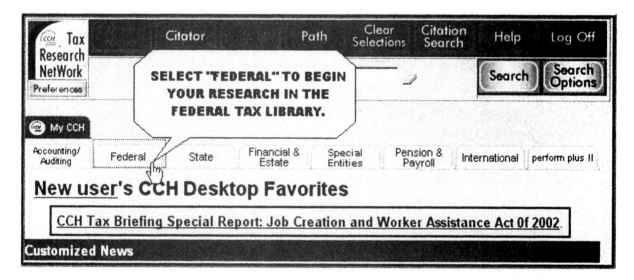

**STEP 2:**

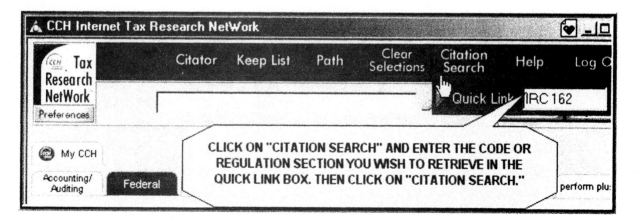

Appendix
B

**STEP 3:**

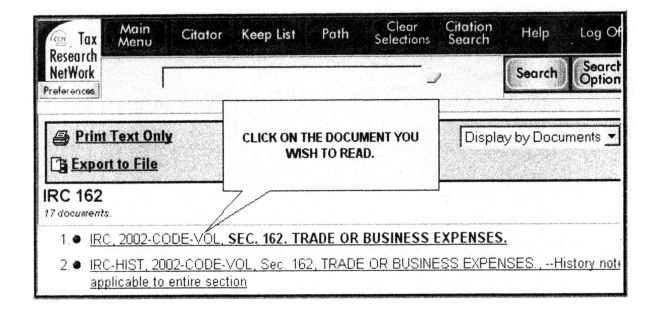

## Research Using CCH *Internet Tax Research NetWork*
## How to Access a Document for Which You Know the Cite

### COURT CASES

**STEP 1:**

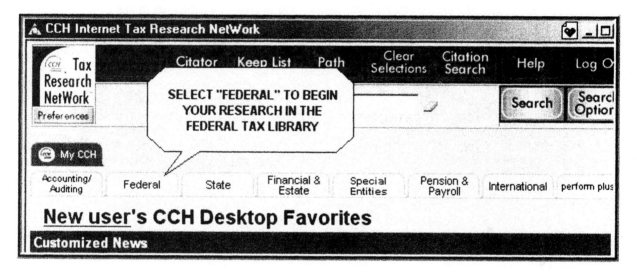

**STEP 2:**

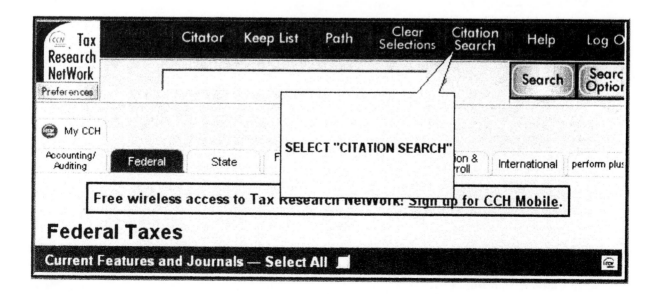

Appendix
B

**STEP 3:**

**CURRENT INTERNAL REVENUE CODE**

SEARCH   IRC Code & Hist. Sec. [          ]

**Cases in FED Current Developments**

SEARCH   [     ] - [ ] USTC ¶ [          ]

**Rulings in FED Current Developments**

SEARCH   [     ] - [ ] CB [          ]

> YOU ARE PROVIDED A TEMPLATE LISTING EACH TYPE OF DOCUMENT IN THE CCH DATABASE. NOTE THAT ALL OF THE BEGINNING ENTRIES REFER ONLY TO THOSE DOCUMENTS FOUND IN ONE OF THE CCH REPORTERS.

**Federal Estate and Gift Tax Guide Reporter**

SEARCH   CCH ¶ [          ]

**Cases in Estate & Gift Tax Rptr New Matters**

SEARCH   [     ] - [ ] USTC ¶ [          ]

**Tax Ct Regulars in Estate & Gift Tax Rptr New Matters**

SEARCH   Tax Ct. Dec. [          ]

**Tax Ct Memos in Estate & Gift Tax Rptr New Matters**

SEARCH   Tax Ct. Dec. [          ]

**Rulings in Estate & Gift Tax Rptr New Matters**

SEARCH   Tech. Advice Mem. No. [          ]

**Fed Excise Tax Reporter**

SEARCH   CCH ¶ [          ]

**Cases in ETR Current Developments**

SEARCH   [     ] - [ ] USTC ¶ [          ]

> TO LOCATE THE APPROPRIATE LINES FOR CASES, YOU MUST SCROLL DOWN UNTIL YOU SEE "U.S. TAX CASES."

**Rulings in ETR Current Developments**

SEARCH   Letter Ruling No. [          ]

**STEP 4**

**U.S. Tax Cases**

| SEARCH | - [ ] USTC |
| SEARCH | CCH |
| SEARCH | US |
| SEARCH | S. Ct. |
| SEARCH | F. 2d. |
| SEARCH | F. 3d. |
| SEARCH | F. Supp. |
| SEARCH | F. Supp.2d |
| SEARCH | Ct. Cl. |
| SEARCH | Cls. Ct. |
| SEARCH | Fed Cl. |
| SEARCH | B.R. |

ALL THE POSSIBLE SOURCES OF CASES ARE PROVIDED IN THIS TEMPLATE WITH THE EXCEPTION OF RIA'S AFTR CITATION. SCROLL DOWN UNTIL YOU LOCATE THE FIELD REPRESENTING THE CITE YOU WISH TO RETRIEVE.

**Tax Court Regulars**

| SEARCH | Tax Ct. Dec. |
| SEARCH | TC No. |
| SEARCH | 100 TC 215 |

ENTER THE CITATION NUMBERS IN THE APPROPRIATE FIELDS. CLICK ON THE SEARCH BUTTON TO THE LEFT OF THE FIELD TO RETRIEVE THE FULL TEXT OF THE COURT CASE.

**Tax Court Memoranda**

| SEARCH | Tax Ct. Dec. |
| SEARCH | TCM |
| SEARCH | TC Memo - |

**Tax Court Small Tax Cases**

| SEARCH | T.C. Summary Opinion - |

**Board of Tax Appeals Regulars and Memoranda**

| Appendix B | Research Using CCH *Internet Tax Research NetWork* How to Access a Document for Which You Know the Cite |
|---|---|

## REVENUE RULINGS

**STEP 1:**

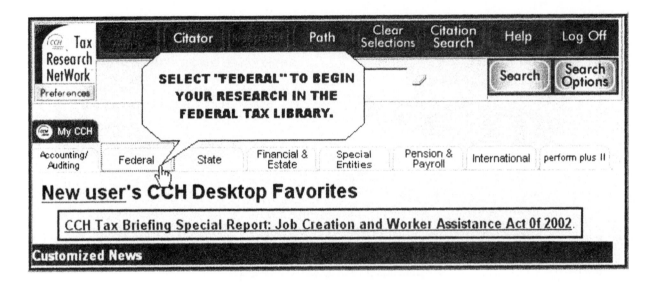

**STEP 2:**

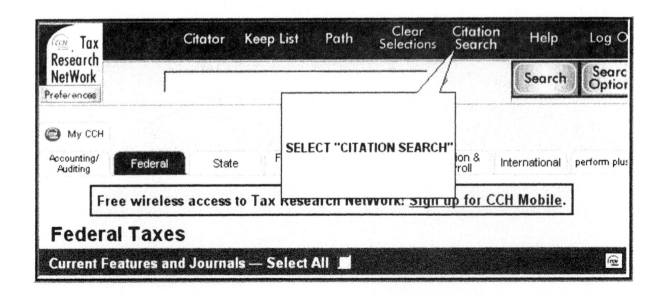

STEP 3:

**CURRENT INTERNAL REVENUE CODE**

[SEARCH]  IRC Code & Hist. Sec. [                ]

**Cases in FED Current Developments**

[SEARCH]  [        ] - [        ] USTC ¶ [        ]

**Rulings in FED Current Developments**

[SEARCH]  [        ] - [        ] CB [        ]

> YOU ARE PROVIDED A TEMPLATE LISTING
> EACH TYPE OF DOCUMENT IN THE CCH
> DATABASE. NOTE THAT ALL OF THE
> BEGINNING ENTRIES REFER ONLY TO THOSE
> DOCUMENTS FOUND IN ONE OF THE CCH
> REPORTERS.

**Federal Estate and Gift Tax Guide Reporter**

[SEARCH]  CCH ¶ [                ]

**Cases in Estate & Gift Tax Rptr New Matters**

[SEARCH]  [        ] - [        ] USTC ¶ [                ]

**Tax Ct Regulars in Estate & Gift Tax Rptr New Matters**

[SEARCH]  Tax Ct. Dec. [                ]

**Tax Ct Memos in Estate & Gift Tax Rptr New Matters**

[SEARCH]  Tax Ct. Dec. [                ]

**Rulings in Estate & Gift Tax Rptr New Matters**

[SEARCH]  Tech. Advice Mem. No. [                ]

**Fed Excise Tax Reporter**

[SEARCH]  CCH ¶ [                ]

**Cases in ETR Current Developments**

[SEARCH]  [        ] - [        ] USTC ¶ [        ]

> TO LOCATE THE APPROPRIATE LINES FOR
> RULINGS, YOU MUST SCROLL DOWN UNTIL
> YOU SEE "RULINGS."

**Rulings in ETR Current Developments**

[SEARCH]  Letter Ruling No. [                ]

**Appendix B**

**STEP 4:**

## U.S. Tax Cases

| | | |
|---|---|---|
| SEARCH | - USTC | |
| SEARCH | CCH | |
| SEARCH | US | |
| SEARCH | S. Ct. | |
| SEARCH | F. 2d. | |
| SEARCH | F. 3d. | |
| SEARCH | F. Supp. | |
| SEARCH | F. Supp.2d | |
| SEARCH | Ct. Cl. | |
| SEARCH | Cls. Ct. | |
| SEARCH | Fed Cl. | |
| SEARCH | B.R. | |

THIS PORTION OF THE TEMPLATE PROVIDES THE FIELDS NECESSARY TO LOCATE CASES. CONTINUE SCROLLING UNTIL YOU LOCATE "RULINGS AND OTHER DOCUMENTS."

## Tax Court Regulars

| | |
|---|---|
| SEARCH | Tax Ct. Dec. |
| SEARCH | TC No. |
| SEARCH | TC |

## Tax Court Memoranda

| | |
|---|---|
| SEARCH | Tax Ct. Dec. |
| SEARCH | TCM |
| SEARCH | TC Memo - |

## Tax Court Small Tax Cases

| | |
|---|---|
| SEARCH | T.C. Summary Opinion - |

## Board of Tax Appeals Regulars and Memoranda

**STEP 5:**

## LTRs & IRS Positions (including TAMs and FSAs)

SEARCH   LTR or TAM No.

SEARCH   Gen. Counsel Memo No.

SEARCH   Action on Decision No CC- [   ] - [   ]

SEARCH   Technical Memo No.

SEARCH   Litigation Guideline (Pre-1999)

SEARCH   Litigation Guideline (Post-1998)

SEARCH   Service Ctr Advice (Pre-1999)

SEARCH   Service Ctr Advice (Post-1998)

SEARCH   Field Service Advice (Pre-1999) [   ] - [   ]

SEARCH   Field Service Advice (Post-1998)

SEARCH   Chief Counsel Advice (Post-1998)

SEARCH   Chief Counsel Advice (Pre-1999)

SEARCH   IRS Positions Reports, CCH ¶

## ADVANCE RELEASE Documents

SEARCH   [   ] ARD [   ] - [   ]

> ON THIS SCREEN, NOTE THAT THIS IS WHERE YOU WILL FIND THE APPROPRIATE FIELD IF YOU ARE TRYING TO LOCATE A SPECIFIC LETTER RULING. CONTINUE SCROLLING UNTIL YOU LOCATE "RULINGS AND OTHER DOCUMENTS."

**Appendix
B**      **STEP 6:**

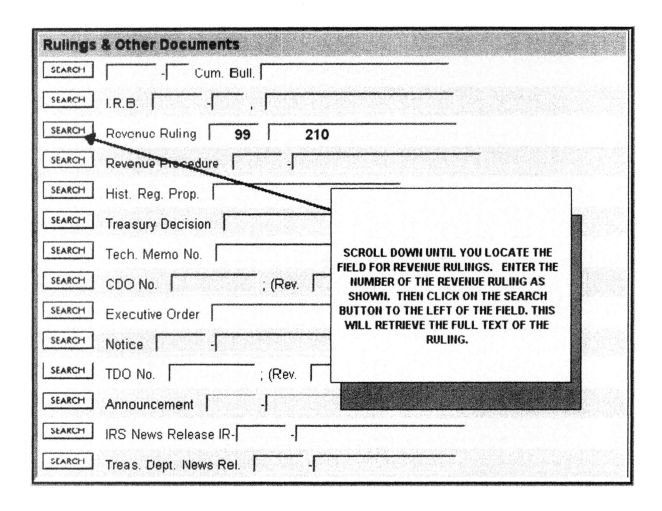

### Rulings & Other Documents

| SEARCH | | - | Cum. Bull. | |
| SEARCH | I.R.B. | - | , | |
| SEARCH | Revenue Ruling | **99** | **210** | |
| SEARCH | Revenue Procedure | - | |
| SEARCH | Hist. Reg. Prop. | |
| SEARCH | Treasury Decision | |
| SEARCH | Tech. Memo No. | |
| SEARCH | CDO No. | ; (Rev. | |
| SEARCH | Executive Order | |
| SEARCH | Notice | - | |
| SEARCH | TDO No. | ; (Rev. | |
| SEARCH | Announcement | - | |
| SEARCH | IRS News Release IR- | - | |
| SEARCH | Treas. Dept. News Rel. | - | |

SCROLL DOWN UNTIL YOU LOCATE THE FIELD FOR REVENUE RULINGS. ENTER THE NUMBER OF THE REVENUE RULING AS SHOWN. THEN CLICK ON THE SEARCH BUTTON TO THE LEFT OF THE FIELD. THIS WILL RETRIEVE THE FULL TEXT OF THE RULING.

## Research Using CCH *Internet Tax Research NetWork*
## How to Locate a Court Case for Which
## You Only Know the Name

**STEP 1:**

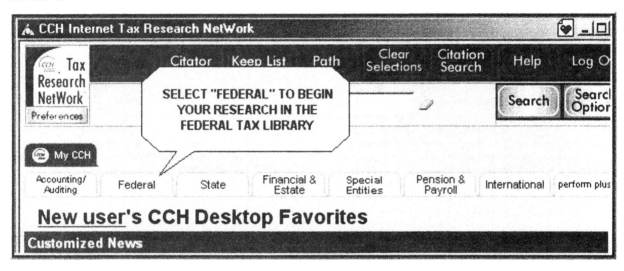

**STEPS 2-4:**

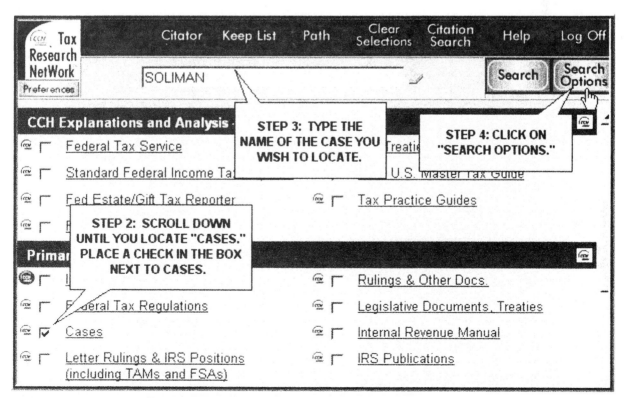

**Appendix B**    **STEP 5:**

Tax Research NetWork    Preferences

| Main Menu | Citator | Keep List | Path | Clear Selections | Citation Search | Help | Log Of |
|---|---|---|---|---|---|---|---|

SOLIMAN                                        [Search] [Search Option]

**Search Method:**
Any Term ▼

**Search results:**
Return 50 documents
☑ Sort results by relevance
☐ Display words around hits in results list
☑ Automatically apply thesaurus

To view synonyms of terms, type terms in the field below and click on the View Synonyms button.

[                    ]    View Synonyms

No Synonyms

**Select Recent Searches:**
[                    ▼]

SCROLL DOWN SCREEN TO "SEARCH IN WHICH PART OF A DOCUMENT." SELECT "CASE-NAME" WHICH WILL LIMIT THE RESULTS TO ONLY THOSE CASES WITH "SOLIMAN" IN THE CASE NAME.

NOTE THAT THIS INFORMATION CONFIRMS THE DATABASE IN WHICH YOU ARE SEARCHING

**Search latest news:**
[                    ▼]
⯈ **Favorite Searches**
⯈ **Search Tips**

**Limit search to the following types of documents:**
☑ **ALL Types**
☐ U.S. Supreme Court
☐ U.S. Appeals Courts
☐ U.S. District Courts
☐ U.S. Court of Claims
☐ U.S. Claims Court
☐ U.S. Bankruptcy Court
☐ Miscellaneous Courts
☐ Tax Court Regulars
☐ Tax Court Memoranda
☐ Board of Tax Appeals Regulars
☐ Board of Tax Appeals Memoranda
☐ Tax Court - Small Tax Cases

**Date Restrictions:**
                    Month    Day    Year
None ▼  [          ▼] [    ] . [    ]

**Search in which part of a document:**
case-name ▼

[ARCH PREFERENCES]    [SEARCH NOW]

You are searching:[U.S. Tax Cases 2, U.S. Tax Cases 1, TC Regulars Current, TC Regulars Archive 1942-1998, Tax Court Memoranda 1/99 - Current, Tax Court Memoranda 1942 - 1998, Tax Court Small Tax Cases, BTA Regulars and Memoranda]

**STEP 6:**

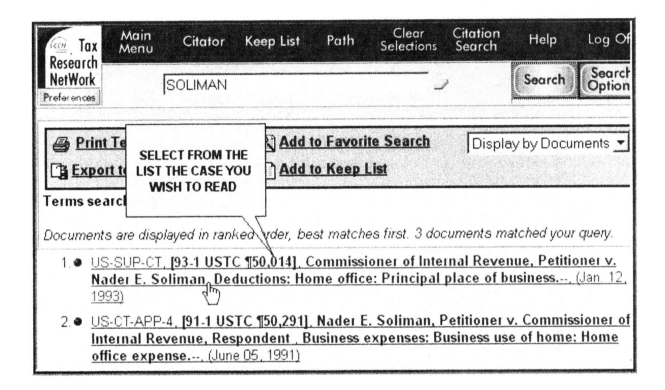

Appendix
B

# Research Using CCH *Internet Tax Research NetWork*
## How to check the validity of an authority – "citating"

### Citing a Case or Revenue Ruling for Which You Know the Cite

**STEP 1:**

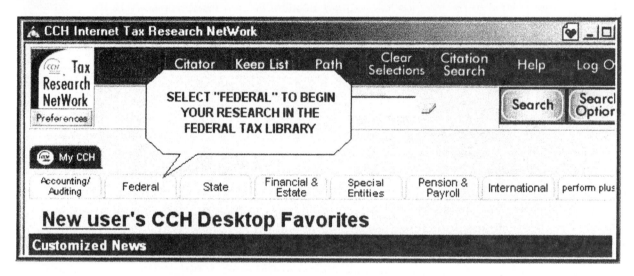

**STEP 2:**

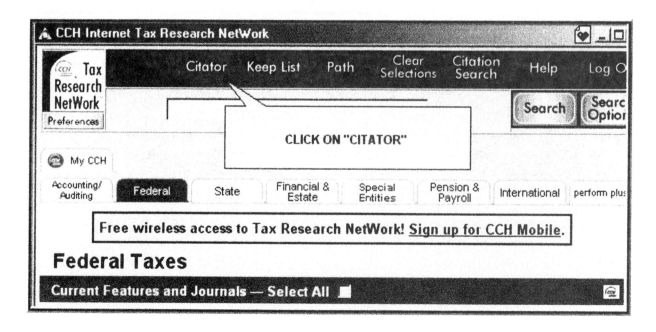

**STEP 3:**

Appendix
B

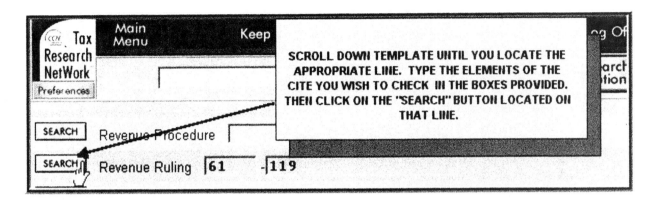

**STEP 4:**

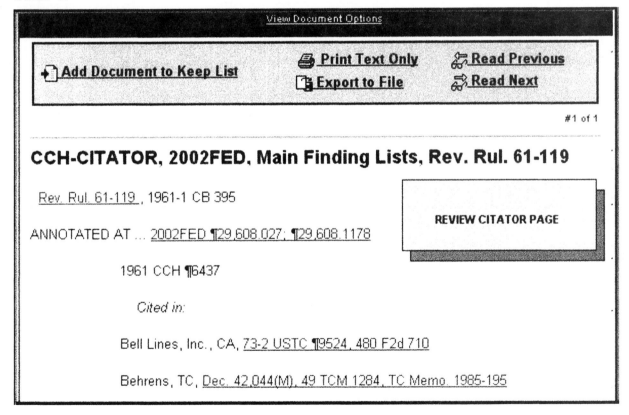

| Appendix B | **Research Using CCH *Internet Tax Research NetWork*** **How to check the validity of an authority – "citating"** |
|---|---|

**Citating a Case or Revenue Ruling from the Document Itself**

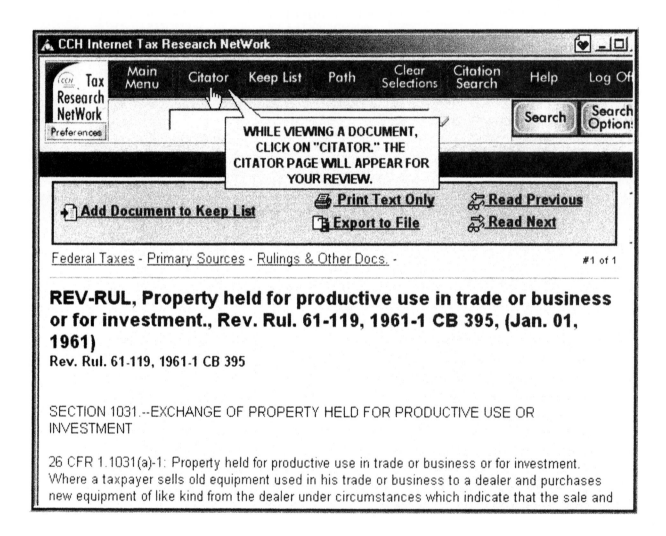

## Research Using CCH *Internet Tax Research NetWork*

### SAMPLE RESEARCH PROJECT

Your client has just had an expensive face-lift and asks you to
determine whether the expenses for the surgery are deductible.

## USING THE INDEX

**STEP 1:**

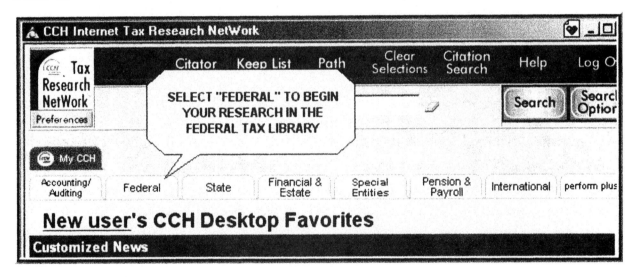

**STEP 2:**

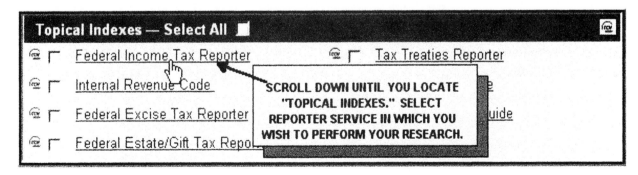

**Appendix B**

**STEP 3:**

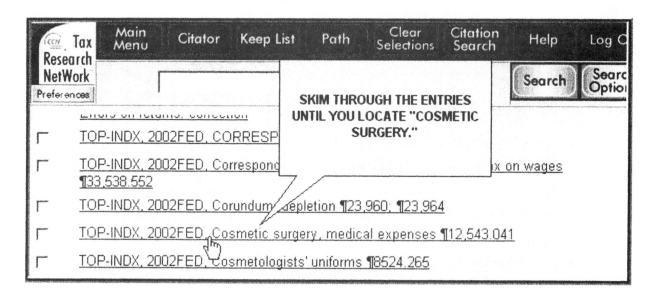

Federal Taxes - Topical Indexes -

**Federal Income Tax Reporter— Select All** ◼

☐    A [413]

☐    B [274]

☐    C [706]

☐    D [339]

☐    E [251]

SELECT THE LETTER "C" FOR "COSMETIC SURGERY." (ALTHOUGH YOU MIGHT ALSO TRY "F" FOR FACE-LIFT," THERE IS NO SUCH ENTRY.)

**STEP 4:**

Tax Research NetWork    Main Menu   Citator   Keep List   Path   Clear Selections   Citation Search   Help   Log O

Preferences                                                                 Search   Searc Optio

SKIM THROUGH THE ENTRIES UNTIL YOU LOCATE "COSMETIC SURGERY."

☐    TOP-INDX, 2002FED, CORRESP

☐    TOP-INDX, 2002FED, Correspond                    x on wages ¶33,538.552

☐    TOP-INDX, 2002FED, Corundum, depletion ¶23,960; ¶23,964

☐    TOP-INDX, 2002FED, Cosmetic surgery, medical expenses ¶12,543.041

☐    TOP-INDX, 2002FED, Cosmetologists' uniforms ¶8524.265

**STEP 5:**

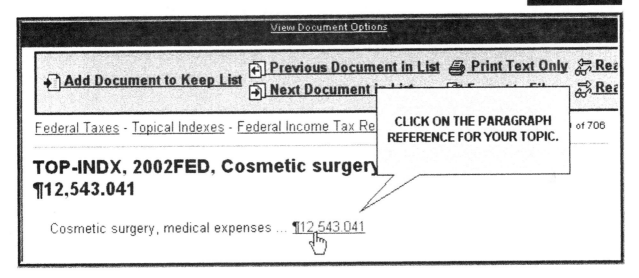

**STEP 6:**

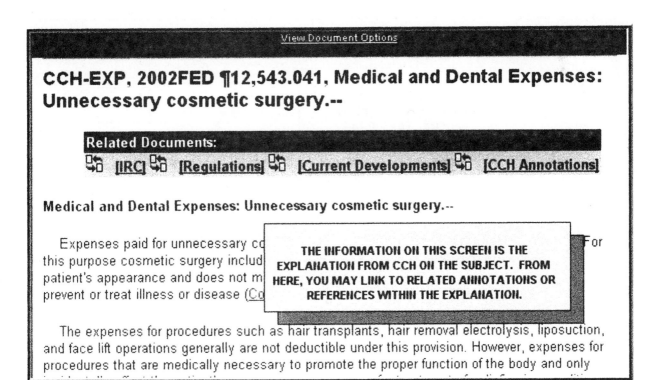

<table>
<tr><td>Appendix<br>B</td><td>**Research Using CCH *Internet Tax Research NetWork***</td></tr>
</table>

## SAMPLE RESEARCH PROJECT

Your client has just had an expensive face-lift and asks you to determine whether the expenses for the surgery are deductible.

## USING THE TABLE OF CONTENTS

## STEP 1:

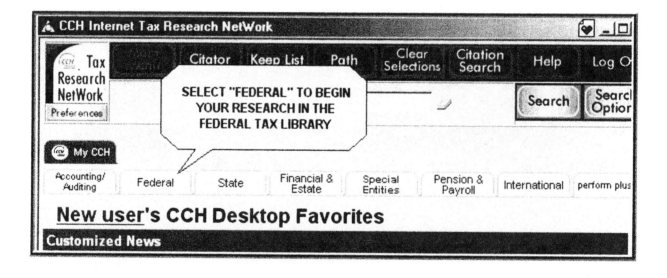

**STEP 2:**

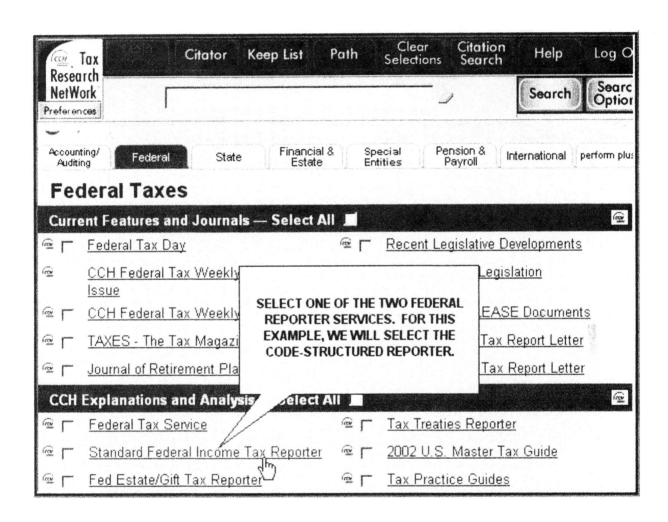

Appendix
B

**STEP 3:**

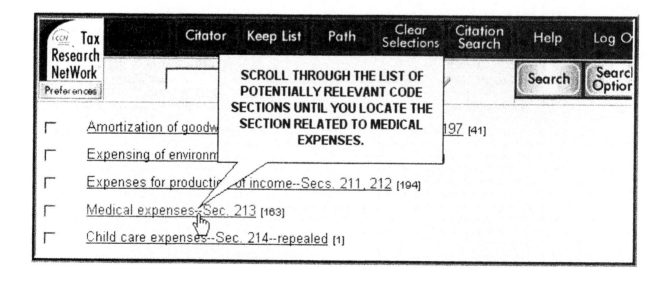

| | |
|---|---|
| | Accounting/ Auditing |
| | Federal |
| | State |
| | Financial & Estate |
| | Special Entities |
| | Pension & Payroll |
| | International |
| | perform plu: |

Federal Taxes - CCH Explanations and Analysis -

**Standard Federal Income Tax Reporter— Select All** ■

☐    Tax planning [302]

☐    Tax treaties and conventions [469]

☐    Calendar, rates and tables ~~~~~~~~~~~~~~~~~~~rotests [728]

☐    Filing status, exemptions, ~~~~~~~~~~~~~~-153 [424]

☐    Credits--Secs. 21-52 [1290]

☐    Minimum tax, environment~~~~~~~~~~~~s. 53-59B [265]

☐    Income and exclusions--S~~~~s. 61-150 [4316]

☐    Deductions--Secs. 161-291 [9914]

☐    Corporate distributions--Secs. 301-386 [2718]

> SCROLL DOWN UNTIL YOU LOCATE THE MOST APPROPRIATE CATEGORY.

**STEP 4:**

| | Citator | Keep List | Path | Clear Selections | Citation Search | Help | Log O |
|---|---|---|---|---|---|---|---|

Tax Research NetWork
Preferences

[Search] [Searcl Option]

☐    Amortization of goodw~~~~~~~~~~~197 [41]

☐    Expensing of environm~~~~~~~

☐    Expenses for production of income--Secs. 211, 212 [194]

☐    Medical expenses--Sec. 213 [163]

☐    Child care expenses--Sec. 214--repealed [1]

> SCROLL THROUGH THE LIST OF POTENTIALLY RELEVANT CODE SECTIONS UNTIL YOU LOCATE THE SECTION RELATED TO MEDICAL EXPENSES.

**STEP 5:**

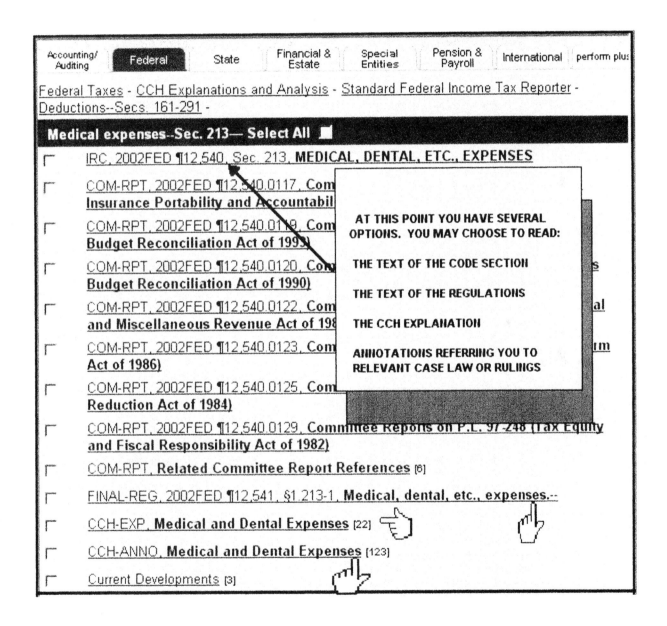

| Appendix B |
| --- |

# Research Using CCH *Internet Tax Research NetWork*

## SAMPLE RESEARCH PROJECT

Your client has just had an expensive face-lift and asks you to determine whether the expenses for the surgery are deductible.

## SEARCHING

**STEP 1:**

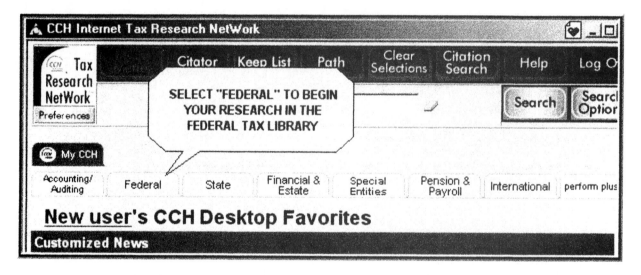

**STEPS 2 - 4:**

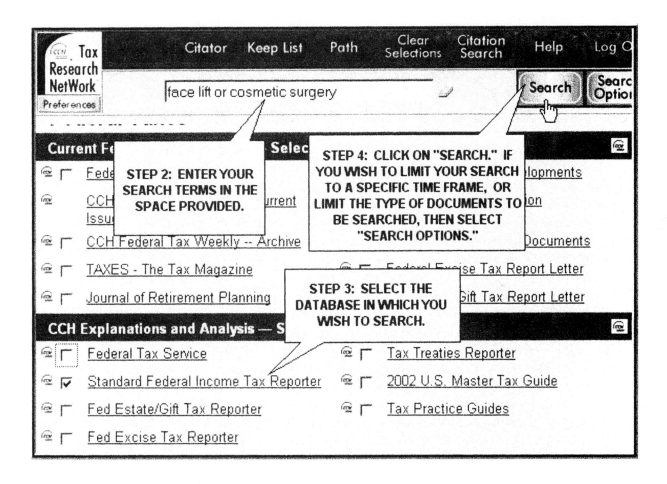

Appendix
B

# Research Using CCH *Internet Tax Research NetWork*

# USEFUL TOOLS

## Location Guide:

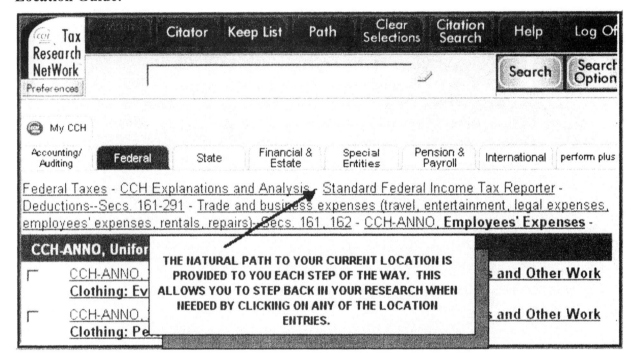

## History of Your Research Path:

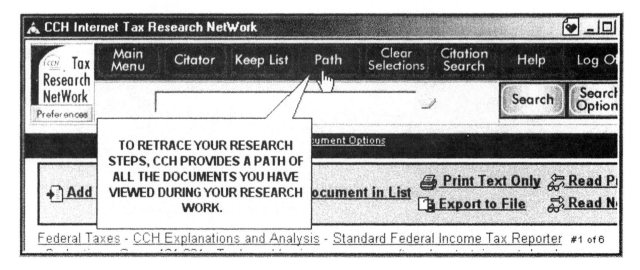

**Research Using CCH *Internet Tax Research NetWork***

## USEFUL TOOLS

## Keeping a Document for Later Review:

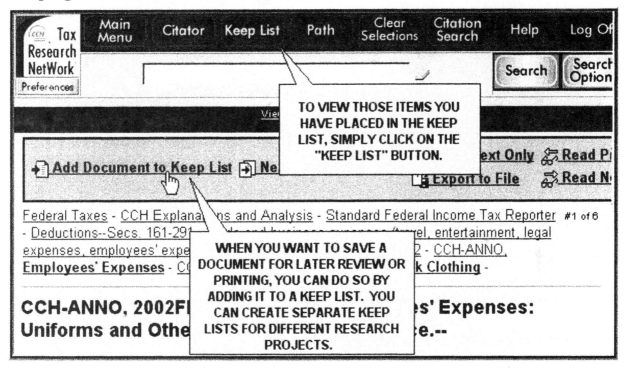

Appendix
C

# Research Using RIA *Checkpoint*
# THE MAIN MENU

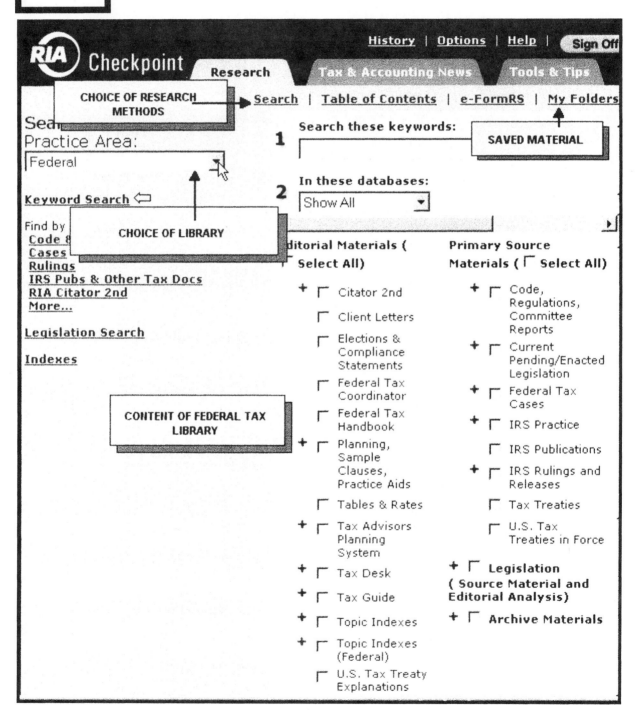

**Research Using RIA *Checkpoint***
**How to Access a Document For Which You Know The Cite**

### THE INTERNAL REVENUE CODE
### AND TREASURY REGULATIONS

**STEP 1:**

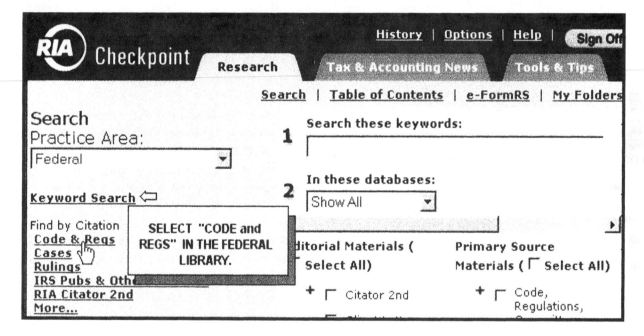

**STEP 2:**

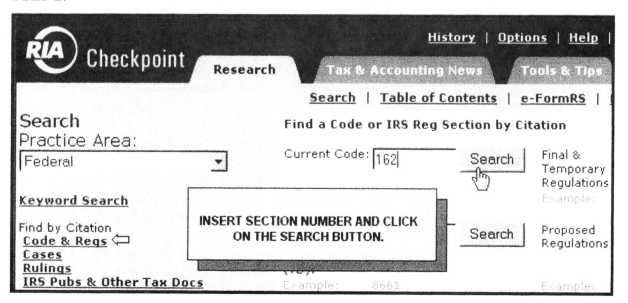

**Appendix C**

**STEP 3:**

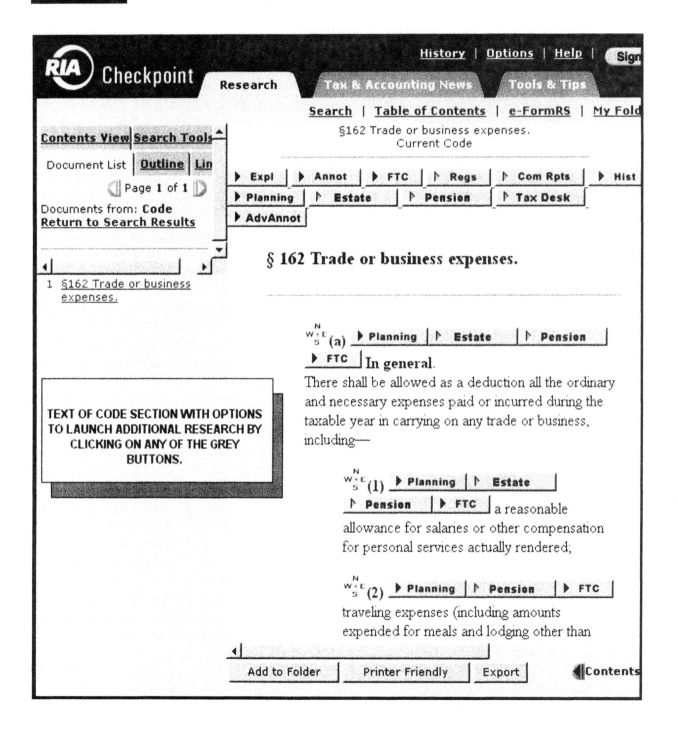

## Research Using RIA *Checkpoint*

## How to Access a Document for Which You Know the Cite

### COURT CASES

**STEP 1:**

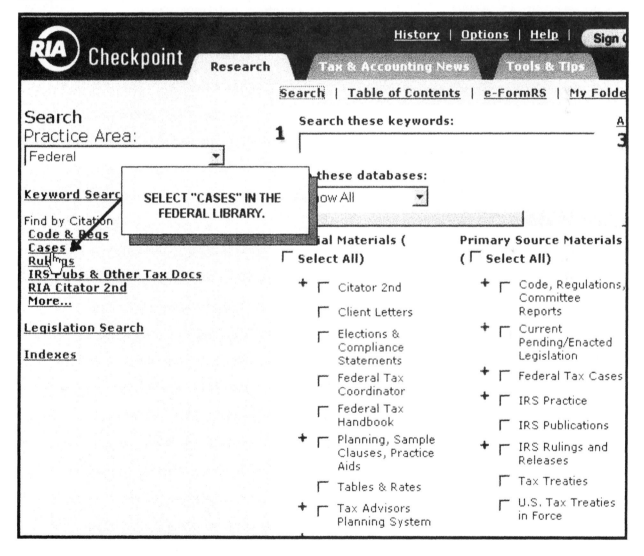

**Appendix C**

**STEPS 2-3:**

**Find a Case by Citation**

American Federal Tax Reports (1860 - Prese[t]

- ⦿ AFTR 2d  ○ AFTR
- ○ S. Ct.  ○ U.S.
- ○ F. 3d  ○ F. 2d
- ○ F.  ○ F. Supp. 2d
- ○ F. Supp  ○ USTC

**STEP 2: SELECT APPROPRIATE SOURCE OF CASE.  NOTE ALL SOURCES, INCLUDING CCH'S USTC, ARE PROVIDED.**

| 12 | 5581 | Search |

Enter Case Name:

Example:

**STEP 3:  INSERT CITE ELEMENTS IN THE FIELDS PROVIDED. THEN CLICK ON THE SEARCH BUTTON.**

Search

Tax Court & Board   Decisions (1928 - Present)

Example: TC Memo 1970-13

Enter Case Name: _____  Search

Example:        Aurora Village Shopping

Tax Court & Board of Tax Appeals Reported Decisions (1924 - Present)
TC or T.C. No. or BTA  _____  Search

Example: 107 TC 301

Enter Case Name: _____  Search

Example:        International Multifoods Corp.

Tax Court Summary Opinions
_____  Search

Example: TC Summary Opinion 2001-129

Enter Case Name: _____  Search

STEP 4:

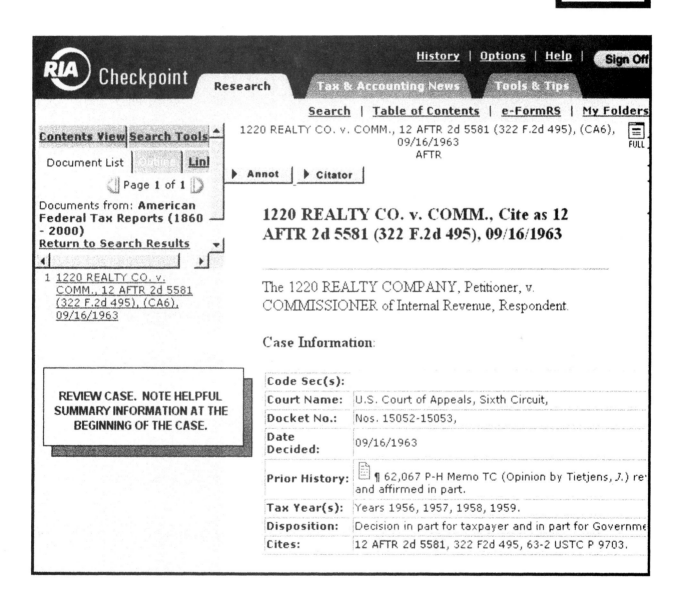

REVIEW CASE. NOTE HELPFUL
SUMMARY INFORMATION AT THE
BEGINNING OF THE CASE.

| Appendix C |
|---|

**Research Using RIA *Checkpoint***
**How to Access a Document for Which You Know the Cite**

## REVENUE RULINGS

**STEP 1:**

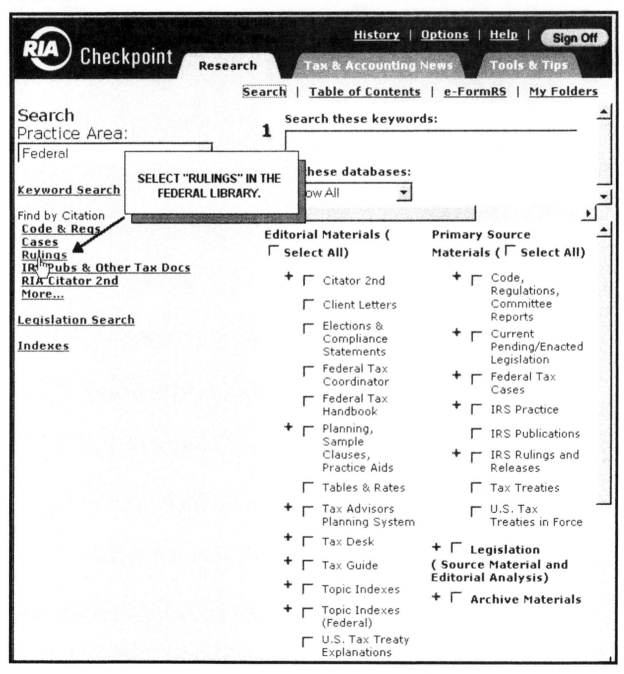

**STEP 2:**

**Find a Ruling by Citation    [Back to Top]**

Revenue Rulings: | 62-180 |    Search     Revenue Procedures: | |    Search

Example:    99-7 or                        Example:    99-10 or
            2000-4 or 00-4                             2000-4 or 00-4

Announcements: | |    Search     Notices: | |    Search

Example:    99-11 or                       Example:    99-12 or
            2000-4 or 00-4                             2000-4 or 00-4

Private Letter     | |    Search
Rulings/TAM:                                          INSERT RULING NUMBER IN FIELD
Example:    9611048 or                                PROVIDED.  CLICK ON SEARCH BUTTON       ch
            199908039                                 NEXT TO FIELD.

---

**Find IRS Pubs and Other Tax Documents by Citation    [Back to Top]**

IRS Publications: | |    Search     Field Service    | |    Search
                                    Advice:

Example:    17                         Example:    1-9913006 or
                                                   1999-687

Tax Court Rule: | |    Search     Treasury Dept.  | |    Search
                                  Circular 230:

Example:    31(a)                     Example:    10.50

IRS Information   | |    Search
Release:

**Appendix C**

**Research Using RIA *Checkpoint***

**How to Locate a Court Case for Which
You Only Know the Name**

**STEP 1:**

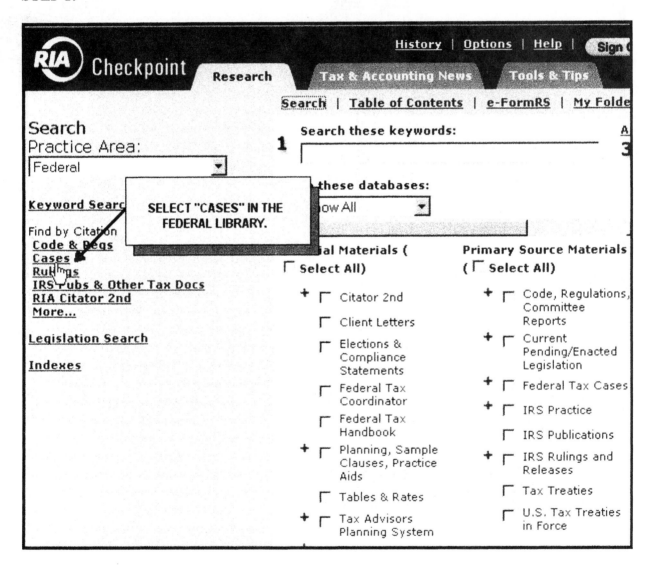

**STEP 2:**

**Find a Case by Citation** **[Back to T**

American Federal Tax Reports (1860 - P

SCROLL DOWN UNTIL YOU LOCATE THE
APPROPRIATE FIELD. NOTE THAT TAX COURT
CASES ARE NOT IN THE AFTR SOURCES.
RATHER, THEY ARE FOUND BELOW. WHEN
SEARCHING FOR A TC CASE, IT DOES NOT
MATTER WHICH AFTR CIRCLE IS CHECKED.

- ⚬ AFTR 2d  ⚬ AFTR
- ⚬ S. Ct.  ⚬ U.S.
- ⚬ F. 3d  ⚬ F. 2d
- ⚬ F.  ⚬ F. Supp. 2
- ⚬ F. Supp  ⦿ USTC

[ Search ]

Enter Case Name: [ ] [ Search ]

Example:  South Louisiana Bank

Tax Court & Board of Tax Appeals Memorandum Decisions (1928 - Present)

[ Search ]

Example: TC Memo 1970-25

ENTER CASE NAME (TAXPAYER NAME
ONLY). THEN CLICK ON THE SEARCH
BUTTON NEXT TO THE FIELD.

Enter Case Name: [ ]

Example:  Aurora Village Shopping

Tax Court & Board of Tax Appeals Reported Decisions (1924 - Present)

TC or T.C. No. or BTA [ Search ]

Example: 107 TC 301

Enter Case Name: [ DRAPPER ] [ Search ]

Example:  International Multifoods Corp.

**Appendix
C**

## Research Using RIA *Checkpoint*

## How to check the validity of an authority – "citating"
### Citing a Case or Revenue Ruling for Which You Know the Cite

**STEP 1:**

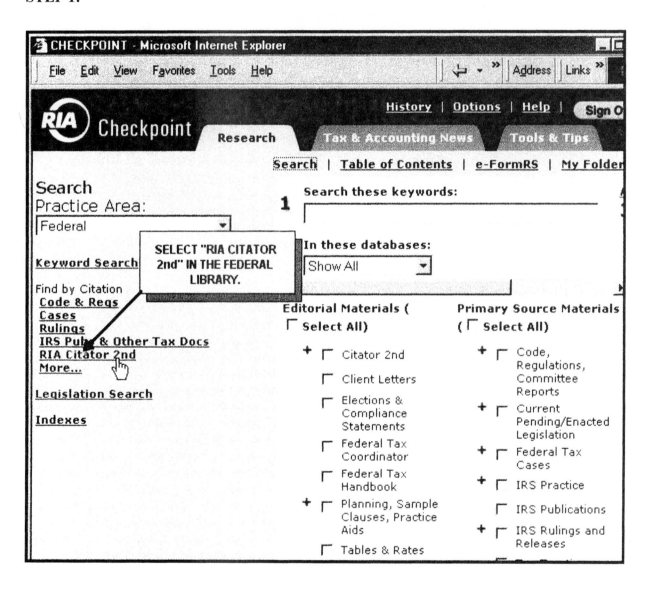

**STEP 2:**

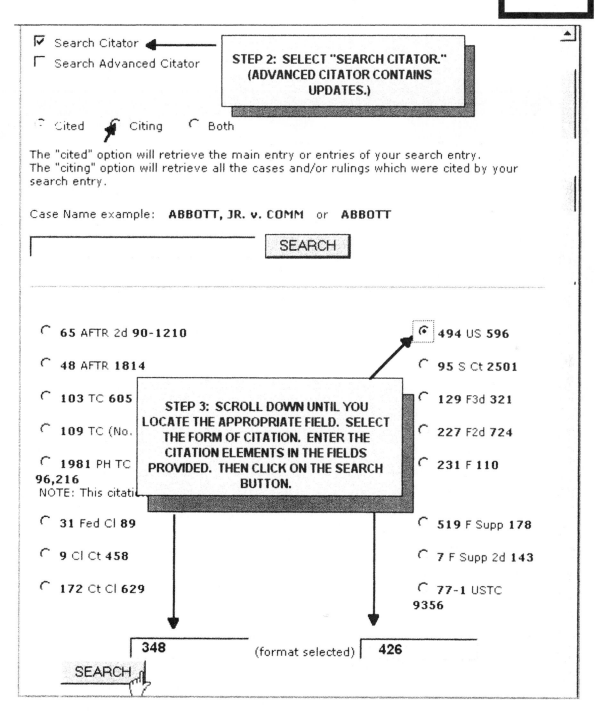

☑  Search Citator

☐  Search Advanced Citator

**STEP 2: SELECT "SEARCH CITATOR."
(ADVANCED CITATOR CONTAINS
UPDATES.)**

○ Cited    ○ Citing    ○ Both

The "cited" option will retrieve the main entry or entries of your search entry.
The "citing" option will retrieve all the cases and/or rulings which were cited by your
search entry.

Case Name example:   **ABBOTT, JR. v. COMM**   or   **ABBOTT**

[                                  ]   | SEARCH |

○  65 AFTR 2d **90-1210**                        ⊙  **494** US **596**

○  48 AFTR **1814**                               ○  **95** S Ct **2501**

○  **103** TC **605**                             ○  **129** F3d **321**

**STEP 3: SCROLL DOWN UNTIL YOU
LOCATE THE APPROPRIATE FIELD.  SELECT
THE FORM OF CITATION.  ENTER THE
CITATION ELEMENTS IN THE FIELDS
PROVIDED.  THEN CLICK ON THE SEARCH
BUTTON.**

○  **109** TC (No.                                ○  **227** F2d **724**

○  **1981** PH TC                                 ○  **231** F **110**
**96,216**
NOTE: This citati

○  **31** Fed Cl **89**                           ○  **519** F Supp **178**

○  **9** Cl Ct **458**                            ○  **7** F Supp 2d **143**

○  **172** Ct Cl **629**                          ○  **77-1** USTC
**9356**

| **348** |  (format selected) | **426** |

| SEARCH |

Appendix
C

**STEP 3:**

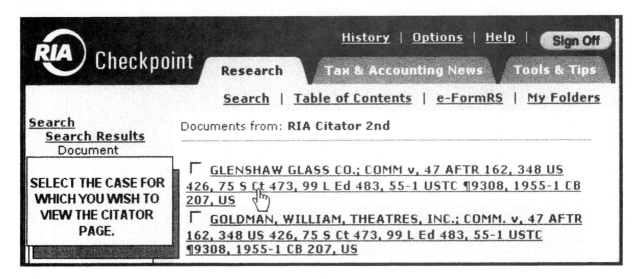

**STEP 4:**

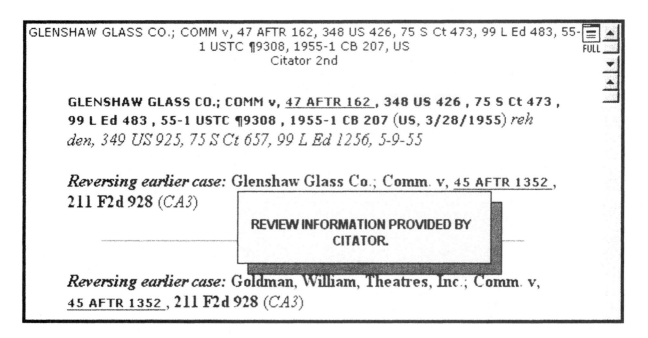

# Research Using RIA *Checkpoint*

## How to check the validity of an authority – "citating"

### Citating a Case or Revenue Ruling from the Document Itself

COMMISSIONER OF INTERNAL REV. v. GLENSHAW GLASS CO., 47 AFTR 162 (75 S.Ct. 473), (S Ct), 03/28/1955
AFTR

▶ Annot   ▶ FTC   ▶ Citator ◀

WHILE IN A CASE OR REVENUE RULING, LOCATE THE CITATOR BUTTON AT THE TOP OF THE CASE. CLICK TO RETRIEVE CITATOR PAGE.

## COMMISSIONER OF INTERN. GLENSHAW GLASS CO., Cite S.Ct. 473), 03/28/1955

COMMISSIONER OF INTERNAL REVENUE, Petitioner, v. GLENSHAW GLASS COMPANY and William Goldman Theatres, Inc.

### Case Information:

| Code Sec(s): | |
|---|---|
| Court Name: | U.S. Supreme Court. |
| Docket No.: | No. 199. |
| Date Argued: | 02/28/1955 |
| Date Decided: | 03/28/1955Rehearing Denied May 9, 1955. |
| Disposition: | |
| Related Proceedings: | See 349 U.S. 925, 75 S.Ct. 657. |
| Cites: | 47 AFTR 162, 348 US 426, 75 S Ct 473, 99 L Ed 483, 55-1 |

| Appendix C |
|---|

## Research Using RIA *Checkpoint*

## SAMPLE RESEARCH PROJECT

Your client has just had an expensive face-lift and asks you to determine whether the expenses for the surgery are deductible.

## USING THE INDEX

**STEP 1:**

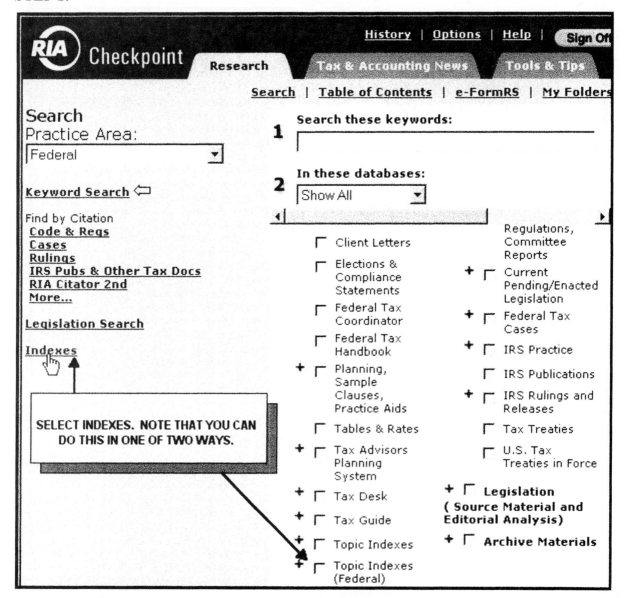

SELECT INDEXES. NOTE THAT YOU CAN DO THIS IN ONE OF TWO WAYS.

**STEP 2:**

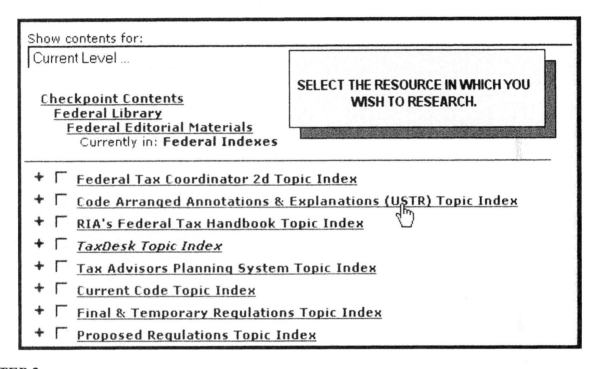

**STEP 3:**

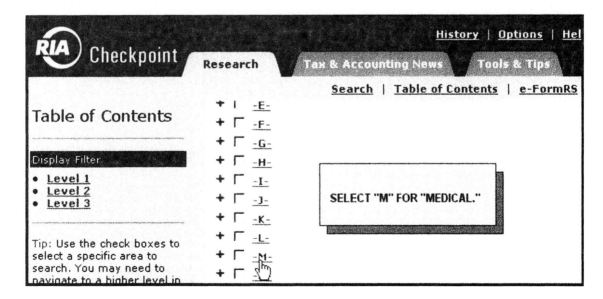

Appendix
C

STEP 4:

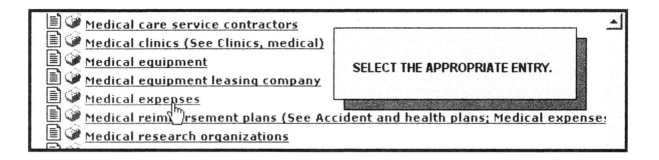

STEP 5:

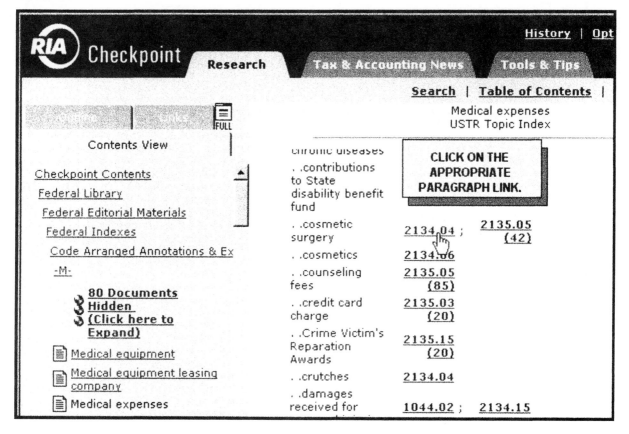

## Research Using RIA *Checkpoint*

## SAMPLE RESEARCH PROJECT

> Your client has just had an expensive face-lift and asks you to
> determine whether the expenses for the surgery are deductible.

## USING THE TABLE OF CONTENTS

**STEP 1:**

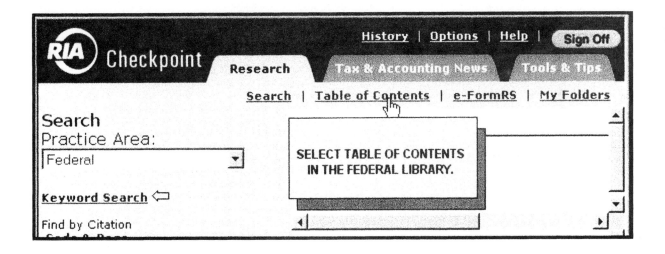

Appendix
C

**STEP 2:**

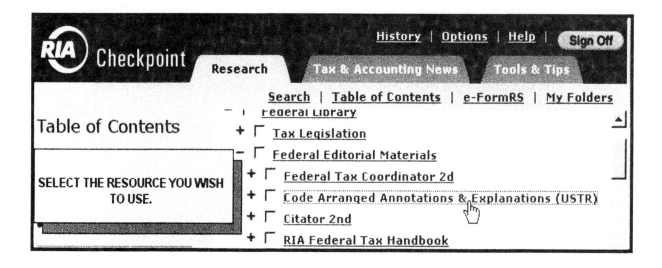

**STEP 3:**

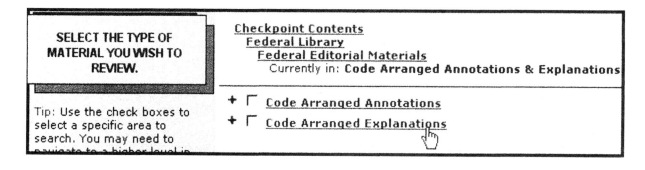

**STEP 4:**

+ ☐ <u>Overviews - Income</u>
+ ☐ <u>Income</u>
+ ☐ <u>Overviews - Estate and Gift</u>
+ ☐ <u>Estate & Gift</u>

> **SELECT THE APPROPRIATE SUBJECT MATTER.**

**STEP 5:**

<u>Checkpoint Contents</u>
  <u>Federal Library</u>
    <u>Federal Editorial Materials</u>
      <u>Code Arranged Annotations & Explanations (USTR)</u>
        <u>Code Arranged Explanations</u>
        Currently in: **Income**

+ ☐ <u>Determination of Tax Liability (¶14 -- ¶59B8.4)</u>
+ ☐ <u>Gross Income -- Taxable Income (¶614 -- ¶684)</u>
+ ☐ <u>Alimony Annuities (¶714 -- ¶904)</u>
+ ☐ <u>Exclusions (¶1014 -- ¶1394)</u>
+ ☐ <u>Tax-Exempt Bonds Personal Exemptio</u>
+ ☐ <u>Business Expenses (¶1614 -- ¶1624)</u>
+ ☐ <u>Interest Deductions Taxes (¶1634 -- ¶</u>
+ ☐ <u>Losses Bad Debts (¶1654 -- ¶1664)</u>
+ ☐ <u>Depreciation (¶1674 -- ¶1694)</u>
+ ☐ <u>Charitable Contributions (¶1704 -- ¶1714)</u>
+ ☐ <u>Net Operating Losses Other Business Expenses (¶1724 -- ¶1984)</u>
+ ☐ <u>Additional Individual Deductions (¶2114 -- ¶2228.40)</u>
+ ☐ <u>Special Corporate Deductions (¶2414 -- ¶2914)</u>

> **SELECT THE APPROPRIATE TOPIC.**

**Appendix C**

**STEPS 6 -7:**

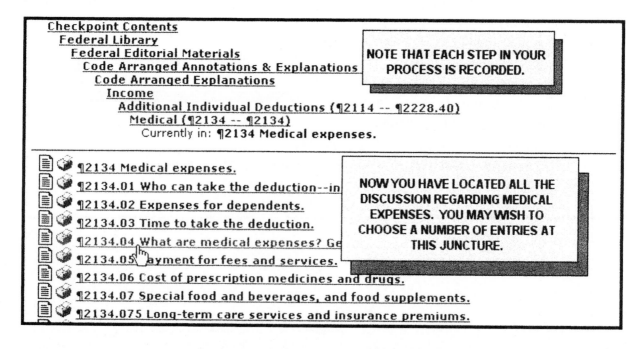

+ ☐ <u>Nonbusiness Expenses (¶2114 -- ¶2124</u>

+ ☐ <u>Medical (¶2134 -- ¶2134)</u>

+ ☐ <u>Other Deductions ¶2154 -- ¶2228.40)</u>

> **CONTINUE SELECTING THE APPROPRIATE TOPICS.**

---

<u>Checkpoint Contents</u>
   <u>Federal Library</u>
      <u>Federal Editorial Materials</u>
         <u>Code Arranged Annotations & Explanations (USTR)</u>
            <u>Code Arranged Explanations</u>
               <u>Income</u>
                  <u>Additional Individual Deductions (¶2114 -- ¶2228.40)</u>
                    Currently in: **Medical (¶2134 -- ¶2134)**

+ ☐ <u>¶2134 Medical expenses.</u>

**STEP 8:**

<u>Checkpoint Contents</u>
   <u>Federal Library</u>
      <u>Federal Editorial Materials</u>
         <u>Code Arranged Annotations & Explanations</u>
            <u>Code Arranged Explanations</u>
               <u>Income</u>
                  <u>Additional Individual Deductions (¶2114 -- ¶2228.40)</u>
                    <u>Medical (¶2134 -- ¶2134)</u>
                      Currently in: **¶2134 Medical expenses.**

> **NOTE THAT EACH STEP IN YOUR PROCESS IS RECORDED.**

📄🔍 <u>¶2134 Medical expenses.</u>

📄🔍 <u>¶2134.01 Who can take the deduction--in</u>

📄🔍 <u>¶2134.02 Expenses for dependents.</u>

📄🔍 <u>¶2134.03 Time to take the deduction.</u>

📄🔍 <u>¶2134.04 What are medical expenses? Ge</u>

📄🔍 <u>¶2134.05 ayment for fees and services.</u>

📄🔍 <u>¶2134.06 Cost of prescription medicines and drugs.</u>

📄🔍 <u>¶2134.07 Special food and beverages, and food supplements.</u>

📄🔍 <u>¶2134.075 Long-term care services and insurance premiums.</u>

> **NOW YOU HAVE LOCATED ALL THE DISCUSSION REGARDING MEDICAL EXPENSES. YOU MAY WISH TO CHOOSE A NUMBER OF ENTRIES AT THIS JUNCTURE.**

## Research Using RIA *Checkpoint*
### SAMPLE RESEARCH PROJECT

Your client has just had an expensive face-lift and asks you to
determine whether the expenses for the surgery are deductible.

## USING SEARCHING

**STEPS 1-3:**

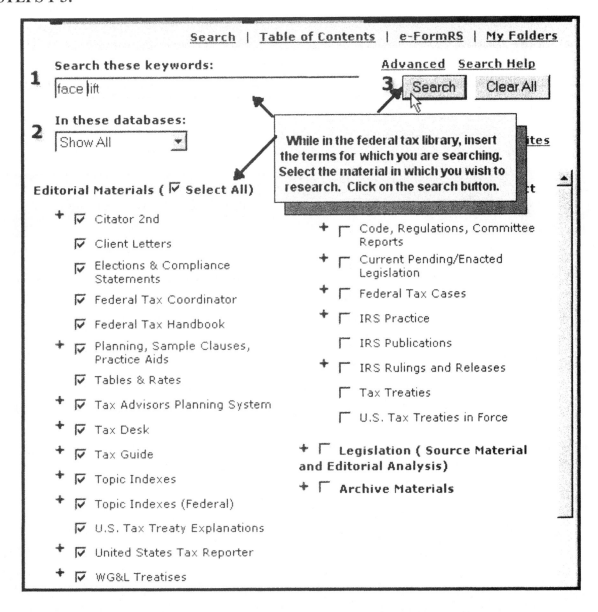

Search | Table of Contents | e-FormRS | My Folders

**1** Search these keywords:

face lift

Advanced   Search Help

**3** Search    Clear All

**2** In these databases:

Show All

While in the federal tax library, insert
the terms for which you are searching.
Select the material in which you wish to
research. Click on the search button.

**Editorial Materials ( ☑ Select All)**

+ ☑ Citator 2nd

☑ Client Letters

☑ Elections & Compliance
Statements

☑ Federal Tax Coordinator

☑ Federal Tax Handbook

+ ☑ Planning, Sample Clauses,
Practice Aids

☑ Tables & Rates

+ ☑ Tax Advisors Planning System

+ ☑ Tax Desk

+ ☑ Tax Guide

+ ☑ Topic Indexes

+ ☑ Topic Indexes (Federal)

☑ U.S. Tax Treaty Explanations

+ ☑ United States Tax Reporter

+ ☑ WG&L Treatises

+ ☐ Code, Regulations, Committee
Reports

+ ☐ Current Pending/Enacted
Legislation

+ ☐ Federal Tax Cases

+ ☐ IRS Practice

☐ IRS Publications

+ ☐ IRS Rulings and Releases

☐ Tax Treaties

☐ U.S. Tax Treaties in Force

+ ☐ **Legislation ( Source Material
and Editorial Analysis)**

+ ☐ **Archive Materials**

Appendix
C

STEP 4:

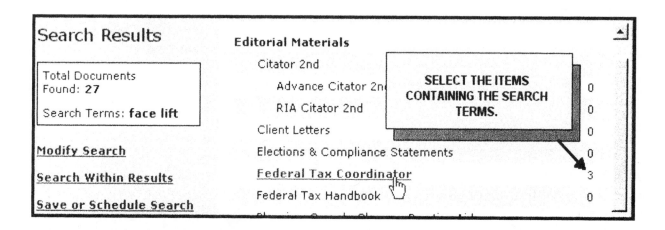

STEP 5:

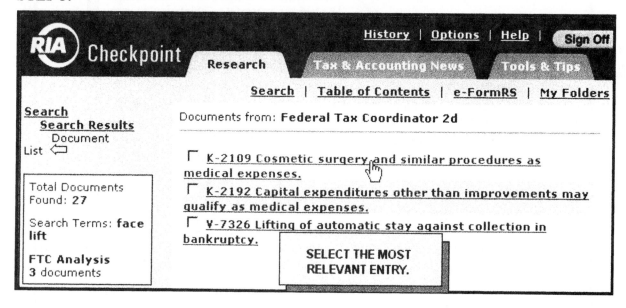

**Research Using RIA** *Checkpoint*

## USEFUL TOOLS

## Location Guide:

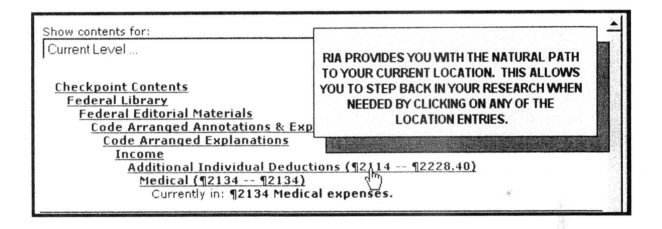

**Research Using RIA *Checkpoint***

**USEFUL TOOLS**
**History of Your Research Path:**

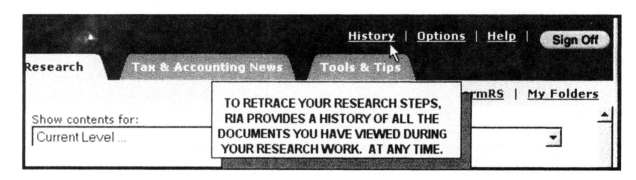

| Name: 4/10/2002 11:15 PM | | Starts: 4/10/2002 11:15 PM Last Access: *in progress…* | | |
|---|---|---|---|---|
| **Event** | **Research Event** | **Notes** | **Information** | **Date*** |
| 🔍 💾 | **162**<br>(1 documents) | | Code | 4/10/2002<br>11:26 PM |
| 📄 ☐ | **§162 Trade or business expenses.** | | Code | 4/10/2002<br>11:27 PM |
| 🔍 💾 | **12 5561**<br>(0 documents) | | American Federal Tax<br>Reports (1860 - 2000);<br>American Federal Tax<br>Reports (Current Year) | 4/10/2002<br>11:35 PM |
| 🔍 💾 | **12 5581**<br>(1 documents) | | American Federal Tax<br>Reports (1860 - 2000);<br>American Federal Tax<br>Reports (Current Year) | 4/10/2002<br>11:36 PM |
| 📄 ☐ | **1220 REALTY CO. v. COMM., 12 AFTR<br>2d 5581 (322 F.2d 495), (CA6),<br>09/16/1963** | | American Federal Tax<br>Reports (1860 - 2000) | 4/10/2002<br>11:37 PM |
| 🔍 💾 | **62-180**<br>(1 documents) | | Revenue Rulings (1954 -<br>Present) | 4/10/2002<br>11:42 PM |
| 📄 ☐ | **Rev. Rul. 62-180, 1962-2 CB 52 -- IRC<br>Sec(s). 162** | | Revenue Rulings (1954 -<br>Present) | 4/10/2002<br>11:43 PM |
| 🔍 💾 | **348 426**<br>(2 documents) | | RIA Citator 2nd | 4/10/2002<br>11:50 PM |

Callout in top figure: TO RETRACE YOUR RESEARCH STEPS, RIA PROVIDES A HISTORY OF ALL THE DOCUMENTS YOU HAVE VIEWED DURING YOUR RESEARCH WORK. AT ANY TIME.

Callout in bottom figure: YOUR RESEARCH HISTORY CONTAINS EACH DOCUMENT VIEWED AS WELL AS START TIME OF RESEARCH.

**Research Using RIA *Checkpoint***
**USEFUL TOOLS**
**Keeping a Document for Later Review:**

Appendix
C

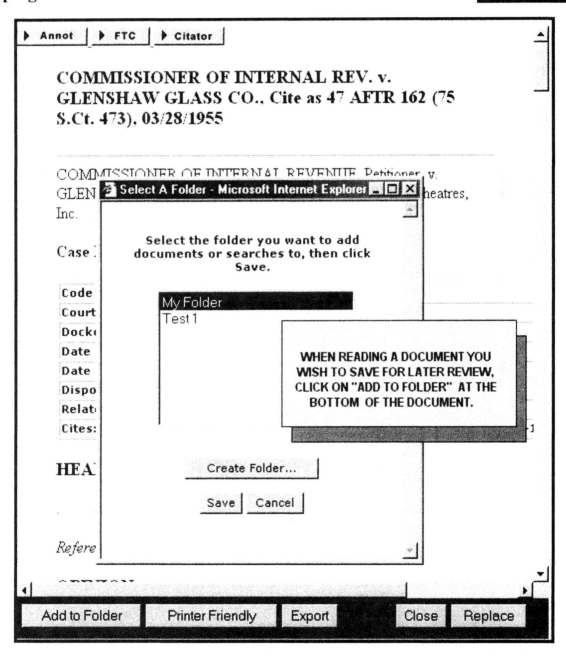

| Appendix D | **Research Using Tax Analysts' *TaxBase*** |

## THE MAIN MENU

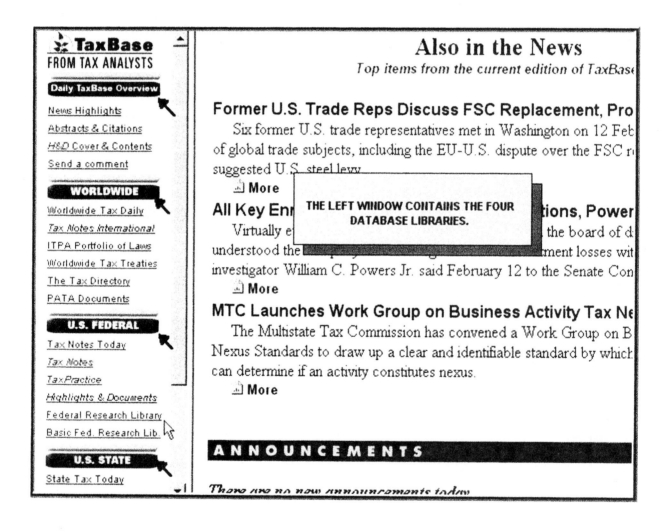

# Research Using Tax Analysts' *TaxBase*

# How to Access a Document for Which You Know the Cite

# The Internal Revenue Code and Treasury Regulations

## STEP 1:

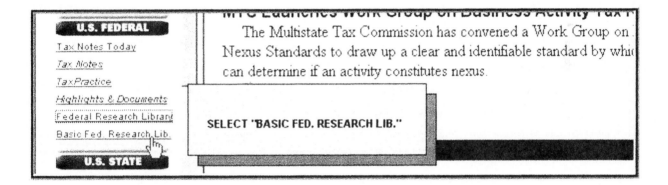

## STEP 2:

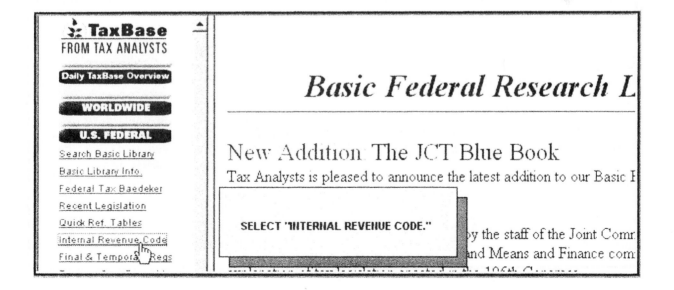

**Appendix D**

**STEP 3:**

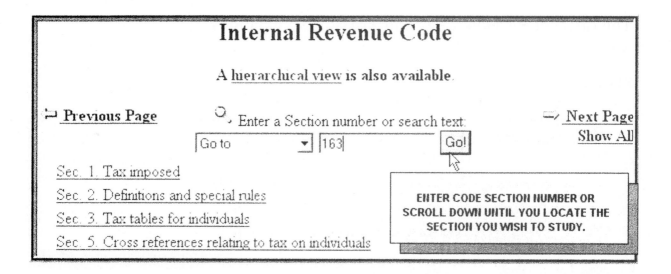

**STEP 4:**

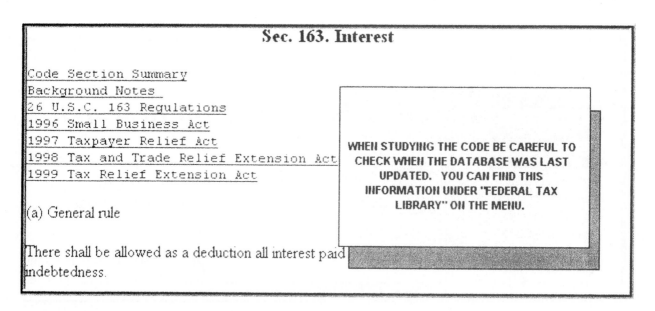

# Research Using Tax Analysts' *TaxBase*

## How to Access a Document for Which You Know the Cite

## REVENUE RULINGS

**STEP 1:** (Note: You cannot access a case by its citation.  Cases may only be accessed by case name).

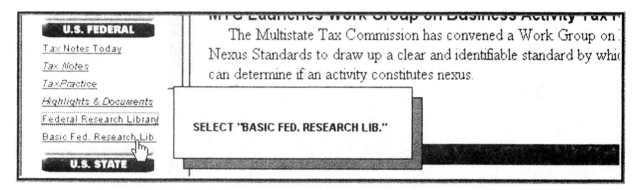

**STEPS 2-3:** (Note that you will not be able to citate the ruling using this database.)

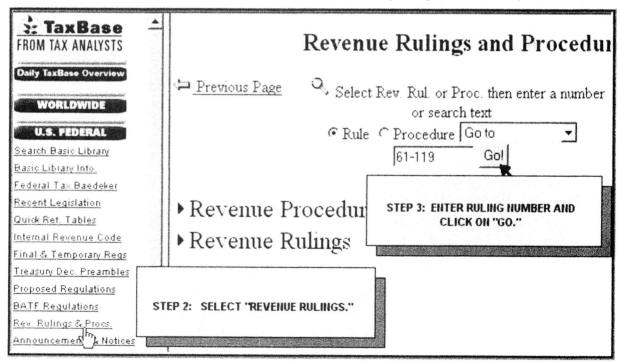

| Appendix D | Research Using Tax Analysts' *TaxBase* |
|---|---|

## How to Locate a Court Case for Which You Only Know the Name

**STEP 1:**

# Research Using Tax Analysts' *TaxBase*

**STEPS 2-5:**

**Appendix
D**

**STEP 6:**

---

### United States Supreme Court

COMMISSIONER OF INTERNAL REVENUE,
Petitioner

v.

NADER E. SOLIMAN

Docket No. 91-998
Date of Decision: January 12, 1993
Judge: Kennedy, Anthony

**REVIEW CASE.  YOU DO
NOT HAVE ACCESS TO A
CITATOR IN THIS
DATABASE.**

Tax Analysts Citation: 1993 TNT 9-1
Parallel Citations: 71 AFTR2d 93-350

---

## Research Using Tax Analysts' *TaxBase*

## SAMPLE RESEARCH PROJECT

Your client has just had an expensive face-lift and asks you to determine whether the expenses for the surgery are deductible.

## USING TABLE OF CONTENTS
(Note: There is no index in this database.)

**STEPS 1-2:**

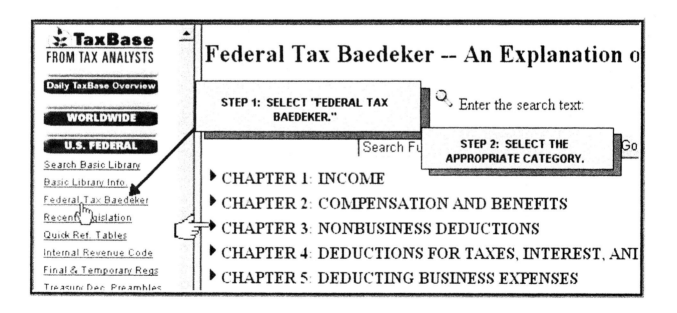

**Appendix D**

**STEP 3:**

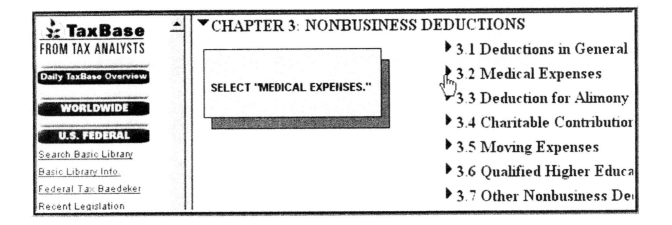

**STEP 4:**

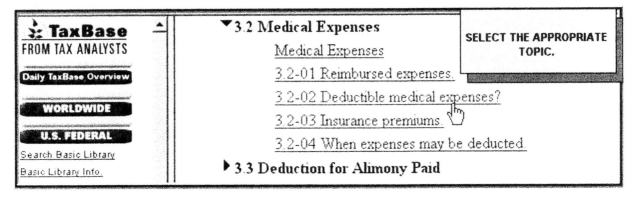

**STEP 5:**

per right for each individual. (IRC
seeking medical care also may clair

STUDY TEXT. NOTE THAT THIS RESOURCE
DOES NOT REFER TO CASE LAW.

**Deductible and nondeductible e**
deductions will be denied? Here are some examples.

Unnecessary cosmetic surgery -- not deductible. Cosmetic surgery includes a
improving the patient's appearance that does not meaningfully promote the pro
or prevent or treat illness or disease. (IRC section 213(d)(9))

Birth control pills prescribed by a physician -- deductible. (Rev. Rul. 73-200,

Legal abortion -- deductible. (Rev. Rul. 73-201, 1973-1 C.B. 140, clarified
9 IRB 4) But payments for illegal abortions or other illegal operations or treat
(Reg. section 1.213-1(e)(1)(ii))

**Appendix D**

### Research Using Tax Analysts' *TaxBase*

### SAMPLE RESEARCH PROJECT

Your client has just had an expensive face-lift and asks you to determine whether the expenses for the surgery are deductible.

## USING SEARCHING

**STEPS 1- 3:**

**TaxBase**
FROM TAX ANALYSTS

Daily TaxBase Overview

WORLDWIDE

U.S. FEDERAL

Search Basic Library
Basic Library Info.
Federal Tax Baedeker
Recent Legislation
Quick Ref. Tables
Internal Revenue Code
Final & Temporary Regs
Treasury Dec. Preamble

*Searching only the Basic Federal*

STEP 1:  SELECT "SEARCH BASIC
         LIBRARY" FROM THE MENU.
STEP 2:  ENTER TERMS TO BE SEARCHED.
STEP 3:  SELECT DATABASE TO SEARCH.

For help with searching, please see

Search for the following word(s) or numbers:

Cosmetic Surgery                    Search

**Databases To Search**

☑ *Search All Basic Federal Research Library Databases*

**STEP 4:**

# TaxBase Search Results for
# "Cosmetic Surgery"

**Internal Revenue Code -- 1 document found**

Sec. 213. Medical, dental, etc., expenses

SELECT THE DOCUMENTS YOU WISH
TO READ.

**IRS Final and Temporary Regulations - No Documents found**

**IRS Proposed Regulations - No Documents found**

**IRS Regulatory Agenda - No Documents found**

**Revenue Rulings and Procedures - No Documents found**

**Announcements and Notices - No Documents found**

**Tax Information Publications -- 2 documents found**

GUIDE TO FREE TAX SERVICES For Tax Year 1999

Appendix
E

# State Tax Research Using CCH *Internet Tax Research NetWork*

## STEP 1:

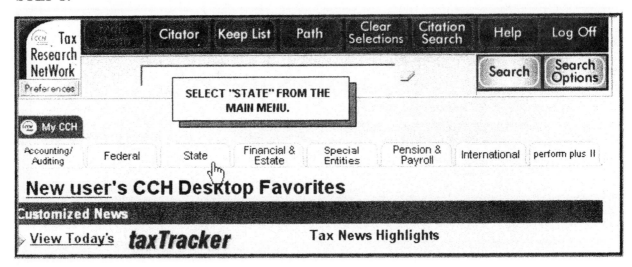

## STEP 2:

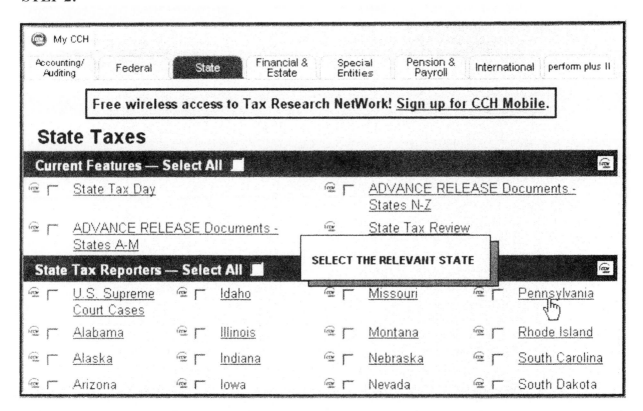

**STEP 3:**

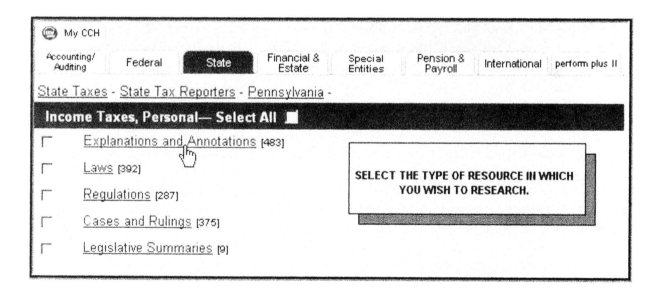

State Taxes - State Tax Reporters -

**Pennsylvania— Select All** ◼

    Administration (see Practice and Procedure) [no documents]

☐  Cigarettes, Tobacco [190]

☐  Franchise/Capital Stock Taxes [846]

☐  Income Taxes, Corporate [1672]

☐  Income Taxes, Personal [1546]

☐  Incorporation and Qualification [248]

> SCROLL THROUGH THE MENU AND SELECT THE MOST PERTINENT ENTRY.

**STEP 4:**

🔵 My CCH

| Accounting/ Auditing | Federal | State | Financial & Estate | Special Entities | Pension & Payroll | International | perform plus II |

State Taxes - State Tax Reporters - Pennsylvania -

**Income Taxes, Personal— Select All** ◼

☐  Explanations and Annotations [483]

☐  Laws [392]

☐  Regulations [287]

☐  Cases and Rulings [375]

☐  Legislative Summaries [9]

> SELECT THE TYPE OF RESOURCE IN WHICH YOU WISH TO RESEARCH.

**Appendix E**

## STEP 5:

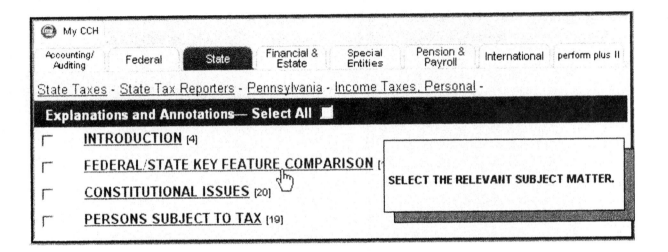

## STEP 6:

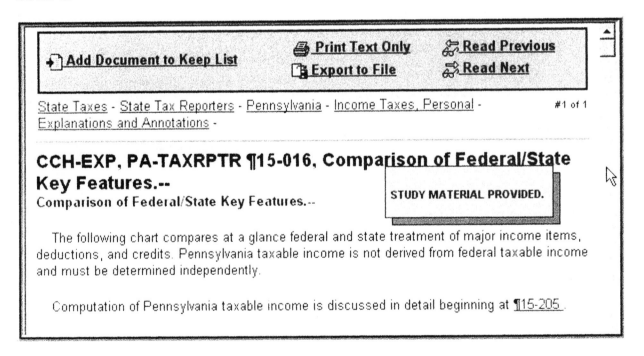

## State Tax Research Using RIA *CHECKPOINT*

**STEP 1:**

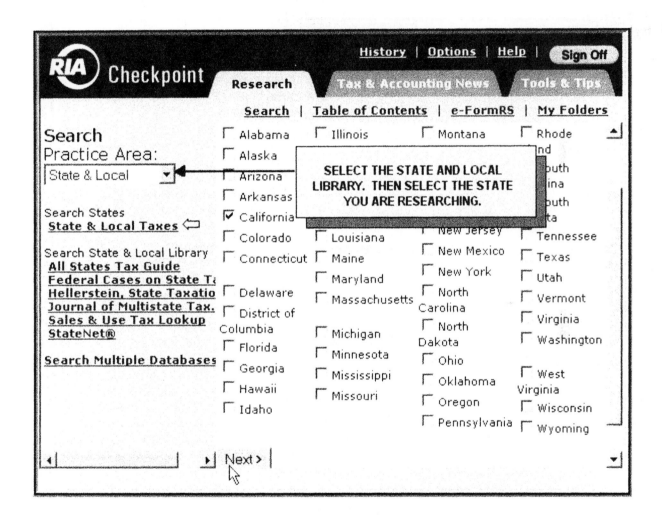

**Appendix F**

**STEP 2:**

☑ Estate & Gift Taxes

☑ Fuels & Minerals Taxes

☑ General Administrative Provisions

☑ Initial Taxes

☑ Licenses & Occu Taxes

☑ Limited Liability Companies

☑ Limited Liability Partnerships

☑ Personal Income

**SELECT THE RELEVANT SUBJECT MATTER AND DOCUMENT TYPE. IF YOU WISH TO SEARCH FOR CERTAIN KEY WORDS, INSERT THOSE WORDS IN THE FIELD PROVIDED.  THEN CLICK ON THE SEARCH BUTTON.**

Select Document Type(s):   | Select All | | Deselect All |

☐ Statutes

☑ Explanations

☐ Forms Instructions

☐ Official Material

☐ List of Approved Laws

☐ Regulations

☐ Annotations

☐ Federal Cases

☐ State Cases

☐ State & Local Weekly Newsletter

☐ Legislative Highlights

☐ Rates

☐ Rulings

☐ Attorney General Opinions

Search these Keywords:                                        **Advanced**

| Net operating loss |                         | Search |

**STEP 3:**

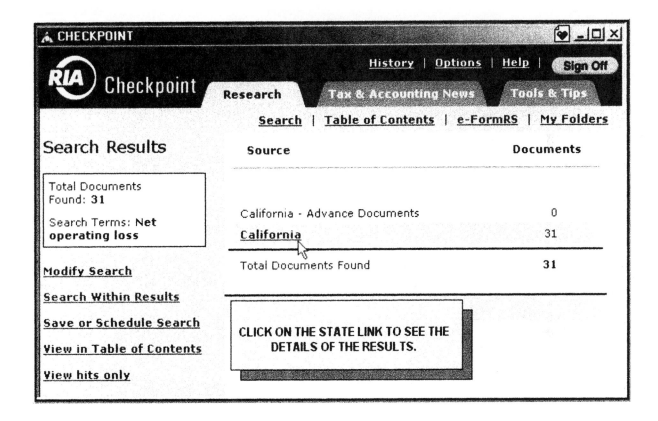

**Appendix F**

**STEP 4:**

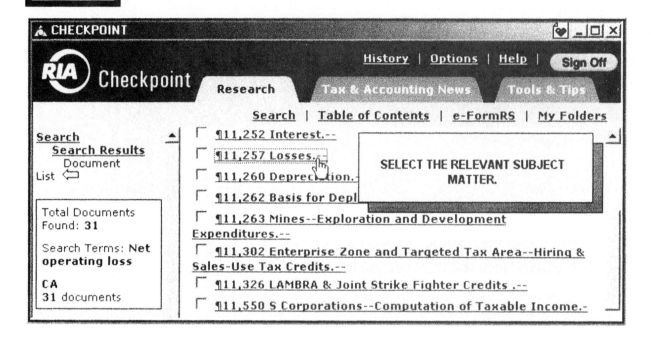

**STEP 5:**

Appendix
F

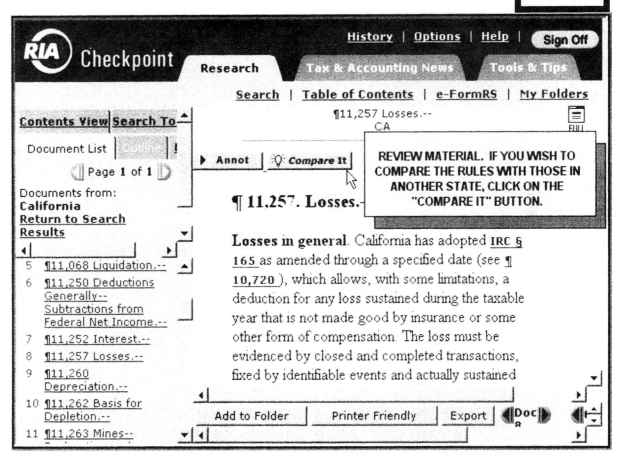

**STEP 6:**

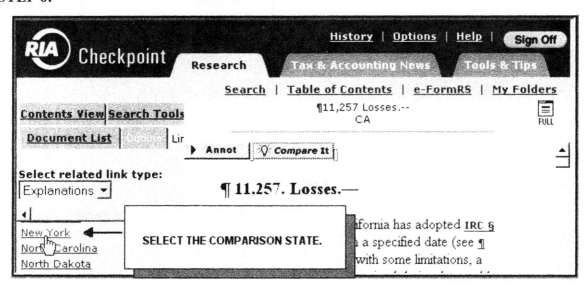

---

**Appendix
G**

# State Research Using Tax Analysts' *TaxBase*

**STEP 1:**

**STEP 2:**                          **STEP 3:**

                          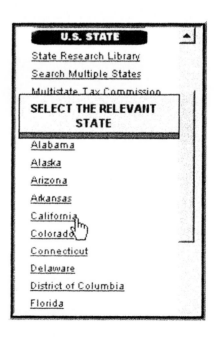

**STEP 4:**

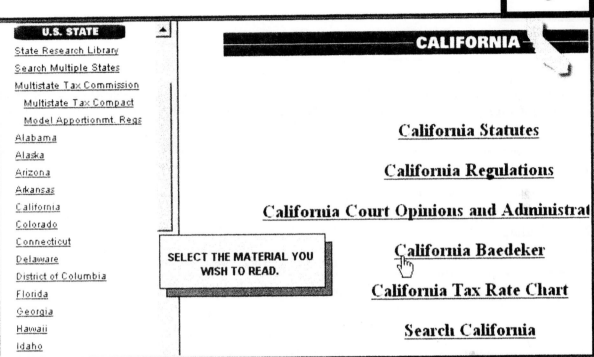

**STEP 5:**

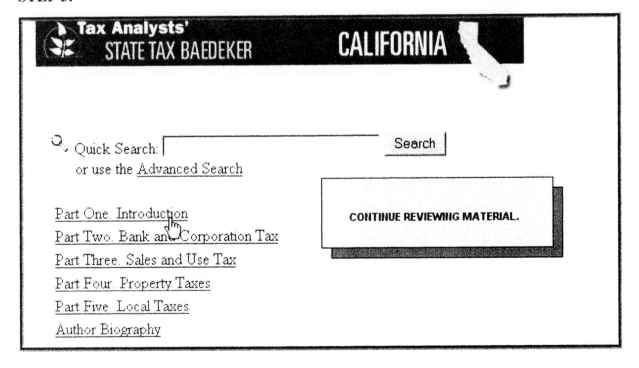

<table>
<tr><td>Appendix<br>H</td><td colspan="2"><h2>Citation Examples</h2></td></tr>
</table>

| Internal Revenue Code | IRC §101(c)(3)(B)(i)(II) | |
|---|---|---|
| Treasury Regulation | Treas. Reg. §1.371-1(a)(4) | |
| Revenue Ruling | Rev. Rul. 75-320, 1975-2 CB 105 | |
| | Rev. Rul. 98-5, IRB 1998-15, 20 | |
| Revenue Procedure | Rev. Proc. 96-1, 1996-1 CB 5 | |
| | Rev. Proc. 99-5, IRB 1999-4, 50 | |
| Letter Ruling | Letter Ruling 98-34-210 | |
| | Letter Ruling 9834210 | |
| Technical Advice Memorandum | TAM 9723400 | |
| | TAM 97-23-400 | |
| IRS Announcement | Announcement 84-9, IRB, 1984-1, 3 | |
| General Counsel Memorandum | GCM 42,789 | |
| Tax Court Regular Case | Name, 100 TC __, No. 5 (1992) | |
| | Name, 100 TC 405 (1992) | |
| Tax Court Memorandum Case | (CCH case book):  Name, 70 TCM 500 (1998) | |
| | (RIA case book):   Name, 1998 P-H Memo TC ¶98,005 | |
| District Court Case | Official:          Name, 800 F.Supp. 300 (SDNY, 1992) | |
| | (CCH case book):  Name, 92-2 USTC ¶500 (SDNY, 1992) | |
| | (RIA case book):   Name, 50 AFTR2d 92-6000 (SDNY, 1992) | |

| Court of Claims Case | Official: | Name, 10 Fed.Cl. 200 (1992) |
|---|---|---|
| | (CCH case book) | Name, 92-2 USTC ¶500 (Cls. Crt.) |
| | (RIA case book): | Name, 50 AFTR2d 92-6000 (Cls. Crt. (1992) |
| Appellate Court Case: | Official: | Name, 100 F.2d. 500 (1992) |
| | (CCH case book): | Name, 92-2 USTC ¶500 (CA 2, 1992) |
| | (RIA case book): | Name, 50 AFTR2d 92-6000 (CA 2, 1992) |
| Supreme Court Case: | Official: | Name, 50 U.S. 200 (1992) |
| | (CCH case book): | Name, 92-2 USTC ¶500 (S.Ct., 1992) |
| | (RIA case book): | Name, 50 AFTR2d 92-6000 (S.Ct., 1992) |

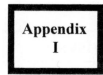

**Appendix I**

# Useful Tax Resource Internet Addresses

## Helpful Gateway Sites

There is a large number of free Web sites available to the general public that provide primary source tax materials. Because the addresses frequently change and grow, the most efficient way to access these materials is through one of the several "gateway" sites. These sites organize the tax material available on the Web and provide direct links to the various sites. Some of them include:

- ❏    www.taxsites.com (maintained by Dennis Schmidt)
- ❏    www.willyancey.com (maintained by Will Yancey)
- ❏    www.abanet.org/tax/sites.html (maintained by ABA Tax Section)

## Selected Tax Publishers' Web Sites (paid subscribers only)

- ❏    tax.cchgroup.com (Commerce Clearing House)
- ❏    www.checkpoint.riag.com (Research Institute of America)
- ❏    taxbase.tax.org (Tax Analysts)

## Selected Web Sites Providing Free Text of the Internal Revenue Code

- ❏    www4.law.cornell.edu/uscode/26
- ❏    tax.cchgroup.com/freecoderegs
- ❏    www.fourmilab.ch/ustax/ustax.html
- ❏    law.house.gov
- ❏    uscode.house.gov/title_26.htm

Code of Federal Regulations
Title 31, Volume 1, Parts 0 to 199
Revised as of July 1, 2000
From the U.S. Government Printing Office via GPO Access
CITE: 31CFR10.0

**Appendix
J**

## TITLE 31 - MONETARY OFFICES, DEPARTMENT OF THE TREASURY
## PART 10--PRACTICE BEFORE THE INTERNAL REVENUE SERVICE

**Appendix
J**

**Appendix J**

## Sec. 10.0  Scope of part.

This part contains rules governing the recognition of attorneys, certified public accountants, enrolled agents, and other persons representing clients before the Internal Revenue Service. Subpart A of this part sets forth rules relating to authority to practice before the Internal Revenue Service; subpart B of this part prescribes the duties and restrictions relating to such practice; subpart C of this part contains rules relating to disciplinary proceedings; subpart D of this part contains rules applicable to disqualification of appraisers; and Subpart E of this part contains general provisions, including provisions relating to the availability of official records.

[59 FR 31526, June 20, 1994]

## SUBPART A--RULES GOVERNING AUTHORITY TO PRACTICE

## Sec. 10.1  Director of Practice.

(a) Establishment of office. There is established in the Office of the Secretary of the Treasury the office of Director of Practice. The Director of Practice shall be appointed by the Secretary of the Treasury.

(b) Duties. The Director of Practice shall act upon applications for enrollment to practice before the Internal Revenue Service; institute and provide for the conduct of disciplinary proceedings relating to attorneys, certified public accountants, enrolled agents, enrolled actuaries and appraisers; make inquiries with respect to matters under his jurisdiction; and perform such other duties as are necessary or appropriate to carry out his functions under this part or as are prescribed by the Secretary of the Treasury.

(c) Acting Director. The Secretary of the Treasury will designate an officer or employee of the Treasury Department to act as Director of Practice in the event of the absence of the director or of a vacancy in that office.

[31 FR 10773, Aug. 13, 1966, as amended at 51 FR 2878, Jan. 22, 1986]

**Appendix J**

## Sec. 10.2  Definitions.

As used in this part, except where the context clearly indicates otherwise: (a) Attorney means any person who is a member in good standing of the bar of the highest court of any State, possession, territory, Commonwealth, or the District of Columbia.

(b) Certified Public Accountant means any person who is duly qualified to practice as a certified public accountant in any State, possession, territory, Commonwealth, or the District of Columbia.

(c) Commissioner refers to the Commissioner of Internal Revenue.

(d) Director refers to the Director of Practice.

(e) Practice before the Internal Revenue Service comprehends all matters connected with a presentation to the Internal Revenue Service or any of its officers or employees relating to a client's rights, privileges, or liabilities under laws or regulations administered by the Internal Revenue Service. Such presentations include preparing and filing necessary documents, corresponding and communicating with the Internal Revenue Service, and representing a client at conferences, hearings, and meetings.

(f) Practitioner means any individual described in Sec. 10.3 (a), (b), (c), or (d) of this part.

(g) A return includes an amended return and a claim for refund.

(h) Service means the Internal Revenue Service.

[59 FR 31526, June 20, 1994]

## Sec. 10.3  Who may practice.

(a) Attorneys. Any attorney who is not currently under suspension or disbarment from practice before the Internal Revenue Service may practice before the Service upon filing with the Service a written declaration that he or she is currently qualified as an attorney and is authorized to represent the particular party on whose behalf he or she acts.

(b) Certified public accountants. Any certified public accountant who is not currently under suspension or disbarment from practice before the Internal Revenue Service may practice before the Service upon filing with the Service a written declaration that he or she is currently qualified as a certified public accountant and is authorized to represent the particular party on whose behalf he or she acts.

(c) Enrolled agents. Any person enrolled as an agent pursuant to this part may practice before the Internal Revenue Service.

(d) Enrolled actuaries. (1) Any individual who is enrolled as an actuary by the Joint Board for the Enrollment of Actuaries pursuant to 29 U.S.C. 1242 may practice before the Internal Revenue Service upon filing with the Service a written declaration that he/she is currently qualified as an enrolled actuary and is authorized to represent the particular party on whose behalf he/she acts. Practice as an enrolled actuary is limited to representation with respect to issues involving the following statutory provisions. Internal Revenue Code (Title 26 U.S.C.) sections: 401 (qualification of employee plans), 403(a) (relating to whether an annuity plan meets the requirements of section 404(a)(2)), 404 (deductibility of employer contributions), 405 (qualification of bond purchase plans), 412 (funding requirements for certain employee plans), 413 (application of qualification requirements to collectively bargained plans and to plans maintained by more than one employer), 414 (containing definitions and special rules relating to the employee plan area), 4971 (relating to excise taxes payable as a result of an accumulated funding deficiency under section 412), 6057 (annual registration of plans), 6058 (information required in connection with certain plans of deferred compensation), 6059 (periodic report of actuary), 6652(e) (failure to file annual registration and other notifications by pension plan), 6652(f) (failure to file information required in connection with certain plans of deferred compensation), 6692 (failure to file actuarial report), 7805(b) (relating to the extent, if any, to which an Internal Revenue Service ruling or determination letter coming under the herein listed statutory provisions shall be applied without retroactive effect); and 29 U.S.C. 1083 (relating to waiver of funding for nonqualified plans).

(2) An individual who practices before the Internal Revenue Service pursuant to this subsection shall be subject to the provisions of this part in the same manner as attorneys, certified public accountants and enrolled agents.

(e) Others. Any individual qualifying under Sec. 10.5(c) or Sec. 10.7 is eligible to practice before the Internal Revenue Service to the extent provided in those sections.

(f) Government officers and employees, and others. An individual, including an officer or employee of the executive, legislative, or judicial branch of the United States Government; officer or employee of the District of Columbia; Member of Congress; or Resident Commissioner, may not practice before the Service if such practice would violate 18 U.S.C. 203 or 205.

(g) State officers and employees. No officer or employee of any State, or subdivision thereof, whose duties require him to pass upon, investigate, or deal with tax matters of such State or subdivision, may practice before the Service, if such State employment may disclose facts or information applicable to Federal tax matters.

[31 FR 10773, Aug. 13, 1966, as amended at 35 FR 13205, Aug. 19, 1970; 36 FR 8671, May 11, 1971; 44 FR 4946, Jan. 24, 1979; 59 FR 31526, June 20, 1994]

### Sec. 10.4  Eligibility for enrollment.

(a) Enrollment upon examination. The Director of Practice may grant enrollment to an applicant who demonstrates special competence in tax matters by written examination administered by the Internal Revenue Service and who has not engaged in any conduct which would justify the suspension or disbarment of any attorney, certified public accountant, or enrolled agent under the provisions of this part.

(b) Enrollment of former Internal Revenue Service employees. The Director of Practice may grant enrollment to an applicant who has not engaged in any conduct which would justify the suspension or disbarment of any attorney, certified public accountant, or enrolled agent under the provisions of this part and who, by virtue of his past service and technical experience in the

**Appendix J**

Internal Revenue Service has qualified for such enrollment, as follows:

(1) Application for enrollment on account of former employment in the Internal Revenue Service shall be made to the Director of Practice. Each applicant will be supplied a form by the Director of Practice, which shall indicate the information required respecting the applicant's qualifications. In addition to the applicant's name, address, citizenship, age, educational experience, etc., such information shall specifically include a detailed account of the applicant's employment in the Internal Revenue Service, which account shall show (i) positions held, (ii) date of each appointment and termination thereof, (iii) nature of services rendered in each position, with particular reference to the degree of technical experience involved, and (iv) name of supervisor in such positions, together with such other information regarding the experience and training of the applicant as may be relevant.

(2) Upon receipt of each such application, it shall be transmitted to the appropriate officer of the Internal Revenue Service with the request that a detailed report of the nature and rating of the applicant's services in the Internal Revenue Service, accompanied by the recommendation of the superior officer in the particular unit or division of the Internal Revenue Service that such employment does or does not qualify the applicant technically or otherwise for the desired authorization, be furnished to the Director of Practice.

(3) In examining the qualification of an applicant for enrollment on account of employment in the Internal Revenue Service, the Director of Practice will be governed by the following policies:

(i) Enrollment on account of such employment may be of unlimited scope or may be limited to permit the presentation of matters only of the particular class or only before the particular unit or division of the Internal Revenue Service for which his former employment in the Internal Revenue Service has qualified the applicant.

(ii) Application for enrollment on account of employment in the Internal Revenue Service must be made within 3 years from the date of separation from such employment.

(iii) It shall be requisite for enrollment on account of such employment that the applicant shall have had a minimum of 5 years continuous employment in the Service during which he shall have been regularly engaged in applying and interpreting the provisions of the Internal Revenue Code and the regulations thereunder relating to income, estate, gift, employment, or excise taxes.

(iv) For the purposes of paragraph (b)(3)(iii) of this section an aggregate of 10 or more years of employment, at least 3 of which occurred within the 5 years preceding the date of application, shall be deemed the equivalent of 5 years continuous employment.

(c) Natural persons. Enrollment to practice may be granted only to natural persons.

[31 FR 10773, Aug. 13, 1966, as amended at 35 FR 13205, Aug. 19, 1970; 42 FR 38352, July 28, 1977; 51 FR 2878, Jan. 22, 1986; 59 FR 31526, June 20, 1994]

### Sec. 10.5  Application for enrollment.

(a) Form; fee. An applicant for enrollment shall file with the Director of Practice of Internal Revenue an application on Form 23, properly executed under oath or affirmation. Such application shall be accompanied by a check or money order in the amount set forth on Form

23, payable to the Internal Revenue Service, which amount shall constitute a fee which shall be charged to each applicant for enrollment. The fee shall be retained by the United States whether or not the applicant is granted enrollment.

(b) Additional information; examination. The Director of Practice, as a condition to consideration of an application for enrollment, may require the applicant to file additional information and to submit to any written or oral examination under oath or otherwise. The Director of Practice shall, upon written request, afford an applicant the opportunity to be heard with respect to his application for enrollment.

(c) Temporary recognition. Upon receipt of a properly executed application, the Director of Practice may grant the applicant temporary recognition to practice pending a determination as to whether enrollment to practice should be granted. Such temporary recognition shall not be granted if the application is not regular on its face; if the information stated therein, if true, is not sufficient to warrant enrollment to practice; if there is any information before the Director of Practice which indicates that the statements in the application are untrue; or which indicates that the applicant would not otherwise qualify for enrollment. Issuance of temporary recognition shall not constitute enrollment to practice or a finding of eligibility for enrollment, and the temporary recognition may be withdrawn at any time by the Director of Practice.

(d) Appeal from denial of application. The Director of Practice, in denying an application for enrollment, shall inform the applicant as to the reason(s) therefor. The applicant may, within 30 days after receipt of the notice of denial, file a written appeal therefrom, together with his/her reasons in support thereof, to the Secretary of the Treasury. A decision on the appeal will be rendered by the Secretary of the Treasury as soon as practicable.

(Sec. 501, Pub. L. 82-137, 65 Stat. 290; 31 U.S.C. 483a)

[31 FR 10773, Aug. 13, 1966, as amended at 42 FR 38352, July 28, 1977; 51 FR 2878 Jan. 22, 1986]

## Sec. 10.6  Enrollment.

(a) Roster. The Director of Practice shall maintain rosters of all individuals:

(1) Who have been granted active enrollment to practice before the Internal Revenue Service;

(2) Whose enrollment has been placed in an inactive status for failure to meet the requirements for renewal of enrollment;

(3) Whose enrollment has been placed in an inactive retirement status;

(4) Who have been disbarred or suspended from practice before the Internal Revenue Service;

(5) Whose offer of consent to resignation from enrollment to practice before the Internal Revenue Service has been accepted by the Director of Practice under Sec. 10.55 of this part; and

(6) Whose application for enrollment has been denied.

(b) Enrollment card. The Director of Practice will issue an enrollment card to each individual whose application for enrollment to practice before the Internal Revenue Service is approved after the effective date of this regulation. Each such enrollment card will be valid for the period stated

**Appendix
J**

thereon. Enrollment cards issued individuals before February 1, 1987 shall become invalid after March 31, 1987. An individual having an invalid enrollment card is not eligible to practice before the Internal Revenue Service.

(c) Term of enrollment. Active enrollment to practice before the Internal Revenue Service is accorded each individual enrolled, so long as renewal of enrollment is effected as provided in this part.

(d) Renewal of enrollment. To maintain active enrollment to practice before the Internal Revenue Service, each individual enrolled is required to have his/her enrollment renewed as set forth herein. Failure by an individual to receive notification from the Director of Practice of the renewal requirement will not be justification for circumvention of such requirement.

(1) All individuals enrolled to practice before the Internal Revenue Service before November 1, 1986 shall apply for renewal of enrollment during the period between November 1, 1986 and January 31, 1987. Those who receive initial enrollment between November 1, 1986 and January 31, 1987 shall apply for renewal of enrollment by March 1, 1987. The first effective date of renewal will be April 1, 1987.

(2) Thereafter, applications for renewal will be required between November 1, 1989 and January 31, 1990, and between November 1 and January 31 of every third year subsequent thereto. Those who receive initial enrollment during the renewal application period shall apply for renewal of enrollment by March 1 of the renewal year. The effective date of renewed enrollment will be April 1, 1990, and April 1 of every third year subsequent thereto.

(3) The Director of Practice will notify the individual of renewal of enrollment and will issue a card evidencing such renewal.

(4) A reasonable nonrefundable fee may be charged for each application for renewal of enrollment filed with the Director of Practice.

(5) Forms required for renewal may be obtained from the Director of Practice, Internal Revenue Service, Washington, DC 20224.

(e) Condition for renewal: Continuing Professional Education. In order to qualify for renewal of enrollment, an individual enrolled to practice before the Internal Revenue Service must certify, on the application for renewal form prescribed by the Director of Practice, that he/she has satisfied the following continuing professional education requirements.

(1) For renewed enrollment effective April 1, 1987. (i) A minimum of 24 hours of continuing education credit must be completed between January 1, 1986 and January 31, 1987.

(ii) An individual who receives initial enrollment between January 1, 1986 and January 31, 1987 is exempt from the continuing education requirement for the renewal of enrollment effective April 1, 1987, but is required to file a timely application for renewal of enrollment.

(2) For renewed enrollment effective April 1, 1990 and every third year thereafter. (i) A minimum of 72 hours of continuing education credit must be completed between February 1, 1987 and January 31, 1990, and during each three year period subsequent thereto. Each such three year period is known as an enrollment cycle.

(ii) A minimum of 16 hours of continuing education credit must be completed in each year of an enrollment cycle.

(iii) An individual who receives initial enrollment during an enrollment cycle must complete two

(2) hours of qualifying continuing education credit for each month enrolled during such enrollment cycle. Enrollment for any part of a month is considered enrollment for the entire month.

(f) Qualifying continuing education--(1) General. To qualify for continuing education credit, a course of learning must:

(i) Be a qualifying program designed to enhance the professional knowledge of an individual in Federal taxation or Federal tax related matters, i.e. programs comprised of current subject matter in Federal taxation or Federal tax related matters to include accounting, financial management, business computer science and taxation; and

(ii) Be conducted by a qualifying sponsor.

(2) Qualifying programs--(i) Formal programs. Formal programs qualify as continuing education programs if they:

(A) Require attendance;

(B) Require that the program be conducted by a qualified instructor, discussion leader or speaker, i.e. a person whose background training, education and/or experience is appropriate for instructing or leading a discussion on the subject matter of the particular program; and

(C) Require a written outline and/or textbook and certificate of attendance provided by the sponsor, all of which must be retained by the attendee for a three year period following renewal of enrollment.

(ii) Correspondence or individual study programs (including taped programs). Qualifying continuing education programs include correspondence or individual study programs completed on an individual basis by the enrolled individual and conducted by qualifying sponsors. The allowable credit hours for such programs will be measured on a basis comparable to the measurement of a seminar or course for credit in an accredited educational institution. Such programs qualify as continuing education programs if they:

(A) Require registration of the participants by the sponsor;

(B) Provide a means for measuring completion by the participants (e.g., written examination); and

(C) Require a written outline and/or textbook and certificate of completion provided by the sponsor which must be retained by the participant for a three year period following renewal of enrollment.

(iii) Serving as an instructor, discussion leader or speaker.

(A) One hour of continuing education credit will be awarded for each contact hour completed as an instructor, discussion leader or speaker at an educational program which meets the continuing education requirements of this part.

(B) Two hours of continuing education credit will be awarded for actual subject preparation time for each contact hour completed as an instructor, discussion leader or speaker at such programs. It will be the responsibility of the individual claiming such credit to maintain records to verify preparation time.

(C) The maximum credit for instruction and preparation may not exceed 50% of the

**Appendix
J**

continuing education requirement for an enrollment cycle.

(D) Presentation of the same subject matter in an instructor, discussion leader or speaker capacity more than one time during an enrollment cycle will not qualify for continuing education credit.

(iv) Credit for published articles, books, etc.

(A) Continuing education credit will be awarded for publications on Federal taxation or Federal tax related matters to include accounting, financial management, business computer science, and taxation, provided the content of such publications is current and designed for the enhancement of the professional knowledge of an individual enrolled to practice before the Internal Revenue Service.

(B) The credit allowed will be on the basis of one hour credit for each hour of preparation time for the material. It will be the responsibility of the person claiming the credit to maintain records to verify preparation time.

(C) The maximum credit for publications may not exceed 25% of the continuing education requirement of any enrollment cycle.

(3) Periodic examination. Individuals may establish eligibility for renewal of enrollment for any enrollment cycle by:

(i) Achieving a passing score on each part of the Special Enrollment Examination administered under this part during the three year period prior to renewal; and

(ii) Completing a minimum of 16 hours of qualifying continuing education during the last year of an enrollment cycle.

(g) Sponsors. (1) Sponsors are those responsible for presenting programs.

(2) To qualify as a sponsor, a program presenter must:

(i) Be an accredited educational institution;

(ii) Be recognized for continuing education purposes by the licensing body of any State, possession, territory, Commonwealth, or the District of Columbia responsible for the issuance of a license in the field of accounting or law;

(iii) Be recognized by the Director of Practice as a professional organization or society whose programs include offering continuing professional education opportunities in subject matter within the scope of this part; or

(iv) File a sponsor agreement with the Director of Practice to obtain approval of the program as a qualified continuing education program.

(3) A qualifying sponsor must ensure the program complies with the following requirements:

(i) Programs must be developed by individual(s) qualified in the subject matter;

(ii) Program subject matter must be current;

(iii) Instructors, discussion leaders, and speakers must be qualified with respect to program content;

(iv) Programs must include some means for evaluation of technical content and presentation;

(v) Certificates of completion must be provided those who have successfully completed the program; and

(vi) Records must be maintained by the sponsor to verify completion of the program and attendance by each participant. Such records must be retained for a period of three years following completion of the program. In the case of continuous conferences, conventions, and the like, records must be maintained to verify completion of the program and attendance by each participant at each segment of the program.

**Appendix J**

(4) Professional organizations or societies wishing to be considered as qualified sponsors shall request such status of the Director of Practice and furnish information in support of the request together with any further information deemed necessary by the Director of Practice.

(5) Sponsor agreements and qualified professional organization or society sponsors approved by the Director of Practice shall remain in effect for one enrollment cycle. The names of such sponsors will be published on a periodic basis.

(h) Measurement of continuing education coursework. (1) All continuing education programs will be measured in terms of contact hours. The shortest recognized program will be one contact hour.

(2) A contact hour is 50 minutes of continuous participation in a program. Credit is granted only for a full contact hour, i.e. 50 minutes or multiples thereof. For example, a program lasting more than 50 minutes but less than 100 minutes will count as one contact hour.

(3) Individual segments at continuous conferences, conventions and the like will be considered one total program. For example, two 90-minute segments (180 minutes) at a continuous conference will count as three contact hours.

(4) For university or college courses, each semester hour credit will equal 15 contact hours and a quarter hour credit will equal 10 contact hours.

(i) Recordkeeping requirements. (1) Each individual applying for renewal shall retain for a period of three years following the date of renewal of enrollment the information required with regard to qualifying continuing professional education credit hours. Such information shall include:

(i) The name of the sponsoring organization;

(ii) The location of the program;

(iii) The title of the program and description of its content, e.g., course syllabi and/or textbook;

(iv) The dates attended;

(v) The credit hours claimed;

(vi) The name(s) of the instructor(s), discussion leader(s), or speaker(s), if appropriate; and

(vii) The certificate of completion and/or signed statement of the hours of attendance obtained from the sponsor.

(2) To receive continuing education credit for service completed as an instructor, discussion leader, or speaker, the following information must be maintained for a period of three years following the date of renewal of enrollment:

(i) The name of the sponsoring organization;

(ii) The location of the program;

(iii) The title of the program and description of its content;

(iv) The dates of the program; and

(v) The credit hours claimed.

(3) To receive continuing education credit for publications, the following information must be maintained for a period of three years following the date of renewal of enrollment:

(i) The publisher;

(ii) The title of the publication;

(iii) A copy of the publication; and

(iv) The date of publication.

(j) Waivers. (1) Waiver from the continuing education requirements for a given period may be granted by the Director of Practice for the following reasons:

(i) Health, which prevented compliance with the continuing education requirements;

(ii) Extended active military duty;

(iii) Absence from the United States for an extended period of time due to employment or other reasons, provided the individual does not practice before the Internal Revenue Service during such absence; and

(iv) Other compelling reasons, which will be considered on a case-by-case basis.

(2) A request for waiver must be accompanied by appropriate documentation. The individual will be required to furnish any additional documentation or explanation deemed necessary by the Director of Practice. Examples of appropriate documentation could be a medical certificate, military orders, etc.

(3) A request for waiver must be filed no later than the last day of the renewal application period.

(4) If a request for waiver is not approved, the individual will be so notified by the Director of Practice and placed on a roster of inactive enrolled individuals.

(5) If a request for waiver is approved, the individual will be so notified and issued a card evidencing such renewal.

(6) Those who are granted waivers are required to file timely applications for renewal of enrollment.

(k) Failure to comply. (1) Compliance by an individual with the requirements of this part shall be determined by the Director of Practice. An individual who fails to meet the requirements of eligibility for renewal of enrollment will be notified by the Director of Practice at his/her last known address by first class mail. The notice will state the basis for the non-compliance and will provide the individual an opportunity to furnish in writing information relating to the matter within 60 days of the date of the notice. Such information will be considered by the Director of Practice in making a final determination as to eligibility for renewal of enrollment.

(2) The Director of Practice may require any individual, by first class mail to his/her last known mailing address, to provide copies of any records required to be maintained under this part. The Director of Practice may disallow any continuing professional education hours claimed if the individual concerned fails to comply with such requirement.

(3) An individual who has not filed a timely application for renewal of enrollment, who has not made a timely response to the notice of non-compliance with the renewal requirements, or who has not satisfied the requirements of eligibility for renewal will be placed on a roster of inactive enrolled individuals for a period of three years. During this time, the individual will be ineligible to practice before the Internal Revenue Service.

(4) During inactive enrollment status or at any other time an individual is ineligible to practice before the Internal Revenue Service, such individual shall not in any manner, directly or indirectly, indicate he or she is enrolled to practice before the Internal Revenue Service, or use

the term ``enrolled agent,'' the designation ``E. A.,'' or other form of reference to eligibility to practice before the Internal Revenue Service.

(5) An individual placed in an inactive status may satisfy the requirements for renewal of enrollment during his/her period of inactive enrollment. If such satisfaction includes completing the continuing education requirement, a minimum of 16 hours of qualifying continuing education hours must be completed in the 12 month period preceding the date on which the renewal application is filed. Continuing education credit under this subsection may not be used to satisfy the requirements of the enrollment cycle in which the individual has been placed back on the active roster.

(6) An individual placed in an inactive status must file an application for renewal of enrollment and satisfy the requirements for renewal as set forth in this section within three years of being placed in an inactive status. The name of such individual otherwise will be removed from the inactive enrollment roster and his/her enrollment will terminate. Eligibility for enrollment must then be reestablished by the individual as provided in this part.   (7) Inactive enrollment status is not available to an individual who is the subject of a discipline matter in the Office of Director of Practice.

(l) Inactive retirement status. An individual who no longer practices before the Internal Revenue Service may request being placed in an inactive status at any time and such individual will be placed in an inactive retirement status. The individual will be ineligible to practice before the Internal Revenue Service. Such individual must file a timely application for renewal of enrollment at each applicable renewal or enrollment as provided in this part. An individual who is placed in an inactive retirement status may be reinstated to an active enrollment status upon filing an application for renewal of enrollment and providing evidence of the completion of the required continuing professional education hours for the enrollment cycle. Inactive retirement status is not available to an individual who is the subject to a discipline matter in the Office of Director of Practice.

(m) Renewal while under suspension or disbarment. An individual who is ineligible to practice before the Internal Revenue Service by virtue of disciplinary action is required to meet the requirements for renewal of enrollment during the period of ineligibility.

(n) Verification. The Director of Practice may review the continuing education records of an enrolled individual and/or qualified sponsor in a manner deemed appropriate to determine compliance with the requirements and standards for renewal of enrollment as provided in this part.

(Approved by the Office of Management and Budget under control number 1545-0946)

[51 FR 2878, Jan. 22, 1986]

## Sec. 10.7  Representing oneself; participating in rulemaking; limited practice; special appearances; and return preparation.

(a) Representing oneself. Individuals may appear on their own behalf before the Internal

**Appendix J**

Revenue Service provided they present satisfactory identification.

(b) Participating in rulemaking. Individuals may participate in rulemaking as provided by the Administrative Procedure Act. See 5 U.S.C. 553.

(c) Limited practice--(1) In general. Subject to the limitations in paragraph (c)(2) of this section, an individual who is not a practitioner may represent a taxpayer before the Internal Revenue Service in the circumstances described in this paragraph (c)(1), even if the taxpayer is not present, provided the individual presents satisfactory identification and proof of his or her authority to represent the taxpayer. The circumstances described in this paragraph (c)(1) are as follows:

(i) An individual may represent a member of his or her immediate family.

(ii) A regular full-time employee of an individual employer may represent the employer.

(iii) A general partner or a regular full-time employee of a partnership may represent the partnership.

(iv) A bona fide officer or a regular full-time employee of a corporation (including a parent, subsidiary, or other affiliated corporation), association, or organized group may represent the corporation, association, or organized group.

(v) A trustee, receiver, guardian, personal representative, administrator, executor, or regular full-time employee of a trust, receivership, guardianship, or estate may represent the trust, receivership, guardianship, or estate.

(vi) An officer or a regular employee of a governmental unit, agency, or authority may represent the governmental unit, agency, or authority in the course of his or her official duties.

(vii) An individual may represent any individual or entity before personnel of the Internal Revenue Service who are outside of the United States.

(viii) An individual who prepares and signs a taxpayer's return as the preparer, or who prepares a return but is not required (by the instructions to the return or regulations) to sign the return, may represent the taxpayer before officers and employees of the Examination Division of the Internal Revenue Service with respect to the tax liability of the taxpayer for the taxable year or period covered by that return.

(2) Limitations. (i) An individual who is under suspension or disbarment from practice before the Internal Revenue Service may not engage in limited practice before the Service under Sec. 10.7(c)(1).

(ii) The Director, after notice and opportunity for a conference, may deny eligibility to engage in limited practice before the Internal Revenue Service under Sec. 10.7(c)(1) to any individual who has engaged in conduct that would justify suspending or disbarring a practitioner from practice before the Service.

(iii) An individual who represents a taxpayer under the authority of Sec. 10.7(c)(1)(viii) is subject to such rules of general applicability regarding standards of conduct, the extent of his or her authority, and other matters as the Director prescribes.

(d) Special appearances. The Director, subject to such conditions as he or she deems appropriate, may authorize an individual who is not otherwise eligible to practice before the Service to represent another person in a particular matter.

(e) Preparing tax returns and furnishing information. An individual may prepare a tax return, appear as a witness for the taxpayer before the Internal Revenue Service, or furnish information at the request of the Service or any of its officers or employees.

[59 FR 31526, June 20, 1994]

### Sec. 10.8  Customhouse brokers.

Nothing contained in the regulations in this part shall be deemed to affect or limit the right of a customhouse broker, licensed as such by the Commissioner of Customs in accordance with the regulations prescribed therefor, in any customs district in which he is so licensed, at the office of the District Director of Internal Revenue or before the National Office of the Internal Revenue Service, to act as a representative in respect to any matters relating specifically to the importation or exportation of merchandise under the customs or internal revenue laws, for any person for whom he has acted as a customhouse broker.

## SUBPART B--DUTIES AND RESTRICTIONS RELATING TO PRACTICE BEFORE THE INTERNAL REVENUE SERVICE

### Sec. 10.20  Information to be furnished.

(a) To the Internal Revenue Service. No attorney, certified public accountant, enrolled agent, or enrolled actuary shall neglect or refuse promptly to submit records or information in any matter before the Internal Revenue Service, upon proper and lawful request by a duly authorized officer or employee of the Internal Revenue Service, or shall interfere, or attempt to interfere, with any proper and lawful effort by the Internal Revenue Service or its officers or employees to obtain any such record or information, unless he believes in good faith and on reasonable grounds that such record or information is privileged or that the request for, or effort to obtain, such record or information is of doubtful legality.

(b) To the Director of Practice. It shall be the duty of an attorney or certified public accountant, who practices before the Internal Revenue Service, or enrolled agent, when requested by the Director of Practice, to provide the Director with any information he may have concerning violation of the regulations in this part by any person, and to testify thereto in any proceeding instituted under this part for the disbarment or suspension of an attorney, certified public accountant, enrolled agent, or enrolled actuary, unless he believes in good faith and on reasonable grounds that such information is privileged or that the request therefor is of doubtful legality.

[31 FR 10773, Aug. 13, 1966, as amended at 57 FR 41095, Sept. 9, 1992]

### Sec. 10.21  Knowledge of client's omission.

Each attorney, certified public accountant, enrolled agent, or enrolled actuary who, having been retained by a client with respect to a matter administered by the Internal Revenue Service, knows that the client has not complied with the revenue laws of the United States or has made an error in or omission from any return, document, affidavit, or other paper which the client is

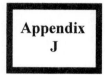
**Appendix J**

required by the revenue laws of the United States to execute, shall advise the client promptly of the fact of such noncompliance, error, or omission.

[42 FR 38352, July 28, 1977, as amended at 57 FR 41095, Sept. 9, 1992]

## Sec. 10.22  Diligence as to accuracy.

Each attorney, certified public accountant, enrolled agent, or enrolled actuary shall exercise due diligence:

(a) In preparing or assisting in the preparation of, approving, and filing returns, documents, affidavits, and other papers relating to Internal Revenue Service matters;

(b) In determining the correctness of oral or written representations made by him to the Department of the Treasury; and

(c) In determining the correctness of oral or written representations made by him to clients with reference to any matter administered by the Internal Revenue Service.

[35 FR 13205, Aug. 19, 1970, as amended at 42 FR 38352, July 28, 1977;
57 FR 41095, Sept. 9, 1992]

## Sec. 10.23  Prompt disposition of pending matters.

No attorney, certified public accountant, enrolled agent, or enrolled actuary shall unreasonably delay the prompt disposition of any matter before the Internal Revenue Service.

## Sec. 10.24  Assistance from disbarred or suspended persons and former Internal Revenue Service employees.

No attorney, certified public accountant, enrolled agent, or enrolled actuary shall, in practice before the Internal Revenue Service, knowingly and directly or indirectly:

(a) Employ or accept assistance from any person who is under disbarment or suspension from practice before the Internal Revenue Service.

(b) Accept employment as associate, correspondent, or subagent from, or share fees with, any such person.

(c) Accept assistance from any former government employee where the provisions of Sec. 10.26 of these regulations or any Federal law would be violated.

[44 FR 4943, Jan. 24, 1979, as amended at 57 FR 41095, Sept. 9, 1992]

## Sec. 10.25  Practice by partners of Government employees.

No partner of an officer or employee of the executive branch of the U.S. Government, of any independent agency of the United States, or of the District of Columbia, shall represent anyone in any matter administered by the Internal Revenue Service in which such officer or employee of the Government participates or has participated personally and substantially as a Government employee or which is the subject of his official responsibility.

[31 FR 10773, Aug. 13, 1966, as amended at 35 FR 13205, Aug. 19, 1970]

### Sec. 10.26  Practice by former Government employees, their partners and their associates.

(a) Definitions. For purposes of Sec. 10.26. (1) Assist means to act in such a way as to advise, furnish information to or otherwise aid another person, directly or indirectly.

(2) Government employee is an officer or employee of the United States or any agency of the United States, including a special government employee as defined in 18 U.S.C. 202(a), or of the District of Columbia, or of any State, or a member of Congress or of any State legislature.

(3) Member of a firm is a sole practitioner or an employee or associate thereof, or a partner, stockholder, associate, affiliate or employee of a partnership, joint venture, corporation, professional association or other affiliation of two or more practitioners who represent non-Government parties.

(4) Practitioner includes any individual described in Sec. 10.3(e).

(5) Official responsibility means the direct administrative or operating authority, whether intermediate or final, and either exercisable alone or with others, and either personally or through subordinates, to approve, disapprove, or otherwise direct Government action, with or without knowledge of the action.

(6) Participate or participation means substantial involvement as a Government employee by making decisions, or preparing or reviewing documents with or without the right to exercise a judgment of approval or disapproval, or participating in conferences or investigations, or rendering advice of a substantial nature.

(7) Rule includes Treasury Regulations, whether issued or under preparation for issuance as Notices of Proposed Rule Making or as Treasury Decisions, and revenue rulings and revenue procedures published in the Internal Revenue bulletin. Rule shall not include a transaction as defined in paragraph (a)(9) of this section.

(8) Transaction means any decision, determination, finding, letter ruling, technical advice, contract or approval or disapproval thereof, relating to a particular factual situation or situations involving a specific party or parties whose rights, privileges, or liabilities under laws or regulations administered by the Internal Revenue Service, or other legal rights, are determined or immediately affected therein and to which the United States is a party or in which it has a direct and substantial interest, whether or not the same taxable periods are involved. Transaction does not include rule as defined in paragraph (a)(7) of this section.

(b) General rules. (1) No former Government employee shall, subsequent to his Government employment, represent anyone in any matter administered by the Internal Revenue Service if the representation would violate 18 U.S.C. 207 (a) or (b) of any other laws of the United States.

(2) No former Government employee who participated in a transaction shall, subsequent to his Government employment, represent or knowingly assist, in that

transaction, any person who is or was a specific party to that transaction.

(3) No former Government employee who within a period of one year prior to the termination of his Government employment had official responsibility for a transaction shall, within one year after his Government employment is ended, represent or knowingly assist in that transaction any person who is or was a specific party to that transaction.

(4) No former Government employee shall, within one year after his Government employment is ended, appear before any employee of the Treasury Department in connection with the publication, withdrawal, amendment, modification, or interpretation of a rule in the development of which the former Government employee participated or for which, within a period of one year prior to the termination of his Government employment, he had official responsibility. However, this subparagraph does not preclude such former employee for appearing on his own behalf or from representing a taxpayer before the Internal Revenue Service in connection with a transaction involving the application or interpretation of such a rule with respect to that transaction: Provided, That such former employee shall not utilize or disclose any confidential information acquired by the former employee in the development of the rule, and shall not contend that the rule is invalid or illegal. In addition, this subparagraph does not preclude such former employee from otherwise advising or acting for any person.

(c) Firm representation. (1) No member of a firm of which a former Government employee is a member may represent or knowingly assist a person who was or is a specific party in any transaction with respect to which the restrictions of paragraph (b)(1) (other than 18 U.S.C. 207 (b)) or (b)(2) of this section apply to the former Government employee, in that transaction, unless:

(i) No member of the firm who had knowledge of the participation by the Government employee in the transaction initiated discussions with the Government employee concerning his becoming a member of the firm until his Government employment is ended or six months after the
termination of his participation in the transaction, whichever is earlier;

(ii) The former Government employee did not initiate any discussions concerning becoming a member of the firm while participating in the transaction or, if such discussions were initiated, they conformed with the requirements of 18 U.S.C. 208(b); and

(iii) The firm isolates the former Government employee in such a way that he does not assist in the representation.

(2) No member of a firm of which a former Government employee is a member may represent or knowingly assist a person who was or is a specific party in any transaction with respect to which the restrictions of paragraph (b)(3) of this section apply to the former employee, in that transaction unless the firm isolates the former Government employee in such a way that he does not assist in the representation.

(3) When isolation of the former Government employee is required under paragraph (c)(1) or (c)(2) of this section, a statement affirming the fact of such isolation shall be executed under oath by the former Government employee and by a member of the firm acting on behalf of the firm, and shall be filed with the Director of Practice and in such other place and in the manner prescribed by regulation. This statement shall clearly identify the firm, the former Government

employee, and the transaction or transactions requiring such isolation.

(d) Pending representation. Practice by former Government employees, their partners and associates with respect to representation in specific matters where actual representation commenced before publication of this regulation is governed by the regulations set forth in the June 1972 amendments to the regulations of this part (published at 37 FR 11676): Provided, that the burden of showing that representation commenced before publication is with the former Government employees, their partners and associates.

[42 FR 38352, July 28, 1977, as amended at 57 FR 41095, Sept. 9, 1992; 59 FR 31527, June 20, 1994]

### Sec. 10.27  Notaries.

No attorney, certified public accountant, enrolled agent, or enrolled actuary as notary public shall with respect to any matter administered by the Internal Revenue Service take acknowledgments, administer oaths, certify papers, or perform any official act in connection with matters in which he is employed as counsel, attorney, or agent, or in which he may be in any way interested before the Internal Revenue Service (26 Op. Atty. Gen. 236).

[31 FR 10773, Aug. 13, 1966, as amended at 57 FR 41095, Sept. 9, 1992]

### Sec. 10.28  Fees.

(a) Generally. A practitioner may not charge an unconscionable fee for representing a client in a matter before the Internal Revenue Service.

(b) Contingent fees for return preparation. A practitioner may not charge a contingent fee for preparing an original return. A practitioner may charge a contingent fee for preparing an amended return or a claim for refund (other than a claim for refund made on an original return) if the practitioner reasonably anticipates at the time the fee arrangement is entered into that the amended return or claim will receive substantive review by the Service. A contingent fee includes a fee that is based on a percentage of the refund shown on a return or a percentage of the taxes saved, or that otherwise depends on the specific result attained.

[59 FR 31527, June 20, 1994]

### Sec. 10.29  Conflicting interests.

No attorney, certified public accountant, enrolled agent, or enrolled actuary shall represent conflicting interests in his practice before the Internal Revenue Service, except by express consent of all directly interested parties after full disclosure has been made.

[31 FR 10773, Aug. 13, 1966, as amended at 57 FR 41095, Sept. 9, 1992]

```
┌─────────────┐
│  Appendix   │
│     J       │
└─────────────┘
```

### Sec. 10.30  Solicitation.

(a) Advertising and solicitation restrictions. (1) No attorney, certified public accountant, enrolled agent, enrolled actuary, or other individual eligible to practice before the Internal Revenue Service shall, with respect to any Internal Revenue Service matter, in any way use or participate in the use of any form of public communication containing (i) A false, fraudulent, unduly influencing, coercive, or unfair statement or claim; or (ii) a misleading or deceptive statement or claim. Enrolled agents, in describing their professional designation, may not utilize the term of art "certified" or indicate an employer/employee relationship with the Internal Revenue Service. Examples of acceptable descriptions are ``enrolled to represent taxpayers before the Internal Revenue Service," "enrolled to practice before the Internal Revenue Service," and "admitted to practice before the Internal Revenue Service." Enrolled agents and enrolled actuaries may abbreviate such designation to either EA or E.A.

(2) No attorney, certified public accountant, enrolled agent, enrolled actuary, or other individual eligible to practice before the Internal Revenue Service shall make, directly or indirectly, an uninvited solicitation of employment in matters related to the Internal Revenue Service. Solicitation includes, but is not limited to, in-person contacts and telephone communications. This restriction does not apply to (i) Seeking new business from an existing or former client in a related matter; (ii) communications with family members; (iii) making the availability of professional services known to other practitioners, so long as the person or firm contacted is not a potential client; (iv) solicitation by mailings; or (v) non-coercive in-person solicitation by those eligible to practice before the Internal Revenue Service while acting as an employee, member, or officer of an exempt organization listed in sections 501(c)(3) or (4) of the Internal Revenue Code of 1954 (26 U.S.C.). Any targeted direct mail solicitation, i.e. a mailing to those whose unique circumstances are the basis for the solicitation, distributed by or on behalf of an attorney, certified public accountant, enrolled agency, enrolled actuary, or other individual eligible to practice before the Internal Revenue Service shall be clearly marked as such in capital letters on the envelope and at the top of the first page of such mailing. In addition, all such solicitations must clearly identify the source of the information used in choosing the recipient.

(b) Fee information. (1) Attorney, certified public accountant, enrolled agent, or enrolled actuary and other individuals eligible to practice before the Internal Revenue Service may disseminate the following fee information:

(i) Fixed fees for specific routine services.

(ii) Hourly rates.

(iii) Range of fees for particular services.

(iv) Fee charged for an initial consultation.

Any statement of fee information concerning matters in which costs may be incurred shall include a statement disclosing whether clients will be responsible for such costs.

(2) Attorney, certified public accountant, enrolled agent, or enrolled actuary and other individuals eligible to practice before the Internal Revenue Service may also publish the availability of a written schedule of fees.

(3) Attorney, certified public accountant, enrolled agent, or enrolled actuary and other

individuals eligible to practice before the Internal Revenue Service shall be
bound to charge the hourly rate, the fixed fee for specific routine services, the
range of fees for particular services, or the fee for an initial consultation
published for a reasonable period of time, but no less than thirty days from the
last publication of such hourly rate or fees.

**Appendix J**

(c) Communications. Communication, including fee information, may include professional
lists, telephone directories, print media, mailings, radio and television, and any other method:
Provided, that the method chosen does not cause the communication to become untruthful,
deceptive, unduly influencing or otherwise in violation of these regulations. It shall be construed
as a violation of these regulations for a practitioner to persist in attempting to contact a
prospective client, if such client has made known to the practitioner a desire not to be solicited.
In the case of radio and television broadcasting, the broadcast shall be pre-recorded and the
practitioner shall retain a recording of the actual audio transmission. In the case of direct mail
communications, the practitioner shall retain a copy of the actual mailing, along with a list or
other description of persons to whom the communication was mailed or otherwise distributed.
Such copy shall be retained by the practitioner for a period of at least 36 months from the date of
the last transmission or use.

(d) Improper associations. An attorney, certified public accountant, enrolled agent, or enrolled
actuary may in matters related to the Internal Revenue Service, employ or accept employment or
assistance as an associate, correspondent, or subagent from, or share fees with, any person or
entity who, to the knowledge of the practitioner, obtains clients or otherwise practices in a
manner forbidden under this section: Provided, That a practitioner does not, directly or indirectly,
act or hold himself out as an Internal Revenue Service practitioner in connection with that
relationship. Nothing herein shall prohibit an attorney, certified public accountant, or enrolled
agent from practice before the Internal Revenue Service in a capacity other than that described
above.

[44 FR 4943, Jan. 24, 1979, as amended at 57 FR 41095, Sept. 9, 1992]

**Sec. 10.31  Negotiation of taxpayer refund checks.**

No attorney, certified public accountant, enrolled agent, or enrolled actuary who is an income
tax return preparer shall endorse or otherwise negotiate any check made in respect of income
taxes which is issued to a taxpayer other than the attorney, certified public accountant or enrolled
agent.

[42 FR 38353, July 28, 1977, as amended at 57 FR 41095, Sept. 9, 1992]
**Sec. 10.32  Practice of law.**

Nothing in the regulations in this part shall be construed as authorizing persons not members
of the bar to practice law.

[31 FR 10773, Aug. 13, 1966. Redesignated at 42 FR 38353, July 28, 1977]

**Appendix J**

### Sec. 10.33  Tax shelter opinions.

(a) Tax shelter opinions and offering materials. A practitioner who provides a tax shelter opinion analyzing the Federal tax effects of a tax shelter investment shall comply with each of the following requirements:

(1) Factual matters. (i) The practitioner must make inquiry as to all relevant facts, be satisfied that the material facts are accurately and completely described in the offering materials, and assure that any representations as to future activities are clearly identified, reasonable and complete.

(ii) A practitioner may not accept as true asserted facts pertaining to the tax shelter which he/she should not, based on his/her background and knowledge, reasonably believe to be true. However, a practitioner need not conduct an audit or independent verification of the asserted facts, or assume that a client's statement of the facts cannot be relied upon, unless he/she has reason to believe that any relevant facts asserted to him/her are untrue.

(iii) If the fair market value of property or the expected financial performance of an investment is relevant to the tax shelter, a practitioner may not accept an appraisal or financial projection as support for the matters claimed therein unless:

(A) The appraisal or financial projection makes sense on its face;

(B) The practitioner reasonably believes that the person making the appraisal or financial projection is competent to do so and is not of dubious reputation; and

(C) The appraisal is based on the definition of fair market value prescribed under the relevant Federal tax provisions.

(iv) If the fair market value of purchased property is to be established by reference to its stated purchase price, the practitioner must examine the terms and conditions upon which the property was (or is to be) purchased to determine whether the stated purchase price reasonably may be considered to be its fair market value.

(2) Relate law to facts. The practitioner must relate the law to the actual facts and, when addressing issues based on future activities, clearly identify what facts are assumed.

(3) Identification of material issues. The practitioner must ascertain that all material Federal tax issues have been considered, and that all of those issues which involve the reasonable possibility of a challenge by the Internal Revenue Service have been fully and fairly addressed in the offering materials.

(4) Opinion on each material issue. Where possible, the practitioner must provide an opinion whether it is more likely than not that an investor will prevail on the merits of each material tax issue presented by the offering which involves a reasonable possibility of a challenge by the Internal Revenue Service. Where such an opinion cannot be given with respect to any material tax issue, the opinion should fully describe the reasons for the practitioner's inability to opine as to the likely outcome.

(5) Overall evaluation. (i) Where possible, the practitioner must provide an overall evaluation whether the material tax benefits in the aggregate more likely than not will be realized. Where such an overall evaluation cannot be given, the opinion should fully describe the reasons for the practitioner's inability to make an overall evaluation. Opinions concluding that an overall

evaluation cannot be provided will be given special scrutiny to determine if the stated reasons are adequate.

(ii) A favorable overall evaluation may not be rendered unless it is based on a conclusion that substantially more than half of the material tax benefits, in terms of their financial impact on a typical investor, more likely than not will be realized if challenged by the Internal Revenue Service.

(iii) If it is not possible to give an overall evaluation, or if the overall evaluation is that the material tax benefits in the aggregate will not be realized, the fact that the practitioner's opinion does not constitute a favorable overall evaluation, or that it is an unfavorable overall evaluation, must be clearly and prominently disclosed in the offering materials.

(iv) The following examples illustrate the principles of this paragraph:

Example (1). A limited partnership acquires real property in a sale-leaseback transaction. The principal tax benefits offered to investing partners consist of depreciation and interest deductions. Lesser tax benefits are offered to investors by reason of several deductions under Internal Revenue Code section 162 (ordinary and necessary business expenses). If a practitioner concludes that it is more likely than not that the partnership will not be treated as the owner of the property for tax purposes (which is required to allow the interest and depreciation deductions), then he/she may not opine to the effect that it is more likely than not that the material tax benefits in the aggregate will be realized, regardless of whether favorable opinions may be given with respect to the deductions claimed under Code section 162.

Example (2). A corporation electing under subchapter S of the Internal Revenue Code is formed to engage in research and development activities. The offering materials forecast that deductions for research and experimental expenditures equal to 75% of the total investment in the corporation will be available during the first two years of the corporation's operations, other expenses will account for another 15% of the total investment, and that little or no gross income will be received by the corporation during this period. The practitioner concludes that it is more likely than not that deductions for research and experimental expenditures will be allowable. The practitioner may render an opinion to the effect that based on this conclusion, it is more likely than not that the material tax benefits in the aggregate will be realized, regardless of whether he/she can opine that it is more likely than not that any of the other tax benefits will be achieved.

Example (3). An investment program is established to acquire offsetting positions in commodities contracts. The objective of the program is to close the loss positions in year one and to close the profit positions in year two. The principal tax benefit offered by the program is a loss in the first year, coupled with the deferral of offsetting gain until the following year. The practitioner concludes that the losses will not be deductible in year one. Accordingly, he/she may not render an opinion to the effect that it is more likely than not that the material tax benefits in the aggregate will be realized, regardless of the fact that he/she is of the opinion that losses not allowable in year one will be allowable in year two, because the principal tax benefit offered is a one-year deferral of income.

Example (4). A limited partnership is formed to acquire, own and operate residential rental real estate. The offering material forecasts gross income of $2,000,000 and total deductions of $10,000,000, resulting in net losses of $8,000,000 over the first six taxable years. Of the total deductions, depreciation and interest are projected to be $7,000,000, and other deductions

$3,000,000. The practitioner concludes that it is more likely than not that all of the depreciation and interest deductions will be allowable, and that it is more likely than not that the other deductions will not be allowed. The practitioner may render an opinion to the effect that it is more likely than not that the material tax benefits in the aggregate will be realized.

(6) Description of opinion. The practitioner must assure that the offering materials correctly and fairly represent the nature and extent of the tax shelter opinion.

(b) Reliance on other opinions--(1) In general. A practitioner may provide an opinion on less than all of the material tax issues only if:

(i) At least one other competent practitioner provides an opinion on the likely outcome with respect to all of the other material tax issues which involve a reasonable possibility of challenge by the Internal Revenue Service, and an overall evaluation whether the material tax benefits in the aggregate more likely than not will be realized, which is disseminated in the same manner as the practitioner's opinion; and

(ii) The practitioner, upon reviewing such other opinions and any offering materials, has no reason to believe that the standards of paragraph (a) of this section have not been complied with. Notwithstanding the foregoing, a practitioner who has not been retained to provide an overall evaluation whether the material tax benefits in the aggregate more likely than not will be realized may issue an opinion on less than all the material tax issues only if he/she has no reason to believe, based on his/her knowledge and experience, that the overall evaluation given by the practitioner who furnishes the overall evaluation is incorrect on its face.

(2) Forecasts and projections. A practitioner who is associated with forecasts or projections relating to or based upon the tax consequences of the tax shelter offering that are included in the offering materials, or are disseminated to potential investors other than the practitioner's clients, may rely on the opinion of another practitioner as to any or all material tax issues, provided that the practitioner who desires to rely on the other opinion has no reason to believe that the standards of paragraph (a) of this section have not been complied with by the practitioner rendering such other opinion, and the requirements of paragraph (b)(1) of this section are satisfied. The practitioner's report shall disclose any material tax issue not covered by, or incorrectly opined upon, by the other opinion, and shall set forth his/her opinion with respect to each such issue in a manner that satisfies the requirements of paragraph (a) of this section.

(c) Definitions. For purposes of this section:

(1) Practitioner includes any individual described in Sec. 10.3(e).

(2) A tax shelter, as the term is used in this section, is an investment which has as a significant and intended feature for Federal income or excise tax purposes either of the following attributes:

(i) Deductions in excess of income from the investment being available in any year to reduce income from other sources in that year, or

(ii) Credits in excess of the tax attributable to the income from the investment being available in any year to offset taxes on income from other sources in that year. Excluded from the term are municipal bonds; annuities; family trusts (but not including schemes or arrangements that are marketed to the public other than in a direct practitioner-client relationship); qualified retirement plans; individual retirement accounts; stock option plans; securities issued in a corporate reorganization; mineral development ventures, if the only tax benefit would be percentage depletion; and real estate where it is anticipated that in no year is it likely that deductions will exceed gross income from the investment in that year, or that tax credits will exceed the tax attributable to gross income from the investment in that year. Whether an investment is intended to have tax shelter features depends on the objective facts and circumstances of each case. Significant weight will be given to the features described in the offering materials to determine whether the investment is a tax shelter.

(3) A tax shelter opinion, as the term is used in this section, is advice by a practitioner concerning the Federal tax aspects of a tax shelter either appearing or referred to in the offering materials, or used or referred to in connection with sales promotion efforts, and directed to persons other than the client who engaged the practitioner to give the advice. The term includes the tax aspects or tax risks portion of the offering materials prepared by or at the direction of a practitioner, whether or not a separate opinion letter is issued or whether or not the practitioner's name is referred to in the offering materials or in connection with the sales promotion efforts. In addition, a financial forecast or projection prepared by a practitioner is a tax shelter opinion if it is predicated on assumptions regarding Federal tax aspects of the investment, and it meets the other requirements of the first sentence of this paragraph. The term does not, however, include rendering advice solely to the offeror or reviewing parts of the offering materials, so long as neither the name of the practitioner, nor the fact that a practitioner has rendered advice concerning the tax aspects, is referred to in the offering materials or in connection with the sales promotion efforts.

(4) A material tax issue as the term is used in this section is

(i) Any Federal income or excise tax issue relating to a tax shelter that would make a significant contribution toward sheltering from Federal taxes income from other sources by providing deductions in excess of the income from the tax shelter investment in any year, or tax credits available to offset tax liabilities in excess of the tax attributable to the tax shelter investment in any year;

(ii) Any other Federal income or excise tax issue relating to a tax shelter that could have a significant impact (either beneficial or adverse) on a tax shelter investor under any reasonably foreseeable circumstances (e.g., depreciation or investment tax credit recapture, availability of long-term capital gain treatment, or realization of taxable income in excess of cash flow, upon sale or other disposition of the tax shelter investment); and

(iii) The potential applicability of penalties, additions to tax, or interest charges that reasonably could be asserted against a tax shelter investor by the Internal Revenue Service with respect to the tax shelter. The determination of what is material is to be made in good faith by the practitioner, based on information available at the time the offering materials are circulated.

(d) For purposes of advising the Director of Practice whether an individual may have violated Sec. 10.33, the Director of Practice is authorized to establish an Advisory Committee, composed of at least five individuals authorized to practice before the Internal Revenue Service. Under procedures established by the Director of Practice, such Advisory Committee shall, at the request of the Director of Practice, review and make recommendations with regard to alleged violations of Sec. 10.33.

<table>
<tr><td>

**Appendix
J**

</td><td>

(Sec. 3, 23 Stat. 258, secs. 2-12, 60 Stat. 237 et seq.; 5 U.S.C. 301;
31 U.S.C. 330; 31 U.S.C. 321 (Reorg. Plan No. 26 of 1950, 15 FR 4935, 64
Stat. 1280, 3 CFR, 1949-53 Comp., p. 1017))

</td></tr>
</table>

[49 FR 6722, Feb. 23, 1984; 49 FR 7116, Feb. 27, 1984; 59 FR 31527, 31528, June 20, 1994]

### Sec. 10.34  Standards for advising with respect to tax return positions and for preparing or signing returns.

(a) Standards of conduct--(1) Realistic possibility standard. A practitioner may not sign a return as a preparer if the practitioner determines that the return contains a position that does not have a realistic possibility of being sustained on its merits (the realistic possibility standard) unless the position is not frivolous and is adequately disclosed to the Service. A practitioner may not advise a client to take a position on a return, or prepare the portion of a return on which a position is taken, unless--

(i) The practitioner determines that the position satisfies the realistic possibility standard; or

(ii) The position is not frivolous and the practitioner advises the client of any opportunity to avoid the accuracy-related penalty in section 6662 of the Internal Revenue Code of 1986 by adequately disclosing the position and of the requirements for adequate disclosure.

(2) Advising clients on potential penalties. A practitioner advising a client to take a position on a return, or preparing or signing a return as a preparer, must inform the client of the penalties reasonably likely to apply to the client with respect to the position advised, prepared, or reported. The practitioner also must inform the client of any opportunity to avoid any such penalty by disclosure, if relevant, and of the requirements for adequate disclosure. This paragraph (a)(2) applies even if the practitioner is not subject to a penalty with respect to the position.

(3) Relying on information furnished by clients. A practitioner advising a client to take a position on a return, or preparing or signing a return as a preparer, generally may rely in good faith without verification upon information furnished by the client. However, the practitioner may not ignore the implications of information furnished to, or actually known by, the practitioner, and must make reasonable inquiries if the information as furnished appears to be incorrect, inconsistent, or incomplete.

(4) Definitions. For purposes of this section:

(i) Realistic possibility. A position is considered to have a realistic possibility of being sustained on its merits if a reasonable and well-informed analysis by a person knowledgeable in the tax law would lead such a person to conclude that the position has approximately a one in three, or greater, likelihood of being sustained on its merits. The authorities described in 26 CFR 1.6662-4(d)(3)(iii), or any successor provision, of the substantial understatement penalty regulations may be taken into account for purposes of this analysis. The possibility that a position will not be challenged by the Service (e.g., because the taxpayer's return may not be audited or because the issue may not be raised on audit) may not be taken into account.

(ii) Frivolous. A position is frivolous if it is patently improper.

(b) Standard of discipline. As provided in Sec. 10.52, only violations of this section that are willful, reckless, or a result of gross incompetence will subject a practitioner to suspension or disbarment from practice before the Service.

[59 FR 31527, June 20, 1994]

## SUBPART C--RULES APPLICABLE TO DISCIPLINARY PROCEEDINGS

### Sec. 10.50 Authority to disbar or suspend.

Pursuant to 31 U.S.C. 330(b), the Secretary of the Treasury after notice and an opportunity for a proceeding, may suspend or disbar any practitioner from practice before the Internal Revenue Service. The Secretary may take such action against any practitioner who is shown to be incompetent or disreputable, who refuses to comply with any regulation in this part, or who, with intent to defraud, willfully and knowingly misleads or threatens a client or prospective client.

[59 FR 31528, June 20, 1994]

### Sec. 10.51 Disreputable conduct.

Disreputable conduct for which an attorney, certified public accountant, enrolled agent, or enrolled actuary may be disbarred or suspended from practice before the Internal Revenue Service includes, but is not limited to:

(a) Conviction of any criminal offense under the revenue laws of the United States, or of any offense involving dishonesty, or breach of trust.

(b) Giving false or misleading information, or participating in any way in the giving of false or misleading information to the Department of the Treasury or any officer or employee thereof, or to any tribunal authorized to pass upon Federal tax matters, in connection with any matter pending or likely to be pending before them, knowing such information to be false or misleading. Facts or other matters contained in testimony, Federal tax returns, financial statements, applications for enrollment, affidavits, declarations, or any other document or statement, written or oral, are included in the term ``information."

(c) Solicitation of employment as prohibited under Sec. 10.30, the use of false or misleading representations with intent to deceive a client or prospective client in order to procure employment, or intimating that the practitioner is able improperly to obtain special consideration or action from the Internal Revenue Service or officer or employee thereof.

(d) Willfully failing to make Federal tax return in violation of the revenue laws of the United States, or evading, attempting to evade, or participating in any way in evading or attempting to evade any Federal tax or payment thereof, knowingly counseling or suggesting to a client or prospective client an illegal plan to evade Federal taxes or payment thereof, or concealing assets of himself or another to evade Federal taxes or payment thereof.

(e) Misappropriation of, or failure properly and promptly to remit funds received from a client for the purpose of payment of taxes or other obligations due the United States.

**Appendix J**

(f) Directly or indirectly attempting to influence, or offering or agreeing to attempt to influence, the official action of any officer or employee of the Internal Revenue Service by the use of threats, false accusations, duress or coercion, by the offer of any special inducement or promise of advantage or by the bestowing of any gift, favor or thing of value.

(g) Disbarment or suspension from practice as an attorney, certified public accountant, public accountant, or actuary by any duly constituted authority of any State, possession, territory, Commonwealth, the District of Columbia, any Federal court of record or any Federal agency, body or board.

(h) Knowingly aiding and abetting another person to practice before the Internal Revenue Service during a period of suspension, disbarment, or ineligibility of such other person. Maintaining a partnership for the practice of law, accountancy, or other related professional service with a person who is under disbarment from practice before the Service shall be presumed to be a violation of this provision.

(i) Contemptuous conduct in connection with practice before the Internal Revenue Service, including the use of abusive language, making false accusations and statements knowing them to be false, or circulating or publishing malicious or libelous matter.

(j) Giving a false opinion, knowingly, recklessly, or through gross incompetence, including an opinion which is intentionally or recklessly misleading, or a pattern of providing incompetent opinions on questions arising under the Federal tax laws. False opinions described in this paragraph include those which reflect or result from a knowing misstatement of fact or law; from an assertion of a position known to be unwarranted under existing law; from counseling or assisting in conduct known to be illegal or fraudulent; from concealment of matters required by law to be revealed; or from conscious disregard of information indicating that material facts expressed in the tax opinion or offering material are false or misleading. For purposes of this paragraph, reckless conduct is a highly unreasonable omission or misrepresentation involving an extreme departure from the standards of ordinary care that a practitioner should observe under the circumstances. A pattern of conduct is a factor that will be taken into account in determining whether a practitioner acted knowingly, recklessly, or through gross incompetence. Gross incompetence includes conduct that reflects gross indifference, preparation which is grossly inadequate under the circumstances, and a consistent failure to perform obligations to the client.

(Sec. 3, 23 Stat. 258, secs. 2-12, 60 Stat. 237 et seq.; 5 U.S.C. 301; 31 U.S.C. 330; 31 U.S.C. 321 (Reorg. Plan No. 26 of 1950, 15 FR 4935, 64 Stat. 1280, 3 CFR, 1949-53 Comp., p. 1017))

[31 FR 10773, Aug. 13, 1966, as amended at 35 FR 13205, Aug. 19, 1970; 42 FR 38353, July 28, 1977; 44 FR 4946, Jan. 24, 1979; 49 FR 6723, Feb. 23, 1984; 57 FR 41095, Sept. 9, 1992; 59 FR 31528, June 20, 1994]

### Sec. 10.52  Violation of regulations.

A practitioner may be disbarred or suspended from practice before the Internal Revenue Service for any of the following:

(a) Willfully violating any of the regulations contained in this part.

(b) Recklessly or through gross incompetence (within the meaning of Sec. 10.51(j)) violating Sec. 10.33 or Sec. 10.34 of this part.

[59 FR 31528, June 20, 1994]

### Sec. 10.53  Receipt of information concerning attorney, certified public accountant, enrolled agent, or enrolled actuary.

If an officer or employee of the Internal Revenue Service has reason to believe that an attorney, certified public accountant, enrolled agent, or enrolled actuary has violated any provision of this part, or if any such officer or employee receives information to that effect, he shall promptly make a written report thereof, which report or a copy thereof shall be forwarded to the Director of Practice. If any other person has information of such violations, he may make a report thereof to the Director of Practice or to any officer or employee of the Internal Revenue Service.

[31 FR 10773, Aug. 13, 1966, as amended at 57 FR 41095, Sept. 9, 1992]

### Sec. 10.54  Institution of proceeding.

Whenever the Director of Practice has reason to believe that any attorney, certified public accountant, enrolled agent, or enrolled actuary has violated any provision of the laws or regulations governing practice before the Internal Revenue Service, he may reprimand such person or institute a proceeding for disbarment or suspension of such person. The proceeding shall be instituted by a complaint which names the respondent and is signed by the Director of Practice and filed in his office. Except in cases of willfulness, or where time, the nature of the proceeding, or the public interest does not permit, a proceeding will not be instituted under this section until facts or conduct which may warrant such action have been called to the attention of the proposed respondent in writing and he has been accorded opportunity to demonstrate or achieve compliance with all lawful requirements.

[31 FR 10773, Aug. 13, 1966, as amended at 57 FR 41095, Sept. 9, 1992]

### Sec. 10.55  Conferences.

(a) In general. The Director of Practice may confer with an attorney, certified public accountant, enrolled agent, or enrolled actuary concerning allegations of misconduct irrespective of whether a proceeding for disbarment or suspension has been instituted against him. If such conference results in a stipulation in connection with a proceeding in which such person is the

**Appendix J**

respondent, the stipulation may be entered in the record at the instance of either party to the proceeding.

(b) Resignation or voluntary suspension. An attorney, certified public accountant, enrolled agent, or enrolled actuary, in order to avoid the institution or conclusion of a disbarment or suspension proceeding, may offer his consent to suspension from practice before the Internal Revenue Service. An enrolled agent may also offer his resignation. The Director of Practice, in his discretion, may accept the offered resignation of an enrolled agent and may suspend an attorney, certified public accountant, or enrolled agent in accordance with the consent offered.

[31 FR 10773, Aug. 13, 1966, as amended at 35 FR 13206, Aug. 19, 1970; 57 FR 41095, Sept. 9, 1992]

### Sec. 10.56  Contents of complaint.

(a) Charges. A complaint shall give a plain and concise description of the allegations which constitute the basis for the proceeding. A complaint shall be deemed sufficient if it fairly informs the respondent of the charges against him so that he is able to prepare his defense.

(b) Demand for answer. In the complaint, or in a separate paper attached to the complaint, notification shall be given of the place and time within which the respondent shall file his answer, which time shall not be less than 15 days from the date of service of the complaint, and notice shall be given that a decision by default may be rendered against the respondent in the event he fails to file his answer as required.

[31 FR 10773, Aug. 13, 1966, as amended at 42 FR 38353, July 28, 1977]

### Sec. 10.57  Service of complaint and other papers.

(a) Complaint. The complaint or a copy thereof may be served upon the respondent by certified mail, or first-class mail as hereinafter provided; by delivering it to the respondent or his attorney or agent of record either in person or by leaving it at the office or place of business of the respondent, attorney or agent; or in any other manner which has been agreed to by the respondent. Where the service is by certified mail, the return post office receipt duly signed by or on behalf of the respondent shall be proof of service. If the certified matter is not claimed or accepted by the respondent and is returned undelivered, complete service may be made upon the respondent by mailing the complaint to him by first-class mail, addressed to him at the address under which he is enrolled or at the last address known to the Director of Practice. If service is made upon the respondent or his attorney or agent of record in person or by leaving the complaint at the office or place of business of the respondent, attorney or agent, the verified return by the person making service, setting forth the manner of service, shall be proof of such service.

(b) Service of papers other than complaint. Any paper other than the complaint may be served upon an attorney, certified public accountant, or enrolled agent as provided in paragraph (a) of this section or by mailing the paper by first-class mail to the respondent at the last address known to the Director of Practice, or by mailing the paper by first-class mail to the respondent's attorney or agent of record. Such mailing shall constitute complete service. Notices may be served upon the respondent or his attorney or agent of record by telegraph.

(c) Filing of papers. Whenever the filing of a paper is required or permitted in connection with a disbarment or suspension proceeding, and the place of filing is not specified by this subpart or by rule or order of the Administrative Law Judge, the paper shall be filed with the Director of Practice, Treasury Department, Washington, DC 20220. All papers shall be filed in duplicate.

[Dept. Circ. 230, Rev., 31 FR 10773, Aug. 13, 1966, as amended at 31 FR 13992, Nov. 2, 1966; 42 FR 38354, July 28, 1977]

## Sec. 10.58  Answer.

(a) Filing. The respondent's answer shall be filed in writing within the time specified in the complaint or notice of institution of the proceeding, unless on application the time is extended by the Director of Practice or the Administrative Law Judge. The answer shall be filed in duplicate with the Director of Practice.

(b) Contents. The answer shall contain a statement of facts which constitute the grounds of defense, and it shall specifically admit or deny each allegation set forth in the complaint, except that the respondent shall not deny a material allegation in the complaint which he knows to be true, or state that he is without sufficient information to form a belief when in fact he possesses such information. The respondent may also state affirmatively special matters of defense.

(c) Failure to deny or answer allegations in the complaint. Every allegation in the complaint which is not denied in the answer shall be deemed to be admitted and may be considered as proved, and no further evidence in respect of such allegation need be adduced at a hearing. Failure to file an answer within the time prescribed in the notice to the respondent, except as the time for answer is extended by the Director of Practice or the Administrative Law Judge, shall constitute an admission of the allegations of the complaint and a waiver of hearing, and the Examiner may make his decision by default without a hearing or further procedure.

[31 FR 10773, Aug. 13, 1966, as amended at 42 FR 38354, July 28, 1977]

## Sec. 10.59  Supplemental charges.

If it appears that the respondent in his answer, falsely and in bad faith, denies a material allegation of fact in the complaint or states that the respondent has no knowledge sufficient to form a belief, when he in fact possesses such information, or if it appears that the respondent has knowingly introduced false testimony during proceedings for his disbarment or suspension, the Director of Practice may thereupon file supplemental charges against the respondent. Such supplemental charges may be tried with other charges in the case, provided the respondent is

**Appendix J**

given due notice thereof and is afforded an opportunity to prepare a defense thereto.

### Sec. 10.60  Reply to answer.

No reply to the respondent's answer shall be required, and new matter in the answer shall be deemed to be denied, but the Director of Practice may file a reply in his discretion or at the request of the Administrative Law Judge.

[31 FR 10773, Aug. 13, 1966 as amended at 42 FR 38354, July 28, 1977]

### Sec. 10.61  Proof; variance; amendment of pleadings.

In the case of a variance between the allegations in a pleading and the evidence adduced in support of the pleading, the Examiner may order or authorize amendment of the pleading to conform to the evidence: Provided, That the party who would otherwise be prejudiced by the amendment is given reasonable opportunity to meet the allegations of the pleading as amended; and the Administrative Law Judge shall make findings on any issue presented by the pleadings as so amended.

[31 FR 10773, Aug. 13, 1966, as amended at 42 FR 38354, July 28, 1977]

### Sec. 10.62  Motions and requests.

Motions and requests may be filed with the Director of Practice or with the Administrative Law Judge.

[31 FR 10773, Aug. 13, 1966, as amended at 42 FR 38354, July 28, 1977]

### Sec. 10.63  Representation.

A respondent or proposed respondent may appear in person or he may be represented by counsel or other representative who need not be enrolled to practice before the Internal Revenue Service. The Director may be represented by an attorney or other employee of the Internal Revenue Service.

### Sec. 10.64  Administrative Law Judge.

(a) Appointment. An Administrative Law Judge appointed as provided by 5 U.S.C. 3105 (1966), shall conduct proceedings upon complaints for the disbarment or suspension of attorneys, certified public accountants, or enrolled agents.

(b) Powers of Examiner. Among other powers, the Examiner shall have authority, in connection with any disbarment or suspension proceeding assigned or referred to him, to do the following:

(1) Administer oaths and affirmations;

(2) Make rulings upon motions and requests, which rulings may not be appealed from prior to the close of a hearing except, at the discretion of the Administrative Law Judge, in extraordinary circumstances;

(3) Determine the time and place of hearing and regulate its course and conduct;

(4) Adopt rules of procedure and modify the same from time to time as occasion requires for the orderly disposition of proceedings;

(5) Rule upon offers of proof, receive relevant evidence, and examine witnesses;

(6) Take or authorize the taking of depositions;

(7) Receive and consider oral or written argument on facts or law;

(8) Hold or provide for the holding of conferences for the settlement or simplification of the issues by consent of the parties;

(9) Perform such acts and take such measures as are necessary or appropriate to the efficient conduct of any proceeding; and

(10) Make initial decisions.

[31 FR 10773, Aug. 13, 1966, as amended at 42 FR 38353, 38354, July 28, 1977]

## Sec. 10.65  Hearings.

(a) In general. An Administrative Law Judge will preside at the hearing on a complaint furnished under Sec. 10.54 for the disbarment or suspension of a practitioner. Hearings will be stenographically recorded and transcribed and the testimony of witnesses will be taken under oath or affirmation. Hearings will be conducted pursuant to 5 U.S.C. 556. A hearing in a proceeding requested under Sec. 10.76(g) will be conducted de novo.

(b) Failure to appear. If either party to the proceeding fails to appear at the hearing, after due notice thereof has been sent to him, he shall be deemed to have waived the right to a hearing and the Administrative Law Judge may make his decision against the absent party by default.

[31 FR 10773, Aug. 13, 1966, as amended at 42 FR 38354, July 28, 1977; 59 FR 31528, June 20, 1994]

## Sec. 10.66  Evidence.

(a) In general. The rules of evidence prevailing in courts of law and equity are not controlling in hearings on complaints for the disbarment or suspension of attorneys, certified public accountants, and enrolled agents. However, the Administrative Law Judge shall exclude evidence which is irrelevant, immaterial, or unduly repetitious.

(b) Depositions. The deposition of any witness taken pursuant to Sec. 10.67 may be admitted.

(c) Proof of documents. Official documents, records, and papers of the Internal Revenue

**Appendix
J**

Service and the Office of Director of Practice shall be admissible in evidence without the production of an officer or employee to authenticate them. Any such documents, records, and papers may be evidenced by a copy attested or identified by an officer or employee of the Internal Revenue Service or the Treasury Department, as the case may be.

(d) Exhibits. If any document, record, or other paper is introduced in evidence as an exhibit, the Administrative Law Judge may authorize the withdrawal of the exhibit subject to any conditions which he deems proper.

(e) Objections. Objections to evidence shall be in short form, stating the grounds of objection relied upon, and the record shall not include argument thereon, except as ordered by the Administrative Law Judge. Rulings on such objections shall be a part of the record. No exception to the ruling is necessary to preserve the rights of the parties.

[31 FR 10773, Aug. 13, 1966, as amended at 35 FR 13206, Aug. 19, 1970; 42 FR 38354, July 28, 1977]

## Sec. 10.67  Depositions.

Depositions for use at a hearing may, with the written approval of the Administrative Law Judge be taken by either the Director of Practice or the respondent or their duly authorized representatives. Depositions may be taken upon oral or written interrogatories, upon not less than 10 days' written notice to the other party before any officer duly authorized to administer an oath for general purposes or before an officer or employee of the Internal Revenue Service who is authorized to administer an oath in internal revenue matters. Such notice shall state the names of the witnesses and the time and place where the depositions are to be taken. The requirement of 10 days' notice may be waived by the parties in writing, and depositions may then be taken from the persons and at the times and places mutually agreed to by the parties. When a deposition is taken upon written interrogatories, any cross-examination shall be upon written interrogatories. Copies of such written interrogatories shall be served upon the other party with the notice, and copies of any written cross-interrogation shall be mailed or delivered to the opposing party at least 5 days before the date of taking the depositions, unless the parties mutually agree otherwise. A party upon whose behalf a deposition is taken must file it with the Administrative Law Judge and serve one copy upon the opposing party. Expenses in the reporting of depositions shall be borne by the party at whose instance the deposition is taken.

[31 FR 10773, Aug. 13, 1966, as amended at 42 FR 38354, July 28, 1977]

## Sec. 10.68  Transcript.

In cases where the hearing is stenographically reported by a Government contract reported, copies of the transcript may be obtained from the reporter at rates not to exceed the maximum rates fixed by contract between the Government and the reporter. Where the hearing is stenographically reported by a regular employee of the Internal Revenue Service, a copy thereof will be supplied to the respondent either without charge or upon the payment of a reasonable fee. Copies of exhibits introduced at the hearing or at the taking or depositions will be supplied to the parties upon the payment of a reasonable fee (Sec. 501, Pub. L. 82-137, 65 Stat. 290 (31 U.S.C. 483a)).

Appendix
J

[31 FR 10773, Aug. 13, 1966, as amended at 42 FR 38354, July 28, 1977]

### Sec. 10.69  Proposed findings and conclusions.

Except in cases where the respondent has failed to answer the complaint or where a party has failed to appear at the hearing, the Administrative Law Judge prior to making his decision, shall afford the parties a reasonable opportunity to submit proposed findings and conclusions and supporting reasons therefor.

[31 FR 10773, Aug. 13, 1966, as amended at 42 FR 38354, July 28, 1977]

### Sec. 10.70  Decision of the Administrative Law Judge.

As soon as practicable after the conclusion of a hearing and the receipt of any proposed findings and conclusions timely submitted by the parties, the Administrative Law Judge shall make the initial decision in the case. The decision shall include (a) a statement of findings and conclusions, as well as the reasons or basis therefor, upon all the material issues of fact, law, or discretion presented on the record, and (b) an order of disbarment, suspension, or reprimand or an order of dismissal of the complaint. The Administrative Law Judge shall file the decision with the Director of Practice and shall transmit a copy thereof to the respondent or his attorney of record. In the absence of an appeal to the Secretary of the Treasury, or review of the decision upon motion of the Secretary, the decision of the Administrative Law Judge shall without further proceedings become the decisions of the Secretary of the Treasury 30 days from the date of the Administrative Law Judge's decision.

[31 FR 10773, Aug. 13, 1966, as amended at 42 FR 38354, July 28, 1977]

### Sec. 10.71  Appeal to the Secretary.

Within 30 days from the date of the Administrative Law Judge's decision, either party may appeal to the Secretary of the Treasury. The appeal shall be filed with the Director of Practice in duplicate and shall include exceptions to the decision of the Administrative Law Judge and supporting reasons for such exceptions. If an appeal is filed by the Director of Practice, he shall transmit a copy thereof to the respondent. Within 30 days after receipt of an appeal or copy thereof, the other party may file a reply brief in duplicate with the Director of Practice. If the reply brief is filed by the Director, he shall transmit a copy of it to the respondent. Upon the filing of an appeal and a reply brief, if any, the Director of Practice shall transmit the entire record to the Secretary of the Treasury.

[31 FR 10773, Aug. 13, 1966, as amended at 42 FR 38354, July 28, 1977]

### Sec. 10.72  Decision of the Secretary.

On appeal from or review of the initial decision of the Administrative Law Judge, the Secretary of the Treasury will make the agency decision. In making his decision the Secretary of the Treasury will review the record or such portions thereof as may be cited by the parties to permit limiting of the issues. A copy of the Secretary's decision shall be transmitted to the respondent by the Director of Practice.

[31 FR 10773, Aug. 13, 1966, as amended at 42 FR 38354, July 28, 1977]

### Sec. 10.73  Effect of disbarment or suspension; surrender of card.

In case the final order against the respondent is for disbarment, the respondent shall not thereafter be permitted to practice before the Internal Revenue Service unless and until authorized to do so by the Director of Practice pursuant to Sec. 10.75. In case the final order against the respondent is for suspension, the respondent shall not thereafter be permitted to practice before the Internal Revenue Service during the period of suspension. If an enrolled agent is disbarred or suspended, he shall surrender his enrollment card to the Director of Practice for cancellation, in the case of disbarment, or for retention during the period of suspension.

### Sec. 10.74  Notice of disbarment or suspension.

Upon the issuance of a final order disbarring or suspending an attorney, certified public accountant, or enrolled agent, the Director of Practice shall give notice thereof to appropriate officers and employees of the Internal Revenue Service and to interested departments and agencies of the Federal Government. Notice in such manner as the Director of Practice may determine may be given to the proper authorities of the State by which the disbarred or suspended person was licensed to practice as an attorney or accountant.

### Sec. 10.75  Petition for reinstatement.

The Director of Practice may entertain a petition for reinstatement from any person disbarred from practice before the Internal Revenue Service after the expiration of 5 years following such disbarment. Reinstatement may not be granted unless the Director of Practice is satisfied that the petitioner, thereafter, is not likely to conduct himself contrary to the regulations in this part, and that granting such reinstatement would not be contrary to the public interest.

[31 FR 10773, Aug. 13, 1966, as amended at 35 FR 13206, Aug. 19, 1970]

## Sec. 10.76  Expedited suspension upon criminal conviction or loss of license for cause.

(a) When applicable. Whenever the Director has reason to believe that a practitioner is described in paragraph (b) of this section, the Director may institute a proceeding under this section to suspend the practitioner from practice before the Service.

(b) To whom applicable. This section applies to any practitioner who, within 5 years of the date a complaint instituting a proceeding under this section is served–

(1) Has had his or her license to practice as an attorney, certified public accountant, or actuary suspended or revoked for cause (not including a failure to pay a professional licensing fee) by any authority or court, agency, body, or board described in Sec. 10.51(g); or

(2) Has been convicted of any crime under title 26 of the United States Code, or a felony under title 18 of the United States Code involving dishonesty or breach of trust.

(c) Instituting a proceeding. A proceeding under this section will be instituted by a complaint that names the respondent, is signed by the Director, is filed in the Director's office, and is served according to the rules set forth in Sec. 10.57(a). The complaint must give a plain and concise description of the allegations that constitute the basis for the proceeding. The complaint, or a separate paper attached to the complaint, must notify the respondent--

(1) Of the place and due date for filing an answer;

(2) That a decision by default may be rendered if the respondent fails to file an answer as required;

(3) That the respondent may request a conference with the Director to address the merits of the complaint and that any such request must be made in the answer; and

(4) That the respondent may be suspended either immediately following the expiration of the period by which an answer must be filed or, if a conference is requested, immediately following the conference.

(d) Answer. The answer to a complaint described in this section must be filed no later than 30 calendar days following the date the complaint is served, unless the Director extends the time for filing. The answer must be filed in accordance with the rules set forth in Sec. 10.58, except as otherwise provided in this section. A respondent is entitled to a conference with the Director only if the conference is requested in a timely filed answer. If a request for a conference is not made in the answer or the answer is not timely filed, the respondent will be deemed to have waived his or her right to a conference and the Director may suspend such respondent at any time following the date on which the answer was due.

(e) Conference. The Director or his or her designee will preside at a conference described in this section. The conference will be held at a place and time selected by the Director, but no sooner than 14 calendar days after the date by which the answer must be filed with the Director, unless the respondent agrees to an earlier date. An authorized representative may represent the respondent at the conference. Following the conference, upon a finding that the respondent is described in paragraph (b) of this section, or upon the respondent's failure to appear at the conference either personally or through an authorized representative, the Director may immediately suspend the respondent from practice before the Service.

| Appendix J |
| --- |

(f) Duration of suspension. A suspension under this section will commence on the date that written notice of the suspension is issued. A practitioner's suspension will remain effective until the earlier of the following--

(1) The Director lifts the suspension after determining that the practitioner is no longer described in paragraph (b) of this section or for any other reason; or

(2) The suspension is lifted by an Administrative Law Judge or the Secretary of the Treasury in a proceeding referred to in paragraph (g) of this section and instituted under Sec. 10.54.

(g) Proceeding instituted under Sec. 10.54. If the Director suspends a practitioner under this Sec. 10.76, the practitioner may ask the Director to issue a complaint under Sec. 10.54. The request must be made in writing within 2 years from the date on which the practitioner's suspension commences. The Director must issue a complaint requested under this paragraph within 30 calendar days of receiving the request.

[59 FR 31528, June 20, 1994]

### Sec. 10.77 Authority to disqualify; effect of disqualification.

Source: 50 FR 42016, Oct. 17, 1985, unless otherwise noted.

(a) Authority to disqualify. Pursuant to section 156 of the Deficit Reduction Act of 1984, 98 Stat. 695, amending 31 U.S.C. 330, the Secretary of the Treasury, after due notice and opportunity for hearing may disqualify any appraiser with respect to whom a penalty has been assessed after July 18, 1984, under section 6701(a) of the Internal Revenue Code of 1954, as amended (26 U.S.C. 6701(a)).

(b) Effect of disqualification. If any appraiser is disqualified pursuant to 31 U.S.C. 330 and this subpart:

(1) Appraisals by such appraiser shall not have any probative effect in any administrative proceeding before the Department of the Treasury or the Internal Revenue Service; and

(2) Such appraiser shall be barred from presenting evidence or testimony in any such administrative proceeding. Paragraph (b)(1) of this section shall apply to appraisals made by such appraiser after the effective date of disqualification, but shall not apply to appraisals made by the appraiser on or before such date. Notwithstanding the foregoing sentence, an appraisal otherwise barred from admission into evidence pursuant to paragraph (b)(1) of this section may be admitted into evidence solely for the purpose of determining the taxpayer's reliance in good faith on such appraisal. Paragraph (b)(2) of this section shall apply to the presentation of testimony or evidence in any administrative proceeding after the date of such disqualification, regardless of whether such testimony or evidence would pertain to an appraisal made prior to such date.

## SUBPART D--RULES APPLICABLE TO DISQUALIFICATION OF APPRAISERS

### Sec. 10.78 Institution of proceeding.

(a) In general. Whenever the Director of Practice is advised or becomes aware that a penalty has been assessed against an appraiser under 26 U.S.C. 6701(a), he/she may reprimand such person or institute a proceeding for disqualification of such appraiser through the filing of a complaint. Irrespective of whether a proceeding for disqualification has been instituted against an appraiser, the Director of Practice may confer with an appraiser against whom such a penalty has been assessed concerning such penalty.

(b) Voluntary disqualification. In order to avoid the initiation or conclusion of a disqualification proceeding, an appraiser may offer his/her consent to disqualification. The Director of Practice, in his/her discretion, may disqualify an appraiser in accordance with the consent offered.

### Sec. 10.79 Contents of complaint.

(a) Charges. A proceeding for disqualification of an appraiser shall be instituted through the filing of a complaint, which shall give a plain and concise description of the allegations that constitute the basis for the proceeding. A complaint shall be deemed sufficient if it refers to the penalty previously imposed on the respondent under section 6701(a) of the Internal Revenue Code of 1954, as amended (26 U.S.C. 6701(a)), and advises him/her of the institution of the proceeding.

(b) Demand for answer. In the complaint, or in a separate paper attached to the complaint, notification shall be given of the place and time within which the respondent shall file his/her answer, which time shall not be less than 15 days from the date of service of the complaint, and notice shall be given that a decision by default may be rendered against the respondent in the event there is failure to file an answer.

### Sec. 10.80 Service of complaint and other papers.

(a) Complaint. The complaint or a copy thereof may be served upon the respondent by certified mail, or first-class mail as hereinafter provided, by delivering it to the respondent or his/her attorney or agent of record either in person or by leaving it at the office or place of business of the respondent, attorney or agent, or in any other manner that has been agreed to by the respondent. Where the service is by certified mail, the return post office receipt duly signed by or on behalf of the respondent shall be proof of service. If the certified mail is not claimed or accepted by the respondent and is returned undelivered, complete service may be made by mailing the complaint to the respondent by first-class mail, addressed to the respondent at the last address known to the Director of Practice. If service is made upon the respondent in person or by leaving the complaint at the office or place of business of the respondent, the verified return by the person making service, setting forth the manner of service, shall be proof of such service.

(b) Service of papers other than complaint. Any paper other than the complaint may be served as provided in paragraph (a) of this section or by mailing the paper by first-class mail to the respondent at the last address known to the Director of Practice, or by mailing the paper by first-class mail to the respondent's attorney or agent of record. Such mailing shall constitute complete service. Notices may be served upon the respondent or his/her attorney or agent of record by telegraph.

(c) Filing of papers. Whenever the filing of a paper is required or permitted in connection with a disqualification proceeding under this subpart or by rule or order of the Administrative Law Judge, the paper shall be filed with the Director of Practice, Treasury Department, Internal Revenue Service, Washington, DC 29224. All papers shall be filed in duplicate.

## Sec. 10.81  Answer.

(a) Filing. The respondent's answer shall be filed in writing within the time specified in the complaint or notice of institution of the proceeding, unless on application the time is extended by the Director of Practice or the Administrative Law Judge. The answer shall be filed in duplicate with the Director of Practice.

(b) Contents. The answer shall contain a statement of facts that constitute the grounds of defense, and it shall specifically admit or deny each allegation set forth in the complaint, except that the respondent shall not deny a material allegation in the complaint that he/she knows to be true, or state that he/she is without sufficient information to form a belief when in fact he/she possesses such information.

(c) Failure to deny or answer allegations in the complaint. Every allegation in the complaint which is not denied in the answer shall be deemed to be admitted and may be considered as proved, and no further evidence in respect of such allegation need be adduced at a hearing. Failure to file an answer within the time prescribed in the notice to the respondent, except as the time for answer is extended by the Director of Practice or the Administrative Law Judge, shall constitute an admission of the allegations of the complaint and a waiver of hearing, and the Administrative Law Judge may make his/her decision by default without a hearing or further procedure.

## Sec. 10.82  Supplemental charges.

If it appears that the respondent in his/her answer, falsely and in bad faith, denies a material allegation of fact in the complaint or states that the respondent has no knowledge sufficient to form a belief, when he/she in fact possesses such information, or if it appears that the respondent has knowingly introduced false testimony during proceedings for his/her disqualification, the Director of Practice may thereupon file supplemental charges against the respondent. Such supplemental charges may be tried with other charges in the case, provided the respondent is given due notice thereof and is afforded an opportunity to prepare a defense thereto.

## Sec. 10.83  Reply to answer.

No reply to the respondent's answer shall be required, and any new matter in the answer shall be deemed to be denied, but the Director of Practice may file a reply in his/her discretion or at the request of the Administrative Law Judge.

### Sec. 10.84  Proof, variance, amendment of pleadings.

In the case of a variance between the allegations in a pleading and the evidence adduced in support of the pleading, the Administrative Law Judge may order or authorize amendment of the pleading to conform to the evidence; provided, that the party who would otherwise be prejudiced by the amendment is given reasonable opportunity to meet the allegations of the pleading as amended, and the Administrative Law Judge shall make findings on any issue presented by the pleadings as so amended.

### Sec. 10.85  Motions and requests.

Motions and requests may be filed with the Director of Practice or with the Administrative Law Judge.

### Sec. 10.86  Representation.

A respondent may appear in person or may be represented by counsel or other representative. The Director of Practice may be represented by an attorney or other employee of the Department of the Treasury.

### Sec. 10.87  Administrative Law Judge.

(a) Appointment. An Administrative Law Judge appointed as provided by 5 U.S.C. 3105, shall conduct proceedings upon complaints for the disqualification of appraisers.

(b) Powers of Administrative Law Judge. Among other powers, the Administrative Law Judge shall have authority, in connection with any disqualification proceeding assigned or referred to him/her, to do the following:

(1) Administer oaths and affirmations;

(2) Make rulings upon motions and requests, which rulings may not be appealed from prior to the close of a hearing except at the discretion of the Administrative Law Judge, in extraordinary circumstances;

(3) Determine the time and place of hearing and regulate its course and conduct;

(4) Adopt rules of procedure and modify the same from time to time as occasion requires for the orderly disposition of proceedings;

(5) Rule upon offers of proof, receive relevant evidence, and examine witnesses;

(6) Take or authorize the taking of depositions;

(7) Receive and consider oral or written argument on facts or law;

(8) Hold or provide for the holding of conferences for the settlement or simplification of the

**Appendix J**

issues by consent of the parties;

    (9) Perform such acts and take such measures as are necessary or appropriate to the efficient conduct of any proceeding; and

    (10) Make initial decisions.

## Sec. 10.88  Hearings.

  (a) In general. The Administrative Law Judge shall preside at the hearing on a complaint for the disqualification of an appraiser. Hearings shall be stenographically recorded and transcribed and the testimony of witnesses shall be taken under oath or affirmation. Hearings will be conducted pursuant to 5 U.S.C. 556.

  (b) Failure to appear. If either party to the proceeding fails to appear at the hearing after due notice thereof has been sent to him/her, the right to a hearing shall be deemed to have been waived and the Administrative Law Judge may make a decision by default against the absent party.

## Sec. 10.89  Evidence.

  (a) In general. The rules of evidence prevailing in courts of law and equity are not controlling in hearings on complaints for the disqualification of appraisers. However, the Administrative Law Judge shall exclude evidence which is irrelevant, immaterial, or unduly repetitious.

  (b) Depositions. The deposition of any witness taken pursuant to Sec. 10.90 may be admitted.

  (c) Proof of documents. Official documents, records, and papers of the Internal Revenue Service or the Department of the Treasury shall be admissible in evidence without the production of an officer or employee to authenticate them. Any such documents, records, and papers may be evidenced by a copy attested or identified by an officer or employee of the Internal Revenue Service or the Department of the Treasury, as the case may be.

  (d) Exhibits. If any document, record, or other paper is introduced in evidence as an exhibit, the Administrative Law Judge may authorize the withdrawal of the exhibit subject to any conditions which he/she deems proper.

  (e) Objections. Objections to evidence shall be in short form, stating the grounds of objection relied upon, and the record shall not include argument thereon, except as ordered by the Administrative Law Judge. Rulings on such objections shall be a part of the record. No exception to the ruling is necessary to preserve the rights of the parties.

## Sec. 10.90  Depositions.

  Depositions for use at a hearing may, with the written approval of the Administrative Law Judge, be taken either by the Director of Practice or the respondent or their duly authorized representatives. Depositions may be taken upon oral or written interrogatories, upon not less than 10 days' written notice to the other party before any officer duly authorized to administer an oath for general purposes or before an officer or employee of the Internal Revenue Service who is authorized to administer an oath in internal revenue matters. Such notice shall state the names of the witnesses and the time and place where the depositions are to be taken. The requirement of 10 days' notice may be waived by the parties in writing, and depositions may then be taken from the persons and at the times and places mutually agreed to by the parties. When a deposition is taken upon written interrogatories, any cross-examination shall be upon written interrogatories. Copies of such written interrogatories shall be served upon the other party with the notice, and copies of any written cross-interrogation shall be mailed or delivered to the opposing party at least 5 days before the date of taking the depositions, unless the parties mutually agree otherwise. A party upon whose behalf a deposition is taken must file it with the Administrative Law Judge and serve one copy upon the opposing party. Expenses in the reporting of depositions shall be borne by the party at whose instance the deposition is taken.

**Appendix J**

## Sec. 10.91  Transcript.

In cases where the hearing is stenographically reported by a Government contract reporter, copies of the transcript may be obtained from the reporter at rates not to exceed the maximum rates fixed by contract between the Government and the reporter. Where a hearing is stenographically reported by a regular employee of the Internal Revenue Service, a copy thereof will be supplied to the respondent either without charge or upon the payment of a reasonable fee. Copies of exhibits introduced at the hearing or at the taking of depositions will be supplied to the parties upon the payment of a reasonable fee (Sec. 501, Pub. L. 82-137, 65 Stat. 290 (31 U.S.C. 483a)).

## Sec. 10.90  Depositions.

Depositions for use at a hearing may, with the written approval of the Administrative Law Judge, be taken either by the Director of Practice or the respondent or their duly authorized representatives. Depositions may be taken upon oral or written interrogatories, upon not less than 10 days' written notice to the other party before any officer duly authorized to administer an oath for general purposes or before an officer or employee of the Internal Revenue Service who is authorized to administer an oath in internal revenue matters. Such notice shall state the names of the witnesses and the time and place where the depositions are to be taken. The requirement of 10 days' notice may be waived by the parties in writing, and depositions may then be taken from the persons and at the times and places mutually agreed to by the parties. When a deposition is taken upon written interrogatories, any cross-examination shall be upon written interrogatories. Copies of such written interrogatories shall be served upon the other party with the notice, and copies of any written cross-interrogation shall be mailed or delivered to the opposing party at least 5 days before the date of taking the depositions, unless the parties mutually agree otherwise. A party upon whose behalf a deposition is taken must file it with the Administrative Law Judge and serve one copy upon the opposing party. Expenses in the reporting of depositions shall be borne by the party at whose instance the deposition is taken.

## Sec. 10.92  Proposed findings and conclusions.

Appendix
J

　　　　Except in cases where the respondent has failed to answer the complaint or where a party has failed to appear at the hearing, the Administrative Law Judge, prior to making a decision, shall afford the parties a reasonable opportunity to submit proposed findings and conclusions and supporting reasons therefor.

### Sec. 10.93  Decision of the Administrative Law Judge.

As soon as practicable after the conclusion of a hearing and the receipt of any proposed findings and conclusions timely submitted by the parties, the Administrative Law Judge shall make the initial decision in the case. The decision shall include (a) a statement of findings and conclusions, as well as the reasons or basis therefor, upon all the material issues of fact, law, or discretion presented on the record, and (b) an order of disqualification or an order of dismissal of the complaint. The Administrative Law Judge shall file the decision with the Director of Practice and shall transmit a copy thereof to the respondent or his attorney of record. In the absence of an appeal to the Secretary of the Treasury, or review of the decision upon motion of the Secretary, the decision of the Administrative Law Judge shall without further proceedings become the decision of the Secretary of the Treasury 30 days from the date of the Administrative Law Judge's decision.

### Sec. 10.94  Appeal to the Secretary.

Within 30 days from the date of the Administrative Law Judge's decision, either party may appeal such decision to the Secretary of the Treasury. If an appeal is by the respondent, the appeal shall be filed with the Director of Practice in duplicate and shall include exceptions to the decision of the Administrative Law Judge and supporting reasons for such exceptions. If an appeal is filed by the Director of Practice, a copy thereof shall be transmitted to the respondent. Within 30 days after receipt of an appeal or copy thereof, the other party may file a reply brief in duplicate with the Director of Practice. If the reply brief is filed by the Director, a copy shall be transmitted to the respondent. Upon the filing of an appeal and a reply brief, if any, the Director of Practice shall transmit the entire record to the Secretary of the Treasury.

### Sec. 10.95  Decision of the Secretary.

On appeal from or review of the initial decision of the Administrative Law Judge, the Secretary of the Treasury shall make the agency decision. In making such decision, the Secretary of the Treasury will review the record or such portions thereof as may be cited by the parties. A copy of the Secretary's decision shall be transmitted to the respondent by the Director of Practice.

### Sec. 10.96  Final order.

Upon the issuance of a final order disqualifying an appraiser, the Director of Practice shall give notice thereof to appropriate officers and employees of the Internal Revenue Service and to interested departments and agencies of the Federal Government.

## Sec. 10.97  Petition for reinstatement.

The Director of Practice may entertain a petition for reinstatement from any disqualified appraiser after the expiration of 5 years following such disqualification. Reinstatement may not be granted unless the Director of Practice is satisfied that the petitioner, thereafter, is not likely to conduct himself/herself contrary to 26 U.S.C. 6701(a), and that granting such reinstatement would not be contrary to the public interest.

## Sec. 10.98  Records.

(a) Availability. There are made available to public inspection at the Office of Director of Practice the roster of all persons enrolled to practice, the roster of all persons disbarred or suspended from practice, and the roster of all disqualified appraisers. Other records may be disclosed upon specific request, in accordance with the disclosure regulations of the Internal Revenue Service and the Treasury Department.

(b) Disciplinary procedures. A request by a practitioner that a hearing in a disciplinary proceeding concerning him be public, and that the record thereof be made available for inspection by interested persons may be granted if agreement is reached by stipulation in advance to protect from disclosure tax information which is confidential, in accordance with the applicable statutes and regulations.

[31 FR 10773, Aug. 13, 1966. Redesignated at 50 FR 42016, Oct. 17, 1985, and amended at 50 FR 42018, Oct. 17, 1985]

## SUBPART E--GENERAL PROVISIONS

## Sec. 10.100  Saving clause.

Any proceeding for the disbarment or suspension of an attorney, certified public accountant, or enrolled agent, instituted but not closed prior to the effective date of these revised regulations, shall not be affected by such regulations. Any proceeding under this part based on conduct engaged in prior to the effective date of these regulations may be instituted subsequent to such effective date.

[50 FR 42019, Oct. 17, 1985]

## Sec. 10.101  Special orders.

The Secretary of the Treasury reserves the power to issue such special orders as he may deem proper in any cases within the purview of this part.
[31 FR 10773, Aug. 13, 1966. Redesignated at 50 FR 42016, Oct. 17, 1985]

**Appendix K**

August 2000

# 1-8

Statements on Standards for Tax Services

Issued by the Tax Executive Committee

*Copyright © 2000 by*
*American Institute of Certified Public Accountants, Inc.,*
*New York, NY 10036-8775*

*All rights reserved. For information about the procedure for requesting permission*
*to make copies of any part this work, please call the AICPA Copyright Permissions*
*Hotline at 201-938-3245. A Permissions Request Form for emailing requests is*
*available at www.aicpa.org by clicking on the copyright notice on any page. Otherwise,*
*requests should be written and mailed to the Permissions Department, AICPA,*
*Harborside Financial Center, 201 Plaza Three, Jersey City, NJ 07311-3881.*

*1 2 3 4 5 6 7 8 9 0  TD  0 9 8 7 6 5 4 3 2 1 0*

# Contents of Statements

# Preface

1.    Practice standards are the hallmark of calling one's self a professional. Members should fulfill their responsibilities as professionals by instituting and maintaining standards against which their professional performance can be measured. Compliance with professional standards of tax practice also confirms the public's awareness of the professionalism that is associated with CPAs as well as the AICPA.

2.    This publication sets forth ethical tax practice standards for members of the AICPA: Statements on Standards for Tax Services (SSTSs or Statements). Although other standards of tax practice exist, most notably Treasury Department Circular No. 230 and penalty provisions of the Internal Revenue Code (IRC), those standards are limited in that (1) Circular No. 230 does not provide the depth of guidance contained in these Statements, (2) the IRC penalty provisions apply only to income-tax return preparation, and (3) both Circular No. 230 and the penalty provisions apply only to federal tax practice.

3.    The SSTSs have been written in as simple and objective a manner as possible. However, by their nature, ethical standards provide for an appropriate range of behavior that recognizes the need for interpretations to meet a broad range of personal and professional situations. The SSTSs recognize this need by, in some sections, providing relatively subjective rules and by leaving certain terms undefined. These terms and concepts are generally rooted in tax concepts, and therefore should be readily understood by tax practitioners. It is, therefore, recognized that the enforcement of these rules, as part of the AICPA's Code of Professional Conduct Rule 201, General Standards, and Rule 202, Compliance With Standards, will be undertaken with flexibility in mind and handled on a case-by-case basis. Members are expected to comply with them.

## History

4.    The SSTSs have their origin in the Statements on Responsibilities in Tax Practice (SRTPs), which provided a body of advisory opinions on good tax practice. The guidelines as originally set forth in the SRTPs had come to play a much more important role than most members realized. The courts, Internal Revenue Service,

state accountancy boards, and other professional organizations recognized and relied on the SRTPs as the appropriate articulation of professional conduct in a CPA's tax practice. The SRTPs, in and of themselves, had become de facto enforceable standards of professional practice, because state disciplinary organizations and malpractice cases in effect regularly held CPAs accountable for failure to follow the SRTPs when their professional practice conduct failed to meet the prescribed guidelines of conduct.

5.     The AICPA's Tax Executive Committee concluded that appropriate action entailed issuance of tax practice standards that would become a part of the Institute's Code of Professional Conduct. At its July 1999 meeting, the AICPA Board of Directors approved support of the executive committee's initiative and placed the matter on the agenda of the October 1999 meeting of the Institute's governing Council. On October 19, 1999, Council approved designating the Tax Executive Committee as a standard-setting body, thus authorizing that committee to promulgate standards of tax practice. These SSTSs, largely mirroring the SRTPs, are the result.

6.     The SRTPs were originally issued between 1964 and 1977. The first nine SRTPs and the Introduction were codified in 1976; the tenth SRTP was issued in 1977. The original SRTPs concerning the CPA's responsibility to sign the return (SRTPs No. 1, *Signature of Preparers*, and No. 2, *Signature of Reviewer: Assumption of Preparer's Responsibility*) were withdrawn in 1982 after Treasury Department regulations were issued adopting substantially the same standards for all tax return preparers. The sixth and seventh SRTPs, concerning the responsibility of a CPA who becomes aware of an error, were revised in 1991. The first Interpretation of the SRTPs, Interpretation 1-1, "Realistic Possibility Standard," was approved in December 1990. The SSTSs and Interpretation supersede and replace the SRTPs and their Interpretation 1-1 effective October 31, 2000. Although the number and names of the SSTSs, and the substance of the rules contained in each of them, remain the same as in the SRTPs, the language has been edited to both clarify and reflect the enforceable nature of the SSTSs. In addition, because the applicability of these standards is not limited to federal income-tax practice, the language has been changed to mirror the broader scope.

## Ongoing Process

7.    The following Statements on Standards for Tax Services and Interpretation 1-1 to Statement No. 1, "Realistic Possibility Standard," reflect the AICPA's standards of tax practice and delineate members' responsibilities to taxpayers, the public, the government, and the profession. The Statements are intended to be part of an ongoing process that may require changes to and interpretations of current SSTSs in recognition of the accelerating rate of change in tax laws and the continued importance of tax practice to members.

8.    The Tax Executive Committee promulgates SSTSs. Even though the 1999-2000 Tax Executive Committee approved this version, acknowledgment is also due to the many members whose efforts over the years went into the development of the original statements.

# Statement on Standards for Tax Services No. 1, Tax Return Positions

## Introduction

1.   This Statement sets forth the applicable standards for members when recommending tax return positions and preparing or signing tax returns (including amended returns, claims for refund, and information returns) filed with any taxing authority. For purposes of these standards, a *tax return position* is (*a*) a position reflected on the tax return as to which the taxpayer has been specifically advised by a member or (*b*) a position about which a member has knowledge of all material facts and, on the basis of those facts, has concluded whether the position is appropriate. For purposes of these standards, a *taxpayer* is a client, a member's employer, or any other third-party recipient of tax services.

## Statement

2.   The following standards apply to a member when providing professional services that involve tax return positions:

*a*.  A member should not recommend that a tax return position be taken with respect to any item unless the member has a good-faith belief that the position has a realistic possibility of being sustained administratively or judicially on its merits if challenged.

*b*.  A member should not prepare or sign a return that the member is aware takes a position that the member may not recommend under the standard expressed in paragraph 2*a*.

*c*.  Notwithstanding paragraph 2*a*, a member may recommend a tax return position that the member concludes is not frivolous as long as the member advises the taxpayer to appropriately disclose. Notwithstanding paragraph 2*b*, the member may prepare or sign a return that reflects a position that the member concludes is not frivolous as long as the position is appropriately disclosed.

*d*.  When recommending tax return positions and when preparing or signing a return on which a tax return position is taken, a member should, when relevant, advise the taxpayer regarding potential penalty consequences of such tax return position and the opportunity, if any, to avoid such penalties through disclosure.

3.    A member should not recommend a tax return position or prepare or sign a return reflecting a position that the member knows—

a.  Exploits the audit selection process of a taxing authority.

b.  Serves as a mere arguing position advanced solely to obtain leverage in the bargaining process of settlement negotiation with a taxing authority.

4.    When recommending a tax return position, a member has both the right and responsibility to be an advocate for the taxpayer with respect to any position satisfying the aforementioned standards.

## Explanation

5.    Our self-assessment tax system can function effectively only if taxpayers file tax returns that are true, correct, and complete. A tax return is primarily a taxpayer's representation of facts, and the taxpayer has the final responsibility for positions taken on the return.

6.    In addition to a duty to the taxpayer, a member has a duty to the tax system. However, it is well established that the taxpayer has no obligation to pay more taxes than are legally owed, and a member has a duty to the taxpayer to assist in achieving that result. The standards contained in paragraphs 2, 3, and 4 recognize the members' responsibilities to both taxpayers and to the tax system.

7.    In order to meet the standards contained in paragraph 2, a member should in good faith believe that the tax return position is warranted in existing law or can be supported by a good-faith argument for an extension, modification, or reversal of existing law. For example, in reaching such a conclusion, a member may consider a well-reasoned construction of the applicable statute, well-reasoned articles or treatises, or pronouncements issued by the applicable taxing authority, regardless of whether such sources would be treated as *authority* under Internal Revenue Code section 6662 and the regulations thereunder. A position would not fail to meet these standards merely because it is later abandoned for practical or procedural considerations during an administrative hearing or in the litigation process.

8.    If a member has a good-faith belief that more than one tax return position meets the standards set forth in paragraph 2, a member's advice concerning alternative acceptable positions may include a discussion of the likelihood that each such position might or might not cause the taxpayer's tax return to be examined and whether the position would be challenged in an examination. In such circumstances, such advice is not a violation of paragraph 3a.

9.    In some cases, a member may conclude that a tax return position is not warranted under the standard set forth in paragraph 2a. A taxpayer may, however, still wish to take such a position. Under such circumstances, the taxpayer should have the opportunity to take such a position, and the member may prepare and sign the return provided the position is appropriately disclosed on the return or claim for refund and the position is not frivolous. A frivolous position is one that is knowingly advanced in bad faith and is patently improper.

10.    A member's determination of whether information is appropriately disclosed by the taxpayer should be based on the facts and circumstances of the particular case and the authorities regarding disclosure in the applicable taxing jurisdiction. If a member recommending a position, but not engaged to prepare or sign the related tax return, advises the taxpayer concerning appropriate disclosure of the position, then the member shall be deemed to meet these standards.

11.    If particular facts and circumstances lead a member to believe that a taxpayer penalty might be asserted, the member should so advise the taxpayer and should discuss with the taxpayer the opportunity to avoid such penalty by disclosing the position on the tax return. Although a member should advise the taxpayer with respect to disclosure, it is the taxpayer's responsibility to decide whether and how to disclose.

12.    For purposes of this Statement, preparation of a tax return includes giving advice on events that have occurred at the time the advice is given if the advice is directly relevant to determining the existence, character, or amount of a schedule, entry, or other portion of a tax return.

**12**

# Interpretation No. 1-1, "Realistic Possibility Standard" of Statement on Standards for Tax Services No. 1, *Tax Return Positions*

## Background

1.   Statement on Standards for Tax Services (SSTS) No. 1, *Tax Return Positions,* contains the standards a member should follow in recommending tax return positions and in preparing or signing tax returns. In general, a member should have a good-faith belief that the tax return position being recommended has a realistic possibility of being sustained administratively or judicially on its merits, if challenged. The standard contained in SSTS No. 1, paragraph 2*a,* is referred to here as the realistic possibility standard. If a member concludes that a tax return position does not meet the realistic possibility standard:

*a.* The member may still recommend the position to the taxpayer if the position is not frivolous, and the member recommends appropriate disclosure of the position; or

*b.* The member may still prepare or sign a tax return containing the position, if the position is not frivolous, and the position is appropriately disclosed.

2.   A *frivolous position* is one that is knowingly advanced in bad faith and is patently improper (see SSTS No. 1, paragraph 9). A member's determination of whether information is appropriately disclosed on a tax return or claim for refund is based on the facts and circumstances of the particular case and the authorities regarding disclosure in the applicable jurisdiction (see SSTS No. 1, paragraph 10).

3.   If a member believes there is a possibility that a tax return position might result in penalties being asserted against a taxpayer, the member should so advise the taxpayer and should discuss with the taxpayer the opportunity, if any, of avoiding such penalties through disclosure (see SSTS No. 1, paragraph 11). Such advice may be given orally.

## General Interpretation

4.   To meet the realistic possibility standard, a member should have a good-faith belief that the position is warranted by existing law or can be supported by a good-faith argument for an extension, modification, or reversal of the existing law through the administrative or judicial process. Such a belief should be based on reasonable interpretations of the tax law. A member should not take into account the likelihood of audit or detection when determining whether this standard has been met (see SSTS No. 1, paragraphs 3*a* and 8).

5.   The realistic possibility standard is less stringent than the substantial authority standard and the more likely than not standard that apply under the Internal Revenue Code (IRC) to substantial understatements of liability by taxpayers. The realistic possibility standard is stricter than the reasonable basis standard that is in the IRC.

6.   In determining whether a tax return position meets the realistic possibility standard, a member may rely on authorities in addition to those evaluated when determining whether substantial authority exists under IRC section 6662. Accordingly, a member may rely on well-reasoned treatises, articles in recognized professional tax publications, and other reference tools and sources of tax analyses commonly used by tax advisers and preparers of returns.

7.   In determining whether a realistic possibility exists, a member should do all of the following:

- Establish relevant background facts
- Distill the appropriate questions from those facts
- Search for authoritative answers to those questions
- Resolve the questions by weighing the authorities uncovered by that search
- Arrive at a conclusion supported by the authorities

8.   A member should consider the weight of each authority to conclude whether a position meets the realistic possibility standard. In determining the weight of an authority, a member should consider its persuasiveness, relevance, and source. Thus, the type of authority is a significant factor. Other important factors include whether the facts stated by the authority are distinguishable from those of the tax-

payer and whether the authority contains an analysis of the issue or merely states a conclusion.

9.   The realistic possibility standard may be met despite the absence of certain types of authority. For example, a member may conclude that the realistic possibility standard has been met when the position is supported only by a well-reasoned construction of the applicable statutory provision.

10.   In determining whether the realistic possibility standard has been met, the extent of research required is left to the professional judgment of the member with respect to all the facts and circumstances known to the member. A member may conclude that more than one position meets the realistic possibility standard.

## Specific Illustrations

11.   The following illustrations deal with general fact patterns. Accordingly, the application of the guidance discussed in the General Interpretation section to variations in such general facts or to particular facts or circumstances may lead to different conclusions. In each illustration there is no authority other than that indicated.

12.   *Illustration 1.* A taxpayer has engaged in a transaction that is adversely affected by a new statutory provision. Prior law supports a position favorable to the taxpayer. The taxpayer believes, and the member concurs, that the new statute is inequitable as applied to the taxpayer's situation. The statute is constitutional, clearly drafted, and unambiguous. The legislative history discussing the new statute contains general comments that do not specifically address the taxpayer's situation.

13.   *Conclusion.* The member should recommend the return position supported by the new statute. A position contrary to a constitutional, clear, and unambiguous statute would ordinarily be considered a frivolous position.

14.   *Illustration 2.* The facts are the same as in illustration 1 except that the legislative history discussing the new statute specifically addresses the taxpayer's situation and supports a position favorable to the taxpayer.

15. *Conclusion.* In a case where the statute is clearly and unambiguously against the taxpayer's position but a contrary position exists based on legislative history specifically addressing the taxpayer's situation, a return position based either on the statutory language or on the legislative history satisfies the realistic possibility standard.

16. *Illustration 3.* The facts are the same as in illustration 1 except that the legislative history can be interpreted to provide some evidence or authority in support of the taxpayer's position; however, the legislative history does not specifically address the situation.

17. *Conclusion.* In a case where the statute is clear and unambiguous, a contrary position based on an interpretation of the legislative history that does not explicitly address the taxpayer's situation does not meet the realistic possibility standard. However, because the legislative history provides some support or evidence for the taxpayer's position, such a return position is not frivolous. A member may recommend the position to the taxpayer if the member also recommends appropriate disclosure.

18. *Illustration 4.* A taxpayer is faced with an issue involving the interpretation of a new statute. Following its passage, the statute was widely recognized to contain a drafting error, and a technical correction proposal has been introduced. The taxing authority issues a pronouncement indicating how it will administer the provision. The pronouncement interprets the statute in accordance with the proposed technical correction.

19. *Conclusion.* Return positions based on either the existing statutory language or the taxing authority pronouncement satisfy the realistic possibility standard.

20. *Illustration 5.* The facts are the same as in illustration 4 except that no taxing authority pronouncement has been issued.

21. *Conclusion.* In the absence of a taxing authority pronouncement interpreting the statute in accordance with the technical correction, only a return position based on the existing statutory language will meet the realistic possibility standard. A return position based on the proposed technical correction may be recommended if it is appropriately disclosed, since it is not frivolous.

22. *Illustration 6.* A taxpayer is seeking advice from a member regarding a recently amended statute. The member has reviewed the

statute, the legislative history that specifically addresses the issue, and a recently published notice issued by the taxing authority. The member has concluded in good faith that, based on the statute and the legislative history, the taxing authority's position as stated in the notice does not reflect legislative intent.

23. *Conclusion.* The member may recommend the position supported by the statute and the legislative history because it meets the realistic possibility standard.

24. *Illustration 7.* The facts are the same as in illustration 6 except that the taxing authority pronouncement is a temporary regulation.

25. *Conclusion.* In determining whether the position meets the realistic possibility standard, a member should determine the weight to be given the regulation by analyzing factors such as whether the regulation is legislative or interpretative, or if it is inconsistent with the statute. If a member concludes that the position does not meet the realistic possibility standard, because it is not frivolous, the position may nevertheless be recommended if the member also recommends appropriate disclosure.

26. *Illustration 8.* A tax form published by a taxing authority is incorrect, but completion of the form as published provides a benefit to the taxpayer. The member knows that the taxing authority has published an announcement acknowledging the error.

27. *Conclusion.* In these circumstances, a return position in accordance with the published form is a frivolous position.

28. *Illustration 9.* A taxpayer wants to take a position that a member has concluded is frivolous. The taxpayer maintains that even if the taxing authority examines the return, the issue will not be raised.

29. *Conclusion.* The member should not consider the likelihood of audit or detection when determining whether the realistic possibility standard has been met. The member should not prepare or sign a return that contains a frivolous position even if it is disclosed.

30. *Illustration 10.* A statute is passed requiring the capitalization of certain expenditures. The taxpayer believes, and the member concurs, that to comply fully, the taxpayer will need to acquire new computer hardware and software and implement a number of new accounting procedures. The taxpayer and member agree that the costs of full compliance will be significantly greater than the result-

ing increase in tax due under the new provision. Because of these cost considerations, the taxpayer makes no effort to comply. The taxpayer wants the member to prepare and sign a return on which the new requirement is simply ignored.

31. *Conclusion*. The return position desired by the taxpayer is frivolous, and the member should neither prepare nor sign the return.

32. *Illustration 11*. The facts are the same as in illustration 10 except that a taxpayer has made a good-faith effort to comply with the law by calculating an estimate of expenditures to be capitalized under the new provision.

33. *Conclusion*. In this situation, the realistic possibility standard has been met. When using estimates in the preparation of a return, a member should refer to SSTS No. 4, *Use of Estimates*.

34. *Illustration 12*. On a given issue, a member has located and weighed two authorities concerning the treatment of a particular expenditure. A taxing authority has issued an administrative ruling that required the expenditure to be capitalized and amortized over several years. On the other hand, a court opinion permitted the current deduction of the expenditure. The member has concluded that these are the relevant authorities, considered the source of both authorities, and concluded that both are persuasive and relevant.

35. *Conclusion*. The realistic possibility standard is met by either position.

36. *Illustration 13*. A tax statute is silent on the treatment of an item under the statute. However, the legislative history explaining the statute directs the taxing authority to issue regulations that will require a specific treatment of the item. No regulations have been issued at the time the member must recommend a position on the tax treatment of the item.

37. *Conclusion*. The member may recommend the position supported by the legislative history because it meets the realistic possibility standard.

38. *Illustration 14*. A taxpayer wants to take a position that a member concludes meets the realistic possibility standard based on an assumption regarding an underlying nontax legal issue. The member recommends that the taxpayer seek advice from its legal counsel, and the taxpayer's attorney gives an opinion on the nontax legal issue.

39. *Conclusion.* A member may in general rely on a legal opinion on a nontax legal issue. A member should, however, use professional judgment when relying on a legal opinion. If, on its face, the opinion of the taxpayer's attorney appears to be unreasonable, unsubstantiated, or unwarranted, a member should consult his or her attorney before relying on the opinion.

40. *Illustration 15.* A taxpayer has obtained from its attorney an opinion on the tax treatment of an item and requests that a member rely on the opinion.

41. *Conclusion.* The authorities on which a member may rely include well-reasoned sources of tax analysis. If a member is satisfied about the source, relevance, and persuasiveness of the legal opinion, a member may rely on that opinion when determining whether the realistic possibility standard has been met.

# Statement on Standards for Tax Services No. 2, Answers to Questions on Returns

## Introduction

1.   This Statement sets forth the applicable standards for members when signing the preparer's declaration on a tax return if one or more questions on the return have not been answered. The term *questions* includes requests for information on the return, in the instructions, or in the regulations, whether or not stated in the form of a question.

## Statement

2.   A member should make a reasonable effort to obtain from the taxpayer the information necessary to provide appropriate answers to all questions on a tax return before signing as preparer.

## Explanation

3.   It is recognized that the questions on tax returns are not of uniform importance, and often they are not applicable to the particular taxpayer. Nevertheless, there are at least two reasons why a member should be satisfied that a reasonable effort has been made to obtain information to provide appropriate answers to the questions on the return that are applicable to a taxpayer.

*a*. A question may be of importance in determining taxable income or loss, or the tax liability shown on the return, in which circumstance an omission may detract from the quality of the return.

*b*. A member often must sign a preparer's declaration stating that the return is true, correct, and complete.

4.   Reasonable grounds may exist for omitting an answer to a question applicable to a taxpayer. For example, reasonable grounds may include the following:

a. The information is not readily available and the answer is not significant in terms of taxable income or loss, or the tax liability shown on the return.

b. Genuine uncertainty exists regarding the meaning of the question in relation to the particular return.

c. The answer to the question is voluminous; in such cases, a statement should be made on the return that the data will be supplied upon examination.

5.   A member should not omit an answer merely because it might prove disadvantageous to a taxpayer.

6.   If reasonable grounds exist for omission of an answer to an applicable question, a taxpayer is not required to provide on the return an explanation of the reason for the omission. In this connection, a member should consider whether the omission of an answer to a question may cause the return to be deemed incomplete.

# Statement on Standards for Tax Services No. 3, Certain Procedural Aspects of Preparing Returns

## Introduction

1.   This Statement sets forth the applicable standards for members concerning the obligation to examine or verify certain supporting data or to consider information related to another taxpayer when preparing a taxpayer's tax return.

## Statement

2.   In preparing or signing a return, a member may in good faith rely, without verification, on information furnished by the taxpayer or by third parties. However, a member should not ignore the implications of information furnished and should make reasonable inquiries if the information furnished appears to be incorrect, incomplete, or inconsistent either on its face or on the basis of other facts known to a member. Further, a member should refer to the taxpayer's returns for one or more prior years whenever feasible.

3.   If the tax law or regulations impose a condition with respect to deductibility or other tax treatment of an item, such as taxpayer maintenance of books and records or substantiating documentation to support the reported deduction or tax treatment, a member should make appropriate inquiries to determine to the member's satisfaction whether such condition has been met.

4.   When preparing a tax return, a member should consider information actually known to that member from the tax return of another taxpayer if the information is relevant to that tax return and its consideration is necessary to properly prepare that tax return. In using such information, a member should consider any limitations imposed by any law or rule relating to confidentiality.

## Explanation

5.   The preparer's declaration on a tax return often states that the information contained therein is true, correct, and complete to the best of the preparer's knowledge and belief based on all information known by the preparer. This type of reference should be understood to include information furnished by the taxpayer or by third parties to a member in connection with the preparation of the return.

6.   The preparer's declaration does not require a member to examine or verify supporting data. However, a distinction should be made between (a) the need either to determine by inquiry that a specifically required condition, such as maintaining books and records or substantiating documentation, has been satisfied or to obtain information when the material furnished appears to be incorrect or incomplete and (b) the need for a member to examine underlying information. In fulfilling his or her obligation to exercise due diligence in preparing a return, a member may rely on information furnished by the taxpayer unless it appears to be incorrect, incomplete, or inconsistent. Although a member has certain responsibilities in exercising due diligence in preparing a return, the taxpayer has the ultimate responsibility for the contents of the return. Thus, if the taxpayer presents unsupported data in the form of lists of tax information, such as dividends and interest received, charitable contributions, and medical expenses, such information may be used in the preparation of a tax return without verification unless it appears to be incorrect, incomplete, or inconsistent either on its face or on the basis of other facts known to a member.

7.   Even though there is no requirement to examine underlying documentation, a member should encourage the taxpayer to provide supporting data where appropriate. For example, a member should encourage the taxpayer to submit underlying documents for use in tax return preparation to permit full consideration of income and deductions arising from security transactions and from pass-through entities, such as estates, trusts, partnerships, and S corporations.

8.   The source of information provided to a member by a taxpayer for use in preparing the return is often a pass-through entity, such as a limited partnership, in which the taxpayer has an interest but is not involved in management. A member may accept the infor-

mation provided by the pass-through entity without further inquiry, unless there is reason to believe it is incorrect, incomplete, or inconsistent, either on its face or on the basis of other facts known to the member. In some instances, it may be appropriate for a member to advise the taxpayer to ascertain the nature and amount of possible exposure to tax deficiencies, interest, and penalties, by contact with management of the pass-through entity.

9.   A member should make use of a taxpayer's returns for one or more prior years in preparing the current return whenever feasible. Reference to prior returns and discussion of prior-year tax determinations with the taxpayer should provide information to determine the taxpayer's general tax status, avoid the omission or duplication of items, and afford a basis for the treatment of similar or related transactions. As with the examination of information supplied for the current year's return, the extent of comparison of the details of income and deduction between years depends on the particular circumstances.

24

# Statement on Standards for Tax Services No. 4, Use of Estimates

## Introduction

1.    This Statement sets forth the applicable standards for members when using the taxpayer's estimates in the preparation of a tax return. A member may advise on estimates used in the preparation of a tax return, but the taxpayer has the responsibility to provide the estimated data. Appraisals or valuations are not considered estimates for purposes of this Statement.

## Statement

2.    Unless prohibited by statute or by rule, a member may use the taxpayer's estimates in the preparation of a tax return if it is not practical to obtain exact data and if the member determines that the estimates are reasonable based on the facts and circumstances known to the member. If the taxpayer's estimates are used, they should be presented in a manner that does not imply greater accuracy than exists.

## Explanation

3.    Accounting requires the exercise of professional judgment and, in many instances, the use of approximations based on judgment. The application of such accounting judgments, as long as not in conflict with methods set forth by a taxing authority, is acceptable. These judgments are not estimates within the purview of this Statement. For example, a federal income tax regulation provides that if all other conditions for accrual are met, the exact amount of income or expense need not be known or ascertained at year end if the amount can be determined with reasonable accuracy.

4.    When the taxpayer's records do not accurately reflect information related to small expenditures, accuracy in recording some data may be difficult to achieve. Therefore, the use of estimates by a taxpayer in determining the amount to be deducted for such items may be appropriate.

5.   When records are missing or precise information about a transaction is not available at the time the return must be filed, a member may prepare a tax return using a taxpayer's estimates of the missing data.

6.   Estimated amounts should not be presented in a manner that provides a misleading impression about the degree of factual accuracy.

7.   Specific disclosure that an estimate is used for an item in the return is not generally required; however, such disclosure should be made in unusual circumstances where nondisclosure might mislead the taxing authority regarding the degree of accuracy of the return as a whole. Some examples of unusual circumstances include the following:

*a.* A taxpayer has died or is ill at the time the return must be filed.

*b.* A taxpayer has not received a Schedule K-1 for a pass-through entity at the time the tax return is to be filed.

*c.* There is litigation pending (for example, a bankruptcy proceeding) that bears on the return.

*d.* Fire or computer failure has destroyed the relevant records.

26

# Statement on Standards for Tax Services No. 5, Departure From a Position Previously Concluded in an Administrative Proceeding or Court Decision

## Introduction

1. This Statement sets forth the applicable standards for members in recommending a tax return position that departs from the position determined in an administrative proceeding or in a court decision with respect to the taxpayer's prior return.

2. For purposes of this Statement, *administrative proceeding* also includes an examination by a taxing authority or an appeals conference relating to a return or a claim for refund.

3. For purposes of this Statement, *court decision* means a decision by any court having jurisdiction over tax matters.

## Statement

4. The tax return position with respect to an item as determined in an administrative proceeding or court decision does not restrict a member from recommending a different tax position in a later year's return, unless the taxpayer is bound to a specified treatment in the later year, such as by a formal closing agreement. Therefore, as provided in Statement on Standards for Tax Services (SSTS) No. 1, *Tax Return Positions*, the member may recommend a tax return position or prepare or sign a tax return that departs from the treatment of an item as concluded in an administrative proceeding or court decision with respect to a prior return of the taxpayer.

## Explanation

5. If an administrative proceeding or court decision has resulted in a determination concerning a specific tax treatment of an

item in a prior year's return, a member will usually recommend this same tax treatment in subsequent years. However, departures from consistent treatment may be justified under such circumstances as the following:

a. Taxing authorities tend to act consistently in the disposition of an item that was the subject of a prior administrative proceeding but generally are not bound to do so. Similarly, a taxpayer is not bound to follow the tax treatment of an item as consented to in an earlier administrative proceeding.

b. The determination in the administrative proceeding or the court's decision may have been caused by a lack of documentation. Supporting data for the later year may be appropriate.

c. A taxpayer may have yielded in the administrative proceeding for settlement purposes or not appealed the court decision, even though the position met the standards in SSTS No. 1.

d. Court decisions, rulings, or other authorities that are more favorable to a taxpayer's current position may have developed since the prior administrative proceeding was concluded or the prior court decision was rendered.

6. The consent in an earlier administrative proceeding and the existence of an unfavorable court decision are factors that the member should consider in evaluating whether the standards in SSTS No. 1 are met.

28

# Statement on Standards for Tax Services No. 6, Knowledge of Error: Return Preparation

## Introduction

1.    This Statement sets forth the applicable standards for a member who becomes aware of an error in a taxpayer's previously filed tax return or of a taxpayer's failure to file a required tax return. As used herein, the term error includes any position, omission, or method of accounting that, at the time the return is filed, fails to meet the standards set out in Statement on Standards for Tax Services (SSTS) No. 1, *Tax Return Positions*. The term *error* also includes a position taken on a prior year's return that no longer meets these standards due to legislation, judicial decisions, or administrative pronouncements having retroactive effect. However, an error does not include an item that has an insignificant effect on the taxpayer's tax liability.

2.    This Statement applies whether or not the member prepared or signed the return that contains the error.

## Statement

3.    A member should inform the taxpayer promptly upon becoming aware of an error in a previously filed return or upon becoming aware of a taxpayer's failure to file a required return. A member should recommend the corrective measures to be taken. Such recommendation may be given orally. The member is not obligated to inform the taxing authority, and a member may not do so without the taxpayer's permission, except when required by law.

4.    If a member is requested to prepare the current year's return and the taxpayer has not taken appropriate action to correct an error in a prior year's return, the member should consider whether to withdraw from preparing the return and whether to continue a professional or employment relationship with the taxpayer. If the member does prepare such current year's return, the member should take reasonable steps to ensure that the error is not repeated.

# Explanation

5.    While performing services for a taxpayer, a member may become aware of an error in a previously filed return or may become aware that the taxpayer failed to file a required return. The member should advise the taxpayer of the error and the measures to be taken. Such recommendation may be given orally. If the member believes that the taxpayer could be charged with fraud or other criminal misconduct, the taxpayer should be advised to consult legal counsel before taking any action.

6.    It is the taxpayer's responsibility to decide whether to correct the error. If the taxpayer does not correct an error, a member should consider whether to continue a professional or employment relationship with the taxpayer. While recognizing that the taxpayer may not be required by statute to correct an error by filing an amended return, a member should consider whether a taxpayer's decision not to file an amended return may predict future behavior that might require termination of the relationship. The potential for violating Code of Professional Conduct rule 301 (relating to the member's confidential client relationship), the tax law and regulations, or laws on privileged communications, and other considerations may create a conflict between the member's interests and those of the taxpayer. Therefore, a member should consider consulting with his or her own legal counsel before deciding upon recommendations to the taxpayer and whether to continue a professional or employment relationship with the taxpayer.

7.    If a member decides to continue a professional or employment relationship with the taxpayer and is requested to prepare a tax return for a year subsequent to that in which the error occurred, the member should take reasonable steps to ensure that the error is not repeated. If the subsequent year's tax return cannot be prepared without perpetuating the error, the member should consider withdrawal from the return preparation. If a member learns that the taxpayer is using an erroneous method of accounting and it is past the due date to request permission to change to a method meeting the standards of SSTS No. 1, the member may sign a tax return for the current year, providing the tax return includes appropriate disclosure of the use of the erroneous method.

8.    Whether an error has no more than an insignificant effect on the taxpayer's tax liability is left to the professional judgment of the member based on all the facts and circumstances known to the member. In judging whether an erroneous method of accounting has more than an insignificant effect, a member should consider the method's cumulative effect and its effect on the current year's tax return.

9.    If a member becomes aware of the error while performing services for a taxpayer that do not involve tax return preparation, the member's responsibility is to advise the taxpayer of the existence of the error and to recommend that the error be discussed with the taxpayer's tax return preparer. Such recommendation may be given orally.

# Statement on Standards for Tax Services No. 7, Knowledge of Error: Administrative Proceedings

## Introduction

1.   This Statement sets forth the applicable standards for a member who becomes aware of an error in a return that is the subject of an administrative proceeding, such as an examination by a taxing authority or an appeals conference. The term *administrative proceeding* does not include a criminal proceeding. As used herein, the term *error* includes any position, omission, or method of accounting that, at the time the return is filed, fails to meet the standards set out in Statement on Standards for Tax Services (SSTS) No. 1, *Tax Return Positions*. The term *error* also includes a position taken on a prior year's return that no longer meets these standards due to legislation, judicial decisions, or administrative pronouncements having retroactive effect. However, an error does not include an item that has an insignificant effect on the taxpayer's tax liability.

2.   This Statement applies whether or not the member prepared or signed the return that contains the error. Special considerations may apply when a member has been engaged by legal counsel to provide assistance in a matter relating to the counsel's client.

## Statement

3.   If a member is representing a taxpayer in an administrative proceeding with respect to a return that contains an error of which the member is aware, the member should inform the taxpayer promptly upon becoming aware of the error. The member should recommend the corrective measures to be taken. Such recommendation may be given orally. A member is neither obligated to inform the taxing authority nor allowed to do so without the taxpayer's permission, except where required by law.

4.   A member should request the taxpayer's agreement to disclose the error to the taxing authority. Lacking such agreement, the member should consider whether to withdraw from representing

the taxpayer in the administrative proceeding and whether to continue a professional or employment relationship with the taxpayer.

## Explanation

5.   When the member is engaged to represent the taxpayer before a taxing authority in an administrative proceeding with respect to a return containing an error of which the member is aware, the member should advise the taxpayer to disclose the error to the taxing authority. Such recommendation may be given orally. If the member believes that the taxpayer could be charged with fraud or other criminal misconduct, the taxpayer should be advised to consult legal counsel before taking any action.

6.   It is the taxpayer's responsibility to decide whether to correct the error. If the taxpayer does not correct an error, a member should consider whether to withdraw from representing the taxpayer in the administrative proceeding and whether to continue a professional or employment relationship with the taxpayer. While recognizing that the taxpayer may not be required by statute to correct an error by filing an amended return, a member should consider whether a taxpayer's decision not to file an amended return may predict future behavior that might require termination of the relationship. Moreover, a member should consider consulting with his or her own legal counsel before deciding on recommendations to the taxpayer and whether to continue a professional or employment relationship with the taxpayer. The potential for violating Code of Professional Conduct rule 301 (relating to the member's confidential client relationship), the tax law and regulations, laws on privileged communications, potential adverse impact on a taxpayer of a member's withdrawal, and other considerations may create a conflict between the member's interests and those of the taxpayer.

7.   Once disclosure is agreed on, it should not be delayed to such a degree that the taxpayer or member might be considered to have failed to act in good faith or to have, in effect, provided misleading information. In any event, disclosure should be made before the conclusion of the administrative proceeding.

8.  Whether an error has an insignificant effect on the taxpayer's tax liability is left to the professional judgment of the member based on all the facts and circumstances known to the member. In judging whether an erroneous method of accounting has more than an insignificant effect, a member should consider the method's cumulative effect and its effect on the return that is the subject of the administrative proceeding.

34

# Statement on Standards for Tax Services No. 8, Form and Content of Advice to Taxpayers

## Introduction

1.    This Statement sets forth the applicable standards for members concerning certain aspects of providing advice to a taxpayer and considers the circumstances in which a member has a responsibility to communicate with a taxpayer when subsequent developments affect advice previously provided. The Statement does not, however, cover a member's responsibilities when the expectation is that the advice rendered is likely to be relied on by parties other than the taxpayer.

## Statement

2.    A member should use judgment to ensure that tax advice provided to a taxpayer reflects professional competence and appropriately serves the taxpayer's needs. A member is not required to follow a standard format or guidelines in communicating written or oral advice to a taxpayer.

3.    A member should assume that tax advice provided to a taxpayer will affect the manner in which the matters or transactions considered would be reported on the taxpayer's tax returns. Thus, for all tax advice given to a taxpayer, a member should follow the standards in Statement on Standards for Tax Services (SSTS) No. 1, *Tax Return Positions.*

4.    A member has no obligation to communicate with a taxpayer when subsequent developments affect advice previously provided with respect to significant matters, except while assisting a taxpayer in implementing procedures or plans associated with the advice provided or when a member undertakes this obligation by specific agreement.

# Explanation

5.    Tax advice is recognized as a valuable service provided by members. The form of advice may be oral or written and the subject matter may range from routine to complex. Because the range of advice is so extensive and because advice should meet the specific needs of a taxpayer, neither a standard format nor guidelines for communicating or documenting advice to the taxpayer can be established to cover all situations.

6.    Although oral advice may serve a taxpayer's needs appropriately in routine matters or in well-defined areas, written communications are recommended in important, unusual, or complicated transactions. The member may use professional judgment about whether, subsequently, to document oral advice in writing.

7.    In deciding on the form of advice provided to a taxpayer, a member should exercise professional judgment and should consider such factors as the following:

*a*.  The importance of the transaction and amounts involved

*b*.  The specific or general nature of the taxpayer's inquiry

*c*.  The time available for development and submission of the advice

*d*.  The technical complications presented

*e*.  The existence of authorities and precedents

*f*.  The tax sophistication of the taxpayer

*g*.  The need to seek other professional advice

8.    A member may assist a taxpayer in implementing procedures or plans associated with the advice offered. When providing such assistance, the member should review and revise such advice as warranted by new developments and factors affecting the transaction.

9.    Sometimes a member is requested to provide tax advice but does not assist in implementing the plans adopted. Although such developments as legislative or administrative changes or future judicial interpretations may affect the advice previously provided, a member cannot be expected to communicate subsequent developments that affect such advice unless the member undertakes this obligation by specific agreement with the taxpayer.

10.  Taxpayers should be informed that advice reflects professional judgment based on an existing situation and that subsequent developments could affect previous professional advice. Members may use precautionary language to the effect that their advice is based on facts as stated and authorities that are subject to change.

11.  In providing tax advice, a member should be cognizant of applicable confidentiality privileges.

*These Statements on Standards for Tax Services and Interpretation were unanimously adopted by the assenting votes of the twenty voting members of the twenty-one-member Tax Executive Committee.*

## Tax Executive Committee (1999-2000)

| | |
|---|---|
| David A. Lifson, *Chair* | Jeffrey A. Porter |
| Pamela J. Pecarich, *Vice Chair* | Thomas J. Purcell, III |
| Ward M. Bukofsky | Jeffrey L. Raymon |
| Joseph Cammarata | Frederick H. Rothman |
| Stephen R. Corrick | Barry D. Roy |
| Anna C. Fowler | Jane T. Rubin |
| Jill Gansler | Douglas P. Stives |
| Diane P. Herndon | Philip J. Wiesner |
| Ronald S. Katch | Claude R. Wilson, Jr. |
| Allan I. Kruger | Robert A. Zarzar |
| Susan W. Martin | |

## SRTP Enforceability Task Force

| | |
|---|---|
| J. Edward Swails, *Chair* | Michael E. Mares |
| Alan R. Einhorn | Dan L. Mendelson |
| John C. Gardner | Daniel A. Noakes |
| Ronald S. Katch | William C. Potter |

## AICPA Staff

| | |
|---|---|
| Gerald W. Padwe | Edward S. Karl |
| *Vice President* | *Director* |
| *Taxation* | *Taxation* |

*The AICPA gratefully acknowledges the contributions of William A. Tate, Jean L. Rothbarth, and Leonard Podolin, former chairs of the Responsibilities in Tax Practice Committee; A. M. (Tony) Komlyn and Wilber Van Scoik, former members of the Committee; and Carol B. Ferguson, AICPA Technical Manager.*

**Note:** *Statements on Standards for Tax Services are issued by the Tax Executive Committee, the senior technical body of the Institute designated to promulgate standards of tax practice. Rules 201 and 202 of the Institute's Code of Professional Conduct require compliance with these standards.*

# INDEX